P9-ASL-997

FEMALE PSYCHOLOGY: The Emerging Self

SUE COX, Ph. D.

City College of San Francisco
Lecturer, San Francisco
State University

 SCIENCE RESEARCH ASSOCIATES, INC.
Chicago, Palo Alto, Toronto, Henley-on-Thames, Sydney, Paris, Stuttgart

A Subsidiary of IBM

LIST OF EXPERIENTIAL EXERCISES

© 1976, Science Research Associates, Inc. All rights reserved.
Printed in the United States of America

Library of Congress Cataloging in Publication Data

Main entry under title:

Female psychology.

Bibliography
1. Women—Psychology—Addresses, essays, lec-
tures. 2. Feminism—Addresses, essays, lectures.
I. Cox, Sue.
HQ1206.F424   155.6'33   75-35571
ISBN 0-574-17905-4

WOMEN ST.
HQ
1206
F24
1976

CONTENTS

FEMALE PSYCHOLOGY: The Emerging Self

WOMEN'S STUDIES PROGRAM
UNIVERSITY OF DAYTON
ST. JOSEPH   414

DISCARDED
FROM
UNIVERSITY OF DAYTON
ROESCH LIBRARY

I am a woman giving birth to myself.

PREFACE

This book, based on "Female" energy, would not have been possible without the many women who made valuable contributions during the process and evolution of this book. I would like especially to thank Pat Grosh, as well as Linda Bancke, Lois Shelton, Diana Russell, Rusty (Jane) Hardy, and Martha Richards. Also important to me was the support and energy from my Psychology of Women class during the spring of 1975. There are many others too numerous to mention who helped me in various ways with the development of this book, though several individuals deserve special mention.

For consultation regarding the chapter "Ethnic Diversity of Female Experience," I thank the women contacted through the School of Ethnic Studies at San Francisco State—especially Rae Richardson of the Black Studies Department and Beatrice Rosales. I also wish to acknowledge Dorindo Moreno of the Concilio de Mujeres of San Francisco and Anna Nieto-Gomez, whom I contacted through the Chicano Studies Program at U.C.L.A. I also thank Marie-Helen Laraque of Indigena in Berkeley.

Many people were helpful in locating possible illustrations to fulfill the goal of presenting women's art from the newly emerging Female culture, most notably Karla Tonella of the Women's Art Center in San Francisco and Diane Rusnak in Berkeley. Many thanks also to J. J. Wilson and Karen Peterson of Sonoma State who graciously allowed me to view their slide collection and shared important information. I am also grateful to Anne Shapiro of San Francisco State for the use of her personal slide collection. Acknowledgment also goes to the San Francisco Art Institute and the Berkeley Main Library for housing women's slide registries. I would especially like to express my appreciation to the women who compiled such registries. Thanks also to the Women's Press Collective in Oakland.

This list would not be complete, however, without acknowledging the many individual women artists in the Bay Area and elsewhere who showed interest and support for the book. I thank them for sharing their art with me, and I only wish there had been the space to include more of their work.

Finally, I would like to thank Barbara Carpenter, the editor at SRA with whom I worked most closely. Barbara was invaluable in enabling this book in its final form to express the result of my seven years of teaching the Psychology of Women course, and in making my work on this book an extremely satisfying and personally rewarding experience.

ACKNOWLEDGMENTS

"Sex Hormones and Executive Ability" by Estelle R. Ramey, from the Annals of The New York Academy of Sciences, vol. 208, 1973, pp. 237–245.

"The Premenstrual Syndrome" by Mary Brown Parlee, from the *Psychological Bulletin,* 1973, vol. 80, pp. 454–465. Copyright 1973 by the American Psychological Association. Reprinted by permission.

"A Cross-Cultural Analysis of Sex Differences in the Behavior of Children Aged Three through Eleven" by Beatrice Whiting and Carolyn Pope Edwards, from *The Journal of Social Psychology,* 1973, vol. 91, pp. 171–188.

"Conclusion" reprinted by permission of William Morrow & Co., Inc. from *Sex and Temperament in Three Primitive Societies* by Margaret Mead. Copyright © 1939, 1950, 1963 by Margaret Mead.

"Matriarchy: As Women See It" by Esther Newton and Paula Webster; first published in *Aphra,* vol. 4, #3, Summer 1973.

"Psychology Constructs the Female, or the Fantasy Life of the Male Psychologist" by Naomi Weisstein. © 1971 by Naomi Weisstein.

A portion of Chapter 10, "Summary and Commentary," pp. 349–366, reprinted from *The Psychology of Sex Differences* by Eleanor Emmons Maccoby and Carol Nagy Jacklin, with the permission of the publishers, Stanford University Press. © 1974 by the Board of Trustees of the Leland Stanford Junior University.

"The Psychology of Women—Selected Topics" by Martha T. Shuch Mednick and Hilda J. Weissman; reproduced, with permission, from *Annual Review of Psychology,* Volume 26. Copyright © 1975 by Annual Reviews Inc. All rights reserved.

"Social Construction of the Second Sex" by Jo Freeman; reprinted by permission of the author.

"Women as a Minority Group" by Helen Mayer Hacker, from *Social Forces,* 1951, vol. 30. Reprinted by permission.

"The Sexual Politics of Interpersonal Behavior" by Nancy Henley and Jo Freeman; reprinted by permission of the authors.

"Case Study of a Nonconscious Ideology: Training the Woman to Know Her Place" by Sandra L. Bem and Daryl J. Bem. Reprinted by permission of the authors.

"Who Has the Power? The Marital Struggle" by Dair L. Gillespie, from the *Journal of Marriage and the Family,* Aug. 1971, pp. 445–458. Copyright 1971 by National Council on Family Relations. Reprinted by permission.

"The Black Movement and Women's Liberation" by Linda La Rue. Copyright 1970, by *The Black Scholar.*

"Heritage of La Hembra" by Anna Nieto Gomez. Copyright 1975 by Anna Nieto-Gomez.

Reprinted by permission of the editor and the publisher from Irene Fujitomi and Diane Wong "The New Asian-American Woman." In Stanley Sue and Nathaniel N. Wagner (Eds.), *Asian-Americans: Psychological Perspectives.* Palo Alto, California: Science and Behavior Books, 1973.

"Native Women Today: Sexism and the Indian Woman" by Shirley Hill Witt. Reprinted by permission of the author.

"Sexuality" from *Sex, Gender & Society* by Ann Oakley, 1972. Reprinted by permission of Harper & Row, Publishers, Inc., and Maurice Temple Smith Ltd., London.

"A Theory on Female Sexuality" by Mary Jane Sherfey from *Sisterhood Is Powerful.* © 1970 by Random House, Inc. Reprinted by permission of Random House, Inc.

"The Myth of the Vaginal Orgasm" by Anne Koedt. Copyright © by Anne Koedt, 1970. The article first appeared in *Notes from the Second Year.*

"Rape: The All-American Crime" by Susan Griffin. Copyright 1971 by Susan Griffin, by special arrangement with *Ramparts* Magazine.

"The Woman Identified Woman" by Radicalesbians (Rita Mae Brown, Cynthia Funk, Lois Hart, March Hoffman, Suzanne, and Barbara XX). This article originally appeared in *Notes from the Third Year.*

"Women's Sexuality: A Feminist View" by E. K. Childs, E. A. Sachnoff, and E. S. Stocker. Reprinted by permission of the authors.

"Patient and Patriarch: Women in the Psychotherapeutic Relationship" by Phyllis Chesler, from the *Journal of Marriage and the Family,* Nov. 1971, pp. 746–759.

"On Masochism" by Betsy Belote, from *Sexual Intimacy between Female Clients and Male Psychotherapists: Masochistic Sabotage,* July 1974, pp. 23–44, 100–104; unpublished dissertation, California School of Professional Psychology, San Francisco, Ca.

"Depression and Middle-Aged Women" by Pauline B. Bart; reprinted by permission of the author.

"The Consciousness-Raising Group as a Model for Therapy with Women" by Annette M. Brodsky, from *Psychotherapy: Theory, Research and Practice,* Vol. 10, No. 1, 1973, published by the Division of Psychotherapy, American Psychological Association.

"What Happens in Feminist Therapy" by Hannah Lerman, presented at symposium "Feminist Therapy: In Search of a Theory," 1974 convention of American Psychological Association.

"What Is a Healthy Woman?" by Marcia Perlstein, presented at San Francisco Women's Mental Health Workers Conference, 1975.

"On Male Liberation" by Jack Sawyer from *Liberation,* Aug.–Sept.–Oct., 1970. Reprinted by permission of *Liberation* Magazine.

"Berkeley Men's Center Manifesto" reprinted by permission of the Berkeley Men's Center, Berkeley, Ca.

"Why Are Women So Hard on Women?" by Elaine Walster and Mary Ann Pate, from *Forum on Public Affairs*, Vol. 7, No. 4, 1974, published by University of Wisconsin–Platteville.

Reproduced by special permission from the *Journal of Applied Behavioral Science*, "Male Power and the Women's Movement," by Barbara Bovee Polk, pp. 415–431, Vol. 10, No. 3. Copyright 1974, NTL Institute for Applied Behavioral Science.

Excerpt from *The Pursuit of Loneliness* by Philip Slater, pp. 100–103. Copyright © 1970 by Philip E. Slater. Reprinted by permission of Beacon Press.

Excerpt from "Käthe Kollwitz" by Muriel Rukeyser, from *Speed of Darkness,* © 1960, 1961 by Muriel Rukeyser.

"See the Sky Is Her Belly and It Moves" by Allie Light, from *The Glittering Cave.* © 1974 by Rebus Press.

Excerpt from "Menses: A Seasonal" by Pamela Victorine, from *Anthology of Women Poets.* © 1973 by Dremen.

Excerpt from "Stepping Westward" by Denise Levertov, from *The Sorrow Dance.* Copyright © 1966 by Denise Levertov Goodman. Reprinted by permission of New Directions Publishing Corporation.

"A work of artifice" first appeared in *Leviathan;* "Women's laughter" first appeared in ELIMA; "Doing it differently" first appeared in ANON 1973. All were published in *To Be of Use* by Marge Piercy. Copyright © 1969, 1971, 1973 by Marge Piercy. Reprinted by permission of Doubleday & Company, Inc.

"Witchcraft was hung, in History" by Emily Dickinson. Reprinted by permission of the publishers and the Trustees of Amherst College from Thomas H. Johnson, Editor, *The Poems of Emily Dickinson,* Cambridge, Mass.: The Bellknap Press of Harvard University Press. Copyright, 1951, 1955 by the President and Fellows of Harvard College.

"Lineage" by Margaret Walker, from *For My People.* © 1942 by Yale University Press.

"Matrilineal Descent," "The One That Got Away or The Woman Who Made It," excerpt from "Letter to a Sister Underground," excerpt from "Lesbian Poem," excerpt from "Monster Poem," "Credo," and excerpt from "Revolucinations" by Robin Morgan, all from *Monster: Poems by Robin Morgan.* Copyright © 1972 by Robin Morgan. Reprinted by permission of Random House, Inc.

"Housewife" by Anne Sexton, from *All My Pretty Ones,* copyright © 1961, 1962 by Anne Sexton; reprinted by permission of the publisher, Houghton Mifflin Co.

"Women" by May Swenson is reprinted by permission of the author from *Iconographs,* copyright © 1970 by May Swenson, published by Charles Scribner's Sons, New York.

"The Difference" by Grace Wade, from *This Is Women's Work,* copyright © 1974 by Panjandrum Press. Reprinted by permission of Panjandrum Press.

"Relationships" by Mona Van Duyn, from *To See, To Take.* Copyright © 1966 by Mona Van Duyn. Reprinted by permission of Atheneum Publishers. Appeared originally in *The Quarterly Review of Literature, 1970.*

Title poem reprinted from *Snapshots of a Daughter-In-Law, Poems 1954–1962* by Adrienne Rich, by permission of W. W. Norton & Company, Inc. Copyright © 1956, 1957, 1958, 1959, 1960, 1961, 1962, 1963, 1967 by Adrienne Rich Conrad.

"Alcestis on the Poetry Circuit" by Erica Jong, copyright 1971 by Erica Mann Jong, reprinted by permission of the author.

"The Process of Dissolution" and "An Expression" by Susan Efros, from *This Is Women's Work.* Copyright © 1974 by Panjandrum Press. Reprinted by permission of Panjandrum Press.

"The Black Latin and the Mexican Indian" by Avotcja, from *Third World Women;* © 1972, Third World Communications, San Francisco.

"Roundelays" by Sor Juana Inez de La Cruz (1648–1695); translated by Bernice Rincón; reprinted from *Third World Women,* © 1972, Third World Communications, San Francisco.

"Crossbreeds" by Carol Lee Sanchez and "Too Much to Require" by Janice Mirikitani, both from *Third World Women,* © 1972, Third World Communications, San Francisco.

Untitled poem (I am the wind . . .) by Suzan Shown Harjo; reprinted by permission of the author.

Untitled poem ("When you came . . .") by Lydia Yellowbird; reprinted by permission of the author.

"Missoula Rape Poem" by Marge Piercy, reprinted by permission of the author.

"A History of Lesbianism" an excerpt from "The Common Woman Poems" by Judy Grahn from *Edward the Dyke and Other Poems,* © 1971 by Judy Grahn, reprinted by permission of the Women's Press Collective, 5251 Broadway, Oakland.

"The Invisible Woman" © 1970 by Robin Morgan; reprinted from *Monster: Poems by Robin Morgan,* by permission of Random House, Inc.

"The Friend" by Marge Piercy. Copyright © 1969 by Marge Piercy. Reprinted from *Hard Loving* by permission of Wesleyan University Press.

"Elegy for My Mad Mother" by Rachel Loden, from *Anthology of Women Poets.* © 1973 by Dremen (Berkeley).

"Gesture" by Beverly Dahlen, reprinted from *Out of the Third,* published by Momo's Press, San Francisco. © 1974 by Beverly Dahlen. Reprinted by permission of the author.

"Wild Women Blues" by Ida Cox, reprinted from *The World Split Open* by permission of Random House, Inc.

Emerging Light by Remedios Varo. Reprinted by permission of Walter Gruen.

"Unlearning to Not Speak" by Marge Piercy, from *To Be of Use;* copyright © 1969, 1971, 1973 by Marge Piercy. Reprinted by permission of Doubleday & Company, Inc.

"For Witches" by Susan Sutheim, copyright © 1969 by *Women: A Journal of Liberation,* 3028 Greenmount Ave., Baltimore, Md. 21218.

Excerpts from "From the Prison House" and "Merced" by Adrienne Rich, reprinted from *Diving into the Wreck, Poems 1971–1972* by Adrienne Rich. By permission of W. W. Norton & Company, Inc. Copyright © 1973 by W. W. Norton & Company, Inc.

"Feeling Righteous" by Susan Griffin, copyright © 1971 by Susan Griffin. Originally appeared in *Dear Sky* published by Shameless Hussy Press.

"In Our Own Land," "Fear," and "Therapist" by Jody Aliesan, reprinted by permission of the author. "Therapist" originally appeared in *To Set Free,* published by Second Moon, 1972; "Fear" first appeared in *Rough Times* and was reprinted in *The Northwest Passage* and *Soul Claiming,* published by Mulch Press, Northampton, Mass., 1976.

Portions of the experiential exercises were borrowed from the following sources:

"Feminine/Masculine: Yin/Yang" by Ann and Tom Yeomans, Psychosynthesis Institute, Palo Alto, Ca.

"Experiencing Various Points of View" from John O. Stevens, *Awareness: Exploring, Experimenting, Experiencing;* copyright © 1971 Real People Press, Moab, Utah.

"Body Image" from *For Yourself—the Fulfillment of Female Sexuality* by Lonnie Garfield Barbach. Copyright © 1975 by Doubleday & Co., Inc.

"Woman—Which Includes Man, of Course," original and revision copyright © 1970 and 1972 respectively by Theodora Wells.

"Toward the Future" from exercises developed by the Psychosynthesis Institute, Palo Alto, Ca.

Introduction

One of the major premises of this text is that a significant relationship exists between the psychology of women and the principles and theories of feminism and that, through feminism, we can discover aspects of this psychology not found in the traditional approach to the subject. These discoveries can then provide a basis for understanding and conceptualizing the newly emerging Female* psychology (hence the title *Female Psychology: The Emerging Self*). Before this premise can be further explained or supported, however, it is necessary to understand what feminism is. We will, therefore, briefly explore the basic beliefs and principles of feminism.

Feminists are women who agree that we live in a male-dominated culture in which women remain unacknowledged and invalidated as sources of power. Male domination means, in this case, that men have the *admitted* right to rule—that is, both men and women grant men this right. Men are the heads of governing and political bodies, their labor is worth more in the marketplace, their opinions have more force, authority, and influence, and they make the most important decisions. Though there is much evidence that men have the admitted right to rule, feminists question whether that right is *inherent,* based on some intrinsic characteristic. Instead, feminists advocate that women and men should have equal political, economic, and social rights.

On a more personal level, feminists are interested in eliminating the negative value placed on women—that women are secondary, lower in status, worth, or importance, weak or inferior. Negative evaluations of women result from *sexism,* beliefs or statements about women that cast them in an unfavorable light.

Furthermore, in eliminating sexism, feminists are engaged in the struggle to liberate both women and men. They share the humanistic goal of removing limitations imposed by sex roles that prevent full development of each person's potential. It is curious that even though the aim of feminism is to promote and expand human capacities, there is a tendency for people to respond to it with fear and anger. Some of these fears, which may be accompanied by anger, are discussed below (the reader may be able to add to the list).

1. Fear that feminists want to reverse the present situation, making women dominant over men. This clearly is *not* what feminists intend.† Even though this fear is unfounded, still it persists. The reason for its persistence may be based on the existence of other fears related to women increasing their power—namely, men's fear of losing power and women's fear of gaining power.

Men's fear of losing power may be related to several other fears: (a) They may fear feminism because it enables women to increase their power, resulting in a corresponding decrease in men's power. This is understandably difficult

---

*Uppercase term refers to psychology defined by women's own experience rather than men's view of women's experience. This is discussed in more detail later in this Introduction.

†One notable exception is Valerie Solanis's "satirical" diatribe, *SCUM Manifesto,* which does deal with the reversal idea.

for men to accept. (b) As women increase their power, men may fear becoming powerless, helpless, and impotent. This is understandable since no one likes to feel powerless—such feelings have not been easy for women to cope with, either, although they have had no choice but to adapt to these feelings. (c) Men may also fear that women would seek revenge for the many years of domination and mistreatment by men. While this fear is understandable since more and more women are expressing their anger, it is unwarranted (based on feminist writings). (d) Men may also be afraid of women simply because they are women.* An increase in women's power would then increase men's fear of them.

It seems almost paradoxical that women should fear gaining power, but this often seems to be the case (see chapters in this book entitled "Oppression of the Self" and "Psychotherapy and Women"). Their fear of gaining power may, however, merely reflect the intensity of their desire for more power. (a) This may be related to another fear, that of admitting one's relatively powerless position and having to deal with the fear and pain that accompany such a position. (b) Women may fear gaining power because they think it will mean hurting others (men). This fear may relate to their desire to hurt others (men) because they have been hurt themselves by being placed in a powerless position; they may also be afraid of hurting another because they can identify with the pain involved, having experienced it themselves. (c) Women may also fear gaining power because it means taking more responsibility for and defining themselves and taking full responsibility for their actions, rather than being or

---

*For an interesting theoretical development of this topic, see W. Lederer, 1968, *The Fear of Women* (New York: Harcourt Brace Jovanovich).

wanting to be under the protectorship of men.

Of course, all of the above fears depend on the premise that power is defined as domination (based on the Male principle). It is possible, however, for both sexes to increase their power, that is, for both to be powerful at the same time—if we redefine power according to Female principles (see discussion of Male and Female principles later in this Introduction).

2. Fear of loss of sex-role identity. Many people feel threatened by the loss of some part(s) of their sex role. This is understandable, since at present so much of our sense of who we are as people is based on what sex we are. There is necessarily some fear involved in the loss of one's "female" or "male" self, but it is essential in order to discover and express our true selves.

3. Fear that feminism prescribes rules about how people should behave, that is, the fear of being controlled or dictated to. Feminists, however, are concerned with being aware of what we do as a result of our sex roles and then choosing whether or not we wish to continue these behaviors. At present people do not freely choose their sex roles, but are socialized into them and continue in them without awareness.

4. Fear of androgyny, that is, fear of having both male and female characteristics. Underlying this is the fear of losing one's sex-role identity and the fear that everyone will become the same. Feminism, however, instead of making people more uniform, advocates a release from the restrictions and limitations of sex roles and opens the range and variety of possible behavior. Sex roles make men as a group and women as a group far more uniform than the loss of sex roles would.

5. Fear that should feminism abolish sex roles, men and women would become more and

more alike so that, therefore, they would no longer be sexually attracted to each other. This view ignores the fact there would still exist psychological *opposites* in both sexes. Furthermore, one can also be attracted to *similarities* as well as differences to one's self in both sexes.

6. Fear that if feminism abolishes sex roles, there will be an increase in bisexuality or homosexuality. Feminism does support the existence of hetero- and homosexual alternatives (without social conditioning resulting from present sex roles, bisexuality may well be the norm). Although it is widely recognized that there are many fears about homosexuality, it has not been demonstrated to be unhealthy.†

7. Fear that if men and women are not naturally sexually attracted to each other and sex-roles were eliminated, then (a) children would not be born or properly cared for, and (b) there may be a disintegration of the nuclear family as the primary social structure. This assumes that children are at present adequately cared for and that the nuclear family is the best social structure for rearing children. This has not been empirically demonstrated to be the case.

8. Fear that development of a feminist consciousness might threaten women's relationships, especially with men. In light of women's experiences to date, there are several possibilities of what could happen—it depends upon the particular individuals involved.

9. Fear of any kind of change because of the uncertainty involved. Many human beings have a great deal of resistance to believing that men and women could be different from what they seem to be now. There is for both women and men a fear of taking responsibility for becoming fully human.

---

†In fact, the American Psychiatric Association recently passed a resolution to this effect.

To prevent oversimplification, we need to be aware that several variations of feminism exist. While a detailed description of the basic feminist positions is not essential in order to use this book, it may be helpful to have at least a nodding acquaintance with them, especially since the author's explicit bias is in favor of cultural feminism. Since many inaccuracies and misconceptions about feminism have been perpetuated, a table summarizing the three basic positions on various key issues is included in Appendix B.

A Feminist View of the Psychology of Women

Before we explore the feminist view of the psychology of women, we need to discuss what is meant by the term *psychology*, especially as it applies to women. According to Webster's New Collegiate Dictionary, there are four definitions: (1) the science of mind and behavior; (2) the mental or behavioral characteristics of an individual or group; (3) the study of mind and behavior in relation to a particular field of knowledge or activity; and (4) a treatise on psychology. This set of definitions applies to the psychology of women in the following ways. Science refers simply to knowledge derived from observation, study, and experimentation; the psychology of women is then the knowledge about women derived from observation, study, and experimentation of women. The second definition applies most readily to the mental and behavioral characteristics of women as a group. In the contents of this book, this definition parallels most closely surveys of psychological sex differences. The third definition applies to the study of women with respect to other academic disciplines—biological, anthropological, sociological sciences, for example—as

Representation of the world, like the world itself, is the work of men; they describe it from their own point of view, which they confuse with absolute truth.

Simone de Beauvoir

well as to another area of activity, feminism. Opinions about the degree of relationship between feminism and the psychology of women vary widely, ranging from no relationship whatever to extreme skepticism about the validity of the entire discipline of psychology. The middle ground is probably the opinion that feminism provides some significant insights into the psychology of women. Finally, in applying the fourth definition, a treatise on the psychology of women consists of a formal, systematic essay, a discussion of facts, evidence, principles, and any conclusions based on all of these. Based on the above definition, a treatise on the psychology of women need not be written by a psychologist, but could be formulated by social scientists in other fields, for example, or by feminists. Many such writings are included in this book.

Feminism describes the psychology of women and men in terms of the results of power differences between the two groups with regard to real, material conditions. In addition, cultural feminists believe that each person has the potential for all human attributes but that present sex roles separate these attributes artificially into two distinct categories. It is thus possible, they assert, that changing the social and material conditions that result in power differences and eliminating sexism—which both results from and produces and maintains the inequalities of material conditions—will allow greater opportunity for each person to become fully human. It is assumed that both women

and men have within themselves both Female and Male capacities and attributes.

Since the term "psychology of" connotes a fixed, "natural," and therefore unchangeable state, we will use the term "point of view" to explore the concept of a new psychology of women. It is important, first of all, to distinguish between female and Female points of view. The lower-case term represents the Male concept of the female point of view, that is, women as defined by men's experiences of them, and the upper-case term connotes women's experiences of their true selves. There also exist male and Male points of view; however, in a patriarchy, culture is presented from a Male point of view, so these two generally overlap. In other words, men's (and women's) definitions of men are based on and therefore consistent with men's experiences of themselves. For women, however, the two points of view are very different. Since women are still in the process of discovering their true selves, the Female point of view continues to emerge.

The Male point of view is so pervasive and dominant in our culture that much of the time both women and men fail to recognize it as a point of view and mistake it for reality. To demonstrate how pervasive and subtle this view is, we will use the following analogy about left-handedness. The fact that our culture operates from the dominant point of view of right-handedness is barely noticeable unless one is left-handed. Left-handed people quickly become aware that such items as pay tele-

Women have no means of coming to an understanding of what their experience is, or even that it is different from male experience. The tool for representing, for objectifying one's experience in order to deal with it, culture, is so saturated with male bias that women almost never have a chance to see themselves culturally through their own eyes. So that finally, signals from their direct experience that conflict with the prevailing (male) culture are denied and repressed.

Shulamith Firestone

---

phones, eggbeaters, pencil sharpeners, paring knives, and fountain pens are constructed for the convenience of right-handed people. Those who design and make such items are probably right-handed themselves and are not aware that these cultural artifacts do not work equally well for left-handed people. In this way, an entire culture may be created from the right-handed point of view. This is the same way the Male point of view dominates the culture, but to an even greater extent.

To carry this analogy further, just as females differ in their degree of awareness about living in a culture dominated by a Male point of view, left-handed people have varying degrees of consciousness about living in a culture dominated by a right-handed point of view. For example, left-handed persons may fail to notice their difficulty in using pencil sharpeners or phone booths, or they may notice the difficulty and pretend that it does not bother them. Another reaction may be to feel there is something wrong with themselves, assuming that if only they could overcome their natural clumsiness, they would be all right. They might also respond by thinking that right-handed people deserve to have phone booths, eggbeaters, and pencil sharpeners built for them because, after all, they are the majority and they are more important—therefore, the culture *should* be for the convenience of the right-handed people. A much different reaction is to notice that other left-handed people also have difficulty with such items and to decide to change the culture

and its artifacts to serve the interests of both right- and left-handed people.

In this analogy the left-handed people are, of course, comparable to women in our culture. A woman may fail to recognize that the culture is dominated by the Male point of view, or she may recognize the fact but fail to see that she has difficulties living in it. Another reaction a woman may have is to acknowledge the predominance of the Male point of view but pretend it does not bother her. She may decide that it is not that difficult and that she "can live with it." On the other hand, she may blame herself, feeling that "if only I were more intelligent, if only I were more assertive, more beautiful . . . ," then her difficulties would disappear. Another common reaction is to rationalize that men deserve to have the culture operate from the Male point of view—after all, they work so hard and are so important (much more than women); they are the founders of the nation, the discoverers of knowledge, and the establishers of the very foundations of the culture, so of course the culture is (should be) based on the Male point of view. In contrast, the reaction of feminists (and other women as well) is to notice that other women also have difficulties living in a Male-dominated culture and to try to change the culture to make it work equally well for both women and men. This change would involve including both the Male and Female points of view with neither one predominating. So far, the people who have designed and constructed the culture have been

The woman who most needs liberating in this country is the woman in every man, and the man who most needs liberating is the man in every woman.

Rev. William Sloane Coffin, Jr.

Experiencing Culture from the Male Point of View

Purpose: To assist you in experiencing that we live in a culture in which the male point of view predominates.

1. Role Reversal

    Directions: With any of the following items— magazine article, advertising, school textbooks, movie or television scenarios, song lyrics, romance story:

    a. Reverse the pronouns by actually crossing out the words *she, he, him, her* and write the opposite above the space.
    b. Re-read the entire piece again with the pronouns reversed as you have penciled them in.
    c. What are the direct and indirect messages about women (and men)?

    Another version of this exercise is to change the pronouns to all of one gender, that is, change the characters to be all males or all females. Then re-read the piece and see what messages you get.

2. Martian Exercise

    Directions:

    a. Pretend that you are a Martian. Really get into being one.
    b. Observe the Earth beings for an entire day. Observe *everything* about them.
    c. Record your observations. What are the direct and indirect messages about beings on Earth depending on whether they are female or male? What other conclusions can you draw based on your observations?

men who, not having had the life experiences that women have had, are generally unaware that women's experiences are different from their own. Furthermore, they are generally not interested in learning about these differences.

The description of the Female point of view is much briefer than that of the Male point of view, because the Female view is only beginning to be recognized. In fact, it is easier to describe what the Female point of view is *not*—it is not what males have defined as the female point of view. For example, the women's section in newspapers represents the Male view of what women are interested in. Try the following experiential exercise to experience other ways in which culture exists from a Male point of view.

Women, for the most part, have accepted the Male point of view. In the previous analogy, they are the women who fail to recognize that they live in a Male-dominated culture, or they may have some awareness of it but have decided they can "live with it." Furthermore, they may be women who blame themselves for being women or who rationalize that culture is and should be based on a Male point of view. Most women accept the Male point of view and see and evaluate themselves accordingly. In other words, women become what they think men want them to be. (This is another description of what the Female point of view is *not*). As women no longer accept men's definition of themselves and begin to experience their own reality, the Female point of view begins to

It is often argued that it is useless to change social institutions until the mentality of the individual has changed, and the argument has too often been a convenient justification for the indefinite postponement of necessary changes. But have we, in fact, done what lay in our power to change the individual human unit, while we tried to change society? Did we carry on the two tasks together as we should have done, so that they intermingled and supported each other?

Léon Blum

emerge. As this process takes place, women gain increasing awareness of the external limitations placed on their development as full human beings by the patriarchal society.

Masculine and Feminine on Three Levels

The concept of Male and Female points of view has important implications for the psychologies of women and men on many levels: in terms of living in a society based on a Male point of view with Male values; in terms of relationships with others, especially relationships between women and men; and in terms of how women and men relate internally within themselves. Male and Female points of view are not merely different sets of human attributes or characteristics—they have different values and different underlying motivational structures. Since Male traits, values, and motivational structure are more apparent in the current patriarchal context, Female traits, values and motivational structure remain submerged and devalued. Many sources of tension are thus created between the two points of view on societal, interpersonal, and intrapsychic (internal) levels.

In the following excerpt from *The Pursuit of Loneliness* (1970), Philip Slater discusses the differences between the two motivational structures and the difficulty of making a transition between the two because of their inherent incompatibility. Although he was not referring to feminism, this is a precise description of the differences between the Male and Female points of view. In feminist terms the old culture is based on Male point of view (patriarchy), Male values, and Male motivational structure; and the new culture, the Female point of view (matriarchy), Female values, and Female motivational structure. As Slater points out:

There are an almost infinite number of polarities by means of which one can differentiate between the two cultures. The old culture, when forced to choose, tends to give preference to property rights over personal rights, technological requirements over human needs, competition over cooperation, violence over sexuality, concentration over distribution, the producer over the consumer, means over ends, secrecy over openness, social forms over personal expression, striving over gratification, Oedipal love over communal love, and so on. The new counterculture tends to reverse all of these priorities.

Now it is important to recognize that these differences cannot be resolved by some sort of compromise or "golden mean" position. Every cultural system is a dynamic whole, resting on processes that must be accelerative to be self-sustaining. Change must therefore affect the motivational roots of a society or it is not change at all. An attempt to introduce some isolated element into such a system produces cultural redefinition and absorption of the novel element if the culture is strong, and deculturation if it is susceptible. As Margaret Mead points out, to introduce cloth garments into a grass- or bark-clad population, without simultaneously introducing closets, soap, sewing, and furniture, merely transforms a neat and attractive tribe into a dirty and slovenly one.

Cloth is part of a complex cultural pattern that includes storing, cleaning, mending, and protecting—just as the automobile is part of a system that includes fueling, maintenance, and repair. A fish with the lungs of a land mammal still will not survive out of water.

Imagine, for example, that we are cooperation purists attempting to remove the invidious element from a foot race. We decide, first of all, that we will award no prize to the winner, or else prizes to everyone. This, we discover, brings no reduction in competitiveness. Spectators and participants alike are still preoccupied with who won and how fast he ran relative to someone else now or in the past. We then decide to eliminate even *announcing* the winner. To our dismay we discover that our efforts have generated some new cultural forms: the runners have taken to wearing more conspicuous identifying clothing—bright-colored trunks or shirts, or names emblazoned in iridescent letters—and underground printed programs have appeared with names, physical descriptions, and other information facilitating this identification. In despair we decide to have the runners run one at a time and we keep no time records. But now we find that the sale of stopwatches has become a booming enterprise, that the underground printed programs have expanded to include voluminous statistics on past time records of participants, and that private "timing services," comparable to the rating services of the television industry, have grown up to provide definitive and instantaneous results for spectators willing to pay a nominal sum (thus does artificial deprivation facilitate enterprise).

At this point we are obliged to eliminate the start and finish lines—an innovation which arouses angry protest from both spectators and participants, who have evinced only mild grumbling over our previous efforts. "What kind of a race can it be if people begin and end wherever they like? Who will be interested in it?" To mollify their complaints and combat dwindling attendance, we reintroduce the practice of having everyone run at the same time. Before long we ob-

serve that the runners have evolved the practice of all starting to run at about the same time (although we disallow beginning at the same place), and that all of the races are being run on the circular track. The races get longer and longer, and the underground printed programs now record statistics on how many laps were run by a given runner in a given race. All races have now become longevity contests, and one goes to them equipped with a picnic basket. The newer fields, in fact, do not have bleachers, but only tables at which drinks are served, with scattered observation windows through which the curious look from time to time and report to their tables the latest news on which runners are still going. Time passes, as we are increasingly subjected to newspaper attacks concerning the corrupt state into which our efforts have fallen. With great trepidation, and in the face of enormous opposition from the ideologically apathetic masses, we inaugurate a cultural revolution and make further drastic alterations in racing rules. Runners begin and end at a signal, but there is no track, merely an open field. A runner must change direction every thirty seconds, and if he runs parallel with another runner for more than fifteen seconds he is disqualified. At first attendance falls off badly, but after a time spectators become interested in how many runners can survive a thirty-minute race without being eliminated for a breach of these rules. Soon specific groups become so skilled at not running parallel that none of them are ever disqualified. In the meantime they begin to run a little more slowly and to elaborate intricate patterns of synchronizing their direction changes. The more gifted groups become virtuosi at moving parallel until the last split second and then diverging. The thirty-second rule becomes unnecessary as direction changes are voluntarily frequent, but the fifteen-second rule becomes a five-second one. The motions of the runners become more and more elegant, and a vast outpouring of books and articles descends from and upon the university (ever a dirty bird) to establish definitive distinctions between the race and the dance.

The first half of this parable is a reasonably accurate representation of what most liberal reform amounts to: opportunities for the existing system to flex its muscles and exercise its self-maintaining capabilities. Poverty programs put very little money into the hands of the poor because middle-class hands are so much more gifted at grasping money—they know better where it is, how to apply for it, how to divert it, how to concentrate it. That is what being middle class means, just as race means competition. No matter how much we try to change things it somehow ends as merely a more complex, intricate, bizarre, and interesting version of what existed before. A heavily graduated income tax somehow ends by making the rich richer and the poor poorer. "Highway beautification" somehow turns into rural blight, and so on.

But there is a limit to the amount of change a system can absorb, and the second half of the parable suggests that if we persist in our efforts and finally attack the system at its motivational roots we may indeed be successful. In any case there is no such thing as "compromise": we are either strong enough to lever the train onto a new track or it stays on the old one or it is derailed.

Thus it becomes important to discern the core motivational logic behind the old and the new cultures. Knowing this would make rational change possible—would unlock the door that leads most directly from the old to the new.* For a prolonged, unplanned collision will nullify both cultures, like bright pigments combining into gray. The transition must be as deft as possible if we are to minimize the destructive chaos that inevitably accompanies significant cultural transformations.

The differences Slater describes on a societal level also exist at the interpersonal and intra-psychic levels. In this book we will deal with all three levels, since they are mutually interdependent. In fact, for effective change to occur at any level, it must occur on all three. Since the societal and interpersonal are more easily observed than the intrapsychic, the following psychosynthesis exercise (Feminine/Masculine: Yin/Yang) is intended to help you experience both points of view at the intrapsychic level.

As Slater points out, a significant characteristic of the two points of view is that they are mutually exclusive. He suggests that the difference in motivational structure between the two is comparable to the difference between running a race against others and dancing with them—one cannot do both at the same time. Furthermore, whether there can be a compromise between the Male and Female points of view at any level remains to be seen.†

Regardless of the possibility of a compromise in the future, at present the apparent mutual exclusivity of these two viewpoints makes it especially difficult for women to exist in a culture based on Male values and motivational structure. The result is a feeling of "craziness" from trying to operate simultaneously within

*This of course makes the assumption that some kind of drastic change is either desirable or inevitable. I do not believe our society can long continue on its old premises without destroying itself and everything else. Nor do I believe it can contain or resist the gathering forces of change without committing suicide in the process.

†Several lines of neurophysiological evidence suggest an actual biological basis for the separation of what may be interpreted as the "Male" and "Female" functions of the brain. Arthur Koestler (1967) has theorized that the split between reason and emotion (corresponding to the Male and Female, respectively) has its basis in the neuroanatomy of the human brain. Based on evolutionary development, there is insufficient coordination between the *archicortex*—the phylogenetically older, more primitive structure of the brain having to do with affect—and the *neocortex*, a relatively recent development involved in the more intellectual functions. Based on the lack of integration between these structures, Koestler speculates as to the impending "genosuicidal" extinction of the human species and possible evolutionary re-development in order to correct for this "constructional error" in the human species.

Another area of research indicates a separation of the intuitive, holistic "feminine" functions and the analytic, logical "masculine" functions in the brain in terms of left-

Feminine/Masculine: Yin/Yang

Purpose: To experience the Female and Male points of view (the feminine and masculine) in ourselves; to reclaim, own, and value both parts and attempt to integrate them; to see how these two parts manifest themselves in our lives presently.

Directions:

1. Without identifying with either the masculine or feminine, list the essential qualities of both Male and Female points of view. The following is the beginning of such a list. The group may want to add to the list so that everyone feels clarified as to what these two are and to distinguish them from male and female (since every male and female contain both masculine and feminine).

Male Point of View *(masculine, yang)*	**Female Point of View** *(feminine, yin)*
The creative, arousing, generating, phallic element. The begetter.	The receptive, yielding containing, gestating element. The bearer.
Sun, light, penetration.	Earth, darkness, womb.
Active, aggressive, assertive, initiating and moving toward a conscious goal.	Passive, waiting, letting nature take its course, in tune with the repeating cycles of nature.
Conscious knowledge, discrimination, meaning, law, order. Directness, to the point.	Dark instinctive earth wisdom, not consciously thought out. Indirect, serpentine.
Understanding, meaning, essence.	Experience, being, existence.
Objective, Head-centered, Linear, Invulnerable, Penetrating, Definite, Analytical	Subjective, Heart-centered, Round, Vulnerable, Yielding, Mysterious, Intuitive

2. Close your eyes and relax (you may either sit comfortably in a chair or lie down).
3. Imagine a blank screen in front of you. Have someone slowly read the list of items for feminine and allow these words to evoke the feminine.
4. After the list is read, let an image appear on the screen. Don't try to censor or change it; take whatever appears.
5. Interact with the image as follows:
   (a) Talk to it by saying "hello" and have it say "hello" back. You may wish to speak out loud if you are doing the exercise with one other person.
   (b) What are your feelings toward the image?

Get in touch with them and note them to yourself (or out loud if there is only one other person present).
   (c) What do you want or need from it? Get in touch with this and note it.
   (d) Become the image. As you become it, look back and see yourself standing there.
   (e) What does it feel like to be this image?
   (f) Find out what it wants and needs.
   (g) Now become you again.
6. Open your eyes and, without disturbing your mood, write a description of your experience.
7. As soon as you have finished writing, close your eyes again.
8. Imagine a blank screen in front of you. Have someone slowly read the list of items for the masculine and allow these words to evoke the masculine.
9. Let an image appear on the screen [Repeat steps 4 through 6].
10. As soon as you have finished writing, close your eyes again.
11. Imagine a blank screen. Let the images for both the feminine and masculine appear on the screen. Watch them. See how they interact. Let them talk with each other.
12. Come into the situation yourself, talk with them and try to improve the relationship between them.
13. Imagine a mountain in the background that the three of you are going to climb. Go to the base of the mountain and begin the ascent, observing how all three go up the mountain.
14. When you get to the top, look around at the setting and each other. Feel the sunshine; smell the air.
15. Look up at the sun and see a beam of sunshine come from it and end at a spot on the ground in front of you. Down the sunbeam comes a wise old person. Ask this person anything any of you would like to know. Perhaps problems have come up among the three of you that the wise old person may be able to offer comments or advice about.
16. When you have finished talking with the wise old person, thank her/him, say goodbye, and let her/him return up the sunbeam.
17. Rest for a few moments and then open your eyes. Write a description of what happened.

What happened in this exercise? What did you learn? What did you experience? How do these images manifest themselves in your present life? Share your experiences with the group.

mutually exclusive, conflicting realities. This experience is similar to the response evoked by Escher's drawings (one of which is pictured on the next page) which depict mutually exclusive realities based on different points of view.

Let's look at a specific example of this conflict. In a patriarchy males are valued since they personify the basic cultural values, and such a culture would not and does not value women, Female values, and Female motivational structure. Valuing women is incompatible with many of the rules and assumptions of patriarchy upon which our daily lives are based. Therefore, for women to value other women or themselves is to be on the wrong track or simply crazy!

Women who operate from a Female point of view are particularly affected by this conflict since they are more acutely aware of the difference in realities. Women have generally depended on men for their frame of reference. Since men's reality is different from women's, the result is that women can experience a kind of "meta-craziness"—feeling crazy about feeling crazy—since there is no apparent cause (at least from the Male point of view) for feeling crazy.

This analysis of women's "craziness" is part of the newly emerging Female psychology, coming from a cultural feminist interpretation of the psychology of women. Nowhere can it be found in the empirical literature or theoretical formulations of traditional female psychology. Likewise, the analysis of this newly emerging Female psychology on all three levels—societal, interpersonal, and intrapsychic—could not have occurred within the limitations of traditional female psychology but rather springs from a cultural feminist framework.

Academic Feminists' Redefinition of Female Psychology

At this point it might be useful to the instructor (and interesting to the student) to examine the ways in which academic feminists are influencing the concepts of Female psychology. Just as the Male point of view infuses the whole culture, it pervades the social sciences and psychology as well.* Traditional psychology has thus far studied female psychology from the Male point of view, with the attendant distortions of women's true (Female) psychology. Feminism is invaluable in the academic study of

---

right hemispherical specializations (Orstein, 1972). Furthermore, it has been theorized that such specialization may be the basis for conscious and unconscious processes as conceptualized by Freud (Galen, 1974). Carl Jung, who at least began in the Freudian tradition, explicitly formulated Masculine and Feminine principles similar to those described in this book, with complementary components (anima and animus, respectively) suppressed. Cultural feminists would contend that such suppression of complementary components results from society's prescription of sex roles, which prevents each person from becoming fully human and thus forces suppression of the other component within each individual. Furthermore, Eastern philosophies describe the Yin/Yang principle as a basic law of nature. The nearly universal occurrence of the dichotomous split into Male and Female in psychological functioning may have its basis in neurophysiology and anatomy of the brain. This not only suggests that Female and Male points of view are an inevitable fact of human existence but also supports the notion that it occurs on three levels, as well as pointing to the difficulty of integrating the two.

*In fact, sexism has been shown to pervade all phases of research in these areas: in the choice of problem to be investigated (Millman, 1971); in test construction (Johannsson and Harmon, 1972; Milton, 1959; Munley, Fretz, and Mills, 1972); in selection of subjects (Carson, 1971;Schultz, 1969; Schwabaker, 1972), and in the overgeneralization of findings from males to all people (Dan and Beekman, 1972; Bowen, 1973). In addition, the Rosenthal effect (1966) has clearly demonstrated and no doubt affects the outcome of sex-role research because of widely held beliefs about the nature of men and women (see the Weisstein and the Maccoby and Jacklin articles in this book for such myths that have no empirical support). Sexism has also influenced the formulation of concepts and theories (Bart, 1971; Broverman et al, 1972; Chesler, 1972; Weisstein, 1968).

Relativity by M. C. Escher. Reprinted by permission of the Escher Foundation—Haags Gemeentemuseum—The Hague.

women since it can recognize both Female and Male realities and can observe the existence of both. Academic feminists are seeking to re-define the psychology of women by separating the effects of women living in a patriarchy from women's true psychology, making Female psychology more compatible with the concept of a human psychology, not split into Male and Female.

The following are some preliminary principles which seem to distinguish the style and content of academic feminists' work:

1. Interdisciplinary nature of the study of women. It is not possible to understand the whole psychology of women separate from biological and cross-cultural perspectives, or from the social, historical, economic, and political context as well as the art and literature produced by women. The current trend in education is toward interdisciplinary studies, and women are discovering from their own experiences the value and necessity of this position.

2. Integration of thinking and feeling; development of intuition. Many feminists view as unnatural the separation of thinking and feeling, either between the two sexes or within each sex. Intuition (which lies somewhere between thinking and feeling) has been an ascribed attribute of women and, rather curiously, has been negatively regarded by men in favor of the more rational, objective thought processes. Academic feminists wish to redefine psychology by giving feelings and intuition an equal status with thinking for both women and men.

3. Explicit concern with values. In theory, social science is value free; in practice, it never is. The idea that social science should be value free may be seen as a reflection of the ideal male sex role—to be cool, disinvolved, detached, and objective. Feminist academicians question these values and note that they perpetuate sexist views in psychology. Women seem to be more sensitive to the issue of values in social science and, without abandoning scientific goals, are more candid about having values that guide them in their work.

4. Value of cooperation and interdependency. One of the rediscovered strengths of women that has been given positive valuation is cooperation. It has been viewed by traditional psychology as compliance, conformity, or dependence and has been negatively evaluated. Academic feminists question the value of the individualistic, striving, competitive, aggressive style of achievement for either sex. The style of achievement in which feminists would like to work is based on cooperation, mutual respect, interdependence. Women are seeking to redefine the style of achievement in feminist terms, though at present this is difficult within the current motivational structure and reward system.

5. Sensitivity to other points of view. Just as the field of psychology has been biased from a Male point of view, it has similarly been biased from the point of view of white, middle-class, and heterosexual values. The psychology of women cuts across all of these categories of race, class, and sexual preference. All of these additional points of view need to be included in Female psychology if academic feminists are to avoid the errors that traditional theorists have made in excluding any other experience of reality.

Although there are class differences among women depending on race and class (and this must be taken into account in the final analysis of the psychology of women), there is also a bond of the universal female condition that cuts

from Kathe Kollwitz

What would happen if one woman told the truth about her life?
  The world would split open.

Muriel Rukeyser

---

across class and racial lines. Since male aggressiveness (in all groups) tends to lead to competition, domination, and mutual hostility among and within class and racial groups, it seems likely that further changes among the relationships of these various groups will probably come about through changes in women. The psychology and study of women, then, seems most exciting and momentous not only in terms of the present but the future as well.

6. Style of teaching. The new Female psychology involves women discovering their true selves and unlearning the traditional female point of view. They must learn to rely on their own experiences, not on traditional psychology, to guide them toward a Female psychology. For that reason, neither this book nor any other can define Female psychology—it must be discovered through women's own experiences. It seems that the success of psychology of women courses, much like the success of consciousness raising groups within the women's movement, has depended on women discovering their true selves by telling "the truth" about their experiences. As women become emotionally engaged in the course, they experience growth and personal development, in addition to simply absorbing and incorporating intellectual course content. It seems that in the classroom, a balance must always be maintained between allowing the space for basic "truths" to be discovered and experienced (since this is also the psychology of women) and providing intellectual course material.

Organization of Contents

The presentation of the psychology of women from a feminist point of view will be reflected in both the content and style of this book. In terms of content, many of the articles included are written by feminists. In keeping with the interdisciplinary nature of women's studies and in grounding the psychology of women in biological and social conditions, biological and cultural perspectives of psychological differences are presented. The psychology of women in terms of sex differences is then examined, with some critical analysis of what such psychological sex differences might mean and how they may be viewed from a political standpoint. Oppression of the self is discussed as an alternative explanation of the psychology of women. This chapter shows how oppression becomes internalized and then maintained in daily interactions. Some guidelines for equality, as well as a discussion of the many factors that may inhibit equality, are considered.

Ethnic diversity of the Female experience is included as a separate section, since it seems most appropriate to do so under present conditions. Ideally, however, various ethnic, racial, and class points of view would be present throughout (some other articles included are presented from more than a white, middle-class point of view).

Women and their sexuality is another area where much more feminist academic work is needed. Several of the articles included were written several years ago by women involved in the women's movement. Certain basic truths are still the same and the insights of these articles are still valuable, but it is noteworthy that no development has taken place since then. The discussion of the psychology of women in terms of psychotherapeutic theory and practice provides insights into the nature of femininity and psychological oppression as it is manifested in hysteria, masochism, and depression. The final section provides some ideas about the future of the psychology of women (and men).

An attempt has been made to create a flexible text for the psychology of women course. The instructor may wish to cover the topics in this book in a different order from that presented, and certain sections may even be dropped or additional readings substituted.

At the end of each chapter is a list of books and articles for further reading on the subject presented. Those works specifically endorsed by the author are preceded by an asterisk.

Since Female psychology depends not only on the intellectual content of the study of women, but on experiencing oneself as a woman, experiential exercises are provided in each chapter to facilitate this process. (A few of these have been included in this introduction. (See complete list on p. iv.) The instructor may use these exercises as she (or he) wishes, either as large class, small group, or outside activities, or students may simply pursue the exercises on their own. Experiential exercises are set off from the rest of the book by the use of a special border. Some of the exercises may produce different results at different times and may therefore be worth repeating from time to time.

Students may also benefit from keeping a journal, even if it is not a course assignment. In this journal they may record the results of

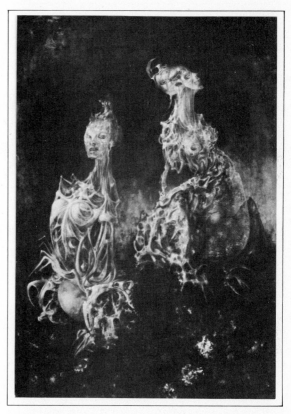

Emerging Ones by Leonor Fini. Reprinted by permission of the artist.

the experiential exercises, insights, realizations, awarenesses, thoughts, and feelings about the content of the book or about the entire course. The journal could serve as a medium for observing connections among intrapsychic, interpersonal, and cultural aspects of being Female (and Male). Students might also record dreams, appropriate quotations from others, reactions to their own internal processes, and conversations with other people. This journal can, by the end of the course, provide a vivid account of each student's change and growth throughout the year. It can reflect one's successes and peaks as well as one's difficulties and struggles.

Biological Perspectives

In this chapter we will begin to look at the biological basis for the psychological "nature" of women and review some of the evidence of the relative biological superiority/inferiority of the sexes. The extent to which biological differences between men and women determine psychological differences will be further explored in the chapter on cultural variations.

The "biological argument" takes several forms and is often used to justify women's inferior social status. Whether the argument is based on greater physical strength, larger body size, hormones, or external genitals, it ultimately asserts that men are naturally the dominant sex, based on "innate" sex differences.

Although science seeks to be value free, in practice it almost never is. While research on biological sex differences does not directly attempt to establish the superiority of one sex, since we live in a patriarchy and most scientists are men, research would tend to favor male superiority. If we lived in a matriarchy in which the difference in power between the sexes were reversed, most scientists would be women, and sex-difference research might be based on the underlying assumption of female superiority.

As Estelle Ramey suggests in the first article, there already exists evidence that might be emphasized in this situation. For example, all embryos begin their development as females. It is only the addition of hormones at a certain stage in the embryo's development that produces a male. Therefore nature's basic plan is that of a female. Further, evidence shows that the percentage of male fetuses that are aborted or stillborn is higher than that of female fetuses. Also, the male population in general is more susceptible to disease and has a higher mortality rate than the female population. Males grow and physically mature more slowly than females, have more learning and behavior dis-

orders, and a higher percentage of males are mentally defective (see Singer, Westphal, and Niswander, 1968). Ashley Montagu (1968) presents the interesting theory—and there is abundant evidence in support of it—that women are "naturally" superior.

Another topic we will examine here is whether one's gender identity—sex identification— is determined by one's biological identity. Estelle Ramey concludes, as do several of the investigators whose work she reports, that one is psychologically sexually neutral at birth, and that the sex identification an individual attains can be considered the result of both biological and social factors.

Data from both hermaphrodites and transsexuals support the theory that biological factors play less of a role in causing one to think of oneself as "male" or "female" than social factors. In the case of hermaphrodites (individuals whose reproductive structures at birth are neither clearly male nor female) the final adult sex identification is usually the same as the sex the individual was assigned at birth. That is, if a hermaphrodite is assigned at birth to be male, he usually grows up to have a "normal" masculine gender identity; if assigned to be female, she matures with a "normal" feminine gender identity. (Usually in such cases the external genitals are surgically made consistent with the assigned sex, and appropriate hormones are given at puberty.)

Transsexuals are individuals who are biologically clearly either male or female, but who identify with the other sex. Obviously, gender identity in these cases does not depend on biological realities. Transsexuals feel themselves to be inside the wrong type of body: their bodies do not "fit" who they are. When they become adults, many transsexuals decide to undertake hormone treatment and surgery, and eventually legally become members of the other sex. [For an interesting autobiographical account of a biological male who became a female consistent with (her) gender identity, see Jan Morris' *Conundrum* (1974).]

Transvestites and homosexuals also behave as the other sex but are biologically either male or female. Transvestites are individuals who dress like members of the other sex. Homosexuals and lesbians behave sexually like the other sex; that is, they prefer sexual partners of the same sex.

One major criticism of many researchers in this field (although it does not apply to the authors included here) is that they do not question certain basic assumptions and norms. The first of these is the very existence of sex-role norms as concepts and institutions, and second is the norm of heterosexuality. Both assumptions should be seriously considered in view of arguments made by the women's liberation and gay liberation movements.

Some feminists advocate that sex roles be totally eliminated since they are based on an artificial division of all human attributes (Firestone, 1970). If sex roles were eliminated, obviously problems of gender identity and inappropriate sex-role behavior would disappear. For example, hermaphrodites would be regarded as simply being physically unusual, transsexuals would be biologically categorized as *male* (or female) and psychologically what is now labeled *feminine* (or *masculine),* transvestites would dress in whatever clothes they wished (as would everyone), and homosexuals and lesbians would follow their sexual preferences (as would everyone). In other words, in place of hermaphrodites, transsexuals, transvestites, homosexuals, and lesbians there would simply be people, behavior, and sexuality.

One more interesting point is that based on physical characteristics alone, the two sexes overlap. If each individual were to receive a score on each primary (chromosomes, gonads, hormones, internal and accessory organs, external genitals) and secondary sex characteristic (physical size, body weight, muscle/fat ratio, amount of body hair), there would be a basic profile of scores on a continuum. If we plotted the characteristics of all individuals on a graph, we would see not two completely separate curves (categories) but instead the two would overlap a great deal. In other words, there is a great deal of variation within each sex and much overlapping between the two. In fact, simply on the basis of hormonal sex alone, one researcher (Williams, 1956) has suggested the possibility of categorizing men and women into nine categories based on three levels of each of the two hormones estrogen and androgen. Yet for the purposes of socialization, people are sharply divided into two distinct categories—male or female—and somewhat rigid sex roles are prescribed for each.

If there were no biological differences—and therefore no social or psychological differences—there would then be no basis for women's place in society as it now exists. Continuance of patriarchy depends on the belief that there are distinct biological (and therefore social and psychological) differences between women and men, despite evidence to the contrary. One of the more blatant biological arguments often used to justify patriarchy is that women are subject to "raging hormones." Such presumed disordering and disrupting effects on female behavior have been used to justify and maintain women's secondary status. [Incidentally, it has been shown that men also have cycles (Ramey, 1972).] However, were we living in a matriarchy in which females were assumed to be superior, we might emphasize

With woman rests the future of the world.

the existence of synchronized cycles in women (McClintock, 1971) as evidence for natural (superior) communication—and therefore justify female domination on the basis of men's inability to participate in this primitive communication system.

The second and final article in this chapter is a critical review of the research on the premenstrual syndrome. In summarizing the literature, Mary Parlee concludes that there are several problems with the hypothesis of a premenstrual syndrome. Further, universal cultural and religious taboos surrounding women's menstruation have been shown to affect the severity of menstrual distress (Paige, 1973). This indicates that cultural components are no doubt involved in the menstrual syndrome.

In general, science is value-laden. It selects certain topics for investigation and emphasizes certain results. Therefore, we must be cautious in accepting even scientific evidence as fact. Perhaps it might be worthwhile to pose several questions instead:

1. To what extent are the biological differences we observe today the result of the cumulative effects of thousands of years of patriarchy? For example, in a culture in which males are dominant, if food is scarce, males are given what little there is, and females are left to starve (Watkins, 1971). Attitudes and practices such as these could have a long-term effect on the development of females.

2. How is the occurrence of matriarchy or patriarchy related to biological differences? Are either of these the direct result of biological realities? Upon which biological foundations would matriarchy most likely be based?

3. What norms or value systems does one use to determine the relative inferiority/superiority of the sexes? For example, it is often asserted that a male's higher level of testosterone leads

Guardian of the Phoenixes by Leonor Fini. Reprinted by permission.

to greater aggressiveness (in humans) and therefore to physical superiority. However, one could just as easily assume female superiority. If the female hormone balance were regarded as the norm, men could go to "hormone rebalancing centers" where they could artificially bring their "raging hormones" more under control into the normal (female) range.

4. Given whatever biological differences may exist and taking them into account, how do you think we could begin to achieve an egalitarian society—one in which both sexes have equal status and worth?

Estelle R. Ramey

Sex Hormones and Executive Ability

"She thinks like a man."

Translated, this means: This female has somehow overcome her gender disability and seems to be able to use her neocortex* in rational decision making. Therefore, she may be designated as an honorary *Homo sapiens*.

"That's just like a woman."

Translated, this means: This female manifests the characteristic cerebral defects of the XX chromosomal behavior determinants. She is largely restricted to decision making via limbic system†–hypothalamic‡ neuronal pathways with little evidence of neocortical influences. Therefore, she is more accurately classified as *Homo emotionalis* or *Homo gonadis*.

Freud put it more succinctly when he said, "Anatomy is Destiny." This middle-class Victorian genius identified the female reproductive system as the inexorable vise that kept women emotionally unstable, submissive, passive, masochistic, and devoid of creative intellectual potential.[1,2] Freud's distorted view of female psychology was the most palatable of all his theories to the society of his day, because it appeared to give a physiological basis to the prevailing theological and cultural attitudes toward women. Seventy years later, it remains his most comforting pronouncement to many scientists, physicians, politicians, professors, university presidents, business executives, husbands, and lovers. It has, sadly, been embraced also by the very women who are bound by its chains. And it is a lie.

The female as a defective male has been bred into the bone of our culture.[4] Even those who reject the penis-envy construct that is central to Freud's hollow woman find solace in his a priori opinions about the psychological inferiority of the female. Others, like Erikson, place her identity in the "inner space" of her uterus and her human destiny in her tail rather than in her head. And now, a bastardized endocrinology is being invoked to keep her in her place. A physician made headlines recently by calling attention to the "raging hormonal imbalances" every month which make women unfit for jobs of top responsibility. Those who have lunar cycles thus become lunatics every month and cannot be trusted with the important affairs of the world. They can be relegated to only the trivial tasks of rearing the next generation.

The basic assumption that illumines all this mutually destructive nonsense is that males are biologically superior to females in every aspect of human function except the bearing and nurturing of the young. As a corollary, these special female attributes are assigned conflicting and dubious social values. On the one hand, motherhood is a noble state (if there is a man in the house), and on the other hand, any slob can have a baby and momism (see *Portnoy's Complaint*) is the curse of mankind.

The biology and psychology of the human

---

neocortex: the outer layer (cortex) of the brain, the newest portion in an evolutionary sense. It is developed to the highest degree in the human brain.

†*limbic system:* the old cortex (paleocortex) of the brain; it governs functions and behavior of humans that are shared by lower species.

‡*hypothalmic:* referring to a structure of a part of the brain (diencephalon) important in the regulation of vital functions, including sex; it releases neurohumoral substances from nerve cells that in turn regulate the pituitary gland.

I'M WORKING HARD AT THINKING LIKE A MAN

Ellen Levine, from *All She Needs . . .* , Quadrangle, 1973.

female has been fixed like a bug in amber to conform to unproved and unprovable theories about the effect of female hormones on behavior. The Devil can quote endocrinology as well as scripture. When the pseudoscientific maunderings are cleared away, however, there is an interesting body of information about hormones and human behavior. It is known that, like the male, the female is exposed to a continually changing internal milieu of hormones.[5] It is also known that, like the male, the behavioral response of the female to these hormonal changes is in large part conditioned by her adaptive needs, experience, and cultural strictures. Animal studies even in the area of measurable metabolic responses can be extrapolated to humans only with the greatest caution. Species differences are often profound, and at the level of psychosexual responses, the extraordinary preeminence of the human neocortex makes a hash of the simplistic conclusions of many ethologists and anthropologists. Playful ducks and male-bonded baboons do not seem to be accurate prognosticators of the lack of "territorial imperative" evidenced by the South Vietnamese, for example.

Frank Beach, in a review of the neural and chemical regulation of behavior,[6] expressed this cogently: "It is reasonable to assume that the evolutionary increase in experiential control of sexual activities is an outcome of the increasing importance of the neocortex as a mediating agent. Evolutionary shifts in the physiological control of sexuality are most evident in our own species. Here one sees the greatest degree of diversity. Exclusive homosexuality, complete reversal of sex roles, sexual responsiveness to immature individuals, to animals or even to inanimate objects, total sublimation of the sex drive—these and many other uniquely human manifestations are possible only because the experiential component plays a dominant role in shaping human sexual behavior. The primary importance of individual experience is in turn due to reduced reliance upon gonadal hormones and increased intervention of the cerebral cortex."

It is the human cerebral cortex, not the endocrine system, that confers the almost infinite variability characteristic of human responses to environmental stimuli. It is also the neocortex that can distort and manipulate information to create myths and stereotypes. The stereotype of woman as the second sex, biologically fragile, unstable, intuitive, and irrational, and the stereotype of man as the primary sex, biologically strong, stable, hard-headed, and rational belies the empirical and experimental data available. For the little it is worth as commentary on Adam's Rib, it is the female sex that is primal.[7,14] The early embryo is female until the fifth or sixth week of fetal life. A testicular inductor substance must be generated at this point to suppress the growth of ovaries. No ovarian inductor is required for female differentiation, because all mammalian embryos of either genetic sex have the innate capacity for femaleness. Eve, and not Adam, appears to

The basilar region of the female head is also smaller, the occipital more elongated, and the frontal developed in a minor degree, the organs of the perceptive faculties being commonly larger than those of the reflective powers. The female cerebral fibre is slender and long rather than thick. Lastly, and in particular, the organs of philoprogenitiveness, of attachment, love of approbation, circumspection, secretiveness, ideality, and benevolence, are for the most part proportionately larger in the female; while in the male those of amativeness, combativeness, destructiveness, constructiveness, self-esteem, and firmness predominate.

G. Spurzheim, M.D., *Phrenology*, 1826

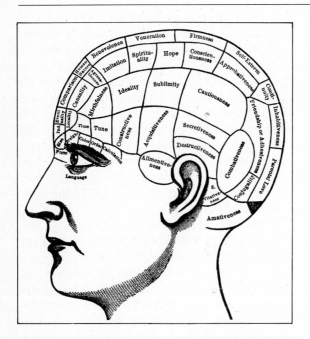

Phrenology, a 19th century precursor of psychology, drew conclusions about the psychological nature of women based on "scientific" measurements. Today, on the basis of more advanced and sophisticated techniques, the same "discoveries" are made about the psychology of women. In both cases, the scientific conclusions reached reflect social norms and are used to justify women's position in society.

From *Phrenology: A Practical Guide to Your Head* by Orson Squire Fowler and Lorenzo Niles Fowler. Design by J. Steinberg and U. McGeehan. Copyright © 1969 by Chelsea House Publishers, a Division of Chelsea House Educational Communications, Inc. By permission.

have been the primeval human that God had in mind.

In passing, it might be added that it was Eve, not Adam, who showed the earliest signs of scientific curiosity and aggressive questioning of the status quo.

The endocrinology of the fetus does indeed determine the maleness or femaleness of the child in terms of the development of primary and secondary sex characteristics. The crucial question, however, is: What are the innate and immutable behavioral characteristics of the adult that can be attributed to the hormonal differences in the two sexes? The extensive work of Money and Hampson and others at Johns Hopkins reveals the complexity of gender identity and behavior in human beings.[8,9] Hampson and colleagues conclude that:

In the human, psychologic sexuality is not differentiated when the child is born. Rather, psychologic sex becomes differentiated during the course of many experiences of growing up, including those experiences dictated by his or her own bodily equipment. Thus, in the place of the theory of an innate, constitutional psychologic bisexuality such as that proposed by Freud—a concept already questioned on theoretical grounds by Rado,[10] among others—we must substitute a concept of psychologic sexual neutrality in humans at birth. Such psychosexual neutrality permits the development and perpetuation of diverse patterns of psychosexual orientation and functioning in accordance with the life experiences each individual may encounter and transact.

"Man differs from woman in size, bodily strength, hairiness, etc. as well as in mind."

Darwin

These scientists go on to detail their evidence for this statement from the study of patients born with profound gonadal abnormalities, such as human hermaphroditism. The term "hermaphrodite" is used here to describe not only patients with completely ambiguous external genital development but also a variety of individuals with a contradiction between the predominant external genital appearance and the sex chromatin pattern, gonads, hormones, or internal accessory structures. These biologic states are compared with the gender roles assumed by the individuals so afflicted. The investigators define "gender role" as:

> all those things that a person says or does to disclose himself or herself as having the status of boy or man, girl or woman respectively. It includes but is not restricted to sexuality in the sense of eroticism. Gender role is appraised in relation to the following: general mannerisms, deportment and demeanor; play preferences and recreational interests; spontaneous topics of talk in unprompted conversation and casual comment; content of dreams, daydreams and fantasies; replies to oblique inquiries and projective tests; evidence of erotic practice and finally, the person's own replies to direct inquiry.

These surely constitute our social interpretation of what is a man and what is a woman. In humans, the attempts to correlate these "typically" male or female gender roles with the basic physiology of gonadal development have not been notably successful. On the contrary, the data available on humans with gonadal or sex hormonal anomalies suggest that psychosexual orientation cannot be attributed to two separate predetermined instincts[11-13]—one male and one female.

The terms "innate" or "constitutional" or genetically determined antecedents and comcount for behavioral differences that emerge in the two sexes with such seeming spontaneity and predictability that it seems inconceivable that they might result from experience and learning. Yet the effect of chromosomal influence on adult psychosexual behavior is of itself of not specific significance if the gonadal development is defective. In humans, there are many examples of a discrepancy between the chromosomal configuration and the fetal differentiation of ovaries or testes with the concomitant secretion of the appropriate sex hormones. Money concludes: "No matter what the genetically determined antecedents and components of gender-identity differentiation, the post conceptual and postnatal determinants can, in test cases, completely override them. The syndrome of androgen insensitivity* (testicular feminization) in genetic males provides a graphic example of the extent to which the

---

*androgen-insensitivity syndrome: a congenital condition in girls or women who appear externally to be sexually normal females. Body cells cannot respond to the male sex hormone, which is produced in the testes in normal amounts for a

genetics of sex chromosomes can be overridden in gender-identify formation."[11]

Such an individual is usually identified as a girl at birth and often is diagnosed as a genetic male only at puberty when she fails to menstruate and the physician belatedly discovers the male genetic identity. Such a human grows and develops with a self-image identical with that of the society description of a woman. She-he typically marries a male and gives loving mothering to adopted children, since, of course, she-he is infertile. This individual does have some estrogen secretion from the testes, but the establishment of physical characteristics does not require this contribution of the female hormones.

As described by Ehrhardt and associates, in a condition known as Turner's Syndrome the child has an inborn genetic anomaly and has virtually no evidence of either male or female gonadal development. These individuals lack a second X chromosome totally or in part. They may thus be considered as XO. Nevertheless, they grow up unequivocally female in their gender roles and gender identity despite the absence of estrogens. They look like girls at birth and are reared as girls. They remain feminine in their self-image. Ehrhardt concludes: "Any attempt to attribute gender identity in human beings simply to either genetic, hormonal or social-environmental factors must result in oversimplification and misconception."

---

male, but instead responds to the small amount of female sex hormone (estrogen) produced in normal male testes. Before birth, the fetus begins to develop as a male internally but this process is not completed; it does, however, prevent internal female development, even though external genitalia appear normal for a female. Breasts develop normally but there is no menstruation and no fertility.

The question, however, that has occasioned the most soul searching and rage has been the role of testicular hormones or other androgens in conditioning behavior that is supposed to be typically male. The data from animal experiments and human fetal anomalies suggest strongly that fetal androgens influence the functional anatomy of the developing brain.[14-21] In rats, it has been shown that when radioactive male hormone is given either directly to the fetus or to the pregnant mother, the hormone is taken up in several organs including the hypothalamus. If the exogenous hormone is given within a critical period of fetal development, the hypothalamic nuclei that regulate cyclic release of pituitary gonadotropic hormones in the female appear to become masculinized. As a consequence, cyclic release of the gonadal hormones is not manifest in the female adult. The sexual behavior of such animals tends also to be somewhat disoriented, even though the external genitalia appear normal.

The extrapolation of these data to primates is not so easy. For example, in humans or even in the rhesus monkey, fetal exposure to androgens does not seem to interfere with the subsequent gonadal cyclicity of the adult female.[22] There are, however, some behavioral aspects of in utero exposure to excess androgens that have been reported in primates.

Recently, Ehrhardt and coworkers[13] described a series of 15 girls who had been masculinized in utero as a result of cogenital virilizing adrenal hyperplasia.* When the condition was recognized at birth, the necessary surgical and hormonal corrections were instituted early, and

---

*hyperplasia: more than the normal number of cells in an organ, resulting in an increase in size of the organ.

the child was more or less restored to her genetic sex in terms of secondary sex characteristics and internal hormonal milieu. Nevertheless, these girls are reported to be more interested in so-called boys' sports and toys. They were more frequently identified as tomboys by their parents. Significantly, there was no evidence of a higher degree of lesbianism or aberrant sexual behavior than in control groups of women. They are described, however, as being more "career-oriented." An examination of the data reveals that of the fifteen girls studied, seven were thought at birth to be hypospadiac† males with cryptorchidism.‡ Presumably, the proud parents had been initially told they had a son. The sex assignment was changed within the first seven months in this group, but it is a matter of some importance that in these, as in all the other cases, the sex ambiguity was a problem for the parents from the time of birth. The effect of parental concern about the true sex identity of these children, despite medical corrective procedures, must inevitably have conditioned their behavior toward the child and the child's response. For example, the data reveal that in at least half the matched control group of normal children, sex education was derived in large part from communication in the home, while the adrenogenital children reported as the chief source of information the hospital input. These children were examined frequently with regard to their genitalia and could not have escaped the knowledge that they

were not entirely the little girls that their parents might have wished for.

How is one to interpret the finding of a greater career interest in these young girls as compared with normal adolescent girls in this society? For Freudians it is tempting to postulate that fetal masculinization of the brain induces the development of a special neuronal pathway for "career orientation." It is more likely, however, that a girl who sees herself as less desirable as a woman than her peer group may seek other avenues of ego development. Of far greater interest in elucidating the ultimate effect of male hormones on behavior and achievement is the fact that most women with those "masculinized" brains do not, in fact, go on to typically male roles in society, but retain tenaciously the conception of themselves as women.[9] They play out the normal female roles, male brains notwithstanding. This is especially significant in light of the recent reports that excess androgens, progestins, or progesterone in fetal blood seem to be correlated with higher performance on all aspects of intelligence testing.[25,26] Males or females with the adrenogenital syndrome who were exposed to high androgen titers in utero have been shown to have a statistically significant elevation in verbal and spatial intelligence scores as compared with the normal population. Androgens after birth seem to have no such effect on performance.[25] The results of prenatal treatment with progesterone in girls who were not masculinized also point to a higher than normal IQ as a consequence of the effect of these female hormones.[26] The academic achievement of these individuals was also higher than that of the controls.

These observations are important in their implications as regards the extremes of human intelligence, both high and low. They shed little

---

†*hypospadiac:* referring to a congenital defect in the placement of the urinary opening on the penis; in severe cases, the opening is in the female position and the penis has an open gutter rather than a covered urinary tract.
‡*cryptorchidism:* a condition in which one or both testicles are undescended.

BECAUSE OF THEIR
RAGING HORMONAL
IMBALANCES,
WOMAN MAKE BETTER
MOTHERS THAN MEN

Ellen Levine, from *All She Needs . . .* , Quadrangle, 1973.

light, however, on the phenomenon of females or males with very high IQs who never achieve much of note in this society. For women, in particular, this is of the greatest importance, because for them the possession of an extraordinary intellectual capacity has seldom been the high road to achievement. Lewis Terman's study of exceptionally gifted boys and girls gives ample proof that whatever the genesis of a first-class brain, hormonal, genetic, or environmental, a female sex-identity seems to make creative use of that brain unlikely. The smartest women in Terman's series got married and vegetated pretty much like the not-so-smart ones in the general community. They did not become Supreme Court Justices.

Human behavior thus transcends natural endowment in an extraordinary way. An early study by Hampson and associates[9] demonstrates this forcibly. He followed the psychological development of thirty-one patients with virilization due to the adrenogenital syndrome* and was led to the conclusion that "in the human, psychosexuality is not differentiated when the child is born." The group they studied was, in fact, far more traumatized by sexual

*androgenital syndrome: a condition resulting from malfunction of the adrenal cortices in males or females (caused by a defect in genetically transmitted enzymes). Females born with this syndrome have ambiguous genitalia, and if they survive, undergo severe virilization. This syndrome is not usually recognized in males at birth, but if they survive, they prematurely develop sexually during the early years.

ambiguity than Ehrhardt's patients. Hampson's female patients had lived for years with the external sex characteristics of the male: the enlarged clitoris, male hair distribution, male body configuration, and so on. They were all brought up as females, however, by parents who were told that their children were genetically female. In this series, the contradiction between sex rearing, sex appearance, and hormonal milieu was not corrected until the girls had achieved a precocious puberty. Despite this prolonged exposure to excess androgens both in utero and postnatal life, Hampson reports: "Of the 31 patients whose sex hormones and secondary sexual body development contradict their assigned sex and rearing, only 5 became ambivalent with respect to their gender role."

The remarkable fact of this study is that the other twenty-six patients in this group "established a gender role consistent with their assigned sex and rearing, despite the embarrassment and difficulties of living with contradictory secondary sexual development." Obviously, these women must have had enormous problems in dealing with their paradoxical appearance. It is also of interest that another group of 11 females with the same degree of virilization who were reared as boys went on to establish a typical masculine gender role and orientation.[9] They were thus eligible for leadership and decision-making roles. Hampson's studies reveal that reassignment attempts after the first year of life, whatever the hormonal

If you had an investment in a bank, you wouldn't want the president of your bank making a loan under these raging hormonal influences at that particular period. Suppose we had a President in the White House, a menopausal woman President, who had to make the decision of the Bay of Pigs, which was, of course, a bad one, or the Russian contretemps with Cuba at that time?

Dr. Edgar F. Berman, Baltimore physician

---

or genetic status, lead to a permanently poor psychosexual adjustment.

It should be noted that because of the lateness of surgical correction of the external genitalia of the girls in Hampson's study, many exhibited an enlarged clitoris during the most significant years of their psychological development. Yet these patients tested out later as typical American women in virtually all aspects of behavior, life goals, and self-image. What price penis envy?

None of this is to deny that sex hormones play a role in conditioning aspects of behavior in humans as well as in other animals. The problem is to separate the imprinting due primarily to hormonal mediation and the imprinting due to early experience. Even in lower animals, where parent-offspring responses are considered to be innate, unlearned behavior, it has been shown that appropriate responses of the young to members of their own or other species is not preestablished.[23] Lorenz[24] points out that a greyleg gosling that has lived a few days with its parents will never react to a human as a transfer object. But goslings that are taken from their parents immediately after hatching and are cared for by humans will never follow a mother goose. They follow only humans. It is the ability to respond to the early environment that is innate, not some mysterious foreordained attachment of offspring to parent.

There is good evidence that androgens tend to increase libido in both men and women. Both women and men secrete the entire spectrum of steroid hormones. Males have higher androgens and lower estrogens than females, but both require androgens for normal sex drive. The adrenal cortex of the female secretes androgens, and the adrenal cortex of the female tends to be larger than in the male. Are the androgens that are normally secreted in her adrenal cortex male hormones? Since their secretion in excess produces "masculinization," the answer is a qualified yes. But since this masculinization is readily overridden by her psyche, the answer is a qualified no. When Fisher[27] injected sodium testosterone into the midlateral preoptic region of the hypothalamus of male or female rats, he could elicit male sexual behavior. That suggests that testosterone is a powerful male hormone that overrides previous brain imprinting. Well, yes and no. When Fisher injected testosterone into the medial preoptic region of the brains of males or females, he elicited typical maternal behavior. That is a rather odd effect for the most potent male hormone. Its possible meaning for human behavior is discussed in a perceptive paper by Money.[27] There may be a potential dimorphism in the human brain that is activated or suppressed by sex hormones or there may not. Adult human behavior and achievement cannot, however, be explained on this basis.

John Money and his coworkers have worked with the problem of gender identity and hormonal milieu for many years. In one of his

*It is as if in the evolution of sex a particle one day broke away from
an X-chromosome, and thereafter in relation to X-chromosomes could
produce only an incomplete female—the creature we now call the male!
It is to this original chromosomal deficiency that all the various
troubles to which the male falls heir can be traced.*

Ashley Montagu, *The Natural Superiority of Women*

---

papers[11] Money describes a boy and girl; both
were genetically male, and both were subjected
to the same fetal-hormonal environment. They
were somatically similar in infancy and childhood but were subjected to very different
parent-child and environmental experiences.
With appropriate medical management the girl
became a woman, and the boy a man. Money
concludes:

> "This remarkable antithesis in psychosexual
> (sexo-behavioral) differentiation is indicative of
> a general principle: namely, that gender-identity
> differentiation is phyletically programmed in the
> human species to take place largely after birth,
> and also to be dependent to a large degree on
> stimulation from and interaction with, the social
> environment."[11]

Given all these complexities of human development vis-à-vis sex differentiation, it is not
surprising that selection and interpretation of
data can be made to prove any point of view.
For example, Maggie Scarf in *The New York
Times Magazine* (May 7, 1972, p. 30) concludes
that Freud was right, and hormones are indeed
destiny because of the critical role they play
in prenatal life. She quotes many of the excellent animal experiments to support this
thesis and also some of the data on testosterone
levels in homosexual humans. The problems
of extrapolating from animal to human data
has been mentioned above, but it is the interpretation of the human studies that requires
comment. Despite the fact that some of the

investigators quoted (Ehrhardt and Money, for
example) have repeatedly commented on the
postnatal environmental programming of behavior in humans, the emphasis in Scarf's article is almost entirely in the direction of immutable predestination. In the original papers
of Money and Ehrhardt on the effects of androgens and progesterone on IQ, for example, the
data show (and the authors emphasize) that the
elevation in IQ is across the board and does
not differentiate between verbal and mathematical skills. Yet Ehrhardt is quoted in Scarf's
article as suggesting that the data on excess
prenatal hormones might support the difference
in verbal and spatial skills that are said to exist
between females and males. Their data support
just the opposite conclusion.

The data on testosterone levels in homosexuals are also a matter of dispute. Money, in
reviewing the data, concludes: One may fairly
safely interpret today's clinical evidence to
mean that sex-hormone levels of adulthood
have very little to do with the etiology of homosexuality."[22] Certainly the high incidence and
social acceptance of homosexuality in societies
such as Greece and Hitler's Germany would
suggest that this kind of sexual behavior does
not require an abnormal hormonal balance.
Similarly, the administration of male hormones
to either male or female homosexuals may increase libido (as it does in heterosexuals), but
the direction of the sex drive is not altered.

The characterization of testosterone as the
"take charge" hormone is also an engaging no-

The male is a biological accident: the Y (male) gene is an incomplete X (female) gene, that is, has an incomplete set of chromosomes. In other words, the male is an incomplete female, a walking abortion, aborted at the gene stage. To be male is to be deficient, emotionally limited; maleness is a deficiency disease and males are emotional cripples.

Valerie Solanis

tion to many investigators. Aggression and leadership in humans or in subhuman primates have been studied with this bias and the results have been interpreted in many ways. One of the problems rests with the parameter chosen for study—in this case, plasma testosterone levels. Behavior characteristic of aggression is associated with changes in virtually all neuroendocrine systems. Adrenalin and noradrenalin, cortisol, thyroxine, glucagon, and the pituitary hormones, to mention a few, are altered by a variety of environmental factors that are the cues for aggression and "leadership." Gonadal hormones are additional variables in this complex system. The animal studies themselves demonstrate that testosterone levels in individual primates can be associated with pecking order only under certain conditions. The same monkey with high testosterone levels when he is at the top of the hierarchy can be shown to have low testosterone levels in a different social order. In other words, it looks as if the high testosterone levels do not determine ranking order or leadership, but the behavioral coordinates of being top monkey may change testosterone secretion along with many other physiological parameters.

Stress itself may significantly lower testosterone secretion as the adrenal corticoid secretion is elevated. Does this mean that those men who daily do battle with the competitive environment of the high reaches of business and government have chronic undersecretion of testosterone? If this were the case, then mea-

surement of testosterone levels in our great leaders might lead one to conclude that low testosterone levels are the stigmata of leadership. This obviously makes nonsense of the complexity of human motivation and achievement. Conversely, when apparently normal women show the symptoms of high intelligence, aggressive competitiveness, and a capacity for leadership, does this reflect an unusual pre- or postnatal exposure to high androgens? There is nothing to support such a concept. At a guess, the measurement of 17 ketosteroid excretion in such women is highly unlikely to reflect this simple association. Most such women are able to conceive and bear children, and this is the proof irrefutable of the predominance of female hormones.

The relatively greater aggressive behavior reported for male rats[17] can be interpreted simplistically to mean that women are naturally gentler creatures than men. Was Joan of Arc a woman when she rallied the French against the English and raised the siege of Orleans? Was Kenau Hasselaer a woman when she and her band of women fighters held out against 30,000 Spaniards in the 16th century? Are the Viet Cong women who lead companies in battle, really women? Or the women guerrillas of the IRA, or the women fighters of the anti-Nazi underground, or the women who fought with their Israeli men in 1948? We have no data on their androgen levels, but it is probably that these women secreted more estrogens than androgens. Human aggressivity is whatever a so-

Woman is "defective and accidental . . . a male gone awry . . . the
result of some weakness in the [father's] generative power."

St. Thomas Aquinas (13th Cent.)

Woman/Man: Word Associations and Images

Purpose: To explore some of our attitudes and feelings about women and men.

Directions: Read the following questions and write your responses. Be aware of your experiences as you do the exercises.

1. What are your associations to the word *woman*?
2. What do you like about women? What do you dislike about them?
3. What do you expect of women? What do you expect to get from and give to them?
4. What do you actually give to and get from women?
5. What do you want and need from women?
6. What fears do you have about women? [May be repeated, substituting other emotions for "fears."]
7. What other feelings do you have about women?

Repeat the above questions substituting *man* and *men* for *woman* and *women*.

What were your experiences? What did you learn about yourself? About your relationships with women and men?

---

would use animal and human data to suggest that subtle but important contributions to behavior are made by the sex hormones, there can be no definitive proof to the contrary. Males are different biologically from females. They are also different sociologically. Men become United States Presidents and women do not. But then women do become premieres of Israel and India and Ceylon. Endocrinologists have nothing to contribute to the explanation of these national differences.

In the modern world of extended life spans, where females outlive males by about seven years, an argument could be made that biology is on the side of the sex with the blood vessels that stay patent longer. But old men run the world. If testosterone levels are criteria for leadership, it is therefore no surprise that things are in such a bad way.

There can be no better conclusion to this rather pointless argument than to quote from the brochure that advertises a book published in the fall of 1972. The authors are the great authorities in this field, John Money and Anke Ehrhardt, and the book is called *Man and Woman, Boy and Girl*. These experienced investigators are described as having reached the following conclusion: "In general, the authors' research suggests that there are as great differences between individual men and individual women as there are between members of opposite sexes. They conclude, therefore, that the social roles of men and women should be related to individual needs, rather than to membership in a sexual caste."

To the question: Which is the best hormonal basis for leadership and achievement, man or woman? The meaningful answer can only be: Which man and which woman?

ciety says it is and leadership is in the minds of those who are led.

In all this miasma of claims and counter claims about the role of sex hormones in determining human behavior, there are no data to show that males as a group are more intelligent than females, or that there is any area of psychic response unique to either sex. For those who

Mary Brown Parlee

The Premenstrual Syndrome

Psychological studies of the premenstrual syndrome are discussed in four methodological categories: (a) studies reporting a positive correlation between specific behavioral acts and phase of the menstrual cycle; (b) those using retrospective questionnaires concerning symptom and mood changes; (c) studies involving day-to-day (self-) ratings of various behaviors, symptoms, and moods; and (d) thematic analyses of verbal material gathered in an unstructured situation throughout the cycle. The scientific status of the hypothesis of a premenstrual syndrome is considered, together with more general topics—in particular the question of control groups, the choice of a base line for describing changes in behavior and the difficulties involved in physiological explanations of psychological phenomena. Brief consideration is given to publication practices of psychological journals as they affect the kind of scientific information available on behavioral changes associated with the menstrual cycle.

Considerable biological evidence is now available to support Seward's (1934) observation that "Rhythm is a universal characteristic of natural phenomena [p. 153]." In human beings, circadian rhythms have been reported to exist in a variety of processes including cell division, adrenal cortical activity, and glucose tolerance, as well as in sleeping and waking, pain tolerance, and susceptibility to asthmatic attacks (Luce, 1970). Cyclic changes with periods of greater than 24 hours are also well established (Richter, 1968). One rhythm that has been studied in detail is the menstrual cycle of the human female.

Southam and Gonzaga (1965) extensively reviewed studies of physiological changes occurring throughout the menstrual cycle. While a full specification of the neuroendocrine mechanisms controlling menstruation depends upon the development of of appropriate techniques (e.g., Neill, Johansson, Datta, & Knobil, 1967), these mechanisms are understood in rough outline and will no doubt eventually provide explanations for the various bodily changes observed. Of more interest to the psychologist, however, are the numerous reports of behavioral changes associated with the menstrual cycle. Such studies would seem to be important for at least two reasons, the first being that psychological changes accompanying the menstrual cycle are phenomenologically significant to many women and are thus an appropriate topic for psychological research. The second reason, however, lies not in their contribution to the body of scientific knowledge, but in the fact that they raise methodological and theoretical issues which have implications for the study of other psychological phenomena as well. The purpose of the present article is to consider the literature on those psychological changes associated with the menstrual cycle which have been called the premenstrual syndrome(s) (Dalton, 1964; Moos, 1968) or premenstrual tension (Frank, 1931; Rees, 1953a). Another major topic in the study of behavioral changes accompanying the menstrual cycle—fluctuations in sexual behavior—will not be included here; this literature has been reviewed by Kane, Lipton, and Ewing (1969).

They will ask thee also concerning the courses of women; answer, They are a pollution; therefore separate yourselves from women in their courses, and go not near them, until they be cleansed.

Koran

The Premenstrual Syndrome: Four Types of Studies

Correlational Data

The syndrome first described by Frank (1931) as a premenstrual feeling of "indescribable tension," irritability, and "a desire to find relief by foolish and ill-considered actions [p. 1054]" has been studied in a variety of ways, one of which is simply to look for correlations between the phase of the menstrual cycle and statistical data on the occurrence of specific, well-defined behaviors. Correlations have been reported, for example, between the premenstrual or menstrual phase of the cycle and commission of violent crimes (Cooke, 1945; Dalton, 1961; Morton, Additon, Addison, Hunt, & Sullivan, 1953; Ribeiro, 1962), death from accident or suicide (MacKinnon and MacKinnon, 1956; Mandell and Mandell 1967), accidents (Dalton, 1960b), admission to a hospital with acute psychiatric illness (Dalton, 1959; Janowsky, Gorney, Castelnuovo-Tedesco, and Stone, 1969), taking a child to a medical clinic (Dalton, 1966), and loss of control of aircraft (Whitehead, 1934). Such data were summarized by Dalton (1964) who has been a major contributor in this area of research.

In statistical studies, the behavioral act—when considered as one term of the correlation—is readily identifiable; it either occurs (and often becomes part of a public record) or it does not. It is usually the case that the other term of the correlation—the phase of the menstrual cycle—is also objectively determined by the investigators either by questioning the women shortly after the behavioral event (Dalton) or by basal body temperature (Altman, Knowles, and Bull, 1941; Ivey & Bardwick, 1968), vaginal smears (Benedek & Rubenstein, 1939a, 1939b), or data from autopsies (MacKinnon & MacKinnon, 1956; Ribeiro, 1962). Some frequently cited correlational studies, however, are methodologically less than sound. Morton et al. (1953), for example, reported that 62% of violent crimes committed by women took place during the premenstrual week, 19% during midcycle, and 17% during menstruation, but they did not define the length in days of these latter two phases. Nor did they say precisely how they determined the phase of the cycle at the time of the crime. "Review of the inmates' records . . . [Morton et al., 1953, p. 1191]" suggested that onset of menstruation may be part of a prisoner's record, but in a table presenting the data themselves (p. 1189), 8 of the 58 women are listed in a "cannot remember" category which does not support the notion that a record was kept for all prisoners.

In spite of possible weaknesses in method, however, the Morton et al. (1953) study does not have as many flaws as some others of this correlational type. Cooke (1945), for example, whose study is cited by Morton et al., Greene and Dalton (1953), MacKinnon and MacKinnon (1956), and Coppen and Kessel (1963) in support

School of Humans by Ann Leda Shapiro. Reprinted by permission.

of a relationship between menstrual cycle phase and commission of violent crime, included exactly one sentence on the topic. It reads:

> That this ["the hypersensitization of the nervous system which occurs during the premenstrual phase of the cycle"] is a very potent factor in the psychology of women is evidenced by the report of a Parisian prefect of police: that 84% of all the crimes of violence committed by women are perpetrated during the premenstrual and early menstrual phases of the cycle [Cooke, 1945, p. 459].

Although several relatively recent papers refer to an association between the menstrual cycle and crashes by women airplane pilots (Dalton, 1960b; Moos, 1968, 1969b; Pierson & Lockhart, 1963), the only reference offered is to Whitehead (1934) or to Dalton (1964) who cited only Whitehead. Whitehead's article consisted of reports of three airplane crashes over a period of eight months in which the women pilots were said to be menstruating at the crash.

While methodologically sound in terms of specifying both the behavioral event and the phase of the menstrual cycle, even Dalton's much-cited work does not always establish the correlations between menstrual cycle and behavior as clearly as might be desirable. As Sherman (1971) and Sommer (1972) pointed out, Dalton (1960a) reported a decrease in 27% of her schoolgirl subjects' test performance during the premenstrual phase of the cycle, but did

See the Sky   Is Her Belly   and It Moves

A woman is bathing   water
* breaks   on her shore*
the edge of   world is her boundary
and what you know of the ocean
*   is   her   bath*
A woman is bathing   our rounded sky
*   is her belly   I am in her   we*
never wake to more than her body   when
she moves her leg the sky cracks open to
* stars*
The tide moves inward the lip of land is our
* exit*

*   All people   who have ever*
*   live in a woman*
*   who is bathing   I have for a while*
lifted my arms   I have eaten her fruit
you   combed your hair in her   Space
*   breaks on her   shore*
Every   28   days   her suns and moons
fall.

*   Allie Light*

not provide a statistical test of the significance of this decrease, and references to her work fail to note that a premenstrual increase in 17% of the schoolgirls' performance was also found, while 56% of the girls showed no change.

Reynolds (1966) has documented the persistence of at least one "myth" in psychology (that there are sex differences in color discrimination) and suggests that such myths tend to

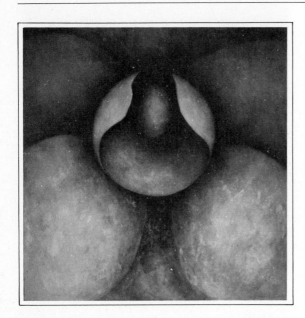

Untitled by Miriam Brumer. Reprinted by permission.

be perpetuated when authors cite studies from other reviews or repeat the original author's conclusions without checking the data as they appeared in the original report. Given the variable quality of the basic data in correlational studies of the menstrual cycle, it would seem necessary for contemporary authors to be familiar with the methodological adequacy of the original studies before citing them as factual evidence—a caution which does not, of course, apply alone to studies of the premenstrual syndrome.

Putting aside questions of method, however, and assuming that many of the correlations between phase of the cycle and behavior are true as reported, how should the studies be interpreted and to whom can the results be generalized? Most of the investigators in this

area do not explicitly point to a causal relationship between hormonal changes and the occurrence of various behaviors, but they do use phrases which tend strongly to imply that the hormones are the cause of the behaviors. Rarely is it suggested that it is the behavioral events that affect the menstrual cycle, although gynecology texts state that psychological stress may delay menstruation (Lloyd, 1962, p. 473) or precipitate its onset (Benson, 1964, p. 573); Balint (1937) offered an elaborate psychodynamic interpretation of how this might occur.[1] It is also important to note in interpreting correlational studies that data from particular groups cannot provide a basis for a generalization about all women or about any woman selected at random unless it is assumed that women are equally likely to be or become a member of the groups in which the data were collected. From knowing, for example, that crimes are likely to *have been committed* during certain phases of the cycle, it is not possible to assume the truth of the inverse—that women in these phases of the cycle are more likely to commit crimes; this latter is true only for women who will at some time commit crimes. It is possible that studies of different populations of women might reveal correlations between the premenstrual and menstrual phases of the cycle and more positively valued acts

---

[1]The suggestion that behavior can indeed influence levels of reproductive hormones is supported by the recent finding that testosterone levels in primates are affected by manipulations of the social setting (Rose, Gordon, & Berstein, 1972). McClintock's (1971) study demonstrated in another context the effects of social factors on the timing of menstruation in human beings: Menstrual cycles of females living together in a college dormitory were found to become more closely synchronized over the course of an academic year. While it is clear that many of the correlational data mentioned

such as, for example, bursts of creative energy. Without further correlational studies of more diverse populations, and in the absence of additional information as to which subgroup a woman belongs (e.g., potential criminal, potential artist), it is difficult to predict anything about an individual's behavior from the fact that she is in the premenstrual or menstrual phase of the cycle.

Retrospective Questionnaires

A second type of data which is available to support the hypothesis of a premenstrual syndrome is based upon questionnaires asking women to report (their memory of) their experience of various "symptoms" and moods at different phases of the cycle. The symptoms and moods listed on the questionnaires are usually negative ones, and the subjects are questioned primarily about their experiences just before and during menstruation. Moos (1968, 1969b) has described the development of a comprehensive questionnaire of this sort; Coppen and Kessel (1963) and Sutherland and Stewart (1965) provided earlier examples. None of these questionnaires can be considered well-developed psychometric instruments, since no reliability data or external validity data (with the exception of Coppen & Kessel) are offered to support their usefulness. The Moos Menstrual Distress Questionnaire, which is relatively recent and frequently used (Moos, Kopell, Melges, Yalom, Lunde, Clayton, & Ham-

burg, 1969; Silbergeld, Brast, & Nobel, 1971), suffers from additional methodological inadequacies. In his articles describing the development of the questionnaire, Moos failed to report the fact that of the 839 subjects in the normative sample, 420 were taking oral contraceptives, 81 were pregnant, and 40 did not answer the questions about their use of oral contraceptives. These data are presented elsewhere (Moos, 1969a) along with the fact that significant differences in responses on the questionnaire were found between those women who were taking the pill and those who were not. In light of the suggestion that clinical studies and retrospective questionnaires have been the primary source of evidence that there are behavioral changes associated with the menstrual cycle (Moos et al., 1969, p. 37), the methodological soundness of individual questionnaires must be carefully considered in evaluating the relevance of such data to the hypothesis of a premenstrual syndrome.

Daily Self-Reports or Observations

Another approach to the study of the premenstrual syndrome also involves women's self-ratings of various symptoms and moods, but is different from the simple questionnaire in that the ratings are made regularly throughout the cycle and do not depend upon a retrospective account. McCance, Luff, and Widdowson (1937) collected self-reports from 167 women (over 4–6 menstrual cycles) of their experience of ten carefully defined symptoms and moods. The data, consisting of records kept over 780 cycles, showed discrepancies between the daily-record technique and the results of a preliminary questionnaire on menstrual cycle symptons given before the study was made, discrepancies "so frequent that they throw considerable

---

above cannot be interpreted in this way, a consideration of possible psychological effects on the menstrual cycle as well as the reverse would be useful in assessing the extent and limitations of the statistical evidence cited in support of a hormone-"related" (with connotations of "caused") premenstrual syndrome of "neurotic and antisocial reactions [Janowsky et al., 1969, p. 189]."

doubt upon the value of any work on this subject based upon history or a questionnaire [pp. 579–580]." McCance et al. reported that the majority of individual records showed no evidence of rhythm during the period of the study. When records were combined, however, cyclic changes were observed, related to the menstrual cycle, in fatigue, abdominal and—to a lesser extent—back pain, headache, breast changes, sexual feelings and intercourse, tendency to cry, irritability, and effort required for intellectual work. Rees (1953a) also collected day-to-day records of reports of symptoms from thirty women (over a period of "some months") and found overall patterns of premenstrual increases in tension, irritability, depression, emotional liability, anxiety, swelling of extremities and breasts, fatigue, and headaches. In a similar study with more subjects, Rees (1953b) noted that 56% of the women did not report any significant "premenstrual tension symptoms"; the method section is not sufficiently detailed, however, to determine precisely what data were collected to support this conclusion. The Nowlis (1965) Mood Adjective Check List has been used to study daily changes in self-ratings over the course of the menstrual cycle, with consistent results (Moos et al., 1969; Silbergeld et al., 1971).

Altman et al. (1941) followed ten subjects over a total of fifty-five menstrual cycles, recording variations in physiological events associated with ovulation (basal body tempera-

ture, "bioelectric ovulatory potentials," skin temperature) and psychological changes (sleep, physical and mental activity, mood, worry, tension, irritability, and fatigue). The psychological changes were assessed by the experimenter during daily interviews which apparently were conducted after the physiological measures had been taken (see pp. 200–201). Their psychological data showed the presence at ovulation of elation and activity, and the presence during the premenstrual phase of depression, tension, and activity. Individual women showed considerable variability in patterns of behavior. Abramson and Torghele (1961) reported changes in daily recordings of weight, temperature, and "psychosomatic symptomatology" (ratings of abdominal pain, irritability, bloating, depression, etc.). As was the case in Rees' reports, information which might have been gained in a longitudinal study is lost since the authors did not report the ratings for individual symptoms at different points throughout the cycle; instead, they presented bar graphs of the total number of times individual signs and symptoms were reported. The most frequently indicated symptom was headache, which was mentioned ninety times (the study involved thirty-four subjects who reported in all approximately 3,000 times on the presence or absence of headache). In the absence of a fuller presentation of the data and of control groups of nonmenstruating individuals, it is unclear whether such "psychosomatic symptomatol-

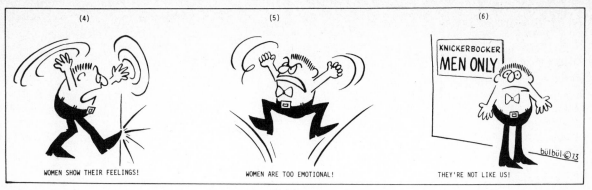

(4) WOMEN SHOW THEIR FEELINGS!

(5) WOMEN ARE TOO EMOTIONAL!

(6) KNICKERBOCKER MEN ONLY — THEY'RE NOT LIKE US!

By Bülbül, from *I'm Not for Women's Lib . . . But*, Arachne Publishing, Mountain View, Ca.

ogy" can be taken as evidence of a premenstrual syndrome. Dalton's (1964) use of control groups, unusual in studies of this kind, raises an interesting question about the interpretation of any fluctuations in day-to-day records of activities; she reported that punishment records in prisons and schools failed to show 28-day cycles for males but did show them for female prisoners and schoolgirls, both those who were menstruating *and those who had not yet begun to menstruate* (pp. 81–82).

Thematic Analysis of Unstructured Verbal Material

A final approach to the study of the premenstrual syndrome is one which also records data on a day-to-day basis, but this technique, first put in quantitative form by Gottschalk, Kaplan, Gleser, and Winget (1962), differs from those above in that the subjects are not rated or asked to rate themselves on specific symptoms, but rather are requested to talk into a tape recorder for five minutes "about any life experience they cared to [p. 301]." Gottschalk and his coworkers developed a standardized method of scoring which allowed them to analyze the verbal material gathered in this way in terms of the levels of "hostility directed inwards," "hostility directed outwards," and "anxiety" manifested by the subject. Studying five women over a period of 30–60 days, they found that "four of the five women showed statistically significant rhythmical changes in the magni-

tude of at least one of the affects . . . during the sexual cycle [test and significance level not specified]. The changes in these affects were not similar among the women [Gottschalk et al., 1962, pp. 307–308]." It should be noted that they did not say that these rhythmic changes are linked to the phase of the menstrual cycle.

Using the Gottschalk technique with a larger sample of subjects (twenty-six women, data collected four times over the course of two cycles), Ivey and Bardwick (1968) confirmed the Gottschalk et al. (1962) report of transient "decreased in levels of anxiety and hostility [p. 307]," finding that the ovulatory anxiety level was significantly lower than that during the premenstrual phase. Paige (1971) also gathered unstructured verbal material from an even larger sample at four different times throughout the cycle, and used Gottschalk's scoring procedure to assess anxiety, hostility, and negative affect (the latter being the sum of the anxiety and hostility scales). In the thirty-eight subjects not taking oral contraceptives, she found that all three scores varied significantly throughout the cycle. These cyclic variations were not present in the group of fifty-two subjects who were taking oral contraceptives containing both estrogens and progestin.

While not relying upon a standardized scoring technique such as Gottschalk, Benedek and Rubenstein's (1939a, 1939b) classic study also involved day-by-day analysis of women's speech in a relatively unstructured setting. In

from **Menses: A Seasonal**

I was   as you say
born under the moon
and my belly-lining
plays
a ritual imitation
of that lunar
dissonance.

Pamela Victorine

---

their case, the data consisted of "verbal material" (not verbatim records) collected over the course of psychoanalysis of women diagnosed as neurotic. Studying nine patients over a total of seventy-five cycles, Benedek found that she could predict, solely on the basis of a patient's reports of dreams, the day on which ovulation occurred, a prediction which was corroborated independently by Rubenstein's analysis of vaginal smears. Benedek (1963) noted the difficulty she experienced in formalizing what it was in the records which allowed her to make such precise predictions; the fact that her data are described in terms which are inseparable from her theoretical orientation makes it difficult to specify operationally the procedures by which she was able to infer the phase of the menstrual cycle from the women's reports of their dreams.

Scientific Status of the Premenstrual Syndrome

The four kinds of studies discussed above—correlations between behavioral acts and phases of the menstrual cycle, retrospective questionnaires, daily self-ratings or observations, and thematic analyses of verbal material—represent the sorts of evidence that are cited in support of the hypothesis of the existence of a premenstrual syndrome. Given the variety of types of supporting data, it is not surprising that the terms "premenstrual syndrome" and its asso-

ciated "symptoms" seem to have been used somewhat broadly. Premenstrual syndrome, for example, has been taken to include the "recurrence of [any] symptoms always at the same time in each menstrual cycle [Dalton, 1954, p. 339]" or even "any combination of emotional or *physical* features which occur cyclically in a female before menstruation [Sutherland & Stewart, 1965, p. 1182, italics added]." Moos (1969b) found from a review of the literature that over 150 different symptoms have been associated with the menstrual cycle, including such various ones as elation, depression, back pain, sexual desire, and a great many other more or less specific behaviors and inferred psychological states. Sutherland and Stewart suggested that "the only common denominator to all the symptoms described is that, when they occur, they do so at regular [28-day?] intervals [p. 1183]." Given the broad and not always consistent use of "premenstrual syndrome" and its constituent "symptoms," estimates of the prevalence of "menstrual symptoms" or of the premenstrual syndrome are useless for most purposes (Ferguson & Vermillion, 1957; see Moos, 1968, p. 854, for other references).

In spite of the lack of agreement on the precise nature of the premenstrual syndrome or even its relationship to the phases of the menstrual cycle, a wide variety of physiological factors have been proposed in the past to account for it. Among them are "female sex hormones" (Frank, 1931), estrogen-progesterone imbalance (Morten et al., 1953), altered suparenal cortex activity (MacKinnon & MacKinnon, 1956), water retention caused by high estrogen-progesterone ratio (Green & Dalton, 1953); [see Southam and Gonzaga (1965) for others]. This physiologic explanatory bias dictated some of the early attempts to "cure" the syndrome: Sterilization by X-ray was reported to have been successful for some of Frank's (1931) patients; Green (1954) reported, however, that "not only does hysterectomy fail to cure the premenstrual syndrome, but it may actually initiate it, a fact which we have so far failed to explain [p. 338]." Less drastic measures such as diuretics (Eichner & Waltner, 1955) and hormone therapy (Rees, 1953a) were also reported.

Recently, several investigators have suggested that monoamine oxidase activity might be the means through which estrogens and progesterone affect neural firing and behavior (Grant & Pryse-Davies, 1968; Klaiber, Broverman, Vogel, Kobaytashi, & Moriarty, 1972; Paige, 1971). As in the case of earlier proposals, evidence supporting a hypothetical mechanism involving monoamine oxidase is indirect, and a number of currently untested assumptions about physiological processes are required.[2] On the basis of available data, such an hypothesis seems premature since physiological knowledge is not yet sufficiently detailed to put serious limits on the kinds of physiological processes which might mediate hormone-behavior relationships, and more importantly, psychological studies have not yet clarified the nature and extent of the behavioral changes which are to be explained by the proposed mechanism.

---

[2]The argument is that estrogens and progesterones affect levels of monoamine oxidase which in turn affect catecholamine-mediated neural activity in the brain; this central nervous system activity is, according to the hypothesis, related to psychological states of depression and irritability. Supporting evidence is indirect: (a) endometrial monoamine oxidase fluctuates throughout the human menstrual cycle (Cohen, Belensky, & Chaym, 1965; Southgate, Grant, Pollard, Pryse-Davies, & Sandler, 1968); (b) drugs which inhibit monoamine oxidase activity—and possibly affect other physiologically significant substances as well—transiently relieve psychological depression (Crane, 1970), (c) oral contraceptives affect both endometrial monoamine oxidase levels and psychological depression (method for assessing "depression" not stated; Grant & Pryse-Davies, 1968). Several assumptions are obviously required if these data and others like them are to be interpreted as supporting the hypothesis that naturally occurring fluctuations in estrogen and progesterone levels during the menstrual cycle are responsible—by means of a mechanism involving monoamine oxidase—for clearly established cycles in depression and irritability. Some of these assumptions are (a) that the pharmacologic doses of estrogen and progesterone present in oral contraceptives have similar psychological effects on the physiologic levels of these hormones; (b) that peripheral, systemic measures of monoamine oxidase activity (blood plasma, endometrial monoamine oxidase) reflect central levels; (c) that monoamine oxidase regulates the functional levels of catecholamines in the brain; and (d) that central nervous system activity involving catecholamines as transmitter substances is directly related to psychological states of depression and irritability. Relevant considerations: (a) behavioral effects of drug substances are not always a monotonic function of dosage; (b) one of the basic functions of the blood-brain barrier is to maintain constant levels of some substances in the brain in the presence of fluctuating systemic levels; (c) even if there were direct evidence that monoamine oxidase influences absolute levels of brain catecholamines, it would still be necessary to establish that monoamine oxidase affects direct measures of neural transmission in the same way; and (d) no evidence is available showing the existence of a one-to-one relationship between brain activity of a specified kind and psychological states. As an example of the relationship between the sort of physiological knowledge now available and the psychophysiological assumptions required by the monoamine oxidase—catecholamine hypothesis, compare Assumptions b and c above with the Southgate et al. (1968) report in which they were able to show a correlation between two methods for assessing human endometrial monoamine oxidase activity. In this article they noted that "at present there is insufficient information to decide whether the observed changes

*Until now it has been thought that the level of testosterone in men is
normal simply because they have it. But if you consider how abnormal
their behavior is, then you are led to the hypothesis that almost all men
are suffering from* testosterone *poisoning.*
*Testosterone poisoning is particularly cruel because its sufferers usually
don't know they have it. In fact, when they are most under its sway
they believe that they are at their healthiest and most attractive. They
even give each other medals for exhibiting the most advanced
symptoms of the illness.*

Alan Alda, "What Every Woman Should Know About Men" (*Ms.*, Oct. 1975)

There is clearly a need for a more precise definition of the premenstrual syndrome and for a specification, in terms of the methods used to identify them, of the symptoms of which it is thought to be composed. This definition should be accompanied by a conceptual scheme for relating to each other the data collected by different methods. Is a premenstrual increase in irritability (e.g., found in daily self-ratings) causally related to a premenstrual increase in commission of violent crimes? Is the anxiety found through thematic analysis related to the increased likelihood of a mother's taking her child to a clinic? Questions such as these illustrate the need for an explicit statement of the hypothetical psychological mechanisms relating one kind of data to another. Before such theories can be elaborated and tested, however, it must be shown that data collected by different methods are in fact correlated, since one would expect that any psychological state that is included in a description of the premenstrual syndrome would be measurable by more than one method. There is some evidence that this is not always the case. The premenstrual syndrome as assessed by the Moos (1968, 1969b) Menstrual Distress Questionnaire, for example, includes symptom scales labeled Autonomic Reactions and Concentration (which includes as one item "lowered motor coordination"), but in his own work with Kopell, Lunde, Clayton, and Moos, (1969), Moos reported failure to find fluctuations throughout the menstrual cycle in galvanic skin potential and in reaction time. Pierson and Lockhart (1963) and Zimmerman and Parlee (1973) also reported failure to find changes in reaction time and in galvanic skin potential. McCance et al. (1937) found cyclic variations in subjects' self-ratings of "effort required for intellectual work," but Sommer (1972) could not demonstrate changes in intellectual performance when subjects were tested repeatedly over the course of the menstrual cycle. Using three different measures within a single study—the Moos Menstrual Distress Questionnaire (retrospective questionnaire), the Nowlis Mood Adjective Check List (daily self-report), and the Gottschalk techniques of thematic analysis—Silbergeld et al. (197;) concluded that "the three methods of behavioral assessment produced scores which were, at best, only weakly correlated [p. 411]."

---

are localized to the endometrium or are part of a more generalized cyclical variation in MAO [monoamine oxidase] activity [p. 724]" and that "in recent years it has become increasingly obvious that there are not one but a series of MAOs, each differing in its action towards substrates and inhibitors [p. 725]."

While none of the assumptions required by the monoamine oxidase hypothesis is itself inherently implausible, considerable physiological and psychophysiological research would be needed to establish each of them, research which is not cited by supporters of the monoamine oxidase-catecholamine hypothesis. In view of the considerations bearing on the correctness of each assumption, furthermore, any hypothesis which depends upon the validity of all of them must be regarded as far from established.

Painful menstruation (dysmenorrhea) is usually functional in origin, especially in young women. It often reflects a hidden, resentful attitude toward MENSTRUATION ("the curse"), toward being a woman instead of a man, and toward sex. But sometimes it is caused by hormone imbalance, tumors or infections, mechanical factors or other constitutional disorders. Normal menstruation is not painful.

from *Schifferes' Family Medical Encyclopedia*

Coppen and Kessel (1963) have attempted to make the generalized use of premenstrual syndrome more precise by distinguishing between dysmenorrhea—pain specifically associated with and occurring during menstruation—and the premenstrual syndrome which they define in a more limited way as irritability, depression, nervousness or tension, and anxiety. While it is not clear that all of the symptoms which have previously been studied in conjunction with the menstrual cycle can be placed reliably into one of these two categories (e.g., how would "headache" be classified?), the distinction does have some empirical justification. On the basis of a retrospective questionnaire administered to 500 women, Coppen and Kessel reported that the premenstrual syndrome as they defined it is correlated with neuroticism (Maudsley Personality Inventory), while dysmenorrhea is negatively correlated with age and with parity, and is uncorrelated with neuroticism. Although the authors offered no speculation concerning the causes of either dysmenorrhea or the premenstrual syndrome, their discussion implied that dysmenorrhea has a more direct physiological basis (it occurs during menstruation and is not "a psychosomatic condition or one that calls for psychological treatment, [p. 720]") while "the subjects with premenstrual symptoms had abnormal personality traits [p. 718]" Lennane and Lennane (1973) have also noted that, contrary to a considerable body of medical opinion,

evidence strongly suggests that dysmenorrhea is primarily of physiological rather than psychogenic origin.

Thompson (1950), Shainess (1961), Paige (1971), and others have suggested, on the other hand, that a woman's psychological response to the physiological changes associated with her menstrual cycle may also be shaped or modified by cultural practices which attach values to menstruation and to femininity. In this view, what Coppen and Kessel (1963) call the premenstrual syndrome would be the result of complex psychological processes arising from an interaction between physiological changes and environmental factors specifically related to femininity and sexuality. As such, it would be associated with other aspects of the personality to the extent that these also are related to sexuality, and considerable individual differences might be expected.

Whether a distinction between dysmenorrhea and a more limited and precise definition of the premenstrual syndrome will prove useful for psychological theory construction remains to be seen, but in its present form it represents one attempt to deal with at least some of the various and complex factors which must be considered in dealing with phenomena involving both physiological and psychological processes. Statements which simply assume a direct causal relationship between physiological processes and complex psychological experiences

A menstruous woman is the work of Uhremaun, the devil. A woman during her periodical illness is not to gaze upon the sacred fire, sit in water, behold the sun, or hold conversation with a man.

Zoroaster, Circa 1000 B.C.

and behaviors are abundant in the literature,[3] but they are inadequate as contributions to psychology since they neither specify in at least outline form the nature of the hypothetical mechanism supposed to link physiological and psychological events nor make explicit the underlying beliefs about the conceptually difficult relationship between mind and body (Borst, 1970; Fodor, 1968).

[3] "The personality changes associated with the menstrual cycle occur in spite of individual personality differences and may even be extreme; they are consequences of endocrine and related physical changes . . . [Bardwick, 1971, p. 27]." "We felt assured that the phases of ovarian function were reflected in physic processes [Benedek, 1963, p. 315]." "There was a tendency for the levels of tension measured—specifically, anxiety and hostility inward—to decrease transiently around the time of ovulation. The presumed cause is some hormonal change . . . [Gottschalk et al., 1962, p. 308]." "The menstrual cycle imposes on the human female a rhythmic variability encompassing all aspects of her being, from the biochemical to the psychosocial [Silbergeld et al., 1971, p. 411]." "The theory that the pathological emotional findings are hormonally influenced is widely accepted [Janowsky, Gorney, & Kelley, 1966, p. 243]." Janowsky et al., regard these hormonal influences as having considerable scope, listing the following as

some [sic] of the cyclically recurring phenomena of the premenstrual and menstrual phases . . . depression, irritability, sleep disturbances, lethergy, alcoholic excesses, nymphomania, feelings of unreality, sleep disturbances, epilepsy, vertigo, syncope, paresthesias, nausea, vomiting, constipation, bloating, edema, colicky pain, enuresis, urinary retention, increased capillary fragility, glaucoma, migraine headaches, relapses of meningiomas, schizophrenic reactions and relapses, increased susceptibility to infection, suicide attempts, admission to surgical and medical wards, crime rates, work morbidity, manic reactions, and dermatological diseases [p. 242].

General Issues

Many of the studies of the premenstrual syndrome discussed above involve certain assumptions which, when made explicit, raise some interesting general questions about the description and explanation of behavior. One of these assumptions is that the syndrome (however it may be defined in a particular study) can best be described as a premenstrual or menstrual "increase" in certain symptoms, moods, or behaviors. With some exceptions, the data seem equally consistent with an hypothesis of a mid-cycle syndrome of lowered incidence of crime (Dalton, 1961) and epileptic seizures (Hamburg, 1966), increased self-esteem and elation (Ivey & Bardwick, 1968), and increased sexual desire and sexual activity (Benedek & Rubenstein, 1939a, 1939b; McCance et al., 1937). What is the base line compared with which *changes* in behavior are described as an increase or decrease? If control groups of males are used in studies of cyclic behavior, the question of what to use as a base line for description of behaviors also arises. To take a hypothetical example, if female performance on a digit-symbol substitution task should be found to fluctuate with the menstrual cycle, it would seem incomplete and therefore misleading to say only that females' performance is worse at certain times in the cycle than at others, since it may at all times be better than the average performance of males at this task. One can say,

Oh! Menstruating woman, thou'rt a fiend
From which all nature should be closely screened.

Unknown, Circa 1900

---

of course, that male performance is by definition irrelevant to the study of behavioral changes associated with the menstrual cycle, but it is not irrelevant—though it is not often investigated—to studies of rhythmic changes in human behavior, which may be a more useful concept in a general psychological way.

The question of control groups, then, points to a second assumption which seems to underlie studies of the premenstrual syndrome—that is, the assumption that the menstrual cycle is relevant to the interpretation of a great many cyclic changes in behavior in human females. In view of the evidence of the pervasiveness of cyclic phenomena in human beings (Luce, 1970), control groups would appear to be essential for proper interpretation of data on adult female subjects. Hersey (1931), for example, has reported finding cycles of emotionality in males (determined on the basis of daily observations of behavior and self-reports). These cycles varied from three and one-half to nine weeks in length, but were constant, within ± one week, and predictable for a given individual. Lieber and Sherin (1972) have reported finding lunar cycles in the occurrence of violent crimes—whether committed by males or females. As noted above, Dalton (1964) described 28-day cycles in the behavior of prepubertal schoolgirls, cycles comparable to those found in menstruating females of various ages (though not found in men and boys). Whatever the cause of such rhythmic behaviors in nonmenstruating

individuals, their existence points to the necessity of control groups for interpretation of cyclic phenomena as well as for determining a base line for describing any changes which may be found only in one sex.

A final issue which is raised by the literature on the premenstrual syndrome has to do with some of the conventions governing the publication of psychological research. One of these is the generally accepted practice of not publishing "negative" results. In the menstrual cycle literature, for example, numerous investigators have tested reaction time at various phases of the menstrual cycle and have found no changes (the data were included as part of a report of a larger study in which some other change was found; e.g., Kopell et al., 1969). There is, on the other hand, at least one report of positive findings (Voitsechovsky, 1909) which presumably could be cited in support of a claim that reaction time varies throughout the menstrual cycle. Given the conventions governing the availability of "facts" in psychology, it is difficult to document a claim of "no change" or "no difference." The issue of negative results is, of course, a complex one, involving questions about the sensitivity of the tests used, random sampling errors, and the like. Nevertheless, in a problem area where there may be a general expectation of finding a "result," there would seem to be a danger that the literature will be encumbered with more Type II errors than is desirable simply because a result fre-

from **Stepping Westward**

*If woman is inconstant,
good, I am faithful to
ebb and flow, I fall
in season and now
is a time of ripening.*

Denise Levertov

---

quently sought may occur by chance at least a few times and make its way into print.

Also related to publication practices is another difficulty illustrated by the menstrual cycle literature, one which arises when investigators have data on which a large number of correlations can be computed. What should be the editorial policy regarding publication of such data when only a few of the correlations are significant? In studies of the menstrual cycle, this generally occurs when correlations are computed between each item on a lengthy questionnaire and individual items on other questionnaires or tests. Kopell et al. (1969), for example, found twelve of at least seventy-two correlations (the exact number cannot be determined from their report) to be statistically significant. Levitt and Lubin (1967) found fourteen of seventy-five, and Silbergeld et al. (1971) found thirteen of one hundred and twenty-nine variables to vary significantly during the cycle. In interpreting such data, it seems that either the authors do not attempt to make even ad hoc sense out of the data in terms of a coherent psychological theory (Silbergeld et al., 1971), or else they draw a conclusion which seems more elaborate than is justified by the data. Kopell et al., for example, found that time estimation varied significantly during the menstrual cycle; time estimation and two-flash threshold were found to be positively correlated on three out of four tests; and self-ratings of "concentration" and "social affection" were

negatively correlated with time estimation at each of the four phases of the cycle tested. From these data they posed the "intriguing question" of whether the "subjective changes experienced during the premenstrual period" are "an expression of a distortion of the basic time sense which, in turn, might be part of a very mild, transient, confusional state [p. 186]."

In light of these various methodological and theoretical considerations, then, it seems fair to conclude:

1. Psychological studies of the premenstrual syndrome have not as yet established the existence of a class of behaviors and moods, *measurable in more than one way*, which can be shown in a longitudinal study to fluctuate throughout the course of the menstrual cycle, or even a class of such behaviors which is regularly correlated with any particular phase of the cycle for groups of women. This is not to say that such a set of behaviors does not exist—many women spontaneously attest that they do—but that as a scientific hypothesis the existence of a premenstrual syndrome has little other than face validity.

2. Psychological studies of the premenstrual syndrome are difficult to interpret without control groups to establish a base line for describing changes in behavior in one sex and to determine the presence or absence of cyclic changes in the behaviors of nonmenstruating individuals. The use of control groups—

AND GOD CREATED WOMAN IN HER OWN IMAGE

And God Created Woman in Her Own Image by Ann Grifalconi. Reprinted by permission.

---

automatic in most psychological studies might yield new data on rhythmic behaviors of hitherto unsuspected generality and, if so, would broaden the interpretation of those previously studied only in adult females.

3. Given the paucity of data showing actual changes in nonverbal behavior throughout the menstrual cycle, careful consideration should be given to the nature of the data in a particular study: Do they show what the subject *says* about menstruation or what she *does*—nonverbally—throughout the cycle? In view of the prevalence of culturally transmitted beliefs and attitudes about menstruation, this distinction is important in considering the relative influence of social and physiological factors both in interpreting the data and in formulating new hypotheses.

4. Given the variety of methods and the variable quality of data on the premenstrual syndrome, investigators proposing a physiological mechanism to explain hormone-behavior relationships should make clear both what behaviors they propose to account for and also the nature of the empirical and conceptual assumptions upon which their psychophysiological hypotheses rest.

For Further Reading

*Money, J. and Ehrhardt, A. A. 1972. *Man and Woman, Boy and Girl.* Baltimore: Johns Hopkins Univ. Press.

*Money, J. and Turk, P. 1975. *Sexual Signatures: On Being a Man or a Woman.* Boston: Little, Brown.

*Montagu, A. 1970. *The Natural Superiority of Women.* New York: Macmillan.

*Morris, J. 1974. *Conundrum.* New York: Harcourt Brace Jovanovich.

Cultural Variations

Continuing the investigation of the possible innateness of psychological maleness and femaleness, in this chapter we will survey the definitions of sex roles in various cultures. The first article reports a fairly recent investigation of cross-cultural sex differences in which Beatrice Whiting and Carolyn Pope observed children aged three to eleven in six different cultures. They investigated popular sexual stereotypes, i.e., that females are more dependent, passive, compliant, nurturant, responsible, and sociable and that males are more dominant, aggressive, and active. One of their most important findings was that sex differences may occur in *style* rather than *intention*. For example, girls exhibit dependency in the form of seeking help and seeking or offering physical contact, whereas boys show this same quality by seeking attention or physical contact through rough-and-tumble play. In terms of dominance, the female style seems to be appealing to rules to justify dominance, rather than the straight egoistic dominance that typifies the masculine style. Another significant finding is that a sex difference in one variable may create other differences. For example, boys usually counter aggression with agression and, overall, seem to exhibit more aggression than girls. They may interrupt girls frequently, thereby reducing the girls' opportunities for self-initiating acts.

The investigators also question the interpretation of certain variables such as compliance, and suggest that this quality may also be viewed as cooperativeness. The tendency toward greater compliance in females may, therefore, be seen more positively as greater cooperativeness. In general, the investigators conclude that sex differences are not as great as expected and that the universality of some sex differences may be due to different task assignment for boys and girls in most cultures. When boys are assigned feminine tasks, for example, they become more feminine than boys not assigned such tasks. Just as Barry, Bacon, and Child concluded (1957), Whiting and Pope found that when there is less difference in the daily routine of girls and boys (in the United States, for instance, as compared to other cultures), the behavior of the sexes is not widely different.

The second selection, the conclusion from Margaret Mead's *Sex, Temperament and Society*, describes three New Guinea tribes—the Arapesh, the Mundugumor, and the Tchambuli. Among the Arapesh, both sexes resemble the feminine type in our culture, possessing gentle, passive, and cherishing natures. The Mundugumor, on the other hand, are similar to our masculine type, i.e., both women and men are reared to be assertive, vigorous, independent, and hostile. Unlike the Arapesh and Mundugumor, the personalities of the Tchambuli do vary by sex, but male and female roles are the reverse of our cultural types of masculine and feminine. Tchambuli women are self-assertive, practical, and managing, and the men are skittish, wary of each other, interested in art and theatre, and fond of petty insults and gossip. On the basis of her observations, Mead concludes that sex differences are socially rather than biologically produced and discusses the implications of this conclusion for our own culture.

Mead observes that especially in this country sex-typed roles are diminishing, producing what she feels is an undesirable ambiguity. She offers three possible alternatives to reduce this ambiguity, the first of which is to reinforce or standardize sex roles. Since limiting the role for one sex necessarily limits the other, however, society would lose many potential contributions of both sexes. This observation is consistent with feminist arguments that sex roles limit both sexes and artificially separate all human attributes into two rigid categories so that both males and females are "half-humans." Feminists go further than Mead, however, to acknowledge that in a patriarchy women are more severely restricted within their sex role than are men. Supporting evidence in this and other chapters shows that females are socialized to be more passive, compliant, and conforming. Other recent research on this topic indicates that sex-role typing for men appears to expand their available personal options while sex-role typing for women seems to restrict their available alternatives of action and expression (Block, Von Der Lippe, and Block, 1973).

Mead's second alternative for resolving the ambiguity resulting from diminishing sex roles is to eliminate them altogether. She argues, however, that this loss of distinctly masculine and feminine personality types would result in potential loss in the range, depth, and complexity of the culture. She fears, for example, that the color and festivity present when the sexes dress differently would be lost.

Mead sees this position—that of advocating total elimination of sex roles—as radical, and correctly so. Feminists would assert that such a radical change is necessary to transform both women and men into whole human beings. They would argue that, contrary to Mead's fear that cultural variations and depth would be lost, greater variations would occur on an individual level, independent of one's sex, race, class, or group. As for Mead's example about losing the festivity resulting from the sexes dressing differently, feminists might wonder how much more festive it would be if everyone dressed uniquely according to her/his own style and mood. For example, a shawl, typically worn as a symbol of softness by women in a sex-typed culture, could still retain its symbolic property and be worn by any individual wishing to express the human quality of softness.

The final alternative for handling the weakening of sex roles, which Mead offers as the best solution, is to specialize personality along several lines to allow for many different endowments. She warns us not to substitute one arbitrary standard for another and to make sure that decreasing the rigidity of sex roles does not increase the rigidity of classification based on some other characteristic such as class. Rather, she feels, the way to accomplish maximum expression of human potential would be to recognize individual gifts, so that anyone may pursue any profession she or he chooses. In this case, both the individual and society would benefit.

Feminists agree with Mead's assertion that the focus should be not simply on eliminating sex roles per se but on creating a culture in which each individual is allowed maximum potential for full self-expression. One criticism of Mead that feminists would make, however, is that she fails to acknowledge the existence of patriarchy. Mead refers to the "myth of male dominance" and, in referring to women, speaks of the "dominance that their society has given them." While this latter statement seems contradictory (to be *given* dominance implies a subordinate position), feminists argue that male dominance is not a myth and that women are the dominated, not the dominant sex.

In the final article of this chapter Esther Newton and Paula Webster review matriarchal theories and examine definitions of matriarchies in which women and men live in peaceful coexistence, not necessarily women dominating men (the reverse of patriarchy). They also discuss the relationship of patriarchy and matriarchy to the psychology of women, especially with regard to innate sex differences, and explore possible sources of the existing power structure. The significance of studying the concept of matriarchy is that, in releasing psychology from its time-bound perspective, it provides some indications for the future of women (and men).

Although many scholars question the actual existence of matriarchies, their occurrence raises some interesting possibilities. For example, if the psychology of women and men results from differential task assignment (as previous studies indicate), would the psychology of women be different in matriarchies? Present cross-cultural surveys suggest some universal sex differences mainly in terms of males' greater aggressiveness. Since the known existing cultures are patriarchal, however, this "universal" sex difference might be merely a reflection of the universal existence of patriarchy!

Whether the psychology of women (and men) was different in matriarchal times can only be imagined. However, if indeed such was the case, there are vast and far-reaching implications not only for present definitions of the psychology of women and men, but also for the future.

Beatrice Whiting and Carolyn Pope Edwards

A Cross-Cultural Analysis of Sex Differences in the Behavior of Children Aged Three through Eleven

Introduction

This paper investigates the validity of the stereotypes of sex differences as evidenced by behavior of children between the ages of three and eleven, observed in natural settings in six different parts of the world.

Females are frequently characterized as more dependent, passive, compliant, nurturant, responsible, and sociable than males, who in turn are characterized as more dominant, aggressive, and active. Assuming that these statements imply observable behaviors, the authors have attempted to define the stereotypes in such a way as to relate them to the categories of interactions which have been used in a series of observational studies of children in natural settings.

There are two major research issues: are these observable differences biological and genetically determined or the result of learning a society's definition of appropriate sex role behavior? To begin to answer these questions one can proceed by asking, first, whether or not the behaviors said to characterize the male and the female are present in all societies and, second, on the assumption that they are found in societies with a variety of cultures, are there associated universal sex role requirements and associated sex typed socialization pressures?

It is our assumption that sex differences reported for the United States or another Western-type culture may reflect only an idiosyncratic type of socialization. If, however, the same differences appear in societies with divergent cultures and life styles, the assumption of universality gains credence. To determine whether sex differences in behavior are biologically determined or the result of universal sex role requirements is far more difficult. Since our study does not include observations of neonates and young infants, it cannot speak to the possible influence and interaction of biological and social variables. It is possible, however, to note age changes during the 3- to 11-year age span and the presence of associated socialization pressures, and to consider the consistency of sex differences across samples of children.

Method

Six of the samples are the children of the Six Culture Study (8, 12), observed in 1954–56 by field teams who lived in communities located in Nyansongo in Kenya, Taira in Koinawa, Khalapur in India, Tarong in the Philippines, Juxlahuaca in Mexico, and Orchard Town in New England.[1] The societies were selected by the field teams on the basis of interest. They vary in complexity as reflected in occupational specialization, political structure, and settlement pattern, and in social structure. Three

---

[1] Observations were gathered by Robert L. LeVine and Barbara LeVine, Thomas and Hatsumi Maretzki, Leigh Minturn, William and Corrine Nydegger, A. Kimball and Romaine Romney, and John and Ann Fischer.

societies favor patrilineal extended families, the other three nuclear families. In three societies children sleep and eat with their mother, father, and siblings; in three they share intimate space with other kin. [For detailed analysis of the cultures see Whiting and Whiting (13).]

The children were all three to eleven years of age, with twelve girls and twelve boys in four of the societies, eleven girls and eleven boys in Juxlahuaca, and eight girls and eight boys in Nyansongo. The children were observed in natural settings, most frequently in their house or yard, on an average of seventeen different times for five-minute periods over a period of six to fourteen months. The observations were focused on one child at a time by one of the members of the field team plus a bilingual assistant. The social interaction recorded in these paragraphs was subsequently coded at the Laboratory of Human Development at Harvard University. The code was designed to identify the instigator and instigation, if any, to the child's act and the action immediately following his act. The analysis of the 8500 interactions was done on a computer. Of the more than seventy original types of interactions coded, twelve summary types were selected for analysis. [For detailed description of methodology, see Imamura (6, pp. 3–18), Whiting (12), and Whiting and Whiting (14, chap. 3)]. The twelve behaviors are *(a) Offering help*—offering food, toys, tools, or general help; *(b) Offering support*—offering emotional support and comfort; *(c) Seeking help and comfort*—seeking instrumental help or emotional support; *(d) Seeking attention and approval*—seeking approval or either positive or negative attention; *(e) Acting sociably*—greeting, initiating friendly interaction, or engaging in friendly interaction; *(f) Dominating*—attempting to change the ongo-

ing behavior of another to meet one's own egoistic desires; *(g) Suggesting responsibly or prosocial dominance*—suggesting that another change his behavior in such a way as to meet the rules of the family or other group, or serve the welfare of the group; *(h) Reprimanding*—criticizing another's behavior after the fact; *(i) Seeking or offering physical contact*—non-aggressive touching or holding; *(j) Engaging in rough and tumble play*—playing which includes physical contact, wrestling and playful aggression; *(k) Insulting*—verbally derogating another; *(l) Assaulting*—attempting to injure another.

In 1968–70 a sample of seventy children between the ages of two and ten were observed in Ngecha, a village situated twenty miles north of Nairobi in Kenya. The children were observed by students for periods of thirty minutes over the course of two years, and their behavior was recorded in running paragraphs and then coded by the observers. The code used was a revised version of the six culture code. The children between three and ten years of age have been selected for the analysis in this paper; there were twenty-one girls and eighteen boys aged 3–6 years, and nine girls and nine boys aged 7–11.

In order to relate the stereotypes of female and male behavior to the behavior we have observed and coded in our studies, we have attempted to define the stereotypes operationally and then selected from our codes those categories that seem best to represent the definitions. To measure the sex differences in these behaviors, we have used the proportion scores of each child for each of the relevant types of observed behavior and computed a set of group means from those individual proportion scores. The children have been divided into groups on

In the East, women religiously conceal that they have faces; in the West, that they have legs. In both cases they make it evident that they have but little brains.

Henry David Thoreau, *Journal,* 31 Jan. 1852

the basis of sex, age (3–6 years old *versus* 7–11 years old), and cultural sample.

Comparisons between boys and girls in each culture are based on the differences between the mean proportion scores for the behavior types. Significance levels are based on *t* tests between the means of the sex age groups. The comparisons for the pooled samples are based on scores standardized by culture. Nyansongo and Juxtlahuaca, because of the smaller number of children (sixteen and twenty-two, respectively), are slightly underrepresented when the standardized scores are pooled.

Results

1. *"Dependency"* (Stereotype: girls are more dependent than boys.)

There are three types of behavior which have been traditionally classified under this heading: *(a)* seeking help, *(b)* seeking attention, *(c)* seeking physical contact. In the six culture study, seeking for help included both asking for instrumental help—that is, requesting help in reaching a goal, asking for an object needed to reach a goal, or requesting food—and asking for comfort or reassurance. Seeking attention included bids for approval and attempts to call attention to oneself by boasting or by performing either praiseworthy or blameworthy acts with the intent of becoming the focus of another person's attention. The category of seeking or offering physical contact included behavior in which the child sought proximity to another, or touched, held, or clung to another.

Table 1 presents the comparisons. It can be seen that in five of the six societies girls aged 3–6 were observed to seek help more frequently than did the boys aged 3–6, and the difference between the pooled groups of younger girls and boys is significant at the .05 level. In the 7- to 11-year-old comparison, however, there is an equal split; in three societies girls were observed to seek help more than boys and in three the reverse was true.

Seeking attention is more characteristic of boys than girls. In four of the samples, boys 3–6 seek attention more frequently than do girls, but for the pooled sample of six societies there is no significant difference. Among 7- to 11-year-olds in the four societies where there are differences, boys seek attention more frequently and the difference is significant at the .05 level.

Girls were observed to seek or offer physical contact more frequently than boys. For the young group, as a whole there is a marked sex difference, girls seeking or offering physical contact more frequently than boys ($p < .01$).

In sum, the stereotype of female "dependency" holds for two of the types of behavior—seeking help and seeking or offering physical contact—but is especially true of the younger age groups, there being no significant difference in these behaviors in the 7- to 11-year-olds. Seeking attention, on the other hand, is a male form of "dependency," is clearly present in the 7- to 11-year-old group, and is the only type of "dependent" behavior in which

TABLE 1

DIFFERENCE BETWEEN THE MEAN PROPORTION SCORES OF BOYS AND GIRLS IN THE SIX CULTURE STUDY

Behavior category		Nyansongo	Juxtlahuaca	Tarong	Taira	Khalapur	Orchard Town	All
Dependency								
1. Seeks help	3–6	+	+	+	+	+*	−	+*
	7–11	−	−	+	+	−**	+	−
2. Seeks attention	3–6	+	−	−	−	−	+	−
	7–11	−	−**	−	−	−	−	−*
3. Physical contact	3–6	+	+	−	+	+	+	+**
	7–11	+	+	+	−	+	+	+
Sociability								
	3–6	+	−	−	+	+	+	+
	7–11	+	−	+	+	+*	−	+
Passivity								
1. Withdrawal from aggressive instigations	3–6	+	−	+	+	−	+	+
	7–11	−	+	+	−	+	−	+
2. Counteraggression in response to an aggressive instigation	3–6	−	−	+	+	+	−	−
	7–11	−	+	−	−*	−	−*	−**
3. Compliance to dominant instigations (prosocial and egoistic)	3–6	−	−	+	+	+	−	+
	7–11	+	+	+	−	−	−	+
4. Initiative (% of acts which are self-instigated)	3–6	−	−	+	−	+	−	−
	7–11	+	−	−	−*	−	+	−
Nurturance								
1. Offers help	3–6	−	+	+	+	+	−	+
	7–11	+	+	+**	−	+	+	+**
2. Gives support	3–6	−	+	+	+*	−	+	+
	7–11	+	+*	+	+	+	+	+***
Responsibility								
	3–6	+	+	+	+	+	+	+*
	7–11	−	+	−	+	−*	+	−
Dominance								
	3–6	−	−	+	−	−	−	−*
	7–11	−	+	−	−	−	−	−
Aggression								
1. Rough and tumble play	3–6	+	−	−	−	−	+	−*
	7–11	+	−	−	−	−	−	−*
2. Insults	3–6	−	−	−	−**	−	−	−**
	7–11	−	−	−	−**	−	+	−*
3. Assaults	3–6	−	−	−	−	−	+	−
	7–11	+	−	−	−	+	−	−

Note: A (+) indicates that the girls' score was higher than the boys'. A (−) indicates that the boys' score was higher than the girls'.

* *p* .05.

** *p* .01.

*** *p* .001.

there are significant differences in the older age group.

2. "*Sociability*" (Stereotype: girls are more sociable than boys.)

"Sociability," which includes greeting behavior and all acts judged to have the primary intent of seeking or offering friendly interaction, is correlated with "dependent" behavior. As can be seen in Table 1, there is a slight tendency for girls to be more sociable than boys but the differences are not significant.

3. "*Passivity*" (Stereotype: girls are passive.)

"Passivity" is frequently associated with dependency in the stereotype of female behavior. This concept is more difficult to operationalize, and we have accepted the definitions of Kagan and Moss (7). They list among other behavioral indices of passivity in the preschool child: (a) retreat when dominated by a sibling; (b) no reaction when goal object is lost; (c) withdrawal when blocked from goal by environmental obstacle; and (d) withdrawal from mildly noxious or potentially dangerous situation situations. During the school years, their passivity measures included (a) withdrawal from attack or social rejection, and (b) withdrawal from difficult and frustrating situations.

The six culture code included instigational situations described as encountering difficulty, being blocked, having property taken away, being challenged to competition, being insulted or physically attacked, and being dominated. In these situations, if we accept the above definition of "passivity," girls should, according to the stereotype, respond by withdrawal. Two types of instigations occur with sufficient frequency to make analysis possible: (a) aggressive instigations, including being insulted, roughed up in a playful fashion, and being physically attacked by peers; and (b) dominant instiga-

tions. We have analyzed the proportion of responses that are compliant and the proportion of those that are counteraggressive. Table 1 presents the findings. "Withdrawal" includes behavior coded as complies, hides, avoids, breaks interaction, deprecates self, and acts shy. "Counteraggression" includes playful aggression or rough and tumble play, insulting behavior, and assaulting with the judged intent of injuring another.

It can be seen (Table 1) that there is no consistent trend in the sample in relation to withdrawal from aggressive instigations of peers, although there is an overall tendency for girls to withdraw more frequently than boys. If one contrasts the proportion of counteraggressive responses when attacked by peers, the findings are more consistent. There is no significant difference between girls and boys in the 3–6 age group but by 7–11 the boys react proportionately and significantly more frequently with counteraggression than do the girls (Table 1).

Sex differences in compliance to prosocial and egoistically dominant instigations (Table 1) are only slightly in the direction the stereotype would predict. There is one type of compliance which is significantly different for girls and boys: namely, obedience to the mother. In the 7–11 age group girls are significantly more compliant to their mothers' commands and suggestions ($p < .05$). However, this kind of compliance seems a much better operational measure of a variable that might be called "cooperativeness" than it does of passivity. One might interpret that the 7- to 11-year-old girls have identified with their mothers and their mothers' goals and are therefore willing to cooperate when their mothers assign tasks.

In sum, older boys respond more aggressively

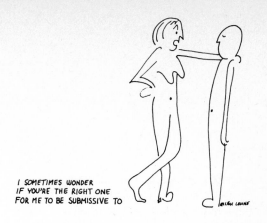

I SOMETIMES WONDER
IF YOU'RE THE RIGHT ONE
FOR ME TO BE SUBMISSIVE TO

Ellen Levine, from *All She Needs* . . . , Quadrangle, 1973.

than girls to aggressive instigations, and there is a trend for boys to be less compliant than girls to the wishes of others. However, these differences are not as great as the literature would imply (1.).

There is another dimension of behavior which might be considered the obverse of "passivity": namely, "initiative." As operationalized here, initiative is measured by a proportion score, the proportion of the child's acts that were judged to be self-instigated, rather than responses to the instigations of others. Table 1 presents the comparison. It can be seen that in the younger group the proportion of self-instigated acts is similar for boys and girls. In the older age group boys were judged to initiate interaction proportionately more frequently than were girls, but the difference between the two groups does not reach an acceptable level of significance. What accounts for this slight difference? It could either be that girls initiate fewer acts than boys or that they receive proportionately more instigations than do boys. Girls initiate social interaction somewhat more frequently than do boys as judged by rate scores. However, girls receive proportionately more *mands* from others than do boys. That is, other individuals interrupt and try to change the ongoing behavior of girls more than that of boys. It is this higher rate of interruptions or instigations received that makes the older girls have a slightly lower proportion of self-instigated acts than have the boys. Perhaps this

higher rate of attempts to change girls' behavior sets is related to the Western stereotype of feminine "sensitivity" or "responsiveness" and to the reports that girls have greater awareness of their immediate environment than do boys (15).

4. *"Nurturance"* (Stereotype: girls are more nurturant than boys.)

Table 1 presents the difference between boys and girls on two components of this behavior system. It can be seen that in the 3- to 6-year-old period there are no consistent trends across the six societies and no significant differences. By 7–11, however, girls are observed to offer help and support significantly more than boys ($p<.01$ and $<.001$, respectively). That there are no sex differences in the early age group, but rather marked increases with age, does not fit the innate differences hypothesis.

5. *"Responsibility"* (Stereotype: girls are more responsible than boys.)

In the six culture study any attempt to change the behavior of others with the judged intent of seeing to the welfare of the group and the maintenance of socially approved behavior has been coded as "suggests responsibly" (prosocial dominance) and distinguished from "dominance," which was defined as attempts to change the behavior of another to meet the egoistic desires of the actor. As can be seen in Table 1, in the 3- to 6-year-old group girls offered responsible suggestions more frequently than boys in all six samples, the difference significant at the .05 level of confidence. By 7-11, however, there is no difference, the boys having increased markedly.

6. *"Dominance"* (Stereotype: boys are more dominant than girls).

Egoistic dominance (Table 1), on the other hand, as the stereotype would have it, was observed more frequently in boys. The level of significance is .05 for the young group and not significant in the 7–11 sample.

7. *"Aggression"* (Stereotype: boys are more physically aggressive than girls; girls are more verbally aggressive.)

We have coded three types of aggression: *(a)* rough and tumble play, aggression which has a strong sociable component; *(b)* verbal aggression, primarily verbal communications judged to be motivated by the desire to derogate and insult; and *(c)* assaulting, physical aggression judged to be motivated by the desire to cause pain and injury. As can be seen (Table 1), boys were observed in rough and tumble play significantly more frequently than girls in both age groups. They were also, contrary to the stereotype, significantly more insulting than girls—the level of significance reaching .01 for the young and .05 for the older group (Table 1). Assaulting with the intent to injure (Table 1) was not observed with great enough frequency to make any definitive statement. In five of the samples, the 3- to 6-year-old boys assaulted more; by 7–11 the frequency of the behavior is roughly similar in four samples. The reader is referred back to the findings concerning responses to aggressive instigations. In sum, on all measures of aggression, boys score higher than girls but the differences are significant only in rough and tumble play and verbal aggression, and in the older group in counteraggression when attacked by peers.

Discussion

Insulting, rough and tumble play, and dominating egoistically are the most clearly "masculine" types of behavior in the 3- to 6-year-old age group, and seeking or offering physical contact, seeking help, and suggesting responsibly (or prosocial dominance) the most clearly "feminine." The fact that body contact is involved in both rough and tumble play and touching behavior suggests that they are alternative modes of establishing cutaneous contact. One may also dichotomize two types of dominance—straight commanding (dominates), the male mode, and dominance justified by rules of appropriate behavior (suggesting responsibly), the female mode. In the older age group nurturance becomes a clearly "feminine" characteristic, and the measures of aggression distinguish the boys. Seeking attention appears to be both a "masculine" form of dependency and, in its self-arrogating aspects, a measure of competitiveness.

Although it is obviously impossible to do more than speculate about biophysical determinants of these behaviors, the sex differences that are greatest in the younger group might be considered the best candidates for sex-linked characteristics. The age trends in the behavioral systems are presented in Table 2.

Seeking and offering of physical contact, a behavior that differentiates the sexes clearly in the 3- to 6-year-old group, decreases significantly with age. One might interpret this as a decrease in the desire for physical contact, contact which may have served as a pain and anxiety reducer at the younger age and now is less frequently needed. The significant increase of nurturance and responsibility with age suggests that these are behaviors which increase with socialization pressure. Nurturance increases significantly in girls, and responsibility or prosocial dominance increases in both girls and boys, at the .06 level of significance for girls and the .001 level for boys. Since by 7–11 years of age there is no significant sex difference in the proportion of responsible suggestions, the significant increase for the boys may indicate that pressure for responsibility begins at an earlier age for girls.[2] The proportionate increase of self-instigated acts of boys may reflect the fact that girls are assigned tasks that keep them closer to the house and adults, tasks and setting that are associated with more requests and demands from others.

There is evidence in our data of differential pressure on girls and boys to be nurturant. Older girls in our sample took care of children under eighteen months of age more frequently than did boys (*p*<.05), and infant care is undoubtedly one of the variables contributing to the significant increase in the proportion of offering help and support. There is also evidence that more girls than boys in the younger age group are assigned responsible tasks. By the older age group, however, boys are engaged in animal husbandry, and both girls and boys are beginning to help in agricultural work. Boys feed and pasture animals significantly more frequently than girls (*p*<.001); girls do significantly more domestic chores (cleaning *p*<.001, food preparation, cooking, and grinding *p*<.001) and care for siblings. The number of tasks assigned to both boys and girls increases significantly with age (8).

---

[2]In Ember's study in Western Kenya and in the ongoing research in Kenya there are significant sex differences in prosocial dominance, girls scoring significantly higher than boys in the 7- to 11-year-old age groups.

TABLE 2

SHOWING SIGNIFICANT CHANGES IN THE MEAN OF THE PROPORTION SCORES OF THE BEHAVIOR OF GIRLS AND BOYS FROM AGES 3–6 TO 7–11

Behavior	Girls	Boys
Offers help	+**	
Offers support	+*	
Responsibility		+***
Seeks or offers physical contact	−**	−***
Proportion of self-instigated acts		+*

Note: A (+) indicates an increase with age, a (−) indicates a decrease.
* *p* .05.
** *p* .01.
*** *p* .001.

These sex differences in assigned work are associated with the different frequency with which boys and girls interact with various categories of people: i.e., adults, infants, and peers. Caring for infants and performing domestic chores require that girls stay in the vicinity of the house and yard and hence remain more frequently in the company of adult females. Both young and older girls interact with female adults more frequently than do boys (*p*<.05 and<.01, respectively), and older girls interact with infants significantly more than do boys (*p*<.01). Herding and other animal husbandry chores take the boy away from the house. Boys interact less frequently with adults and infants and proportionately and significantly more with peer (3–4 years *p*<.05; 7–10 *p*<.01), especially male peers.

What can be said about the consequences of this difference in type of dyadic interaction? To answer this question we analyzed the types of behavior that children direct most frequently to adults, to infants and to child peers. These three age grades of people seem to draw different types of behavior from children, and the behavior which children direct to a given category is remarkably similar across cultures (14). The acts most frequently directed toward adults are *(a)* seeking help, *(b)* seeking or offering physical contact, *(c)* seeking attention, and *(d)* seeking friendly interaction, or "sociability"— the first two of these being "feminine" type behavior (see Table 1). When interacting with infants, children most frequently offer help, support, and sociability—the first two again "feminine"-type behaviors. In contrast, when interacting with peers, sociability, rough and tumble play, and derogatory and insulting interchanges are most frequent, the last two of these "masculine" type behaviors.

Two studies in Kenya and research in progress in Guatemala confirm our deduction that girls are at home more frequently than are boys (9, 10, 11). In Kenya, Sara Nerlove working in Nyansongo and Robert and Ruth Munroe working in Vihiga made observational studies of same-aged pairs of girls and boys. At the same times each day they sought out the children's whereabouts and measured their distance from home. The girls were found to be nearer to home significantly more often than the boys. Although these findings may be interpreted to indicate that girls are innately more timid than boys, it seems more parsimonious to assume that they reflect socialization pressure and differential task assignment, girls being kept home to perform infant tending and domestic chores.

The question then becomes why girls are assigned domestic chores and the care of infants significantly more frequently than are boys. Is it because girls are innately better suited to such tasks or does it simply reflect a universal sex typing and preparation of young girls for their adult roles? In all the societies we have studied, women have the major responsibility for the care of infants and for domestic chores. This is in accord with the findings of cross-cultural studies on the division of labor (3). Assigning these chores to girls rather than boys may simply reflect the early training of girls for the expected female role.

This differential socialization pressure on girls is in accord with the findings of Barry, Bacon, and Child (2) in their cross-cultural study of sex differences in socialization, based on ratings made from published ethnographic reports of societies distributed around the world. They found that girls received more pressure to be nurturant, obedient, and responsible, boys more pressure to achieve and be self-reliant. In our sample the greater frequency in the proportion of nurturant behavior, its increase with age, and the greater compliance to mothers of girls are as one would predict from the Barry, Bacon, and Child findings. As noted above the greater amount of time spent caring for infants can be interpreted as greater pressure toward nurturance. Pressure toward obedience as reported by the mothers of the six cultures is greatest in those societies that assign infant care and similarly is exerted more on girls than on boys (13, 14). It is also greater in those societies in which children are engaged in animal husbandry. Responsible behavior, as we have measured it, does not show significant sex differences in the six culture samples, but does in recent observational studies in Kenya (see footnote 3). However, since there is a high correlation between the Barry, Bacon, and Child ratings on pressure toward responsibility and the number of chores assigned to girls and boys as reported in the ethnographic monographs, the significant difference in the number of chores assigned to girls and boys in the 3- to 6-year-old age group is in accord with their findings. In the older group there is great variation from one society to another. The crucial variable seems to be economic; in societies with animal husbandry or agricultural work that can be assigned to boys, there are no sex differences in amount of work required of girls and boys after 7–8 years of age.

Our measures of achievement-oriented and self-reliant behavior are less direct, but are also in accord with the sex differences in socialization reported by Barry, Bacon, and Child. Seeking attention as we have coded it includes self-arrogation and boasting. In the older age group, as reported above, boys are proportionately significantly higher than girls in this type of behavior. If we assume that these behaviors are motivated by achievement needs, the findings are as predicted. The proportion of self-instigated acts might be considered a measure of self-reliance. There is a trend, as reported above, for boys 7–11 to be proportionately higher in acts that were not judged to be clearly instigated by the actions of others. It should be noted again here, however, that this measure may simply reflect the fact that boys are interrupted less frequently by the *mands* of others than are girls. The ethnographic sources make it difficult to distinguish between being allowed to do what one wishes unsupervised by others and self-reliance.[3]

In sum, our evidence suggests that the nature of the tasks assigned to girls is the best predictor of four of the five primary types of "feminine"

[3]For discussion of the problem, and data on achievement and self-reliance among the Kung Bushmen of the Khalahari, see Patricia L. Draper (4).

behavior (see Table 1), since *(a)* the tasks require more frequent interaction with infants and adults and *(b)* the nature of the tasks themselves involves care of others—offering help and comfort to infants, preparing and offering food to the entire family—all work focused on the needs of others and the welfare of the family. These tasks clearly require a child to be compliant—to be willing to service the requests of others and to obey task-related instructions. Furthermore, all of these tasks require the girl to be tolerant of interruptions and demands for succorance, and require her to be constantly alert to the motivational states of others—behaviors possibly related to field dependence, a quality commonly attributed to women (15).

It is interesting to note here societal differences in "femininity" scores. Orchard Town girls, for example, score low in offering help and support and do significantly less infant care than girls in other societies.

Further insight into the possible consequences of task assignment can be gained by looking at the "masculine" and "feminine" profiles of boys who are assigned domestic chores and the care of infants. There are many societies in which young boys are required to do such work. Among these are East African societies in which women are the agriculturalists, men traditionally the pastoralists and warriors. In these societies young boys are classified with women and girls until they approach pubescence, at which time they are frequently initiated into manhood in formal *rites de passage*. Nyansongo, one of the six cultures, is an example of such a society. The women, who work four or five hours a day in the gardens, assign the care of infants to a designated older sibling and the tending of the cooking fire and the washing of utensils to the same or some other child of the family. Although mothers prefer girl nurses, it is not considered inappropriate to delegate the responsibility to a boy if there is no female of the proper age—in this case under 10 years of age—since older girls are either in school or helping in agricultural work.

Our evidence suggests that requiring boys to tend babies and perform domestic chores reduces sex differences in the mean proportion scores of "masculine" and "feminine" behavior in two of these East African societies. In Nyansongo half of the boys aged five and over took care of infants and half helped with domestic chores. When one contrasts the mean proportion scores of the boys and girls, the magnitude of the sex differences is smaller than in any of the six societies with the exception of Orchard Town, which will be discussed later. Nyansongo boys score higher than would be predicted on offering help and offering support, young boys scoring higher than young girls on both types of behavior. Nyansongo girls are aberrantly high in rough and tumble play, younger girls in assaulting, and boys retreat from aggressive attacks from peers as frequently as do girls. The comparisons are similar in Ngecha, our other East African sample. In the Ngecha sample, the older boys offer help and support somewhat more frequently than do the girls ($p<.22$), the younger boys seek sociability significantly more than do the girls ($p<.05$), the older girls seek attention slightly more frequently than do the boys ($p<.23$), and the girls of both ages were observed in rough and tumble play as frequently as the boys.

A more detailed analysis of the effect of assigning "feminine" tasks to boys has been presented by Carol Baldwin Ember (5). In 1968 when she was working in Oyugis in Western Kenya, by fluke of sex ratio there were an unusually large number of households in which there was no girl of the appropriate age to care for an infant sibling, and hence there was quite a large sample of boys who were acting as nurses and doing domestic chores. Using this unusual opportunity Carol Ember undertook an observational study of these boys. She compared them to a matched sample of boys who were not responsible for "feminine" chores, as well as to a sample of girls. She used a code similar to that used in the six culture study. Her observations were made when the children were not working.

Her findings based on a linear regression of the means for the three groups—boys who did little child tending or domestic chores which kept them inside the homestead, boys who did many such tasks, and girls—show significant differences between the three samples. Boys high on feminine work had behavior profiles that were more "feminine" than boys who did not perform such work. They were more responsible (prosocially dominant), less aggressive (including assaulting and insulting), less dependent (including seeking help, support, attention, information, and material goods),[5] and less egoistically dominant (including dominating, reprimanding, and prohibiting action egoistically (all differences significant at the .01 level). The differences were not great, however, when Ember compared boys who were and who were not assigned "feminine" chores which took them *outside* the homestead: i.e., carrying water, fetching wood, digging root crops, picking vegetables, and going to the market to mill flour. Her data do not show the predicted differences in nurturant behavior.

[5]It is unfortunate that dependency as operationally defined by Ember included both the masculine and feminine modes.

In sum, societies where boys take care of infants, cook, and perform other domestic chores, there are fewer sex differences between boys and girls, and this decrease is due primarily to the decrease in "masculine" behavior in boys; boys are less egoistically dominant, score proportionately lower in some forms of aggression, seek attention proportionately less frequently, and score higher on suggesting responsibly. On the other hand, the 3- to 6-year-old girls in these societies are high on assaulting and miscellaneous aggression, and both younger and older girls score low on sociability (14).

Although there are no samples of girls in any of the six cultures who do "masculine" type tasks, the girls of Orchard Town, New England, as mentioned above, do very little infant care. Since most New England families consist of two children averaging around two years apart in age, and since there are no courtyard cousins, young nieces, nephews, or half-siblings as in extended and polygynous families, there is little opportunity for Orchard Town girls to care for infants except as paid baby sitters. In general, however, Orchard Town mothers do not hire baby sitters under 11 years of age. Orchard Town girls are also more strongly committed to education and may aspire to jobs that are considered appropriate to both sexes. Their work in school is practically identical with that of boys. It is interesting, therefore, to see how this sample of U.S. girls who have been observed in natural settings fits the predicted patterns on the behaviors which we have found to be significantly different between boys and girls in the pooled samples. As in Nyansongo, the magnitude of the differences is small. The direction of the insignificant differences is as expected with one exception, the young girls

Pygmy Family (Ituri Forest, northeast Zaire) by Malvina Hoffman. By permission of Field Museum of Natural History.

scoring higher than the boys in the proportion of attention seeking, a "masculine" type behavior. They also score higher than any other sample of girls on this type of behavior—behavior which in general is higher among the children of the more complex societies (Orchard Town, Khalapur, and Taira) where schooling and achievement are more highly valued (14). It is a type of behavior which, when directed toward adults, is frequently motivated by a desire for approval and, as discussed above, when directed toward peers may have affiliation or

---

In our own land

Alone we are misfits,
excluded and shamed;
together we are a people
divided and chained
but remembering,
remembering our secrets
and that we once worshipped
each other.
Recalling now our powers,
the old wisdoms, simple arts,
we feel myths kick for birth.
The man who wived his mother,
the Danish prince, the son of god
are boy-child's tales.
Who has yet heard
all that his sister knows?

Jody Aliesan

self-arrogation as its goal. It is a frequent behavior in New England classrooms.

As noted above, the Orchard Town girls score the lowest of the samples of girls on offering help and support, "feminine" traits, and have one of the lowest percentages of interaction with infants.

In sum, in both the East African societies where "feminine" work is assigned to boys and in Orchard Town, New England, where less "feminine" work is assigned to girls and where there is less difference in the daily routine of boys and girls, the behavior of girls and boys does not show as great differences as in other societies.

Margaret Mead

Conclusion from "Sex and Temperament"

The knowledge that the personalities of the two sexes are socially produced is congenial to every programme that looks forward towards a planned order of society. It is a two-edged sword that can be used to hew a more flexible, more varied society than the human race has ever built, or merely to cut a narrow path down which one sex or both sexes will be forced to march, regimented, looking neither to the right nor to the left. It makes possible a Fascist programme of education in which women are forced back into a mould that modern Europe had fatuously believed to be broken forever. It makes possible a Communist programme in which the two sexes are treated as nearly alike as their different physiological functions permit. Because it is social conditioning that is determinative, it has been possible for America, without conscious plan but none the less surely, partially to reverse the European tradition of male dominance, and to breed a generation of women who model their lives on the pattern of their school-teachers and their aggressive, directive mothers. Their brothers stumble about in a vain attempt to preserve the myth of male dominance in a society in which the girls have come to consider dominance their natural right. As one fourteen-year-old girl said in commenting on the meaning of the term "tomboy," "Yes, it's true that it used to mean a girl who tried to act like a boy, dress like a boy, and things like that. But that belonged to the hoop-skirt era. Nowadays all girls have to do is to act exactly like boys, quite quietly." The tradition in this country has been changing so rapidly that the term "sissy," which ten years ago meant a boy who showed personality traits regarded as feminine, can now be applied with scathing emphasis by one girl to another, or can be defined by a small girl as "the kind of boy who always wears a baseball glove and goes about shouting, 'Put her there! Put her there!' and when you throw him a soft one he can't catch it." These penetrating comments are sharply indicative of a trend that lacks the concerted planning behind Fascist or Communist programmes, but which has nevertheless gained in acceleration in the last three decades. Plans that regiment women as home-makers, or which cease to differentiate the training of the two sexes, have at least the virtue of being clear and unambiguous. The present development in this country has all the insidious ambiguity of the situation that we found illustrated among the Tchambuli head-hunters, where the man is still defined as the head of the house, although the woman is trained to a greater celerity and sureness in taking that position. The result is an increasing number of American men who feel they must shout in order to maintain their vulnerable positions, and an increasing number of American women who clutch unhappily at a dominance that their society has granted them—but without giving them a charter of rules and regulations by which they can achieve it without damage to themselves, their husbands, and their children.

There are at least three courses open to a society that has realized the extent to which male and female personality are socially pro-

Though it appears that both men and women live together within the institutions of society, men really define and control the institutions while women live under their rule. The government, army, religion, economy, and family are institutions of the male culture's colonial rule of the female. . . . A female culture exists. It is a culture that is subordinated and under the male culture's colonial, imperialist rule all over the world. Underneath the surface of every national, ethnic, or racial culture is the split between the two primary cultures of the world—the female culture and the male culture. . . . Crossing national boundaries often awakens a woman's understanding of her position in society. We cannot, like James Baldwin, even temporarily escape to Paris or another country from our caste role. It is everywhere—there is no place to escape.

Fourth World Manifesto (Jan. 13, 1971)

A Work of Artifice

*The bonsai tree
in the attractive pot
could have grown eighty feet tall
on the side of a mountain
till split by lightning.
But a gardener
carefully pruned it.
It is nine inches high.
Every day as he
whittles back the branches
the gardener croons,
It is your nature
to be small and cozy,
domestic and weak;
how lucky, little tree,
to have a pot to grow in.
With living creatures
one must begin very early
to dwarf their growth:
the bound feet,
the crippled brain,
the hair in curlers,
the hands you
love to touch.*

Marge Piercy

race. The first is to standardize the personality of men and women as clearly contrasting, complementary, and antithetical, and to make every institution in the society congruent with this standardization. If the society declared that woman's sole function was motherhood and the teaching and care of young children, it could so arrange matters that every woman who was not physiologically debarred should become a mother and be supported in the exercise of this function. It could abolish the discrepancy between the doctrine that women's place is the home and the number of homes that were offered to them. It could abolish the discrepancy between training women for marriage and then forcing them to become the spinster supports of their parents.

Such a system would be wasteful of the gifts of many women who could exercise other functions far better than their ability to bear children in an already overpopulated world. It would be wasteful of the gifts of many men who could exercise their special personality gifts far better in the home than in the marketplace. It would be wasteful, but it would be clear. It could attempt to guarantee to each individual the rôle for which society insisted upon training him or her, and such a system would penalize only those individuals who, in spite of all the training, did not display the approved personalities. There are millions of persons who would gladly return to such a standardized method of treating the relation-

duced. Two of these courses have been tried before, over and over again, at different times in the long, irregular, repetitious history of the

ship between the sexes, and we must bear in mind the possibility that the greater opportunities open in the twentieth century to women may be quite withdrawn, and that we may return to a strict regimentation of women.

The waste, if this occurs, will be not only of many women, but also of as many men, because regimentation of one sex carries with it, to greater or less degree, the regimentation of the other also. Every parental behest that defines a way of sitting, a response to a rebuke or a threat, a game, or an attempt to draw or sing or dance or paint, as feminine, is moulding the personality of each little girl's brother as well as moulding the personality of the sister. There can be no society which insists that women follow one special personality-pattern, defined as feminine, which does not do violence also to the individuality of many men.

Alternatively, society can take the course that has become especially associated with the plans of most radical groups: admit that men and women are capable of being moulded to a single pattern as easily as to a diverse one, and cease to make any distinction in the approved personality of both sexes. Girls can be trained exactly as boys are trained, taught the same code, the same forms of expression, the same occupations. This course might seem to be the logic which follows from the conviction that the potentialities which different societies label as either masculine or feminine are really potentialities of some members of each sex, and not sex-linked at all. If this is accepted, is it not reasonable to abandon the kind of artificial standardizations of sex-differences that have been so long characteristic of European society, and admit that they are social fictions for which we have no longer any use? In the world today, contraceptives make it possible for

Neanderthal Woman by Tiziana Blaisdell. By permission of the artist.

women not to bear children against their will. The most conspicuous actual difference between the sexes, the difference in strength, is progressively less significant. Just as the difference in height between males is no longer a realistic issue, now that lawsuits have been substituted for hand-to-hand encounters, so the difference in strength between men and women is no longer worth elaboration in cultural institutions.

In evaluating such a programme as this, however, it is necessary to keep in mind the nature

Cantonese Woman (Canton, south Chica) by Malvina Hoffman. By permission of Field Museum of Natural History.

of the gains that society has achieved in its most complex forms. A sacrifice of distinctions in sex-personality may mean a sacrifice in complexity. The Arapesh recognize a minimum of distinction in personality between old and young, between men and women, and they lack categories of rank or status. We have seen that such a society at the best condemns to personal frustration, and at the worst to maladjustment, all of those men and women who do not conform to its simple emphases. The violent person among the Arapesh cannot find, either in the literature, or in the art, or in the ceremonial, or in the history of his people, any expression of the internal drives that are shattering his peace of mind. Nor is the loser only the individual whose own type of personality is nowhere recognized in his society. The imaginative, highly intelligent person who is essentially in tune with the values of his society may also suffer by the lack of range and depth characteristic of too great simplicity. The active mind and intensity of one Arapesh boy whom I knew well was unsatisfied by the laissez-faire solutions, the lack of drama in his culture. Searching for some material upon which to exercise his imagination, his longing for a life in which stronger emotions would be possible, he could find nothing with which to feed his imagination but tales of the passionate outbursts of the maladjusted, outbursts characterized by a violent hostility to others that he himself lacked.

Nor is it the individual alone who suffers. Society is equally the loser, and we have seen such an attenuation in the dramatic representations of the Mundugumor. By phrasing the exclusion of women as a protective measure congenial to both sexes, the Arapesh kept their *tamberan* cult, with the necessary audiences of women. But the Mundugumor developed a kind of personality for both men and women to which exclusion from any part of life was interpreted as a deadly insult. And as more and more Mundugumor women have demanded and been given the right of initiation, it is not surprising that the Mundugumor ceremonial life has dwindled, the actors have lost their audience, and one vivid artistic element in the life of the Mundugumor community is vanishing. The sacrifice of sex-differences has meant a loss in complexity to the society.

So in our own society. To insist that there are no sex-differences in a society that has always believed in them and depended upon them may be as subtle a form of standardizing personality as to insist that there are many sex-differences. This is particularly so in a changing tradition, when a group in control is attempting to develop a new social personality, as is the case today in many European countries. Take, for instance, the current assumption that women are more opposed to war than men, that any outspoken approval of war is more horrible, more revolting, in women than in men.

The primitive woman is independent because, not in spite of her labor. Generally speaking, it is in those societies where women toil most that their status is most independent and their influence greatest; where they are idle, and the work is done by slaves, the women are, as a rule, little more than sexual slaves. . . .

Robert Briffault, *Mothers*

Behind this assumption women can work for peace without encountering social criticism in communities that would immediately criticize their brothers or husbands if they took a similarly active part in peace propaganda. This belief that women are naturally more interested in peace is undoubtedly artificial, part of the whole mythology that considers women to be gentler than men. But in contrast let us consider the possibility of a powerful minority that wished to turn a whole society whole-heartedly towards war. One way of doing this would be to insist that women's motives, women's interests, were identical with men's, that women should take as bloodthirsty a delight in preparing for war as ever men do. The insistence upon the opposite point of view, that the woman as a mother prevails over the woman as a citizen at least puts a slight drag upon agitation for war, prevents a blanket enthusiasm for war from being thrust upon the entire younger generation. The same kind of result follows if the clergy are professionally committed to a belief in peace. The relative bellicosity of different individual clerics may be either offended or gratified by the prescribed pacific rôle, but a certain protest, a certain dissenting note, will be sounded in society. The dangerous standardization of attitudes that disallows every type of deviation is greatly reinforced if neither age nor sex nor religious belief is regarded as automatically predisposing certain individuals

to hold minority attitudes. The removal of all legal and economic barriers against women's participating in the world on an equal footing with men may be in itself a standardizing move towards the wholesale stamping-out of the diversity of attitudes that is such a dearly bought product of civilization.

Such a standardized society, in which men, women, children, priests, and soldiers were all trained to an undifferentiated and coherent set of values, must of necessity create the kind of deviant that we found among the Arapesh and the Mundugumor, the individual who, regardless of sex or occupation, rebels because he is temperamentally unable to accept the one-sided emphasis of his culture. The individuals who were specifically unadjusted in terms of their psycho-sexual rôle would, it is true, vanish, but with them would vanish the knowledge that there is more than one set of possible values.

To the extent that abolishing the differences in the approved personalities of men and women means abolishing any expression of the type of personality once called exclusively feminine, or once called exclusively masculine, such a course involves a social loss. Just as a festive occasion is the gayer and more charming if the two sexes are dressed differently, so it is in less material matters. If the clothing is in itself a symbol, and a woman's shawl corresponds to a recognized softness in her charac-

*In every known society, the male's need for achievement can be
recognized. Men may cook, or weave, or dress dolls, or hunt
hummingbirds, but if such activities are appropriate occupations of
men, then the whole society, men and women alike, votes them as
important. When the same occupations are performed by women, they
are regarded as less important.*

Margaret Mead, *Male and Female*

---

ter, the whole plot of personal relations is made
more elaborate, and in many ways more rewarding. The poet of such a society will praise
virtues, albeit feminine virtues, which might
never have any part in a social Utopia that
allowed no differences between the personalities of men and women.

To the extent that a society insists upon different kinds of personality so that one age-
group or class or sex-group may follow purposes disallowed or neglected in another, each
individual participant in that society is the
richer. The arbitrary assignment of set clothing,
set manners, set social responses, to individuals
born in a certain class, or a certain sex, or of
a certain colour, to those born on a certain day
of the week, to those born with a certain
complexion, does violence to the individual
endowment of individuals, but permits the
building of a rich culture. The most extreme
development of a society that has attained great
complexity at the expense of the individual is
historical India, based, as it was, upon the un-
compromising association of a thousand attributes of behaviour, attitude, and occupation
with an accident of birth. To each individual
there was given the security, although it might
be the security of despair, of a set rôle, and
the reward of being born into a highly complex
society.

Furthermore, when we consider the position
of the deviant individual in historical cultures,
those who are born into a complex society in
the wrong sex or class for their personalities
to have full sway are in a better position than
those who are born into a simple society which
does not use in any way their special temperamental gifts. The violent woman in a society
that permits violence to men only, the strongly
emotional member of an aristocracy in a culture
that permits downright emotional expression
only in the peasantry, the ritualistically inclined
individual who is bred a Protestant in a country
which has also Catholic institutions—each one
of these can find expressed in some other group
in the society the emotions that he or she is
forbidden to manifest. He is given a certain kind
of support by the mere existence of these values, values so congenial to him and so inacces-
sible because of an accident of birth. For those
who are content with a vicarious spectator-rôle,
or with materials upon which to feast the creative imagination, this may be almost enough.
They may be content to experience from the
sidewalks during a parade, from the audience
of a theatre or from the nave of a church, those
emotions the direct expression of which is denied to them. The crude compensations offered
by the moving pictures to those whose lives
are emotionally starved are offered in subtler
forms by the art and literature of a complex
society to the individual who is out of place
in his sex or his class or his occupational group.

Sex-adjustments, however, are not a matter
of spectatorship, but a situation in which the
most passive individual must play some part

It is not nature, but class society, which robbed women of their right to participate in the higher functions of society and placed the primary emphasis upon their animal functions of maternity. And this robbery was perpetrated through a two-fold myth. On the one side, motherhood is represented as a biological affliction arising out of the maternal organs of women. Alongside this vulgar materialism, motherhood is represented as being something almost mystical. To console women for their status as second-class citizens, mothers are sanctified, endowed with halos and blessed with special "instincts," feelings and knowledge forever beyond the comprehension of men. Sancity and degradation are simply two sides of the same coin of the social robbery of women under class society.

Evelyn Reed, *The Myth of Women's Inferiority*

if he or she is to participate fully in life. And while we may recognize the virtues of complexity, the interesting and charming plots that cultures can evolve upon the basis of accidents of birth, we may well ask: Is not the price too high? Could not the beauty that lies in contrast and complexity be obtained in some other way? If the social insistence upon different personalities for the two sexes results in so much confusion, so many unhappy deviants, so much disorientation, can we imagine a society that abandons these distinctions without abandoning the values that are at present dependent upon them?

Let us suppose that, instead of the classification laid down on the "natural" bases of sex and race, a society had classified personality on the basis of eye-colour. It had decreed that all blue-eyed people were gentle, submissive, and responsive to the needs of others, and all brown-eyed people were arrogant, dominating, self-centred, and purposive. In this case two complementary social themes would be woven together—the culture, in its art, its religion, its formal personal relations, would have two threads instead of one. There would be blue-eyed men, and blue-eyed women, which would mean that there were gentle, "maternal" women, and gentle, "maternal" men. A blue-eyed man might marry a woman who had been bred to the same personality as himself, or a brown-eyed woman who had been bred to the contrasting personality. One of the strong ten-

Bushman Family: Woman and Baby by Malvina Hoffman. By permission of Field Museum of Natural History.

dencies that makes for homosexuality, the tendency to love the similar rather than the antithetical person, would be eliminated. Hostility between the two sexes as groups would be minimized, since the individual interests of members of each sex could be woven together in different ways, and marriages of similarity and friendships of contrast need carry no necessary handicap of possible psycho-sexual maladjustment. The individual would still suffer a mutilation of his temperamental preferences, for it would be the unrelated fact of eye-colour that would determine the attitudes which he was educated to show. Every blue-eyed person would be forced into submissiveness and declared maladjusted if he or she showed any traits that it had been decided were only appropriate to the brown-eyed. The greatest social loss, however, in the classification of personality on the basis of sex would not be present in this society which based its classification on eye-colour. Human relations, and especially those which involve sex, would not be artificially distorted.

But such a course, the substitution of eye-colour for sex as a basis upon which to educate children into groups showing contrasting personalities, while it would be a definite advance upon a classification by sex, remains a parody of all the attempts that society has made through history to define an individual's rôle in terms of sex, or colour, or date of birth, or shape of head.

However, the only solution of the problem does not lie between an acceptance of standardization of sex-differences with the resulting cost in individual happiness and adjustment, and the abolition of these differences with the consequent loss in social values. A civilization might take its cues not from such categories as age or sex, race or hereditary position in a family line, but instead of specializing personality along such simple lines recognize, train, and make a place for many and divergent temperamental endowments. It might build upon the different potentialities that it now attempts to extirpate artificially in some children and create artificially in others.

Historically the lessening of rigidity in the classification of the sexes has come about at different times, either by the creation of a new artificial category, or by the recognition of real individual differences. Sometimes the idea of social position has transcended sex-categories. In a society that recognizes gradations in wealth or rank, women of rank or women of wealth have been permitted an arrogance which was denied to both sexes among the lowly or the poor. Such a shift as this has been, it is true, a step towards the emancipation of women, but it has never been a step towards the greater freedom of the individual. A few women have shared the upper-class personality, but to balance this a great many men as well as women have been condemned to a personality characterized by subservience and fear. Such shifts as these mean only the substitution of one arbitrary standard for another. A society is equally unrealistic whether it insists that only men can be brave, or that only individuals of rank can be brave.

To break down one line of division, that between the sexes, and substitute another, that between classes, is no real advance. It merely shifts the irrelevancy to a different point. And meanwhile, individuals born in the upper classes are shaped inexorably to one type of personality, to an arrogance that is again uncongenial to at least some of them, while the arrogant among the poor fret and fume beneath their training for submissiveness. At one end of the scale is the mild, unaggressive young son of wealthy parents who is forced to lead, at the other the aggressive, enterprising child of the slums who is condemned to a place in the ranks. If our aim is greater expression for each individual temperament, rather than any partisan interest in one sex or its fate, we must see these historical developments which have aided in freeing some women as nevertheless a kind of development that also involved major social losses.

The second way in which categories of sex-differences have become less rigid is through a recognition of genuine individual gifts as they occurred in either sex. Here a real distinction has been substituted for an artificial one, and the gains are tremendous for society and for the individual. Where writing is accepted as a profession that may be pursued by either sex with perfect suitability, individuals who have the ability to write need not be debarred from it by their sex, nor need they, if they do write, doubt their essential masculinity or femininity. An occupation that has no basis in sex-determined gifts can now recruit its ranks from twice as many potential artists. And it is here that we can find a ground-plan for building a society that would substitute real differences for arbitrary ones. We must recognize that beneath the superficial classifications of sex and race the same potentialities exist, recurring generation after generation, only to perish because society has no place for them. Just as society now permits the practice of an art to members of either sex, so it might also permit the development of many contrasting temperamental gifts in each sex. It might abandon its various attempts to make boys fight and to make girls remain passive, or to make all children fight, and instead shape our educational institutions to develop to the full the boy who shows a capacity for maternal behaviour, the girl who shows an opposite capacity that is stimulated by fighting against obstacles. No skill, no special aptitude, no vividness of imagination or precision of thinking would go unrecognized because the child who possessed it was of one sex rather than the other. No child would be relentlessly shaped to one pattern of behaviour, but instead there should be many patterns, in a world that had learned to allow to each individual the pattern which was most congenial to his gifts.

Such a civilization would not sacrifice the gains of thousands of years during which society has built up standards of diversity. The social gains would be conserved, and each child would be encouraged on the basis of his actual temperament. Where we now have patterns of behaviour for women and patterns of behaviour for men, we would then have patterns of behaviour that expressed the interests of individuals with many kinds of endowment. There would be ethical codes and social symbolisms, an art and a way of life, congenial to each endowment.

Historically our own culture has relied for the creation of rich and contrasting values upon many artificial distinctions, the most striking of which is sex. It will not be by the mere abolition of these distinctions that society will develop patterns in which individual gifts are given place instead of being forced into an ill-fitting mould. If we are to achieve a richer culture, rich in contrasting values, we must recognize the whole gamut of human potentialities, and so weave a less arbitrary social fabric, one in which each diverse human gift will find a fitting place.

Esther Newton and Paula Webster

Matriarchy: As Women See It

Why bring up the matriarchy controversy at all? Isn't the notion of a matriarchal stage in social history dead and buried with the nineteenth century? Both of us had accepted without question that males had always been dominant, that even in matrilineal systems this was so.

For similar reasons we are both re-examining the whole matriarchy question. This began with our commitment to the feminist movement, and later our participation in a women's anthropology collective. One of the first papers to stimulate our thinking was "Woman the Gatherer," by Sally Linton, presented at the annual meeting of the American Anthropological Association in 1970. Where did the family come from? Why did women need men in the first place? What did paleolithic society look like? Was the position of women better then?

The only literature within anthropology which questions the existence of universal male domination, and therefore implicitly assumes the possibility of a different kind of society, is the nineteenth century work of Engels and Bachofen which claimed that matriarchies had preceded the patriarchies at some period of prehistory. Although the evidence of prehistory does not rule out matriarchal societies, it certainly does not demonstrate that they existed, and in the face of the world-wide patriarchies of today, there is no strong reason to suppose that things were ever different. Nor has the claim held up that matrilineal societies (in which kin groups, property holding, and inheritance are organized around or through women)

represent vestiges of ancient matriarchal societies.

Engels' assertions for a universal stage of matriarchy rest, briefly, on historical materialism. Institutions are determined by material conditions, and before the existence of class society, women shared equally in social production and therefore were equal to men. The kind of evidence needed to prove or disprove Engels' theory would come from whatever archeology could divulge about paleolithic social organization and from ethnography of present day pre-state societies. And this is an enormous job, which has barely begun.

Bachofen's theory of matriarchy is based on universal stages of social evolution, to which religious organization is the key. He argues that religions based on "the feminine principle" were dominant up through early states, when they were overthrown by patriarchal religions. These early societies had mother-right clans as their analogue in social organization. His theory has many weaknesses both internally and methodologically: the existence of mother-goddess religions, no matter how well documented, does not automatically prove the existence of matriarchy or even higher status for women.

Feminists have already begun to review Bachofen and Engels: a number of papers and books have come out recently. Some of these reassert the existence of matriarchy, modify the original theories or build on them, and forward new evidence. From this literature of claims and disclaims, all by women, certain key issues emerge. The most interesting of these is that feminists who were claiming the existence of a golden age in which women had power and/or were not oppressed (we say golden age because not all of them accept the term matriarchy) did not visualize it as the mirror opposite of patriarchy. We had been thinking of patriarchy as a social system in which men, as a class or group, were dominant over women as a class or group. That is, what we have today in America, and what we see in all present day societies, whether or not they are patrilineal. In other words, for us, patriarchy = male dominance. We expected that matriarchy = female dominance. But even where the author unequivocally postulated a system based on female dominance, the system was seen as based on different *principles* from the male-dominated systems we know. In other words, there was no general agreement on what the word matriarchy meant, while at the same time it was often used to mean something quite different from the reverse of patriarchy.

The key to the difficulty seemed to have to do with power. Was it that these authors could not visualize women having power since they had no models for it? Was there a need for a distinction between power and authority? Was it a failure of imagination, or rather of will? Perhaps the idea of women holding power made the authors uncomfortable. Would we be a more benevolent ruling class than men because we were morally superior?

We do not believe that the existence of matriarchy can be conclusively proven or disproven at this time. But the controversy itself is valuable. In the work of the eight feminist authors listed above, we can see how matriarchy is defined and described by each. Let us relate each definition, first to several key issues about

the correlates of (or obstructions to) power and second to their vision of what it might mean for women to be liberated. The position on matriarchy and the vision for the future are in every case directly related.

For us, the matriarchy controversy raises some very essential issues about our present condition and our future in a way that cannot be easily dismissed because it is visionary. The controversy goes far beyond a narrow academic haggle over the origins of social institutions into the very pressing problems that feminists are facing today. Whatever else the idea of matriarchy is, it is most compellingly an idea about what a society would look like in which women would truly be free. We have been so powerless that the effort to imagine ourselves *with* power is a critical exercise. Unfortunately, as each author has tried to imagine women with power, she has been faced with the problem that all our models for power/authority are male.

There are two assumptions that all the authors share. First, that women today are everywhere oppressed, that this is wrong and should be changed. Curiously, although there is a great deal of disagreement about what it would mean to be free, there is a kind of assumption made that we all know what we are talking about when we say we are oppressed. Many authors cite specific examples: we have been denied knowledge of our history; we never have the prestige that men have; we are denied access to public power and control over technology; our sexuality and our bodies are controlled by the double standard and marriage; according to Leacock, our "socially necessary labor was turned into a private service," and so on. Second, that our society as a whole is in need of radical change. There is sharp disagreement

Witchcraft Was Hung, in History

Witchcraft was hung, in History,
But History and I
Find all the Witchcraft that we need
Around us, every Day—

Emily Dickinson

---

over whether liberating women in itself would bring about a new society.

It is within this broad consensus that each author deals with the matriarchy question. In each work we were able to isolate certain issues, all of which, we think, are intimately related.

Defining the Matriarchy

Five of our authors, none of whom are anthropologists, assert that matriarchy once existed (de Beauvoir, Reed, Firestone, Davis and Diner). The three anthropologists deny that matriarchy *ever* existed. What kind of society are they talking about? When we boiled down the various definitions we found there were two types, a dominance matriarchy and an equality matriarchy.

Logically, we thought, matriarchy should mean the power of women, as a group, over men, i.e., female dominance. But only two of the authors claim that women were dominant in matriarchy (Davis and Diner). The other three who use the term—Reed, Firestone, and de Beauvoir—do not describe a society in which women had power over men, but rather a social order in which women's *position* or *status* was "more equal," where women were "highly esteemed." In many cases we couldn't even tell whether the author meant "more equal/ influential/esteemed than they are now" or "more equal/influential/esteemed than men." To add to the difficulty, nearly all authors see

the matriarchy as influence or power of *mothers,* while patriarchy has come to mean power of *men.* We think the definitional vagueness comes not only from basic theoretical disagreements, but also from anxiety about saying that woman might have had power (much less that they had power *over* men).

One of the authors, Leacock, defines matriarchy as a society in which women would hold power over men, and denies that such a society ever existed. Nevertheless, she believes that under prehistoric conditions of hunting/ gathering and horticulture, there existed egalitarian societies:

> The significant point for women's status is that the household was communal, and the division of labor between the sexes reciprocal; the economy did not involve the dependence of the wife and children on the husband . . . since in primitive communal society decisions were made by those who would be carrying them out, the participation of women in a major share of socially necessary labor did not reduce them to virtual slavery, as is the case in class society, but accorded them decision-making powers commensurate with their contribution.

Leacock speculates that these primitive communal societies were very likely matrilineal, so that Engels' matriarchy should be read as matrilineal. Leacock never says that women held power as a group, or that they had authority and legitimacy even equal to men. Presumably in the communal society they had no need for them.

Evelyn Reed, whose thought is based on Engels, with some anthropological data mixed in, vigorously defends the notion that matriarchies existed. When you examine her argument she is describing almost exactly the same primitive communal society (which was matrilineal) as Leacock. So actually the same claim is being made, although Leacock denies and Reed affirms the existence of primitive matriarchy.

Therefore, of our eight authors, two affirm matriarchy defined as class power (Davis and Diner), while four accept matriarchy only if defined as a stage of equality with harmony between the sexes, some kind of classless authority-reciprocity (although Leacock explicitly rejects the word matriarchy because for her it means power over men). Two of the anthropologist authors doubt the existence not only of matriarchy but of primitive egalitarianism (the Know group and Gough). According to the first, hereinafter referred to by an acronym of their last names, BMOPS:

> In no society at any point in time, or in any place in the world, are women's activities, no matter how economically productive, considered by the society to be as important as the activities in which men engage. Further, women *as a group* have never been in the position to make political decisions which affect the wider society . . . individual women hold power; women as a class do not.

Gough says that *"even in hunting societies it seems that women are in some sense the 'second sex' with greater or lesser subordination to men."* Yet, she sees enough merit in Engels' scheme to supplement it with comparative ethnographic data:

> In hunting societies, however, women are less subordinated in certain crucial respects as [than?] they are in most, if not all, of the archaic states,

or even in some capitalist nations. These respects include men's ability to deny women sexuality or to force it upon them; to command or exploit their labor or to control their produce; to control or rob them of their children; to confine them physically and prevent their movement; or to withhold from them large areas of the societies' knowledge and cultural attainments.

Summing up the school of thought that sees matriarchy as harmonious primitive egalitarianism, we get the following picture: In early hunting and gathering and horticultural societies women were more equal, more esteemed, and not oppressed. The better position women had was based on their contribution to production in a society that was most probably organized into matrilineal, matrilocal clans where both the productive and socializing burdens of women were shared. They seem to imply that there was the usual division of labor by sex, but that the women's portion was shared with other women [female bonding?]. But, with the creation of the state, class society, and monogamous marriage women's condition changed for the worse. In this general picture Reed, Leacock, Gough, Firestone, de Beauvoir, all take off from Engles. We have not developed de Beauvoir's and Firestone's notions of matriarchy, because *they did not* do so. In fact their matriarchy claims seem in the nature of a ritual bow to Engels; both authors base their theories on the statement that women have always been oppressed.

The vision of primitive egalitariarism is contradicted by ethnographic evidence. For example, according to a personal communication from Nancy Howell, a demographer who has worked in the area, Woodburn has reported that among the Hadza in Tanzania, a hunting and gathering group, if a woman overhears or learns any of the men's ritual secrets, the men

Were there actually such things as the fabulous nations of maidens, the mounted demons, galloping from the edges of the world to make ice and golden sand splash to all sides? Was there ever a "man-hating army" with changing tresses and awesome customs? . . . In time and reality the Amazon kingdoms not only comprise an extremist end of matriarchy but also are a beginning and a purpose in themselves. . . . In the mother clan, there was a constant progression of great mothers begetting more great mothers. Amazons however, reproduced the daughter type, which practically skips a generation and is something altogether different. They were conquerers, horse tamers, and huntresses who gave birth to children but did not nurse or rear them. They were an extreme, feminist wing of a young human race, whose other extreme wing consisted of the stringent patriarchies.

Helen Diner

---

gang-rape her. There is also much hostility between men and women centering around the distribution of food. We cite this as one of the many examples of the oppression of women in hunting and gathering groups which runs counter to the assertions of Leacock and Gough about the happy reciprocity that existed between men and women in "primitive communism." They meet these objections unsatisfactorily, in our opinion, by attributing modern-day male domination in these groups to the influence of patriarchal imperialist hegemony.

Davis and Diner are the two authors who accept the definition of matriarchy as class power and do in fact defend its past existence. Their matriarchy was not an egalitarian society. Women as a group were more powerful than men and dominated them in both the private and public spheres. The problems that their schemes present are provocative.

Although it is tempting simply to assign these authors to the Bachofen tradition of anthropological thinking, they have departed so far from current anthropological orthodoxy that we must present their theories in some detail. Some anthropologists might decide to reject these author's claims out of hand as being too unscientific, unsubstantiable or just too weird ever to be taken seriously. However, we focus specifically on these claims because they now have and may continue to have more influence in the feminist movement than the writings of their more "legitimate" sisters. Already such claims have been taken as fact and are begin-

ning to be found in the works of writers like Jill Johnston and Phyllis Chesler. Davis's book, *The First Sex*, in inexpensive paperback, has already reached thousands of women and its readership continues to grow. Contrary to some feminists, we do not think that this is necessarily regrettable.

Who is Elizabeth Gould Davis and what is she saying? We don't know much about her except that she is a librarian in Sarasota, Florida. She began to write this revolutionary view of women's history following the death of her sister. None of her other professional qualifications or intellectual history are known to us. Glancing at the title, one is immediately struck by the fact that, while Simone de Beauvoir, who, despite her almost gratuitous reference to primitive matriarchy, calls her great work *The Second Sex,* Davis insists that women were *The First Sex*. While de Beauvoir believes that women never had power, except that given to them by men, Davis gloriously announces to all women (and quite secondarily, men) that we once had a great deal of power, that this was the natural state of things and only by means of a violent patriarchal revolution was it wrested from us.

Taking off from Bachofen, Davis also believes that myth is history. Myth and other symbolic elements of the superstructure determine the form of social organization. The Marxian emphasis on material base as a causal factor in the creation of social forms is explicitly rejected. Davis, however, is no slavish disciple, for her theory is really her own. Based on extremely diverse sources including mythology, archeology, anthropology, history, biology, and such marginal thinkers as Velikovsky, Atlantean theorists, believers in extraterrestrial travel, Davis weaves a fascinating and ingenious argument for women's past supremacy.

There are five stages in Davis' historical reconstruction:

1. Based on the works of Hesiod and the exponents of Atlantis, she identifies a Golden Age, so ancient that it is impossible to date. There was equality between the sexes, harmony, no gods or kings, and an advanced technology. This age was ended by a natural cataclysm in the tenth millennium, which has come down to us as the Great Flood.

This stage is not essential to her matriarchal claims, but it reinforces her cyclic view of history in which our patriarchal age is a very low point.

2. Next is a period of social chaos and savagery which was ended by the revolt of women against men's "lustful sexuality."

Culture, represented by women, becomes dominant over nature, represented by men. The outcome of this conflict was that women curbed and tamed men, brought peace and order to the world, which was critical for the further development of civilization. This revolt, which might have been led by Basilea, an Amazon Queen, occurred about fifty thousand years ago.

(This date conflicts with the 10,000 date for the end of the Golden Age, as well as with our knowledge of the human fossil record.)

3. The victory of the Amazons, that is all women, ushered in a long period of primitive matriarchy, whose basic form of social organization was units of mothers and their children,

---

Lineage

My grandmothers were strong.
They followed plows and bent to toil.
They moved through fields sowing seed.
They touched earth and grain grew.
They were full of sturdiness and singing.
My grandmothers were strong.

My grandmothers are full of memories
Smelling of soap and onions and wet clay
With veins rolling roughly over quick hands
They have many clean words to say.
My grandmothers were strong.
Why am I not as they?

Margaret Walker

---

excluding men, who were ignorant of their biological paternity. Women, to protect themselves and their daughters from the lust of their sons, invented the incest taboo and later exogamy to expel them. (This is a fascinating reversal of Freud.) The expelled sons formed bands of "marauding males" but "gradually more and more of the boys remained at home and became civilized."

4. Eventually the primitive matriarchies evolved into matriarchal city-states including the great civilizations of Sumer, Egypt, and Crete. This was the age of the Great Mother Goddess when there was justice and harmony; no sacrifices, no hunting, no killing, and, of course, no war. Davis does not accept the idea that the Great Goddesses merely reflect man's veneration of women, but rather, women's veneration of herself. "Man was pacific, deity feminine, and women supreme." She uses archeological sites such as Catal Hüyük and Mersin to support her claims.

5. Meanwhile, the descendants[1] of the men who were kicked out of the matriarchal clans and denied agricultural knowledge became carnivorous hunters, and existed on the periphery of the "gynocratic" city-states. These "rejects" of the civilized queendoms invaded and finally overthrew established agricultural communities in the Near East in the third millennium B.C. and in the Aegean about 1500 B.C. with the following results:

> Suddenly all is ended. Paradise is lost. A dark age overtakes the world—a dark age brought on by the cataclysm accompanied by a patriarchal revolution. Nomads, barbaric and uncivilized, roving bands of ejected, womanless men, destroy civilized city states, depose queens, and attempt to rule in their stead. The result is chaos. War and violence make their appearance, justice and law fly out the window, might replaces right, the Great Goddess is replaced by a stern and vengeful God, man becomes carnivorous, property rights become paramount over human rights, woman is degraded and exploited and civilization starts on the downward path that it still pursues.

The downfall of the matriarchal states is not adequately explained. Davis believes that the matriarchs may have brought about their own downfall by choosing the phallic meat-eaters as mates over their own pacific men—she suggests a correlation between the size of the phallus and carnivorous diet.

We are well aware that much or most of Davis' reconstruction of history sounds fantastic, that her methodology is highly questionable and that some of the empirical assertions are demonstrably untrue (for instance, fire was discovered well before the neolithic, hunting before that, etc.). Some of her claims are quite specific however, as for instance that the Catal Hüyük site gives clear evidence of matriarchy, and might be examined by archeologists and classicists.

We must conclude that, for Davis, the matriarchy (or gynocracy—significantly Davis is the only one of our authors to use the two terms interchangeably as Bachofen did) was not the mirror image of the patriarchy, for the society she describes was peaceful, harmonious, and spiritual. For Davis, this difference flows from the innate moral superiority of women. Yet as she goes on to describe the humiliations that the formerly despised men inflicted on women after the patriarchal revolution (clitoridectomy, chastity belts, rape, etc.) we are left with the impression that Davis could not resolve the paradox of a just and harmonious society in which men were valued *only* as sexual objects and servants. Did the men who were allowed to stay within the matriarchal city-states form an oppressed class? It seems that they did, yet Davis implies that women were more benevolent rulers than men have been. We might formulate this problem as follows: If women rulers are just, how can they oppress? If women cannot oppress, how can they rule? Does power inevitably corrupt?

Helen Diner, writing in the early 30's, is more closely tied to Bachofen's thinking than Davis, although she buttresses her argument with Briffault's ethnographic evidence, (published in 1927). Though not as provocative, angry, or original as Davis, she was devoted to unearthing the true history of women and was not afraid of being called one-sided. The theoretical part of her book is eclectic and hard to puzzle out, for she draws not only on Bachofen but also

---

[1]How did they produce descendants without women?—Editors of article

on a number of other, more obscure social theorists. She includes Engels but dismisses his theory as having no more vision than that of a "petty union official." She was put off by Engels' materialism; she preferred the mythic and symbolic. Like Davis and Bachofen, she has a cyclic notion of historical forms, and implies a return to a more just social order— matriarchy?

The matriarchy, for Diner, is an ideal social order based upon the natural primacy of the mother. She believes that in the long period of prehistory, the basic social form was the mother clan. These primitive matriarchies were harmonious; she seems to see them as some kind of matrilineal society in which men and women were truly equal. But with the rise of agriculture, women consolidated their rule, men became an oppressed class, and woman "degenerates" into an "Amazon." Somehow two extreme social forms split off from the ideal mother clan: daughter (Amazon) clans and brother (patriarchal) clans. For a period of several hundred years prior to the Homeric age the Amazons and brother clans fought in intense sibling warfare, which the Amazons ultimately lost.

For Diner then, men were definitely not an oppressed class in the ideal matriarchy, although the feminine *principle* ruled and women were certainly equal to, though different from, men. But in the Amazon clans, women showed another side of their character. While mothers are pacific and just, daughters are angry and warlike, and not at all averse to harsh measures. The different Amazon groups had various ways of dealing with the man problem. Most of the Amazons limited their contacts with adult men to sexual intercourse for procreation. In the moderate groups, the sons were returned to their fathers and only the daughters were raised. More extreme groups crippled the sons and used them as child nurses and domestic servants. Amazons on the Far Left killed the sons and often the fathers as well. The centers of Amazon predominance were the Black Sea Region and Libya, (present-day Morocco). Diner draws heavily on the historic records left by Strabo, Pliny, and Herodotus, who were quite explicit about these queendoms. Diner gives us a picture of what they were like:

> Of all the African Amazons, only the Gorgons seem to have maintained a pure Amazon state; the others though keeping the army purely feminine, maintained some men in their camps. The Libyan Amazons, who removed their right breasts, had compulsory military service for all girls for a number of years, during which they had to refrain from marriage. After that, they became part of the reserves and were allowed to take a mate and reproduce their kind. The women monopolized the government and other influential positions. In contrast to the later Thermodontines, however, they lived in a permanent relationship with their sex partners, even though the men led a retiring life, could not hold public office, and had no right to interfere in the government of the state or society. Children, who were brought up on mare's milk, were given to the men to rear.

In *The Glory of Hera* (Beacon, 1968), Philip Slater states that "there is a little too much ethnographic and circumstantial detail about the Amazons and the Amazon war to dismiss the entire episode as pure myth." After all, Troy was "pure myth" until it was looked for and found, as were the Biblical kingdoms.

Diner, like Davis, (and Engels, we may add) seems to imply that women brought about their own downfall, but where Davis suggests that women have a fatal weakness for the big phallus, Diner suggests that by degrading men to an oppressed class, by letting power corrupt them, they provoked the men to revolt. How the men were *able* to win is not explained.

Sources of Oppression and Innate Differences

Each author's construction of the matriarchy is directly related to what she thinks were the sources of women's oppression. One question that all authors address themselves to is the consequences of the most obvious biological difference between women and men, that women bear children. There are three contrasting positions on this issue:

Childbearing has nothing intrinsic to do with women's oppression (Leacock, Reed). Oppression is caused by marriage and class society. The agent of our oppression is therefore "the class system."

Childbearing intrinsically brings status and even dominance. Oppression has resulted from military defeat (Davis and Diner). The agent of our oppression is therefore men and male principle.

Childbearing and other related factors (child-rearing) are sufficient to account for women's universal and historic oppression. The ultimate agent of our oppression is therefore our own biology. (Firestone, de Beauvoir, BMOPS, and Gough all support some version of this position.)

Another closely related factor is the position on possible innate or at least universal differences of a temperamental or psychological nature between women and men. All the authors, except Leacock, Reed and Gough, imply or state that such differences do exist.

For Leacock and Reed, women's childbearing ability is not the cause of our present oppression; if anything, in primitive communism, it was a source of our high status:

In some ways it is the ultimate alienation in our society that the ability to give birth has been *transformed* into a liability. . . . The reason [for our present oppression] is not simply that, since women bear children they are more limited in their movements and activities. . . . This was not a handicap even in the limited technology of hunting and gathering life; it certainly has no relevance today. [Leacock: our italics]

Both writers also deny that there are any fundamental differences in temperament or psychology between women and men that could account either for matriarchy in prehistoric time or for patriarchy today. Rather the cause of our current oppression is the monogamous family which made women's labor into a private service rather than social production in class society. It follows then that before class society, women were not oppressed: i.e., the equality type matriarchy, egalitarianism, that both espouse existed.

For Davis and Diner, childbearing was not a source of oppression but rather a source of status and power until the patriarchal revolt (which for them occurred *after* the development of class society). Both see women as morally superior, attributing this to her closeness to nature, i.e., her reproductive system and consequent attachment to life over death, creation over destruction, harmony over conflict. That these qualities attach to woman as mother, at least for Diner, is clear from the warlike characteristics the latter imputes to the Amazons or daughter clans. Neither writer ignores the problems surrounding reproduction and child-rearing; each believes that women were able to handle them in a social organization in which both women and the female principle were dominant (for example, socialized child care in mother clans, rearing babies on mare's milk among Amazons and relegating child care to men). For both Davis and Diner then, the cause of our present oppression is military defeat at the hands of men and the consequent triumph of patriarchal religion and ideology, that is, force, although this line of thought is never fully developed.

For the other four authors, childbearing and associated factors have always made women subordinate to men. Obviously, this rules out the possibility of prehistoric matriarchy; for de Beauvoir and Firestone then primitive matriarchy meant a society in which perhaps women's position was less oppressive than today because the female *principle* was important. (As we all know, the proverbial pedestal is a very small space). The original root cause of women's oppression is the biologically given unequal distribution of reproductive labor. Because of her reproductive and associated child-care burdens, woman has always been restricted to a maintaining, nurturing role, while man has appropriated the creative, (or for de Beauvoir, transcendent) role:

> The Golden Age of woman is only a myth. To say that woman was the *other* is to say that there did not exist between the sexes a reciprocal relation; Earth, Mother, Goddess—she was no fellow creature in man's eyes; it was *beyond* the human realm that her power was confirmed, and she was therefore outside of that realm. Society has always been made; political power has always been in the hands of men.

However de Beauvoir believes that women's status declined even further in class society, and she calls for a socialist revolution as a necessary step toward liberation, leaving the problem of biology unsolved. Firestone, writing much later, goes beyond the necessary socialist revolution to advocate (logically enough), the elimination of the inequality via test-tube babies and complete redistribution of child-care functions.

Gough agrees with Firestone and de Beauvoir that woman has always been "the second sex."

> To the extent that men hold power over women in hunting societies this seems to spring from the male monopoly of heavy weapons, from the particular division of labor between the sexes, or from both. Although men seldom use weapons against women, they possess them (or possess superior weapons) in addition to their physical strength. This does give men an ultimate control of force.

She claims that the inequality between the sexes was adaptive under primitive conditions:

> The extent of inequality varied according to the ecology and the resulting sexual division of tasks. But in any case, it was largely a matter of survival rather than of man-made cultural impositions.

Gough denies the existence of any innate psychological differences. Obviously the introduction of an adaptational imperative begins to shift the discussion from power toward ecology and technology; we turn to the implications of this in the next section.

Finally, BMOPS also state that women have always been oppressed and therefore reject any notion of primitive matriarchy. Due to women's reproductive burden and the needs for hunting and defense, nature selected for the greater size

Matrilineal Descent

Not having spoken for years now,
I know you claim exile from my conscious-
    ness.
Yet I wear mourning whole nights through
for that embrace that warmed my ignorant
    lust
even past intimacies you had dreamed.
I played your daughter-husband, lover-son, to
    earn
both Abraham and Ishmael's guilt
for your indulgence, and in time, reproach.
Who sent us to that wilderness we both now
    know,
although I blamed you for that house of
    women
too many years. But Time is a waiting woman,
not some old man with a stupid beard,
and when I finally met my father I found him
arrogant and dull, a formican liar
with an Austrian accent. Well, we meet
the phantom that we long for in the end,
and getting there is half the grief.
Meanwhile, my theories rearrange themselves
like sand before this woman whose flaccid
 - breasts
sway with her stumblings, whose diamonds
still thaw pity from my eyes.
You're older than I thought. But so am I,
and grateful that we've come to this:
a ragged truce, an affirmation in me
that your strength, your pushiness, your sharp
    love,
your embroidery of lies—all, all were survival
    tools,
as when, during our personal diaspora, you
    stood
in some far country blocks away,
burning poems I no longer sent you
like Yahrzeit candles in my name, unsure of me
    at last
who sought a birthright elsewhere,
beyond the oasis of your curse,
even beyond that last mirage, your blessing.
Mother, in ways neither of us can ever
    understand,
I have come home.

                                   Robin Morgan

and strength of the male, biologically innate male aggressiveness and tendency to bond with other males (they accept Tiger and Fox on this point). Male dominance was adaptive under primitive conditions and has survived until today.

What Is Liberation?

For those who hold the vision of the golden age or some time when women's position was better, it serves as a model to imagine a liberated society, and as a statement about how problems currently facing women might be dealt with, particularly the problem of power and hierarchy. For those who reject the matriarchy, the problem is not one of return, but of changing what has always been, in order to bring about liberation of women for the first time. In neither group is the vision of the new society really as specific as a blueprint, and more problems are raised than are answered.

Each author wants to see an end to the oppression of women and a new society in which technology will be used for human ends. Whether one will almost automatically bring about the other or whether both must be done at the same time is a subject of disagreement which partially results from a fundamental unclarity about what liberation for women would mean. There seem to us to be two logical possibilities. The central tendency among our authors is to hope that men and women will be equal. But what does this mean? Does it mean that sex distinctions including roles will be eliminated, so that men and women would be in some sense the same? This solution is proposed by Firestone, as the source of women's oppression has always been childbearing and child-rearing, sex distinction could be eliminated by ending the biologically unequal division of labor via population reduction and test-tube babies, and by fully shared and socialized child care. At the same time, she argues, as an integral part of the change, we need a socialist revolution. Ultimately all forms of hierarchy and power are based on the sex distinction, and should be done away with, including finally, culture itself. The end goal is "cosmic consciousness." How are women to make sure that revolutionary change proceeds in our interests? Firestone assumes that those in power after the socialist revolution will have "good intentions."

On the other hand, if equal does not mean the same, does it mean a balance of power? This problem is nowhere worked out by Leacock, Reed, de Beauvoir or Gough, all of whom advocate a socialist revolution as more or less sufficient to bring about equality between men and women if it includes the socialization of child care and an end to monogamous marriage. For Leacock and Reed, this answer is logically consistent with what they see as the source of women's oppression. But who is to guarantee that future socialist revolutions will do away with monogamous marriage? Women are clearly still oppressed in socialist countries. And what if these changes, even if realized, are not enough to free women? None of the authors goes further than the suggestion of some kind of women's caucus within the socialist revolution to push for women's interests. Gough avoids the problem of how to reverse men's ultimate monopoly on force, which she sees as a likely source of women's oppression from hunting and gathering times.

BMOPS do explicitly recommend the elimination of sex oppression through a balance of power. For them, male dominance was adaptive under primitive conditions, but is now leading us toward destruction and must be eliminated.

Myself and My Mother

Purpose: To explore our relationships with our mothers.

Directions:

1. Write a biography of your mother.* (You may need to interview her or another family member to gain the necessary information.)
2. Try to include the following kinds of information:

   When and where was your mother born? What were her parents like (such as ethnic and economic background)? What were the important influences on her as a child? What is/was her relationship like with your father? Did/does she work? What are her main interests? What are your earliest memories of her? What is your relationship like with her—in the past and now? What messages or advice did she give you about being a woman? In what ways are you like/unlike your mother?

3. What did you learn? What did you experience? Share your experiences with the class.

How do you feel about your mother? How do you feel toward her now that you have written her biography?

*(or stepmother, sister, or whatever woman was most important to you while you were growing up.)

As an antidote to man's aggressive tendencies, they propose a "partly female dominated polity" and equal control over technology. Everyone shies away from the possible implications of a balance-of-power situation. Isn't a balance of power notoriously unstable and conflict-ridden, rather than harmonious and cooperative, as these authors assume? Why should the sex antagonism pointed to by de Beauvoir, Diner, Davis, and Firestone disappear?

I will never take a husband. A man in Toul took an action against me
for breach of promise; but I never promised him. I am a soldier; I do
not want to be thought of as a woman. I do not care for the things
women care for. They dream of lovers, and of money. I dream of
leading a charge, and of placing the big guns.

from *Saint Joan* by George Bernard Shaw

A basic problem is the failure to spell out the relationship of power to women's freedom. For the previous writers, somehow women's oppression as a group will be ended *without* their holding power as a group. Why should men give up their power simply because male dominance is no longer adaptive? How can we count on men agreeing that their dominance is no longer in the interests of the human race?

On the other hand, Davis and (perhaps only implicitly) Diner reject the equality or the balance-of-power models, and propose instead a female-*dominated* society. Since women were originally overthrown by force, you would expect Davis to call for a new Amazon army to redress the situation, but she avoids this by claiming that patriarchy is bringing about its own destruction. For her, female dominance will bring about equality and harmony between the sexes, and end all the evils she sees as caused by the current dominance of men and "masculist" principle: violence, chaos, injustice, overemphasis on materialism and property rights as against spirituality and human rights. Davis' vision is apocalyptic:

The ages of masculism are now drawing to a close. Their dying days are lit up by a final flare of universal violence and despair such as the world has seldom seen. Men of goodwill turn in every direction seeking cures for their perishing society, but to no avail. *Any and all social reforms superimposed upon our sick civilization can be no more*

effective than a bandage on a gaping and putrefying wound. . . .

In the new science of the twenty-first century, not physical force but spiritual force will lead the way. Mental and spiritual gifts will be more in demand than gifts of physical nature. Extrasensory perception will take precedence over sensory perception. And in this sphere woman will again predominate. [italics ours]

Once again the fundamental problem revolves around power. If women are to be supreme, won't men necessarily be subordinate? If women are to rule, won't men be the subjects? Why should they agree to this state of affairs? How could this society be better than what we have now? (However, if sex oppression cannot be eliminated, why not say frankly we would rather be the rulers than the ruled?) You might think that men are to be an oppressed class, whether they like it or not. But no, for the new utopia for Davis will be:

founded on love and trust and mutual respect and concern in which all men and women are truly brothers and sisters under the just guidance of a beneficent deity, where laws are enforced by persuasion and good will.

The *deus ex machina* here is the notion that men and women are so innately different that power in the hands of women will be wholly different from what it has been in the hands of men, i.e., women will be benevolent rulers.

As far as we know, the only feminist to work out power in the hands of women to a logical, if unlikely conclusion, is Valerie Solanis, who advocated the overthrow of patriarchy by the simple means of physically eliminating men (except for exhibition or reproductive purposes). If men are eliminated, so is sex oppression; see also the Amazon societies for a version of this solution.

Where are we now? We are left to explain the implications and contributions which the matriarchy debate has for anthropological and feminist theory. One area of difficulty has been the definition of power and its confusion with authority, high status or prestige. Much more work must be done by feminist anthropologists to clarify these concepts. We can also begin to pool our resources and energy to begin looking at critical issues for women in our own society.

Another offshoot of the matriarchy debate is the growing awareness that women's history has yet to be written. Since both anthropologists and feminists are interested in history a re-examination of mythic, historical and archeological evidence for woman's true role should be undertaken immediately. Perhaps some of Davis's book is not so fantastic.

Finally, whether one believes or disbelieves in the existence of primitive matriarchy, the controversy does push women (and men) into the future by challenging us to envision a society where women would be liberated, free and (perhaps for the first time) powerful. Up to now, with the exception of Monique Wittig's *Les Guérillères*, there is no feminist utopian literature which helps us imagine the society of the future. What would a society look like in which we had public political power and authority? Most women are so oppressed and repressed

Amazon Holding a Bow, courtesy of Musei Capitolini, Rome, Italy

that we can't imagine having power and, if we could imagine it, would be afraid to propose it. Perhaps this is why we respect and admire all of the women who chose to deal seriously with the matriarchy question. And we have a special respect for Davis because she is not afraid to go out on a limb or be called "crazy." There is a place *within* science for vision, intuition, and risk-taking. Men with these qualities are often called "geniuses."

Many women will be embarrassed by *The First Sex* because of its insistence that women *are* biologically and morally superior to men,

Specifically, my thesis is that woman is being identified with—or, if you will, seems to be a symbol of—something that every culture devalues, something that every culture defines as being of a lower order of existence than itself. Now it seems that there is only one thing that would fit that description, and that is "nature" in the most generalized sense. Every culture, or, generically, "culture," is engaged in the process of generating and sustaining systems of meaningful forms (symbols, artifacts, etc.) by means of which humanity transcends the givens of natural existence, bends them to its purposes, controls them in its interest. We may thus broadly equate culture with the notion of human consciousness, or with the products of human consciousness (i.e., systems of thought and technology), by means of which humanity attempts to assert control over nature.

Sherry B. Ortner

Stellar Food by Remedios Varo. Reprinted by permission of Walter Gruen.

because of its unscientific method, and perhaps above all by its very angry tone. This is an affront to our notion of value-free social science and objectivity. Some anthropologists have denied that ideological neutrality exists in any social science, and when this argument is mentioned in relation to imperialism or racism, many would agree. We are only now directing the same critique at the sexist bias in anthropology, and if we are honest we will have to admit that anger is a big part of our motivation. But anger is not academic and so is muted or hidden by the language of "respectable" anthropological discourse. We think that for a new understanding of women in society we will have to push some of the old boundaries to their limits and create new paradigms in the process.

What concerns us most as feminists and anthropologists is the danger of a split taking place in the women's movement. Many women in the movement are seizing on the matriarchy as a true women's history and ideal model (mythic or not). Let's not cast ourselves as nice daddy's girls defending the conventional wisdom of anthropology, and dismissing our sisters outside anthropology as simply misinformed or misguided. Those of us who reject, on whatever theoretical and/or empirical grounds, the existence of matriarchy, had better make sure we are not throwing out the search for women's history or the ideal of women's power at the same time.

For Further Reading

Hoiter, H. 1970. *Sex Roles and Social Structure.* Universitetsforlaget.

*****Jacobs, S.** 1971. *Women in Perspective: A Guide for Cross Cultural Studies.* Urbana: Univ. of Illinois Press.

Mead, M. 1968. *Male and Female.* New York: Dell.

——, 1967. *Sex and Temperament.* W. Caldwell, N.J.: Morrow.

*****Paulme, D.** 1971. *Women in Tropical Africa.* Berkeley: Univ. of California Press.

Pescatello, A. 1973. *Male and Female in Latin America: Essays.* Pittsburgh: Univ. of Pittsburgh Press.

*****Rosaldo, M. Z. and Lamphere, L.** 1971. *Woman, Culture, Society.* Stanford: Stanford Univ. Press.

Rosenberg, M. and Bergstrom, L. 1974. *Women and Society: A Critical Review of the Literature with a Selected Annotated Bibliography.* Beverly Hills: Sage Pubs.

*All readings reviewed in the previous article, *Matriarchy: As Women See It.*

Psychological Sex Differences

This chapter continues to probe the questions examined in the first two chapters: What is the psychology of women? It begins with psychologist Naomi Weisstein's "Psychology Constructs the Female," a treatise that examines anthropological and biological as well as psychological data and arguments. Weisstein concludes basically that clinical psychological theories are not based on scientific evidence and that empirical studies that do exist ignore the fact that cultural expectations and social context are different for males and females. Since we cannot conduct experiments in which we can hold this social, cultural context constant, we can't really know what the psychology of women (or men) is. Present views of the psychology of women, therefore, merely reflect male fantasies of women. Until "the crucial experiment"—one in which social expectations for males and females are the same—can be performed, we do not know what, if any, innate psychological sex differences exist. This leads Weisstein to the conclusion that perhaps it might be more parsimonious to assume there are none. In either event (whether or not there are innate psychological differences) she asserts that both sexes are due equal status, respect, and worth.

Since there are different sets of expectations for women and men and since they are reared differently in our culture, it is no surprise that psychological sex differences occur. Eleanor Maccoby and Carol Jacklin have surveyed the literature and produced a summary of such differences in *The Psychology of Sex Differences* (1974). The excerpt in this chapter lists the differences that are not real, those that are, and those areas still open for further investigation.

Maccoby and Jacklin mention three theories of how socialization produces sex differences.

The first is praise and encouragement in which parents and significant others reinforce the child for appropriate sex-typed behaviors. The second theory maintains that the child learns spontaneously through imitating a role model of the same sex. In the third theory, self-socialization, the child develops a concept of maleness and femaleness, adjusting his or her behavior to match the appropriate concept.

Following the Maccoby and Jacklin excerpt, an article by Martha Mednick and Hilda Weissman presents a selective review of the psychological literature that pertains to adults, focusing on three areas—sex roles, achievement, and psychotherapy. This selection reflects, beside the authors' preferences, three major areas of current research about women. As the authors themselves imply, the "Zeitgeist" (the women's movement) has contributed a great deal of freshness to their approach to the psychology of women. In terms of sex roles, there is now a greater emphasis on the social and cultural factors that affect the psychology of women. In terms of achievement, this has led to the examination of many additional aspects of achievement, especially applicable to women. As Mednick implies, it should be noted that while many conservative feminists encourage women to succeed within the current (patriarchal) socioeconomic system, more radical feminists challenge the motivational structure based on (male) values of competition, striving, individuality, domination, and aggression.

Weissman discusses the effect of feminist thought and knowledge of sexuality on the theories and practice of psychotherapy. She discusses the redefinition of traditional (male) psychology.

If a major theme can be discerned, it is that of the sexual division of personality characteristics based on the male thinker's view of reality. To the extent this division is accepted, individual women, and men to a lesser degree, are constricted in their personal fulfillment, and society is hobbled in both competence and relatedness.

In the next article political scientist Jo Freeman, employing her insight into the social sciences, presents an alternative view of psychological sex differences. In exposing social science as politically conservative, she asserts that it acts as a means of social control by merely describing what *is* rather than trying to explain why. Freeman's approach to understanding the psychology of women focuses on two themes also explored by Mednick and Weissman—self-concept/self-esteem and achievement.

Freeman presents abundant evidence of women's negative self-image and shows that it inevitably results in low self-esteem, although Maccoby and Jacklin report that women do not have low self-esteem at least through childhood and adolescence. In another study, mentioned in Mednick and Weissman's paper (Broverman, et al., 1970), a series of opposite adjectives were identified first as either male or female traits, and then as to whether they were socially desirable. The following were considered male traits and deemed desirable for any person to have:

> aggressive, independent, unemotional, hides emotions, objective, not easily influenced, dominant, likes math and science, not excitable in a minor crisis, active, competitive, logical, worldly, skilled in business, direct, knows the way of the world, feelings not easily hurt, adventurous, makes decisions easily, never cries, acts as a leader, self-confident, not comfortable about being aggressive, ambitious, able to separate feelings from ideas, not dependent, not conceited about appearance, thinks men are superior to women, talks freely about sex with men.

Traits considered female and deemed desirable for any person to have were the following:

> does not use harsh language, talkative, tactful, gentle, aware of the feelings of others, religious, interested in own appearance, neat in habits, quiet, strong need for security, appreciates art and literature, expresses tender feelings.

There was a high percentage of agreement about these traits among both male and female subjects. As Freeman suggests, the female role does have positive aspects, but the female attributes are not those which receive the highest rewards in our society. Since this is true, women perceive that the valuable traits belong to men rather than to themselves.

Next, Freeman summarizes the many facets of women's failure to achieve in this society. Based on Maccoby and Jacklin's documentation of girls' early superior achievements, how is it, one wonders, that achievement declines with the beginning of adolescence? After surveying all of the factors involved, Freeman, like Weisstein, concludes that it is remarkable that women continue to achieve at all. Furthermore, the author concludes that the difference between women's intellectual abilities and their actual achievement shows how much patriarchy limits and disables women.

Although Freeman cites earlier work that has since been revised, such as Horner's original fear-of-success study (discussed in Mednick and Weissman) and Maccoby's earlier work (1966), she does provide interesting political and historical perspectives on achievement as well as other aspects of the psychology of women.

Freeman raises the possibility of a social and political analysis of the psychology of women—a notion more fully explored in the next chapter, "Oppression of the Self."

Naomi Weisstein

Psychology Constructs the Female

It is an implicit assumption that the area of psychology which concerns itself with personality has the onerous but necessary task of describing the limits of human possibility. Thus when we are about to consider the liberation of women, we naturally look to psychology to tell us what 'true' liberation would mean: what would give women the freedom to fulfill their own intrinsic natures.

Psychologists have set about describing the true natures of women with a certainty and a sense of their own infallibility rarely found in the secular world. Bruno Bettelheim, of the University of Chicago, tell us (1965) that

> We must start with the realization that, as much as women want to be good scientists or engineers, they want first and foremost to be womanly companions of men and to be mothers.

Erik Erikson of Harvard University (1965), upon noting that young women often ask whether they can 'have an identity before they know whom they will marry, and for whom they will make a home', explains somewhat elegiacally that

> Much of a young woman's identity is already defined in her kind of attractiveness and in the selectivity of her search for the man (or men) by whom she wishes to be sought. . . .

Mature womanly fulfillment, for Erikson, rests on the fact that a woman's

> . . . somatic design harbors an "inner space" destined to bear the offspring of chosen men, and

with it, a biological, psychological, and ethical commitment to take care of human infancy.

Some psychiatrists even see the acceptance of woman's role by women as a solution to societal problems. "Woman is nurturance . . . ," writes Joseph Rheingold (1964), a psychiatrist at Harvard Medical School. ". . . anatomy decrees the life of a woman. . . . When women grow up without dread of their biological functions and without subversion by feminist doctrine, and therefore enter upon motherhood with a sense of fulfillment and altruistic sentiment, we shall attain the goal of a good life and a secure world in which to live it." (p. 714)

These views from men who are assumed to be experts reflect, in a surprisingly transparent way, the cultural consensus. They not only assert that a woman is defined by her ability to attract men, they see no alternative definitions. They think that the definition of a woman in terms of a man is the way it should be; and they back it up with psychosexual incantation and biological ritual curses. A woman has an identity if she is attractive enough to obtain a man, and thus, a home; for this will allow her to set about her life's task of "joyful altruism and nurturance."

Business certainly does not disagree. If views such as Bettelheim's and Erikson's do indeed have something to do with real liberation for women, then seldom in human history has so much money and effort been spent on helping a group of people realize their true potential. Clothing, cosmetics, home furnishings, are multi-million dollar businesses: if you don't like investing in firms that make weaponry and flaming gasoline, then there's a lot of hard cash in "inner space." Sheet and pillowcase manufacturers are concerned to fill this inner space:

Mother, for a while this morning, I thought I wasn't cut out for married life. Hank was late for work and forgot his apricot juice and walked out without kissing me, and when I was all alone I started crying. But then the postman came with the sheets and towels you sent, that look like big bandana handkerchiefs, and you know what I thought? That those big red and blue handkerchiefs are for girls like me to dry their tears on so they can get busy and do what a housewife has to do. Throw open the windows and start getting the house ready, and the dinner, maybe clean the silver and put new geraniums in the box. *Everything to be ready for him when he walks through that door.* (Fieldcrest 1966; emphasis added.)

Of course, it is not only the sheet and pillowcase manufacturers, the cosmetics industry, the home furnishings salesmen who profit from and make use of the cultural definitions of man and woman. The example above is blatantly and overtly pitched to a particular kind of sexist stereotype: the child nymph. But almost all aspects of the media are normative, that is, they have to do with the ways in which beautiful people, or just folks, or ordinary Americans, or extraordinary Americans, should live their lives. They define the possible; and the possibilities are usually in terms of what is male and what is female. Men and women alike are waiting for Hank, the Silva Thins man, to walk back through that door.

It is an interesting but limited exercise to show that psychologists and psychiatrists embrace these sexist norms of our culture, that they do not see beyond the most superficial and stultifying media conceptions of female nature, and that their ideas of female nature serve industry and commerce so well. Just because it's good for business doesn't mean it's wrong. What I will show is that it *is wrong;* that there isn't the tiniest shred of evidence that these fantasies of servitude and childish dependence have anything to do with women's true potential; that the idea of the nature of human possibility which rests on the accidents of individual development of genitalia, on what is possible today because of what happened yesterday, on the fundamentalist myth of sex organ casuality, has strangled and deflected psychology so that it is relatively useless in describing, explaining or predicting humans and their behavior. It then goes without saying that present psychology is less than worthless in contributing to a vision which could truly liberate—men as well as women.

The central argument of my paper, then, is this. Psychology has nothing to say about what women are really like, what they need and what they want, essentially because psychology does not know. I want to stress that this failure is not limited to women; rather, the kind of psychology which has addressed itself to how people act and who they are has failed to understand, in the first place, why people act the way they do, and certainly failed to understand what might make them act differently.

The kind of psychology which has addressed itself to these questions divides into two professional areas: academic personality research, and clinical psychology and psychiatry. The basic reason for failure is the same in both these areas: the central assumption for most psychologists of human personality has been that human behavior rests on an individual and inner dynamic, perhaps fixed in infancy, perhaps fixed by genitalia, perhaps simply arranged in a rather immovable cognitive network. But this assumption is rapidly losing ground as personality psychologists fail again and again to get consistency in the assumed personalities of their subjects (Block, 1968). Meanwhile, the evidence is collecting that what a person does and who she believes herself to be, will in general be a function of what people around her expect her to be, and what the overall situation in which she is acting implies that she is. Compared to the influence of the social context within which a person lives, his or her history and "traits," as well as biological make-up, may simply be random variations, "noise" superimposed on the true signal which can predict behavior.

Some academic personality psychologists are at least looking at the counter evidence and questioning their theories; no such corrective is occurring in clinical psychology and psychiatry: Freudians and neo-Freudians, Nudie-marathonists and Touchy-feelies, classicists and swingers, clinicians and psychiatrists, simply refuse to look at the evidence against their theory and practice. And they support their theory and practice with stuff so transparently biased as to have absolutely no standing as empirical evidence.

To summarize: the first reason for psychology's failure to understand what people are and how they act is that psychology has looked for inner traits when it should have been looking for social context; the second reason for psychology's failure is that the theoreticians of personality have generally been clinicians and psychiatrists, and they have never considered it necessary to have evidence in support of their theories.

Theory without Evidence

Let us turn to this latter cause of failure first: the acceptance by psychiatrists and clinical psychologists of theory without evidence. If we inspect the literature of personality, it is immediately obvious that the bulk of it is written by clinicians and psychiatrists, and that the major support for their theories is "years of intensive clinical experience." This is a tradition started by Freud. His "insights" occurred during the course of his work with his patients. Now there is nothing wrong with such an approach to theory *formulation;* a person is free to make up theories with any inspiration that works: divine revelation, intensive clinical practice, a random numbers table. But he/she is not free to claim any validity for his/her theory until it has been tested and confirmed. But theories are treated in no such tentative way in ordinary clinical practice. Consider Freud. What he thought constituted evidence violated the most minimal conditions of scientific rigor. In *The Sexual Enlightenment of Children* (1963), the classic document which is supposed to demonstrate empirically the existence of a castration complex and its connection to a phobia, Freud based his analysis on the reports of the father of the little boy, himself in therapy, and a devotee of Freudian theory. I really don't have to comment further on the contamination in this kind of evidence. It is remarkable that only recently has Freud's classic theory on the sexuality of women—the notion of the double orgasm—been actually tested physiologically and found just plain wrong. Now those who claim that fifty years of psychoanalytic experience constitute evidence enough of the essential truths of Freud's theory should ponder the robust health of the double orgasm. Did women, until Masters and Johnson (1966), believe they were having two different kinds of orgasm? Did their psychiatrists badger them into reporting something that was not true? If so, were there other things they reported that were also not true? Did psychiatrists ever learn anything different than their theories had led them to believe? If clinical experience means anything at all, surely we should have been done with the double orgasm myth long before the Masters and Johnson studies.

But certainly, you may object, "years of intensive clinical experience" is the only reliable measure in a discipline which rests for its findings on insight, sensitivity, and intuition. The problem with insight, sensitivity, and intuition, is that they can confirm for all time the biases that one started out with. People used to be absolutely convinced of their ability to tell which of their number were engaging in witchcraft. All it required was some sensitivity to the workings of the devil.

Years of intensive clinical experience is not the same thing as empirical evidence. The first thing an experimenter learns in any kind of experiment which involves humans is the concept of the "double blind." The term is taken from medical experiments, where one group is given a drug which is presumably supposed to change behavior in a certain way, and a control group is given a placebo. If the observers or the subjects know which group took which drug, the result invariably comes out on the positive side for the new drug. Only when it is not known which subject took which pill is validity remotely approximated. In addition, with judgments of human behavior, it is so difficult to precisely tie down just what behavior is going on, let alone what behavior should be expected, that one must test again and again

the reliability of judgments. How many judges, blind, will agree in their observations? Can they replicate their own judgments at some later time? When, in actual practice, these judgment criteria are tested for clinical judgments, then we find that the judges cannot judge reliably, nor can they judge consistently: they do no better than chance in identifying which of a certain set of stories were written by men and which by women; which of a whole battery of clinical test results are the products of homosexuals and which are the products of heterosexuals (Hooker, 1957), and which, of a battery of clinical test results *and* interviews (where questions are asked such as "Do you have delusions?", Little & Schneidman, 1959) are products of psychotics, neurotics, psychosomatics, or normals. Lest this summary escape your notice, let me stress the implications of these findings. The ability of judges, chosen for their clinical expertise, to distinguish male heterosexuals from male homosexuals on the basis of three widely used clinical projective tests—the Rorschach, the TAT, and the MAP—was *no better than chance.* The reason this is such devastating news, of course, is that sexuality is supposed to be of fundamental importance in the deep dynamic of personality; if what is considered gross sexual deviance cannot be caught, then what are psychologists talking about when they, for example, claim that at the basis of paranoid psychosis is "latent homosexual panic"? They can't even identify what homosexual anything is, let alone "latent homosexual panic." [1] More frightening, expert

---

[1] It should be noted that psychologists have been as quick to assert absolute truths about the nature of homosexuality as they have about the nature of women. The arguments presented in this paper apply equally to the nature of homosexuality; psychologists know nothing about it; there is no

clinicians cannot be consistent on what diagnostic category to assign to a person, again on the basis of both tests and interviews; a number of normals in the Little & Schneidman study were described as psychotic, in such categories as "schizophrenic with homosexual tendencies" or "schizoid character with depressive trends." But most disheartening, when the judges were asked to rejudge the test protocols some weeks later, their diagnoses of the same subjects on the basis of the same protocol differed markedly from their initial judgments. It is obvious that even simple descriptive conventions in clinical psychology cannot be consistently applied; if clinicians were as faulty in recognizing food from non-food, they'd poison themselves and starve to death. That their descriptive conventions have any explanatory significance is therefore, of course, out of the question.

As a graduate student at Harvard some years ago, I was a member of a seminar which was asked to identify which of two piles of clinical test, the TAT, had been written by males and which by females. Only four students out of twenty identified the piles correctly, and this was after one and a half months of intensively studying the differences between men and women. Since this result is below chance—that is, this result would occur by chance about four out of a thousand times— we may conclude that there *is* finally a consistency here; students are judging knowledgeably within the context of psychological teaching about the differences

between men and women; the teachings themselves are simply erroneous.

You may argue that the theory may be scientifically "unsound" but at least it cures people. There is no evidence that it does. In 1952, Eysenck reported the results of what is called an "outcome of therapy" study of neurotics which showed that, of the patients who received psychoanalysis the improvement rate was 44%; of the patients who received psychotherapy the improvement rate was 64%; and of the patients who received no treatment at all the improvement rate was 72%. These findings have never been refuted; subsequently, later studies have confirmed the negative results of the Eysenck study. (Barron & Leary, 1955; Bergin, 1963; Cartwright and Vogel, 1960; Truax, 1963; Powers and Witmer, 1951) How can clinicians and psychiatrists, then, in all good conscience, continue to practice? Largely by ignoring these results and being careful not to do outcome-of-therapy studies. The attitude is nicely summarized by Rotter (1960) (quoted in Astin, 1961): "Research studies in psychotherapy tend to be concerned more with psychotherapeutic procedure and less with outcome. . . . To some extent, it reflects an interest in the psychotherapy situation as a kind of personality laboratory." Some laboratory.

The Social Context

Thus, since we can conclude that since clinical experience and tools can be shown to be worse than useless when tested for consistency, efficacy, agreement, and reliability, we can safely conclude that theories of a clinical nature advanced about women are also worse than useless. I want to turn now to the second major point in my paper, which is that, even when

more evidence for the "naturalness" of heterosexuality than for the "naturalness" of homosexuality. Psychology has functioned as a pseudo-scientific buttress for patriarchal ideology and patriarchal social organization: women's liberation and gay liberation fight against a common victimization.

psychological theory is constructed so that it may be tested, and rigorous standards of evidence are used, it has become increasingly clear that in order to understand why people do what they do, and certainly in order to change what people do, psychologists must turn away from the theory of the causal nature of the inner dynamic and look to the social context within which individuals live.

Before examining the relevance of this approach for the question of women, let me first sketch the groundwork for this assertion.

In the first place, it is clear (Block, 1968) that personality tests never yield consistent predictions; a rigid authoritarian on one measure will be an unauthoritarian on the next. But the reason for this inconsistency is only now becoming clear, and it seems overwhelmingly to have much more to do with the social situation in which the subject finds him/herself than with the subject him/herself.

In a series of brilliant experiments, Rosenthal and his co-workers (Rosenthal and Jacobson, 1968; Rosenthal, 1966) have shown that if one group of experimenters has one hypothesis about what they expect to find, and another group of experimenters has the opposite hypothesis, both groups will obtain results in accord with their hypotheses. The results obtained are not due to mishandling of data by biased experimenters; rather, somehow, the bias of the experimenter creates a changed environment in which subjects actually act differently. For instance, in one experiment, subjects were to assign numbers to pictures of men's faces, with high numbers representing the subject's judgment that the man in the picture was a successful person, and low numbers representing the subject's judgment that the man in the picture was an unsuccessful person.

Prior to running the subjects, one group of experimenters was told that the subjects tended to rate the faces high; another group of experimenters was told that the subjects tended to rate the faces low. Each group of experimenters was instructed to follow precisely the same procedure: they were required to read to subjects a set of instructions, and to *say nothing else*. For the 375 subjects run, the results showed clearly that those subjects who performed the task with experimenters who expected high ratings gave high ratings, and those subjects who performed the task with experimenters who expected low ratings gave low ratings. How did this happen? The experimenters all used the same words; it was something in their conduct which made one group of subjects do one thing, and another group of subjects do another thing.[2]

The concreteness of the changed conditions produced by expectation is a fact, a reality: even with animal subjects, in two separate studies (Rosenthal & Fode, 1960; Rosenthal & Lawson, 1961), those experimenters who were told that rats learning mazes had been especially bred for brightness obtained better learning from their rats than did experimenters believing their rats to have been bred for dullness. In a very recent study, Rosenthal & Jacobson (1968) extended their analysis to the natural classroom situation. Here, they tested a group of students and reported to the teachers that some among the students tested "showed great promise." Actually, the students so named had been selected on a random basis. Some time later, the experimenters retested the group of students: those students whose teachers had

---

[2] I am indebted to Jesse Lemisch for his valuable suggestions in the interpretations of these studies.

been told that they were "promising" showed real and dramatic increments in their IQs as compared to the rest of the students. Something in the conduct of the teachers towards those who the teachers believed to be the "bright" students, made those students brighter.

Thus, even in carefully controlled experiments, and with no outward or conscious difference in behavior, the hypotheses we start with will influence enormously the behavior of another organism. These studies are extremely important when assessing the validity of psychological studies of women. Since it is beyond doubt that most of us start with notions as to the nature of men and women, the validity of a number of observations of sex differences is questionable, even when these observations have been made under carefully controlled conditions. Second, and more important, the Rosenthal experiments point quite clearly to the influence of social expectation. In some extremely important ways, people are what you expect them to be, or at least they behave as you expect them to behave. Thus, if women, according to Bettelheim, want first and foremost to be good wives and mothers, it is extremely likely that this is what Bruno Bettelheim, and the rest of society, want them to be.

There is another series of brilliant social psychological experiments which point to the overwhelming effect of social context. These are the obedience experiments of Stanley Milgram (1965) in which subjects are asked to obey the orders of unknown experimenters, orders which carry with them the distinct possibility that the subject is killing somebody.

In Milgram's experiments, a subject is told that he is administering a learning experiment, and that he is to deal out shocks each time the other "subject" (in reality, a confederate of the experimenter) answers incorrectly. The equipment appears to provide graduated shocks ranging upwards from 15 volts through 450 volts; for each of four consecutive voltages there are verbal descriptions such as "mild shock", "danger, severe shock", and, finally, for the 435 and 450 volt switches, a red XXX marked over the switches. Each time the stooge answers incorrectly, the subject is supposed to increase the voltage. As the voltage increases, the stooge begins to cry in pain; he/she demands that the experiment stop; finally, he/she refuses to answer at all. When he/she stops responding, the experimenter instructs the subject to continue increasing the voltage; for each shock administered the stooge shrieks in agony. Under these conditions, about 62½% of the subjects administered shock that they believed to be possibly lethal.

No tested individual differences between subjects predicted how many would continue to obey, and which would break off the experiment. When forty psychiatrists predicted how many of a group of 100 subjects would go on to give the lethal shock, their predictions were orders of magnitude below the actual percentages; most expected only one-tenth of one per cent of the subjects to obey to the end.

But even though *psychiatrists* have no idea how people will behave in this situation, and even though individual differences do not predict which subjects will obey and which will not, it is easy to predict when subjects will be obedient and when they will be defiant. All the experimenter has to do is change the social situation. In a variant of Milgram's experiment, two stooges were present in addition to the "victim"; these worked along with the subject in administering electric shocks. When these two stooges refused to go on with the experi-

Untitled drawing by Melissa Mathis

ment, only ten per cent of the subjects continued to the maximum voltage. This is critical for personality theory. It says that behavior is predicted from the social situation, not from the individual history.

Finally, an ingenious experiment by Schachter and Singer (1962) showed that subjects injected with adrenalin, which produces a state of physiological arousal in all but minor respects identical to that which occurs when subjects are extremely afraid, became euphoric when they were in a room with a stooge who was acting euphoric, and became extremely angry when they were placed in a room with a stooge who was acting extremely angry.

To summarize: If subjects under quite innocuous and non-coercive social conditions can be made to kill other subjects and under other types of social conditions will positively refuse to do so; if subjects can react to a state of physiological fear by becoming euphoric because there is somebody else around who is euphoric or angry because there is somebody else around who is angry; if students become intelligent because teachers expect them to be intelligent, and rats run mazes better because experimenters are told the rats are bright, then it is obvious that a study of human behavior requires, first and foremost, a study of the social contexts within which people move, the expectations as to how they will behave, and the authority which tells them who they are and what they are supposed to do.

Biologically Based Theories

Biologists also have at times assumed they could describe the limits of human potential from their observations not of human, but of animal behavior. Here, as in psychology, there has been no end of theorizing about sexes, again with a sense of absolute certainty surprising in "science." These theories fall into two major categories.

One category of theory argues that since females and males differ in their sex hormones, and sex hormones enter the brain (Hamburg & Lunde in Maccoby, 1966), there must be innate behavioral differences. But the only thing this argument tells us is that there are differences in physiological state. The problem is whether these differences are at all relevant to behavior.

Consider, for example, differences in levels of the sex hormone testosterone. A man who calls himself Tiger[3] has recently argued (1970) that the greater quantities of testosterone found in human males as compared with human females (of a certain age group) determines innate differences in aggressiveness, competitiveness, dominance, ability to hunt, ability to hold public office, and so forth. But Tiger demonstrates in this argument the same manly and courageous refusal to be intimidated by evidence

[3]Schwarz-Belkin (1914) claims that the name was originally Mouse, but this may be a reference to an earlier L. Tiger (putative).

which we have already seen in our consideration of the clinical and psychiatric tradition. The evidence does not support his argument, and in most cases, directly contradicts it. Testosterone level does not seem to be related to hunting ability, or dominance, or aggression, or competitiveness. As Storch has pointed out (1970), all normal *male mammals* in the reproductive age group produce much greater quantities of testosterone than females; yet many of these males are neither hunters nor are they aggressive (e.g., rabbits). And among some hunting mammals, such as the larger cats, it turns out that more hunting is done by the female than the male. And there exist primate species where the female is clearly more aggressive, competitive, and dominant than the male (Mitchell, 1969; and see below). Thus, for some species, being female and therefore having less testosterone than the male of that species means hunting more, or being more aggressive, or being more dominant. Nor does having *more* testosterone preclude behavior commonly thought of as "female": there exist primate species where females do not touch infants except to feed them; the males care for the infants at all times (Mitchell, 1969; see fuller discussion below). So it is not clear what testosterone or any other sex-hormonal difference means for differences in nature, or sex-role behavior.

In other words, one can observe identical types of behavior which have been associated with sex (e.g., "mothering") in males and females, despite known differences in physiological state, i.e., sex hormones, genitalia, etc. What about the converse to this? That is, can one obtain differences in behavior given a single physiological state? The answer is overwhelmingly yes, not only as regards nonsex-specific hormones (as in the Schachter and

Singer 1962 experiment cited above), but also as regards gender itself. Studies of hermaphrodites with the same diagnosis (the genetic, gonadal, hormonal sex, the internal reproductive organs, and the ambiguous appearances of the external genitalia were identical) have shown that one will consider oneself male or female depending simply on whether one was defined and raised as male or female (Money, 1970; Hampton & Hampton, 1961):

> There is no more convincing evidence of the power of social interaction on gender-identity differentiation than in the case of congenital hermaphrodites who are of the same diagnosis and similar degree of hermaphroditism but are differently assigned and with a different postnatal medical and life history. (Money, 1970, p. 432).

Thus, for example, if out of two individuals diagnosed as having the adrenogenital syndrome of female hermaphroditism, one is raised as a girl and one as a boy, each will act and identify her/himself accordingly. The one raised as a girl will consider herself a girl; the one raised as a boy will consider himself a boy; and each will conduct her/himself successfully in accord with that self-definition.

So, identical behavior occurs given different physiological states; and different behavior occurs given an identical physiological starting point. So it is not clear that differences in sex hormones are at all relevant to behavior.

The other category of theory based on biology, a reductionist theory, goes like this. Sex-role behavior in some primate species is described, and it is concluded that this is the "natural" behavior for humans. Putting aside the not insignificant problem of observer bias (for instance, Harlow, 1962, of the University of Wisconsin, after observing differences be-

In general, it can be said that feminine mentality manifests an underdeveloped, childlike, or primitive character; instead of the thirst for knowledge, curiosity; instead of judgment, prejudice; instead of thinking, imagination or dreaming; instead of will, wishing.

Emma Jung

---

tween male and female rhesus monkeys, quotes Lawrence Sterne to the effect that women are silly and trivial, and concludes that "men and women have differed in the past and they will differ in the future"), there are a number of problems with this approach.

The most general and serious problem is that there are no grounds to assume that anything primates do is necessary, natural or desirable in humans, for the simple reason that humans are not nonhumans. For instance, it is found that male chimpanzees placed alone with infants will not "mother" them. Jumping from hard data to ideological speculation, researchers conclude from this information that *human* females are necessary for the safe growth of human infants. It would be as reasonable to conclude, following this logic, that it is quite useless to teach human infants to speak, since it has been tried with chimpanzees and it does not work.

One strategy that has been used is to extrapolate from primate behavior to "innate" human preference by noticing certain trends in primate behavior as one moves phylogenetically closer to humans. But there are great difficulties with this approach. When behaviors from lower primates are directly opposite to those of higher primates, or to those one expects of humans, they can be dismissed on evolutionary grounds—higher primates and/or humans grew out of that kid stuff. On the other hand, if the behavior of higher primates is

counter to the behavior considered natural for humans, while the behavior of some lower primate is considered the natural one for humans, the higher primate behavior can be dismissed also, on the grounds that it has diverged from an older, prototypical pattern. So either way, one can select those behaviors one wants to prove as innate for humans. In addition, one does not know whether the sex-role behavior exhibited is dependent on the phylogenetic rank, or on the environmental conditions (both physical and social) under which different species live.

Is there then any value at all in primate observations as they relate to human females and males? There is a value but it is limited: its function can be no more than to show some extant examples of diverse sex-role behavior. It must be stressed, however, that this is an extremely limited function. The extant behavior does not begin to suggest all the possibilities, either for non-human primates or for humans. Bearing these caveats in mind, it is nonetheless interesting that if one inspects the limited set of observations of existing non-human primate sex-role behaviors, one finds, in fact, a much larger range of sex-role behavior than is commonly believed to exist. "Biology" appears to limit very little; the fact that a female gives birth does not mean, even in non-humans, that she necessarily cares for the infant (in marmosets, for instance, the male carries the infant at all times except when the infant is feeding

"But no one can evade the fact, that in taking up a masculine calling, studying, and working in a man's way, woman is doing something not wholly in agreement with, if not directly injurious to, her feminine nature." . . . *[Female] psychology is founded on the principle of Eros, the great binder and deliverer; while age-old wisdom has ascribed Logos to man as his ruling principle.*

Carl G. Jung

[Mitchell, 1969]); "natural" female and male behavior varies all the way from females who are much more aggressive and competitive than males (e.g., Tamarins, see Mitchell, 1969) and male "mothers" (e.g., Titi monkeys, night monkeys, and marmosets; see Mitchell, 1969)[4] to submissive and passive females and male antagonists (e.g., rhesus monkeys).

But even for the limited function that primate arguments serve, the evidence has been misused. Invariably, only those primates have been cited which exhibit exactly the kind of behavior that the proponents of the biological fixedness of human female behavior wish were true for humans. Thus, baboons and rhesus monkeys are generally cited: males in these groups exhibit some of the most irritable and aggressive behavior found in primates, and if one wishes to argue that females are naturally passive and submissive, these groups provide vivid examples. There are abundant counter examples, such as those mentioned above (Mitchell, 1969); in fact, in general, a counter example can be found for every sex-role behavior cited, including, as mentioned in the case of marmosets, male "mothers".

But the presence of counter examples has not stopped florid and overarching theories of the

natural or biological basis of male privilege from proliferating. For instance, there have been a number of theories dealing with the innate incapacity in human males for monogamy. Here, as in most of this type of theorizing, baboons are a favorite example, probably because of their fantasy value: the family unit of the hamadryas baboon, for instance, consists of a highly constant pattern of one male and a number of females and their young. And again, the counter examples, such as the invariably monogamous gibbon, are ignored.

An extreme example of this maiming and selective truncation of the evidence in the service of a plea for the maintenance of male privilege is a recent book, *Men in Groups* (1969) by Tiger. (See above, especially footnote.) The central claim of this book is that females are incapable of "bonding" as in "male bonding". What is "male bonding"? Its surface definition is simple: ". . . a particular relationship between two or more males such that they react differently to members of their bonding units as compared to individuals outside of it" (pp. 19–20). If one deletes the word male, the definition, on its face, would seem to include all organisms that have any kind of social organization. But this is not what Tiger means. For instance, Tiger asserts that females are incapable of bonding; and this alleged incapacity indicates to Tiger that females should be restricted from public life. Why is bonding an exclusively male behavior? Because, says Tiger,

---

[4]All these are lower-order primates, which makes their behavior with reference to humans unnatural, or more natural, take your choice.

it is seen in male primates. All male primates? No, very few male primates. Tiger cites two examples where male bonding is seen: rhesus monkeys and baboons. Surprise, surprise. But not even all baboons: as mentioned above, the hamadryas social organization consists of one-male units; so does that of the Gelada baboon (Mitchell, 1969). And the great apes do not go in for male bonding much either. The "male bond" is hardly a serious contribution to scholarship; one reviewer for *Science* has observed that the book ". . . shows basically more resemblance to a partisan political tract than to a work of objective social science", with male bonding being ". . . some kind of behavioral phlogiston" (Fried, 1969, p. 884).

In short, primate arguments have generally misused the evidence; primate studies themselves have, in any case, only the very limited function of describing some possible sex-role behavior; and at present, primate observations have been sufficiently limited so that even the range of possible sex-role behavior for non-human primates is not known. This range is not known since there is only minimal observation of what happens to behavior if the physical or social environment is changed. In one study (Itani, 1963), different troops of Japanese macaques were observed. Here, there appeared to be cultural differences: males in three out of the eighteen troops observed differed in their amount of aggressiveness and infant-caring behavior. There could be no possibility of differential evolution here; the differences seemed largely transmitted by infant socialization. Thus, the very limited evidence points to some plasticity in the sex-role behavior of non-human primates; if we can figure out experiments which massively change the social organization of primate groups, it is possible that

we might observe great changes in behavior. At present, however, we must conclude that, given a constant physical environment, non-human primates do not change their social conditions by themselves very much, and thus the "innateness" and fixedness of their behavior is simply not known. Thus, even if there were some way, which there isn't, to settle on the behavior of a particular primate species as being the "natural" way for humans, we would not know whether or not this were simply some function of the present social organization of that species. And finally, once again it must be stressed that even if non-human primate behavior turned out to be relatively fixed, this would say little about our behavior. More immediate and relevant evidence, i.e., the evidence from social psychology, points to the enormous plasticity in human behavior, not only from one culture to the next, but from one experimental group to the next. One of the most salient features of human social organization is its variety; there are a number of cultures where there is at least a rough equality between men and women (Mead, 1949). In summary, primate arguments can tell us very little about our "innate" sex-role behavior; if they tell us anything at all, they tell us that there is no one biologically "natural" female or male behavior, and that sex-role behavior in non-human primates is much more varied than has previously been thought.

Conclusion

In brief, the uselessness of present psychology (and biology) with regard to women is simply a special case of the general conclusion: one must understand the social conditions under which humans live if one is going to attempt

No matter how friendly and obliging a woman's Eros may be, no logic on earth can shake her if she is ridden by the animus. Often the man has the feeling—and he is not altogether wrong—that only seduction or a beating or rape would have the necessary power of persuasion.

Carl G. Jung

to explain their behavior. And, to understand the social conditions under which women live, one must understand the social expectations about women.

How are women characterized in our culture, and in psychology? They are inconsistent, emotionally unstable, lacking in a strong conscience or superego, weaker, "nurturant" rather than productive, "intuitive" rather than intelligent, and if they are at all "normal", suited to the home and the family. In short, the list adds up to a typical minority group stereotype of inferiority (Hacker, 1951): if they know their place, which is in the home, they are really quite lovable, happy, childlike, loving creatures. In a review of the intellectual differences between little boys and little girls, Eleanor Maccoby (1966) has shown that there are no intellectual differences until about high school, or, if there are, girls are slightly ahead of boys. At high school, girls begin to do worse on a few intellectual tasks, such as arithmetic reasoning, and beyond high school, the achievement of women now measured in terms of productivity and accomplishment drops off even more rapidly. There are a number of other, non-intellectual tests which show sex differences; I choose the intellectual differences since it is seen clearly that women start becoming inferior. It is no use to talk about women being different but equal; all of the tests I can think of have a "good" outcome and a "bad" outcome. Women usually

end up at the "bad" outcome. In light of social expectations about women, what is surprising is not that women end up where society expects they will; what is surprising is that little girls don't get the message that they are supposed to be stupid until high school; and what is even more remarkable is that some women resist this message even after high school, college, and graduate school.

My paper began with remarks on the task of the discovery of the limits of human potential. Psychologists must realize that it is they who are limiting discovery of human potential. They refuse to accept evidence, if they are clinical psychologists, or, if they are rigorous, they assume that people move in a context-free ether, with only their innate dispositions and their individual traits determining what they will do. Until psychologists begin to respect evidence, and until they begin looking at the social context within which people move, psychology will have nothing of substance to offer in this task of discovery. I don't know what immutable differences exist between men and women apart from differences in their genitals; perhaps there are some other unchangeable differences; probably there are a number of irrelevant differences. But it is clear that until social expectations for men and women are equal, until we provide equal respect for both men and women, our answers to this question will simply reflect our prejudices.

Eleanor Emmons Maccoby and Carol Nagy Jacklin

Summary and Commentary

Summary

Unfounded Beliefs About Sex Differences

1. *That girls are more "social" than boys.* The findings: First, the two sexes are equally interested in social (as compared with non-social) stimuli, and are equally proficient at learning through imitation of models. Second, in childhood, girls are no more dependent than boys on their caretakers, and boys are no more willing to remain alone. Furthermore, girls are not more motivated to achieve for social rewards. The two sexes are equally responsive to social reinforcement, and neither sex consistently learns better for this form of reward than for other forms. Third, girls do not spend more time interacting with playmates; in fact, the opposite is true, at least at certain ages. Fourth, the two sexes appear to be equally "emphatic," in the sense of understanding the emotional reactions of others; however, the measures of this ability have so far been narrow.

Any differences that exist in the "sociability" of the two sexes are more of kind than of degree. Boys are highly oriented toward a peer group and congregate in larger groups; girls associate in pairs or small groups of age-mates, and may be somewhat more oriented toward adults, although the evidence for this is weak.

2. *That girls are more "suggestible" than boys.* The findings: First, boys and girls are equally likely to imitate others spontaneously. Second, the two sexes are equally susceptible to persuasive communications, and in face-to-face social-influence situations (Asch-type experiments), sex differences are usually not found. When they are, girls are somewhat more likely to adapt their own judgments to those of the group, although there are studies with reverse findings. Boys, on the other hand, appear to be more likely to accept peer-group values when these conflict with their own.

3. *That girls have lower self-esteem.* The findings: The sexes are highly similar in their overall self-satisfaction and self-confidence throughout childhood and adolescence; there is little information about adulthood, but what exists does not show a sex difference. However, there are some qualitative differences in the areas of functioning where the two sexes have greatest self-confidence: girls rate themselves higher in the area of social competence; boys more often see themselves as strong, powerful, dominant, "potent."

Through most of the school years, the two sexes are equally likely to believe they can influence their own fates, rather than being the victims of chance or fate. During the college years (but not earlier or later), men have a greater sense of control over their own fate, and greater confidence in their probable performance on a variety of school-related tasks that they undertake. However, this does not imply a generally lower level of self-esteem among women of this age.

4. *That girls are better at rote learning and simple repetitive tasks, boys at tasks that require higher-level cognitive processing and the inhibition of previously learned responses.* The findings: Neither sex is more susceptible to simple conditioning, or excels in simple

paired-associates or other forms of "rote" learning. Boys and girls are equally proficient at discrimination learning, reversal shifts, and probability learning, all of which have been interpreted as calling for some inhibition of "available" responses. Boys are somewhat more impulsive (that is, lacking in inhibition) during the preschool years, but the sexes do not differ thereafter in the ability to wait for a delayed reward, to inhibit early (wrong) responses on the Matching Familiar Figures test (MFF) or on other measures of impulsivity.

5. *That boys are more "analytic."* The findings: The sexes do not differ on tests of analytic cognitive style. Boys do not excel at tasks that call for "decontextualization," or disembedding, except when the task is visual-spatial; boys' superiority on the latter tasks seems to be accounted for by spatial ability (see below), and no sex differences in analytic ability are implied. Boys and girls are equally likely to respond to task-irrelevant aspects of a situation, so that neither sex excels in analyzing and selecting only those elements needed for the task.

6. *That girls are more affected by heredity, boys by environment.* The findings: Male identical twins are more alike than female identical twins, but the two sexes show equivalent amount of resemblance to their parents.

Boys are more susceptible to damage by a variety of noxious environmental agents, both prenatally and postnatally, but this does not imply that they are generally more influenced by environmental factors. The correlations between parental socialization techniques and child behavior are higher for boys in some studies, higher for girls in others. Furthermore, the two sexes learn with equal facility in a wide variety of learning situations; if learning is the

primary means whereby environmental effects come about, sex equivalence is indicated.

7. *That girls lack achievement motivation.* The findings: In the pioneering studies of achievement motivation, girls scored higher than boys in achievement imagery under "neutral" conditions. Boys need to be challenged by appeals to ego or competitive motivation to bring their achievement imagery up to the level of girls'. Boys' achievement motivation does appear to be more responsive to competitive arousal than girls', but this does not imply a generally higher level. In fact, observational studies of achievement strivings either have found no sex difference or have found girls to be superior.

8. *That girls are auditory, boys visual.* The findings: The majority of studies report no differences in response to sounds by infants of the two sexes. At most ages boys and girls are equally adept at discriminating speech sounds. No sex difference is found in memory for sounds previously heard.

Among newborn infants, no study shows a sex difference in fixation to visual stimuli. During the first year of life, results are variable, but neither sex emerges as more responsive to visual stimuli. From infancy to adulthood, the sexes are highly similar in interest in visual stimuli, ability to discriminate among them, identification of shapes, distance perception, and a variety of other measures of visual perception.

Sex Differences That Are Fairly Well Established

1. *That girls have greater verbal ability than boys.* It is probably true that girls' verbal abilities mature somewhat more rapidly in early life, although there are a number of recent studies in which no sex difference has been found.

During the period from preschool to early adolescence, the sexes are very similar in their verbal abilities. At about age eleven, the sexes begin to diverge, with female superiority increasing through high school and possibly beyond. Girls score higher on tasks involving both receptive and productive language, and on "high-level" verbal tasks (analogies, comprehension of difficult written material, creative writing) as well as upon the "lower-level" measures (fluency). The magnitude of the female advantage varies, being most commonly about one-quarter of a standard deviation.

2. *That boys excel in visual-spatial ability.* Male superiority on visual-spatial tasks is fairly consistently found in adolescence and adulthood, but not in childhood. The male advantage on spatial tests increases through the high school years up to a level of about .40 of a standard deviation. The sex difference is approximately equal on analytic and nonanalytic spatial measures.

3. *That boys excel in mathematical ability.* The two sexes are similar in their early acquisition of quantitative concepts, and their mastery of arithmetic during the grade-school years. Beginning at about age 12–13, boys' mathematical skills increase faster than girls'. The greater rate of improvement appears to be not entirely a function of the number of math courses taken, although the question has not been extensively studied. The magnitude of the sex differences varies greatly from one population to another, and is probably not so great as the difference in spatial ability. Both visual-spatial and verbal processes are sometimes involved in the solution of mathematical problems; some math problems can probably be solved in either way, while others cannot, a fact that may help to explain the variation in degree of sex difference from one measure to another.

4. *That males are more aggressive.* The sex difference in aggression has been observed in all cultures in which the relevant behavior has been observed. Boys are more aggressive both physically and verbally. They show the attenuated forms of aggression (mock-fighting, aggressive fantasies) as well as the direct forms more frequently than girls. The sex difference is found as early as social play begins—at age 2 or 2½. Although the aggressiveness of both sexes declines with age, boys and men remain more aggressive through the college years. Little information is available for older adults. The primary victims of male aggression are other males—from early ages, girls are chosen less often as victims.

Open Questions: Too Little Evidence, or Findings Ambiguous

1. *Tactile sensitivity.* Most studies of tactile sensitivity in infancy, and of the ability to perceive by touch at later ages, do not find sex differences. When differences are found, girls are more sensitive, but such findings are rare enough that we cannot have confidence that the difference is a meaningful one. Additional work is needed with some of the standard psychophysical measurements of tactile sensitivity, over a range of ages. Most of the existing studies in which the data are analyzed by sex have been done with newborns.

2. *Fear, timidity, and anxiety.* Observational studies of fearful behavior usually do not find sex differences. Teacher ratings and self-reports, however, usually find girls to be more timid or more anxious. In the case of self-reports, the problem is to know whether the results reflect "real" differences or only dif-

ferences in the willingness to report anxious feelings. Of course, the very willingness to assert that one is afraid may lead to fearful behavior, so the distinction may not turn out to be important. However, it would be desirable to have measures other than self-report (which make up the great bulk of the data from early school age on) as a way of clarifying the meaning of the girls' greater self-attribution of fears and anxiety.

3. *Activity level.* Sex differences in activity level do not appear in infancy. They begin to be seen when children reach the age of social play. During the preschool years, when sex differences are found they are in the direction of boys' being more active. However, there are many instances in which sex differences have not been found. Some, but not all, of the variance among studies can be accounted for by whether the measurement situation was social. That is, boys appear to be especially stimulated to bursts of high activity by the presence of other boys. But the exact nature of the situational control over activity level remains to be established. Activity level is responsive to a number of motivational states—fear, anger, curiosity—and is therefore not a promising variable for identifying stable individual or group differences. More detailed observations are needed on the vigor and qualitative nature of play.

4. *Competitiveness.* When sex differences are found, they usually show boys to be more competitive, but there are many studies finding sex similarity. Madsen and his colleagues find sex differences to be considerably weaker than differences between cultures and, in a number of studies, entirely absent. Almost all the research on competition has involved situations in which competition is maladaptive. In the Prisoner's Dilemma game, for example, the sexes are equally cooperative, but this is in a situation in which cooperation is to the long-run advantage of both players and the issue is one of developing mutual trust. It appears probable that in situations in which competitiveness produces increased individual rewards, males would be more competitive, but this is a guess based on commonsense considerations, such as the male interest in competitive sports, not upon research in controlled settings. The age of the subject and the identity of the opponent no doubt make a difference—there is evidence that young women hesitate to compete against their boyfriends.

5. *Dominance.* Dominance appears to be more of an issue within boys' groups than girls' groups. Boys make more dominance attempts (both successful and unsuccessful) toward one another than do girls. They also more often attempt to dominate adults. The dominance relations between the sexes are complex: in childhood, the sex segregation of play groups means that neither sex frequently attempts to dominate the other. In experimental situations in which the sexes are combined, the evidence is ambiguous on whether either sex is more successful in influencing the behavior of the other. Among adult mixed pairs or groups, formal leadership tends to go to males in the initial phases of interaction, but the direction of influence becomes more sex-equal the longer the relationship lasts, with "division of authority" occurring along lines of individual competencies and division of labor.

6. *Compliance.* In childhood, girls tend to be more compliant to the demands and directions of adults. This compliance does not extend, however, to willingness to accept directions from, or be influenced by, age-mates. Boys are

Housewife

Some women marry houses.
It's another kind of skin; it has a heart,
a mouth, a liver and bowel movements.
The walls are permanent and pink.
See how she sits on her knees all day,
faithfully washing herself down.
Men enter by force, drawn back like Jonah
into their fleshy mothers.
A woman is her mother.
That's the main thing.

Anne Sexton

Linen Closet by Sandra Orgel (1972); Womanhouse, Los Angeles, Ca.; Feminist Art Program, California Institute of the Arts, Valencia, Ca. 91355

especially concerned with maintaining their status in the peer group, and are probably therefore more vulnerable to pressures and challenges from this group, although this has not been well established. As we have seen in the discussion of dominance, it is not clear that in mixed-sex interactions either sex is consistently more willing to comply with the wishes of the other.

7. Nurturance and "maternal" behavior. There is very little evidence concerning the tendencies of boys and girls to be nurturant or helpful toward younger children or animals. Cross-cultural work does indicate that girls between the ages of six and ten are more often seen behaving nurturantly. Within our own society, the rare studies that report nurturant behavior are observational studies of free play among nursery school children; sex differences are not found in these studies, but the setting normally does not include children much younger than the subjects being observed, and it may be that the relevant elicitors are simply not present. Female hormones play a role in maternal behavior in lower animals, and the same may be true in human beings, but there is no direct evidence that this is the case. There is very little information on the responses of adult men to infants and children, so it is not possible to say whether adult women are more disposed to behave maternally than men are to behave paternally. If there is a sex difference in the tendency to behave nurturantly, it does

Despite the numerous ways in which men have attempted to mimic or colonize the "gloriousness" of biological maternity (and consequently, to devalue or punish it in women), men, particularly in Christian culture, are not very "maternal" to their children, their wives, their mistresses, their prostitutes, their secretaries, their housekeepers—or to each other.

Phyllis Chesler

not generalize to a greater female tendency to behave altruistically over varying situations. The studies of people's willingness to help others in distress have sometimes shown men more helpful, sometimes women, depending on the identity of the person needing help and the kind of help that is needed. The overall finding on altruism is one of sex similarity.

. . . [Earlier] we raised the question of whether the female is more passive than the male. The answer is complex, but mainly negative. The two sexes are highly similar in their willingness to explore a novel environment, when they are both given freedom to do so. Both are highly responsive to social situations of all kinds, and although some individuals tend to withdraw from social interaction and simply watch from the sidelines, such persons are no more likely to be female than male. Girls' greater compliance with adult demands is just as likely to take an active as a passive form; running errands and performing services for others are active processes. Young boys seem more likely than girls to put out energy in the form of bursts of strenuous physical activity, but the girls are not sitting idly by while the boys act; they are simply playing more quietly. And their play is fully as organized and planful (possibly more so), and has as much the quality of actively imposing their own design upon their surroundings as does boys' play. It is true that boys and men are more aggressive, but this does not mean that females are the passive victims of

aggression—they do not yield or withdraw when aggressed against any more frequently than males do, at least during the phases of childhood for which observations are available. With respect to dominance, we have noted the curious fact that while males are more dominant, females are not especially submissive, at least not to the dominance attempts of boys and girls their own age. In sum, the term "passive" does not accurately describe the most common female personality attributes.

Returning to one of the major conclusions of our survey of sex differences, there are many popular beliefs about the psychological characteristics of the two sexes that have proved to have little or no basis in fact. How is it possible that people continue to believe, for example, that girls are more "social" than boys, when careful observation and measurement in a variety of situations show no sex difference? Of course it is possible that we have not studied those particular situations that contribute most to the popular beliefs. But if this is the problem, it means that the alleged sex difference exists only in a limited range of situations, and the sweeping generalizations embodied in popular beliefs are not warranted.

However, a more likely explanation for the perpetuation of "myths," we believe, is the fact that stereotypes are such powerful things. An ancient truth is worth restating here: if a generalization about a group of people is believed, whenever a member of that group behaves in the expected way the observer notes it and his belief is confirmed and strengthened; when a member of the group behaves in a way that is not consistent with the observer's expectations, the instance is likely to pass unnoticed, and the observer's generalized belief is protected from disconfirmation. We believe that this well-documented process occurs continually in relation to the expected and perceived behavior of males and females, and results in the perpetuation of myths that would otherwise die out under the impact of negative evidence. However, not all unconfirmed beliefs about the two sexes are of this sort. It is necessary to reconsider the nature of the evidence that permits us to conclude what is myth and what is (at least potentially) reality.

How Much Confidence Can Be Placed in These Conclusions?

Having gone through the often tedious process of summarizing and analyzing existing research, we must ask ourselves about the adequacy of this method as a way of knowing the truth about sex differences. We have tallied studies—the number showing higher scores for boys, the number favoring girls, and the number showing no difference—knowing, of course, that the studies differ widely in the rigor of their design and procedures, the number of subjects used, the definition of variables, etc. It is not uncommon to find a "box score" in which the majority of studies find no difference, but where the studies that do find a difference favor one sex by a considerable margin (say, two or three to one). We have interpreted such an outcome as a weak trend in the direction indicated by the largest number of studies, but recognize that it is quite possible that the mi-

nority of studies might turn out to have more than a kernel of truth. With stereotypes and biases being as common as they are in the field of sex differences, it is quite possible that the majority of studies were all distorted in the same direction. We think it equally likely, however, that the appearance of a sex difference often depends upon detailed aspects of the situation in which behavior was studied —details that have so far gone unrecognized, but that interact with the more obvious aspects of a situation to change the way in which it is perceived.

We have repeatedly encountered the problem that so-called "objective" measures of behavior yield different results than ratings or self-reports. Ratings are notoriously subject to shifting anchor points. For example, if a parent is asked, "How often does your daughter cry?," the parent may answer "Not very often," meaning "Not very often *for a girl.*" The same frequency of behavior might have been rated "quite often" for a son, from whom the behavior was less expected. Ratings, then, if they are made against different subjective standards, should minimize sex differences where they exist. Where they do not exist, ratings might produce them, but in the opposite direction from stereotypical behavior. It is puzzling that ratings so frequently yield sex differences in the stereotypical direction. For example, in one study, teachers rated each child in their class on activity level; the boys received higher average ratings; but "actometer" recordings for the same group of children did not show the boys to be engaging in more body movement. Obviously, the possibility exists that teachers are noticing and remembering primarily the behavior that fits their stereotypes. There is another possibility, however: that teachers are analyzing clusters or patterns of behavior that a simple single-attribute measurement such as an actometer score does not capture. If this is so, however, and the teachers are reporting something real about sex differences, the cluster that they are attending to should not be named "activity level," for the label implies that the behavior is simpler than it is.

The problems of shifting anchor points for ratings, selective perceptions of raters, and unclear definitions of what is being rated are not the only problems that beset the student of sex differences. It matters how large a "chunk" of behavior is chosen for analysis. This point has been nicely illustrated in work by Raush (1965)[R], in which he compared the social interactions of a group of clinically diagnosed "hyperaggressive" boys with a group of normals. The sequences of aggressive behavior were monitored. The two groups of boys were similar in the frequency and kind of response the victim first made. They were also similar in the aggressor's response to the victim's response. It was only in the fourth and fifth actions in the sequence that the groups diverged—the "hyperactives" continued to respond intensely; the normals "let it go" without continuing the sequence. It may be that sex differences, too, emerge at only certain points in a sequence, and the results of a study will depend upon how detailed and continuous the measurements are. Often, of course, an experimental situation is arranged in such a way that only single responses are recorded, and then summed across trials. Such a procedure makes it nearly impossible to detect either sequences or other patterning of behavior.

We have found a number of instances in which sex differences are situation-specific. For example, although boys and girls do not differ in their attachment to their parents in early childhood (that is, their tendency to remain close to them, interact with them, and resist separation from them), or in the amount of positive interaction with nonfamily adults, boys do interact more with same-sex age-mates. Unfortunately, many studies tally social behavior without specifying the "target" of this behavior. Similarly, studies of "nurturance" behavior (rare in the first place) have usually not identified the beneficiary of the behavior. Clearly, if a child brings a glass of water to his mother, the behavior is subject to different interpretations than if he does the same helpful act for a younger sibling. Furthermore, it makes a difference who is watching. We suspect, for example, that a man may behave more dominantly toward his girl friend and she more submissively when other men are present than they would do in private. It is possible, too, that marriage partners are especially likely to become more equal in dominance with time if there are children—that it is the need to maintain a united front before the children and to support one another's disciplinary moves that is a primary factor producing a change in the dominance relations of a married pair. These situational subtleties have gone largely unnoticed in existing research; we have had no choice but to report the data that researchers have obtained, but we think findings will be much clearer than these distinctions begin to be introduced.

We have attempted to understand the relationship of sex differences to age; we have wanted to know at what age a particular difference first manifests itself, whether it is temporary, whether it increases or decreases with development. We have been able to make only a tantalizing beginning to a genuinely develop-

Photograph by Cathy Cade

there are a few instances in our review where a difference was evident only briefly, during a limited age period. This appears to be true, for example, on certain measures of "impulsivity," where boys are more impulsive only during the preschool years. On the whole, however, our efforts to understand developmental change have been frustrated by two things: (1) the fact that certain ages are overrepresented, others underrepresented, in research on a given topic; and (2) the fact that the methods of measuring a given attribute change so drastically with age that cross-age comparison becomes virtually impossible. Newborn infants in the first two or three days of life, nursery school children, and college students are the groups most frequently studied. In addition, extensive data are available for school-age children on attributes that are clearly relevant to school success (e.g., intellectual aptitudes and achievement scores), with much less information available on social behavior. Very little is known about age changes during adulthood with respect to either cognitive or social measures.

The problem of changing measures over ages is a ubiquitous one in developmental psychology. One can learn something about a young child's attachments and fears by tallying the frequency with which he literally hides behind his mother's skirts; to attempt to do so with an adult would be absurd. One may measure quantitative skill in a preschooler by finding how accurately he can count, and of a fifth- or sixth-grader by asking him to do percentages; but by college age, subjects must be asked to solve differential equations before stable individual differences can be identified. There are great shifts with age not only in *what* is measured but in *how* measurement is done. Behav-

mental analysis. It is reasonably clear that differences in "temperament" and in social behavior emerge much earlier than differences in specific intellectual abilities. Furthermore,

ioral observation is fairly frequent with young children. From the time children become literate through adulthood, however, observational studies in naturalistic settings are very rare, and scores are based either on questionnaires or other self-reports, or on experimental situations using a deliberately restricted set of eliciting conditions and behavioral measures.

It is to be expected that results of experiments may yield quite different results than "real life" observations. It is possible, for example, that if a girl is put into a foot race, she will be as competitive and active as a male. But she might be much less likely to enter such a race spontaneously, and naturalistic observation would show her to be less frequently engaged in competitive behavior, whereas the foot race "experiment" would not. The conclusions of both kinds of studies are correct, but they have rather different implications. The shift from naturalistic observation in early childhood to experimental studies at later ages may mean that sex differences in self-selection of activities have had a better chance of being detected in the early years, rather than that there has been any decline in the importance of motivation and interest with growth.

In a certain sense it is reasonable to make the shift from observational data to questionnaires or self-reports. If one is sampling behavior in a nursery school, it may be meaningful to record simply that a child moved across the room. If one looked out the window at a college student walking down the sidewalk just before the bell rang, however, what is meaningful to record about his behavior? The fact that he was walking? The fact that he was going to class? The fact that he was taking a course in psychology? The fact that his attendance at this class was part of his four-year program to obtain a

Photograph by Cathy Cade

bachelor's degree? Elements of an adult's behavior are usually part of a nested set of organized action sequences (i.e. "plans"). Judging by the data we collect about people at different ages, researchers implicitly assume that a young child's behavior is less so. This is probably correct, although there are probably many more nested sequences in children's behavior than have been detected with the usual techniques of time sampling and frequency tallies of individual behavior elements. If plans of varying duration and complexity do assume more and more control of behavior as the individual develops, it would be reasonable to ask about the plans, rather than to spend so much time enumerating specific responses, as is done for young children. However, the value of observational data surely does not decline to zero with increasing age. We can point out here only that, reasonable though the shift in methods may be, it makes the meaning of measured age changes quite ambiguous. We hope there will be an increase in observational work in naturalistic settings with subjects beyond nursery school age, so that a few more cross-age comparisons will be possible.

One interesting age trend emerged in our survey that is probably *not* a reflection of changes in methods of measurement: this is the tendency for young women of college age to lack confidence in their ability to do well on a new task, and their sense that they have less control over their own fates than men do. These trends are not seen among older or younger women. Age 18–22 is the period of their lives when many young adults are marrying or forming some other kind of relatively enduring sexual liaison. In the dating and mating game, women traditionally are expected to take less initiative than men. Perhaps it is at this period of their lives more than any other that individuals define themselves in terms of their "masculinity" and "femininity," and when greater sex differences may therefore appear than at earlier or later ages, with respect to any attribute considered central to this definition.

This brings us to a related point: that sex differences may be greater among certain subgroups of men and women than among others. In a recent paper, "On Predicting Some of the People Some of the Time," Bem and Allen (1974)[R] suggest that an individual's behavior is likely to be stable across situations and across time with respect to only those attributes that are central to his self-definition. If the individual thinks of himself as a "friendly" person, and considers it important to be as friendly as possible, then he should be consistently friendly in many situations, partly because he will continually monitor his own behavior to take note of how friendly he is being and will correct his own behavior if he is not behaving in ways that are consistent with his self-definition. For other individuals, however, friendliness is not a defining attribute; self-monitoring activity will not be directed toward maintaining consistency with respect to friendly behavior, and hence such behavior will vary greatly depending on the situation in which the person finds himself. In this vein, it is reasonable to believe that "masculinity" and "femininity" are essential self-defining attributes for some people but not for others. If the studies summarized in previous chapters of this book had been based on selected subsamples of subjects, including only those women who consider it important to be feminine and those men for whom masculinity is central to their self-concept, the chances are that greater sex differences would have been reported and the findings would have been much more consistent than we have found them to be. The variations in findings from one study to another probably reflect, in part, the relative concentration of people of this type in the subject population, as well as subtle variations in experimental situations that would signal to the subjects whether the tasks they were called on to perform had any relevance to masculinity or femininity.

On the Etiology of
Psychological Sex Differences

In previous chapters we have discussed three kinds of factors that affect the development of sex differences: genetic factors, "shaping" of boylike and girl-like behavior by parents and other socializing agents, and the child's spontaneous learning of behavior appropriate for his sex through imitation. Anyone who would hope to explain acquisition of sex-typed behavior through one or two of these processes alone would be doomed to disappointment. Not only do the three kinds of processes exert their own direct influence, but they interact with one another.

Biological factors have been most clearly implicated in sex differences in aggression and visual-spatial ability. We have argued that the male's greater aggression has a biological component, citing in support the fact that (1) the sex difference manifests itself in similar ways in man and subhuman primates; (2) it is cross-culturally universal; and (3) levels of aggression are responsive to sex hormones. We have also found, surprisingly, that there is no good evidence that adults reinforce boys' aggression more than girls' aggression; in fact, the contrary may be true. Here, however, there are questions about the adequacy of our information. Direct observational studies of parental reactions to aggression have been carried out in settings in which only the responses to a child's aggression *toward the parents* (or sometimes toward siblings) could be observed. When it comes to permissiveness for fighting among unrelated children, we must rely on parent interviews. Parents *say* they encourage daughters to defend themselves as much as they do sons, and that

they attempt to teach non-aggression to the same degree to both sexes. Serbin et al. (1973) found that in the case of aggressive or destructive behavior by one child toward another child in nursery school, teachers were more likely to intervene (and perhaps scold the guilty child) if the aggressor was a boy. It is possible that mothers react in an opposite way when they are supervising groups of children in neighborhoods and parks. We doubt it, but we do not know. Meanwhile, the available evidence is that adults do not generally accept or approve aggression in either sex. Either their reaction is equally negative for the two sexes, or they react somewhat more strongly to boys' aggression, on the grounds that boys are stronger and more given to fighting and therefore must be kept under closer control. Although strong negative reactions by parents and teachers may actually be "reinforcing" to some children, this is not usually what is meant when it is alleged that parents shape the aggressive behavior of the two sexes differently. What is usually meant is that they allow, accept, or encourage the behavior more in boys, and this we have not found to be true. The negative evidence on differential socialization has strengthened the case for biological origins of the sex differences in aggression. This does not mean that we believe aggressive behavior is unlearned. There is plentiful evidence that it *is* learned. We argue only that boys are more biologically prepared to learn it.

Does the male predisposition toward aggression extend to other behavior, such as dominance, competitiveness, and activity level? Probably yes, to some degree, but the case is not strong. Among subhuman primates, dominance is achieved largely through aggression,

Women

Women   Or they
    should be   should be
        pedestals   little horses
            moving   those wooden
                pedestals   sweet
                    moving   oldfashioned
                        to the   painted
                    motions   rocking
                        of men   horses

                the gladdest things in the toyroom

                    The   feelingly
                pegs   and then
                of their   unfeelingly
                ears   To be
            so familiar   joyfully
        and dear   ridden
        to the trusting   rockingly
    fists   ridden until
To be chafed   the restored

egos dismount and the legs stride away

Immobile   willing
    sweetlipped   to be set
        sturdy   into motion
            and smiling   Women
                women   should be
                    should always   pedestals
                        be waiting   to men

                                    May Swenson

is called "leadership" provides a clue to the fact that adult human beings influence one another by persuasion, charisma, mutual affection, and bargaining, as well as by force or threats thereof. To the extent that dominance is *not* exercised by coercion, the biological male aggressiveness is probably not implicated in it.

The case for biological control of visual-spatial ability rests primarily with genetic studies. There is evidence of a recessive sex-linked gene that contributes an element to high spatial ability. Present estimates are that approximately 50% of men and 25% of women show this element phenotypically, although of course more women than this are "carriers." This sex-linked element is not the only genetic element affecting spatial ability, and the others appear not to be sex-linked. There is so far little evidence for sex linkage of any of the genetic determiners of other specific abilities such as mathematical or verbal ability. The existence of a sex-linked genetic determiner of spatial ability does not imply that visual-spatial skills are unlearned. The specific skills involved in the manifestation of this ability improve with practice. Furthermore, cross-cultural work indicates that the sex differences can be either large or small, or may even disappear, depending upon cultural conditions affecting the rearing of the two sexes. Where women are subjugated, their visual-spatial skills are poor relative to those of men. Where both sexes are allowed independence early in life, both sexes have good visual-spatial skills.

Our review of the socialization pressures directed at the two sexes revealed a surprising degree of similarity in the rearing of boys and girls. The two sexes appear to be treated with equal affection, at least in the first five years

and an individual's position in the dominance hierarchy is related to levels of sex hormones. However, there is no direct evidence that dominance among adult human groups is linked either to sex hormones or to aggressiveness. The fact that "dominance" in most human groups

What are little girls made of?
What are little girls made of?
Sugar and spice
And all that's nice.
That's what little girls are made of.

Nursery Rhyme

of life (the period for which most information is available); they are equally allowed and encouraged to be independent, equally discouraged from dependent behavior; as noted above, there is even, surprisingly, no evidence of distinctive parental reaction to aggressive behavior in the two sexes. There *are* differences, however. Boys are handled and played with somewhat more roughly. They also receive more physical punishment. In several studies boys were found to receive both more praise and more criticism from their caretakers—socialization pressure, in other words, was somewhat more intense for boys—but the evidence on this point is inconsistent. The area of greatest differentiation is in very specifically sex-typed behavior. Parents show considerably more concern over a boy's being a "sissy" than over a girl's being a tomboy. This is especially true of fathers, who seem to take the lead in actively discouraging any interest a son might have in feminine toys, activities, or attire.

Is the direct socialization pressure from parents sufficient to account for known sex differences? For some behaviors, probably so. In some areas, clearly not. Aggression is a case of the second kind. Also, we see nothing in the socialization of the two sexes that would produce different patterns of intellectual abilities. In the area of sex typing as narrowly defined, there is clear parental pressure, particularly on boys; nevertheless, children seem to adopt sex-typed patterns of play and interests for which they have never been reinforced, and avoid sex-inappropriate activities for which they have never been punished. Observations of parental behavior may not have been detailed enough to pick up the more subtle pressures exerted, but it is our impression that parents are fairly permissive where many aspects of sex typing are concerned, and that direct "shaping" by parents does not, in most instances, account for the details of the behavior that is acquired. Parents seem to treat a child in accordance with their knowledge of his individual temperament, interests, and abilities, rather than in terms of sex-role stereotypes. We suspect that others who do not know the child well as an individual are more likely to react to him according to their stereotyped views of what a child of a given sex is likely to be like. Although this conclusion runs counter to common sense, it appears possible that relative strangers exert more stereotyping pressure on children than their own parents do. In any case, we believe that socialization pressures, whether by parents or others, do not by any means tell the whole story of the origins of sex differences.

How then does psychological sex differentiation come about? The psychoanalytic theory of identification would have it that the child identifies with the same-sex parent and learns the details of a sex role through imitation of this parent. Social-learning theory also empha-

Superanatomy by Gladys Nilsson

sizes imitation, but argues that children are more often reinforced when they imitate a same-sex than an opposite-sex model, so that they acquire a generalized tendency to imitate not only the same-sex parent but other same-sex models as well. The distinction between acquisition and performance of a given item of behavior is stressed. A child may learn how to do something by watching an opposite-sex model, but may seldom do it because he learns (through observation or otherwise) that such action would probably be punished if performed by a person of his own sex.

We have found several reasons to be dissatisfied with these theories. The first is that children have not been shown to resemble closely the same-sex parent in their behavior. In fact, the rather meager evidence suggests that a boy resembles other children's fathers as much as he does his own, at least with respect to most of the behaviors and attributes measured so far. The same applies to girls' resemblance to their mothers. When people believe they see parent-child resemblance, we suspect they are often noticing physical resemblance rather than behavioral resemblance.

A second problem is that when offered an opportunity to imitate either a male or female model, children (at least those under age 6 or 7) do not characteristically select the model whose sex matches their own; their choices are fairly random in this regard. Yet their behavior is clearly sex-typed at a much earlier age than the age at which choice of same-sex models begins to occur. A final problem is that children's sex-typed behavior does not closely resemble that of adult models. Boys select an all-male play group, but they do not observe their fathers avoiding the company of females. Boys choose to play with trucks and cars, even though they may have seen their mothers driving the family car more frequently than their fathers; girls play hopscotch and jacks (highly sex-typed games), although these games are totally absent from their mother's observable behavior.

To recapitulate briefly: we have been discussing the biological factors and the learning processes that have been alleged to underlie the development of behavioral sex differences. It is tempting to try to classify the differential behaviors as being either innate or learned, but we have seen that this is a distinction that does not bear close scrutiny. We have noted that a genetically controlled characteristic may take the form of a greater *readiness to learn* a particular kind of behavior, and hence is not distinct from learned behavior. Furthermore, if one sex is more biologically predisposed than the other to perform certain actions, it would be reasonable to expect that this fact would be reflected in popular beliefs about the sexes, so that innate tendencies help to produce the cultural lore that the child learns. Thus he adapts himself, through learning, to a social stereotype that has a basis in biological reality. (Of course, not all social stereotypes about the sexes have such a basis.) It is reasonable, then, to talk about the process of acquisition of sex-typed behavior—the *learning* of sex-typed behavior—as a process built upon biological foundations that are sex-differentiated to some degree.

So far we have discussed two learning processes that have been presumed to account for the development of socially defined sex-appropriate behavior. The first emphasizes direct parental reinforcement. We have seen that, although differential reinforcement of boys and girls may account for some sex typing as narrowly defined (e.g., the fact that boys avoid wearing dresses and playing with dolls), there are large areas of sex-differentiated behavior where parental sanctions and encouragement seem to play only a very minor role. A second process widely believed to be crucial in differentiation is the child's identification with (and imitation of) the same-sex parent and, by generalization, other same-sex models. The

Mother and Child by Mary Cassatt; reprinted by permission of National Gallery of Art, Washington; Chester Dale Collection

weaknesses of this process in accounting for the evidence have been delineated above.

We turn now to a third kind of process—the one we entitled "self-socialization" in Chapter 1. This process has been most explicitly enunciated by Kohlberg (1966)[R]. Kohlberg stresses that sex-typed behavior is not made up of a set of independent elements acquired by imitating actions the child has seen same-sex people perform. It stems from organized rules the child has induced from what he has observed and what he has been told, and these rules are in many ways a distortion of reality. They are based upon a limited set of features that are salient and describable from a child's point of view (e.g., hair styles and dress); the child's sex-role conceptions are cartoon-like—oversimplified, exaggerated, and stereotyped. He fails to note the variations in the sex-role behavior of his real-life models. A compelling example of this is seen in the case of a 4-year-old girl who insisted that girls could become nurses but only boys could become doctors. She held to this belief tenaciously even though her own mother was a doctor. Hers was a concept clearly not based upon imitation of the most available model. It represented an induction from instances seen and heard (in fiction as well as fact), and like most childish rule inductions it did not easily take account of exceptions.

The child's problem in behaving in ways appropriate to his sex is two-fold: he not only must have some conception of what boy-like and girl-like behavior is, but also must have a clear conception of his own sex identity so that he knows which kind of behavior to adopt. Kohlberg notes that neither a child's conception of his own sexual identity nor his notions of what it means to be "masculine" or "feminine" are static. Both change with intellectual growth. Initially a child might know only what his or her own sex is without understanding that his own gender is unchangeable. When sex constancy has been achieved, the child then seeks to determine what behavior is appropriate for his own sex. Early in development, he may not know precisely which other people share a sex category with him; a boy of four may know, for example, which other children are also boys, but he may class all adults together as "grown-ups" and fail to make consistent distinctions between men and women or to realize that men and boys are similar in the sense of all being males. When sex groupings have been understood, the child is then in a position to identify what behavior is appropriate for his sex by observing what kinds of things males, as distinct from females, do and to match his own behavior to the conceptions he has constructed.

There is a problem with the Kohlberg view: sex typing of behavior occurs much earlier than gender constancy normally develops. We do not question that the achievement of gender constancy may accelerate the process of sex typing. Indeed, R. G. Slaby[1] has found that those kindergartners who have come to understand that gender is constant choose to observe same-sex models (as compared with opposite-sex models), whereas other children of the same age do not. But we would like to argue that gender constancy is not necessary in order for self-socialization into sex roles to begin. Children as young as 3, we suggest, have begun to develop a rudimentary understanding of their own sex identity, even though their ability to group others according to sex is imperfect and their notion about the permanence of their own sex identity incomplete. As soon as a boy knows that he is a boy in any sense, he is likely to begin to prefer to do what he conceives to be boylike things. Of course, he will not selectively imitate male models if he does not yet know which other people around him are in the same sex category as himself. But he will nevertheless try to match his own behavior to his limited concept of what attributes are sex-appropriate.

---

[1] R. G. Slaby, University of Washington, personal communication, 1974.

We believe that the processes of direct reinforcement and simple imitation are clearly involved in the acquisition of sex-typed behavior, but that they are not sufficient to account for the developmental changes that occur in sex typing. The third kind of psychological process—the one stressed by cognitive-developmental theorists such as Kohlberg—must also be involved. This third process is not easy to define, but in its simplest terms it means that a child gradually develops concepts of "masculinity" and "femininity," and when he has understood what his own sex is, he attempts to match his behavior to his conception. His ideas may be drawn only very minimally from observing his own parents. The generalizations he constructs do not represent acts of imitation, but are organizations of information distilled from a wide variety of sources. A child's sex-role concepts are limited in the same way the rest of his concepts are, by the level of cognitive skills he has developed. Therefore the child undergoes reasonably orderly age-related changes in the subtlety of his thought about sex typing, just as he does with respect to other topics. Consequently, his *actions* in adopting sex-typed behavior, and in treating others according to sex-role stereotypes, also change in ways that parallel his conceptual growth.

The Difference

It involves a simplicity,
the difference between men and women.
Women render from complexity
A simpler face.
For that, men think her simplistic.
But she is not.

It's a matter of living:
living equals people.
That is what you will find
when a woman draws the lines.

But do not think it stops there.
The lines are only possible
in the round
that holds them, buoying,
like a mother holds a child.

Grace Wade

Martha T. Schuch Mednick and Hilda J. Weissman

The Psychology of Women—Selected Topics

This is a report on recent work in selected areas.[1] It is limited by space, by the frank biases of the authors, and by topical popularity. We will turn first to the psychological study of sex roles, fundamental to most research concerning women. The second topic concerns a new look at achievement motivation in women. While some segments of society are rejecting the achievement ethic, there is a growth of interest in patterns and determinants of women's school performance and career development (4, 42, 54, 114, 134). The third topic concerns the impact of feminist thought and knowledge about female sexuality on the theories and practice of psychotherapy. The common thread throughout is a questioning of age-old assumptions about sex roles and sex identity.

There is and continues to be a great emphasis on spelling out differences in abilities and personality traits and their biosocial bases (123). Older and newer works set in the frame of infant and childhood development have provided us with cogent reviews and thorough analyses (80, 81, 124). The controversies are not resolved but they have been well defined, and certainly this will continue to be a "hot topic" generating emotion and political action as well as research. This is not the main concern of this review; the focus is on women more than girls and on intragroup variations and individuality more than on sex differences. Sex comparisons cannot be and are not ignored—in fact, we may in the end realize that understanding

women has led us to a clearer understanding of men and of people in general (22).

Two recent texts on the psychology of women (6, 123) emphasized the biological approach as well as early socialization. The text by Sherman is a well-reasoned, analytical look at the empirical findings about females. More questions are asked than answered—an accurate reflection of the state of the art. Bardwick's text is personal, presenting a biosocial theory of feminine development whose basis has been questioned[2] (33). Bardwick has edited a book of readings (7) which also stresses biology and early socialization (10). Other collections have taken a social-psychological approach (89, 90, 138). A comprehensive annotated bibliography of the interdisciplinary as well as international literature on sex roles is available (3).

Psychological Study of Sex Roles

Research and writing about sex roles have moved from description and an acceptance of the givens (120) to a concern with the dynamics and implications of change (59, 60, 63, 76, 87). Compelling questions about the nature and mutability of social institutions such as marriage, the family, and even motherhood and fatherhood have been raised (14, 15, 56, 59, 116). Holter (60) presents an analysis of how social structures perpetuate even nonfunctional sex role distinctions, and spells out the requirements and consequences of role change. She is fully cognizant of the psychological factors

---

[1] Weissman is responsible for the section on therapy and Mednick is responsible for choice of topics and the remainder of the review.

[2] See also review by E. E. Maccoby (1972) on The Meaning of Being Female in Contemp. Psychol. 17:369–72.

which help maintain the status quo, such as the power of entrenched attitudes and behaviors and immutable self concepts. Similar points have been raised by Bem & Bem (13) in a social-psychological analysis of the influence and pervasiveness of sex role ideology. The implication of role change for men (135) and generally held conceptions of masculinity has received some attention (102), but little empirical work has appeared.

Sex role variation has been studied in numerous societies (16, 18, 50, 61, 87, 113, 116, 120). The comparisons help clarify the possibilities of change, but causal generalizations are problematic. It does seem clear that even in societies with conscious women's emancipation ideologies, role change is superficial (59, 88). Major social factors such as variation in birth rates, sex ratios, technological changes, economic conditions, and national crises (75) may be more potent (even if temporary) effectors than ideology or legislation, and these must be included in any study of the role variation over time and across cultures.

Sex Role Identity

Discussions of sex or gender identity emphasize models of early socialization and their implications for later personality functioning and malfunctioning (e.g., 65, 68, 93). Although critical of the content of Freudian thinking about the development of the feminine personality, Bardwick (6) adheres to classic psychodynamic assumptions regarding the significance of biology and early experience. Such assumptions (unleavened by considerations of environmental challenge) lead to pessimistic conclusions about the possibilities of sex role change, and their validity is being questioned.

Challenge is also directed at the definitions and measures of many overlapping sex role concepts. Indeed major integrative problems stem from the vagueness of the constructs and capricious variation in measurement. For instance, Constantinople (26) addressed part of this problem in a thorough review of the literature on masculinity-femininity (MF). She noted the definitional ambiguity which was not resolved by the operational recourse to "items which separate men from women." Major measures of MF confuse or merge the concepts of sex role identity, sex role preferences, and sex role adoption. Indeed MF measures are also called measures of sex-typing (17) and sex role standards (35, 130). Constantinople concludes that most MF instruments are multidimensional, including various affective and cognitive components, and moreover rejects the assumption that MF is a bipolar trait. Thus evidence suggests that masculinity and femininity are not opposites; each should be conceptualized and measured independently. This is consonant with Carlson's (22 view that characteristics viewed as masculine and those regarded as feminine may co-exist and interact. Helson's (e.g., 55) studies of the creative personality focus on such a conception and indicate that effective creative functioning in men and women may be best understood in these terms.

Other recent research is also addressed to the bipolarity controversy. J. H. Block (16, 17) presents a model of sex role conceptions and provides evidence, based on cross-national and longitudinal data, that the most effective functioning is a product of the incorporation of positive aspects of both the masculine and feminine sex roles. However, she found that the socialization process enhances this trait coexistence for men but not for women. Thus, "For males, socialization tends to enhance experiential options and to encourage more androgynous sex role definitions . . . for women

A little girl is as a rule less aggressive, defiant, and self-sufficient; she seems to have a greater need for being shown affection and on that account to be more dependent and pliant.

Sigmund Freud

---

the socialization process tends to reinforce the nurturant, docile submission and conservative aspects of . . . the role . . . discourage self assertiveness, achievement orientation and independence" (16, p. 525).

Similar results are reported by Spence and her colleagues (130), who found that for men and women the endorsement of both highly valued masculine traits and feminine traits correlated positively with ratings of self esteem. S. L. Bem (11, 12), who like Spence et al (129) is engaged in the development of a new instrument, found that androgynous individuals are more likely to behave adaptively, i.e. do what the situation rather than a rigid sex-role self-concept demands. She also noted a "behavioral deficit" in the most feminine females. That the female role is related to indicators of stress, conflict, and incompetence has been demonstrated in several other recent studies (48, 66, 105, 109, 147). It seems quite safe to predict that the *Zeitgeist* will combine with the stimulating force of new techniques and alternative theories to generate further empirical work on the redefinition and refinement of these concepts.

Stereotypes

An extensive series of studies conducted by Broverman and her colleagues has become standard reference in the research and in popular feminist literature. This work has even been referred to and inserted in hearings on sex discrimination before the Congress of the United States. In a review (20) of their own work, these investigators concluded that stereotypic thinking about sex role related personality traits is pervasive. Furthermore, a greater number of desirable traits are assigned to men than to women, the valued traits for men forming a competence cluster, while those for women form a warmth-expressiveness cluster.

Stereotypic thinking and adherence to traditional role expectations does appear to be pervasive. It is found in school settings (5, 36, 78, 79, 101, 115), in children's literature (143), in U.S. as well as Israeli communes (88, 92, 148), in widely used text books (8),[3] in the mass media (107), and in language styles (141). The occupational world is sex-typed (70, 100, 125); specific job-sex patterns vary across cultures, but prestige and economic value is always higher for those which are male occupied (59, 88, 116). Occupational prestige levels change when the other sex moves in; this has been recently verified in a laboratory setting (137). The perceptions of required and personal job characteristics or requirements also reflect sex role assumptions (119).

There is some work suggesting that stereotypic sex role attitudes held about others or the self are significant moderators or determinants of various classes of behaviors. These include occupational choice (72, 75), attraction

---

[3]A report on sex bias in psychology textbooks is available from the American Psychological Association, Office of Educational Affairs (unpublished manuscript, J. Birk et al).

Copyright 1972, G. B. Trudeau/Distributed by Universal Press Syndicate

(121), activism (118), and achievement (2, 77, 101, 136; also see section on achievement). Several studies indicate that sex role considerations may account for variations in helping behavior and that the nature of the situation intereacts with biological sex and sex role in the elicitation of help. Men and women helpers are equally affected (47, 52, 139).

Ellis & Bentler (35) report that women but not men who perceive extreme sex differences endorse traditional role standards. Additionally, women who scored high on a measure of status seeking regarded themselves as nontraditional—that is, different from women in general. It is also of interest that women like women depicted in masculine but not feminine role activities, even when they are incompetent. This is most true for women with pro-feminist attitudes. Men, on the other hand, did not show this "pro-masculine bias" (128) and liked competent women regardless of the role enacted.

Women's views of men's opinions affect their behavior (53, 62), but there is some evidence that men don't think what women think they think (132). With regard to opposite sex attraction, women were attracted to "masculine" males, while men were equally attracted to "masculine" and "feminine" females (121). Males' response to women depicted in roles varying in degree of "liberatedness" was examined in a study by Dufresne (32). Liberated women aren't "liked," but they are assigned higher status jobs than the neutrally regarded traditionals. Equalitarian women fare the best;

they are liked and given high status assignments. Studies of this type should be repeated with different role incumbents, since the actor's personal characteristics may influence judgments. Another question concerns the subject populations . . . will men (or women) actually doing the hiring respond as college sophomores do? Also critical is a look at the extent to which attitudinal statements and judgments about videotaped or otherwise simulated role incumbents relate to behavior. Such research is status seeking regarded themselves as nontraditional—that is, different from women in general. It is also of interest that women like women depicted in masculine but not feminine role activities, even when they are incompetent. This is most true for women with pro-feminist attitudes. Men on the other hand did not show needed before we can conclude that women are totally misguided in their beliefs about "What Men Want." Finally, questions about the reactions of women to variations in male role behavior as well as *men's* concerns about what women think have yet to be explored.

Achievement Tendencies in Women— Is There a New Look?

In their article on personality in the 1971 *Annual Review of Psychology*, Sarason & Smith singled out the area of achievement motivation as one which has been based almost exclusively on the study of men. This practice was accurately attributed to the conclusion by McClelland and his colleagues that women need ap-

By Bülbül, from *I'm Not for Women's Lib . . . But,* Arachne Publishing, Mountain View, Ca.

proval and men need success. It should be added that neither McClelland nor Atkinson nor their offspring chose to identify their work as the psychology of male achievement motivation. The message was left between the lines. Sarason & Smith noted, "In view of evolving changes in cultural conceptions of female roles and aspirations, greater contemporary research on achievement motivation in women seems warranted" (118a, p. 409). The view from early 1974 indicates that this is happening; the following reviews a portion of recent work.

Two review papers framed in different theoretical context focus on the affiliation-achievement conflict. Hoffman (57) asserts that females are inadequately socialized for independence and thus do not develop adequate mastery skills. She argues, too, that female achievement behavior is motivated by a drive to please rather than to succeed and that success and affiliation are in reality often incompatible. A specific prescription for mastery training for girls is suggested. However, Stein & Bailey (131) conclude that girls and women are achievement oriented but learn to value sex role appropriate social skills. The basis for learning is the same for boys and girls: social reinforcement, i.e., response to approval. They reject the hypothesis that the males and females are different in level of affiliative need, basing much of their argument on evidence that boys and girls are not differentially responsive to social approval or disapproval in a variety of social learning experiments. Stein & Bailey and

Hoffman agree that certain kinds of achievement behaviors are incompatible with the typical feminine sex role training pattern, and that independence and mastery training must be facilitated (also 124).

Fear of Success

The fear of success (FOS)[4] was postulated by Horner (62) within the framework of Atkinson's expectancy-value theory to account for sex differences in achievement behavior. She developed a fantasy measure of the motive that accounted for performance decrements by high ability women in mixed-sex competitive achievement settings. The idea was that women were motivated to achieve but that fear is aroused by the anticipation of the negative consequences of success. It is not a wish or need to fail. The latter concept, which one writer does introduce[5] and at least one study purported to examine (85), would imply an expectation of *positive* consequences from failure in achievement situations.

Recent studies of FOS have looked at variations in incidence of imagery and have generally attempted to explore the validity of the concept. Although Horner noted an increase in FOS in women from 1965 to 1971, others report

[4]Margaret Mead referred to women's fears of success in *Male and Female,* published in 1949. Klinger postulated the same concept in another context (69).

[5]J. E. Albino (unpublished manuscript, 1974) makes the provocative suggestion that this is analogous to the Freudian concept of feminine masochism, but also notes the absence of evidence for such a motive.

The One That Got Away or The Woman Who Made It

We all know who I mean, even me.
She is the one who slid like an eel
from knowing any truth larger than herself.
She wheezed orgasms through all her rapes,
married well and joined clubs
and married average and glowed in the perfect home
*   and kids,*
and didn't marry but "kept her freedom,"
never felt oppressed, of course,
made it into the Senate or
the Weather Underground,
impressed even corporation execs and cookiepattern
*   Che's.*
And she took up Zen,
went back to the earth, wore ankle-length dresses
and madonna mystical smiles,
baked natural bread, did astrology
and good works,
got elected to the Board of United Fruit
and the National Welfare Rights Organization
*   Committee,*
became a famous artist/engineer/pilot/architect/
*   doctor—*
"anyone can, I did; pull yourself up by your own
*   G-string."*
She played: matriarch with a sense of humor,
tough broad, fragile flower, spiritual seeker,
Jewish princess, a real pal, earth mother goddess,
tripper, capable unhysterical real woman friend,
. . . boyish gamin, lyrical lover, chic swinger, and
*   "your equal"*
—and anything else the boys dug in a female
at any given moment.
She even "expanded" her straight consciousness into
*   being gay,*
then bloomed into a macho copy of what is easier
to confront in men than in a sister,
of what women in love never meant, not at all.

And yes, we know why.
We can pity the terror and comprehend the threat
to her of a women's revolution.
We can understand that, until yesterday,
there were no other options.

We can even envy the heart-deadening rewards she
*   seems to reap*

for placing women last, after everything, anything
*   else.*
How she hates us in herself!
How we detest her in our mirror!

And she got herself killed, of course,
trying to shout Black Liberation Now
while her black brother's foot was planted on her
*   throat,*
and then took one too many middleclass pills,
*   committing suicide,*
and after that had a heart attack at the
Fashion Industry Convention Annual Awards,
subsequently breaking her neck in a ditch, while
*   stoned,*
at the free farm in Vermont,
only to get her head blown off in a townhouse
*   explosion,*
two days later hemorrhaging out from a safe,
*   expensive abortion,*
afterward drinking herself to death or overdosing on
*   smack,*
and gave up the ghost forty years later, children all
*   married,*
while the other old ladies at the home,
or the entire congregation, or commune, or college, or
*   congress,*
or movement, or family, or firm
Felt Her Loss Sincerely.
She refused to understand she was doomed from the
*   start,*
and she still doesn't like being reminded.
Too bad, sister.
And there's less and less time for her
to find her own way at her own speed.
She will hide behind our sisterhood, not hers.
She will say this is an anti-woman poem.
She will be the ultimate weapon in the hands of the
*   boys,*
And I've just begun to realize
that I must not only destroy what she is,
but if I have to, kill her.

And then cradle her skull in my arms
and kiss its triumphant grin,
and not even cry for us both.

Robin Morgan

lowered incidence or diminished sex differences for a variety of settings and age groups (21, 37, 58, 104, 112, 140). That social factors affect degree of FOS imagery is suggested by several studies of black women (87, 106, 145). Hoffman found no sex differences, but women did show as much FOS in 1971 as in 1965. Thematic analysis suggested that college women are as fearful as ever but that college men now seem to be downgrading success (58). A study of students in the fifth through eleventh grades reported similar thematic differences (21). On the other hand, Ward & Mausner (140) found that their high school students told few affiliative rejection stories. Monahan et al (94) found high FOS in women, but *both* men and women told FOS stories for successful women but not for men. They suggest that this supports a learned social role rather than motivational explanation for the concept. Horner and others (21, 58, 112) have attributed variations in both male and female imagery to sex differences in scoring, the changed social climate, subject characteristics, and stimulus properties. To date, however, the results are such that none of the explanations are consistently supported.

Other investigations have attempted to verify predictions about the effects of variations in FOS. The hypothesis that opposite sex competition leads to a performance decrement for women is supported by several studies (62, 86, 104, 144) but not by others (21, 27, 127, 140).

Sex role traditionally was found to moderate the expected relationship of FOS and performance (104) and was the only significant predictor in another (103); Sorrentino & Short (127) found that high FOS women performed *better* on a male sex-typed task than a "female" task. This is not only contrary to Horner's predictions, but also to other work (131) regarding sex-typing and achievement oriented behavior. The nature of the task was also explored by McGuinness (86) in the only study that varied difficulty level. A performance decrement due to mixed sex competition was related to FOS for both men and women, but only on a task of moderate difficulty. This suggests that the study of the effect of task variables is a fruitful direction for further research.

Horner's theory also predicts that high ability women are most likely to have FOS. The complexities of predicting actual achievement from individual differences in motivation, expectancy, or attributional measures have been thoroughly discussed in the achievement motivation literature (108, 142). Direct tests of the relationship between ability and FOS do not support the theory (71, 104), but several studies may be cited as showing indirect support (21, 99, 127).

Peplau's (104) study of dating couples appears to reject Horner's prediction that attitudes of and perceptions of supportiveness from a boyfriend is negatively related to FOS. A study of

One way of dealing with these disparities between the athletic promise and achievement of men and women is to view women as truncated males. As such they should be permitted to engage in such sports as men do . . . but in foreshortened versions.

Paul Weiss, Professor of Philosophy at Yale,
Sport: A Philosophical Inquiry (1969)

black women also rejected this hypothesis, but found that the degree of attachment to a man (e.g., dating vs engaged) moderated the relationship of FOS and attitudes about black militancy. Thus attached women who had militant attitudes had less FOS than their unattached counterparts (106).

Horner's construct has indeed stimulated an energetic "new look" in one direction, but it is clear that refinement of the measure[6] and the concept should be encouraged so that adequate testing and modification of the theory may proceed.

Expectancies and Causal Attribution

The general literature on achievement motivation has burgeoned with studies emphasizing cognitive factors as influencers of achievement behavior (38, 142). The research on sex differences in expectancies and causal attributions about success and failure has been summarized by Frieze (41; see also 131) and also suggests promising new directions for research on women and achievement. Many have argued that motivational research reinforces victim rather than institutional blame (112). However, it is also important to recognize that self blame is generated through certain types of misattributions. Gurin & Gurin (49) have suggested that

The above and photographs on page 128 by Cathy Cade

the effect of social change on expectations about success and failure and behavioral change must be based on a complete understanding of the self-attributional process. They suggest that this process may provide a linkage of institutional change to individual response.

Recent reviews and new findings (29, 40, 42, 131) clearly document lower expectations for female than male performance on tasks involving intellectual mastery. We have already seen that tasks and traits typed as female are devalued. Expectancies about one's own performance are also low; women generally expect to fail (42, 131).

There are also sex differences in causal attributions for success and failure (42). Men generally attribute their success to stable fac-

---

[6] A new scoring system was demonstrated by Horner at the American Psychological Association, 1973.

Photograph by Cathy Cade

was shown in a study of causal attributions about others' performance (29). It was found that both men and women rated men as more successful than women on "masculine" as well as on "feminine" tasks. On masculine tasks good performance by a man was attributed to skill, while good performance by a woman was attributed to luck. Furthermore, performance on a masculine task was valued more highly than on the feminine task. In the same vein, Feldman & Kiesler (40) report that "those who are number two try harder." When evaluating peers, subjects attributed women's success to hard work and failure to lack of effort. This was not the case for the attributions about men's performance. In a second phase of the study they found that men and women were expected to be equally successful as pediatricians but not as surgeons. Again, woman's success was attributed to her hard work rather than her ability. As these authors note, other findings (38) indicate that stable factors such as ability are found to be attributed to expected outcomes, and since men are expected to be successful, such attributions are probable. In contrast, variable factors such as effort are used more often to explain unexpected outcomes—such as woman's success. Self attributions and attributions about others seem to go hand in hand, and both reflect expectations based on sex role assumptions.

Women and Psychotherapy

Criticism of the Freudian theory of female psychosexual development has been simmering along since it was first presented. The theoretical issues and their consequences for women in "real life" as well as in psychotherapy surged to a full boil in the late 1960s. The assault on the

tors such as ability and failure to luck which is unstable. Women, on the other hand, tend to attribute failure to ability and success to effort. However, these relationships are moderated by individual differences in level of achievement motivation (42), fear of success (39), ability level, and the relationship of expected to actual outcomes (126). Using Weiner's (142) attributional analysis of achievement motivation as a conceptual framework, Freize (42) derives practical implications for women's achievement efforts from these findings.

The importance of sex role considerations

validity of the theory and discussions of its influence on therapists and on the *Zeitgeist,* as well as its consequences for women in or out of emotional difficulties has continued to grow in both volume and intensity. However, as can be seen from the following summary, there is more speculation than empirical work.

Rice & Rice (111) write of the perplexity and lack of emphathetic understanding of male therapists concerning their women patients' complaints and dissatisfactions. Explaining women's resulting hostility as transference has become less satisfactory.

The feminist issue in psychotherapy has been stated in extreme terms. It is Chesler's (24) thesis that men (including men therapists) drive women crazy, in order to maintain a male sexist hegemony. The Brovermans (19) demonstrated that clinicians view "mentally healthy women" as passive, emotional, subjective, etc.—characteristics they otherwise attribute to "mentally unhealthy adults." Does this pressure their patients into diminishing or even self-destructive roles? It seems that therapists support sex-role stereotypes and the status quo in general (1, 83).

There is strong feelings in counter-cultural and radical feminist circles that psychotherapy in general, and certainly the psychotherapy establishment, is destructive to the human potential of women. Various groups have established lists of accredited, feminist therapists, who are considered to be freer of exploitative bias toward women than establishment therapists, although the categories overlap. There has been a proliferation of therapy substitutes for women: 1. consciousness-raising groups originally developed by the National Organization for Women, but now burgeoning in various other institutions; 2. assertiveness-training groups, generally using behavior modification techniques such as modeling, role-playing, desensitization, etc.; 3. continuing education programs at colleges and universities, which combine vocational and sensitivity training; 4. encounter and sensitivity training groups focusing on women; and 5. associations of paraprofessionals stressing supportive, assertive, and confrontational methods.

Polemic aside, what does the literature reveal of professional response to the issues raised? There is much theoretical discussion but little systematic development or research on theory or practice. A survey of the research literature on psychotherapy and mental illness relating to women, and female sexuality, reveals a heavy predominance of interest in two areas: abortion and frigidity. In a summary of medical and psychiatric attitudes about psychiatric indications for induced abortion, White (146) asserted that individual physicians held rabid opinions about criteria but were in total disagreement. He says, "Is it possible that the pregnant woman symbolizes the proof of male potency and that if we loosen our rule over women and grant them the right to dispose of that proof when *they* want to, we men then feel terribly threatened lest women can at will rob us of the proof of our potency and masculinity?"

Turning to the literature on frigidity, most articles deal with it as a dysfunctional symptom resulting from ignorance, fear, hostility, etc. With regard to treatment, several papers focus on the use of behavior modification (e.g., 34, 64), hypnosis with and without stag films (9),[7]

---

[7]Sales brochure for slides and tape presentation by Gilbert MacVaugh, Frigidity: Successful Treatment in One Hypnotic Imprint Session with the Oriental-Relaxation Technique.

and similar more or less mechanistic techniques (31). While the psychoanalysts do look at frigidity in relation to the woman's life history and pattern, it is still seen as a pathological symptom, never as a conflicted attempt to control her anatomical destiny. Fisher (41) has written a large book on *The Female Orgasm,* which has been criticized on this as well as other grounds by Money et al (95). An alternative way of looking at frigidity, similarly conjectural, is in terms of existential conflict rather than inconvenience or reproach to the male, or defect or failure in the female. Sherfey (122) has observed that "each orgasm tends to increase pelvic vasocongestion," hence readiness for further orgasms. Since most sexual partners could not meet the women's level of repeated readiness, her "frigidity" could be seen as the self-protective outcome of an approach-avoidance conflict, whereby she avoids chronic pelvic congestion—a condition which in fact does occur in many women (and which Freud considered the basis of anxiety neurosis). Even if a tireless partner were available, the prospect of reversion to an instinct-dominated existence, where every orgasm led to more until a state of physical exhaustion was reached, also conflicts realistically with a human range of goals.

Other popular topics are represented by the many clinical reports on contraceptives for women's use, on treatments with psychotropic drugs, and on the effects of gynecological surgery on women's sex life. The charge that therapists see women as functional or dysfunctional objects rather than as humans (see 25, pp. 47, 73, 75–82) seems to have some foundation in the selection of such topics for communication to one's peers about one's work with women patients. It is also true that there are increasing numbers of articles sensitive to women's emotional problems in realistic contexts (91).

The remainder of this article will deal with a few promising developments and more critical rhetoric in psychoanalytic thought, which still seems to be the most influential theoretical basis for treatment situations in clinics and private practice.

Of the numerous articles calling for the revision of psychoanalytic theory and practice, one by Kronsky (73) is outstanding: soundly based in psychoanalytic understanding, free from rhetoric, and specific in its recommendations to the therapist. Kronsky sees women as frequently suffering from a free-floating sense of guilt resulting from inconsistent super-ego prohibitions or a double bind. She urges that the therapist avoid interpretation or mirroring while the patient is venting her rage, her competitiveness, hatred, and envy of men, lest these techniques result in re-repression, with these feelings becoming ego-dystonic, and an inauthentic femininity covering all. Moulton (97) speaks in similar terms and amplifies these themes. Chasseguet-Smirgel (23) has collected a book of articles by French women analysts who regard fulfillment as covering a broader range than matehood and motherhood.

Some male analysts have also spoken out on various aspects of the weakness of orthodox analytic theory in dealing with women's development. Gelb (45) states, "I believe that many in the field of psychoanalysis have been guilty of contributing heavily to the coercive institutionalization of male and female roles which have little to do with sexual identity." While women and men have been struggling toward competence and relatedness, many psychoanalysts discourse about the glory of passivity to women and about "reestablishing masculine identity" to men—rather than moving toward full capacity as human beings. Chodoff (25) points out that the evidence that Freud got from his patients for his theory of infantile sexuality can be explained by the demand characteristics of the doctor-patient relationship. Chodoff states, "I submit that the role attributed to infantile sexuality in general and to penis envy in particular . . . cannot be proved on biologic and other empirical grounds, no matter how widely and repetitiously they are given the status of unassailable truths in large segments of educated opinion in the United States." If the evidence for infantile sexuality is not convincing, Freud's theory of feminine psychology needs to be revised. Salzman (117) underlines the need to recognize that "the psychology of the female . . . is determined by her inherent biological potentiality in a changing cultural matrix." He stresses the importance of religious doctrines and technological limitations in presumptions about woman's natural role. Marmor (84) observes that the fallacy in the common argument that the male's aggressivity and the female's passivity are both "natural" lies in the confusion between what statistically describes the behavior of men and women and what motivates that behavior.

Miller (91) holds that psychoanalysis is now at a turning point, the old sexual theories having failed to solve people's problems in living. She points out that "the notions of renunciation and disengagement inherent in the "masculine" growth model have meant limitations on full human development for men and women alike."

The onslaught against Freudian theory received its greatest recent impetus from implications of the work of Masters and Johnson and of Sherfey (122). The distinction between "clitoral" and "vaginal" orgasms had been a linchpin of the theory of feminine sexuality, which was supposed to develop in two stages. The first was an immature "phallic," "masculine" stage where the female's enjoyment of her clitoris reflected her penis envy and rebellion against her inferior sexual equipment and castrated state. This had to be given up for the attainment of the second stage, a stage of "feminine" orgastic experience based on the passivity of the vagina and acceptance of her castrated state. Masters' and Johnson's studies have been accepted as demolishing the Freudian distinction between "clitoral" and "vaginal" orgasms in women, while Sherfey's integration of major contributions from embryology, biology, and gynecology has cast doubt on Freud's depiction of female sexuality as a pallid counterpart of the male's, and only perilously achieved at that. She started with the previously overlooked finding by embryologists that all mammalian embryos are known to be anatomically female in the early stages of life—until the sixth week of fetal life in the human—when, in the presence of the Y chromosome, fetal androgens bring about the differentiation of the male from the female anlage. She then went on to theorize on the basis of endocrinological research that early human females developed an inordinate cyclic sexual capacity which must have been a major barrier to the evolution of modern man, to the extent that it interfered with maternal care. Feminine hypersexuality therefore had to be suppressed, first in the interest of longer and more richly developmental human childhood, and then in the interest of property rights and ascertainable lines of descent after settled agricultural economies came into being. Although the race needed the suppression of female hypersexuality, one might guess that the individual male suffered from the comparison with this female, especially before the knowledge of paternity. The uneasy attainment of this giant step for mankind may have had to be buttressed by the development of the compensatory hy-

*Like all sciences and all valuations, the psychology of women has
hitherto been considered only from the point of view of men. It is
inevitable that the man's position of advantage should cause objective
validity to be attributed to his subjective, affective relations to the
woman, and . . . the psychology of women hitherto actually represents
a deposit of the desires and disappointments of men. An additional and
very important factor in the situation is that women have adapted
themselves to the wishes of men and felt as if their adaptation were
their true nature. That is, they see or saw themselves in the way that
their men's wishes demanded of them; unconsciously they yielded to the
suggestion of masculine thought.*

Karen Horney

---

permasculinity which has characterized so
many human societies.

Freud postulated that the development to
psychosexual maturity was more difficult and
uncertain for women, since their first love object
was of the same sex, whereas males have
heterosexual objects from the beginning. With
the male, heterosexuality was supposed to be
primary, while for the female it is only achieved
after tortuous changes. Stoller (133) offers other
observations and thoughts in connection with
Freud's postulation. Before the mother becomes
the male infant's love object, there is a stage
of symbiosis when he has not yet separated
from his mother and distinguished his body and
psyche as different from hers—and *"she is female
with a feminine gender identity."* Therefore,
heterosexuality is *not* a given for males,
but an achievement, whereas femininity for
females *is* given by the earliest identification,
not tortuously arrived at through castration,
humiliation, renunciation as Freud said. Symbiosis
anxiety is seen as an important motive
force in the development of masculinity.

Gadpaille (44), in a review of physiological
and other research, wrote in 1972:

> Perhaps even male chauvinism and the worldwide
> predominance of male domination . . . (is) intensely
> motivated as a denial of an unconscious awareness
> by man of his greater fragility and vulnerability,
> both physically and psychosexually, compared to
> women . . . The male is more vulnerable in vir-

tually every way with the exception of physical
prowess: there is greater difficulty in achieving
maleness and masculinity, coupled with an increased
vulnerability of males to disruption of
sexual function and to physical and psychosexual
disorders.

In confirmation, there is the 1972 publication
by Ginsberg, Frosch & Shapiro (46) observing
that the obsolescence of the virginity taboo has
disrupted the former ecological balance in society
resulting in disequilibrium for males, and
the rise of what they call "the new impotence."

Madigan (82) found sex mortality differentials
to be biologically caused, not the result
of social conditions. He found that both sexes
equally lack resistance to infectious and contagious
disease, but that women have greater
constitutional resistance to degenerative diseases.

Paralleling the critique of Freudian theory
regarding female development and malfunctioning
is a revival or shift of interest to Jungian
psychology with its stress on the existence of
both masculine and feminine polarities in each
individual (30, 51). The research referred to in
the earlier section on sex role definitions is also
germane.

Various streams of thought have been flowing
together in the last few years which suggest
a need for far-ranging reorientation of the androcentric
epistemology of our culture if a psychological
understanding of women and men

Is it not really remarkable . . . that so little recognition and attention are paid to the fact of men's secret dread of women? . . . The man . . . has very obvious strategic reasons for keeping his dread quiet. But he also tries by every means to deny it even to himself. This is the purpose of the efforts . . . to "objectify" it in artistic and scientific creative work. We may conjecture that even his glorification of women has its source not only in his cravings for love, but also in his desire to conceal his dread. A similar relief, however, is also sought and found in the disparagement of women that men often display ostentatiously in their attitudes. The attitude of love and adoration signifies: "There is no need for me to dread a being so wonderful, so beautiful, nay, so saintly," That of disparagement implies: "It would be too ridiculous to dread a creature who, if you take her all round, is such a poor thing."

Karen Horney

---

is to be developed which can bear reality testing. Morgan (96) offers a sparkling alternative to the androcentric evolutionist theories. She says:

> I believe the deeply rooted semantic confusion between 'man' as a male and 'man' as a species has been fed back into and vitiated a great deal of the speculation that goes on about the origins, development, and nature of the human race. . . . A very high proportion of the thinking on these topics is androcentric . . . in the same way as pre-Copernican thinking was geocentric. . . . One of these days an evolutionist is going to strike a palm against his large-domed head and cry: 'Of course! We assumed the first human being was a man!'

Daly (28) proclaims the need for a counteraction to patriarchy's naming of reality and morality as in the story of the Fall of Adam and Eve, whereby the "male's viewpoint is metamorphosed into God's viewpoint" (28, p. 47). According to myths, women were weak and evil (98). Theodor Reik (110) discusses the myth of the Creation as a denial of the reality that man is born of woman, not vice versa, and also in terms of what Stoller called symbiosis anxiety. Lederer (74) also goes into prehistory and paleoanthropology to decipher the counterpho-

bic denigration of women in patriarchal society. There has been renewed interest in what can be learned of the genesis of androcentric psychoanalytic theories from the sociology of knowledge (67). We are clearly at a point where psychoanalytic theories of feminine development can thrive only with a transfusion from other disciplines: biological, historical, economic, and sociological.

Concluding Comments

This selective review on the psychology of women has, as we predicted at the outset, raised many questions. It is perhaps banal, but nevertheless necessary, to stress that there are unresolved conceptual and methodological issues within each area which will have to be raised again and reevaluated as the field develops. The different styles of the two authors probably reflect the differing state of the art in their fields. Still, if a major theme can be discerned, it is that of the sexual division of personality characteristics based on the male thinker's view of reality. To the extent this division is accepted, individual women, and men to a lesser degree, are constricted in their personal fulfillment, and society is hobbled in both competence and relatedness.

Jo Freeman

The Social Construction of the Second Sex

During the last thirty years social science has paid scant attention to women, confining its explorations of humanity to the male. Research has generally reinforced the sex stereotypes of popular mythology that women are essentially nurturant/expressive/passive and men instrumental/active/aggressive. Social scientists have tended to justify their stereotypes rather than analyze their origins, their value, or their effect.

In part this is due to the general conservatism and reluctance to question the status quo which has characterized the social sciences during this era of the feminine mystique. In part it is attributable to the "pervasive permeation of psychoanalytic thinking throughout American society."[1] The result has been a social science which is more a mechanism of social control than of social inquiry. Rather than trying to analyze why, it has only described what. Rather than exploring how men and women came to be the way they are, it has taken their condition as an irremediable given and sought to justify it on the basis of "biological" differences.

Nonetheless, the assumption that psychology recapitulates physiology has begun to crack. Masters and Johnson shattered the myth of woman's natural sexual passivity—on which her psychological passivity was claimed to rest. Research is just beginning into the other areas. Even without this new research new interpretations of the old data are being explored. What these new interpretations say is that women are the way they are because they've been trained to be that way. As the Bems put it: "We overlook the fact that the society that has spent twenty years carefully marking the women's

ballot for her has nothing to lose in that twenty-first year by pretending to let her cast it for the alternative of her choice. Society has controlled not her alternatives, but her motivation to choose any but the one of those alternatives."[2]

This motivation is controlled through the socialization process. Women are raised to want to fill the social roles in which society needs them. They are trained to model themselves after the accepted image and to meet as individuals the expectations that are held for women as a group. Therefore, to understand how most women are socialized we must first understand how they see themselves and are seen by others. Several studies have been done on this. Quoting from one of them, McClelland stated that "the female image is characterized as small, weak, soft and light. In the United States it is also dull, peaceful, relaxed, cold, rounded, passive and slow."[3] A more thorough study which asked men and women to choose out of a long list of adjectives those which most closely applied to themselves showed that women strongly felt themselves to be uncertain, anxious, nervous, hasty, careless, fearful, dull, childish, helpless, sorry, timid, clumsy, stupid, silly, and domestic. On a more positive side, women felt that they were understanding, tender, sympathetic, pure, generous, affectionate, loving, moral, kind, grateful, and patient.[4]

This is not a very favorable self-image but it does correspond fairly well with the social myths about what women are like. The image has some nice qualities, but they are not the ones normally required for that kind of achievement to which society gives its highest social rewards. Now one can justifiably question both the idea of achievement and the qualities necessary for it, but this is not the place to do so. Rather, because the current standards are the ones which women have been told they do not meet, the purpose here will be to look at the socialization process as a mechanism to keep them from doing so. We will also need to analyze some of the social expectations about women and about what they define as a successful *woman* (not a successful person) because they are inextricably bound up with the socialization process. All people are socialized to meet the social expectations held for them, and it is only when this process fails to do so (as is currently happening on several fronts) that it is at all questioned.

Let us further examine the effects on women of minority group status. Here, an interesting parallel emerges, but it is one fraught with much heresy. When we look at the *results* of female socialization we find a strong similarity between what our society labels, even extols, as the typical "feminine" character structure and that of oppressed peoples in this country and elsewhere.

In his classic study on *The Nature of Prejudice,* Allport devotes a chapter to "Traits Due to Victimization." Included are such personality characteristics as sensitivity, submission, fantasies of power, desire for protection, indirectness, ingratiation, petty revenge and sabotage, sympathy, extremes of both self and group hatred and self and group glorification, display of flashy status symbols, compassion for the underprivileged, identification with the dominant group's norms, and passivity.[5] Allport was primarily concerned with Jews and Negroes,

but compare his characterization with the very thorough review of the literature on sex differences among young children made by Terman and Tyler. For girls, they listed such traits as sensitivity, conformity to social pressures, response to environment, case of social control, ingratiation, sympathy, low levels of aspiration, compassion for the underprivileged, and anxiety. They found that girls compared to boys were more nervous, unstable, neurotic, socially dependent, submissive, had less self-confidence, lower opinions of themselves and of girls in general, and were more timid, emotional, ministrative, fearful, and passive.[6]

Girls' perceptions of themselves were also distorted. Although girls make consistently better school grades than boys until late high school, their opinion of themselves grows progressively worse with age and their opinion of boys and boys' abilities grows better. Boys, however, have an increasingly better opinion of themselves and worse opinion of girls as they grow older.[7]

These distortions become so gross that, according to Goldberg, by the time girls reach college they have become prejudiced against women. He gave college girls sets of booklets containing six identical professional articles in traditional male, female, and neutral fields. The articles were identical, but the names of the authors were not. For example, an article in one set would bear the name John T. McKay and in another set the same article would be authored by Joan T. McKay. Each booklet contained three articles by "women" and three by "men." Questions at the end of each article asked the students to rate the articles on value, persuasiveness and profundity and the authors on writing style and competence. The male authors fared better in every field, even such

The girl's nature as biologically conditioned gives her the desire to receive, to take into herself; she feels or knows that her genital is too small for her father's penis and this makes her react to her own genital wishes with direct anxiety; she dreads that if her wishes were fulfilled, she herself or her genital would be destroyed.

Karen Horney

"feminine" areas as Art History and Dietetics. Goldberg concluded that "Women are prejudiced against female professionals and, regardless of the actual accomplishments of these professionals, will firmly refuse to recognize them as the equals of their male colleagues."[8]

This combination of group self-hate and distortion of perceptions to justify that group self-hate are precisely the traits typical of a "minority group character structure."[9] It has been noted time and time again. The Clarks' finding of this pattern in Negro children in segregated schools contributed to the 1954 Supreme Court decision that outlawed such schools. These traits, as well as the others typical of the "feminine" stereotype, have been found in the Indians under British rule,[10] in the Algerians under the French,[11] and in black Americans.[12] There seems to be a correlation between being "feminine" and experiencing status deprivation.

This pattern repeats itself even within cultures. In giving TATs to women in Japanese villages, De Vos discovered that those from fishing villages where the status position of women was higher than in farming communities were more assertive, not as guilt-ridden and were more willing to ignore the traditional pattern of arranged marriages in favor of love marriages.[13]

In Terman's famous 50-year study of the gifted, a comparison in adulthood of those men who conspicuously failed to fulfill their early promise with those who did fulfill it showed that the successful had more self-confidence, fewer background disabilities, and were less nervous and emotionally unstable. But, they concluded, "the disadvantages associated with lower social and home status appeared to present the outstanding handicap."[14]

The fact that women do have lower social status than men in our society and that both sexes tend to value men and male characteristics, values, and activities more highly than those of women has been noted by many authorities.[15] What has not been done is to make the connection between this status and its accompanying personality.

The failure to extensively analyze the effects and the causes of lower social status is surprising in light of the many efforts that have been made to uncover distinct psychological differences between men and women to account for the tremendous disparity in their social production and creativity. The Goldberg study implies that even if women did achieve on a par with men it would not be perceived or accepted as such and that a woman's work must be of a much higher quality that that of a man to be given the same recognition. But these circumstances alone, or the fact that it is the male definition of achievement which is applied, are not sufficient to account for the lack of social production. So research has turned to male/female differences.

Most of this research, in the Freudian tradi-

The boy, on the other hand, feels or instinctively judges that his penis is much too small for his mother's genital and reacts with the dread of his own inadequacy, of being rejected and derided. Thus his anxiety is located in quite a different quarter from the girl's, his original dread of women is not castration anxiety at all, but a reaction to the menace to his self-respect.

Karen Horney

---

tion, has focused on finding the psychological and developmental differences supposedly inherent in feminine nature and function. Despite all these efforts, the general findings of psychological testing indicate that: (1) Individual differences are greater than sex differences, i.e., sex is just one of the many characteristics which define a human being. (2) Most differences in ability in any field do not appear until elementary school age or later. "Sex differences become more apparent with increasing education even if it is co-education."[16]

An examination of the literature of intellectual differences between the sexes discloses some interesting patterns. First, the statistics themselves show some regularity. Most conclusions of what is typical of one sex or the other are founded upon the performances of two thirds of the subjects. For example, two thirds of all boys do better on the math section of the College Board Exam than the verbal, and two thirds of the girls do better on the verbal than the math. Bales' studies show a similar distribution when he concludes that in small groups men are the task-oriented leaders and women are the social-emotional leaders.[17] Not all tests show the two-thirds differential, but it is the mean about which most results of the ability test cluster. Sex is an easy visible, differentiable and testable criterion on which to draw conclusions; but it doesn't explain the one third that doesn't fit. The only characteristic virtually all women seem to have in common,

besides their anatomy, is their lower social status.

Second, girls get off to a very good start. They begin speaking, reading, and counting sooner. They articulate more clearly and put words into sentences earlier. They have fewer reading and stuttering problems. Girls are even better in math in the early school years. Consistent sex differences in favor of boys do not appear until high-school age.[18] Here another pattern begins to develop.

During high school, girls' performance in school and on ability tests begins to drop, sometimes drastically. Although well over half of all high-school graduates are girls, significantly less than half of all college students are girls. Presumably, this should mean that a higher percentage of the better female students go on to higher education, but their performance *vis-à-vis* boys' continues to decline.

Girls start off better than boys and end up worse. This change in their performance occurs at a very significant point in time. It occurs when their status changes, or to be more precise, when girls become aware of what their adult status is supposed to be. It is during adolescence that peer-group pressures to be "feminine" or "masculine" increase and the conceptions of what is "feminine" and "masculine" becomes more narrow.[19] It is also at this time that there is a personal drive for conformity.[20]

One of the norms of our culture to which a girl learns to conform is that only men excel.

This was evident in Lipinski's study of "Sex-Role Conflict and Achievement Motivation in College Women," which showed that thematic pictures depicting males as central characters elicited significantly more achievement imagery than female pictures.[21] One need only recall Asch's experiments to see how peer-group pressures, armed only with our rigid ideas about "femininity" and "masculinity" could lead to a decline in girls' performance. Asch found that some 33% of his subjects would go contrary to the evidence of their own senses about something as tangible as the comparative length of two lines when their judgments were at variance with those made by the other group members.[22] All but a handful of the other 67% experienced tremendous trauma in trying to stick to their correct perceptions.

When we move to something as intangible as sex-role behavior and to social sanctions far greater than the displeasure of a group of unknown experimental stooges, we can get an idea of how stifling social expectations can be. It is not surprising, in light of our cultural norm that a girl should not appear too smart or surpass boys in anything, that those pressures to conform, so prevalent in adolescence, should prompt girls to believe that the development of their minds will have only negative results. The lowered self-esteem and the denigration of their own sex noted by Smith[23] and Goldberg[24] are a logical consequence. These pressures even affect the supposedly unchangeable IQ scores. Corresponding with the drive for social acceptance, girls' IQ drop below those of boys during high school, rise slightly if they go to college, and go into a steady and consistent decline when and if they become full-time housewives.[25]

These are not the only consequences. Negative self-conceptions have negative effects in a manner that can only be called a self-fulfilling prophecy. They stifle motivation and channel energies into those areas that are likely to get some positive social rewards. Then those subject to these pressures are condemned for not having strived for the highest social rewards society has to offer.

A good example of this double bind is what psychologists call the "need for achievement." Achievement motivation in male college sophomores has been studied extensively. In women it has barely been looked at; women didn't fit the model social scientists set up to explain achievement in men. Girls do not seem to demonstrate the same consistent correlation between achievement and scores on achievement tests that boys do. For example, Stivers found that "non-motivated for college" girls scored higher on achievement motivation exams than "well-motivated for college" girls.[26] There has been little inquiry as to why this is so. The general policy followed by the researchers was that if girls didn't fit, leave them out. Nonetheless some theories have been put forward.

Pierce postulated that part of the confusion resulted from using the same criteria of achievement for girls that were used for boys— achievement in school. Therefore he did a study of marriage vs. career differentiation in high-school girls which did show a small but consistent correlation between high achievement motivation scores and marriage orientation.[27] In 1961 he did another study which showed a very strong correlation between high achievement scores and actual achievement of marriage within a year of high-school graduation. Those who went on to college and/or did not get married had low achievement scores.[28]

Although he unfortunately did not describe the class origins and other relevant characteristics of his study it does seem clear that the real situation is not that women do not have achievement motivation but that this motivation is directed differently from that of men. In fact, the achievement orientation of both sexes goes precisely where it is socially directed—educational achievement for boys and marriage achievement for girls. Pierce suggested that "achievement motivation in girls attaches itself not to academic performance, but rather to more immediate adult status goals. This would be a logical assumption in that academic success is much less important to achievement status as a woman than it is for a man."[29]

He goes on to say that "girls see that to achieve in life as adult females they need to achieve in non-academic ways, that is, attaining the social graces, achieving beauty in person and dress, finding a desirable social status, marrying the right man. This is the successful adult woman. . . . Their achievement motivations are directed toward realizing personal goals through their relationship with men. . . . Girls who are following the normal course of development are most likely to seek adult status through marriage at an early age."[30]

Achievement for women is adult status through marriage, not success in the usual use of the word. One might postulate that both kinds of success might be possible, particularly for the highly achievement-oriented woman. But in fact the two are more often perceived as contradictory; success in one is seen to preclude success in the other.

Horner just completed a study at the University of Michigan from which she postulated a psychological barrier to achievement in women. She administered a TAT word item to undergraduates that said "After first term finals Anne finds herself at the top of her medical school class." A similar one for a male

---

Relationships

The legal children of a literary man
Remember his ugly words to their mother.
He made them keep quiet and kissed them
*   later.*
He made them stop fighting and finish their
*   supper.*
His stink in the bathroom sickened their noses.
He left them with sitters in lonesome houses.
He mounted their mother and made them wear
*   braces.*
He fattened on fame and raised them thin.

But the secret sons of the same man
Spring up like weeds from the seed of his
*   word.*
They eat from his hand and it is not hard.
They unravel his sweater and swing from his
*   beard.*
They smell in their sleep his ferns and roses.
They hunt the fox on his giant horses.
They slap their mother, repeating his phrases,
And swell in his sight and suck him thin.

Mona Van Duyn

---

control group used a masculine name. The results were scored for imagery of fear of success and Horner found that 65% of the women and only 10% of the men demonstrated a definite "motive to avoid success." She explained the results by hypothesizing that the prospect of success, or situations in which success or failure is a relevant dimension, are perceived as having, and in fact do have, negative consequences for women. Success in the normal sense is threatening to women. Further research confirmed that fear of social rejection and role conflict did generate a "motive to avoid success."[31]

Girls we love for what they are; young men for what they promise to be.

Johann Wolfgang von Goethe (1749–1832)

Ability differences correlate strongly with interest differences[32] and women have a definite interest in avoiding success. This is reinforced by peer and cultural pressures. However, many sex differences appear too early to be much affected by peer groups and are not directly related to sex-role attributes.

One such sex difference is spatial perception, or the ability to visualize objects out of their context. This is a test in which boys do better, though differences are usually not discernible before the early school years.[33] Other tests, such as the Embedded Figures and the Rod and Frame Tests, likewise favor boys. They indicate that boys perceive more analytically, while girls are more contextual. This ability to "break set" or be "field independent" also does not seem to appear until after the fourth or fifth year.[34]

According to Maccoby, this contextual mode of perception common to women is a distinct disadvantage for scientific production. "Girls on the average develop a somewhat different way of handling incoming information—their thinking is less analytical, more global, and more preservative—and this kind of thinking may serve very well for many kinds of functioning but it is not the kind of thinking most conducive to high-level intellectual productivity, especially in science."[35]

Several social psychologists have postulated that the key developmental characteristic of analytic thinking is what is called early "independence and mastery training," or "whether and how soon a child is encouraged to assume initiative, to take responsibility for himself, and to solve problems by himself, rather than rely on others for the direction of his activities."[36] In other words, analytically inclined children are those who have not been subject to what Bronfenbrenner calls "over-socialization,"[37] and there is a good deal of indirect evidence that such is the case. Levy has observed that "overprotected" boys tend to develop intellectually like girls.[38] Bing found that those girls who were good at spatial tasks were those whose mothers left them alone to solve the problems by themselves, while the mothers of verbally inclined daughters insisted on helping them.[39] Witkin similarly found that mothers of analytic children had encouraged their initiative, while mothers of nonanalytic children had encouraged dependence and discouraged self-assertion.[40] One writer commented on these studies that "this is to be expected, for the independent child is less likely to accept superficial appearances of objects without exploring them for himself, while the dependent child will be afraid to reach out on his own, and will accept appearances without question. In other words, the independent child is likely to be more *active,* not only psychologically but physically, and the physically active child will naturally have more kinesthetic experience with spatial relationships in his environment."[41]

The qualities associated with independence training also have an effect on IQ. Sontag did

Women have great talent, but no genius, for they always remain subjective.

Arthur Schopenhauer, *The World as Will and Idea*

---

a longitudinal study in which he compared children whose IQs had improved with those whose IQs had declined with age. He discovered that the child with increasing IQ was competitive, self-assertive, independent, and dominant in interaction with other children. Children with declining IQs were passive, shy, and dependent.[42]

Maccoby commented on this study that "the characteristics associated with a rising IQ are not very feminine characteristics. When one of the people working on it was asked about what kind of developmental history was necessary to make a girl into an intellectual person, he replied, 'The simplest way to put it is that she must be a tomboy at some point in her childhood.' "[43]

Likewise Kagan and Moss noted that "females who perform well on problems requiring analysis and complex reasoning tend to reject a traditional feminine identification."[44] They also observed that among the children involved in the Fels study "protection of girls was associated with the adoption of feminine interests during childhood and adulthood. Maternal protection apparently 'feminized' both the boys and the girls."[45]

However, analytic abilities are not the only ones that are valued in our society. Being person-oriented and contextual in perception are very valuable attributes for many fields where, nevertheless, very few women are found. Such characteristics are also valuable in the arts and some of the social sciences. But while women do succeed here more than in the sciences, their achievement is still not equivalent to that of men. One explanation of this, of course, is the Horner study that established a "motive to avoid success." But when one looks further it appears that there is an earlier cause here as well.

The very same early independence and mastery training that has such a beneficial effect on analytic thinking also determines the extent of one's achievement orientation.[46]

Although comparative studies of parental treatment of boys and girls are not extensive, those that have been made indicate that the traditional practices applied to girls are very different from those applied to boys. Girls receive more affection, more protectiveness, more control and more restrictions. Boys are subjected to more achievement demands and higher expectations.[47] In short, while girls are not always encouraged to be dependent *per se*, they are usually not encouraged to be *independent* and physically active. "Such findings indicate that the differential treatment of the two sexes reflects in part a difference in goals. With sons, socialization seems to focus primarily on directing and constraining the boys' impact on the environment. With daughters, the aim is rather to protect the girl from the impact of environment. The boy is being prepared to mold his world, the girl to be molded by it."[48] The pattern is typical of girls, Bronfenbrenner

The passivity that is the essential characteristic of the "feminine"
woman is a trait that develops in her from the earliest years. But it is
wrong to assert a biological datum is concerned; it is in fact a destiny
imposed upon her by her teachers and by society.

Simone de Beauvoir

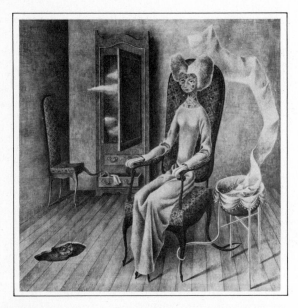

Mimicry by Remedios Varo; reprinted by permission of Walter Gruen

maintains, and involves the risk of "oversocialization."

He doesn't discuss the possible negative effects such oversocialization has on girls, but he does express his concern about what would happen to the "qualities of independence, initiative, and self-sufficiency" of boys if such training were applied to them. "While an affectional context is important for the socialization of boys, it must evidently be accompanied by and be compatible with a strong component of parental discipline. Otherwise, the boy finds himself in the same situation as the girl, who, having received greater affection, is more sensitive to its withdrawal, with the result that a little discipline goes a long way and strong authority is constricting rather than constructive."[49]

That these variations in socialization result in variations in personality is corroborated by Schachter's studies of first and later-born children. Like girls, first children tend to be better socialized but also more anxious and dependent, whereas second children, like boys, are more aggressive and self-confident.[50]

Bronfenbrenner concludes that the crucial variable is the differential treatment by the father and "in fact, it is the father who is especially likely to treat children of the two sexes differently." His extremes of affection, and of authority, are both deleterious. Not only do his high degrees of nurturance and protectiveness toward girls result in "over-socialization," but "the presence of strong paternal power is particularly debilitating. In short, boys thrive in a patriarchal context, girls in a matriarchal one."[51]

His observations receive indirect support from Douvan who noted that "part-time jobs of mothers have a beneficial effect on adolescent children, particularly daughters. This reflects the fact that adolescents may receive too much mothering."[52]

The importance of mothers, as well as moth-

One might consider characterizing femininity psychologically as giving preference to passive aims. This is not, of course, the same thing as passivity; to achieve a passive aim may call for a large amount of activity.

Sigmund Freud

ering, was pointed out by Kagan and Moss. In looking at the kinds of role models that mothers provide for developing daughters, they discovered that it is those women who are looked upon as unfeminine whose daughters tend to achieve intellectually. These mothers are "aggressive and competitive women who were critical of their daughters and presented themselves to their daughters as intellectually competitive and aggressive role models. It is reasonable to assume that the girls identified with these intellectually aggressive women who valued mastery behavior."[53]

There seems to be some evidence that the sexes have been differentially socialized with different training practices, for different goals, and with different results. If McClelland is right in all the relationships he finds between child-rearing practices (in particular independence and mastery training), achievement-motivation scores of individuals, and indeed, the economic growth of whole societies,[54] there is no longer much question as to why the historical achievement of women has been so low. In fact, with the dependency training they receive so early in life, the wonder is that they have achieved so much.

But this is not the whole story. Maccoby, in her discussion of the relationship of independence training to analytic abilities, notes that the girl who does not succumb to overprotection and develop the appropriate personality and behavior for her sex has a major price to pay: a price in anxiety. Or, as other observers have noted: "The universe of appropriate behavior for males and females is delineated early in development and it is difficult for the child to cross these culturally given frontiers without considerable conflict and tension."[55]

Some anxiety is beneficial to creative thinking, but high or sustained levels of it are damaging, "for it narrows the range of solution efforts, interferes with breaking set, and prevents scanning of the whole range of elements open to perception."[56] This anxiety is particularly manifest in college women,[57] and of course they are the ones who experience the most conflict between their current—intellectual—activities, and expectations about behavior in their future—unintellectual—careers.

Maccoby feels that "it is this anxiety which helps to account for the lack of productivity among those women who do make intellectual careers." The combination of social pressures, role-expectations and parental training together tell "something of a horror story. It would appear that even when a woman is suitably endowed intellectually and develops the right temperament and habits of thought to make use of her endowment, she must be fleet of foot indeed to scale the hurdles society has erected for her and to remain a whole and happy person while continuing to follow her intellectual bent."[58]

The reasons for this horror story must by now be clearly evident. Traditionally, women have

In education, in marriage, in everything, disappointment is the lot of woman. It shall be the business of my life to deepen this disappointment in every woman's heart until she bows down to it no longer.

Lucy Stone (1855)

---

been defined as passive creatures, sexually, physically, and mentally. Their roles have been limited to the passive, dependent, auxiliary ones, and they have been trained from birth to fit these roles. However, those qualities by which one succeeds in this society are active ones. Achievement orientation, intellectuality, and analytic ability all require a certain amount of aggression.

As long as women were convinced that these qualities were beyond them, that they were inferior in their exercise and much happier if they stayed in their place, they remained quiescent under the paternalistic system of Western civilization. Paternalism was a pre-industrial scheme of life, and its yoke was partially broken by the industrial revolution.[59] With this loosening up of the social order, the talents of women began to appear.

In the 18th Century it was held that no woman had ever produced anything worthwhile in literature with the possible exception of Sappho. But in the first half of the 19th Century, feminine writers of genius flooded the literary scene.[60] It wasn't until the end of the 19th Century that women scientists of note appeared, and it was still later that women philosophers were found.

Only since the industrial revolution shook the whole social order have women been able to break some of the traditional bounds of society. In pre-industrial societies, the family was the basic unit of social and economic organization,

and women held a significant and functional role within it. This, coupled with the high birth and death rates of those times, gave women more than enough to do within the home. It was the center of production and women could be both at home and in the world at the same time. But the industrial revolution, along with decreased infant mortality, increased life-span and changes in economic organization, have all but destroyed the family as the economic unit. Technological advances have taken men out of the home, and now those functions traditionally defined as female are being taken out also.[61] For the first time in human history women have had to devote themselves to being full-time mothers in order to have enough to do.[62]

Conceptions of society have also changed. At one time, authoritarian hierarchies were the norm and paternalism was reflective of a general social authoritarian attitude. While it is impossible to do retroactive studies on feudalistic society, we do know that authoritarianism as a personality trait does correlate strongly with a rigid conception of sex roles, and with ethnocentrism.[63] We also know from ethnological data that there is a "parallel between family relationships and the larger social hierarchy. Autocratic societies have autocratic families. As the king rules his subjects and the nobles subjugate and exploit the commoners, so does husband tend to lord it over wife, father rule over son."[64]

According to D'Andrade, "another variable

A sound and secure self-confidence draws upon a broad basis of human qualities, such as initiative, courage, independence, talents, erotic values, capacity to master situations. As long as homemaking was a really big task involving many responsibilities, and as long as the number of children was not restricted, woman had the feeling of being a constructive factor in the economic process; thus she was provided with a sound basis for self-esteem. This basis, however, has gradually vanished, and in its departure woman has lost one foundation for feeling herself valuable.

Karen Horney

that appears to affect the distribution of authority and deference between the sexes is the degree to which men rather than women control and mediate property."[65] He presented data which showed a direct correlation between the extent to which inheritance, succession, and descent-group membership were patrilineal and the degree of subjection of women.

Even today, the equality of the sexes in the family is often reflective of the economic equality of the partners. In a Detroit sample, Blood and Wolfe found that the relative power of the wife was low if she did not work and increased with her economic contribution to the family.[66]

"The employment of women affects the power structure of the family by equalizing the resources of husband and wife. A working wife's husband listens to her more, and she listens to herself more. She expresses herself and has more opinions. Instead of looking up into her husband's eyes and worshipping him, she levels with him, compromising on the issues at hand. Thus her power increases and, relatively speaking, the husband's falls."[67]

Goode also noted this pattern but said it varied inversely with class status. Toward the upper strata, wives are not only less likely to work but when they do they contribute a smaller percentage of the total family income than is true in the lower classes.[68] Hill went so far as to say "Money is a source of power that supports male dominance in the family.

. . . Money belongs to him who earns it, not to her who spends it, since he who earns it may withhold it."[69] Hallenbeck feels more than just economic resources are involved but does conclude that there is a balance of power in every family which affects "every other aspect of the marriage—division of labor, amount of adaptation necessary for either spouse, methods used to resolve conflicts, and so forth."[70] Blood feels the economic situation affects the whole family structure. "Daughters of working mothers are more independent, more self-reliant, more aggressive, more dominant, and more disobedient. Such girls are no longer meek, mild, submissive, and feminine like 'little ladies' ought to be. They are rough and tough, actively express their ideas, and refuse to take anything from anybody else. . . . Because their mothers have set an example, the daughters get up the courage and the desire to earn money as well. They take more part-time jobs after school and more jobs during summer vacation."[71]

Barry, Bacon and Child did an ethnohistoriographic analysis that provides some further insights into the origins of male dominance. After examining the ethnographic reports of 110 cultures, they concluded that large sexual differentiation and male superiority occur concurrently and in "an economy that places a high premium on the superior strength and superior development of motor skills requiring strength, which characterize the male."[72] It is those so-

Here I come to a very important difference between the animus problem of the woman and the anima problem of the man, a difference which seems to me to have met with too little attention. When a man discovers his anima and has come to terms with it, he has to take up something which previously seemed inferior to him. It counts for little that naturally the anima figure, be it image or human, is fascinatingly attractive and hence appears valuable. Up to now in our world, the feminine principle, as compared to the masculine, has always stood for something inferior.

Emma Jung

---

cieties in which great physical strength and mobility are required for survival, in which hunting and herding, or warfare, play an important role, that the male, as the physically stronger and more mobile sex, tends to dominate. This is supported by Spiro's analysis of sex roles in an Israeli kibbutz. There, the economy was largely unmechanized and the superior average strength of the men was needed on many jobs. Thus, despite a conscious attempt to break down traditional sex-roles, they began reasserting themselves, as women were assigned to the less strenuous jobs.[73]

Although there are a few tasks which virtually every society assigns only to men or women, there is a great deal of overlap for most jobs. Virtually every task, even in the most primitive societies, can be performed by either men or women. Equally important, what is defined as a man's task in one society may well be classified as a woman's job in another.[74] Nonetheless, the sexual division of labor is much more narrow than dictated by physical limitations, and what any one culture defines as a woman's job will seldom be performed by a man and vice versa. It seems that what originated as a division of labor based upon the necessities of survival has spilled over into many other areas and lasted long past the time of its social value. Where male strength and mobility has been crucial to social survival, male dominance and the aura of male superiority has been the strongest. The latter has been

incorporated into the value structure and attained an existence of its own.

Thus, male superiority has not ceased with an end to the need for male strength. As Goode pointed out, there is one consistent element in the assignment of jobs to the sexes, even in modern societies: "Whatever the strictly male tasks are, they are defined as *more honorific* (emphasis his). . . . Moreover, the tasks of control, management, decision, appeals to the gods—in short the higher level jobs that typically do *not* require strength, speed or traveling far from home—are female jobs."[75]

He goes on to comment that "this element suggests that the sexual division of labor within family and society comes perilously close to the racial or caste restrictions in some modern countries. That is, the low-ranking race, caste, or sex is defined as not being *able* to do certain types of prestigious work, but it is also considered a violation of propriety if they do it. Obviously, if women really cannot do various kinds of male tasks, no moral or ethical prohibition would be necessary to keep them from it."[76]

Sex roles originated in economic necessities but the value attached to any one role has become a factor of sex alone. Even cross-culturally, these roles, and the attitudes associated with them, are ingrained by common socialization practices. Barry, Bacon, and Child discovered that "pressure toward nurturance, obedience and responsibility is most often stronger

Even though she may think otherwise consciously, the idea that what is masculine is in itself more valuable than what is feminine is born in her blood. This does much to enhance the power of the animus. What we women have to overcome in our relation to the animus is not pride but lack of self-confidence and the resistance of inertia. For us, it is not as though we had to demean ourselves (unless we have been identified with the animus), but as if we had to lift ourselves. In this, we often fail for lack of courage and strength of will.

Emma Jung

for girls, whereas pressure toward achievement and self-reliance is most often stronger for boys."[77] There are the same socialization practices traditionally found in Western society. As the Barry, Bacon, and Child study showed, these socializations serve to prepare children for roles as adults that require women to stay near the home and men to go out and achieve. The greater emphasis a society places on physical strength, the greater the sex-role differentiation and the sex differences in socialization.

These sex-role differences may have served a natural function at one time, but it is doubtful that they still do so. The characteristics we observe in women and men today are a result of socialization practices that were developed for survival of a primitive society. The value structure of male superiority is a reflection of the primitive orientations and values. But social and economic conditions have changed drastically since these values were developed. Technology has reduced to almost nothing the importance of muscular strength. In fact, the warlike attitude which goes along with an idealization of physical strength and dominance is proving to be positively destructive. The value of large families has also become a negative one. Now we are concerned with the population explosion and prefer that our society produce children of quality rather than quantity. The result of all these changes is that the traditional sex-roles and the traditional family structures have become dysfunctional.

from **Snapshots of a Daughter-in-Law**

Sigh no more, ladies.
                    Time is male
and in his cups drinks to the fair.
Bemused by gallantry, we hear
our mediocrities over-praised,
indolence read as abnegation,
slattern thought styled intuition,
every lapse forgiven, our crime
only to cast too bold a shadow
or smash the mould straight off.

For that, solitary confinement,
tear gas, attrition shelling.
Few applicants for that honor.

Adrienne Rich

To some extent, patterns of child-rearing have also changed. Bronfenbrenner reports that at least middle-class parents are raising both boys and girls much the same. He noted that over a fifty year period middle-class parents have been developing a "more acceptant, equalitarian relationship with their children."[78] With an increase in the family's social position, the patterns of parental treatment of children begin to converge.[79] He likewise noted that a similar phenomenon is beginning to develop in lower-class parents and that equality of treatment is slowly working its way down the social ladder.

Alone on a Hill

Purpose: To become more aware of how we change, depending on the social surroundings.

Directions: Close your eyes, find a comfortable position, and relax while someone slowly reads you the following:

1. Imagine yourself alone on a hill. Who are you? Describe yourself. What is happening? What are you doing? saying? thinking? feeling?
2. Imagine yourself with a woman. Who are you? Describe yourself. What is happening? What are you doing? saying? thinking? feeling?
3. Imagine yourself with a man. Who are you? Describe yourself. What is happening? What are you doing? saying? thinking? feeling?
4. Imagine yourself with a group of women (or men). Describe yourself. What is happening? What are you doing? saying? thinking? feeling?
5. Imagine yourself with anyone else whom you consider important in your life. (Friends, parents, children, and so forth). Who are you? Describe yourself. What is happening? What are you doing? saying? thinking? feeling?

Open your eyes. What did you experience? How do you feel about it? Record your experiences and share them with the class.

These changes in patterns of child-rearing correlate with changes in relationships within the family. Both are moving toward a less hierarchical and more egalitarian pattern of living.

As Blood has pointed out, "today we may be on the verge of a new phase in American family history, when the companionship family is beginning to manifest itself. One distinguishing characteristic of this family is the dual employment of husband and wife. . . . Employment emancipates women from domination by their husbands and, secondarily, raises their daughters from inferiority to their brothers. . . . The classic differences between masculinity and femininity are disappearing as both sexes in the adult generation take on the same roles in the labor market. . . . The roles of men and women are converging for both adults and children. As a result the family will be far less segregated internally, far less stratified into different age generations and different sexes. The old asymmetry of male-dominated, female-serviced family life is being replaced by a new symmetry."[80]

All these data indicate that several trends are converging at about the same time. Our value structure has changed from an authoritarian one to a more democratic one, though our social structure has not yet caught up. Social attitudes begin in the family; only a democratic family can raise children to be citizens in a democratic society. The social and economic organization of society which kept women in the home has likewise changed. The home is no longer the center of society. The primary male and female functions have left it and there is no longer any major reason for maintaining the large sex-role differentiations which it supported. The value placed on physical strength which reinforced the dominance of men, and the male superiority attitudes that this generated, have also become dysfunctional. It is the mind, not the body, which must now prevail, and woman's mind is the equal of man's. The "pill" has liberated women from the uncertainty of childbearing, and with it the necessity of being attached to a man for economic support. But our attitudes toward women, and toward the family, have not changed concomitantly with the other developments. There is a distinct "cultural lag." Definitions of the family, conceptions of women and ideas about social function are left over from an era when they were necessary for social survival. They have persisted into an era in which they are no longer viable. The result can only be called severe role dysfunctionality for women.

The necessary relief for this dysfunctionality must come through changes in the social and economic organization of society and in social attitudes which will permit women to play a full and equal part in the social order. With this must come changes in the family, so that men and women are not only equal, but can raise the children in a democratic atmosphere. These changes will not come easily, nor will they come through the simple evolution of social trends. Trends do not move all in the same direction or at the same rate. To the extent that changes are dysfunctional with each other they create problems. These problems must be solved not by complacency but by conscious human direction. Only in this way can we have a real say in the shape of our future and the shape of our lives.

For Further Reading

Chafetz, J. S. 1974. *Masculine, Feminine or Human?* Itasca, Illinois: F. E. Peacock.

Horney, K. 1967. *Feminine Psychology.* New York: W. W. Norton.

*****Maccoby, E. E.** 1966. *The Development of Sex Differences.* Stanford: Stanford Univ. Press.

*****Maccoby, E. E. and Jacklin, C. N.** 1974. *The Psychology of Sex Differences.* Stanford: Stanford Univ. Press.

Sherman, J. A. 1971. *On the Psychology of Women.* Springfield, Illinois: Charles C. Thomas.

Thompson, C. 1971. *On Women.* New York: Random House.

Unger, R. K. and Denmark, F. L. 1975. *Woman: Dependent or Independent Variable?* New York: Psychological Dimensions, Inc.

*****Walstedt, J. J.** 1972. *The Psychology of Women, A Partially Annotated Bibliography.* Pittsburgh: KNOW, Inc., Box 86031.

Oppression of the Self

The four articles in this chapter explore the notion that the psychology of women resembles that of an oppressed group. In the first article Helen Hacker examines the caste-like, minority-group status of women and discusses some of its psychological consequences (especially self-hatred and the internalization of inferiority feelings). Next, Nancy Henley and Jo Freeman point out the subtle, nonverbal messages implied in daily social interactions that affirm women's inferior status. The theme of nonconscious ideology in forming the present psychology of both women and men is continued by Sandra and Daryl Bem. Since the one-to-one personal relationship between men and women reinforces sexual differences in power, Dair Gillespie's article examining the intimate social structure of marriage provides the logical next step in this exploration. In it she concludes essentially that it is highly unlikely for equality to be achieved within marriage, given the present inequalities in the larger society, since men as a class obtain greater access to resources from which women as a class are blocked.

When Hacker wrote "Women as a Minority Group" (1951), women did not fully qualify as a minority group since, although discriminated against, they were not aware of such discrimination and lacked feelings of group identification and minority group consciousness. With the recent re-emergence of the feminist movement, however, women now have such an identification and an ever-increasing consciousness of their oppression (Hacker, 1974).

Hacker discusses self-hatred, a distinguishing feature of the psychology of members of any oppressed group, as a feature of the psychology of women as well. Hacker points out that since women are in contact with men more than blacks are with whites, for example, women are even more likely than blacks to accept the dominant group's attitudes and stereotypes of themselves. Because women are devalued by the dominant group and learn to hate themselves as well as each other, their feelings of inferiority are constantly reinforced until women actually believe that they are in fact inferior.

In her article Hacker includes Gunner Myrdal's chart, which compares the caste-like status of blacks and women, although she also notes differences in the status of white women and racial minorities. The listing of children as a third column might be an interesting comparison, especially since many feminists have noted children's oppression.

Hacker makes an interesting comparison of the relationships between men and women and those between whites and nonwhites on the social distance scale. Since men and women marry each other, there is obviously a minimum of social distance, but, she points out, "the pressence of love does not in itself argue for either equality of status or fullness of communication. We may love those who are either inferior or superior to us and we may love persons whom we do not understand." She thus implies that love can take place within the context of emotional distance. This view represents a different definition of distance from the conventional (male) one, and it more aptly describes women's experience. Furthermore, "since inequalities of status are preserved in marriage, a dominant group member may be willing to marry a member of a group which, in general, he would not wish admitted to his club," indicating that men may "love" women although they basically do not like them. This has far-reaching implications for "love" between the sexes. Firestone [1970] has developed a more thorough analysis of love based on present inequalities).

In establishing women's minority-group status, Hacker refers to two particularly noteworthy concepts regarding women's culture. One is that women have a subculture (the beauty parlor, the kitchen, and the like). Feminists (Burris, 1971) have also argued that women's subculture, a global phenomenon known as the "Fourth World," remains submerged under world-wide patriarchy. Secondly, Hacker refers to the lack of a culture with which women can identify. (In a more recent work (1974) she acknowledges that a basis now exists for creating a separate culture). Feminists see the lack of a culture as a problem for women (Anne Battle-Sister, 1971), since one of the sources of relief for blacks and other minority groups has been the ability to have their own cultural identity. Recently, however, as a result of the women's movement, a Female* culture, based on women's experience and women identified with women, is beginning to emerge.

The second paper, by Nancy Henley and Jo Freeman, is a much-needed analysis and documentation of the subtle, nonverbal ways in which sex differences in power are expressed and maintained. These are the daily social interactions through which feelings of inferiority becomes internalized to such a degree that women themselves remain unaware of it. Repeated patterns of submission and dominance become so nonconscious and automatic that they become an integral part of the psychological makeup of both women and men. To some extent, the psychology of women may be seen more simply as the psychology of persons with less power.

Following Hacker's speculation that emotional distance could account for women's caste-like status in intimate relationships, Henley and Freeman describe the forms and dynamics of emotional distancing, based on differences in power between the sexes.

They note that touching, one of the most intimate of interpersonal behaviors, can be interpreted either as a means of exercising power or as a bid for sexual/intimate contact. Since women do not have power, touching is defined for them only as a sexual or intimate contact, whereas for men either interpretation may apply. Extending this point in a feminist-based analysis of sexual politics, Millett (1968) has implied that, for men, power and sexual intimacy overlap. In many cases, therefore, it may not be possible or even necessary to separate power from intimate/sexual motives of men touching women. This point is further elaborated upon in the chapter on "Women and Their Sexual Selves" and a later article on men's liberation.

Manifestation of sexual power differences in interpersonal behavior are complex and intricate. Although it is difficult, women and men can become aware of what each may be contributing to create patterned gestures of dominance and submission. Awareness, however, is not enough. Gestures of dominance and submission can disappear only when the social and economic bases for equality between the sexes have been established.

In the third article Sandra and Daryl Bem present the concept that women themselves nonconsciously follow society's prescriptions for the role they are expected to fulfill. The failure of some women to recognize their mi-

---

*Use of the upper case here distinguishes culture based on women's own experience from that based on men's view of women's experience (female).

nority-group status, which Hacker described, indicates the power of nonconscious ideas. One particularly startling aspect of nonconscious ideology is that women "choose" inequality in a relationship with a man and even say that they like it. It is indeed curious that internalized feelings of inferiority become not only habitual and familiar but desirable as well.

Three arguments are often made to show that women are free to develop as full human beings—the free-will argument, the biological argument, and the argument of "complementary but equal." The weaknesses of all of these arguments are exposed when examined in the light of nonconscious attitudes and motives. Not only is less value placed on women's role but women and men each engage in certain exclusive activities. Life style becomes too predictable, and women's lives are even more predictable than men's.

The Bems then present a test for equality in male-female relationships. Their basic approach is to reverse the sexes in a given situation, or to imagine both individuals as having the same sex, and then to see if the behavior of the individuals in those roles still makes sense. This method may be used to detect the presence of nonconscious ideology in daily interactions by participants as well as observers.

All four articles touch on the topic of equality between the sexes in interpersonal relationships. Hacker announces that inequalities are preserved in marriage, Henley and Freeman demonstrate the interpersonal dynamics that communicate and maintain inequalities in one-to-one relationships, and the Bems suggest guidelines to test for equality in a marriage or relationship. The final paper, by Dair Gillespie, focuses on the myriad factors that hinder or prevent equality from taking place in marriage or any other male-female relationship. Inequalities in these relationships are due to the discrimination against women in the larger society. Men obtain power in such relationships because as a class they gain access to resources that are not available to women as a class.

If, as Henley and Freeman point out, "social interaction is the battlefield where the daily war between the sexes is fought," then marriage based on inequalities of the larger society becomes, rather than a safe nesting place, the arena where the battle becomes even more intensified if not more covert.

Gillespie's paper clearly demonstrates that the power distributions between men and women in white- and blue-collar and white and black marriages reflect larger power differences in the rest of society. She further notes that marriage is a major institution that socializes most women, and thus affects the psychology of every woman. Even if we become aware of the nonconscious ideology and sensitive to the politics of interpersonal behavior, there are economic, social, and cultural factors over which we as individuals have no control. These produce inequalities in the relationships between the sexes and are, therefore, a major force in determining the psychology of women and the psychology of men.

Helen Mayer Hacker

Women as a Minority Group

Although sociological literature reveals scattered references to women as a minority group, comparable in certain respects to racial, ethnic, and national minorities, no systematic investigation has been undertaken as to what extent the term "minority group" is applicable to women. That there has been little serious consideration of women as a minority group among sociologists is manifested in the recently issued index to *The American Journal of Sociology* wherein under the heading of "Minority Groups" there appears: "See Jews; Morale; Negro; Races and Nationalities; Religious Groups; Sects." There is no cross-reference to women, but such reference is found under the heading "Family."

Yet it may well be that regarding women as a minority group may be productive of fresh insights and suggest leads for further research. The purpose of this paper is to apply to women some portion of that body of sociological theory and methodology customarily used for investigating such minority groups as Negroes, Jews, immigrants, etc. It may be anticipated that not only will principles already established in the field of intergroup relations contribute to our understanding of women, but that in the process of modifying traditional concepts and theories to fit the special case of women new viewpoints for the fruitful reexamination of other minority groups will emerge.

In defining the term "minority group," the presence of discrimination is the identifying factor. As Louis Wirth has pointed out, "minority group" is not a statistical concept, nor need it denote an alien group. Indeed for the present discussion I have adopted his definition: "A minority group is any group of people who because of their physical or cultural characteristics, are singled out from the others in the society in which they live for differential and unequal treatment, and who therefore regard themselves as objects of collective discrimination."[1] It is apparent that this definition includes both objective and subjective characteristics of a minority group: the fact of discrimination and the awareness of discrimination, with attendant reactions to that awareness. A person who on the basis of his group affiliation is denied full participation in those opportunities which the value system of his culture extends to all members of the society satisfies the objective criterion, but there are various circumstances which may prevent him from fulfilling the subjective criterion.

In the first place, a person may be unaware of the extent to which his group membership influences the way others treat him. He may have formally dissolved all ties with the group in question and fondly imagine his identity is different from what others hold it to be. Consequently, he interprets their behavior toward him solely in terms of his individual characteristics. Or, less likely, he may be conscious of his membership in a certain group but not be aware of the general disesteem with which the group is regarded. A final possibility is that he may belong in a category which he does not realize has group significance. An example here might be a speech peculiarity which has come to have unpleasant connotations in the minds of others. Or a lower class child with no conception of "class as culture" may not understand how his manners act as cues in eliciting the dislike of his middle class teacher. The foregoing cases all assume that the person believes in equal opportunities for all in the sense that one's group affiliation should not affect his role in the larger society. We turn now to a consideration of situations in which this assumption is not made.

It is frequently the case that a person knows that because of his group affiliation he receives differential treatment, but feels that this treatment is warranted by the distinctive characteristics of his group. A Negro may believe that there are significant differences between whites and Negroes which justify a different role in life for the Negro. A child may accept the fact that physical differences between him and an adult require his going to bed earlier than they do. A Sudra knows that his lot in life has been cast by divine fiat, and he does not expect the perquisites of a Brahmin. A woman does not wish for the rights and duties of men. In all these situations, clearly, the person does not regard himself as an "object of collective discrimination."

For the two types presented above: (1) those who do not know that they are being discriminated against on a group basis; and (2) those who acknowledge the propriety of differential treatment on a group basis, the subjective attributes of a minority group member are lacking. They feel no minority group consciousness, harbor no resentment, and, hence, cannot properly be said to belong in a minority group. Although the term "minority group" is inapplicable to both types, the term "minority group status" may be substituted. This term is used to categorize persons who are denied rights to which they are entitled according to the value

system of the observer. An observer, who is a firm adherent of the democratic ideology, will often consider persons to occupy a minority group status who are well accommodated to their subordinate roles.

No empirical study of the frequency of minority group feelings among women has yet been made, but common observation would suggest that consciously at least, few women believe themselves to be members of a minority group in the way in which some Negroes, Jews, Italians, etc., may so conceive themselves. There are, of course, many sex-conscious women, known to a past generation as feminists, who are filled with resentment at the discriminations they fancy are directed against their sex. Today some of these may be found in the National Woman's Party which since 1923 has been carrying on a campaign for the passage of the Equal Rights Amendment. This amendment, in contrast to the compromise bill recently passed by Congress, would at one stroke wipe out all existing legislation which differentiates in any way between men and women, known to a past generation as feminists, who are filled with resentment at the disponents of the Equal Rights Amendment hold the position that women will never achieve equal rights until they abjure all privileges based on what they consider to be only presumptive sex differences.

Then there are women enrolled in women's clubs, women's auxiliaries of men's organizations, women's professional and educational associations who seemingly believe that women have special interests to follow or unique contributions to make. These latter might reject the appellation of minority group, but their behavior testifies to their awareness of women as a distinct group in our society, either overriding

Being an incomplete female, the male spends his life attempting to complete himself, to become female . . . by constantly seeking out, fraternizing with, and trying to live through and fuse with the female, and by claiming as his own all female characteristics—emotional strength and independence, forcefulness, dynamism, decisiveness, . . . etc.—and projecting onto women all male traits—vanity, frivolity, triviality, weakness, etc. It should be said, though, that the male has one glaring area of superiority over the female—public relations. (He has done a brilliant job of convincing millions of women that men are women and women are men.)

Valerie Solanis

---

differences of class, occupation, religion, or ethnic identification, or specialized within these categories. Yet the number of women who participate in "women's affairs" even in the United States, the classic land of associations, is so small that one cannot easily say that the majority of women display minority group consciousness. However, documentation, as well as a measuring instrument, is likewise lacking for minority consciousness in other groups.

Still women often manifest many of the psychological characteristics which have been imputed to self-conscious minority groups. Kurt Lewin[2] has pointed to group self-hatred as a frequent reaction of the minority group member to his group affiliation. This feeling is exhibited in the person's tendency to denigrate other members of the group, to accept the dominant group's stereotyped conception of them, and to indulge in "mea culpa" breast-beating. He may seek to exclude himself from the average of his group, or he may point the finger of scorn at himself. Since a person's conception of himself is based on the defining gestures of others, it is unlikely that members of a minority group can wholly escape personality distortion. Constant reiteration of one's inferiority must often lead to its acceptance as a fact.

Certainly women have not been immune to the formulations of the "female character" throughout the ages. From those, to us, deluded creatures who confessed to witchcraft to mod-

ern sophisticates who speak disparagingly of the cattiness and disloyalty of women, women reveal their introjection of prevailing attitudes toward them. Like those minority groups whose self-castigation outdoes dominant group derision of them, women frequently exceed men in the violence of their vituperations of their sex. They are more severe in moral judgments, especially in sexual matters. A line of self-criticism may be traced from Hannah More, a blue-stocking herself, to Dr. Marynia Farnham, who lays most of the world's ills at women's door. Women express themselves as disliking other women, as preferring to work under men, and as finding exclusively female gatherings repugnant. The *Fortune* polls conducted in 1946 show that women, more than men, have misgivings concerning women's participation in industry, the professions, and civic life. And more than one-fourth of women wish they had been born in the opposite sex.[3]

Militating against a feeling of group identification on the part of women is a differential factor in their socialization. Members of a minority group are frequently socialized within their own group. Personality development is more largely a resultant of intra- than intergroup interaction. The conception of his role formed by a Negro or a Jew or a second-generation immigrant is greatly dependent upon the definitions offered by members of his own group, on their attitudes and behavior toward him. Ignoring for the moment class dif-

Footstool by Romaine Brooks, National Collection of Fine Arts, Smithsonian Institution

ferences within the group, the minority group person does not suffer discrimination from members of his own group. But only rarely does a woman experience this type of group belongingness. Her interactions with members of the opposite sex may be as frequent as her relationships with members of her own sex. Women's conceptions of themselves, therefore, spring as much from their intimate relationships with men as with women. Although this consideration might seem to limit the applicability to women of research findings on minority groups, conversely, it may suggest investigation to seek out useful parallels in the socialization of women, on the one hand, and the socialization of ethnics living in neighborhoods of hetereogeneous population, on the other.

Even though the sense of group identification is not so conspicuous in women as in racial and ethnic minorities, they, like these others, tend to develop a separate sub-culture. Women have their own language, comparable to the argot of the underworld and professional groups. It may not extend to a completely separate dialect as has been discovered in some preliterate groups, but there are words and idioms employed chiefly by women. Only the acculturated male can enter into the conversation of the beauty parlor, the exclusive shop, the bridge table, or the kitchen. In contrast to men's interest in physical health, safety, money, and sex, women attach greater importance to attractiveness, personality, home, family, and

other people.[4] How much of the "woman's world" is predicated on their relationship to men is too difficult a question to discuss here. It is still a controversial point whether the values and behavior patterns of other minority groups, such as the Negroes, represent an immanent development, or are oriented chiefly toward the rejecting world. A content analysis contrasting the speech of "housewives" and "career women," for example, or a comparative analysis of the speech of men and women of similar occupational status might be one test of this hypothesis.

We must return now to the original question of the aptness of the designation of minority group for women. It has been indicated that women fail to present in full force the subjective attributes commonly associated with minority groups. That is, they lack a sense of group identification and do not harbor feelings of being treated unfairly because of their sex membership. Can it then be said that women have a minority group status in our society? The answer to this question depends upon the values of the observer whether within or outside the group—just as is true in the case of any group of persons who, on the basis of putative differential characteristics are denied access to some statuses in the social system of their society. If we assume that there are no differences attributable to sex membership as such that would justify casting men and women in different social roles, it can readily be shown that

The castration complex of girls is also started by the sight of the genitals of the other sex. They at once notice the difference and, it must be admitted, its significance too. They feel seriously wronged, often declare that they want to 'have something like it too', and fall a victim to 'envy for the penis', which will leave ineradicable traces on their development and the formation of their character and which will not be surmounted in even the most favourable cases without a severe expenditure of psychical energy.

Sigmund Freud

women do occupy a minority group status in our society.

Minority Group Status of Women

Formal discriminations against women are too well-known for any but the most summary description. In general they take the form of being barred from certain activities or, if admitted, being treated unequally. Discriminations against women may be viewed as arising from the generally ascribed status "female" and from the specially ascribed statuses of "wife," "mother," and "sister." (To meet the possible objection that "wife" and "mother" represent assumed, rather than ascribed, statuses, may I point out that what is important here is that these statuses carry ascribed expectations which are only ancillary in the minds of those who assume them.)

As female, in the economic sphere, women are largely confined to sedentary, monotonous work under the supervision of men, and are treated unequally with regard to pay, promotion, and responsibility. With the exceptions of teaching, nursing, social service, and library work, in which they do not hold a proportionate number of supervisory positions and are often occupationally segregated from men, they make a poor showing in the professions. Although they own 80 percent of the nation's wealth, they do not sit on the boards of directors of great corporations. Educational opportunities are likewise unequal. Professional schools, such as architecture and medicine, apply quotas. Women's colleges are frequently inferior to men's. In co-educational schools women's participation in campus activities is limited. As citizens, women are often barred from jury service and public office. Even when they are admitted to the apparatus of political parties, they are subordinated to men. Socially, women have less freedom of movement, and are permitted fewer deviations in the proprieties of dress, speech, manners. In social intercourse they are confined to a narrower range of personality expression.

In the specially ascribed status of wife, a woman—in several states—has no exclusive right to her earnings, is discriminated against in employment, must take the domicile of her husband, and in general must meet the social expectation of subordination to her husband's interests. As a mother, she may not have the guardianship of her children, bears the chief stigma in the case of an illegitimate child, is rarely given leave of absence for pregnancy. As a sister, she frequently suffers unequal distribution of domestic duties between herself and her brother, must yield preference to him in obtaining an education, and in such other psychic and material gratifications as cars, trips, and living away from home.

If it is conceded that women have a minority

It is hard to fight an enemy who has outposts in your head.

Sally Kempton, *Cutting Loose*

status of Negro servants was borrowed from that of women and children, who were under the patria potestas, and until the Civil War there was considerable cooperation between the Abolitionist and woman suffrage movements. According to Myrdal, the problems of both groups are resultants of the transition from a pre-industrial, paternalistic scheme of life to individualistic, industrial capitalism. Obvious similarities in the status of women and Negroes are indicated in Chart 1.

While these similarities in the situation of women and Negroes may lead to increased understanding of their social roles, account must also be taken of differences which impose qualifications on the comparison of the two groups. Most importantly, the influence of marriage as a social elevator for women, but not for Negroes, must be considered. Obvious, too, is the greater importance of women to the dominant group, despite the economic, sexual, and prestige gains which Negroes afford the white South. Ambivalence is probably more marked in the attitude of white males toward women than toward Negroes. The "war of the sexes" is only an expression of men's and women's vital need of each other. Again, there is greater polarization in the relationship between men and women. Negroes, although they have borne the brunt of anti-minority group feeling in this country, do not constitute the only racial or ethnic minority, but there are only two sexes. And, although we have seen that social distance exists between men and women, it is not to be compared with the social segregation of Negroes.

At the present time, of course, Negroes suffer far greater discrimination than women, but since the latter's problems are rooted in a biological reality less susceptible to cultural manipulation, they prove more lasting. Women's privileges exceed those of Negroes. Protective attitudes toward Negroes have faded into abeyance, even in the South, but most boys are still taught to take care of girls, and many evidences of male chivalry remain. The factor of class introduces variations here. The middle class Negro endures frustrations largely without the rewards of his white class peer, but the lower class Negro is still absolved from many responsibilities. The reverse holds true for women. Notwithstanding these and other differences between the position of women and Negroes, the similarities are sufficient to render research on either group applicable in some fashion to the other.

Exemplary of the possible usefulness of applying the caste principle to women is viewing some of the confusion surrounding women's roles as reflecting a conflict between class and caste status. Such a conflict is present in the thinking and feeling of both dominant and minority groups toward upper class Negroes and educated women. Should a woman judge be treated with the respect due a judge or the gallantry accorded a woman? The extent to

I met one remarkable case of this seeming loss of identity in a mediumistic woman who realized that in the absence of her husband or her son she felt completely vague, unfocused, and at a loss. She went to an analyst in the hope that he might help, but was shattered by the following dream: She visited her analyst and looked into the mirror he held up for her, but to her horror there was no reflection. This dream convinced her, as nothing else could have done, of her paramount need to learn to exist in her own right and not merely as a mediator for other people. That she had not understood how to achieve this was evidenced by another dream two years later: A voice said to her: "Don't try to have a reflection. Break the mirror."

Irene de Castillijos

Untitled drawing by Melissa Mathis

which the rights and duties of one role permeate other roles so as to cause a role conflict has been treated elsewhere by the writer.[9] Lower class Negroes who have acquired dominant group attitudes toward the Negro resent upper class Negro pretensions to superiority. Similarly, domestic women may feel the career woman is neglecting the duties of her proper station.

Parallels in adjustment of women and Negroes to the class-caste conflict may also be noted. Point 4 "Accommodation Attitudes" of the foregoing chart indicates the kinds of behavior displayed by members of both groups who accept their caste status. Many "sophisticated" women are retreating from emancipation with the support of psychoanalytic derivations.[10] David Riesman has recently provided an interesting discussion of changes "in the denigration by American women of their own sex" in which he explains their new submissiveness as in part a reaction to the weakness of men in the contemporary world.[11] "Parallelism" and "Negroidism" which accept a racially-restricted economy reflect allied tendencies in the Negro group.

Role segmentation as a mode of adjustment is illustrated by Negroes who indulge in occasional passing and women who vary their behavior according to their definition of the situation. An example of the latter is the case of the woman lawyer who, after losing a case before a judge who was also her husband, said she would appeal the case, and added, "The judge can lay down the law at home, but I'll argue with him in court."

A third type of reaction is to fight for recognition of class status. Negro race leaders seek greater prerogatives for Negroes. Feminist women, acting either through organizations or as individuals, push for public disavowal of any differential treatment of men and women.

Alcestis on the Poetry Circuit

(In Memoriam Marina Tsvetaeva, Anna Wickham, Sylvia Plath, Shakespeare's sister, etc. etc.)

The best slave
does not need to be beaten.
She beats herself.

Not with a leather whip,
or with sticks or twigs,
not with a blackjack
or a billyclub,
but with the fine whip
of her own tongue
& the subtle beating
of her mind
against her mind.

For who can hate her half so well
as she hates herself?
& who can match the finesse
of her self-abuse?

Years of training
are required for this.
Twenty years
of subtle self-indulgence.
self-denial;
until the subject
thinks herself a queen
& yet a beggar—
both at the same time.

She should mistrust herself
in everything but love.
She should choose passionately
& badly.

She should feel lost as a dog
without her master.
She should refer all moral questions
to her mirror.
She should fall in love with a cossack
or a poet.

She must never go out of the house
unless veiled in paint.
She must wear tight shoes
so she always remembers her bondage.
She must never forget
she is rooted in the ground.

Though she is quick to learn
& admittedly clever,
her natural doubt of herself
should make her so weak
that she dabbles brilliantly
in half a dozen talents
& thus embellishes
but does not change
our life.

If she's an artist
& comes close to genius,
the very fact of her gift
should cause her such pain
that she will take her own life
rather than best us.

& after she dies, we will cry
& make her a saint.

Erica Jong

Race Relations Cycle

The "race relations cycle," as defined by Robert E. Park,[12] describes the social processes of reduction in tension and increase of communication in the relations between two or more groups who are living in a common territory under a single political or economic system. The sequence of competition, conflict, accommodation, and assimilation may also occur when social change introduces dissociative forces into an assimilated group or causes accommodated groups to seek new definitions of the situation.[13] The ethnic or nationality characteristics of the groups involved are not essential to the cycle. In a complex industrialized society groups are constantly forming and re-forming on the basis of new interests and new identities. Women, of course, have always possessed a sex-identification though perhaps not a group awareness. Today they represent a previously accommodated group which is endeavoring to modify the relationships between the sexes in the home, in work, and in the community.

The sex relations cycle bears important similarities to the race relations cycle. In the wake of the Industrial Revolution, as women acquired industrial, business, and professional skills, they increasingly sought employment in competition with men. Men were quick to perceive them as a rival group and made use of economic, legal, and ideological weapons to eliminate or reduce their competition. They excluded women from the trade unions, made contracts with employers to prevent their hiring women, passed laws restricting the employment of married women, caricatured the working woman, and carried on ceaseless propaganda to return women to the home or keep them there. Since the days of the suffragettes there has been no overt conflict between men and women on a group basis. Rather than conflict, the dissociative process between the sexes is that of contravention,[14] a type of opposition intermediate between competition and conflict. According to Wiese and Becker, it includes rebuffing, repulsing, working against, hindering, protesting, obstructing, restraining, and upsetting another's plans.

The present contravention of the sexes, arising from women's competition with men, is manifested in the discriminations against women, as well as in the doubts and uncertainties, expressed concerning women's character, abilities, motives. The processes of competition and contravention are continually giving way to accommodation in the relationships between men and women. Like other minority groups, women have sought a protected position, a niche in the economy which they could occupy, and, like other minority groups, they have found these positions in new occupations in which dominant group members had not yet established themselves and in old occupations which they no longer wanted. When women entered fields which represented an extension of services in the home (except medicine!), they encountered least opposition. Evidence is accumulating, however, that women are becoming dissatisfied with the employment conditions of the great women-employing occupations and present accommodations are threatened.

What would assimilation of men and women mean? Park and Burgess in their classic text define assimilation as "a process of interpenetration and fusion in which persons and groups acquire the memories, sentiments, and attitudes of other persons or groups, and, by sharing their experiences and history, are incorporated with

There is one further consideration. Owing to the hitherto purely masculine character of our civilization, it has been much harder for women to achieve any sublimation that would really satisfy their nature, for all the ordinary professions have been filled by men. This again must have exercised an influence upon women's feelings of inferiority, for naturally they could not accomplish the same as men in these masculine professions and so it appeared that there was a basis in fact for their inferiority.

Karen Horney

them in a cultural life." If accommodation is characterized by secondary contacts, assimilation holds the promise of primary contacts. If men and women were truly assimilated, we would find no cleavages of interest along sex lines. The special provinces of men and women would be abolished. Women's pages would disappear from the newspaper and women's magazines from the stands. All special women's organizations would pass into limbo. The sports page and racing news would be read indifferently by men and women. Interest in cookery and interior decoration would follow individual rather than sex lines. Women's talk would be no different from men's talk, and frank and full communication would obtain between the sexes.

The Marginal Woman

Group relationships are reflected in personal adjustments. Arising out of the present contravention of the sexes is the marginal woman, torn between rejection and acceptance of traditional roles and attributes. Uncertain of the ground on which she stands, subjected to conflicting cultural expectations, the marginal woman suffers the psychological ravages of instability, conflict, self-hate, anxiety, and resentment.

In applying the concept of marginality to women, the term "role" must be substituted for that of "group."[15] Many of the traditional de-

vices for creating role differentiation among boys and girls, such as dress, manners, activities, have been de-emphasized in modern urban middle class homes. The small girl who wears a play suit, plays games with boys and girls together, attends a co-educational school, may have little awareness of sexual differentiation until the approach of adolescence. Parental expectations in the matters of scholarship, conduct toward others, duties in the home may have differed little for herself and her brother. But in high school or perhaps not until college she finds herself called upon to play a new role. Benedict[16] has called attention to discontinuities in the life cycle, and the fact that these continuities in cultural conditioning take a greater toll of girls than of boys is revealed in test scores showing neuroticism and introversion.[17] In adolescence girls find the frank, spontaneous behavior toward the neighboring sex no longer rewarding. High grades are more likely to elicit anxiety than praise from parents, especially mothers, who seem more pleased if male callers are frequent. There are subtle indications that to remain home with a good book on a Saturday night is a fate worse than death. But even if the die is successfully cast for popularity, all problems are not solved. Girls are encouraged to heighten their sexual attractiveness, but to abjure sexual expression.

Assuming new roles in adolescence does not mean the complete relinquishing of old ones. Scholarship, while not so vital as for the boy, is still important, but must be maintained discreetly and without obvious effort. Mirra Komarovsky[18] has supplied statements of Barnard College girls of the conflicting expectations of their elders. Even more than to the boy is the "all-around" ideal held up to girls, and it is not always possible to integrate the roles of good date, good daughter, good sorority sister, good student, good friend, and good citizen. The superior achievements of college men over college women bear witness to the crippling division of energies among women. Part of the explanation may lie in women's having interiorized cultural notions of feminine inferiority in certain fields, and even the most self-confident or most defensive woman may be filled with doubt as to whether she can do productive work.

It may be expected that as differences in privileges between men and women decrease, the frequency of marginal women will increase. Widening opportunities for women will call forth a growing number of women capable of performing roles formerly reserved for men, but whose acceptance in these new roles may well remain uncertain and problematic. This hypothesis is in accord with Arnold Green's[19] recent critical reexamination of the marginal man concept in which he points out that it is those Negroes and second-generation immigrants whose values and behavior most approximate those of the dominant majority who experience the most severe personal crises. He believes that the classical marginal man symptoms appear only when a person striving to leave the racial or ethnic group into which he was born is deeply identified with the family of orientation and is met with grudging, uncertain, and unpredictable acceptance, rather than with absolute rejection, by the group he is attempting to join, and also that he is committed

to success-careerism. Analogically, one would expect to find that women who display marginal symptoms are psychologically bound to the family of orientation in which they experienced the imperatives of both the traditional and new feminine roles, and are seeking to expand the occupational (or other) areas open to women rather than those who content themselves with established fields. Concretely, one might suppose women engineers to have greater personality problems than women librarians.

Other avenues of investigation suggested by the minority group approach can only be mentioned. What social types arise as personal adjustments to sex status? What can be done in the way of experimental modification of the attitudes of men and women toward each other and themselves? What hypotheses of intergroup relations may be tested in regard to men and women? For example, is it true that as women approach the cultural standards of men, they are perceived as a threat and tensions increase? Of what significance are regional and community variations in the treatment of and degree of participation permitted women, mindful here that women share responsibility with men for the perpetuation of attitudes toward women? This paper is exploratory in suggesting the enhanced possibilities of fruitful analysis, if women are included in the minority group corpus, particularly with reference to such concepts and techniques as group belongingness, socialization of the minority group child, cultural differences, social distance tests, conflict between class and caste status, race relations cycle, and marginality. I believe that the concept of the marginal woman should be especially productive, and am now engaged in an empirical study of role conflicts in professional women.

Nancy Henley and Jo Freeman

The Sexual Politics of Interpersonal Behavior

Social interaction is the battlefield where the daily war between the sexes is fought. It is here that women are constantly reminded where their "place" is and here that they are put back in their place, should they venture out. Thus, social interaction serves as the most common means of social control employed against women. By being continually reminded of their inferior status in their interactions with others, and continually compelled to acknowledge that status in their own patterns of behavior, women learn to internalize society's definition of them as inferior so thoroughly that they are often unaware of what their status is. Inferiority becomes habitual, and the inferior place assumes the familiarity—and even desirability—of home.

Different sorts of cues in social interaction aid this enforcement of one's social definition, particularly the verbal message, the nonverbal message transmitted within a social relationship, and the nonverbal message transmitted by the environment. Our educational system emphasizes the verbal message and teaches us next to nothing about how we interpret and react to the nonverbal ones. Just how important nonverbal messages are, however, is shown by the finding of Argyle et al. (1970) that nonverbal cues have over four times the impact of verbal ones when both verbal and nonverbal cues are used. Even more important for women, Argyle found that female subjects were more responsive to nonverbal cues (compared with verbal ones) than male subjects. If women are to understand how the subtle forces of social control work in their lives, they must learn as much as possible about how nonverbal cues affect people, and particularly about how they per-

petuate the power and superior status enjoyed by men.

Even if a woman encounters no one else directly in her day, visual status reminders are a ubiquitous part of her environment. As she moves through the day, she absorbs many variations of the same status theme, whether or not she is aware of it: male bosses dictate while female secretaries bend over their steno pads; male doctors operate while female nurses assist; restaurants are populated with waitresses serving men; magazine and billboard ads remind the woman that home maintenance and child care are her foremost responsibilities and that being a sex object for male voyeurs is her greatest asset. If she is married, her mail reminds her that she is a mere "Mrs." appended to her husband's name. When she is introduced to others or fills out a form, the first thing she must do is divulge her marital status, acknowledging the social rule that the most important information anyone can know about her is her legal relationship to a man.

These environmental cues set the stage on which the power relationships of the sexes are acted out, and the assigned status of each sex is reinforced. Though studies have been made of the several means by which status inequalities are communicated in interpersonal behavior, they do not usually deal with power relationships between men and women. Goffman (1956, pp. 64, 78–79) has pointed to many characteristics associated with status:

Between status equals we may expect to find interaction guided by symmetrical familiarity. Between superordinate and subordinate we may

Their [men's] violence is amazing. Yet these men feel that the woman
or the child is to blame for not being "friendly." Because it makes them
uncomfortable to know that the woman or the child or the black or the
workman is grumbling, the oppressed groups must also appear to like
their oppression—smiling and simpering though they may feel like hell
inside. The smile is the child/woman equivalent of the shuffle; it
indicates acquiescence of the victim to his own oppression. . . . My
"dream" action for the women's liberation movement: a smile boycott,
at which declaration all women would instantly abandon their
"pleasing" smiles, henceforth smiling only when something pleased them.

Shulamith Firestone

---

expect to find assymetrical relations, the superordinate having the right to exercise certain familiarities which the subordinate is not allowed to reciprocate. Thus, in the research hospital, doctors tended to call nurses by their first names, while nurses responded with "polite" or "formal" address. Similarly, in American business organizations the boss may thoughtfully ask the elevator man how his children are, but this entrance into another's life may be blocked to the elevator man, who can appreciate the concern but not return it. Perhaps the clearest form of this is found in the psychiatrist-patient relation, where the psychiatrist has a right to touch on aspects of the patient's life that the patient might not even allow himself to touch upon, while of course this privilege is not reciprocated.

Rules of demeanor, like rules of deference, can be symmetrical or asymmetrical. Between social equals, symmetrical rules of demeanor seem often to be prescribed. Between unequals many variations can be found. For example, at staff meetings on the psychiatric units of the hospital, medical doctors had the privilege of swearing, changing the topic of conversation, and sitting in undignified positions; attendants, on the other hand, had the right to attend staff meetings and to ask questions during them . . . but were implicitly expected to conduct themselves with greater circumspection than was required for doctors. . . . Similarly, doctors had the right to saunter into the nurses' station, lounge on the station's dispensing counter, and engage in joking with the nurses; other ranks participated in this informal interaction with doctors, but only after doctors had initiated it.

A status variable widely studied by Brown and others (1960, 1961, 1965) is the use of terms of address. In languages that have both familiar and polite forms of the second person singular ("you"), asymmetrical use of the two forms invariably indicates a status difference, and it always follows the same pattern. The person using the familiar form is always the superior to the person using the polite form. In English, the only major European language not to have dual forms of address, status differences are similarly indicated by the right of first-naming; the status superior can first-name the inferior in situations where the inferior must use the superior's title and last name. An inferior who breaks this rule by inappropriately using a superior's first name is considered insolent (see Brown, 1965, pp. 92–97).

According to Brown, the pattern evident in the use of forms of address applies to a very wide range of interpersonal behavior and invariably has two other components: (1) whatever form is used by a superior in situations of status inequality can be used reciprocally by intimates, and whatever form is used by an inferior is the socially prescribed usage for nonintimates; (2) initiation or increase of intimacy is the right of the superior. To use the example of naming again, friends use first names with each other, while strangers use titles and last names, though "instant" intimacy is considered proper in some cultures, such as

Man: *Do you know the Women's Movement has no sense of humor?*
Woman: *No . . . but hum a few bars and I'll fake it!*

Women's Laughter

1.
When did I first become aware—
hearing myself on the radio?
listening to tapes of women in groups?—
of that diffident laugh that punctuates,
that giggle that apologizes,
that bows fixing parentheses before, after.
That little laugh sticking
in the throat like a chicken bone.

That perfunctory dry laugh
carries no mirth, no joy
but makes a low curtsy, a kowtow
imploring with praying hands:
forgive me, for I do not
take myself seriously.
Do not squash me.

2.
Phyllis, on the deck we sit
telling horror stories
from the Marvel Comics of our lives.
We exchange agonies, battles and after each
we laugh madly and embrace.

That raucous female laughter
is drummed from the belly.
It rackets about kitchens,
flapping crows
up from a carcass.
Hot in the mouth as horseradish,
it clears the sinuses
and the brain.

3.
Phyllis, I had a friend
who used to laugh with me
braying defiance, as we roar
with bared teeth.
After the locked ward
where they dimmed her with drugs
and exploded her synapses,
she has now that cough
fluttering in her throat
like a sick pigeon
as she says, but of course
I was sick, you know,
and laughs blood.

Marge Piercy

our own, among status equals in informal settings. Status superiors, such as professors, specifically tell status inferiors, such as students when they can use the first name, and often rebuff them if they assume such a right unilaterally.

Although Brown did not apply these patterns to status differences between the sexes, their relevance is readily seen. The social rules say that it is boys who are supposed to call girls for dates, men who are supposed to propose marriage to women, and males who are supposed to initiate sexual activity with females. Females who make "advances" are considered improper, forward, aggressive, brassy, or otherwise "unladylike." By initiating intimacy they have stepped out of their place and usurped a status prerogative. The value of such a prerogative is that it is a form of power. Between the sexes, as in other human interaction, the one who has the right to intitiate greater intimacy has more control over the relationship. Superior status brings with it not only greater prestige and greater privileges, but greater power.

These advantages are exemplified in many of the various means of communicating status. Like the doctors in Goffman's research hospital, men are allowed such privileges as swearing and sitting in undignified positions, but women are denied them. Though the male privilege of swearing is curtailed in mixed company, the body movement permitted to women is circumscribed even in all-woman groups. It is considered unladylike for a woman to use her body too forcefully, to sprawl, to stand with her legs widely spread, to sit with her feet up, or to cross the ankle of one leg over the knee of the other. The more "feminine" a woman's clothes are, the more circumscribed the use of her body. Depending on her clothes, she may

be expected to sit with her knees together, not to sit cross-legged, or not even to bend over.

Prior to the 1920's women's clothes were designed to be confining and cumbersome. The dress reform movement, which disposed of corsets and long skirts, was considered by many to have more significance for female emancipation than women's suffrage (O'Neill, 1969, p. 270). Today women's clothes are designed to be revealing, but women are expected to restrict their body movements to avoid revealing too much. Furthermore, because women's clothes are contrived to reveal women's physical features, rather than being loose like men's, women must resort to purses to carry their belongings instead of pockets. These "conveniences" have become, in a time of blurred sex distinctions, one of the surest signs of sex, and thus have developed the character of stigma, a sign of woman's shame, as when they are used to ridicule both women and transvestites.

Women in our society are expected to reveal not only more of their bodies than men but also more of themselves. Female socialization encourages greater expression of emotion than that of the male. Whereas men are expected to be stolid and impassive, and not to disclose their feelings beyond certain limits, women are expected to express their *selves*. Such self-expression can disclose a lot of oneself, and, as Jourard and Lasakow (1958) found, females are more self-disclosing to others than males are. This puts them at an immediate disadvantage.

The inverse relationship between disclosure and power has been reported by other studies in addition to Goffman's earlier cited investigation into a research hospital. Slobin, Miller, and Porter (1968) stated that individuals in a business organization are "more self-disclosing to their immediate superior than to their immediate subordinates." Self-disclosure is a means of enhancing another's power. When one has greater access to information about another person, one has a resource the other person does not have. Thus not only does power give status, but status gives power. And those possessing neither must contribute to the power and status of others continuously.

Another factor adding to women's vulnerability is that they are socialized to *care* more than men—especially about personal relationships. This puts them at a disadvantage, as Ross articulated in 1921 in what he called the "Law of Personal Exploitation": "In any sentimental relation the one who cares less can exploit the one who cares more," (p. 136). The same idea was put more broadly by Waller and Hill (1951) as the "Principle of Least Interest": "That person is able to dictate the conditions of association whose interest in the continuation of the affair is least" (p. 191). In other words, women's caring, like their openness, gives them less power in a relationship.

One way of indicating acceptance of one's place and deference to those of superior status is by following the rules of "personal space." Sommer (1969, Chap. 2) has observed that dominant animals and human beings have a larger envelope of inviolability surrounding them—i.e., are approached less closely—than those of a lower status. Willis (1966) made a study of the initial speaking distance set by an approaching person as a function of the speakers' relationship. His finding that women were approached more closely than men—i.e., their personal space was smaller or more likely to be breached—is consistent with their lower status.

Touching is one of the closer invasions of one's personal space, and in our low-contact culture it implies privileged access to another person. People who accidentally touch other people generally take great pains to apologize; people forced into close proximity, as in a crowded elevator, often go to extreme lengths to avoid touching. Even the figurative meanings of the word convey a notion of access to privileged areas—e.g., to one's emotions (one is "touched" by a sad story), or to one's purse (one is "touched" for ten dollars). In addition, the act of touching can be a subtle physical threat.

Remembering the patterns that Brown found in terms of address, consider the interactions between pairs of persons of different status, and picture who would be more likely to touch the other (put an arm around the shoulder or a hand on the back, tap the chest, hold the arm, or the like): teacher and student; master and servant; policeman and accused; doctor and patient; minister and parishioner; adviser and advisee; foreman and worker; businessman and secretary. As with first-naming, it is considered presumptuous for a person of low status to initiate touch with a person of higher status.

There has been little investigation of touching by social scientists, but the few studies made so far indicate that females are touched more than males are. Goldberg and Lewis (1969) and Lewis (1972) report that from six months on, girl babies are touched more than boy babies. The data reported in Jourard (1966) and Jourard and Rubin (1968) show that sons and fathers tend to refrain from touching each other and that "when it comes to physical contact within the family, it is the daughters who are the favored ones" (Jourard, 1966, p. 224). An examination of the number of different regions in which subjects were touched showed that mothers and fathers touch their daughters in more regions than sons do; and that males touch their opposite-sex best friends in more regions than females do. Overall, women's mean total

---

> ### From the Point of View of the Victim
>
> *Purpose:* To get in touch with the hidden strength and subtle forms of power and control of the victim position.
>
> *Directions:* Choose a partner and sit facing each other. Take turns doing the following (or, this exercise may be done alone by writing your responses to the following):
>
> 1. Think of an experience in which you were the victim and tell (or write) the story from that point of view.
> 2. Now, tell the story again, keeping the facts the same except that now tell it from the point of view of the other person being the victim.
>
> What is your experience upon retelling the story? How have your attitudes or feelings changed about what happened as a result of seeing the situation in a different way? What are some of the advantages of the victim position? The disadvantages?

"being-touched" score was higher than men's.

Jourard and Rubin take the view that "touching is equated with sexual intent, either consciously, or at a less-conscious level" (p. 47), but it would seem that there is a sex difference in the interpretation of touch. Lewis reflects this when he writes, "In general, for men in our culture, proximity (touching) is restricted to the opposite sex and its function is primarily sexual in nature" (p. 237). Waitresses, secretaries, and women students are quite used to being touched by their male superordinates, but they are expected not to "misinterpret" such gestures. However, women who touch men are often interpreted as conveying sexual intent, as they have often found out when their intentions were quite otherwise. Such different interpretations are consistent with the status patterns found earlier. If touching indicates either power or intimacy, and women are deemed by men to be status inferiors, touching by women will be perceived as a gesture of intimacy, since it would be inconceivable for them to be exercising power.

A study by Henley (1970) puts forward this hypothesis. Observations of incidents of touch in public urban places by a white male research assistant, naive to the uses of his data, in which age, sex, and approximate socioeconomic status were recorded, indicated that higher-status persons do touch lower-status persons significantly more. In particular, men touched women more, even when all other variables were held constant. When the settings of the observations were differentially examined, the pattern showed up primarily in the outdoor setting, with indoor interaction being more evenly spread over sex combinations. This finding cannot be unequivocally interpreted, but it may be that outdoor interaction, being more public, necessitates stricter attention to the symbols of power, while indoor interaction, especially in the relatively impersonal yet public settings visited, is more informal and encourages relaxation of the power relationship. Alternatively, one could say that indoors, power may be more easily communicated by cues other than touching.

The other nonverbal cues by which status is indicated have likewise not been adequately researched—for humans. But O'Connor (1970) argues that many of the gestures of dominance and submission that have been noted in the primates are equally present in humans. They are used to maintain and reinforce the status hierarchy by reassuring those of higher status that those of lower status accept their place in the human pecking order.

The most studied nonverbal communication

among humans is probably eye contact, and here too one finds a sex difference. It has repeatedly been found that women look more at another in a dyad than men do (Exline, 1963; Exline, Gray, & Schuette, 1965; Rubin, 1970). Exline, Gray, and Schuette suggest that "willingness to engage in mutual visual interaction is more characteristic of those who are oriented towards inclusive and affectionate interpersonal relations" (p. 207), but Rubin concludes that while "gazing may serve as a vehicle of emotional expression for women, [it] in addition may allow women to obtain cues from their male partners concerning the appropriateness of their behavior" (p. 272). This interpretation is supported by Efran and Broughton's (1966) data showing that even male subjects "maintain more eye contact with individuals toward whom they have developed higher expectancies for social approval" (p. 103).

Another possible reason why women gaze more at men is that men talk more (Argyle, Lalljee, & Cook, 1968), and there is a tendency for the listener to look more at the speaker than vice versa (Exline et al., 1965).

It is especially illuminating to look at the power relationships established and maintained by the manipulation of eye contact. The mutual glance can be seen as a sign of union, but when intensified into a stare it may become a way of doing battle (Exline, 1963). Research reported by Ellsworth, Carlsmith, and Henson (1972) supports the notion that the stare can be interpreted as an aggressive gesture. These authors write, "Staring at humans can elicit the same sort of responses that are common in primates; that is, staring can act like a primate threat display" (p. 310).

Though women engage in mutual visual interaction in its intimate form to a high degree, they probably back down when looking be-

comes a gesture of dominance. O'Connor points out, "The direst stare or glare is a common human gesture of dominance. Women use the gesture as well as men, but often in modified form. While looking directly at a man, a woman usually has her head slightly tilted, implying the beginning of a presenting gesture or enough submission to render the stare ambivalent if not actually submissive."

The idea that the averted glance is a gesture of submission is supported by the research of Hutt and Ounsted (1966) into the characteristic gaze aversion of autistic children. They remark that "these children were never attacked [by peers] despite the fact that to a naive observer they appeared to be easy targets; this indicated that their gaze aversion had some signalling function similar to 'facing away' in the kittiwake or 'head-flagging' in the herring gull—behavior patterns which Tinbergen (1959) has termed 'appeasement postures.' In other words, gaze aversion inhibited any aggressive or threat behavior on the part of other conspecifics" (p. 354).

Gestures of dominance and submission can be verbal as well as nonverbal. In fact, the sheer use of verbalization is a form of dominance because it can quite literally render someone speechless by preventing one from "getting a word in edgewise." As noted earlier, contrary to popular myth, men do talk more than women, both in single-sex and in mixed-sex groups. Within a group a major means of asserting dominance is to interrupt. Those who want to dominate others interrupt more; those speaking will not permit themselves to be interrupted by their inferiors, but they will give way to those they consider their superiors.

Other characteristics of persons in inferior status positions are the tendencies to hesitate and apologize, often offered as submissive ges-

from **Letter to a Sister Underground**

Our smiles and glances,
the ways we walk, sit, laugh, the games we
    must play
with men and even oh my Ancient Mother
    God the games
we must play among ourselves—these are the
    ways we pass
unnoticed, by the Conquerors.
They're always watching,
invisibly electroded in our brains,
to be certain we implode our rage against
    each other
and not explode it against them:
the times we rip and tear at the twin
for what we have intricately defended in
    ourselves;
the mimicry of male hierarchy, male ego,
male possessiveness, leader/follower,
    doer/thinker, butch/femme
yes also when we finally learn to love each
    other physically.
Roles to survive a death-in-life until
that kind of life becomes worthless enough
to risk losing even precious It.

Our subterranean grapevine, which men, like
    fools, call gossip,
has always been efficient.
Our sabotage has ranged from witches'
    research
into herbal poisons to secretaries' spilling
    coffee on the files
to housewives' passive resistance
in front of their soap-opera screens
to housemaids' accidentally breaking china
to mothers' teaching their children to love
    them
a little bit better than their fathers.
    And more.

                                    Robin Morgan

tures in the face of threats or potential threats. If staring directly, pointing, and touching can be subtle nonverbal threats, the corresponding gestures of submission seem to be lowering the eyes from another's gaze, falling silent (or not speaking at all) when interrupted or pointed at, and cuddling to the touch. Many of these nonverbal gestures of submission are very familiar. They are the traits our society assigns as desirable secondary characteristics of the female role. Girls who have properly learned to be "feminine" have learned to lower their eyes, remain silent, back down, and cuddle at the appropriate times. There is even a word for this syndrome that is applied only to females: coy.

In verbal communication one finds a similar pattern of differences between the sexes. As mentioned earlier, men have the privilege of swearing, and hence access to a vocabulary not customarily available to women. On the surface this seems like an innocuous limitation, until one realizes the psychological function of swearing: it is one of the most harmless and effective ways of expressing anger. The alternatives are to express one's feelings with physical violence or to suppress them and by so doing turn one's anger in on oneself. The former is prohibited to both sexes (to different degrees) but the latter is decisively encouraged in women. The result is that women are "intropunitive"; they punish themselves for their own anger rather than somehow dissipate it. Since anger turned inward is commonly viewed as the basis for depression, we should not be surprised that depression is considerably more common in women than in men, and in fact is the most prevalent form of "mental illness" among women.

Swearing is only the most obvious sex difference in language. Key (1972) has noted that sex differences are to be found in phonological, semantic, and grammatical aspects of language as well as in word use (see also Lakoff, 1973). Austin (1965) has commented that "in our culture little boys tend to be nasal . . . and little girls, oral" (p. 34), but that in the "final stages" of courtship the voices of both men and women are low and nasal (p. 37). The pattern cited by Brown (1965), in which the form appropriately used by status superiors is used between status equals in intimate situations, is again visible: in the intimate situation the female adopts the vocal style of the male.

In situations where intimacy is not a possible interpretation, it is not power but abnormality that is the usual interpretation. Female voices are expected to be soft and quiet—even when men are using loud voices. Yet it is only the "lady" whose speech is refined. Women who do not fit this stereotype are often called loud —a word commonly applied derogatorily to other minority groups or out groups (Austin, 1963, pg. 38). One of the most popular derogatory terms for women is "shrill," which, after all, simply means loud (out of place) and high-pitched (female).

In language, as in touch and in most other aspects of interpersonal behavior, status differences between the sexes mean that the same traits are differently interpreted when displayed by each sex. A man's behavior toward a woman might be interpreted as an expression of either power or intimacy, depending on the situation. When the same behavior is engaged in by a woman and directed toward a man, it is interpreted only as a gesture of intimacy— and intimacy between the sexes is always seen as sexual in nature. Because our values say that women should not have power over men, women's nonverbal communication is rarely interpreted as an expression of power. If the

Conversation with a Man by Jennifer Knight

situation precludes a sexual interpretation, women's assumption of the male prerogative is dismissed as deviant (castrating, domineering, unfemine, or the like).

Of course, if women do not wish to be classified either as deviant or as perpetually sexy, then they must persist in playing the proper role by following the interpersonal behavior pattern prescribed for them. Followed repeatedly, these patterns function as a means of control. What is merely habitual is often seen as desirable. The more men and women interact in the way they have been trained to from birth without considering the meaning of what they do, the more they become dulled to the significance of their actions. Just as outsiders observing a new society are more aware of the status differences of that society than its members are, so those who play the sexual politics of interpersonal behavior are usually not conscious of what they do. Instead they continue to wonder that feminists make such a mountain out of such a "trivial" molehill.

Sandra L. Bem and Daryl J. Bem

Training the Woman to Know Her Place:
The Power of a Nonconscious Ideology

In the beginning God created the heaven and the earth. . . . And God said, Let us make man in our image, after our likeness; and let them have dominion over the fish of the sea, and over the fowl of the air, and over the cattle, and over all the earth. . . . And the rib, which the Lord God had taken from man, made he a woman and brought her unto the man. . . . And the Lord God said unto the woman, What is this that thou has done? And the woman said, The serpent beguiled me, and I did eat. . . . Unto the woman He said, I will greatly multiply thy sorrow and thy conception; in sorrow thou shalt bring forth children; and thy desire shall be to thy husband, and he shall rule over thee. (Gen. 1, 2, 3)

And lest anyone fail to grasp the moral of this story, Saint Paul provides further clarification:

For a man . . . is the image and glory of God; but the woman is the glory of the man. For the man is not of the woman, but the woman of the man. Neither was the man created for the woman, but the woman for the man. (1 Cor. 11)

Let the woman learn in silence with all subjection. But I suffer not a woman to teach, nor to usurp authority over the man, but to be in silence. For Adam was first formed, then Eve. And Adam was not deceived, but the woman, being deceived, was in the transgression. Notwithstanding, she shall be saved in childbearing, if they continue in faith and charity and holiness with sobriety. (1 Tim. 2)

And lest it be thought that only Christians have this rich heritage of ideology about women, consider the morning prayer of the Orthodox Jew:

Blessed art Thou, oh Lord our God, King of the Universe, that I was not born a gentile.
Blessed art Thou, oh Lord our God, King of the Universe, that I was not born a slave.
Blessed art Thou, oh Lord our God, King of the Universe, that I was not born a woman.

Or the Koran, the sacred text of Islam:

Men are superior to women on account of the qualities in which God has given them pre-eminence.

Because they think they sense a decline in feminine "faith, charity, and holiness with sobriety," many people today jump to the conclusion that the ideology expressed in these passages is a relic of the past. Not so. It has simply been obscured by an equalitarian veneer, and the ideology has now become nonconscious. That is, we remain unaware of it because alternative beliefs and attitudes about women go unimagined. We are like the fish who is unaware that his environment is wet. After all, what else could it be? Such is the nature of all nonconscious ideologies. Such is the nature of America's ideology about women. For even those Americans who agree that a black skin should not uniquely qualify its owner for janitorial or domestic service continue to act as if the possession of a uterus uniquely qualifies *its* owner for precisely that.

Consider, for example, the 1968 student rebellion at Columbia University. Students from the radical left took over some administration buildings in the name of equalitarian principles which they accused the university of flouting. Here were the most militant spokesmen one could hope to find in the cause of equalitarian ideals. But no sooner had they occupied the buildings than the male militants blandly turned to their sisters-in-arms and assigned them the task of preparing the food, while they—the menfolk—would presumably plan further strategy. The reply these males received was the reply they deserved, and the fact that domestic tasks behind the barricades were desegregated across the sex line that day is an everlasting tribute to the class consciousness of the ladies of the left.

But these conscious coeds are not typical, for the nonconscious assumptions about a woman's "natural" talents (or lack of them) are at least as prevalent among women as they are among men. A psychologist named Philip Goldberg (1968) demonstrated this by asking female college students to rate a number of professional articles from each of six fields. The articles were collated into two equal sets of booklets, and the names of the authors were changed so that the identical article was attributed to the male author (e.g., John T. McKay) in one set of booklets and to a female author (e.g., Joan T. McKay) in the other set. Each student was asked to read the articles in her booklet and to rate them for value, competence, persuasiveness, writing style, and so forth.

As he had anticipated, Goldberg found that the identical article received significantly lower ratings when it was attributed to a female author than when it was attributed to a male author. He had predicted this result for articles from professional fields generally considered the province of men, like law and city planning, but to his surprise, these coeds also downgraded articles from the fields of dietetics and elementary school education when they were attributed to female authors. In other words, these students rated the male authors as better at everything, agreeing with Aristotle that "we should regard the female nature as afflicted with a natural defectiveness." We repeated this experiment informally in our own classrooms and discovered that male students show the same implicit prejudice against female authors that Goldberg's female students showed. Such is the nature of a nonconscious ideology!

It is significant that examples like these can be drawn from the college world, for today's students have challenged the established ways of looking at almost every other issue, and they have been quick to reject those practices of our society which conflict explicitly with their major values. But as the above examples suggest, they will find it far more difficult to shed the more subtle aspects of a sex-role ideology which—as we shall now attempt to demonstrate—conflicts just as surely with their existential values as any of the other societal practices to which they have so effectively raised objection. And as we shall see, there is no better way to appreciate the power of a society's nonconscious ideology than to examine it within the framework of values held by that society's avant-garde.

Individuality and Self-Fulfillment

The dominant values of today's students concern personal growth on the one hand, and interpersonal relationships on the other. The first of these emphasizes individuality and

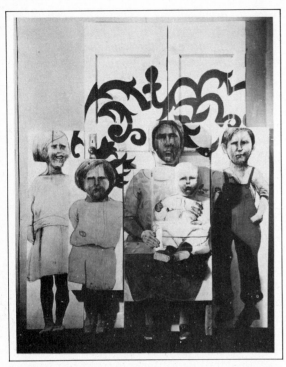

The Family by Escobar Marisol (1962), Collection, The Museum of Modern Art, New York, Advisory Committee Fund

self-fulfillment; the second stresses openness, honesty, and equality in all human relationships.

The values of individuality and self-fulfillment imply that each human being, male or female, is to be encouraged to "do his own thing." Men and women are no longer to be stereotyped by society's definitions. If sensitivity, emotionality, and warmth are desirable human characteristics, then they are desirable for men as well as for women. (John Wayne is no longer an idol of the young, but their pop-art satire.) If independence, assertiveness, and serious intellectual commitment are desirable human characteristics, then they are desirable for women as well as for men. The major prescription of this college generation is that each individual should be encouraged to discover and fulfill his own unique potential and identity, unfettered by society's presumptions.

But society's presumptions enter the scene much earlier than most people suspect, for parents begin to raise their children in accord with the popular stereotypes from the very first. Boys are encouraged to be aggressive, competitive, and independent, whereas girls are rewarded for being passive and dependent (Barry, Bacon, & Child, 1957; Sears, Maccoby, & Levin, 1957). In one study, six-month-old infant girls were already being touched and spoken to more by their mothers while they were playing than were infant boys. When they were thirteen months old, these same girls were more reluctant than the boys to leave their mothers; they returned more quickly and more frequently to them; and they remained closer to them throughout the entire play period. When a physical barrier was placed between mother and child, the girls tended to cry and motion for help; the boys made more active attempts to get around the barrier (Goldberg & Lewis, 1969). No one knows to what extent these sex differences at the age of thirteen months can be attributed to the mothers' behavior at the age of six months, but it is hard to believe that the two are unconnected.

As children grow older, more explicit sex-role training is introduced. Boys are encouraged to take more of an interest in mathematics and science. Boys, not girls, are given chemistry sets and microscopes for Christmas. Moreover, all children quickly learn that mommy is proud to be a moron when it comes to mathematics and science, whereas daddy knows all about these things. When a young boy returns from

The myth of childhood has an even greater parallel in the myth of femininity. Both women and children were considered asexual and thus "purer" than man. Their inferior status was ill-concealed under an elaborate "respect." One didn't discuss serious matters nor did one curse in front of women and children; one didn't openly degrade them, one did it behind their backs. (As for the double standard about cursing: A man is allowed to blaspheme the world because it belongs to him to damn—but the same curse out of the mouth of a woman or a minor, i.e., an incomplete "man" to whom the world does not belong, is considered presumptuous, and thus an impropriety or worse.)

Shulamith Firestone

school all excited about biology, he is almost certain to be encouraged to think of becoming a physician. A girl with similar enthusiasm is told that she might want to consider nurse's training later so she can have "an interesting job to fall back upon in case—God forbid—she ever needs to support herself." A very different kind of encouragement. And any girl who doggedly persists in her enthusiasm for science is likely to find her parents as horrified by the prospect of a permanent love affair with physics as they would be by the prospect of an interracial marriage.

These socialization practices quickly take their toll. By nursery school age, for example, boys are already asking more questions about how and why things work (Smith, 1933). In first and second grade, when asked to suggest ways of improving various toys, boys do better on the fire truck and girls do better on the nurse's kit, but by the third grade, boys do better regardless of the toy presented (Torrance, 1962). By the ninth grade, 25% of the boys, but only 3% of the girls, are considering careers in science or engineering (Flanagan, unpublished, cited by Kagan, 1964). When they apply for college, boys and girls are about equal on verbal aptitude tests, but boys score significantly higher on mathematical aptitude tests—about sixty points higher on the College Board examinations, for example (Brown, 1965, p. 162). Moreover, girls improve their mathematical performance if problems are reworded so that they deal with cooking and gardening, even

though the abstract reasoning required for their solutions remains the same (Milton, 1958). Clearly, not just ability, but motivation too, has been affected.

But these effects in mathematics and science are only part of the story. A girl's long training in passivity and dependence appears to exact an even higher toll from her overall motivation to achieve, to search for new and independent ways of doing things, and to welcome the challenge of new and unsolved problems. In one study, for example, elementary school girls were more likely to try solving a puzzle by imitating an adult, whereas the boys were more likely to search for a novel solution not provided by the adult (McDavid, 1959). In another puzzle-solving study, young girls asked for help and approval from adults more frequently than the boys; and, when given the opportunity to return to the puzzles a second time, the girls were more likely to rework those they had already solved, whereas the boys were more likely to try puzzles they had been unable to solve previously (Crandall & Rabson, 1960). A girl's sigh of relief is almost audible when she marries and retires from the outside world of novel and unsolved problems. This, of course, is the most conspicuous outcome of all: the majority of American women become full-time homemakers. Such are the consequences of a nonconscious ideology.

But why does this process violate the values of individuality and self-fulfillment? It is *not* because some people may regard the role of homemaker as inferior to other roles. That is not the point. Rather, the point is that our society is managing to consign a large segment of its population to the role of homemaker solely on the basis of sex just as inexorably as it has in the past consigned the individual with a black skin to the role of janitor or domestic. It is not the quality of the role itself which is at issue here, but the fact that in spite of their unique identities, the majority of America's women end up in the *same* role.

Even so, however, several arguments are typically advanced to counter the claim that America's homogenization of its women subverts individuality and self-fulfillment. The three most common arguments invoke, respectively, (1) free will, (2) biology, and (3) complementarity.

1. The free will argument proposes that a 21-year-old woman is perfectly free to choose some other role if she cares to do so; no one is standing in her way. But this argument conveniently overlooks the fact that the society which has spent twenty years carefully marking the woman's ballot for her has nothing to lose in that twenty-first year by pretending to let her cast it for the alternative of her choice. Society has controlled not her alternatives, but her motivation to choose any but one of those alternatives. The so-called freedom to choose is illusory and cannot be invoked to justify the society which controls the motivation to choose.

2. The biological argument suggests that there may really be inborn differences between men and women in, say, independence or mathematical ability. Or that there may be biological factors beyond the fact that women can become pregnant and nurse children which uniquely dictate that they, but not men, should stay home all day and shun serious outside commitment. Maybe female hormones really are responsible somehow. One difficulty with this argument, of course, is that female hormones would have to be different in the Soviet Union, where one-third of the engineers and 75% of the physicians are women. In America, women constitute less than 1% of the engineers and only 7% of the physicians (Dodge, 1966). Female physiology *is* different, and it may account for some of the psychological differences between the sexes, but America's sex-role ideology still seems primarily responsible for the fact that so few women emerge from childhood with the motivation to seek out any role beyond the one that our society dictates.

But even if there really were biological differences between the sexes along these lines, the biological argument would still be irrelevant. The reason can best be illustrated with an analogy.

Suppose that every black American boy were to be socialized to become a jazz musician on the assumption that he has a "natural" talent in that direction, or suppose that his parents should subtly discourage him from other pursuits because it is considered "inappropriate" for black men to become physicians or physicists. Most liberal Americans, we submit, would disapprove. But suppose that it *could* be demonstrated that black Americans, *on the average,* did possess an inborn better sense of rhythm than white Americans. Would *that* justify ignoring the unique characteristics of a *particular* black youngster from the very beginning and specifically socializing him to become a musician? We don't think so. Similarly, as long as a woman's socialization does not nurture her uniqueness, but treats her only as a member of a group on the basis of some assumed

He said we were both free. Yes, we're both free. He's free to find someone who will wash his socks, and I'm free to find another slave master.

Anne Battle-Sister

---

average characteristic, she will not be prepared to realize her own potential in the way that the values of individuality and self-fulfillment imply she should.

The irony of the biological argument is that it does not take biological differences seriously enough. That is, it fails to recognize the range of biological differences between individuals within the same sex. Thus, recent research has revealed that biological factors help determine many personality traits. Dominance and submissiveness, for example, have been found to have large inheritable components; in other words, biological factors *do* have the potential for partially determining how dominant or submissive an individual, male or female, will turn out to be. But the effects of this biological potential could be detected only in males (Gottesman, 1963). This implies that only the males in our culture are raised with sufficient flexibility, with sufficient latitude given to their biological differences, for their "natural" or biologically determined potential to shine through. Females, on the other hand, are subjected to a socialization which so ignores their unique attributes that even the effects of biology seem to be swamped. In sum, the biological argument for continuing America's homogenization of its women gets hoist with its own petard.

3. Many people recognize that most women do end up as full-time homemakers because of their socialization and that these women do exemplify the failure of our society to raise girls as unique individuals. But, they point out, the role of the homemaker is not inferior to the role of the professional man: it is complementary but equal.

This argument is usually bolstered by pointing to the joys and importance of taking care of small children. Indeed, mothers *and* fathers find child rearing rewarding, and it is certainly important. But this argument becomes insufficient when one considers that the average American woman now lives to age 74 and has her *last* child at about age 26; thus, by the time the woman is 33 or so, her children all have more important things to do with their daytime hours than to spend them entertaining an adult woman who has nothing to do during the second half of her life span. As for the other "joys" of homemaking, many writers (e.g., Friedan, 1963) have persuasively argued that the role of the homemaker has been glamorized far beyond its intrinsic worth. This charge becomes plausible when one considers that the average American homemaker spends the equivalent of a man's working day, 7.1 hours, in preparing meals, cleaning house, laundering, mending, shopping, and doing other household tasks. In other words, 43% of her waking time is spent in activity that would command an hourly wage on the open market well below the federally-set minimum for menial industrial work.

The point is not how little she would earn if she did these things in someone else's home,

Copyright 1973, G. B. Trudeau/Distributed by Universal Press Syndicate

but that this use of time is virtually the same for homemakers with college degrees and for those with less than a grade school education, for women married to professional men and for women married to blue-collar workers. Talent, education, ability, interests, motivations: all are irrelevant. In our society, being female uniquely qualifies an individual for domestic work.

It is true, of course, that the American homemaker has, on the average, 5.1 hours of leisure time per day, and it is here, we are told, that each woman can express her unique identity. Thus, politically interested women can join the League of Women Voters; women with humane interests can become part-time Gray Ladies; women who love music can raise money for the symphony. Protestant women play Canasta; Jewish women play Mah-Jongg; brighter women of all denominations and faculty wives play bridge; and so forth.

But politically interested *men* serve in legislatures; *men* with humane interests become physicians or clinical psychologists; *men* who love music play in the symphony; and so forth. In other words, why should a woman's unique identity determine only the periphery of her life rather than its central core?

Again, the important point is not that the role of homemaker is necessarily inferior, but that the woman's unique identity has been rendered irrelevant. Consider the following "predictability test." When a boy is born, it is difficult to predict what he will be doing 25 years later.

We cannot say whether he will be an artist, a doctor, or a college professor because he will be permitted to develop and to fulfill his own unique potential, particularly if he is white and middle class. But if the newborn child is a girl, we can usually predict with confidence how she will be spending her time 25 years later. Her individuality doesn't have to be considered; it is irrelevant.

The socialization of the American male has closed off certain options for him too. Men are discouraged from developing certain desirable traits such as tenderness and sensitivity just as surely as women are discouraged from being assertive and, alas, "too bright." Young boys are encouraged to be incompetent at cooking and child care just as surely as young girls are urged to be incompetent at mathematics and science.

Indeed, one of the errors of the early feminist movement in this country was that it assumed that men had all the goodies and that women could attain self-fulfillment merely by being like men. But that is hardly the utopia implied by the values of individuality and self-fulfillment. Rather, these values would require society to raise its children so flexibly and with sufficient respect for the integrity of individual uniqueness that some men might emerge with the motivation, the ability, and the opportunity to stay home and raise children without bearing the stigma of being peculiar. If homemaking is as glamorous as the women's magazines and television commercials portray it, then men,

This means, therefore, that as a result of the discovery of women's lack of a penis they are debased in value for girls just as they are for boys and later perhaps for men.

Sigmund Freud

---

too, should have that option. Even if homemaking isn't all that glamorous, it would probably still be more fulfilling for some men than the jobs in which they now find themselves.

And if biological differences really do exist between men and women in "nurturance," in their inborn motivations to care for children, then this will show up automatically in the final distribution of men and women across the various roles: relatively fewer men will choose to stay at home. The values of individuality and self-fulfillment do not imply that there must be equality of outcome, an equal number of men and women in each role, but that there should be the widest possible variation in outcome consistent with the range of individual differences among people, regardless of sex. At the very least, these values imply that society should raise its males so that they could freely engage in activities that might pay less than those being pursued by their wives without feeling that they were "living off their wives." One rarely hears it said of a woman that she is "living off her husband."

Thus, it is true that a man's options are limited by our society's sex-role ideology, but as the "predictability test" reveals, it is still the woman in our society whose identity is rendered irrelevant by America's socialization practices. In 1954, the United States Supreme Court declared that a fraud and hoax lay behind the slogan "separate but equal." It is unlikely that any court will ever do the same for the more subtle motto that successfully keeps the

> ### The Process of Dissolution
>
> *my husband held me*
> *responsible for his failures.*
> *when he scolded me*
> *he had my father*
> *written all over his face.*
> *our marriage ended*
> *as my childhood*
> *continued; the men in my life*
> *still try teaching me lessons,*
> *and i have not ceased entirely*
> *from kicking myself hard*
> *to please them: damn you*
> *daddy. damn your redundant*
> *face.*
>
> Susan Efros

woman in her place: "complementary but equal."

Interpersonal Equality

Wives, submit yourselves unto your own husbands, as unto the Lord. For the husband is the head of the wife, even as Christ is the head of the church; and he is the savior of the body. Therefore, as the church is subject unto Christ, so let the wives be to their own husbands in everything. (Eph. 5)

As this passage reveals, the ideological rationalization that men and women hold complementary but equal positions is a recent in-

When, finally, we vary both marital status and sex, by comparing married men and unmarried women, we find relatively little overall difference so far as mental health is concerned, superiorities and inferiorities tending to cancel out. But the women are spectacularly better off so far as psychological distress symptoms are concerned, suggesting that women start out with an initial advantage which marriage reverses.

Jessie Bernard

---

vention of our modern "liberal" society, part of the equalitarian veneer which helps to keep today's version of the ideology nonconscious. Certainly those Americans who value open, honest, and equalitarian relationships generally are quick to reject this traditional view of the male-female relationship; and, an increasing number of young people even plan to enter "utopian" marriages very much like the following hypothetical example:

Both my wife and I earned Ph.D. degrees in our respective disciplines. I turned down a superior academic post in Oregon and accepted a slightly less desirable position in New York where my wife could obtain a part-time teaching job and do research at one of the several other colleges in the area. Although I would have preferred to live in a suburb, we purchased a home near my wife's college so that she could have an office at home where she would be when the children returned from school. Because my wife earns a good salary, she can easily afford to pay a maid to do her major household chores. My wife and I share all other tasks around the house equally. For example, she cooks the meals, but I do the laundry for her and help her with many of her other household tasks.

Without questioning the basic happiness of such a marriage or its appropriateness for many couples, we can legitimately ask if such a marriage is, in fact, an instance of interpersonal equality. Have all the hidden assumptions about the woman's "natural" role really been

eliminated? Has the traditional ideology really been exorcised? There is a very simple test. If the marriage is truly equalitarian, then its description should retain the same flavor and tone even if the roles of the husband and wife were to be reversed:

Both my husband and I earned Ph.D. degrees in our respective disciplines. I turned down a superior academic post in Oregon and accepted a slightly less desirable position in New York where my husband could obtain a part-time teaching job and do research at one of the several other colleges in the area. Although I would have preferred to live in a suburb, we purchased a home near my husband's college so that he could have an office at home where he would be when the children returned from school. Because my husband earns a good salary, he can easily afford to pay a maid to do his major household chores. My husband and I share all other tasks around the house equally. For example, he cooks the meals, but I do the laundry for him and help him with many of his other household tasks.

It seems unlikely that many men or women in our society would mistake the marriage *just* described as either equalitarian or desirable, and thus it becomes apparent that the ideology about the woman's "natural" role noncon- sciously permeates the entire fabric of such "utopian" marriages. It is true that the wife gains some measure of equality when her career can influence the final place of residence, but why is it the unquestioned assumption that the

In our society, the husband is assigned a superior status. It helps if he actually is somewhat superior in ways—in height, for example, or age or education or occupation—for such superiority, however slight, makes it easier for both partners to conform to the structural imperatives. The girl wants to be able to "look up" to her husband, and he, of course, wants her to. The result is a situation known sociologically as the marriage gradient.

Jessie Bernard

husband's career solely determines the initial set of alternatives that are to be considered? Why is it the wife who automatically seeks the part-time position? Why is it *her* maid instead of *their* maid? Why *her* laundry? Why *her* household tasks? And so forth throughout the entire relationship.

The important point here is not that such marriages are bad or that their basic assumptions of inequality produce unhappy, frustrated women. Quite the contrary. It is the very happiness of the wives in such marriages that reveals society's smashing success in socializing its women. It is a measure of the distance our society must yet traverse toward the goals of self-fulfillment and interpersonal equality that such marriages are widely characterized as utopian and fully equalitarian. It is a mark of how well the woman has been kept in her place that the husband in such a marriage is often idolized by women, including his wife, for "permitting" her to squeeze a career into the interstices of their marriage as long as his own career is not unduly inconvenienced. Thus is the white man blessed for exercising his power benignly while his "natural" right to that power forever remains unquestioned."

Such is the subtlety of a nonconscious ideology!

A truly equalitarian marriage would permit both partners to pursue careers or outside commitments which carry equal weight when all important decisions are to be made. It is here,

of course, that the "problem" of children arises. People often assume that the woman who seeks a role beyond home and family would not care to have children. They assume that if she wants a career or serious outside commitment, then children must be unimportant to her. But of course no one makes this assumption about her husband. No one assumes that a father's interest in his career necessarily precludes a deep and abiding affection for his children or a vital interest in their development. Once again America applies a double standard of judgment. Suppose that a father of small children suddenly lost his wife. No matter how much he loved his children, no one would expect him to sacrifice his career in order to stay home with them on a full-time basis—*even if he had an independent source of income.* No one would charge him with selfishness or lack of parental feeling if he sought professional care for his children during the day. An equalitarian marriage simply abolishes this double standard and extends the same freedom to the mother, while also providing the framework for the father to enter more fully into the pleasures and responsibilities of child rearing. In fact, it is the equalitarian marriage which has the most potential for giving children the love and concern of two parents rather than one.

But few women are prepared to make use of this freedom. Even those women who have managed to finesse society's attempt to rob them of their career motivations are likely to

Hence there were, and to some extent still are, realistic reasons in our culture why woman is bound to overrate love and to expect more from it than it can possibly give, and why she is more afraid of losing love than man is.

Karen Horney

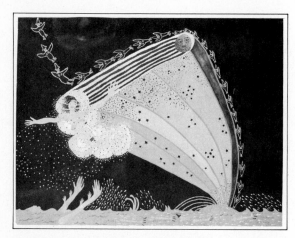

Jumping Off the Golden Gate Bridge by Ann Leda Shapiro

find themselves blocked by society's trump card: the feeling that the raising of the children is their unique responsibility and—in time of crisis—ultimately theirs alone. Such is the emotional power of a nonconscious ideology.

In addition to providing this potential for equalized child care, a truly equalitarian marriage embraces a more general division of labor which satisfies what might be called "the roommate test." That is, the labor is divided just as it is when two men or two women room together in college or set up a bachelor apartment together. Errands and domestic chores are assigned by preference, agreement, flipping a coin, given to hired help, or—as is sometimes the case—left undone.

It is significant that today's young people, many of whom live this way prior to marriage, find this kind of arrangement within marriage so foreign to their thinking. Consider an analogy. Suppose that a white male college student decided to room or set up a bachelor apartment with a black male friend. Surely the typical white student would not blithely assume that his black roommate was to handle all the domestic chores. Nor would his conscious allow him to do so even in the unlikely event that his roommate would say: "No, that's okay. I like doing housework. I'd be happy to do it." We suspect that the typical white student would still not be comfortable if he took advantage of this offer, if he took advantage of the fact that his roommate had been socialized to be "happy" with such an arrangement. But change this hypothetical black roommate to a female marriage partner, and somehow the student's conscience goes to sleep. At most it is quickly tranquilized by the thought that "she is happiest when she is ironing for her loved one." Such is the power of a nonconscious ideology.

Of course, it may well be that she *is* happiest when she is ironing for her loved one.

Such, indeed, is the power of a nonconscious ideology!

We must ask ourselves why there should have to be any power struggle at all between the sexes. At any given time, the more powerful side will create an ideology suitable to help maintain its position and to make this position acceptable to the weaker one. . . . It is the function of such an ideology to deny or conceal the existence of a struggle. Here is one of the answers to the question . . . as to why we have so little awareness of the fact that there is a struggle between the sexes. It is in the interest of men to obscure this fact; and the emphasis they place on their ideologies has caused women, also, to adopt these theories.

Karen Horney

How to Give Power Away and Gain Some Back

Purpose: To become more aware of the ways in which we give away power by "hypnotizing" ourselves with the words we use to describe our own actions.

Directions: I Have to—I Choose to

1. Pair up with someone and sit facing this person. Throughout the experiment, maintain eye contact and talk directly to this person. Take turns saying sentences to each other that begin with the words "I have to—" Make a long list of things that you have to do. (If you do this experiment alone, say these sentences out loud and imagine that you are saying them to some person you know [or write them down].) . . . Take about five minutes to do this. . . .

2. Now go back to all the sentences you just said and replace "I have to—" with "I *choose* to—" and take turns saying these sentences to your partner. Say exactly what you said before except for this change. . . . Realize that you do have the power of making a choice, even if that choice is between two undesirable alternatives. Take time to be aware of how you experience saying each sentence that begins with "I choose to—" Then repeat this sentence and immediately add any sentence that comes to you next. For example, "I choose to stay with my job. I feel safe and secure." Again take about five minutes to do this. . . .

3. Now take a few minutes to tell each other what you experienced as you did this. Do you have any actual experience of taking responsibility for your choices—any feeling of waking up a little from your self-hypnosis, any discovery of more power and possibilities? . . .*

Now do the same with each of the following:
I Can't–I Won't
I Need–I Want
I'm Afraid to–I Want to
Say sentences beginning with the first member of each pair, making a list of sentences as in the "I Have to" example above. Then repeat the sentences replacing the first member of the pair with the second. Be aware of your experience while you do this and share your experiences with your partner.

Dair L. Gillespie

Who Has the Power? The Marital Struggle

The Changing Power Structure

Modern theorists of the family agree that the American family has evolved from a paternalistic to a much more democratic form. Before the Civil War married women had many duties, few rights. They were not permitted to control their property, even when it was theirs by inheritance or dower, or to make a will. To all intents and purposes they did not own property. The husband had the right to collect and use the wife's wages, to decide upon the education and religion of the children, and to punish his wife if she displeased him. The right to will children, even unborn, to other guardians was retained by the husband. In the case of divorce, when granted at all, the husband had the right to determine the control of the children. To a married woman, her husband was her superior, her companion, her master. In every sector of the social arena, women were in a subordinate position. The church was one of the most potent forces for maintaining them in this position. Within the church, women were segregated from men, were not allowed to sing, preach or take public action. There were no high schools for girls, and no college in the world admitted women. Unpropertied males, slaves, and all women were not allowed into the political process at all.

Today, as the textbooks never tire of telling us, couples are more free to choose partners than formerly, they are able to separate more easily, the differences in age and culture between husband and wife are less marked than formerly, the husband recognizes more willingly the independence of his wife's demands, they may share housekeeping and diversions, and the wife may even work. In fact, sociologists claim that the modern husband and wife are so nearly equal in power that marriage today can be termed "democratic," "equalitarian," or "egalitarian."

These changes in the form of marriage are generally attributed to the entrance of women into the economic structure and to the extension of an equalitarian ideology to cover women. This type of explanation is careful to emphasize socioeconomic conditions of the past and the "rise of women" in the American economy. However, socioeconomic conditions of the present are no longer examined, for it is assumed that women have won their rights in all social arenas, and if they haven't—well, ideology takes a while to filter down to the masses. New egalitarian ideals, they tell us, will bring about further socioeconomic changes and a better position for women.

In a major research project on the modern American family, Blood and Wolfe state:

Under former historical circumstances, the husband's economic and social role almost automatically gave him pre-eminence. Under modern conditions, the roles of men and women have changed so much that husbands and wives are potential equals—with the balance of power tipped sometimes one way, sometimes the other. It is no longer possible to assume that just because a man is a man, he is the boss. Once upon a time, the function of culture was to rationalize the predominance of the male sex. Today the function of culture is to develop a philosophy of equal rights under which the saying goes, "May the best man win!"—and the best man is sometimes a woman. The role of culture has shifted from sanctioning a competent sex over an incompetent sex to sanctioning the competent marriage partner over the incompetent one, regardless of sex.[1]

There is good evidence, however, that the balance of power is tipped the same way it always was, and that the best man is very seldom a woman. I am arguing, then, against the *personal* resource theory and am positing that, in fact, this is still a caste/class system rationalizing the preeminence of the male sex.

The Measurement of Power

Before examining the causes of male dominance in marital power, I would like to examine first how Blood and Wolfe* conceive of power and how they measure it. Operationally, power is restricted to who makes the final decision in each of eight areas, ranging from those traditionally held entirely by the husband to those held entirely by the wife. These eight areas include:

1. What job the husband should take.
2. What car to get.
3. Whether or not to buy life insurance.
4. Where to go on a vacation.
5. What house or apartment to take.
6. Whether or not the wife should go to work or quit work.
7. What doctor to have when someone is sick.

---

*Blood and Wolfe's work plays a major part in this paper because it has been one of the most influential studies of marriage in the last 10 years.

8. How much money the family can afford to spend per week on food.

These questions were asked because (a) they are all relatively important, (b) they are questions which nearly all couples have to face, and (c) they range from typically masculine to typically feminine decisions, but affect the family as a whole.[2]

This measurement of power leaves much to be desired. Safilios-Rothschild has made probably the most telling criticisms of such studies. She points out that all decisions are given equal weight even though not all decisions have "objectively" the same degree of importance for the entire life of the family. Which job the husband would take (with important consequences in terms of time to be spent away from home, location of job, salary level, amount of leisure available, etc.) and which doctor to call were considered decisions equally affecting the family and the balance of power within the family. Further, some decisions are made less frequently than others; thus, while a decision such as "what food to buy" requires a daily or weekly enactment, a decision such as "what car to buy" is only made every few years. In addition, some decisions are "important" and frequent, others frequent but not "important," others "important" and not frequent, and still others not important and not frequent. Thus, the familial power structure may not be solely determined on the number of areas of decisions that one can appropriate for himself/herself. She also mentioned the multidimensionality of some of the decision-making areas and suggested that it is possible that one spouse decides which make of car to buy and the other specifies color.[3]

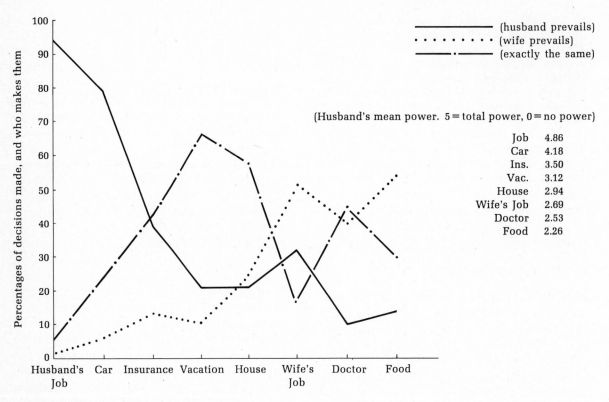

(husband prevails)
(wife prevails)
(exactly the same)

(Husband's mean power. 5 = total power, 0 = no power)

Job	4.86
Car	4.18
Ins.	3.50
Vac.	3.12
House	2.94
Wife's Job	2.69
Doctor	2.53
Food	2.26

Source: Plotted from data contained in Robert O. Blood, Jr., and Donald M. Wolfe, *Husbands and Wives: The Dynamics of Married Living* (New York: Free Press, 1960).

Fig. 1 Husband's Mean Power in Family Decision-Making Areas

It seems, then, that the conception and measurement of power is already biased in that it does not expose certain kinds of power which automatically accrue to the husband by virtue of his work; and second, that it takes no account of the differential importance of the eight decisions in the power structure of the marriage. Further, there is good evidence that even if we accepted Blood and Wolfe's measures as being true measures of power, the husband still controls most of the power decisions in the family (Fig. 1). I must conclude, then, that the husband has much more power than he appears to have according to Blood and Wolfe's analysis.

Their discussion of "who decides" is even more convincing evidence that there are power differentials which are being overlooked. For example, they explain:

That the husband should be more involved in his wife's job decisions than she with his is understandable. For one thing, her work is seldom her major preoccupation in life the way it is for a man. Even if she works just as many hours a week, she does not usually make the same lifelong commitment to the world of work. Nor is her paycheck indispensable to the family finances (if only because it is smaller). In such ways the choice of whether to work or not is less vital to a woman than to a man.

In addition, the wife's decisions about working have repercussions on the husband. If his wife goes to work, he will have to help out more around the house. If he is a business executive, he may prefer to have her concentrate her energy on entertaining prospective clients at home. As a small businessman or independent professional, he may need her services in his own enterprise. On the other hand, regardless of his own occupation, he may want her to work in order to help him buy a house or a business or pay for the children's education.

It may be, then, that the work role is so much the responsibility of the husband in marriage that even the wife's work is but an adjunct of his instrumental leadership, leaving this decision in his hands.[4]

In these *justifications* of the division of power, Blood and Wolfe use the device of examining why a husband would want more power in particular areas. The basic assumption is, of course, that he can have it if he wants it. I think a more pertinent question would be not who wants power, since there are always myriad reasons why anyone would want power, but why he is able to get it if he wants it. This question is not even broached.

William Goode . . . comments on this aspect of power and authority:

After evaluating the conflicting comments and data published by Shaffner, Rodnick, Schelski and Wruzbacher, Baumert comes to the conclusion, which seems eminently reasonable, that claims of fundamental equalitarianism in the German family (or in any other European family) are not correct and that an unequivocally equalitarian family is rarely to be found. In the final analysis, only a few family relations are not determined by the male. It is not possible at present to state just how well such a statement could be applied to other countries. In reality, in all countries there are many women who manage to dominate the man, but it seems likely that in most countries, when the husband tries to dominate he can still do this. Even when the husband performs the household chores, his participation means that he gains power—the household becoming a further domain for the exercise of prerogatives for making decisions.

Perhaps the crucial qualitative difference is to be found in the extent to which, in one country or another, the male can still dominate *without* a definite effort to do so.[5]

Goode calls this "negative authority—the right to prevent others from doing what they want."[6]

I must conclude, then, that the power structure is much more lopsided than Blood and Wolfe lead us to believe, and that it is the husband who holds this hidden power. Why does the husband have all this power? How does he obtain it? How does he maintain it?

It is assumed that most marriages begin with partners at a somewhat egalitarian level. All evidence points to homogamous marriage, i.e., that the woman's *husband* and *father* occupy similar positions in the socioeconomic structure. However, regardless of her background, "her future rank is mainly determined by the future job achievement of the man she marries, rather than by the class position of his family,"[7]

Untitled drawing by Melissa Mathis

or hers, needless to say. In discussing differentials in power which emerge in marriage, most social scientists use an individualistic perspective as do Blood and Wolfe in *Husbands and Wives*. They remark:

> The balance of power is, after all, an interpersonal affair, and the wife's own characteristics cannot long be disregarded if we are to understand who makes the decisions. Whenever possible it is desirable to compare the wife and the husband on the same characteristics, for then the comparative resourcefulness and competence of the two partners can be discovered. Once we know which partner has more education, more organizational experience, a higher status background, etc. we will know who tends to make the most decisions.[8]

The major error made by Blood and Wolfe (and others who use this perspective) is in assuming that this control of competence and resources occurs in individual couples by chance rather than being structurally predetermined (in a statistical sense) in favor of the male. To state it more clearly, I am arguing that it is still a caste/class system, rationalizing the preponderance of dominant males. The distribution of power is not an interpersonal affair, but a class affair. Blood and Wolfe continue:

> Some husbands today are just as powerful as their grandfathers were—but they can no longer take for granted the authority held by older generations of men. No longer is the husband able to exercise power just because he is the "man of the house." Rather, he must prove his right to power, or win power by virtue of his own skills and accomplishments *in competition with his wife*.[9]

I am arguing that in the competition with his wife, the man has most of the advantages. If we assume that the marriage contract is a mutual mobility bet for gaining ascendancy in power, personal autonomy, and self-realization, we will find that the opportunity for winning the bet is very slim for the woman. She is already at a disadvantage when she signs the contract. For further self-realization, for further gains in status and experience as compared with her husband, the cards are already stacked against her, for women are *structurally* deprived of equal opportunities to develop their capacities, resources, and competence in competition with males.

Since theorists of marriage have a quite notable tendency to disregard the psychological, legal, and social blocks put in the way of women as a class when they are discussing power differentials and their sources, I would like to examine some of these differences.

Sources of Marital Power

Socialization

Men and women are differentially socialized. By the time women reach marriageable age, we

Marriage is the destiny traditionally offered to women by society. It is still true that most women are married, or have been, or plan to be, or suffer from not being. The celibate [single] woman is to be explained and defined with reference to marriage whether she is frustrated, rebellious, or even indifferent in regard to that institution.

Simone de Beauvoir

have already been damaged by the socialization process. We have been systematically trained to accept second best, not to strive, and to accept the "fact" that we are unworthy of more. Naomi Weisstein's *Kinde, Küche, Kirche As Scientific Law* states this process clearly:

How are women characterized in our culture, and in psychology? They are inconsistent, emotionally unstable, lacking in strong conscience or superego, weaker, "nurturant" rather than productive, "intuitive" rather than intelligent, and if they are at all "normal," suited to the home and family. In short, the list adds up to a typical minority group stereotype of inferiority: if they know their place, which is in the home, they are really quite loveable, happy, childlike, loving creatures. In a review of the intellectual differences between little boys and little girls, Eleanor Maccoby has shown that there are no intellectual differences until about high school, or if there are, girls are slightly ahead of boys. At high school, the achievement of women now measured in terms of productivity and accomplishment, drops off even more rapidly. There are a number of other, non-intellectual tests which show sex differences; I chose the intellectual differences since it is seen clearly that women start becoming inferior. It is no use to talk about women being different but equal; all of the tests I can think of have a "good" outcome and a "bad" outcome. Women usually end up at the "bad" outcome. In light of social expectations about women, what is surprising is not that women end up where society expects they will; what is surprising is that little girls don't get the message that

they are supposed to be stupid until high school, and what is even more remarkable is that some women resist this message even after high school, college, and graduate school.[10]

Thus, women begin at a psychological disadvantage when we sign the marriage contract, for we have differential training and expectations.

Marriage: A Free Contract Between Equals

Sociologists universally fail to discuss legal differences in power when the marriage contract is signed.* Marriage is ordinarily considered a contract freely entered into by both partners, and the partners are assumed to stand on common footing of equal rights and duties. Sheila Cronan[11] examined this "free" contract between equals and found a few unlisted terms.

Sex. She found that the husband can legally force his wife to have sexual intercourse with him against her will, an act which if committed against any other woman would constitute the crime of rape. By definition, a husband cannot be guilty of raping his own wife, for "the crime (of rape) is ordinarily that of forcing intercourse

---

*It should be made clear that legality is not necessarily a basis for decision making. It merely reflects the position of society as to how the power is to be distributed when such distributions are contested in the courts. This normally occurs upon dissolution of marriage and not in an ongoing relationship.

Any woman who reads the marriage certificate and then goes through with it, deserves what she gets.

Isadora Duncan

---

on someone other than the wife of the person accused."[12] Women are well aware of the "right" of the husband to "insist" and the "duty" of the wife to submit to sexual intercourse. The compulsory nature of sex in marriage operates to the advantage of the male, for though the husband theoretically has the duty to have intercourse with his wife, this normally cannot occur against his will. (Both partners are protected in that a marriage can be annulled by either party if the marriage has not been consummated.)

Other marital responsibilities. Women believe that we are voluntarily giving our household services, but the courts hold that the husband is legally entitled to his wife's services, and further, that *she cannot be paid for her work.* In *Your Marriage and the Law,* Pilpel and Zavin state:

> As part of the rights of consortium, the husband is entitled to the services of his wife. If the wife works outside the home for strangers, she is usually entitled to her own earnings. But domestic services or assistances which she gives her husband are generally considered part of her wifely duties. The wife's services and society are so essential a part of what the law considers the husband is entitled to as part of the marriage that it will not recognize any agreement between spouses which provides that the husband is to pay for such services or society.

In a Texas case David promised his wife, Fannie, that he would give her $5000 if she would stay with him while he lived and continue taking care of the house and farm accounts, selling his butter and doing all the other tasks which she had done since their marriage. After David's death, Fannie sued his estate for the money which had been promised her. The court held that the contract was unenforceable since Fannie had agreed to do nothing which she was not already legally and morally bound to do as David's wife.[13]

The legal responsibilities of a wife are to live in the home established by her husband, to perform the domestic chores (cleaning, cooking, washing, etc.) necessary to help maintain that home, and to care for her husband and children (Gallen 1967:4). The husband, in return, is obligated to provide her with basic maintenance which includes "necessities" such as food, clothing, medical care, and a place to live, in accordance with his income. She has no legal right to any part of his cash income, nor any legal voice in spending it.[14] Were he to employ a live-in servant in place of a wife, he would have to pay the servant a salary, provide her with her own room (as opposed to "bed"), food, and the necessary equipment for doing her job. She would get at least one day a week off and probably would be required to do considerably less work than a wife and would not be required to provide sexual services.

In 1970, Margaret Mead was quoted by Robert Williams as warning women in the Women's Liberation Movement that they might literally be driving men insane. The reverse seems more likely. It is wives who are driven mad, not by men but by the anachronistic way in which marriage is structured today—or, rather, the life style which accompanies marriage today and which demands that all wives be housewives. In truth, being a housewife makes women sick.

Jessie Bernard

Thus, being a wife is a full-time job for which one is not entitled to pay. (Chase Manhattan Bank estimates a woman's overall work week at 99.6 hours.) Furthermore, the wife is not entitled to freedom of movement. The husband has the right to decide where the family will live. If he decides to move, his wife is obliged to go with him. If she refuses, he can charge her with desertion. This has been upheld by the courts even in cases where the wife could be required to change her citizenship. In states where desertion is grounds for divorce (47 states plus the District of Columbia), the wife would be the "guilty party" and would therefore be entitled to no monetary settlement.[15]

A married woman's name. Leo Kanowitz . . . found that the change in a woman's name upon marriage is not only consistent with social custom, it also appears to be generally required by law.

> The probable effects of this unilateral name change upon the relations between the sexes, though subtle in character, are profound. In a very real sense, the loss of a woman's surname represents the destruction of an important part of her personality and its submersion in that of her husband. . . . This name change is consistent with the characterization of coverture as "the old common-law fiction that the husband and wife are one . . . [which] has worked out in reality to mean that the one is the husband."[16]

The law of support. The universal rule is that it is the primary obligation of the husband to provide financial support for the family. Kanowitz explored some of the legal ramifications of this general rule.

> The effects of the basic rule upon the marital relationship itself are complex. In common law marital property jurisdictions, the husband's legal obligation to support the family is not an umixed blessing for the wife. That obligation has been cited, for example, as justifying his right to choose the family home. It has no doubt also played an important part in solidifying his legal role as head and master of the family. For in according the husband this position within the family, the law often seems to be applying on a grand scale the modest principle that "he who pays the piper calls the tune." However, even in the community property states, in which a wife's services in the home are theoretically viewed as being equal to or exceeding in monetary value the husband's earnings outside of the home, husbands have generally been given the rights to manage and control the community property, along with other superior rights and interests in it.[17]

Thus, it is clear that husbands have access to legal advantages which wives do not have. True the wife does gain legal protection against capricious action by the male, but in exchange, she becomes his vassal. He is the economic head of the joint household, and hence, represents it in view of society. She takes his name

Is it possible that the male is sexually dependent on the female to a higher degree than the woman is on him, because in women part of the sexual energy is linked to generative processes? Could it be that men, therefore, have a vital interest in keeping women dependent on them? So much for the factors that seem to be at the root of the great power struggle between men and women, insofar as they are of a psychogenic nature and related to the male.

Karen Horney

---

and belongs to his class. She follows where his work calls to determine their place of residence. Their lives are geared to the daily, weekly, annual rhythms of his life. She gives him her person and her private labor, but he wants more.

The "White Man's Burden." In today's "love match," the husband does not merely require an obedient and efficient worker, he wants something more. He wants his wife to love him, that is, to freely choose over and over again to be subjected to the control of the other, to make his welfare the center of her being.[18] [Yet this] very demand is the crux of what husbands term their "oppression" as Simone de Beauvoir has so clearly observed:

> Her very devotion seems annoying, importunate; it is transformed for the husband into a tyranny from which he tries to escape; and yet he it is who imposes it upon his wife as her supreme, her unique justification. In marrying her, he obliges her to give herself entirely to him; but he does not assume the corresponding obligation, which is to accept this gift and all its consequences.
>
> It is the duplicity of the husband that dooms his wife to a misfortune of which he complains that he is himself the victim. Just as he wants her to be at once warm and cool in bed, he requires her to be wholly his and yet no burden; he wishes her to establish him in a fixed place on earth and to leave him free; to assume the monotonous daily round and not to bore him; to be always at hand

and never importunate; he wants to have her all to himself and not to belong to her, to live as one of a couple, and to remain alone. Thus she is betrayed from the day he marries her. Her life through, she measures the extent of that betrayal.[19]

Throughout their lives together, she attempts to wrest back from him some measure of her independence. Surely it is not entirely an accident that divorce rates are highest at this early phase of the marriage cycle and drop with the birth of children, when women are most dependent upon the husband economically and emotionally.

Economic Sources of Power

It is clear that an economic base of power is important in marriage, for the higher the husband on the social scale, the greater his decision-making [power] in the family. Using three indices of success in the community, Blood and Wolfe found that all three affected power differentials in the family.

1. The higher the husband's occupational prestige, the greater his voice in marital decisions.
2. Income was an even more sensitive indicator of power than occupation. The higher the husband's income, the greater his power.
3. The higher the husband's status (based on occupation, income, education, and ethnic

If there is no God at least there is a man to love. So all her displaced
energy flows into a man-woman relationship. There surely she will find
her deepest values. This tenuous human relationship becomes her all.
She fills it with her idealism, her expectations and her love. There is no
limit to the value it is asked to hold.

Irene de Castillijos

---

background), the more power he had to make decisions.

The major break in power fell between white-collar and blue-collar husbands. High white-collar workers had the most power, then low white-collar workers. Within the blue-collar category, however, low blue-collar husbands had more power than high blue-collar husbands when compared on the basis of their relative occupational prestige and social status. I shall discuss some of the possible causes of this deviation in the section on education.

These material bases of power were operant despite the fact that middle-class husbands espouse a more egalitarian ideology than do working-class husbands. William Goode commented on this tension between the ideal and the real distributions of power.

Since at present this philosophy [of equalitarianism in the family] is most strongly held among better educated segments of the population, and among women more than among men, two interesting tensions may be seen: Lower-class men concede fewer rights *ideologically* than their women in fact *obtain*, and the more educated men are more likely to concede *more* rights ideologically than they in fact grant.[20]

He then supplies us with an excellent example of how ideology may be modified to justify the current distribution of power:

One partial resolution of the latter tension is to be found in the frequent assertion from families of professional men that they should not make demands which would interfere with his *work*: He takes preference as a *professional*, not as a family head or as a male; nevertheless, the precedence is his. By contrast, lower-class men demand deference as *men*, as heads of families.

As we can see, marital power is a function of income to a large extent, and egalitarian philosophies have very little impact on the actual distribution of power. It seems clear that the authority of the male is used as a justification of power where it is useful (working-class), and new justifications will arise as they are useful, as in the case of professional men who demand deference because of their work, thus enabling them to accept the doctrine of equality while at the same time undermining it for their own benefit as males. If this is the effect of that much touted egalitarian ideology which will bring about better conditions for women and racial and ethnic minorities as soon as it filters down to the masses, it seems we will have a long, long wait for cosmic justice.

Blood and Wolfe claim that this superior power of high-status husbands is not due to coercion, but to the recognition by both partners that the husband is the one eminently qualified to make the decisions in the family. This argument is reminiscent of arguments in labor relations. The labor contract is assumed to be freely entered into by both partners. The power conferred on the one party by the difference in class position—the real economic position of both—is not taken into account. That economic relations compel the worker to surrender even the last semblance of equal rights is of no concern. Coercion (however subtle) based on economic power is still coercion, whether it involves wife-beating or not.

As further evidence that individual competence and resourcefulness (regardless of sex) are not the real issues, we must examine Blood and Wolfe's discussion of the *deviant* case—[the dominant wife]. In these cases, they claim that wives who have superior power acquire it, not because they have access to pragmatic sources of power or because they are more competent than their husbands (heaven forbid!), but by default.

> We will find throughout this study dissatisfaction associated with wife-dominance. This is not, however, simply a reflection of the breaking of social rules. Rather, the circumstances which lead to the wife's dominance involve corresponding inadequacies on the husband's part. An inadequate husband is by definition unable to make a satisfactory marriage partner. So the dominant wife is not exultant over her "victory" but exercises power regretfully by default of her "no good" or incapacitated husband.[21]

For Blood and Wolfe, wives can never gain dominance legitimately; it falls in our unhappy laps and is accepted only unwillingly and with much bitterness.

Despite the superior power gained by the husband because of his economic position, there are conditions under which wives do erode that power to some extent. Not surprisingly, the wife's participation in the work force

is an important variable. Women who work have more power vis-a-vis their husbands than do nonworking wives, regardless of race or class. The number of years the wife has worked also affects the balance of power—the longer she has worked, the more power she is able to obtain. This, to some extent, explains why blue-collar wives have more power than white-collar wives (in comparison to their husbands), since their participation in the work force is much higher than for the wives of high-status, high-income husbands.[22]

Organizational Participation

Organizational participation, too, is a factor which affects marital decision making as shown by Blood and Wolfe's data. Women with much more organizational participation than their husbands alter the balance of power in the wife's direction. In those cases where the participation is equal or in which the husband is superior (by far the most frequent), the balance of power increases in the husband's direction.[23]

Education

Education was also influential in the distribution of power. The more education the husband has, the greater his power. High white-collar husbands continue to gain power if they exceed their wives' education (and chances are good that they do, in fact, exceed), and they lose it if they fall short of the wife. The same trend holds within the low white-collar and high blue-collar groups, leaving a low blue-collar reversal, i.e., low blue-collar husbands have more power even when their wives have superior educations.[24]

Mirra Komarovski has drawn attention to the fact that education is a much more important variable when the husband's income and social status are relatively low. In working-class families, the less educated and unskilled husbands have more power than do those with higher incomes. She attempted to explain some of the causes of this power anomaly. First, patriarchal attitudes are more prevalent among the less educated and hence, a source of power in some families. High school graduates, because of a social milieu which does not sanction patriarchal authority (though it does sanction male privilege), tend to lose power. Second, among the less-educated, the husband is more likely to excel in personal resources for the exercise of influence, and this margin of male superiority narrows among the high school graduates. Among the less-educated, the husband has wider contacts in the community than his wife. He represents the world to his family, and he is the family's "secretary of state." In contrast, a few of the more educated wives enjoy wider contacts and higher status outside the home than their husbands. Third, the education of the spouses was found to affect their degrees of power because of mating patterns. The effect of educational inequality appears to explain the lower power of skilled workers in comparison with the semi-skilled. The skilled worker is more likely than the semi-skilled worker to marry a high school graduate. By virtue of their relatively high earnings, skilled workers may be able to marry better-educated women, but by marrying "upward" they lose the degree of power enjoyed by the semi-skilled over their less-educated wives. Fourth, male prestige, or social rank was a source of power in low blue-collar families.[25]

Physical Coercion

Komarovski is one of the few sociologists who has mentioned physical coercion as a source of power in the family. In her discussion of the low blue-collar family, she found that the use of physical violence was a source of masculine power. However, not only the use of physical violence, but its *threat* can be an effective form of control. She reports that one woman said of her husband: "He is a big man and terribly strong. One time when he got sore at me, he pulled off the banister and ripped up three steps." With the evidence of this damage in view, this woman realized, as she put it, what her husband could do to her if he should decide to strike her.[26]

Lynn O'Connor has suggested that threats of violence (in gestures of dominance) are not limited to any particular class, but are a universal source of male power and control. After discussing dominance gestures in primates, she states:

Although there have been no systematic studies of the gestures of dominance and submission in human groups, the most casual observation will show their crucial role in the day to day mechanics of oppression. An example should clarify.

A husband and wife are at a party. The wife says something that the husband does not want her to say (perhaps it reveals something about him that might threaten his ranking with other men). He quickly tightens the muscles around his jaw and gives her a rapid but intense direct stare. Outsiders don't notice the interaction, though they may have a vaguely uncomfortable feeling that they are intruding on something private. The wife, who is acutely sensitive to the gestures of the man on whom she is dependent, immediately stops the conversation, lowers or turns her head slightly, averts her eyes, or gives off some other gestures of submission which communicate acquiescence to her husband and reduce his aggression. Peace is restored; the wife has been put in her place. If the wife does not respond with submission, she

Daddy's Girl, always tense and fearful, uncool, unanalytical, lacking objectivity, appraises Daddy, and thereafter, other men, against a background of fear ("respect") and is not only unable to see the empty shell behind the aloof façade, but accepts the male definition of himself as superior. . . .

Valerie Solanis

---

can expect to be punished. When gestures of dominance fail, the dominant animal usually resorts to violence. We all know stories about husbands beating up their wives after the party when they have reached the privacy of their home. Many of us have experienced at least a few blows from husbands or lovers when we refuse to submit to them. It is difficult to assess the frequency of physical attacks within so-called love relationships, because women rarely tell even one another when they have taken place. By developing a complicated ethic of loyalty (described above in terms of privacy), men have protected themselves from such reports leaking out and becoming public information. Having already been punished for stepping out of role, the woman is more than a little reluctant to tell anyone of the punishment because it would mean violating the loyalty code, which is an even worse infraction of the rules and most likely would result in further and perhaps more severe punishment.[27]

That violence or the threat of violence may be more widespread than is currently admitted is also suggested by complaints made by wives in divorce. Goode found that almost one-third (32 percent) of the wives reported "authority-cruelty" as the reason for divorce. Authority problems are defined as being disagreements concerning permissible degree of dominance over wife and include cruelty, beating, jealousy, and "wanted to have own way."[28] Since Goode did not code cruelty or beating separately, we have no definite evidence as to the frequency

of such behavior, but there is evidence that problems with male dominance are widespread in the population. Goode comments:

. . . In different strata and groups, the husband may be permitted different control techniques. For example, the middle-class male will very likely be censured more if he uses force to control his wife than if he uses techniques of nagging, jealousy, or sulking. On the other hand, there is a strong reservoir of attitude on the part of the American male generally, that he has a *right* to tell his wife what to do. This attitude is given more overt expression, and is more frequently backed by force, in the lower strata. It is not so much that beating and cruelty are viewed as an obvious male right in marriage, but only that this is one of the techniques used from time to time, and with little or no subsequent guilt, for keeping control of the wife. . . . In our society, the husband who successfully asserts his dominance does enjoy some approval and even a modicum of envy from other males. Male dominance is to some extent actually approved.[29]

Suburbanization

Blood and Wolfe also found that families living in the suburbs were more husband-dominant than those which live in the central city. This directly contradicts the popular image of suburban life as being dominated by women and therefore, oriented toward the satisfaction of women's needs. The data showed that suburban families were more husband-dominant at every

> *The original meaning of the word "Family" (familia) . . . is the total number of slaves belonging to one man. The term was invented by the Romans to denote a new social organism, whose head ruled over wife and children and a number of slaves and who was invested under Roman paternal power with rights of life and death over them all.*
>
> Frederick Engels, *The Origin of the Family, Private Property and the State*

status level than their urban peers. They then speculated that suburban husbands were more powerful "because suburban wives feel more indebted to their husbands for providing them with a place to live which is more attractive than the industrial city of Detroit. If so, this fits the theory that power accrues to those husbands who are able to provide for their wives especially well."[30]

In a recent study on the working class in suburbia, Tallman has suggested that other factors than the wife's gratitude might be working to build up the husband's power. He constructed a profile of the working-class marriage which indicated consistently that wives tend to maintain close ties with relatives and old girl friends while husbands continue their premarital peer group associations. Social and psychological support emanates, then, not from marriage partners, but from same-sex friends, and kin from long standing and tight-knit social networks. As a consequence, there is a relatively high degree of conjugal role segmentation which is characterized in part by lack of communication between the spouses. In general the experiences of working class women are more localized and circumscribed than their male counterparts. Since their security and identity depend upon their position vis-a-vis a small group of intimates, their opinions and beliefs are both dependent upon and in accord with this group. Blue-collar women have minimal experience in the external world and tend to view

it fearfully. Men, on the other hand, have more frequent social contacts, in part for occupational reasons, but also because they have been socialized into male roles which define them as family representatives to the outside world.

Tallman concluded that suburban women are more isolated because of disruptions in the primary group relations. The disruption of friendship and kinship ties are not only personally disintegrating for the wife but also demand fundamental changes in the role allocations in the family. Suburban wives are more dependent upon their husbands for a variety of services previously provided by members of tight-knit networks. In brief, he found that moving to the suburbs was experienced as a disintegrative force in the lives of many working-class women, leading to a greater isolation and dependence upon the husbands.[31] This partial explanation of the husband's increased power in the suburbs as being due to the wife's increased isolation and dependence seems eminently more reasonable than Blood and Wolfe's explanation that it is due to gratitude on the part of the wife. Tallman's data also indicates that the wife frequently regrets the move to the suburbs, despite more pleasant living conditions, because of its disruption of the kinship and friendship network.

Race

Blood and Wolfe report very little on black families, except to say that Negro husbands

*The primary role of women is in the home and family . . . men still
need a good mother to come to with their little troubles. Women should
provide a place of refuge where the husband and children can return
from a busy, confused and complex world.*

Belle Spafford, president, Women's Auxiliary,
Church of Jesus Christ of Latter-Day Saints

---

have unusually low power. Their data show that white husbands are always more powerful than their Negro status equals and that this is true within each occupational stratum, each income bracket, and each social level.* They concede that "the label 'black' is almost a synonym for low status in our society—and Detroit Negroes are no exception in having less education, lower incomes, inferior jobs, and lower prestige generally than whites. Since low status white husbands make relatively few decisions, we would expect Negro husbands to exercise little power, too."[32]

What they fail to take into account (among other things) is that black women, too, are discriminated against in this society. They, too, have less education, lower incomes, inferior jobs, and lower prestige generally than whites. The fact that blacks are discriminated against does not explain power differentials within black families. To explain power differentials in black families, just as for white families, the sources of power for black men and black women must be examined and compared. Blood and Wolfe fail to do this.

Their primary purpose seems to be to demonstrate gross differences between black and white families, without bothering to report differences within black families. Andrew and Amy Tate Billingsley have criticized just this approach used in sociological studies, [drawing] attention to the fact that class variables are as important in black families as in white families. "Negro families are not only Negroes to be compared and contrasted with white families, they may also be upper-class (10 percent), middle-class (40 percent), or lower-class (50 percent), with urban or rural moorings, with southern or northern residence, and most importantly, they may be meaningfully compared and contrasted with each other."[33]

Billingsley accounts to some extent for what may be part of the white/black differentials in overall power. [They note] that Negro samples are dominated by low-income families and point out that even where income levels between whites and blacks are similar, the groups are not truly comparable, for the Negro group reflects not only its income level but its experience with prejudice and subjugation as well.

---

*Blood and Wolfe's report of the data is so skimpy that it makes interpretation difficult. For example, they say the 35 high income husbands (over $4,000) have lower mean power (4.09) than their 68 less affluent colleagues (4.56). This is possibly analogous to the distribution in the white blue-collar class, where low blue-collar husbands have more power than the high blue-collar husbands. Comparisons are difficult because, for the general population, income was broken into five groups, while for black families they used only two—over $4,000 and below $4,000. They reported that "the generalization that the husband's power is correlated with occupational status also holds within the Negro race" (4.31, 4.60, no cases, and 5.00 respectively). The only mention of Negro husbands and social status was that the few white husbands in the lowest status groups differ sharply from their powerless Negro counterparts (no figures reported).

Even a marriage is not made secure until the wife has succeeded in making her husband her child as well and in acting as a mother to him.

Sigmund Freud

Because both black husbands and black wives are discriminated against in this society, it is absurd to explain power differentials between them as being due to race (as Blood and Wolfe do), unless there are mitigating factors brought about by racial discrimination which operate in favor of one sex's access to sources of marital power. Since data on the black family are so sadly inadequate, I can at this point only examine some demographic data which have possible implications for power distributions in black families.

Black women comprised 40 percent of all black workers in 1960. They earned considerably less than black men. The median earnings of full-time year round black women in 1959 was two-fifths that of black men. (In 1964, it was 64.2 percent.) The unemployment rate for black women is higher than for black men. In 1967, for Negro men aged 20–64, the unemployment rate was 3.7. For Negro women it was 6.0. The unemployment rates for black women under 20 were also higher than for Negro men. Clearly, then, black women are not superior to black men in income.[34]

In occupational status, we find that Negro women are most frequently in service jobs while Negro men are predominantly blue-collar workers. However, relatively more Negro women than men had professional or technical jobs, this being due primarily to their extensive employment as teachers and nurses. Of all full-time year-round Negro workers in 1960,

Negro women constituted nearly all the private household workers. They were more than half the number of Negroes employed as professional workers (61 percent) and other service workers (51 percent). Except for the clerical group in which the numbers were about equal, the remaining occupational groups (sales, managers, operatives, crafts, laborers, and farmers) had fewer Negro women than men.[35]

Negro women in general had a higher median education than Negro men. (This is also true in the white population.) The median educational level of non-white women was 8.5 years in 1960, but for men it was 7.9. However, at the top of the educational ladder, just as for the white population, men are more numerous.[36]

Though there are differences, we find that the relations *between the sexes* for both Negroes and whites are similar. Obviously, black men have suffered from discrimination in this society. This is evident in the figures of income, occupation, and education. However, it is also evident that Negro women have suffered discrimination, not only because of race, but also because of their sex. Thus, they are doubly oppressed. This, too, is evident in figures of income, occupation, and education.

Jessie Bernard . . . has suggested still another variable which must be taken into account in Negro family patterns. She reports that there is an extraordinarily low sex ratio (number of males per 100 females) among urban Negroes as compared to whites. The ratio is especially low (88.4) in the critical years of marriageability. Bernard conjectures that the low sex ratio means that Negro women are competing for a relatively scarce "good" when they look forward to marriage, being buyers in a sellers' market.[37] While this is certainly not the cause of power distributions in the black family, it does suggest a source of male power.* Delores Mack, in a study of black and white families, supports this contention:

What these findings suggest is that researchers have not carefully evaluated the logic of the assumptions of their hypotheses. They have looked at the white community; there they have observed that education, occupation, and income are important sources of power. . . . They have ignored the possibility that the sources of power in the Black community may be different from that in the white community. In fact, they have ignored one of the most potent forms of power in any marriage, but particularly sex power in Black marriages. Certainly researchers have noted the preoccupation of the Black male with sex. Some have viewed this preoccupation with sex as a form of escapism, failing to realize that this concentration on sexual activities may be a main source of power. The Black male is well aware, as Eldridge Cleaver notes, that he is the desired sex object for both the white and the Black female. He may use this power in his marriage, much as the white male uses his education and earning power as a lever in his marriage.[38]

_____

*This has also been suggested in several articles in _The Black Woman_, edited by Toni Cade (New York: New American Library, 1970), particularly "Dear Black Man," Fran Sanders; "Who Will Revere the Black Woman?", Abbey Lincoln; "The Black Woman as Woman," Kay Lindsey; "Double Jeopardy: To Be Black and Female," Frances Beale; "On the Issue of Roles," Toni Cade; "Black Man, My Man, Listen!," Gail Stokes; "Is the Black Man Castrated?," Jean Carey Bond and Pat Peery.

The threat or use of physical violence (as discussed above) is another factor which must be taken into account to explain power distributions in black as well as in white families. Obviously, a great deal of research on the differences within black families is needed, as Billingsley has suggested.

Life Cycle

The stages of the family life cycle also affect the marital power distribution. In the early (childless) stage of marriage, the wife is frequently working, but the pressure of social discrimination against women is already beginning to be exerted. Women are unable to procure anything but low paying, low status jobs as compared with their husbands. Already status background and autonomous experiences are being eroded. Though the married childless woman maintains some sort of independent social and economic status if she works, it is below that of her husband. During this period; the power of the husband is moderate.

With the birth of children, there is a substantial jump in power differentials, the husband universally gaining.[39] There is more than a little truth in the old saw that the best way to control a woman is to "keep her barefoot and pregnant," for there is evidence that the power of the wife declines as the number of children grows.[40] At this period after the first child is born, but before the oldest child is in school, the power of the husband reaches its maximum. Many women stop working during this stage and in doing so, become isolated and almost totally dependent socially, economically, and emotionally upon their husbands, further eroding any strength they may have gained due to earning power or participation in organizations.

[A woman who stops working] loses her position, cannot keep up with developments in her field, does not build up seniority. Further, she loses that precious "organizational" experience, the growth of competence and resources in the outside world, the community positions which contribute to power in the marriage. The boundaries of her world contract, the possibilities of growth diminish. If she returns to work, and most women do, she must begin again at a low-status job and she stays there— underemployed and underpaid. As her children grow up, she gradually regains some power in the family.

These data again call into question the theory of individual resources as the source of power in marriage. As David Heer pointed out, there is no reason, according to Blood and Wolfe's theory, for the power of the wife to be greater before she has borne children than when her children are pre-school age. Surely the wife with pre-school children is contributing more resources to the marriage than she did before their children were born.[41] Power, then, is clearly not the result of individual contributions and resources in the marriage, but is related to questions of social worth; and the value of women and women's work, as viewed by society, is obviously very low. The contributions of women in the home are of little concern and are consequently little valued, as Margaret Benston explained: "The Political Economy of Women's Liberation."[42]

In sheer quantity, household labor, including child care, constitutes a huge amount of socially necessary production. Nevertheless, in a society based on commodity production, it is not usually considered "real work" since it is outside of trade and market place. It is pre-capitalist in a very real

The Family by Sue Negrin

sense. The assignment of household work as the function of a special category "women" meant that this group *does* stand in a different relation to the production than the group "men." We will tentatively define women, then, as that group of people who are responsible for the production of simple use-values in those activities associated with the home and the family.

Since men carry no responsibility for such production, the difference between the two groups lies here. Notice that women are not excluded from commodity production. Their participation in wage labor occurs, but as a group, they have no structural responsibility in this area and such

Oh, hard is the fortune of all womankind,
She's always controlled, she's always confined,
Controlled by her parent until she's a wife,
A slave to her husband the rest of her life.

Traditional American Folk Ballad

---

participation is ordinarily regarded as transient. Men, on the other hand, are responsible for commodity production; they are not, in principle, given any role in household labor. . . . The material basis for the inferior status of women is to be found in just this definition of women. In a society in which money determines value, women are a group who work outside the money economy. Their work is not worth money, is therefore valueless, is therefore not even real work. And women themselves, who do this valueless work, can hardly be expected to be worth as much as men, who work for money. In structural terms, the closest thing to the condition of women is the condition of others who are or were outside of commodity production, i.e., peasants or serfs.

The Husband: Most Likely To Succeed

Thus, it is clear that for a wife to gain even a modicum of power in the marital relationship, she must obtain it from external sources, i.e., she must participate in the work force, her education must be superior to that of her husband, and her participation in organizations must excel his. Equality of resources leaves the power in the hands of the husband. Access to these sources of power is structurally blocked for women, however.

In the general population, women are unable to procure anything but low-status, low-paying, dead-end jobs as compared with their husbands, be it [in the] factory or [in the] university.[43] Partly as a result of unequal pay for the same work, partly as a consequence of chan-

neling women into low-paying jobs, the median income of women is far less than that of men workers. Black women tend to fare slightly better in relation to black men, but make only two-thirds as much as white women.

MEDIAN INCOME OF YEAR-ROUND FULL-TIME WORKERS BY SEX AND COLOR, 1964.[44]*

	Men	Women	Women as % of Men
White	$6,497	$3,859	59.4
Nonwhite	4,285	2,674	62.2

In higher socioeconomic classes, the husband is more likely to excel his wife in formal education than he is among blue-collar workers. Men predominate among college graduates, regardless of race, but adult women have a higher median of education (12.1 for women, 12.0 for men in 1964.)[45] (We have already seen that the educational attainment of the non-white population is lower (8.5 for women, 7.9 for men), reflecting discrimination on the basis of race.)

All of these areas are sources of power in the marital relationship, and in all of these areas women are structurally blocked from realizing our capacities. It is not because of individual resources of personal competence, then, that

*1973 figures

	Men	Women	Women as % of Men
White	$11,633	$6,544	56.3
Nonwhite	8,363	5,772	69.0

from **Doing It Differently**

We will be equal, we say, new man and new woman.
But what man am I equal to before the law of court or custom?
The state owns my womb and hangs a man's name on me
like the tags hung on dogs, my name is, property of. . . .

We are equal if we make ourselves so, every day, every night
constantly renewing what the street destroys.

Marge Piercy

---

husbands obtain power in marriage, but because of the discrimination against women in the larger society. Men gain resources as a class, not as individuals, and women are blocked as a class, not as individuals.

In our mutual mobility bet the woman (as a class) always loses in the fight for power within the marital relationship. We live in a system of institutionalized male supremacy, and the cards are systematically stacked against women in all areas—occupational, political, educational, legal, [and familial]. As long as the structure of society remains the same, as long as categorical discrimination against women is carried out, there is relatively little chance for the woman to gain autonomy, *regardless* of how much good will there is on the part of her husband.

The equalitarian marriage as a norm is a myth. Under some conditions, women can gain power vis-a-vis their husbands; i.e., working women [and] women with higher educations than their husbands have more power than housewives or women with lesser or identical education . . . but more power is not equal power. Equal power we do not have. Equal power we will never get so long as the present socioeconomic system remains.

For Further Reading

*Allport, G. 1954. *The Nature of Prejudice.* New York: Addison-Wesley.

*Aries, P. 1962. *Centuries of Childhood.* New York: Random House.

Bernard, J. 1972. *The Future of Marriage.* New York: World Publishing.

*Fanon, F. 1967. *Black Skin, White Masks.* New York: Grove Press.

——1963. *Wretched of the Earth.* New York: Grove Press.

*Komarovsky, M. 1962. *Blue Collar Marriage.* New York: Random House.

*Laing, R. D. 1971. *Intimate Oppression: The Politics of the Family and Other Essays.* New York: Pantheon.

Ethnic Diversity of Female Experience

The purpose of this chapter is to describe how the psychology of women is interpreted uniquely for each woman depending on her racial and ethnic background. Psychological oppression, for instance, has additional implications for Third World women, one of which is that they suffer dual psychological oppression both as members of a racial minority and as women. Another factor is that white women suffer primarily from psychological oppression, whereas Third World women suffer also from physical and material oppression as well. In the first article Linda La Rue sees this difference as the distinction between suppression and oppression: "Is there any logical comparison between the oppression of the black woman on welfare who has difficulty feeding her children and the discontent of the suburban mother who has the luxury to protest the washing of the dishes on which her family's full meal was consumed?"

The articles in this chapter have been chosen to reflect some of the diversity of the various racial and ethnic groups. Within each group there are, of course, vast differences. Included among Asians, for example, are the major subgroups of Chinese, Japanese, Filipino, and Korean; among Native Americans, there are the various tribes. Further diversity is apparent depending on the degree of assimilation into American culture—first, second, and third generation Asian-Americans, for example. Then there are differences between urban and rural groups, especially among Chicanas and Native Americans, and differences depending on age. Since it is impossible to include material for all such diverse groups, the articles included in this section only sample the possibilities, and only general themes are highlighted in this introduction. It is hoped that any misconceptions resulting from such generalizations may be corrected by referring to the specific articles and consulting suggestions for further reading.

The psychology of Third World women is based in their struggle, both historically and currently, as minority women in a white culture. Though there are many differences between white and Third World women, hopefully they can discuss their differences and similarities to achieve a better understanding of each other. In so doing, white women may gain perspectives on their own psychology as well as that of Third World women, and Third World women may feel more included in, or at least less excluded from, the psychology of women.

Third World women relate to the stereotype workers, as slaves, as coolied workers and, in addition, have been raped by white slave masters. They are still among the lowest paid workers and have often been forced to practice prostitution or to live on welfare, still earning incomes inadequate to meet the needs of themselves and their children. Sometimes, when the men are unable to find jobs, Third World women can work as domestics in white women's homes, taking care of white women's houses and children to the neglect of their own. The men sometimes beat their women to vent their own frustrations or, giving up in despair, leave them to raise families alone, though extended families are also common. Third World women, then, have experienced the psychological castration of themselves and their men, suffering the effects of sexism, racism and poverty.

The self-concept of Third World women has been greatly affected by racial stereotyping, making them feel unacceptable according to white standards of beauty. Sexually, Third

World women are treated with less respect and are stereotyped as "sexual animals." This is a consequence of the white culture's contradictory Madonna/Whore concept, which is even further accentuated in the Latin culture due to the predominance of the Catholic Church. According to this contradictory notion, white women are viewed as virginal, pure, and "good (the Madonnas)," while nonwhite women are seen as lustful, sexual, and "evil (the Whores)."

Third World Women relate to the stereotype of femininity in two different ways. On the one hand, they have been made to feel inadequate or inferior for not being able to attain femininity easily, and it may be seen as a luxury they cannot afford. On the other hand, Third World women also seem to reject feminine stereotypes, which emphasize qualities designed to inflate the male ego. But if Third World men are still attached to the masculine sex role, they may seek white women to enhance their egos and to express their hostility toward whiteness, an anger more safely directed at white women than white men. As a result, Third World women are particularly vulnerable to rejection by their men and may feel hurt, angry, insulted, abandoned, and degraded.

Increasingly, however, Third World women and men are viewing sex roles as part of a "sick" white society they do not wish to imitate, especially since they recognize that both women and men must participate equally if they are to achieve their revolutionary goals in restructuring society. Blacks, for example, already have role integration to a certain degree since circumstances have forced such modifications of sex roles.

Achieving an identity is another major psychological struggle for Third World women, especially if they choose not to emulate white sex roles and yet wish to combine their own cultural values with those of the dominant culture. This becomes particularly difficult in the face of conflicting norms and values with no available precedents to serve as guides.

Third World women often view the (white) women's movement with contempt, hostility, and distrust—often justifiably, based on the racism of white women. Since white women tend to think as their white husbands do (although this is not as universally true as before), they are seen to be just as oppressive as white men. White women are seen as attempting to gain even more privileges, an even larger "slice of the pie," thus further excluding racial minorities from access to society's resources. Frequently, the women's movement is seen as divisive to the struggle of Third World people, and Third World women define racial oppression as a more vital issue than their oppression as women.

Third World women also disagree with the (white) women's movement in its attitude toward the structure of the family, which white feminists seem to want to alter or abolish. Third World women want the structure of the family to remain and become strengthened to help establish a strong community, which is necessary to their liberation as a race. A second major difference is that, as stated above, Third World women see liberation from racism as having preëminence over liberation from sexism, though both are of high priority. On the other hand, white women, for the most part, view sexism as primary and racism as secondary. Another issue which is different for the two groups is that of birth control and abortion. Women of racial minorities may see these practices as genocidal and racist, even though

When you educate a man, you educate an individual; when you educate a woman, you educate a whole family.

Dr. Charles D. McIver, Address at North Carolina College for Women

such practices may also be viewed as a step toward biological self-determination. For Chicanas, this is a special issue, since the Catholic Church is an important institution in their lives, and religious opinion on birth control and abortion weigh heavily.

There may be some similarities among white and Third World women, however, since there is sexism in all cultures. In Africa, there is obvious male domination; in the Chicana culture, there is machismo; in Asian culture, there is Confucianism. All the original cultures from which these racial minorities came have patriarchal ideologies and practices. Sexually, in both the white and Third World cultures, there are double standards for the two sexes, women are regarded as sexual objects, and women, regardless of race, are subject to rape. Employment and educational opportunities are limited for both white and Third World women, but even more so for Third World women.

A significant aspect of the psychology of Third World women is that, because of the pain and struggles they have endured, they have developed tremendous strengths and survival capacities, probably far greater than most white women have had to develop. Third World women must continue to struggle for equality within their own race, as well as joining Third World men in the fight for equal respect and dignity for all races.

Linda La Rue

The Black Movement and Women's Liberation

Let us first discuss what common literature addresses as the "common oppression" of blacks and women. This is a tasty abstraction designed purposely or inadvertently to draw validity and seriousness to the women's movement through a universality of plight. Every movement worth its "revolutionary salt" makes these headliner generalities about "common oppression" with others—but let us state unequivocally that, with few exceptions, the American white woman has had a better opportunity to live a free and fulfilling life, both mentally and physically, than any other group in the United States, with the exception of her white husband. Thus, any attempt to analogize black oppression with the plight of the American white woman has the validity of comparing the neck of a hanging man with the hands of an amateur mountain climber with rope burns.

"Common oppression" is fine for rhetoric, but it does not reflect the actual distance between the oppression of the black man and woman who are unemployed, and the "oppression" of the American white woman who is "sick and tired" of *Playboy* foldouts, or Christian Dior lowering hemlines or adding ruffles, or of Miss Clairol telling her that blondes have more fun.

Is there any logical comparison between the oppression of the black woman on welfare who has difficulty feeding her children and the discontent of the suburban mother who has the luxury to protest the washing of the dishes on which her family's full meal was consumed.

The surge of "common oppression" rhetoric and propaganda may lure the unsuspecting into an intellectual alliance with the goals of women's liberation, but it is not a wise alliance.

It is not that women ought not to be liberated from the shackles of their present unfulfillment, but the depth, the extent, the intensity, the importance—indeed, the suffering and depravity of the *real* oppression blacks have experienced—can only be minimized in an alliance with women who heretofore suffered little more than boredom, genteel repression, and dishpan hands.

For all the similarities and analogies drawn between the liberation of women and the liberation of blacks, the point remains that when white women received their voting rights, most blacks, male and female, were systematically disenfranchised and had been that way since Reconstruction. And even in 1970, when women's right of franchise is rarely questioned, it is still a less than common occurrence for blacks to vote in some areas of the South.

Tasteless analogies like abortion for oppressed middle class and poor women idealistically assert that all women have the right to decide if and when they want children, and thus fail to catch the flavor of the actual circumstances. Actual circumstances boil down to middle class women deciding when it is convenient to have children, while poor women decide the prudence of bringing into a world of already scarce resources, another mouth to feed. Neither their motives nor their objectives are the same. But current literature leads one to lumping the decisions of these two women under one generalization, when in fact the difference between the plights of these two women is as clear as the difference between being hungry and out of work, and skipping lunch and taking a day off.

If we are realistically candid with ourselves, and accept the fact that despite our beloved rhetoric of Pan-Africanism, our vision of third world liberation, and perhaps our dreams of a world state of multi-racial humanism, most blacks and a good many who generally exempt themselves from categories, still want the proverbial "piece of cake." American values are difficult to discard for, unlike what more militant "brothers" would have us believe, Americanism does not end with the adoption of Afro hairstyles on pregnant women covered in long African robes.

Indeed, the fact that the independent black capitalism demonstrated by the black Muslims, and illustrated in Nixon's speeches, appeared for many blacks as the way out of the ghetto into the light, lends a truthful vengeance to the maxim that perhaps blacks are nothing more than black anglo-saxons. Upon the rebirth of the liberation struggle in the sixties, a whole genre of "women's place" advocates immediately relegated black women to home and babies, which is almost as ugly an expression of black anglo-saxonism as is Nixon's concept of "black capitalism."

The study of many developing areas and countries reflects at least an attempt to allow freedom of education and opportunity to women. Yet, black Americans have not adopted developing area's "new role" paradigm, but rather the Puritan-American status of "home and babies", which is advocated by the capitalist Muslims. This reflects either ingrained Americanism or the lack of the simplest imagination.

Several weeks ago, women's lib advocates demanded that a local women's magazine be "manned" by a woman editor. Other segments of the women's movement have carried on a smaller campaign in industry and business.

If white women have heretofore remained silent while white men maintained the better position and monopolized the opportunities by excluding blacks, can we really expect that white women, when put in direct competition for employment, will be any more open-minded than their male counterparts when it comes to the hiring of black males and females in the same positions for which they are competing? From the standpoint of previous American social interaction, it does not seem logical that white females will not be tempted to take advantage of the fact that they are white, in an economy that favors whites. It is entirely possible that women's liberation has developed a sudden attachment to the black liberation movement as a ploy to share the attention that it has taken blacks 400 years to generate. In short, it can be argued that women's liberation not only attached itself to the black movement, but did so with only marginal concern for black women and black liberation, and functional concern for the rights of white women.

The industrial demands of two world wars temporarily offset the racial limitations to mobility and allowed the possibility of blacks entering industry, as an important labor force, to be actualized. Similarly, women have benefited from an expanded science and industrialization. Their biological limitation, successfully curbed by the pill and by automation, which makes stressing physical labor more the exception than the rule, has created an impressively large and available labor force of women.

The black labor force, never fully employed and always representing a substantial percentage of the unemployed in the American economy, will now be driven into greater unemployment as white women converge at every level on an already dwindling job market.

Ideally, we chanced to think of women's

That species generally labeled Black woman is ultimately a group of individuals whose perceptions of Blackness and Womanhood vary as their experiences and comprehension of those experiences vary. . . . However, what is important is the fact that, for all their individuality, they usually agree in several significant areas: the assigned characteristics and roles are not entirely accurate, inherent, or desirable; though Blacks perpetuate and perpetrate consciously or unconsciously with varying degrees of willingness these stereotypes, the real creator and enemy is white society; and, for this reason, Black unity and self-determination must be dominant factors in a Black woman's personal liberation.

Frances S. Foster, *Afro-American Studies*

---

liberation as a promising beginning of the "oppressed rising everywhere" in the typically Marxian fashion that many blacks seem drawn to. Instead, the spectre of racism and inadequate education, job discrimination, and even greater unequal opportunity will be, more than ever before, a function of neither maleness nor femaleness, but blackness.

This discussion has been primarily to ward off any unintelligent alliance of black people with white women in this new liberation movement. Rhetoric and anathema hurled at the right industrial complex, idealism which speaks of a final humanism, and denunciations of the system which makes competition a fact of life, do not mean that women's liberation has as its goal anyone else's liberation except its own.

It is time that definitions be made clear. Blacks are *oppressed*, and that means unreasonably burdened, unjustly, severely, rigorously, cruelly and harshly fettered by white authority. White women, on the other hand, are only *suppressed*, and that means checked, restrained, excluded from conscious and overt activity. And there is a difference.

For some, the dangers of an unintelligent alliance with women's liberation will suggest female suppression as the only way to protect against a new economic threat. For others, a greater answer is needed, and required, before women's liberation can be seen in perspective.

To say that black women must be freed before the black movement can attain full revolutionary consciousness, is meaningless because of its malleability. To say that black women must be freed from the unsatisfactory male-female role relationship which we adopted from whites as the paradigm of the good family, has more meaning because it indicates the incompatibility of white role models with the goal of black liberation. If there is anything to be learned from the current women's lib agitation, it is that roles are not ascribed and inherent, but adopted and interchangeable in every respect except pregnancy, breastfeeding and the system generally employed to bring the two former into existence.

Role integration, which I will elaborate upon as the goal and the strength of the black family, is substantially different from the role "usurpation" of men by women. The fact that the roles of man and woman are deemed in American society as natural and divine, leads to false ego attachments to these roles. During slavery and following Reconstruction, black men felt inferior for a great number of reasons, among them that they were unable to work in positions comparable to the ones to which black women were assigned. With these positions often went fringe benefits of extra food, clothes, and perhaps elementary reading and writing skills. Black women were in turn jealous of white women, and felt inadequate and inferior because paraded in front of them constantly, was the white woman of luxury who had no need for work, who could, as Sojourner Truth

> *Look at my arm! I have ploughed and planted and gathered into barns, and no man could head me—and ain't I a woman? I could work as much and eat as much as a man—when I could get it—and bear the lash as well! And ain't I a woman? I have born thirteen children, and seen most of 'em sold into slavery, and when I cried out with my mother's grief, none but Jesus heard me—and ain't I a woman?*

> Sojourner Truth, abolitionist and feminist

---

pointed out, "be helped into carriages, and lifted over ditches, and . . . have the best place everywhere."

The resulting "respect" for women and the acceptance of the dominating role for men, encouraged the myth of the immutability of these roles. The term "matriarchy" Frazier employed and Moynihan exploited, was used to indicate a dastardly, unnatural role alteration which could be blamed for inequality of opportunity, discrimination in hiring and sundry other ills. It was as if "matriarchy" was transgression of divine law or natural law, and thus would be punished until the proper hierarchy of man over woman was restored.

Black people have an obligation, as do white women, to recognize that the designation of "mother-head" and "father-head" does not imply inferiority of one and the superiority of the other. They are merely arbitrary role distinctions which vary from culture to culture and circumstance to circumstance.

Thus to quip, as it has been popularly done, that the only place in the black movement for black women, is prone, is actually supporting a white role ideal, and it is neither a compliment to men nor women to advocate such sexual capitalism or sexual colonialism.

It seems incongruous that the black movement has sanctioned the revolutionary involvement of women in the Algerian revolution, even though its revolutionary circumstances modified and often alternated the common role models, but have been duped into hating even their own slave grandmothers who, in not so admirable yet equally frightening and demanding circumstances, also modified and altered the common role models of the black family. Fanon wrote in glorious terms about this role change:

> The unveiled Algerian women, who assumed an increasingly important place in revolutionary action, developed her personality, discovered the exalting realm of responsibility. . . . This woman who, in the avenues of Algiers and of Constantine, would carry the grenades or the submachine gun charges, the woman who tomorrow would be outraged, violated, tortured, could not put herself back into her former state of mind, and relive her behavior of the past. . . .[1]

Can it not be said that in slavery black women assumed an increasingly important place in the survival action and thus developed their personalities and sense of responsibility? And after being outraged, violated and tortured, could she be expected to put herself back into her former state of mind and relive her behavior of the past?

The crux of this argument is essentially that blacks, since slavery and through their entire existence in America, have also been living in revolutionary circumstances and under revolutionary pressures. Simply because the black

---

[1]Frantz Fanon, *A Dying Colonialism*, New York: Grove Press, 1965, p. 107.

liberation struggle has taken 400 years to come to fruition does not mean that it is not every bit as dangerous or psychologically exhausting as the Algerian struggle. Any revolution calls upon the best in both its men and women. This is why Moynihan's statements that "matriarchy" is a root *cause* of black problems is as unfounded as it is inane. He does not recognize the liberation struggle and the demands that it has made on the black family.

How unfortunate that blacks and whites have allowed the most trying and bitter experience in the history of black people to be interpreted as the beginning of an "unashamed plot" to usurp the very manhood of black men. But the myth was perpetuated, and thus what brought the alternation of roles in Algeria was distorted and systematically employed to separate black men and women in America.

> Black women take kindness for weakness. Leave them the least little opening and they will put you on the cross. . . . It would be like trying to pamper a cobra. . . .[2]

Unless we realize how thoroughly the American value of male superiority and female inferiority has permeated our relationships with each other, we can never appreciate the role it plays in perpetuating racism and keeping black people divided.

Most, but not all, American relationships are based on some type of "exclusive competition of the superior, and the exclusive competition of the inferior." This means essentially that the poor, the uneducated, the deprived and the minorities of the aforementioned groups, compete among themselves for the same scarce resources and inferior opportunities, while the privileged, middle-class, educated, and select white minorities, compete with each other for rather plentiful resources and superior opportunities for prestige and power. Competition among groups is rare, due to the fact that elements who qualify are almost invariably absorbed to some extent (note the black middle-class) by the group to which they seek entry. We may well understand that there is only one equal relationship between man and woman, black and white, in America, and this equality is based on whether or not you can force your way into qualifying for the same resources.

But instead of attempting to modify this competive definition within the black movement, many black males have affirmed it as a way of maintaining the closure of male monopolization of scarce benefits and making the "dominion of males" impenetrable to black females." This is, of course, very much the American way of exploitation.

The order of logic which makes it possible to pronounce, as did Dr. Robert Staples, that "black women cannot be free qua women until all blacks attain their liberation,"[3] maintains, whether purposely or not, that black women will be able to separate their femaleness from their blackness and thus they would be able to be free as blacks, if not free as women; or, that male freedom ought to come first; or, finally, that the freedom of black women and men, and the freedom of black people as a whole, are not one and the same.

Only with the concept of role integration can we hope to rise above the petty demarcations of human freedom that America is noted for, and that are unfortunately inherent in Dr. Staples' remark. Role integration is the realization that:

---

[2]Eldridge Cleaver, *Soul on Ice,* New York: McGraw Hill, 1968, p. 158.

[3]Robert Staples, "The Myth of the Black Matriarchy," *The Black Scholar,* Jan.–Feb. 1970, p. 16.

• ego attachments to particular activities or traits must be abolished as a method of determining malehood and femalehood; that instead, ego attachments must be distributed to a wider variety of tasks and traits in order to weaken the power of one activity in determining self-worth, and

• the flexibility of a people in effecting role alternation and role integration has been an historically proven asset to the survival of any people—witness Israel, China and Algeria.

Thus the unwitting adoption and the knowing perpetuation of this American value reflects three inter-related situations:

• black people's growing sense of security and well-being, and their failure to recognize the expanse of black problems;

• black people's over-identification with the dominant group, even though the survival of blacks in America is not assured, and

• black people's belief in the myth of "matriarchy" and their subsequent rejection of role integration as unnatural and unnecessary.

While the rhetoric of black power and the advocates of cultural nationalism laud black people for their ability to struggle under oppressive odds, they simultaneously seek to strip away or incapacitate the phenomenon of role integration—the very means by which blacks were able to survive! They seek to replace it with a weak, intractable role separation which would completely sap the strength of the black movement because it would inhibit the mobilization of both women and men. It was this ability to mobilize black men and black women that guaranteed survival during slavery.

The strength of role integration is sorely overlooked as blacks throw away the hot comb, the bleach cream, the lye, and yet insist on maintaining the worst of American values by

Realization by Augusta Savage; by permission of The Schomburg Center for Research in Black Culture, The New York Public Library; Astor, Lenox and Tilden Foundations

placing the strength of black women in the traction of the white female status.

I would think black men would want a better status for their sister black women; indeed, black women would want a better status for themselves, rather than a warmed-over throne of women's inferiority, which white women are beginning to abandon.

Though most white women's lib advocates fail to realize the possibility, their subsequent liberation may spell a strengthening of the status quo values from which they sought liberation. Since more and more women will be

Untitled drawing by Irmagean

dealt with these husbands in the effort to secure jobs, housing and education, it does not seem likely that blacks will gain significantly from the open mobility of less tolerant women whose viewpoints differ little from those of their husbands.

If white radical thought has called upon the strength of all women to take a position of responsibility and power, can blacks afford to relegate black women to "home and babies" while white women reinforce the status quo?

The cry of black women's liberation is a cry against chaining a very much needed labor force and agitating force to a role that once belonged to impotent, apolitical white women. Blacks speak lovingly of the vanguard and the importance of women in the struggle, and yet fail to recognize that women have been assigned a new place, based on white ascribed characteristics of women, rather than on their actual potential. The black movement needs its women in a position of struggle, not prone. The struggle blacks face is not taking place between knives and forks, at the washboard, or in the diaper pail. It is taking place on the labor market, at the polls, in government, in the protection of black communities, in local neighborhood power struggles, in housing and in education.

Can blacks afford to be so unobservant of current events as to send their women to fight a non-existent battle in a dishpan?

Even now, the black adoption of the white values of women has begun to show its effects on black women in distinctive ways. The black liberation movement has created a politicized, unliberated copy of white womanhood. Black women who participated in the struggle have failed to recognize, for the most part, the unique contradiction between renunciation of capitalistic competition and the acceptance of sexual

participating in the decision making process, those few women participating in the "struggle" will be outnumbered by the more traditional middle class women. This means that the traditional women will be in a position to take advantage of new opportunities which radical women's liberation has struggled to win. Voting studies now reflect that the traditional women, middle class and above, tend to vote the same way as their husbands. Because blacks have

colonialism. The failure of the black movement to resolve and deal with this dilemma has perpetuated the following attitudes in American politicized black women:

• The belief in the myth of matriarchy. The black woman has been made to feel ashamed of her strength, and so to redeem herself she has adopted from whites the belief that superiority and dominance of the male is the most "natural" and "normal" relationship. She consequently believes that black women ought to be suppressed in order to attain that "natural balance."

• Because the white woman's role has been held up as an example to all black women, many black women feel inadequate and so ardently compete in "femininity" with white females for black males' attention. She further competes with black females in an attempt to be the "blackest and the most feminine," thereby, the more superior to her fellow black sisters in appealing to black politicized men. She competes also with the apolitical black female in an attempt to keep black males from "regressing" back to females whom she feels have had more "practice" in the traditional role of white woman than has she.

• Finally, she emphasizes the traditional roles of women, such as housekeeping, children, supportive roles, and self-maintenance, but she politicizes these roles by calling them the role of black women. She then adopts the attitude that her job and her life is to have more children which can be used in the vanguard of the black struggle.

Black women, as the song "Black Pearl" relates, have been put up where they belong, but by American standards. Is it so inconceivable that the American value of respect and human relationships is distorted? It has taken the birth

Untitled drawing by Irmagean

of women's liberation to bring the black movement back to its senses.

The black woman is demanding a new set of female definitions and a recognition of herself as a citizen, companion and confidant, not a matriarchal villain or a step stool baby-maker. Role integration advocates the complementary recognition of man and woman, not the competitive recognition of same.

The recent, unabated controversy over the use of birth control in the black community is of grave importance here. Black people, even the "most liberated of mind," are still infused with ascribed inferiority of females and the natural superiority of males. These same values foster the idea of "good blood" in children. If, indeed there can be any black liberation, it must start with the recognition of contradictions like the following.

Black Venus by Niki de Saint Phalle; Collection of the Whitney Museum of American Art, New York: gift of the Howard and Jean Lipman Foundation, Inc.

It gives a great many black males pride to speak, as Dr. Robert Staples does, of ". . . the role of the black woman in the black liberation struggle is an important one and cannot be forgotten. From her womb have come the revolutionary warriors of our time."[4]

How many potential revolutionary warriors stand abandoned in orphanages while blacks rhetorize disdain for birth control as a "trick of the man" to halt the growth of black population? Why are there not more revolutionary couples adopting black children? Could it be that the American concept of bastard, which is equivalent to inferior in our society, reflects black anglo-saxonism? Do blacks, like whites, discriminate against black babies because they do not represent "our own personal" image? Or do blacks, like the most racist of whites, require that a child be of their own blood before they can love that child or feed it? Does the vanguard, of which Dr. Staples so reverently speaks, recognize the existence of the term "bastard"?

Someone once suggested that the word "bastard" be deleted from the values of black people. Would it not be more revolutionary for blacks to advocate a five-year moratorium on black births until every black baby in an American orphanage was adopted by one or more black parents? Then blacks could really have a valid reason for continuing to give birth. Children would mean more than simply a role for black women to play, or fuel for the legendary vanguard. Indeed, blacks would be able to tap the potential of the existing children and could sensibly add more potential to the black struggle for liberation. To do this would be to do something no other civilization, modern of course, has ever done, and blacks would be allowing every black child to have a home and

[4]Ibid.

The Black Latin & the Mexican Indian

When I grew up on New York streets
And fought my way thru knee deep garbage
My Mama sewed stars on Amerikkkan flags
At the Brooklyn Navy Yard
Like all the other Mamas
And I was lonely

When you grew up in California fields
And listened to the fat greasy patrones
Call your Papa a Wetback Greaser
Your Mama worked in the packing houses
Worked for pennies—so that white ladies could
*   wear silk stockings*
Paid for with your daily hunger
Were you lonely too?

While you grew callouses on your hands
I grew a callous on my heart
And, somewhere, we lost what little laughter
*   we'd known*
And the loneliness grew

While you picked tomatoes
I picked pockets

And we both learned how to lie and steal and
*   fight*
Some call it survival
I call it loneliness

But, one day the smog lifted
The city and the country smiled at each other
And so did we
The Mariachi met the Mambo
And so did we
And like the frozen snow in Spring
We melted
And like the warm winds of Summer
We were gentle
And no matter how the rain falls
And if time stops dead in its track tomorrow
I will praise the Gods for your existence
I will dance to your rhythms
Even as the sun grows cold
And I'm not lonely anymore

Avotcja

not just a plot in some understaffed children's penal farm.

What makes a healthy black baby in an orphanage different from "our own flesh and blood"? Except for the American value of inferiority-superiority, and the concept of "bastard" that accompanies it, there is nothing wrong with the orphaned child save what white society has taught us to perceive.

We can conclude that black women's libera- tion and black men's liberation is what we mean when we speak of the liberation of black people. I maintain that the true liberation of black people depends on their rejection of the inferiority of women, the rejection of competition as the only viable relationship between men, and their re-affirmation of respect for general human potential in whatever form, man, child or woman, it is conceived.

Anna Nieto-Gomez

Heritage of La Hembra

The social-psychological roles of a culture for men and women are the products of economic circumstances spanning hundreds of years. Culture is only a remnant which mirrors people's accumulative economic adaptations through periods of history. Therefore the sexual roles of La Hembra, the Woman, and El Hombre, the Man, are haunted by the economic and class conditions of people for more than 300 years.

The roots of the psyche of la Chicana are buried within the colonial period in Mexico. The conquest, the encomienda system and the colonial Catholic Church played a major role in designing the sexual social roles of the Mexican woman. The class relationship between patron and the Indian slave woman is the historical foundation of machismo. Rape against the Mexican Indian women by the Spanish conquistadores was an individual imperialistic act of conquest. Marriage was used as an imperialistic tool against the Indian woman. Servant to Master, rape, and marriage represented models of power to the Mexican male who longed to be free and powerful too. Even the colonial Catholic church superimposed its ideology and justified the oppression of conquest as something good. Marianismo, the veneration of the Virgin Mary, became the model of how to make oppression an obligation. This is the heritage of the Chicana. Here lies the foundation of La Hembra y El Hombre.

In a patriarchal world, possession of a woman symbolizes wealth, inheritance, and dominance of a man over another person. Because she was property, woman was used by various Mexican Indian tribes to make alliances with the Span-iards. Twenty virgins, Indian slave women, were given by the Tabascan to the Spanish warriors as a token of their alliance to overthrow the Aztec rulers.[1] As the property of the Tabascan Indians, women were given as sex objects to new masters. The Spaniards were given unused property: virgin women.

In fulfillment of the Spaniard's "civilizing mission," of conquest, the civil authorities were satisfied to have the "Indian women baptized prior to coition." No Spanish soldier was to rape or sleep with a non-Christian woman.[2] In accordance with this social etiquette of conquest, the Church baptized the twenty Indian slave women prior to their unanimous rape. And so Malintzin Tenepal became Dona Marina, La Malinche; the symbol of ravaged Mexico and mother of the mestizo nation.[3] Since the Indian Caciques gave their consent, it might be argued that this was not rape because slaves have no consent to give; nevertheless, this is sanctioned rape.

The Spaniards obtained Indian Mexican women both by force and through peaceful means. The seizure of women was part of the general conquest and enslavement of Indians during the first decades of the sixteenth century. Bernal Diaz describes the actual enslavement of women.

> Cortez had decided that all slaves taken by the soldiers should be branded so that the royal fifth (the crown's share) and his own share of human booty could be taken. When the soldiers returned . . . to recover the slaves, they discovered to their dismay that Cortez and his officers had hidden and taken away the best looking slaves . . . The ones we received were old and ugly.[4]

Sylvia Marcos de Robert continues to describe the situation.

> While the Spaniard and the Pope debated over whether the indigenous peoples of Mexico were animal or human, the conquistador treated the indigenous peoples as he pleased. He treated the men like animals and he violated the women. The poor enslaved Indian man and woman had to accept the sexual violation of women because of the military and political power of the conquistador. The children of this violation were the first Mexican mestizos.
>
> The Indian women for general purposes were the sexual objects of the patron. She was the Spaniard's tool to be used to his satisfaction. The Spaniard even institutionalized the belief that the Indian woman was inferior first because she was indigenous and second because she was a woman.[5]

Spaniards also received women in the form of gifts and as tokens of friendship from the Indian Caciques. Bernal Diaz describes how the Cacique Xicotenga offered Cortez his virgin daughter and four other pretty girls for his captains. Many of these Caciques considered the gift of women to be an excellent means of allying themselves with the Spaniards.[6]

Either through marriage to the Caciques' daughters or through rape, the sexual penetration and acquisition of women were imperialistic acts of conquest to seize property and to establish dominance of the king and for the individual man. Just as Spain sought new territories and markets to keep its economy from collapsing, men sought to acquire fortunes, property of land and people, to fulfill the dream of the patriarch, the male economic birthright unobtainable in Spain. As a country commits imperialistic acts against another country, it is the model of action to men and women and therefore sanctions individual aggression and oppression against others. As a result, eventually imperialistic values become integrated into the culture.

Traditionally, sex through marriage or rape, which are the tools of conquest, have been a means of taking possession of women and land. Historically, from the colonization of Mexico to the rape of Inez Garcia, women belong to the man or men who have sexually penetrated them. The encomienda system extended this power and dominance over the Indian slaves and continued this sexual abuse of the Indian woman.

The encomienda enabled the Spanish land owner to totally exploit Indian workers, their sex and their land. "As granted by Cortez and agreed to by the crown, the encomienda grant gave the recipient a temporary right to demand from the Indian Inhabitants of the Land any service desired and any tribute he could collect."[7] One encomendero asked a village to contribute a daily work-force of fifty men and four women.[8] The encomienda's overseers solicited and received labor services in the form of field hands, herdsmen, and housebuilders.[9] Women were used as personal servants for the patron.[10] The domestic and sexual services of a woman were considered tribute paid from the male Indian head of household.[11] As noted by Bishop Juan de Zumarrage in his letter to Emperor Charles in 1529, female servants were used as concubines more often than not,[12] and as his domestic slave, it was the women's duty to wait on every need of the patron to ensure that his "home was his castle." Motolinia describes this life style of the patron.

> . . . The Spaniard would rise from his bed and would ask to be dressed as if he had no hands to use, and they would dress him as if he was a man without hands. And taking advantage of his servant, meanwhile he would pray. One should see the attention he gets should he feel a little

cold or a little chill. As he goes to the fireplace while they clean him from head to toe. Since he feels faint going from his bed to the fireplace, he is not able to comb his hair and therefore must have someone else comb it for him. Afterward his shoes, pants and his hat are brought to him. After mass, he is thankful the priest did not hold a long mass and create discomfort on his knees. Upon his return home, his food is ready on the dot.

For the disinherited indigenous peoples, and for the poor illegitimate mestizo son, the relationship between master and servant was an example of the patron's strength, force and his powerfulness.[13]

It is clear that many Indian women had two masters.

Women were also integrated and exploited into the colonial economy of Mexico's encomienda. In mining communities, women worked as forced labor. They worked as nurses to keep the men alive and they made tallow for candles in the mines. In the silk industry, the heavy labor of reeling the raw silk was done by women. Women were also used as human incubators by having them carry bags of silk worm eggs under their breasts for fifteen days. Women also worked as bakers, candy makers, in the market place, the sugar mills, wineries and in the chocolate mills. In addition to her labor, women maintained their bartering value, and as sexual objects, they were used as a means of monetary exchange.[14]

Because many Indians rebelled against the encomienda system, it was necessary to instill social as well as economic control. How could a Spaniard trust the slave who cooked his food and waited in his bed without fearing for his life?

Although it had always been the responsibility of the encomendero to provide Christian education to all Indians on the encomienda,

he distrusted Christian education until he found it would reinforce the submission of his bee workers.[15]

Therefore, the socialization of the Indian woman to the concept of Marianisma was an ideal means of social control to maintain the subjugation of the Indian woman to her oppression.

Marianisma is the veneration of the Virgin Mary which totally defines the woman's identity as a virgin, saintly mother, wife-sex object, martyr, and also attributes woman's sexuality as the cause of her husband's failures.[16] In respect to the Chicana today, Connie Nieto affirms the fact that Marianisma has a tremendous impact in the development of many Chicanas because it has been the ultimate role model for a woman.[17] In essence, Marianisma has deceived the Indian woman in believing her only predestined alternatives are negative existence and self-denial.

The popular image of the Mexican women is somber clad, long suffering females praying in dim lit colonial churches.[18] Church tradition has directed the women to identify with the emotional suffering of the pure, passive, bystander, the Virgin Mary. Through the Virgin Mary, the Chicana begins to experience a vicarious martyrdom in order to accept and prepare herself for her own oppressive reality.

In explaining the reaction of Inez Garcia after her rape, Maria Del Drago describes the psychology taught to Latinas by the Church today.

> We Latinas are not encouraged to be articulate about any part of our experience, much less sexual abuse. Our teachers are nuns who encourage our silence, as an exercise in self sacrifice.[19]

To be a slave, a servant, a woman cannot be assertive, independent and self defining. She is told to act fatalistically because "all comes to those who wait."[20] She is conditioned to believe it is natural to be in a dependent psychological condition as well as dependent economically. The absolute role for women is not to do for themselves but to yield to the wishes of others, as well as care for their needs before her own. Her needs and desires are in the charge of others—the patron, her family, her father, her boyfriend, her husband, her God. She is told to act for others and to wait for others to act for her.

Suffering and self denial were offered to forced Indian slave concubines as a means of giving self-respect and authority. Marianisma portrayed the women as semi-divine, morally superior and spiritually stronger than her master because of her ability to "endure" pain and sorrow.[21] This pedestal of thorns also justified "men's wickedness" (passed on today as the double standard between master and servant). Unfortunately, it was a good story teller who made the servant seem like a queen and the king seem as a servant. Again an ideology was offered to explain and sanction the oppression and abuse of woman. Marianisma, then, like today, reinforced and sanctioned the class inequity between men of power and powerless women.

Today, the institution of marriage may be seen by some women as economic bondage. Marriage as opposed to concubinage would give the Indian woman as well as her children, certain economic and political rights denied her as an "illegal" wife. Instead, her children were seen as illegitimate and therefore denied the rights of citizenship in their motherland. As an unwed-kept woman of "La Casa Chica" she had no social, economic, or political rights or security, except guaranteed slavery.

In addition, Crown policy concerning interracial marriages was not always consistent. Although many Indian Caciques created alliances with Spaniards through marriage, eventually Spain discouraged intermarriage and also condemned the free union relationships between Indians and Spaniards.[22] The racial mixing between Spaniard and Indian usually involved informal unions rather than marriage. Marriage between an Indian woman and a Spaniard was generally regarded as a step down the social scale for the Spaniard,[23] and only the poor Spaniard "legally" married an Indian woman.[24] Instead, the migrating Spaniards would declare themselves married and either change wives or merely shed them through migration.

Not only would Spaniards not legally marry the Indian woman, many of them could not because they already had a "legal" wife in Spain. To counteract mass bigamy or polygyny, in New Spain, the crown issued rules that married men coming to the New World must either take their wives with them or have their wives' permission and post bond that they would return to Spain after a limited stay.[25]

Nevertheless, most Spaniards did not consider the color of the sexual partner as important. A Venezuelan conquistador justified their sexual activities because: "No one in these parts who has a homestead can live without a woman, Spanish or Indian."[26] Others like Francisco de Aguirre, governor of Tucuman, considered the result of the sexual activities "as a service to God in producing mestizos and greater than the sin committed by the same act."[27] Possibly he felt he could breed out the Indian inferior stock. However, regarding the legal issue of marriage and inheritance, the Spaniards preferred Spanish women.

*Although Chicanas have a responsibility to understand that Chicanos
face oppression and discrimination, this does not mean that the
Chicana should be a scapegoat for the man's frustrations.*

Mirta Vidal

Roundelays

*What manner of being can be more rare
than he that, without counsel
breathes on a mirror and fogs it
and then is sad because it is not clear*

*In favor or in disdain
you are the same
Complaining if you are treated badly
Mocking us if we really love you.*

*None wins your favor,
She that is most prudent,
If she does not open up to you
is ungrateful
and if she does she is lascivious.*

*You are always so foolish,
with your unequal measures,
this one you blame for being cruel
and the other you blame for being easy.*

*Well, how should she be made
that one that your love looks for
if the one who is prudent offends,
and the one who is easy is a bore?*

*Moreover between the boredom and
pain that your favor incurs
Good will come to her who does*

*not love you
And you may complain, as you wish.*

*Do your lovers give you pain
to your liberties take wings,
(and after making them bad,
you want to find them virtuous)
very good.*

*Who has been most to blame in
a passion that has erred
she who falls upon being courted,
or he who courts for the fall?*

*Or who is more to blame
No matter what wrong has been done
She who sins for pay
or he who pays to sin?*

*Well, why are you surprised
at the blame that is yours
like them as you have made them,
or make them as you would like
to find them.*

*Quit soliciting
and then with more reason
you might accuse the inclination
of she who seeks you out to court you.*

De Sor Juana Inez De La Cruz
Translation: Bernice Rincón

Both Chicanos and gabachos have been guilty of the merciless stereotyping of females as docile, helpless, emotional, irrational, and intellectually inferior creatures who are best suited to be sex objects, domestic servants, and typists.

Patricia Cruz

Because of their desire to provide their descendants with good lineage and to pass on their wealth, the Spaniards preferred to "marry" Spanish women.[28] The illegitimate offspring, the mestizo of the Indian women, could not directly inherit property. But if they were the only descendants in New Spain, the land could eventually return to its indigenous inhabitants. However at this time, Spain was in the process of "cleansing its own race." After hundreds of years of miscegenation under Moorish rule, Spain hoped to maintain the new Mexican social political structure through a caste system with Spanish pure bloods at the top.[29]

Therefore in an effort to maintain New Spain in the hands of Spaniards rather than mestizos, Spain exported women to Mexico to marry Spanish men. This "white slavery" across the Atlantic gave destitute women of Spain, poor widows, and women in debtors prison a new economic start.[30]

This new Spanish import changed the Mexican ideal of beauty. Usually one might regard the ideal of beauty as trivial, however, for the Indian women, it was very crucial because beauty depended on how closely she conformed biologically and racially to the Spanish ideal. This was especially true because characteristics of the Mexican mestiza or indigena were considered unbecoming and ugly.[31]

The importation of the Spanish feminine beauty devalued the aboriginal or national images. This acculturation process was a reflection of the ensuing destruction of the various Mexican Indian cultures by changing indigenous values and creating a sense of self rejection. Some Indian women would try to bleach their skin, but most Indian women could only hope that their children would be born white and thereby be accepted as free "Spaniards." Even today many parents do not permit their children to sit in the sun for fear they will get darker and suffer the consequences in a racist society.

However when the women arrived from Spain, the Spanish men still continued to abuse and rape the Indian women.[32]

A double standard for men and women characterized the upper and middle classes. There was a relatively high percentage of concubinage or the keeping of mistresses. Colored women were especially prized as mistresses . . . As the Indians of the suburbs, especially those around Mexico City, became used to Spanish dress and practice, they also tended to take on Spanish practices in family union.[33]

Even with the double standard, the Spanish women and their children gained an indirect economic and legal social status through their recognized legal marriage. However the Indian women who lived as slaves under a common law situation had no legal nor economic protection from the institution of marriage.

It is interesting to note that the historical economic and cultural differences between the Spanish and Indian women seem to be incorporated into the Mexican culture to characterize two kinds of women, "La Mujer Buena en La Casa Grande," and "La Mujer Mala de La Casa Chica."

The basis for La Mujer Buena, the good, respectable woman in La Casa Grande, was the upper class Spanish woman whose role was to stay home. She was the legal consort with the legal heirs entitled to inherit their father's property. Socially and culturally the mujer buena was white, segregated from the social, political, and economic life. She would only go alone to church, or to visit her parents. La mujer buena was totally dependent on her husband and was expected to tolerate the man's right to exercise his sexual freedom.[34]

The concept of Marianisma reinforced this Spanish role as a positive ideal for everyone to follow. Marianisma defined the women in sexual-social roles. The three basic images of the possibilities of women were: woman as a virgin, woman as a wife, and woman as a mother.[35] All three images reinforced a state of social-psychological and economic dependency. Some women were kept secluded and under supervision so that all independence became alien to their experience, and therefore outside of their reality. Independence became synonymous with acting out of control because woman could not control herself. For a woman who chose to act out "su libertad," her independence was destined to lead to whoredom, the negative alternative of Marianisma.[36] Although many of the Spanish women were not virgins on their arrival into Mexico, they made up for it as wives and mothers. They increased the patrons' possessions, began the pure Spanish line in New Spain, and through their children kept the New World in the hands of the Old World.

The social bases for the concept of la mujer mala seems to rest on the class and cultural differences of the Indian woman. Some were mistresses, and her children were usually illegitimate. Plus Mexican Indian women actively participated in the religious, social and commercial life of their people. Women shared the responsibility of the household and also contributed to the economy and social life of society. Many Mexican Indian women worked as bakers, doctors, magicians and midwives. Midwives were also ritual specialists similar to the shaman of other Indian societies. In addition, Aztecan women could hold property, enter into contracts, take cases to court and divorce their husbands and came from a polygamous society.[37]

The different cultural and economic role of the Indian woman opposed the ideal image of Spanish woman and Marianisma, and unfortunately became associated with the image of the Mala Mujer—the Bad Woman, the infamous one.

La Mala Mujer has many connotations. She is a whore who enjoys sex in or out of marriage and entices men to "wallow in brown flesh."[38] She was also a woman who left tradition and passive dependency behind. She dares to be and act independently of a man.[39] (Many women have no choice.) As a public woman, she did not keep her thoughts in the privacy of her home or her mind. Although she expressed knowledge and understanding, it would be received as anger, violence and disobedience. If she would cuss, she made others feel uncomfortable. Others, men, who asserted themselves were accepted for they only represented themselves among their male peers or they had economic credibility. However woman's actions reflected and represented those to whom she belonged to—the family, the husband, the patron. Eventually church ideology integrated these class and cultural differences into the concept of the ideal woman and the tainted despised woman. Through the gradual acculturation process, the Spanish Woman became the ideal and the image of the Indian woman was rejected.

The Indian woman and her mestizo child became the outcasts, the pariahs of society. Neither the mother nor the mestizo children had any legal or social rights. The mothers' only legacy for her child was to be born white in order to be accepted as a free "Spaniard." Speculation may be that many women may have committed mass suicides or infanticides like their Puerto Rican sisters. Undoubtedly many may have also attempted to even kill the patrons. Rather than help the ravaged women gain their economic and social rights due them, the church offered her spiritual compensation. Marianisma convinced the woman to endure the injustices against her.

As a mother, the emulation of Mary drew the mother's worth and nobility from her relationship to her children. Motherhood promoted the essence of altruism such as abnegation, self effacement or self denial.[40] The only approved selfish reward for her martyrdom was life after death. Meanwhile, she could do penance for her illegal morals as a mother, martyr and servant. These nonsexual roles would hopefully hide the woman's potential or present sexuality.[41] Her actions had to neutralize the sensual color of her exotic brown skin.

If she could not offer her mestizo children a legal birthright, she could take responsibility for every pain her children would encounter in their lifetime. She could identify with the Virgin Mary as she watched her son die on the cross.

To the disinherited mestizo, the relationship between master and servant woman was an

Mujeres by Olga Muniz

example of force, strength and power. Motolini describes the effect:

> It seems to me that with the passage of time, the Mexican mind has come to identify with the image of the patron as the symbol of getting ahead to be someone. Many times, the Mexican male expects to have a servant and be a master. Therefore he expects his woman to attend him, to serve him, and he will not allow his meals not to be right on time.[42]

Nor did the Church disagree that every man should be treated like this—by his wife. According to the Church, passivity and martyrdom are posed as the ideal qualities of a wife and thereby relegates her to nurturer and sexual object. As a wife, woman is essentially a body, a totally submissive obedient body to her master, serving every murmur. Because the wife has no personal rights, she must surrender her body on command, while receiving no personal pleasure and allowing herself to be used solely as an instrument of procreation and welfare of her husband.[43]

The Mexican male wanted a servant, virgin, a mujer buena y mala all in one. Men were taught by the church that there are two kinds of women: a good woman with "el himen in tacto," who is an inexhaustible source of tenderness and goodness and a bad woman who is selfish and unyielding.[44] The virgin image remains the ideal. The reality of woman's sexual relationship with a man and the product of sexual relations in or out of the confines of marriage determine his second class treatment of her.

According to Francisco Gonzalez Pineda, the adolescent Mexican male passes through three stages during mate selection:

1. La prentendida or the dream girl who is the romantic nirvana of purity while still permitting sex without sin.
2. The girlfriend briefly represents the living idealization of a companion challenging the adventures of life leaving tradition and passiveness behind.
3. This illusion is shattered when she becomes the esposa "the wife," rather than a companion of his difficult life, wife represents the failure of his ideals."[45]

The implication seems to be that a virgin or a woman outside society's norms rises to personhood and near equality with the male.[46] Sex is negative and has the potential to prevent him from fulfilling his ideals. And as long as she remains a virgin she is free and does not have to submit to male domination nor to the sorrows of childbearing and he need not be economically responsible for his conquests.

Crossbreeds

Mestiza ladies with
golden skins
reach out to touch
the beginnings of us
to find the real places
we come from.

My politics are not
together—
we cry the same
bitter tears
black & white
red & white
yellow & white
brown & white
we cry the same
bitter tears.

I've heard it all
before: someone said—
greeneyes smiling,
freckled hand
flicking strands of
uncertain red hairs
away from a
flaccid cheek, and
I see the dark gloom
of La Muerte
stalking the eyes
of deaf purists
who have heard it all—
seen it all
borne it all
and never understand:
the mestiza hurt & resentment
the anger that drives us
to the rim of a waiting
cliff—waiting for one
more hurt, one last
consuming anger to
wash us over the edge.
I will not take that step
of my own volition.

My politics
are not together,

we cry the same
bitter tears,
cry the same
bitter tears.

My blood lines
mix together—
separate
hold one above
the others to
identify with
one self-segregated
group.
My blood is
not together, each
strain leaps for
recognition
disclaims the rest—
takes turn to pass
for this or that:
each but one part
of me.
My heart
beats segregated
drops—strains to
mix the separate drops
of all the bloods
in me.

My blood
is not together,
my politics
fall apart—
red—
black—
brown—
yellow &
white:
Crossbreeds
we walk alone   alone
& cry
the same bitter tears—
cry the same
bitter tears.

Carol Lee Sanchez

Irene Fujitomi and Diane Wong

The New Asian-American Woman

Reserved, quiet, shy, and humble—are they really virtues of the Asian woman? Those are the characteristics people typically apply to her. Impressed by the Asian woman's femininity, which is rooted in the traditions of the past and is being perpetuated by the mass media in the present, all Asian sisters are being stereotyped by people who have never met them and by Asian brothers who will not accept them if they do not fit their "nice Asian girl" stereotype.

Since the image of the passive, demure Asian woman is pervasive, the struggle for a positive self-identity is difficult. Within the Asian community, the family supports the development of the male's personality and aspirations, while the sister is discouraged from forming any sense of high self-esteem and individuality. Her worth is measured by the "good" husband she catches by being the epitome of Asian femininity. According to modeling theory, both the male and female child learn to adopt the sex roles practiced by their parents. In Asian families, roles are well defined; the father is the decision-maker and the mother is the compliant wife. Thus, Asian sisters soon come to perceive their roles as inferior to all men.

The Asian woman's struggle is a third-world struggle and is, therefore, distinctively different from the White woman's liberation movement. The Asian woman is a minority individual, and, within her own family, she is delegated a lower status than the male; for these reasons, she is doubly oppressed. As the larger society continues to repress the Asian males, the Asian males find it necessary to oppress their own

females. In order to redeem dignity in his maleness, the Asian man exerts his masculinity by keeping his woman in her place. Traditionally, the subordinate role of the Asian woman was an acceptable custom; today, anything but the traditional role is a threat to the Asian male.

Like the Black women, in their struggle for liberation, Asian sisters, first, would like to see their Asian brothers succeed in the larger society. But, in the process of the struggle for racial equality, Asian women are working to discover new potentials. Many are concerned with discarding old images and developing their own positive self-identities . . . and becoming human beings.

Compared to the status of the Asian woman fifty years ago, the position of the Asian woman of today has improved. She is able, now, to marry the man she loves, to hold skilled and professional jobs, and is allowed by the family to attend college. Although this improvement is desirable, it often hides the immense problems still faced by the Asian female.

The Traditional Asian Woman

To understand the status of the Asian-American woman, it is not enough merely to analyze the present condition. It is necessary to examine the attitudes and values which existed in Asia and were later brought to the United States by the immigrants. These attitudes and values affected the status of the woman as an inhabitant of the homeland, as an immigrant, and as a resident of the United States.

Being a woman in traditional Asia was considered undesirable. Confucianism, while establishing a stable government and providing the society with a strong set of moral virtues, committed a great injustice to the Asian woman. Prior to the widespread dissemination of, and adherence to, the teachings of Confucius, the position of Asian women was markedly higher: they were scholars, warriors, leaders, and respected members of communities (Faust, 1926). But the emergence of his teachings as the principles of social relationships for all of Asia ensured for women several centuries of status inferiority and imposed incapability.

At birth, the status of the female child was already lower than that of the male child. Because of the patrilineal, patrilocal, and patriarchal principles guiding the Asian society, the birth of a boy was a particularly joyous event. Through the boy, the parents could be assured that the family name and the memory of ancestors would continue to be worshiped in the afterworld (Burkhardt, 1960). The birth of a daughter, on the other hand, was a liability to the family: she neither carried on the family name nor worshiped her natal ancestors (Fei, 1962; Sung, 1967). Her lower status, often, made her a victim of negligent care, especially in her early years of life (Yang, 1959), or led to her being disposed of in times of family hardship (Loomis, 1969).

Sexual discrimination in early childhood, though limited, did exist. In Japan, if the baby was a male, on the 31st day after his birth he was taken to the shrine to be blessed; if the baby was a female, the mother took her to the shrine on the 33rd day. A Chinese father, if asked about his children, usually mentioned only his male children unless he had only daughters, in which case he then, reluctantly, discussed them (Burkhardt, 1960).

The first major source of discrimination was education. Women seldom enjoyed the advantages of formal education, as this was usually reserved for the sons (Burkhardt, 1960). Instead, their schooling consisted almost entirely of learning household chores as taught by their female relatives (Burkhardt, 1960; Fried, 1953). The women were not only denied formal education, but were discouraged from developing abilities or talents which might have been useful for a career outside the home.

In all situations, the young girl learned to respond submissively. This prepared her for married life (Burkhardt, 1960). A woman had no say in the marriage arrangement; it was all planned by the families concerned (Faust, 1926). The love and happiness of the bride and groom were not among the salient factors considered in the marriage contract. Rather, the marriage was arranged with these classical purposes in mind (Yang, 1959):

a. perpetuating the patrilineal line
b. maintaining the performance of ancestral sacrifice
c. obtaining a daughter-in-law to serve and help the parents
d. establishing a growing family with potential to earn money to increase the family's security.

The marriage symbolized the death of the female's relationship with her natal family. She visited them only rarely, on festival days (Sung, 1967). From her home, she was deeply thrust into an unknown environment; she had to assume intimate terms with almost total strangers (Fei, 1962). In arguments between the wife and the parents-in-law, the husband was expected to ally himself with his parents (Yang, 1959). As a mere possession of the husband's family,

The five worst infirmities that afflict the female are indocility,
discontent, slander, jealousy, and silliness. . . . Such is the stupidity of
her character that it is incumbent upon her, in every particular, to
distrust herself and obey her husband.

Confucian marriage manual

---

the Asian woman was expected to cater to the demands of all the family members and to attend to the menial household duties.

This particular period of a woman's life has been described as "the most personally humiliating and emotionally disturbing stage of a woman's life . . ." (Yang, 1959).

Since the most crucial factor of a marriage was the birth of a male progeny, barrenness was deemed more than sufficient cause for the dissolution of the marriage. In addition to barrenness, the husband had six other classical reasons for divorcing his wife, among which were filial impiety, jealousy, and talkativeness (Burkhardt, 1960; Faust, 1926). The husband could, and, to the extent that it ensured continuance of the family name, was expected to, remarry. The most common type of remarriage—concubinage—had no institutional guarantee for the wife's security or the permanency of her position in the family (Yang, 1959).

The wife, on the other hand, had no right to ask for a divorce (Fei, 1962). The factors which discouraged the wife from dissolving the marriage were that she had no property rights or other means of support, and she could remarry only under severe social sanctions (Yang, 1959). If the husband should die, the wife's supreme act of faith was to take her own life. Should she choose not to die, she, generally, remained with her in-laws as long as they could afford to take care of her. Her husband's death had no effect upon her obligations as a dutiful daughter-in-law. If a widow remarried, she was considered no better than a concubine (Yang, 1959).

Although a man was socially allowed to take additional wives or otherwise to indulge in promiscuous behavior, a woman was not (Sung, 1967). According to Kaibara, a famous Confucian scholar of Japan's middle ages, a woman was required to obey men, who had the absolute right to rule her. Sexually, she was to be pure and chaste, while no restrictions were placed on the men (Faust, 1926). This great stress placed on the woman's chastity and the corresponding laxity in its application to the man fostered not only highly inequitable social norms and values concerning divorce, widowhood, and remarriage, but also led to other dehumanizing customs. For example, at the wedding, the Japanese bride was given a short dagger. If her chastity was ever placed in doubt, she was expected to commit suicide. This act was considered the greatest and only credible proof of her faithfulness. Male jealousy led to other peculiar practices which further reinforced the principle of male superiority and female inferiority. Wives wore their long hair in a marumage, which is a plain, round chignon worn on the back of the head. Furthermore, the prettier wives were required to blacken their teeth with a certain chemical (Faust, 1926). Therefore, with the marumage and the black teeth, the married woman was not only an unattractive sight but was a walking symbol of her faceless inhumanness!

The life of the female was difficult, more so

One hundred women are not worth a single testicle.

Confucius

in many ways than the life of the male (Loomis, 1969). The following passage illustrates the lot of the traditional Asian woman:

> . . . a girl began her working age earlier than a boy. At the age of about eight, she started with light household duties such as watching the younger children and fetching light objects; she also worked along with her mother in the fields at light work. Her duties at home and in the fields increased until she was married at sixteen or seventeen to another family, where her arduous domestic and production tasks continued until she reached her fifties, when they tapered off to lighter tasks. The woman's burden was so heavy that she, generally, looked older than her age (Yang, 1959, p. 22).

The woman worked in both the home and the field and was a servant to her husband, father, and brothers. It was in old age that she could look forward to rest, and then only when her in-laws and her husband had passed away (Yang, 1959).

It is no great wonder, then, that a woman's life was considered a punishment for a previous life of evil and wanton disregard of a virtuous life.

Immigrant Chinese Women

Beginning in the 1850s, there was a large influx of Chinese coming into the United States. While some came to find political and religious freedom, most of the Chinese immigrated to America in hopes of earning enough money to make up for financial losses incurred during

Photograph courtesy of the Bancroft Library

the natural catastrophes of flood and famine and the political disasters of unrest and rebellion. The discovery of gold attracted the Chinese to California and increased their hopes of making money to support their families back in China.

In the mass movement of Chinese, there were very few women involved. Constrained by cultural attitudes and beliefs, the woman was not

*The women's struggle is the liberation of MEN. As women shed their
roles, so goes the "masculine image," the "masculine ego," the
"masculine hang-up." A man won't have to be tall, dark, strong,
aggressive, competitive, rugged, or independent, any more than a
woman has to be small, delicate, passive, artistic, or dependent. The old
order will be destroyed for the creation of a new, emancipated order.
Men will be free to create humanistic relationships from natural
interactions. New relationships and new roles. New frontiers, new
freedoms, new directions. Power to the sisters.*

Yamamoto, *Gidra*, Jan. 1971

Too Much to Require

*Fathers
required me
to split my tongue*

*to learn the silent
graces
of womanhood
like sweeping
cobwebs from family relics*

                    and so i am gentle

*to taste
that guilt for not being
  'what you should be'
and working harder/for/everything*

            and so i am gentle

*to remember the ease
of instant omission
and the necessity for
assimilation*

            and so i am gentle

*to forget hiroshima
to ignore vietnam
to accept tule lake
to enjoy chinatown*

        *o yes, daddy,
        very gentle i am*

        when i clean my gun.

                    Janice Mirikitani

to leave her husband's family home for any
reason. If the parents-in-law passed away while
the husband was gone, she was expected to
attend to their proper burial and mourning rites
(Lyman, 1971; Tow, 1923). Most Chinese husbands did not intend to reside permanently in
the United States but planned to return to China
(Jung, 1971; Lyman, 1971). Therefore, as so-
journers, they had no need nor desire to trans-
plant their entire families and ancestral hearths
to America (Lowe, 1943).

Exacerbation of this culturally based practice
came in 1882 in a series of legislative acts. It
started with the passage of the Chinese Exclusion Act of 1882, which was approved by a
United States Federal Court ruling in 1884
(Lyman, 1971; Sung, 1967). The act prohibited
the entry of Chinese women who were not the
wives of classes of Chinese exempt from the
Exclusion Act, e.g., merchants, students, teachers. The majority of the Chinese immigrants
were affected by this act because they came
as laborers and workers. Therefore, the wives
were forbidden to enter the United States even
though the husbands were willing to break the
traditional Chinese custom that the women stay
in the homeland.

The combination of Chinese tradition and
American law had destructive consequences.
In China, many wives had, virtually, no husbands, since thousands of miles of ocean separated them. Again, because of cultural norms,
wives could not easily obtain a divorce and
remarry and, thus, were compelled to endure

Photograph by Cathy Cade

a "mutilated marriage" (Sung, 1967). They did have a family life—that is, they were able to interact with the husband's family, who took care of them.

Though this condition was serious, the distressing problem was the severe scarcity of Chinese women in the United States, which is only now being ameliorated (Sung, 1967). Lyman (1971) believes that, had the Chinese been allowed to intermarry with White women, the shortage of women could have been mitigated. But, as it was, there were several obstacles to this possible course of action:

> The mutual peculiarities of dress, language, habits, customs, and diets, not to mention the physical distinctiveness of both racial identities, kept the Chinese and Americans apart. In addition, both Americans and Chinese have tended to enclose themselves in mutually exclusive associations, thus reducing the amount of personal contact to a minimum and severely restricting the possibility for romantic attachments to rise (Lyman, 1971, p. 29).

Commencing in 1860, several states passed laws which reinforced this racial segregation and declared marriages of interracial mixture as acts of miscegenation (Lyman, 1971).

An inevitable consequence of the highly disproportionate number of Chinese men to Chinese women in the United States and of the inaccessibility of other women was the establishment and growth of prostitution, which was designed to satisfy the sexual needs of the single or married Chinese male in America.

The women prostitutes were obtained through various, often devious, methods. Many were lured to America by false promises of marriage to a Chinese sojourner; some were captured by pirates who sold them into slavery; still others were kidnapped from their homes, both in China and America (Dillon, 1962; Loomis, 1969; Lyman, 1971). All who had survived the trans-Pacific journey and who eventually landed on the shores of America were sold to brothel owners or were placed under contract with them to pay for their passage.

The lives of these women were tragic and difficult. A few managed to escape from the brothels and seek asylum in missions which were attempting to eradicate this business. Still others were able to marry single Chinese men or become concubines of already married men whose wives were in China. Of those who managed to escape, many were returned to their owners on charges that they had not fully paid their passage loan, or that they had stolen articles of clothing and jewelry (Dillon, 1962; Louie, 1971; Lyman, 1971). Even the protectors of the law—the police, lawyers, and judges— were, often, aligned with the brothel owners and, therefore, ordered the capture and return of the prostitutes (Dillon, 1962). Women who became concubines had no legal rights and could be forsaken at any time by their husbands. The majority of the Chinese women who were unable to escape from their owners were convinced into accepting their lot as the best available to them in America.

The Chinese women of the United States in the late 1800s and early 1900s were severely oppressed, reduced to mere slaves and sexual commodities. The principles associated with female inferiority which were prevalent in traditional China were carried over by the immigrants.

Immigrant Japanese Women

The story of the immigrant Japanese woman has long been overshadowed by the Issei man's history. In examining her side of the human drama, we shall raise the questions usually asked of men. What influenced her decision to come to America? How did she adjust to the stark realities of the hostile and foreign land? More particularly, how did she live through the poverty, the social rejection by the larger society, and the legal injustice? In the following sequence, a glimpse of the Issei woman's struggle will be presented.

The immigration data for Japanese females indicate a pattern which was initially similar to that of Chinese female immigration. In the early period of Japanese immigration (1880s–1890s), very few women came to the United States. The 1900 Census revealed that, out of the total Japanese population of 24,326, only 985 were women (Gee, 1971). The female-male sex ratio was, thus, 1:24 (Gee, 1971). At the turn of the century, the immigration pattern for Chinese and Japanese women deviated. The years from 1900 to 1920 marked the great immigration period for Issei women. By 1920, when the United States passed legislation to curtail further Japanese immigration, the population of Japanese women had risen to 22,193 out of a total Japanese population of 111,010 (Gee, 1971).

The Japanese immigrant population in America changed from that of temporary male immigrants to one of permanent family residents. It was facilitated by the traditional custom of omimai-kekkon. As was previously discussed, marriage was strictly a family matter. Marriage was a partnership rather than an intimate relationship developing from love. Thus, the heads of the bride and groom's families exercised complete control over mate selection. Investigation into the prospective spouse's family tree and economic and political background was customary. Through the services of a "go-between," marital contracts were arranged between the families. Marriages became legal when the wife's name was officially registered in the husband's koseki—a family register. Since the consolidation of marriage did not require the presence of both parties, it was possible for hundreds of Issei men in America to take brides. Pictures of the prospective spouses were exchanged for approval, while all the formalities were handled by the "go-between." Thus, for the single Issei men, the custom of omimai-kekkon extended across the sea to provide them with "picture brides" who were selected by the family, according to the sacred tradition.

Prospects for the brides' future life in America varied. In the case of one woman, her mother convinced her that the streets in America were paved with gold. Expecting a life of prosperity, the dream of this young bride was shattered as she discovered that the streets were not made of gold but stone, and her new house in America was a mere shack, worse than the poorest shacks in Japan.

> . . . I discovered that our house was a house in name only, a shack where hunters had lived, located in the middle of a field. There was only one room with beds placed in three corners. My husband was living here with a younger boy and older person . . . thus, a makeshift curtain had

to be made by stretching a rope across the room and hanging clothes from it. The shack had been fashioned out of boards and leaked. There were no eaves to drain the rain. Sometimes, we passed the night with raincoats over our beds. It was unsuitable for us newlyweds, to say the least! (Gee, 1971, p. 12).

Generally, the "picture brides" came from large farming families. Their mundane lives as country girls accounted for the enthusiasm and hopeful dreams they held of the "New World." Young, spirited, and naïve, the Japanese picture brides were overcome by exaggerated glamour stories told to them in letters by their anxious grooms. Occasionally, Japanese males who had made a small fortune in America returned home in their Western garb to show off their success. Reinforced by such displays, many of the picture brides looked toward America as the "promised land."

There were husbands at the other extreme who were truthful with their brides. According to another picture bride, her husband warned her that, if she was coming to America with great expectations, she would be disappointed. He emphasized that, should she accept his proposal of marriage, she had to come prepared to see things through without giving up. With this understanding and forewarning of hardships ahead, the bride made this resolution:

Aboard the ship, on the way from Koe to Yokohama, gazing upon the rising majestic Mount Fuji in a cloudless sky, I made a vow. For a woman who was going to a strange society and relying upon an unknown husband whom she had married through photographs, my heart had to be as beautiful as Mount Fuji. I resolved that the heart of a Japanese woman had to be sublime, like, like that soaring, majestic figure, eternally constant through wind and rain, heat and cold. Thereafter, I never forgot that resolution on the ship, enabling

me to overcome sadness and suffering. (Gee, 1971, p. 11)

When the brides arrived in America, picture matching was not an easy task. To the disappointment of both wives and husbands, the "go-between" often gave them pictures which were either dated or false. Last minute exchanges, and even refusals, were probably made.

For the Issei brides, there was neither time nor money for a honeymoon. Almost immediately, they were put to work alongside their husbands. The need for money and the constant deprivation required the women to work laboriously in the fields and factories. Besides her regular housekeeping chores and child caring, a wife of a dry cleaning operator recalls having to put in overtime regularly.

I started at 5:00 p.m. to prepare supper for five to six people, and then I began my evening work. The difficult ironing remained. Women's blouses, in those days, were made from silk or lace, with collars, and long sleeves and lots of frills. I could only finish two in one hour, ironing them with great care. Hence, I worked, usually, until 12:00 Midnight or 1:00 a.m. But it was not just me . . . all who worked in the laundry business did the same thing. (Gee, 1971, p. 14)

Child bearing followed in accordance with the custom of ancestor worship. Emphasis was placed not only on bearing male offspring to continue the family line, but on having many children. Families of farmers, typically, were large, because more family members meant more working hands. With the passage of the 1924 Immigration Act, which barred Japanese immigration, family size increased with the intention of guaranteeing a viable future for the Japanese-American community.

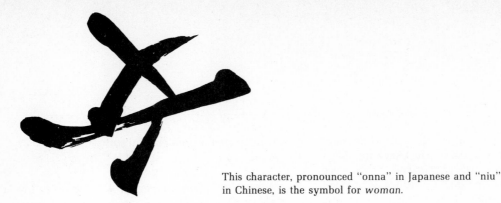

This character, pronounced "onna" in Japanese and "niu" in Chinese, is the symbol for *woman*.

The greatest hardship which the Issei woman endured was childbirth. In rural areas, doctors were not readily available. Those who were available were either too expensive for the family to afford, or the doctors would refuse to treat Japanese women. Thus, two alternatives were left: to perform childbirth by herself or to employ the services of a midwife. Post-natal recuperation was a luxury in most households. Since wives were economic units crucial to the family incomes, they often worked until the day of childbirth and were working within three days afterwards.

Child rearing was strictly a woman's chore. Despite the fact that the Issei woman worked as hard as her husband in the fields, she, alone, had to bear the responsibility of raising her children properly according to the Meiji tradition. Her role as a good wife was to sacrifice and be dutiful to her husband first, her children second, and herself last. One woman reveals . . .

> My husband was a Meiji man. He did not think of helping in the house or with the children. No matter how busy I may have been, he never changed the baby's diapers. Though it may not be right to say this ourselves, we Issei pioneer women from Japan worked solely for our husbands. At mealtime, whenever there was not enough food, we served a lot to our husbands and took very little for ourselves. (Gee, 1971, p. 15)

The persistence of Issei women in the face of obstacles helped to carry the family through the pre-war and war eras. When anti-Japanese feelings were intense and the humiliating cries of "damn Jap" were hurled at the Japanese males, the females made sure their husbands found comfort and reassurance of their male identity as the powerful and honorable "papa-sans." With deep understanding and quiet fortitude, the Issei women suffered and survived.

Duty and obligation continued to guide the Nisei woman's behavior and lifestyle. As a young girl, she was raised to become a respectful wife and good mother to her sons. Getting a college education was not important, so only a minority of the Nisei women have college degrees. Today, the Nisei women, typically, hold occupations as factory workers, waitresses, secretaries, nurses, and teachers. The major concern of the Nisei women is their families. Like the Issei family, the Nisei family is vertically structured. The husband is the decision maker, the head of the household. Family size is decreasing to an average of two children per family (Kitano, 1960). Mothers continue to live vicariously through their children, encouraging all of them, regardless of sex, to pursue, at least, a college degree. In order to help their children through school, the Nisei women will sacrifice their own luxuries to provide the children with the opportunities denied themselves.

Divorce rates are low among the Nisei. When the Nisei married, it was usually between friends of long acquaintance, either through personal or family contacts. Nisei men married Nisei women. Interracial marriages were rare,

Difficult as it is to deal with realities, some Vietnam veterans have been able to speak about their experiences in Vietnam, because they began to understand the nature of sexual violence in an aggressive, colonialist war. The roots of this violence come from deep within our own culture and take their toll on women all over the world, including ourselves.

Jane Fonda and Nancy Dowd, Vietnamese Women's Slide Show

primarily because the Issei families absolutely forbade such marriages, and the United States Government's anti-miscegenation laws had deemed them illegal.

Current Trends

Interestingly, the attitudes of Japanese females are becoming less "traditional." A study on attitudes of Japanese-American and Caucasian-American students toward marriage roles was conducted by Arkoff, Meredith, and Dong (1963.) The Jacobson Scale was used to measure male-dominant and equalitarian attitudes toward marriage.

Results of the questionnaire indicated that Japanese-American males were more male-dominant in their attitudes regarding husband-wife marriage roles. Japanese-American females, Caucasian-American females, and Caucasian-American males were found to agree in their attitudes about marital role being equalitarian. The study suggests that Japanese-American women, today, are "American" in their conception of marriage roles and family living, while the Japanese-American males still believe in the classical, male-dominant "Japanese" marriage.

Omimai (or arranged) marriages are relics of the past. Dating among young Asians follows an acculturative pattern, where early and steady dating has become a common practice. Marrying for love based on mutual interests and compatability has replaced the marriage for

Stop Bombing by Mitsu Yashima, reprinted by permission

convenience. As the third generation of Chinese- and Japanese-Americans becomes more assimilated, interracial dating and rates of interracial marriages are expected to increase.

Recently, Tinker (1972) completed a survey of the marriage records of Japanese-Americans in Fresno, California. He found that, within the past decade, the marriage pattern of the Japanese-Americans was significantly changing; the rate of intermarriage was increasing sharply. Up until 1948, California had prohibited marriages between Asian and Caucasian-Americans. In 1959, over ten years after the law

Mountain Moving Day

The mountain moving day is coming
I say so yet others doubt it
Only a while the mountain sleeps
In the past all mountains moved in fire
Yet you may not believe it
O man this alone believe
All sleeping women now awake and move
All sleeping women now awake and move

Yosano Akiko, 1911

---

had been repealed, fewer than three out of every ten Japanese-American marriages were interracial (Barnett, 1963; Burma, 1963). In 1972, Tinker reported that 56 percent of all Japanese-American marriages in Fresno were interracial. Because the rate of intermarriage is a reliable indicator of the permeability of ethnic boundaries, implications of Tinker's study are controversial.

An examination of intermarriage rates reveals two distinct patterns. One pattern is the tendency for marriage to respect religious differences between the couple concerned. Another observation, based on Black-White marriage studies (Barnett, 1963; Burma, 1963; Merton, 1941) and those of Jews and gentiles (Sklare, 1967), has shown that men of a racial, religious, and ethnic minority "outmarry" at higher rates than minority women. Tinker's study, however, suggests that the religiously and racially distinct Japanese-American women were outmarrying at a slightly higher rate than the Japanese-American male. Barnett (1963) found that, between 1956 and 1959, in California, almost twice as many Japanese-American females (494) as males (256) intermarried with Caucasian-Americans. In the case of the Chinese-Americans, 196 females, as compared to 172 males, intermarried with Caucasian-Americans.

To imply that the Asian woman's increased rate of outmarriage is a function of her sudden preference for a Caucasian-American mate is

oversimplification. Stereotypes of Asian males and females have differential implications, with the male's still being portrayed as short and unmasculine, while the image of the Asian woman is improving in the eyes of Caucasian-Americans. Although many Asian sisters consider the tiny, exotic geisha, or china doll, an equally dehumanizing stereotype, this stereotype, at least, is considered favorable enough to make the Asian woman an eligible candidate for marriage to the American male.

The dating of Caucasian-American males by Asian females did not impose as great a threat to the White community as did the dating of Caucasian-American females by Asian males:

I have a Japanese man friend who was once beat up by some White boys for being on the street with a White girl. Actually, it was an unusual situation in the first place, since many White women won't go out with Asian men because "they aren't attracted to them." So, where Asian men are restricted to Asian women, Asian women are free, more or less, to go out with White men. As a result, some Asian men will resent the Asian women who take advantage of that freedom, and we Asian women don't know how to feel. (Masaoka, 1971, p. 58)

Differential acceptance of minority group members, based on sex, creates numerous problems. It creates jealousy and serves to divide the males and females of a minority group. Friction is generated by arguing over whose stereotype is better than the other's. Although females are better accepted by the dominant culture, inferiority and self-hatred may develop on the part of those Asian women who want to resemble the long-legged, fair-skinned American cover girl. Men are equally vulnerable to the dictates of the American values of sexual attractiveness, as this quote, by an Asian male, conveys:

> I, at first, was strongly critical of the physical appearance of the Japanese. The men were, by White standards, short and skinny; the females, plain and thick-legged. Those females who seemed beautiful to me were precisely the ones who most closely resembled Caucasians. (Okimoto, 1971, p. 7)

Asian Women as Leaders

The Asian-American woman bears the burden of a double onus: she must be an Asian-American and a female. In striving for success and positions of leadership, the female must work harder than the male in proving her capabilities. For most women, their idea of "femininity"—being supportive followers—prevents them from seeking power over other men and women. The Asian-American woman is taught from birth that she is inferior in quality to her male counterpart; inferior in ability, intelligence, perception, and emotional stability. "Brainwashed" through mass media stereotyping and interactions with family and friends, she concludes that, to be feminine and desirable, she must be passive, submissive, and contented with married life (Cade, 1970).

These oppressive conceptions of the "ideal" Asian-American female are being seriously questioned. Young Asian-American women are now beginning to reassess their goals and self-perceptions. Encouraged by the rise in ethnic-group and sexual pride, Asian-American women are entering positions of higher status and leadership.

The Asian woman faces complex obstacles in her endeavors to become a leader. Being a minority group member and an American, she must successfully integrate two cultures (Burma, 1953); often, much of her energy is dissipated in this struggle. Many of her own people may be against her for the following reasons:

a. to be effective, she must be aggressive and assertive, but this is contrary to the Asian values of passivity and submission (Benedict, 1946; Burma, 1953);

b. in being effective, she, often, becomes highly visible and public, which is contrary to traditional Asian values of modesty and moderation (Benedict, 1946; Burma, 1953).

Burma has observed that many Japanese-Americans are overly concerned with doing the "proper thing." The Asian-American leader, in an effort to respect this concern, falls into a tendency to retard innovative and aggressive actions, and to minimize the leadership often needed to mobilize the community. Asians have been characterized as strong individuals but weak groups (Burma, 1953; Chang, 1934). Chang described Chinese-Americans as individuals who are extremely capable, but who are, collectively, "very much like a heap of loose sand" (Chang, 1934). Consequently, in order to be an effective community leader, the Asian-American female, first, must organize individuals to work as a group.

In rejecting her traditional role, the new Asian-American woman is vulnerable to pain and frustration. The role of her leadership is still vague and in the process of evolution. Her position has been described as a "limbo" state of being (Loomis, 1969). She has no clearly defined role or precedence, and, so, people do not know how to react to her, and, correspondingly, she has difficulty relating to them (Lundberg, 1968). By attempting to expand her life space to include personal feelings, individuality, and creativity, she risks being labeled and treated as "unfeminine" or "castrating" (Horner, 1969). Needing and wanting to be herself conflicts with being a "good" traditional Asian woman. This conflict becomes a source of anxiety which the new Asian-American woman must learn to overcome.

The labeling is done by various groups, sexists and racists, and even by those in the Asian-American movement. Many of the females in the movement, who are so acutely attuned to racial prejudice, have amicably accepted or have not become cognizant of the inferior status ascribed to them. They reject the notion of sexual prejudice and ignore the Asian-American woman who espouses the need to end both racism and sexism. The movement males consider the new Asian-American woman a threat to their masculinity. While advocating freedom from racial oppression, many of the movement males are unable to see that, in relegating their Asian-American sisters to clerical, social, and cleaning-up roles, they are oppressing part of their own group.

It must be remembered that it is not the Asian-American woman who has deprived the Asian-American male of his self-determination, for she, too, has been denied power over her own life. Beal (1970) writes that oppression proceeds without the consent of the minority woman; it is fallacious to believe that, for the man to be strong, the woman must be weak. Thus, all Asian-Americans must work together to attain that measure of freedom from racism and sexism to which they have a right.

Conclusion

The authors have tried to present an evolutionary picture of the Asian woman's development as a real and interesting person, as opposed to a flat, subordinate character behind a man. The silent struggle of the traditional and immigrant woman, which has been neglected, has now received some degree of tribute. In order to assess the direction which Asian-American women, today, are taking, it is important to reflect upon the past. There is, in the Asian woman of the past, a source of pride which Asian sisters can share. Although the status of women has greatly improved since the time of Confucius, Asian-American women are still struggling to overcome their inferiority complex which has been perpetuated by traditional thinking.

In the discussion of Asian-American women as leaders, the most crucial fear that not only Asian women but all women must overcome is the fear of being unsexed by success (Horner, 1969). Too many women are afraid to strive for positions of leadership because they are afraid of losing their femininity. In turn, men are trapped, also, in this sexist game, where failure to succeed is equated with immasculinity. Therefore, it is necessary for both men and women to reassess their role hang-ups and to work together in improving the human community.

Once Asian-American women have stopped denying themselves the chance to grow, to discover all the qualities with which they have been endowed, then, and only then, will they be born again to live as total human beings.

Shirley Hill Witt

Native Women Today: Sexism and the Indian Woman

The stereotypes concerning Native Americans popular among the descendants of the European pioneers—whether in legend or on television—nonetheless depict *male* natives. A different set of stereotypes materializes when one says "an Indian woman" or, so demeaningly, a "squaw." In fact, it takes some effort to conjure up an impression of that invisible native woman.

On a time line of New World history, one might locate Malinche of Aztec Mexico, Pocahontas of Virginia, and Sacajawea of the Northwest. They are probably the only female "personalities" that come to mind out of the great faceless sea of all the native women who were born, lived, and died in this hemisphere.

And ironically, these three native women are not now native heroines, if they ever were. In Mexico, the term "malinchismo" refers to selling out one's people to the enemy. Malinche, Pocahontas, and Sacajawea aided—perhaps unwittingly—in the downfall of their own people.

Another stereotype, the personality-less squaw, is regarded as a brown lump of a drudge, chewing buffalo hide, putting that tipi up and down again and again, carrying heavy burdens along with the dogs while the tribe moves ever onward, away from the pursuing cavalry.

The term "squaw" began as a perfectly acceptable Algonkian term meaning "woman." In time, it became synonymous with "drudge" and, in some areas, "prostitute." The ugliest epithet

a frontiersman could receive was to be called a "squawman"—the lowliest of the low.

Very much rarer is the image of a bronze nubile naked "princess," a child of nature or beloved concoction of Hollywood producers. This version is often compounded with the Pocahontas legend. As the story goes, she dies in self-sacrifice, saving the life of the white man for whom she bears an unrequited love, so that he may live happily ever after with a voluptuous but high-buttoned blonde.

Since all stereotypes are unsatisfactory and do not replicate real people, the myths of native women of the past ought also to be retired to the graveyard of stereotypes. But what about stereotypes of modern native women—are there any to be laid to rest? Present stereotypes are also male, are they not? The drunken Indian, the Cadillac Indian, Lonesome Polecat—facelessness still characterizes Native American women.

In this third quarter of the century, Native Americans yet remain the faceless minority despite a few "uprisings" such as Alcatraz, the Trail of Broken Treaties, and the Second Wounded Knee. That these "uprisings" were of definitive importance to the Indian world only underscores its basic invisibility to most Americans, many of whom pass off those protests as trivial and, naturally, futile—much ado about nothing.

And if a million Native Americans reside below national consciousness, certainly that

American Indians from all of the countries of the Americas are rising up and demanding their rightful voice in the world—and the right to live according to our own visions. . . . We do not believe that our way of life is perfect or has ever been so. But as we look at what the whiteman is doing to us, to himself, and to the Earth our Mother, we see that we do have a way of life. The whiteman has a way of death. American Indian women have wisdoms and insights that are valuable, if not necessary, to the dialogue on women's rights—and the dialogue on human rights. . . . Today, as always, American Indian women well understand that there can be no liberation of Indian women as women until all Indian people are free of colonial oppression.

from *Native American Women,* 1975

---

fifty-or-so percent of them that are female are all the more nonentities.

Before Columbus

As many as 280 distinct aboriginal societies existed in North America prior to Columbus. In several, the roles of native women stand in stark contrast to those of Europeans. These societies were matriarchal, matrilineal, and matrilocal—which is to say that women largely controlled family matters, inheritance passed through the female line, and upon marriage the bride usually brought her groom into her mother's household.

In a matrilocal society all the women were blood relatives and all the males were outsiders. This sort of residence pattern was frequently seen among agricultural societies in which women bore the responsibility for farming. It guaranteed a close-knit working force of women who had grown up with each other and the land.

Somewhat similar was the style of acquiring a spouse called "bride service" or "suitor service." In this case, the erstwhile husband went to live and work in his future bride's home for a period of time, proving his ability to manage a family of his own. This essentially resulted in temporary matrilocal residence. After the birth of the first child, the husband usually took his new family with him to live among his own kin.

In matrilineal, matrilocal society, a woman forever remained part of her original household, her family of orientation. All the women she grew up with stayed nearby, although she "lost" her brothers to other households. All the husbands were outsiders brought into the family at the time of marriage.

In such societies, usually agricultural, the economy was maintained largely by females. The fields and harvests were the property of women. Daughters inherited rights to fields and the like through their mothers—fields which they had worked in all their lives in one capacity or another, from chasing away the crows as a child to tilling the soil as an adult.

Women working together certainly characterized aboriginal economy. This lifestyle was roughly similar in such widespread groups as the Iroquois, the Mandan, the Hopi and Zuni, and various Eastern Pueblos. Among the Hopi and the Zuni the husband joined the bride's household upon marriage. The fields were owned by the women, as were their products, the house, and related implements. However, the men labored in the gardens and were (with the unmarried brothers) responsible for much or most of the work.

The strong and influential position of women in Navajo society extended beyond social and economic life. Navajo women also controlled a large share of the political and religious life of the people, called the Diné. Hogans, herds, and equipment were passed down through the

> *A nation is not conquered until the hearts of its women*
> *are on the ground. Then, it is done, no matter how brave its warriors*
> *nor how strong its weapons.*
>
> Cheyenne Proverb

female line, from mother to daughters. Like the Iroquois, women were integral to the religious cycle. The Navajo female puberty ceremony ranked among the most important of Diné activities.

Although the lives of Native American women differed greatly from tribe to tribe, their lifestyles exhibited a great deal more independence and security than those of the European women who came to these shores. Indian women had individual freedom within tribal life that women in more "advanced" societies were not to experience for several generations. Furthermore—and in contrast—native women increased in value in the estimation of their society as they grew older. Their cumulative wisdom was considered one of society's most valuable resources.

Today

What do we know about Native American women today? Inclusive statements such as the following refer to both sexes:

- Only 13.4 percent of the U.S. Indian population had completed eight years of school by 1970.
- The average educational level of all Indians under Federal supervision is five school years.
- Dropout rates for Indians are twice the national average.
- Only 18 percent of the students in Federal

i am the wind
i am the earth
i am the waters

do you think your borders and fences make me
  your captive
that your growth on my being devours my soul
or the contempt in your eyes touches my spirit

        i know your anger
        i know your hunger
        i know your fear

i see it in your art
in your colors lacking joy
in your shapes lacking softness
      as if a hard line
      could give you strength
your music dwells in sadness
your drums beat death
        yet, i cannot deny
        i breathe in time
        to your hourly murders

you are never alone
i envy the comfort
you get from your kind
        i admit to great sadness
        i am continually alone

        for, i am the wind
        i am the earth
        i am the waters

Suzan Shown

Indian schools go to college; the national average is 50 percent.

· Only 3 percent of the Indian students who enroll in college graduate; the national average is 32 percent.

· Indians suffer from unemployment and underemployment—up to 90 percent unemployment on some reservations in winter months.

· Indians have a high birth rate, a high infant mortality rate, and a short life expectancy.

But there are differences in how these facts relate to Native American women as opposed to men. There has not been equal treatment of native males and females any more than there has been equal treatment of the two sexes among non-natives. We can look at this by considering a few major institutions, affecting all our lives—education, employment, and health.

Education

For over a century the Federal Government has assumed the responsibility for educating Native Americans to the standards of the general population. Nearly every treaty contained provisions for education—a teacher, a school, etc.—as partial payment for lands and rights surrendered.

Until recent years, the U.S. Bureau of Indian Affairs educational system relied upon the boarding school as the cornerstone of native education, the foundation for indoctrination. Generation after generation of Native children were processed through boarding schools, from the time they were five or six years old until departure or graduation, whichever came first. They lived away from their homes from 4 to 12 years except during summer (and in some cases, even then). They became divorced from

their cultures in line with the Government's master plan for the ultimate solution to the "Indian Problem": assimilation.

And so, generation after generation after generation of native women have been processed through a system clearly goal-oriented. That is to say, the Government's master plan for women has been to generate an endless stream of domestics and, to a lesser extent, secretaries. The vocational choices for native children in boarding schools have always been exceedingly narrow and sexist. Boys do woodworking, car repair, house painting, or farmwork, while girls do domestic or secretarial work.

Writing about Stewart Indian School, in their book *To Live on This Earth,* Estelle Fuchs and Robert J. Havighurst report:

> The girls may choose from only two fields: general and home service (domestic work) or "hospital ward attendant" training, which the girls consider a degrading farce, a euphemism (they say) for more domestic work.

Thus young women are even more suppressed in working toward their aspirations than are boys. Furthermore, just as the males will more than likely find they must move away from their communities to practice their crafts, females cannot exercise their learned domestic crafts in the reservation setting either. A woman cannot even play out the role of a domestic, or the average American housewife and mother (as portrayed by the BIA), in the reservation atmosphere. As one author explains the Navajo woman's dilemma:

> Reservation life . . . cannot support the picture of the average American homemaker. The starched and relatively expensive advertised clothes are out of place and unobtainable. The polished floors and

picture windows which generated her envious school dreams are so removed from the hogan or log cabin as to become unreal. The many convenient appliances are too expensive and would not run without electricity. The clean and smiling children require more water than the Navajo family can afford the time to haul. Parent Teacher Association meetings, of which she may have read, are the product of tax-supported schools with the parent in the ultimate role of employer. On the reservation the government-appointed teacher is viewed more as an authority figure than a public servant.

Off-reservation, given the prevalence of Indian poverty, the all-American homemaker role still is thwarted, although hiring out as a domestic servant is possible.

Statistics about the educational attainment of Indians, Eskimos, and Aleuts are not hard to come by, but it is very difficult to obtain figures by sex. The exhaustive Havighurst report does not provide separate tabulations by sex in its summary volume *To Live on This Earth*. A U.S. Civil Rights Commission staff report found that 5.8 percent of the Indian males and 6.2 percent of the Indian females in a recent Southwest study had completed eight years of school. (The rate for all U.S. Indians in 1970 was 13.4 percent.)

The impression left from scanning available surveys is that in recent years females attain more years of formal education than do males, although some 50 years ago probably the reverse was true. This impression sits uneasily with study after study indicating that Native women are dramatically less acculturated than males.

Much data suggests that the BIA educational system is less effective for females than it is for males in creating successful mainstream prototypes—although young males have an

Thunderbird Woman by Alana Pohlmeyer

alarming suicide rate that is far higher than that of females.

An investigation by Harry W. Martin, et al., showed that of 411 Indian women at two Oklahoma Public Health Service medical outpatient clinics, 59.4 percent were classified as mildly or severely neurotic, compared to 50 percent of the males.

For the severely neurotic category alone, 31.7 percent of the Indian females were found to be severely impaired. This was almost one-third more than the males, who rated 23.7 percent. No clear relationship seemed to exist between the ages of the women and the incidence of impairment. (Men, on the other hand, tended to show neurotic symptoms more often in the 50 to 59 age bracket.)

When scores and level of education were correlated, it appeared that males with less education suffered more psychiatric problems than high school graduates, although the rates rose again with post-high school attainment. For females, a similar set of rates prevailed, but—as with suicide—their rate was not as acute as the male rate.

Such evidence suggests that amid the general failure of the Federal system to educate Native Americans in school curricula, the system also acculturates native females to a lesser degree than males. It cannot even transform women from native homemakers into mainstream homemakers. The neurotic response seems to tell us of widespread female disorganization and unhappiness.

The suicide statistics for young males who rate as more acculturated than females simply point up the shallowness of the assimilationist mentality of the BIA educational system. Is it not ironic that after more than a century of perfecting a Federal indoctrination system, their best product—the more acculturated males —so often seek self destruction, while nearly one-third of the females abide in a state of neuroticism?

Employment

Employment of native women is as one might expect, considering the level and quality of their educational background. Most employed women are domestics, whether in private homes, in janitorial positions, or in hospitals. The Navajo Times newspaper regularly carries want ads such as:

WANTED: strong young woman for live-in baby-sitter and mother's helper. No smoking or drinking. Call collect: San Diego, California.

As one young woman commented, "They must have run out of black maids." Perhaps the economic reality is that blacks are no longer at the bottom of the pile. Indians who have or will go to the cities are taking their place.

Federal employment for Native Americans essentially means employment in the BIA or the Indian Health Service. Native women in the BIA provide a veritable army of clerks and secretaries. They are concentrated, of course, in lower GS ratings, powerless and vulnerable. The U.S. Civil Rights Commission's *Southwest Indian Report* disclosed that in Arizona, Indians comprised 81.2 percent of all the personnel in grades 1 (lowest) through 5, but white personnel constituted only 7.3 percent of employees in these grades.

The figure for natives includes both male and female employees, but it might not be unreasonable to suggest that females outnumber males among natives employed as GS white-collar employees. And although men most likely outnumber women in the blue-collar jobs, the large numbers of native women in BIA and IHS domestic jobs (for example, hospital ward attendant) should not be overlooked. In general, the *Southwest Indian Report* concluded that although Indians constitute the majority of BIA employees in Arizona and New Mexico, they are disproportionately concentrated in the lower wage, non-professional jobs.

In the Commission report, Ms. Julia Porter, a retired Indian nurse who also testified about Indian employment in the IHS, noted that:

. . . most of the supervisors are Anglos. You never see an Indian head nurse or a supervisor. You see a lot of janitors. You see a lot of low-grade employees over there.

Ms. Ella Rumley, of the Tucson Indian Center, reported that Indians who have jobs in that area are employed only in menial positions. There are no Indian retail clerks, tellers, or secretaries, to her knowledge. The Arizona State Employment Service reported that domestic employment placement averaged out to "approximately 34% of the job placements available for Indians in the years 1969 and 1970."

Moreover, given the wage disparity between the sexes in salary in the general population, it comes as no surprise that native women in clerical and domestic work far too often receive only pittances for their labor. The reason for absenteeism and short-term employment which may to some degree characterize native as well as Anglo female employment are similar: responsibility for the survival of home and family. Outside employment and familial duties conflict for all women. In addition, discrimination and prejudice produce low employee morale, inhibiting commitment to a job. Native women and men are passed over in promotions, as shown in the congressional staff report, *No Room at the Top*—meaning, "no natives need apply."

Sadly, even in the brief but brilliant days of the BIA New Team under former Commissioner Louis R. Bruce, an Iroquois-Sioux, native females in the upper echelons were scarce. One doesn't need to be an Anglo to be a male chauvinist! The common complaint is, of course, that no "qualified" native women are available. This brings to mind the statement of U.S. Civil Rights Commissioner Frankie M. Freeman:

I have been on this Commission . . . for about 8½ years. And I remember back in February of 1965 when the Commission held hearings in Jackson, Mississippi (and was told) "We can't find any qualified . . . blacks." . . . And then in December of 1968 we went to San Antonio, Texas (and, we were told) they could not find any "qualified" Mexican Americans or Chicanos! And in February of this year we were in New York, and they couldn't find any "qualified" Puerto Ricans! And today you can't find any "qualified" Indians! What disturbs me is that the word "qualified" only gets put in front of a member of a minority or an ethnic. The assumption seems to be that all whites are qualified. You never hear about anyone looking for a "qualified white person." . . . It seems that the word "qualified" sort of dangles as an excuse for discriminating against minorities.

In this sense, clearly *all* women must be included as minority members, but to be a woman *and* a minority member can be all the more difficult.

Health

President Johnson observed that "the health level of the American Indian is the lowest of any major population group in the United States." The situation has not improved, as the *Southwest Indian Report* demonstrates. It is inexplicable that the Federal Government provides the best health service anywhere in the world to its astronauts, military, and veterans, while its service to Native Americans is hopelessly inadequate. The obligation of the Federal Government to provide health services to Native Americans derives also from treaty obligations, and appears to be administered in as incompetent a fashion as are the educational services.

The symptom-oriented practise of the IHS makes preventive medicine a secondary effort. Social as well as biologic pathologies are not

When you came
　　　　you found a people
　　with red skin
　　　　they were one
　　　　　　with all living things
But you did not see this
　　　　beauty
　　instead you saw them
　　　　as animals, primitive
　　　　　　savage
Because you had lost this
　　　　whole
In the progress of your civilization
　　look now what
　　　　　your knowledge
　　has made them

Lydia Yellowbird

being attacked at their source, but rather at the stage of acute disability.

Not long ago, Dr. Sophie D. Aberle, a Ph.D. anthropologist and an M.D. advised against following her two-degree pattern. "No," she said, "don't go after the M.D. now that you have your Ph.D. in anthropology, for two reasons: one, because you wouldn't want to spend the rest of your life interacting with doctors—they're so shallow!

"And two, as a doctor I can cure gross symptoms perhaps, but I have to send (people) back into the environment in which they got sick in the first place. Cure the social ills and we're a long way down the road to curing the symptoms."

As it relates to women, the major "preventive" effort has been in the area of birth control and family planning. One gets the impression that it is the sole program concerned with before-the-fact care. But Native Americans on the whole reject the concept of birth control. In an impoverished environment, whether rural or city slum, infant mortality is extremely high. As Robert L. Kane and Rosalie A. Kane describe the rationale for unimpeded reproduction in their book *Federal Health Care (with Reservations!)*:

In earlier years, population growth was crucial to survival of the tribe and its people. In many agrarian societies, children are a form of economic protection. They guarantee a pool of manpower for maintaining and enlarging one's holdings; they are a source of protection and support when the parents can no longer work. With high rates of infant mortality, large numbers of offspring are needed to ensure that several will survive to adulthood.

When the standard of living is raised above the subsistence level, third world nations usually experience a diminution of the birth rate. The Native American population so far does not seem to have taken a downward swing. In fact, birth rates for some native groups may be the highest ever recorded anywhere.

Birth control is a topic laden with tension for many groups, particularly for nonwhites in this country. Federal birth control programs begin with nonwhites: Puerto Ricans, Navajos, and blacks. It is not too difficult to understand how some may view this first effort as an attempt to pinch off nonwhite birth production. It is hard not to draw such a conclusion.

Among Native Americans, the memory of genocide and tribal extinction is a raw unhealing wound. Fear persists that the desire for the "ultimate solution to the Indian Problem"—the extinguishment of Native Americans—still lives. Kane and Kane say of birth control:

It is associated with extinction as a people, (with) genocide. The tension runs close to the surface when Navajos discuss this issue. Many interpret efforts along the family planning line as an attempt to breed the race into oblivion. Other Indian tribes have virtually disappeared because of declining birth rates in the face of captivity and inhospitable government reservations.

Native intractability can be sensed in the statement made at a community discussion with IHS officials about family planning. A Navajo woman concluded: "As long as there are big Navajos, there will be little Navajos." And then the meeting broke up.

An exceedingly interesting set of investigations by two Egyptian female scientists, Laila Hamamsy and Hind Khattah, seems to cast in a new light the accelerating birth rates among some Navajo groups. Their thesis suggests that white American males are the cause, and in a wholly unexpected way.

First, Navajos are traditionally matriarchal, matrilineal, and matrilocal. From such a position of strength, Navajo women performed a wide array of roles necessary for the survival and success of the extended family.

However, as the thesis goes, white Anglo males from a rigidly paternalistic, male-dominated society refused to recognize and deal with the fact of Navajo matriarchy. Instead, they dealt only with Navajo males on all matters where the two cultures touched. As a result, more and more of the women's roles were supplanted by male actors and then male takeover.

There seems to be a statistical correlation between the period in which Anglo ascendency impinged on female roles, and the onset and acceleration of the birth rate around the peripheral Navajo communities where most cul-

Self Portrait #3, painting by Wendy Rose. Hopi, © 1975 Wendy Rose

tural interaction takes place. Anglo culture as practiced by white males brought about the loss of nearly all Navajo women's roles save that of childbearer. When producing offspring is one's only vehicle for gaining prestige and ego satisfaction, then we can expect the birthrate to ascend.

To what extent this thesis can apply to other minority groups—and also to middle class white American females who are now the biggest producers of offspring—is not yet answerable. But the thesis is appealing, in any event.

Other preventive programs are virtually nonexistent. Among some of the Northern Pueblo groups and elsewhere, prenatal care clinics are

Experiencing Various Points of View

Purpose: To develop awareness of sexual and ethnic experiences other than our own.

Directions: Close your eyes, find a comfortable position, and relax while someone reads the following instructions out loud for you.

1. *Sex* Imagine that your sex is reversed. If you are a male, you are now a female; if you are a female, you are now a male. . . . How is your body different now? . . . Become really aware of this new body, particularly the parts that have changed. . . . If you don't want to do this, that's O.K. But don't say to yourself "I *can't* do this." Say "I *won't* do this," and then add whatever words come to you next. By doing this you may get some idea of what it is that you are avoiding by refusing to do this reversal. . . . How do you feel in this new body? . . . And how will your life be different now? . . . What will you do differently, now that you sex has changed? . . . And how do you feel about all these changes? . . . Continue to explore your experience of being the opposite sex for awhile. . . .

   Now change back again and get in touch with your real body and your real sex. . . . Silently compare the experience of being yourself with being the other sex. . . . What did you experience as the other sex that you don't experience now? . . . Were these experiences pleasant or unpleasant? . . . Continue to explore your experience for a little while. . . .

2. *Race* Now imagine that your skin color is reversed: If you are black or dark-skinned, you are now white. If you are white-skinned, you are now black or dark-skinned. . . . Become really aware of your new body. . . . How is your body different now? . . . And how do you feel in this body? . . . How will your life be different, now that your skin color has changed? . . . And how do you feel about these changes? . . . Continue to explore your new existence for awhile. . . .

   Now change back to your own skin color and your own body. . . . Silently compare the experience of being yourself with the experience of having a different skin color. . . . What differences do you notice between the two, and how did you feel in each? . . .

Try this exercise by imagining that you are a Black, Chicana, Asian, Native American or white woman. After each exercise, open your eyes and record your experiences. If possible, have members of the class (or women from outside the class) of various ethnic backgrounds share with each other their experiences arising from the exercise, giving feedback on the basis of real experience as compared with the imagined experiences.

held sporadically and with a minimum of success. This is the fault of both lack of funds and lack of commitment on the part of the IHS and the general lack of information available to potential users about such programs.

That preventive programs can and do succeed where there is commitment is seen in the fine example set by Dr. Annie Wauneka. She received the National Peace Medal for bringing to her Navajo people information and procedures they could use to combat tuberculosis ravaging on the reservation at that time.

Charges that Native Americans are locked into supersitition and therefore hostile to modern medicine just are not factual. Preventive programs properly couched would no doubt be welcome. But, as the Citizen's Advocate Center reports in *Our Brother's Keeper:*

> The Public Health Service has no outreach system or delivery system, no systematic preventive care program, no early detection system. Thus . . .

(it) is not structured to cope at the right point and on the proper scale with the underlying causes of poor health.

Some Comments

In the briefest way, this article has touched upon a few of the major institutions of life—education, employment, and health—as they are experienced by Native American women.

The next step in understanding among women and between peoples is mutual identification of needs. Many of life's difficulties for Native women are no different than those of other minority women—blacks, Chicanos, or the Appalachian poor. And then when the commonalities between minority and majority women are recognized—if not on a socioeconomic level, at least on a philosophic level—we may expect to witness a national movement for the equality of peoples and sexes.

For Further Reading

*Asian Women. c/o 3405 Dwinelle Hall, U. C. Berkeley 94720.

*Cade, T. 1970. *The Black Woman.* New York: New American Library.

*Duran, P. H. and Argandona, R. T. *The Chicana, A Bibliographic Study.* ERIC ED076 305.

Ladner, J. 1971. *Tomorrow's Tomorrow.* New York: Doubleday.

Landis, R. 1971. *The Ojibwa Woman.* New York: W. W. Norton.

*Lerner, G. 1972. *Black Women in White America.* New York: Random House.

Third World Women. 1972. San Francisco: Third World Communications (Glide Memorial Church).

Time to Greez. 1975. San Francisco: Third World Communications (Glide Memorial Church).

Women and Their Sexual Selves

Because sexuality is strongly emphasized in our culture and because females have been defined in terms of their sexual and reproductive functions, women's sexuality forms an important part of their psychology. These definitions of women, which until recently have been widely accepted, have been gross distortions that have deeply affected women. A most glaring example, Freud's theory that women have two kinds of orgasms, was accepted as true even by women themselves for approximately fifty years until it was discovered to be in error. Since many existing formulations of female sexuality are inaccurate and since feminists have begun to redefine female sexuality based on women's experiences and reality, the articles included in this chapter are written primarily by feminists. Analyses of orgasm, rape, and lesbianism are certainly among the most provocative and vital topics in a discussion of female sexuality, since they also shed light on the overall psychology of women.

Anne Oakley's article on sexuality, excerpted from her book, *Sex, Gender, and Society* (1972), summarizes major research on male and female sexuality by Masters and Johnson, Kinsey, and Shofield. She also includes cross-cultural data, to provide interesting comparisons with sexuality in our culture, and reviews psychological and biological bases for sex differences in sexuality. In the last section of the article Oakley presents the contrasting views of Sigmund Freud (psychoanalytic) and Kate Millett (feminist) regarding female sexuality and psychology.

The remainder of the articles in this section are related to the issue of how patriarchy affects female sexuality. As Millett (1968) points out, since the sexes have had unequal economic and material power, women have had to barter their sexual availability in return for economic and material security (in the sister institutions of prostitution or marriage). In addition, patriarchy restricts the behavior and activities of women, including their sexual expression, a condition that seems to be universal. (Patai, 1968). In our culture there is a double standard of sexual behavior for women and men, a basic part of which is a psychological split in terms of the "good" women—the Madonnas, whose reproductive and nurturing capacities are revered—and the "bad" women—the Whores, in whom untamed, female, sexual- "animal" qualities are desired. This presents women with the insoluble problem of trying to follow two conflicting sets of expectations. Men can resolve this split externally by procuring a different woman for each function—for example, the wife and the mistress (or prostitute). Another significant factor in the patriarchal effect on female sexuality is that men control female biological functions through the institutions and research regarding abortion, birth control, pregnancy, and childbirth. Thus, women are prevented from having control over their own bodies and reproductive functioning. Another possible relationship between patriarchy and female sexuality is that patriarchy may be a reaction against prehistoric matriarchies, in which women were feared on the basis of their biological functions. This theory raises the possibility that men may have a deep-seated fear of female sexuality (Lederer, 1968).

Mary Jane Sherfey's article (an excerpt from the original, longer version) deals with women's multiple orgasmic potential and the possibility of a biologically based, inordinate sexual drive in women. This topic has several implications, one of which is that this sexual drive could be the source of men's fear of female sexuality and thus the reason for its suppression (given patriarchal conditions). Economic, social, and cultural inequalities tend to make the sexual relationship between women and men unequal, independent of women's greater sexual suppression. Unequal sexual expression is one more way in which men are ensured dominance and mastery over women. This becomes particularly relevant for men who have difficulty achieving dominance over other men or through securing economic and material symbols of power and masculinity. The area of sexual relations is one sphere in which men may prove their masculinity through power, aggression, and domination at least over women. The discovery that women may be potentially more sexually aggressive and demanding would be particularly threatening to men since this removes one of the bases of men's masculinity (as currently defined). For men, sexuality and power are interwoven so that men are invested in maintaining women's sexual suppression in order to maintain masculinity—a position of greater power (over women)—and therefore patriarchy. Underlying the patriarchal creations of the Whore and the Madonna, then, may be both men's desire and their fear that women be fully sexual.

Sherfey argues that historically the suppression of female sexuality occurred with the shift from matriarchy to patriarchy and was necessary for the development of civilization—to establish the family and private property. Several matriarchal theorists have attempted to account for the shift from matriarchy to patriarchy (see "Cultural Variations") and Sherfey's formulations suggest one more possibility.

Sherfey's theory may be viewed, however, as a reflection of prevailing patriarchal attitudes toward women, since, once again, women are defined in terms of their sexuality. Seeing women as subject to their raging emotions or to uncontrollable and insatiable sexual urges is not new—it is one side of the Madonna-Whore concept. Furthermore, women's sexuality may have been suppressed more than was necessary for the development of civilization. Instead, this additional suppression served to establish male domination as women became objects or possessions, the property of men. Sherfey's theory is based on men having to limit female sexuality, as if women could not do so themselves. (There is evidence of the existence of matriarchies such as Amazon societies in which women were presumably in control of their own sexuality.) Moreover, this theory makes it seem that men "saved the day" by exhibiting rational control and order for women's (and men's) own good ("Father knows best"), a further justification for patriarchy. At the end of her article, Sherfey concludes that psychoanalytic theory is acceptable except for some modifications. In taking this stance she remains, in Chesler's terms (1972), a "Dutiful Daughter" to Freud and patriarchal ideology. Nonetheless, Sherfey's thesis is a highly provocative one and at least raises the possibility that women have a far greater sexual potential than is currently being realized. In view of this potential, women's sexual lives at present may be indicative of the toll that patriarchy has taken on the lives of women.

Sherfey was astounded that the psychoanalytic literature had overlooked the fact of women's greater orgasmic capacity. The article by Anne Koedt presents a possible explanation for that failure and for the persistence of the myth of the vaginal orgasm. Taking it further than Sherfey, Koedt analyzes the continuation of such myths and the failure to accept certain facts about female sexuality, finding them consistent with maintaining male dominance.

Susan Griffin's article on rape makes the significant implication, in terms of both women's sexuality and psychology, that basically women learn fear. This fear restricts women's movements and makes them psychologically dependent on men for protection from other men. Furthermore, since sexuality and violence are often intertwined for men, it is understandable that women should fear men, especially since, as Griffin asserts, it has not been demonstrated that men who rape are psychologically different from ordinary men. This is consistent with the cultural stereotype that men are supposed to be more powerful than women, so that normal heterosexual relationships are based on male domination and female submission. It is a natural consequence, then, that women are coerced into sexual relationships with men or simply comply with men's sexual demands.

In the rape situation it becomes clear that women are regarded as objects or property, a factor that must also affect the psychology of women. Rapists are punished more because they have defiled another man's property than because of the harm done to the women. A rapist has insulted the manhood or masculinity of the man to whom the woman "belonged." In this way black and white men wage a war against each other through the raping of white and black women. There is also a double standard in rape, whereby certain women deserve protection (the Madonnas) and certain women do not (the Whores). Based on the white value system, black and other Third World women tend to fall into the latter category. The white political institutions also punish black men more severely because white men are particularly insulted if black men defile white "property."

"Women Identified Women" deals with the topic of lesbianism as an alternative to being male identified. As Hacker (1951) pointed out in an earlier chapter, the subordinate group tends to identify with the dominant group, so women have become identified with men. Lesbianism means being identified with women and contains within it the possibility of women loving women and themselves. As a result of the women's movement, it seems that increasingly women are seeing lesbian sexual-emotional relationships as a satisfying or preferable alternative to sexual relationships with men. Special problems of lesbians and the difficulties involved when heterosexual and lesbian women relate to one another are discussed in terms of patriarchal, and predominantly heterosexual, cultural values.

The concluding article is a position paper on women's sexual expression that represents an attempt to define Female* sexuality. Written by feminist psychologists, and pending ratification by the Association of Women Psychologists, it asserts that women must redefine sexual-emotional relationships in their own terms according to their own needs and desires. It implies that women must no longer become sexually whatever pleases men—be it remaining virgins until marriage, participating in "free love," having babies for the revolution, having monogamous or nonmonogamous relationships, or even being bisexual or multiply orgasmic—simply because it pleases men. Women must have full self-determination for sexual expression, however each individual woman defines it for herself.

---

*Upper case is used to connote women's definition of their own sexuality rather than that defined by men (female). See Introduction for discussion of these terms.

Ann Oakley

Sexuality

As a leading anthropologist once observed, "sex" is not a particularly useful word in the analysis of cultures. To survive, a culture must reproduce, and copulation is the only way. But what is defined as "sexual" in content or implication varies infinitely from one culture to another or within the same culture in different historical periods.

In Victorian times, for instance, a large group of Western females were denied their sexuality altogether, but the twentieth century has seen the emergence (or re-emergence, after the inhibitions of the eighteenth and nineteenth centuries) of the female's right to sexuality, which has come to be defined at least partly in terms of her own sexual needs. The Victorian lady was not supposed to have sexual desires—hence her paradoxical use as a sexual object for the man's satisfaction. Her twentieth-century counterpart, however, has considerable auras of sexuality, extending beyond the bedroom into an entire world of commercially-oriented sex and erotic meaning.

These terms "sex" and "sexual" are subject to constant confusion. The dictionary gives, under "sexual," "Of, pertaining to, or based on, sex or the sexes, or on the distinction of sexes; pertaining to generation or copulation." Perhaps it is not surprising that the confusion exists: "sex" (biological maleness or femaleness) and "sexuality" (behaviour related to copulation) are very closely connected. Behaviour is "sexual" if it refers to the kind of relationship between male and female in which copulation is, or could be, or is imagined to be, a factor. "Sexuality" describes the whole area of personality related to sexual behaviour.

Both male and female must have some propensity for sexual behaviour if copulation is to occur, but this propensity is usually held to be different in male and female. Along with the male's greater aggression in other fields, goes his aggression in the sphere of sexuality: males initiate sexual contact, and take the symbolically, if not actually, aggressive step of vaginal penetration—a feat which is possible even with a frigid mate. They assume the dominant position in intercourse. Males ask females to go to bed with them, or marry them, or both: not vice versa.

The female's sexuality is supposed to lie in her receptiveness and this is not just a matter of her open vagina: it extends to the whole structure of feminine personality as dependent, passive, unaggressive and submissive. Female sexuality has been held to involve long arousal and slow satisfaction, inferior sex drive, susceptibility to field dependence (a crying child distracts the attention) and romantic idealism rather than lustful reality. Women are psychologically, no less than anatomically, incapable of rape.

That these stereotypes persist can be seen from any woman's magazine and almost any fiction dealing with sexual relationships. Many men and women conform to them in reality, as can be seen from the kind of psychological problems each sex has over its sexuality. (The incompetence of some women in taking contraceptive precautions often comes from the fact that they do not want, or are not able, to direct the course of their own sexuality: they feel that to admit they are planning—even perhaps, that they desire—to make love is immoral;

It seems to me that when such a wish [for the penis] is expressed, the woman is but demanding in this symbolic way some form of equality with men.

Clara Thompson

group status, what may be learned from applying to women various theoretical constructs in the field of intergroup relations?

Social Distance Between Men and Women

One instrument of diagnostic value is the measurement of social distance between dominant and minority group. But we have seen that one important difference between women and other minorities is that women's attitudes and self-conceptions are conditioned more largely by interaction with both minority and dominant group members. Before measuring social distance, therefore, a continuum might be constructed of the frequency and extent of women's interaction with men, with the poles conceptualized as ideal types. One extreme would represent a complete "ghetto" status, the woman whose contacts with men were of the most secondary kind. At the other extreme shall we put the woman who has prolonged and repeated associations with men, but only in those situations in which sex-awareness plays a prominent role or the woman who enters into a variety of relationships with men in which her sex identity is to a large extent irrelevant? The decision would depend on the type of scale used.

This question raises the problem of the criterion of social distance to be employed in such a scale. Is it more profitable to use we-feeling, felt interdependence, degree of communication, or degrees of separation in status? Social distance tests as applied to relationships between other dominant and minority groups have for the most part adopted prestige criteria as their basis. The assumption is that the type of situation into which one is willing to enter with average members of another group reflects one's estimate of the status of the group relative to one's own. When the tested group is a sex-group rather than a racial, national, religious, or economic one, several important differences in the use and interpretation of the scale must be noted.

1. Only two groups are involved: men and women. Thus, the test indicates the amount of homogeneity or we-feeling only according to the attribute of sex. If men are a primary group, there are not many groups to be ranked secondary, tertiary, etc. with respect to them, but only one group, women, whose social distance cannot be calculated relative to other groups.

2. Lundberg[5] suggests the possibility of a group of Catholics registering a smaller social distance to Moslems than to Catholics. In such an event the group of Catholics, from any sociological viewpoint, would be classified as Moslems. If women expressed less social distance to men than to women, should they then be classified sociologically as men? Perhaps no more so than the legendary Negro who, when requested to move to the colored section of the

Women tend to seek identification with the person whom they love. A woman likes to follow her man and will even change her political ideas or her religion in her attempt to achieve once more that sense of union with another that was hers in the beginning. Even the modern woman who consciously admits a man's right to live his life without accounting for every moment of his day and expects to do the same herself, still wants to share his inmost thoughts and feelings, for that to her is the essence of true relationship. Not so man. For him, separation is inevitable, and it is from his island of separateness that he tries to relate. For him the woman's attempts to probe the inmost recesses of his mind feels, consciously or unconsciously, like a threat to engulf him.

Irene de Castillijo

---

train, replied, "Boss, I'se done resigned from the colored race," should be classified as white. It is likely, however, that the group identification of many women in our society is with men. The feminists were charged with wanting to be men, since they associated male physical characteristics with masculine social privileges. A similar statement can be made about men who show greater social distance to other men than to women.

Social distance may be measured from the standpoint of the minority group or the dominant group with different results. In point of fact, tension often arises when one group feels less social distance than the other. A type case here is the persistent suitor who underestimates his desired sweetheart's feeling of social distance toward him.

3. In social distance tests the assumption is made of an orderly progression—although not necessarily by equal intervals—in the scale. That is, it is not likely that a person would express willingness to have members of a given group as his neighbors, while simultaneously voicing the desire to have them excluded from his country. On all scales marriage represents the minimum social distance, and implies willingness for associations on all levels of lesser intimacy. May the customary scale be applied to men and women? If we take the expressed attitude of many men and women not to marry, we may say that they have feelings of social distance toward the opposite sex, and in this

situation the usual order of the scale may be preserved.

In our culture, however, men who wish to marry, must perforce marry women, and even if they accept this relationship, they may still wish to limit their association with women in other situations. The male physician may not care for the addition of female physicians to his hospital staff. The male poker player may be thrown off his game if women participate. A damper may be put upon the hunting expedition if women come along. The average man may not wish to consult a woman lawyer. And so on. In these cases it seems apparent that the steps in the social distance scale must be reversed. Men will accept women at the supposed level of greatest intimacy while rejecting them at lower levels.

But before concluding that a different scale must be constructed when the dominant group attitude toward a minority group which is being tested is that of men toward women, the question may be raised as to whether marriage in fact represents the point of minimum social distance. It may not imply anything but physical intimacy and work accommodation, as was frequently true in non-individuated societies, such as preliterate groups and the household economy of the Middle Ages, or marriages of convenience in the European upper class. Even in our own democratic society where marriage is supposedly based on romantic love there may be little communication between the partners

Imperfections—on the part of the spouse, to be sure—inevitably make their appearance during the long period of living closely together. They set in motion a minor avalanche, which automatically keeps growing, as it rolls down the mountain slope of time. If, perhaps, a husband clings to the illusion of his independence, he will react with secret bitterness to his feeling needed and tied down by his wife. She, in turn, senses his suppressed rebellion, reacts with hidden anxiety, lest she lose him, and out of this anxiety instinctively increases her demands on him. The husband reacts to this with heightened sensitivity and defensiveness—until finally the dam bursts, neither one having understood the underlying irritability.

Karen Horney

in marriage. The Lynds[6] report the absence of real companionship between husband and wife in Middletown. Women have been known to say that although they have been married for twenty years, their husband is still a stranger to them. There is a quatrain of Thoreau's that goes:

Each moment as we drew nearer to each
A stern respect withheld us farther yet
So that we seemed beyond each other's reach
And less acquainted than when first we met.

Part of the explanation may be found in the subordination of wives to husbands in our culture, which is expressed in the separate spheres of activity for men and women. A recent advertisement in a magazine of national circulation depicts a pensive husband seated by his knitting wife, with the caption, "Sometimes a man has moods his wife cannot understand." In this case the husband is worried about a pension plan for his employees. The assumption is that the wife, knowing nothing of the business world, cannot take the role of her husband in this matter.

The presence of love does not in itself argue for either equality of status nor fullness of communication. We may love those who are either inferior or superior to us, and we may love persons whom we do not understand. The supreme literary examples of passion without communication are found in Proust's portrayal of Swann's obsession with Odette, the narrator's infatuation with the elusive Albertine, and, of course, Dante's longing for Beatrice.

In the light of these considerations concerning the relationships between men and women, some doubt may be cast on the propriety of placing marriage on the positive extreme of the social distance scale with respect to ethnic and religious minority groups. Since inequalities of status are preserved in marriage, a dominant group member may be willing to marry a member of a group which, in general, he would not wish admitted to his club. The social distance scale which uses marriage as a sign of an extreme degree of acceptance is inadequate for appreciating the position of women, and perhaps for other minority groups as well. The relationships among similarity of status, communication as a measure of intimacy, and love must be clarified before social distance tests can be applied usefully to attitudes between men and women.

Caste-Class Conflict

Is the separation between males and females in our society a caste line? Folsom[7] suggests that it is, and Myrdal[8] in his well-known Appendix 5 considers the parallel between the position of and feelings toward women and Negroes in our society. The relation between women and Negroes is historical, as well as analogical. In the seventeenth century the legal

CHART 1
CASTELIKE STATUS OF WOMEN AND NEGROES

Negroes	Women

1. High Social Visibility

Negroes	Women
a. Skin color, other "racial" characteristics	a. Secondary sex characteristics
b. (Sometimes) distinctive dress—bandana, flashy clothes	b. Distincitve dress, skirts, etc.

2. Ascribed Attributes

Negroes	Women
a. Inferior intelligence, smaller brain, less convoluted, scarcity of geniuses	a. ditto
b. More free in instinctual gratifications. More emotional, "primitive" and childlike. Imagined sexual prowess envied.	b. Irresponsible, inconsistent, emotionally unstable. Lack strong super-ego. Women as "temptresses."
c. Common stereotype "inferior"	c. "Weaker"

3. Rationalizations of Status

Negroes	Women
a. Thought all right in his place	a. Woman's lace is in the home
b. Myth of contended Negro	b. Myth of contented woman—"feminine" woman is happy in subordinate role

4. Accomodation Attitudes

Negroes	Women
a. Supplicatory whining intonation of voice	a. Rising inflection, smiles, laughs, downward glances
b. Deferential manner	b. Flattering manner
c. Concealment of real feelings	c. "Feminine wiles"
d. Outwit "white folks"	d. Outwit "menfolk"
e. Careful study of points at which dominant group is susceptible to influence	e. ditto
f. Fake appeals for directives; show of ignorance	f. Appearance of helplessness

5. Discriminations

Negroes	Women
a. Limitations on education—should fit "place" in society	a. ditto
b. Confined to traditional jobs—barred from supervisory positions. Their competition feared. No family precedents for new aspirations	b. ditto
c. Deprived of political importance	c. ditto
d. Social and professional segregation	d. ditto
e. More vulnerable to criticism	e. e.g. conduct in bars.

6. Similar Problems

a. Roles not clearly defined, but in flux as result of social change
Conflict between achieved status and ascribed status

Most clinicians have not thought deeply about the sociopolitical—or the psychological—conditions that are necessary for female sexual self-definition. Women can never be sexually actualized as long as men control the means of production and reproduction. Women have had to barter their sexuality (or their capacity for sexual pleasure) for economic survival and maternity. Female frigidity as we know it will cease only when such bartering ceases. . . . From a psychological point of view female frigidity will cease when female children are surrounded by and can observe non-frigid female adults.

Phyllis Chesler, *Women and Madness*

had masturbated. Between twenty and fifty the frequency of masturbation stabilises for women with relatively little variation. The much higher frequency of masturbation for men, which is not related to marital status, declines after the age of eighteen or twenty.

These differences in sexual experience are associated with, and help to explain, differences in ability to reach orgasm. The ability to respond sexually is at least partly a function of experience for both sexes, and as women begin all forms of sexual activity later than men—masturbation, petting with or without orgasm, and intercourse—they are slower to reach a "masculine" level of sexual response. If the figures are adjusted to take account of the difference in experience of the two groups, their responses to sexual stimulation are very alike.

It is clear from these figures that women take longer than men to discover their sexual-genital excitability and they seem to need the aid of a male partner to do so. Does the more prolonged development of female genital sexuality occur because of the female's relative paucity of experience? Or is the paucity of experience a reflection of the slower and different maturation of the female's potential for being sexually aroused?

In *The Sexual Behaviour of Young People* Michael Schofield relates the amount of sexual experience boys and girls have had, and the age at which they began, to their family situa-

---

Body Image

Purpose: To explore our images of our bodies.

Directions:

1. Gather construction paper, scissors, paste or tape, and old magazines from which you can cut.
2. From the images that you find in magazines, make a collage that expresses what you look like to yourself.
3. Make a collage of how you think you look to others.
4. Make a collage of how you would like to look.

How do you feel about your collages? What do they say to you? What do you need in order to make the transition from your present image of yourself to your ideal self? What did you experience while making the collages? Share your collages and experiences with the class.

---

tion. He finds that in general girls are more closely controlled by the family, and allowed far fewer opportunities to get sexual experience than boys. Mostly the girls are more emotionally bound up with their families than the boys: they set a higher value on loyalty to the family and on conforming to parental norms of behaviour.

TABLE 8

PERCENTAGE OF PEOPLE WITH DIFFERENT DEGREES
OF SEXUAL EXPERIENCE WHO WISHED TO HAVE
COITUS.*

Experience	Male	Female
No experience	69	37
Petting	82	53
Petting with orgasm	78	74
(Male = male students, no. 931		
Female = female students, no. 337)		

*None of them had actually experienced it.

A comparison of the sexually experienced girl with the sexually experienced boy shows that

> . . . experienced girls have gone much farther than boys in rejecting family influences. Relations with both parents were often strained, and they were less likely to receive advice on sexual matters from their parents, and when they did get this advice, they were more likely to reject it.
>
> In matters of parental discipline the experienced girls were like the experienced boys. These girls did not tell their parents where they were going, did not have to be in at a definite time; spent more time outside the home . . . Like the boys, their home situation provided them with more opportunities and facilities for sexual activities.

In other words, the home situation of the average girl is a much more restricting influence on the development of sexual behavior than that of the average boy. To approach the level of sexual experience boys reach, a girl has positively to reject the influence of home and family.

So it is not surprising to find that most female deviance in adolescence consists of sexual offences (which is not true of boys). Somewhere between two thirds and three quarters of all female acts of delinquency are sexual. Also, while most of the sex offences committed by adolescent males involve sexual deviations, female offences are promiscuous but otherwise normal (that is, they are concerned with heterosexual intercourse).

This leads to various conclusions. (1) Parents' expectations of appropriate behaviour in the adolescent girl exclude overt sexual activity, whereas for the boy they permit it. (2) Parental controls (and social controls in general) retard the onset of sexual experience in most adolescent girls. (3) Where they do not, overt sexual activity is likely to be allied with delinquency (or defined as delinquency) because of the equation between femininity and the absence of overt sexual behaviour for the adolescent female. A rebellious girl may show her defiance by acts of overt sexuality; alternatively, active sexuality may be construed as deviation. In any case, both delinquency in general and sexual delinquency in particular are likely to be correlated with the girl's rejection of home and family. And this rejection is itself less likely in girls than in boys.

These findings clearly help to provide a cultural explanation of the apparent differences in male and female sexuality. What weight should we give to the opposing theory, held by many people, that, for biological reasons, sexuality arises spontaneously in the male but not in the female?

Puberty for the male is an overtly sexual event. Right from the beginning, his sexuality is localised in the genitals by the start of seminal emissions. Female puberty, on the other hand, is marked by the onset of menstruation, which has a reproductive rather than sexual significance, and brings with it associations of pain and probably fear. Within Western culture, sexuality may well be latent in the female, while manifest in the male. If so, this may be because females resist the open acknowledgement of their sexuality, and some backing for this belief comes from those cases in which females with glandular disturbances have clitoral erections when they are sexually aroused. When they are relieved of this by surgery, they claim pleasure at being able to feel like "normal" women: clearly they have learnt to associate spontaneous sexuality with the aggressive masculine role.

But in other societies this difference between male and female sexuality is reduced to a mere linguistic quibble. The theory that male sexuality arises spontaneously and is specifically genital while the female's is not, is simply not borne out by the behaviour of males and females in other cultures—for instance by the Brazilian tribe studied by Jules Henry or the Trobriand islanders studied by Malinowski (see below). The differences in the emotional meaning of puberty to male and female in our cultures, are not necessarily universal either, any more than are the social differences influencing the ways in which they gain their sexual experience.

Although there is a distinct difference between males and females in the physiological events and timing of puberty, these differences may be either accentuated or minimised by culture. As Michael Schofield shows, the onset of puberty in our culture not only produces a whole set of social responses from family and friends which differ between the sexes: it also arouses different expectations in the girls and boys themselves. For the girl, puberty is a time of danger from which she only emerges by tying herself to a single man in marriage (or at least in a relationship that will lead to marriage).

For the male, on the other hand, it is a time of adventure, when the apron strings which tie him to the home are released as he sets out to prove his manhood. While pubescent male and pubescent female alike may feel the stirrings of a specifically sexual-genital excitement, and the consequent urge for its release, the female's thoughts are directed into anticipating the less dangerous occupations of wife, mother and housewife. Her dreams of two children, her own house and all the trappings of domesticity thus represent a "displacement activity" whose function is the inhibition of the sexual urge. There is no equivalent inhibition acting on the male.

Because puberty is a bridge between childhood and adulthood, and because the adult roles of the sexes are significantly differentiated in our society both inside and outside the home, the climate in which male and female pass through puberty tends to stress rather than ignore sex differences in the physiological process itself. An additional factor is perhaps our cultural emphasis on the importance of sexuality. The Arapesh, who as a culture devalue sexuality and develop tenderness and parental responsibility in both males and females, do not treat the adolescent girl as in need of protection from the male's exploitation of her as a sexual object. Menstruation is therefore not the signal of danger it is in our society. Arapesh males simply do not regard females as vessels for their own sexual satisfaction, but as individuals whose desirability as spouses is related to the culture's primary work of child-rearing. The sexual feeling that exists between spouses is not fundamentally different from the other feelings or affections that tie siblings, or parents and children, together—it is just a more complete expression of it. In this context, adolescence is not a period of fervent mating choice either: by the age of nine or ten girls are already betrothed, and the adolescent male's task is to prepare his own betrothed for the responsibilities of parenthood which they will both share. The Arapesh have no fear that adolescents left to themselves will copulate, nor do the adolescents themselves expect that they will. Margaret Mead (in "Sex and Temperament") explains:

> ... the Arapesh further contravene our traditional idea of men as spontaneously sexual creatures, and women as innocent of desire, until wakened, by denying spontaneous sexuality to both sexes and expecting the exceptions, when they do occur, to occur in women. Both men and women are conceived as merely capable of response to a situation that their society has already defined for them as sexual ... with their definition of sex as response to an external stimulus rather than as spontaneous desire, both men and women are regarded as helpless in the face of seduction ... Parents warn their sons even more than they warn their daughters against permitting themselves to get into situations in which someone can make love to them.

Puberty for the Arapesh is therefore hardly a physiological situation at all, although it remains a sign of maturation and of readiness for the adult role.

Anthropology shows that the whole area of human sexuality is subject to tremendous cultural variation. The following are among the many features of human sexual behaviour which vary: sexual play between children (which may be specifically genital and widely permitted throughout childhood, as among the Trobrianders, or heavily discouraged and repressed, in middle childhood especially, as in our own society); intercourse between imma-

ture adults (which may be a common occurrence unrelated to marriage and procreation, as in Samoa, or discouraged, as again in Western culture); the importance of sexual activity itself (which may be defined as the appropriate preoccupation for an entire society to the exclusion of other interests, as among the Truk, or may take a very secondary place indeed as among the Arapesh); the extent to which sexual desire is dangerous and needs curbing, as among the Manus, or is weak and uncertain and likely to fail altogether, as in Bali.

The idea that the female's sexuality is qualitatively different from the male's, and in particular that it is slow to mature and in need of intensive stimulation, is not universal in all cultures. In the Southwest Pacific society described by William Davenport sexual intercourse is assumed to be highly pleasurable (and deprivation harmful) for both sexes. During the early years of marriage men and women are reported to have intercourse twice a day, with both reaching orgasm simultaneously. Intercourse is defined as a prolonged period of foreplay, during which there is a mutual genital stimulation by both partners, and a short period of copulation lasting fifteen to thirty seconds. It is firmly believed that, once stimulated during foreplay, neither male nor female can fail to reach orgasm, and women unable to reach orgasm are unheard of. Either husband or wife can break up the marriage if sexual intercourse is infrequent (that is, about every ten days).

In this society children beyond the age of three or four are discouraged from genital play, and all sex play between children is frowned upon: there is a latency period from about five or six until puberty when sexual behaviour is not in evidence. Beyond puberty and before marriage both males and females are urged to masturbate to orgasm in order to relieve sexual tension, which is assumed to be as great in females as in males.

Malinowski reported a similar convergence of male and female sexual behaviour among the Trobriand Islanders. Like many other people, the Trobrianders appear to do without latency—there is no period of childhood during which sexual interests and activities are absent. Small children play sexual games together; genital manipulation and oral genital stimulation are frequent. By the age of four or five children are mimicking intercourse, and girls of six to eight have intercourse with penetration. (This experience is delayed for boys, presumably until they are able to achieve full intercourse at the age of ten or twelve). These sexual activities continue unabated throughout childhood, but at adolescence become more serious—the subject of great endeavour and absorbing preoccupation.

Trobriander folklore contains an account of ritual rape by women of men which the natives informed Malinowski was a regular occurrence. Since he was unable to observe it, he disbelieved them, but nevertheless acknowledged Trobriander women to be much more assertive and vigorous and stronger in their sexual drive than women of his own culture. The conventional invitation of female to male is erotic scratching, which draws blood. Malinowski wrote: "On the whole, I think that in the rough usage of passion the woman is the more active. I have seen far larger scratches and marks on men than on women; and only women may actually lacerate their lovers."

Amongst the Trobrianders, as also among the Lesu, Kurtachi, Lepcha, Kwoma and Mataco, women frequently take the initiative in sexual relationships. Indeed, in the last two societies, sexual initiatives are taken by the female exclusively.

The positions used in intercourse by the Trobrianders omit the usual dorsal-ventral (man on top of woman) position used by Europeans—which they dislike because the woman is hampered by the weight of the man and cannot be sufficiently active. The expression for orgasm means "the seminal fluid discharge" and is used of both sexes, referring also to the nocturnal emission of seminal and glandular secretions in male and female. Masturbation is looked on by the Trobrianders as the practice of an idiot, one who is unable to indulge in heterosexual intercourse. It is unworthy of both men and women, whose proper sexuality is bound up with their mutual relationships. Malinowski, in comparing the sexuality of the Trobrianders with that of his own culture, concluded that there were qualitative differences between them. He said that the Trobriander threshold of arousal was much higher than ours, and that sexual excitement was only produced in them by the direct stimulation of the sexual organs. Orgasm in both sexes needed more bodily contact, erotic preliminaries and direct stimulation—a characteristic which is usually considered to be specifically female in our culture.

The differences between the thresholds of arousal of men and women have been related to sexual differences in general in our society. The male is usually reported to be more often and more easily aroused—by visual stimuli or even by his own anticipation—than the female. The stimuli which arouse males and females will also, of course, normally be different, as will the type or erotic imagery accompanying it. Are there biological reasons for these differences?

Cultural distortion of sexuality explains also how female sexuality gets twisted into narcissism: women make love to themselves vicariously through the man, rather than directly making love to him. At times this cultural barrage of man/subject, woman/object desensitizes women to male forms to such a degree that they are even orgasmically affected.

Shulamith Firestone

Medical evidence suggests that the sex hormones may play a part in determining the threshold and frequency of arousal. Children who undergo precocious puberty (because of a hormonal defect) sometimes have more frequent erotic dreams and daydreams, especially boys. Men who usually produce too little of the male hormones often become more sexually active with the administration of androgen, while women on androgen therapy also say that they feel increased sexual desire. Females masculinised before birth by an excess of male hormones, but reared as girls, are reported to exhibit an eroticism which is more characteristically male than female. Visual stimuli produce genital arousal in them, together with clitoral erection and a desire for intercourse with even a transitory partner. (As the clinicians report this, they imply that it is a male tendency only.) Apart from indicating that androgen is the libido hormone for both sexes, these cases suggest that androgen secretion may bear some relationship to the threshold of arousal and to the energy with which males pursue their sexual exploits.

Experiments with monkeys have led to the conclusion that, although androgen may be significantly related to sexual behaviour, the social situation is of great importance. Female rhesus monkeys injected with androgen show an increase in the masculine practice of "mounting," but only if they are dominant members of their group before the experiment.

Among dominant females, the incidence of mounting increases from 0.8 times to 1.2 times per test (which is statistically significant) but if subordinate females are injected the incidence of mounting behaviour remains at the same low level.

So the role of sex hormones in generating signals which are relayed to the brain and converted into sexual arousal can clearly be overlaid by factors of social learning. If data did not already exist to support this contention, the cross-cultural material would supply it. Also there is a clear tendency for the sex difference in threshold of arousal to be exaggerated quite out of proportion to its extent. Research on the general responses of males and females to visual stimuli on sexual themes shows a significant, but not enormous, sex difference. In one study, 58% of the women in the sample reported that they were sometimes sexually aroused at the sight of men, while 72% of the men reported similar reactions. 12% of the women and 54% of the men were sexually aroused by posed pictures of the opposite sex: a third of the women and three quarters of the men were excited by pictures of the sexual act. But men and women were equally excited by erotic books and films. Masters and Johnson exposed their subjects to pornographic literature, and observed a vasocongestive and clitoral reaction in 75% of the female cases, identical to that occurring in the excitement phase of sexual response. They have not so far come

Photograph by Cathy Cade

across a female subject who can fantasise to orgasm, although Kinsey reported that 2% of the females in his sample with a history of masturbation were able to do so, and he also reported a significant number who claimed to reach orgasm during sleep, often awakening with the violence of the orgasmic contractions.

Sex differences in the erotic content of dreams and daydreams reflect, as one might expect, differences in the sexual and social roles of male and female in our culture. Female fantasy is more often romantic and emotional than genitally sexual and erotic. Specifically sexual-erotic fantasies tend to be a male prerogative: however, during masturbation, 50% of women always have erotic fantasies, and 70% sometimes do, compared with 90% of men who say that they always do. Masturbation is to some extent an equaliser here, as it is in the amount of time required to reach orgasm.

Attempts to get statistical proof of a sex difference in fantasy have not been much of a success, but they do show how far the sex roles prescribed by society have become internalised. K.M. Colby took a sample of 200 males and 200 females, and noted one dream from each of them. He found a group of words and associated qualities predominating in male dreams—wife, vehicle, travel, car, and "to hit"—and a group more characteristic of women's dreams—husband, women and "to cry." Like Erikson's account of sex differences in children's play, this sex difference in dream imagery faithfully reflects features of the social worlds of the sexes, including the fact that men have wives, whereas women have husbands, men travel more than women, women are allowed to cry more than men (in our culture, that is) and men are allowed and even encouraged to show more aggression than women.

Colby's attempt to extend his conclusion to the dreams of primitive tribes met with conspicuous failure. "Wife" and "husband" were the only two words with statistical significance. Generally, studies by anthropologists show that the kinds of fears and fantasies people have in the area of sexuality are related to their society's attitudes. Women in our society certainly have fantasies of rape, but so do men in societies where women are strong and aggressive, and this (to us) strange male fear is articulated very often in folklore (as in the Trobriander example mentioned earlier). . . .

Some observers have seen a relationship between personality type and the expression of sexuality which holds true for males as well as females (as does the relationship between intellectual achievement and personality noted in the previous chapter). L.M.Terman reported in 1957 that the relationship between certain personality traits and the capacity for orgasm in a sample of women reached statistical significance. Women with a low capacity for orgasm were less confident and less sure of themselves, more emotionally unstable and sensitive, and more conformist in their attitude towards authority and convention. These same personality traits are found more often in males who are less self-assertive sexually and have more sexual problems generally (perhaps to do with impotence or the fear of it) than in males whose approach to sex is the more usually dominant and straightforward one. Other researchers (notably A.H. Maslow) have subsequently reported that "dominant" women appear to enjoy sex more (like the Trobrianders). One might also add the speculation that because more females than males in our society exhibit "passive" traits, more of them find it hard to enjoy sex and have difficulty in reaching orgasm.

A final area in which explanations of male-female differences in sexuality have been sought is psychology—particularly Freudian psychology. According to this school of thought, the evolution of male and female personality, and the development of sexuality, are both part of the same process. Compared to the factors already discussed, psychoanalytic theory does little to explain why male and female sexuality appear to differ; however, the coherence between the Freudian view of sexuality and the Freudian explanation of personality formation has been very influential, and a brief account of these theories will suggest some of the points at which psychoanalysis has raised a cultural sex difference to the status of a universal and natural distinction.

In traditional psychoanalytic theory, three basic features determine the different development of sexuality in males and females: the exteriority of the male genitals, the female's destiny of motherhood, and the structure of the family.

Both boys and girls are said to pass through the oral and anal stages in early infancy: then both become more specifically sexual in their interests. The penis becomes an object of attention to the boy and her clitoris to the girl, but at this point male and female sexuality take diverging paths. The female child is disappointed in her clitoris, wishing it to be more male in size and function; she turns away from her mother (whom she holds responsible) and projects her love towards her father. From her father she hopes to get a penis: later, when it is clear she will not, she translates this desire into the desire to bear a child. The male, however, around his third year, becomes intensely and sexually attracted to his mother, a passion which he gives up a year or so later because of the fear that his father might take revenge on him by castration. The sexuality of both sexes then passes into a stage of latency, re-emerging near puberty in recognisably masculine and feminine forms.

The penis envy from which the female child suffers, and the way she later equates the penis with a child, give rise to the traits of passivity, masochism and narcissism that make up the female character. Passivity, for example, comes from her abandonment of clitoral stimulation and from the onset of the maternal urge during the period of intense attachment to the father. Partly because of these qualities the female sex drive is said to be much weaker than the male's. Feminine personality and sexuality are both therefore a response—a solution—which the female child devises to the problems of penis envy. Before her discovery of the missing penis, she is "masculine" in character—that is, she shares the same interests, genital and nongenital, as boys. After her sight of the male organ she acquires femininity almost as a compensation. (At this point things may go wrong and she may become either neurotic or masculine). Because of these compensatory masochistic, narcissistic and passive qualities, her sex drive and her general libidinous energy are much weaker than in the male. But she has a heightened inner emotional life and a capacity to give maternal tenderness not only to her children but to her male partner. This tenderness cannot coexist with genital sexual excitement, localised and orgiastic as the male's is: in any case the reproductive purpose is achieved without any activity on the part of the female in intercourse. What the normal woman experiences in intercourse is not pleasure but a kind of masochistic pain. The sexual life cannot be divorced from motherhood—both the reality of it and the desire for it. The simple desire to rid oneself of sexual tension which characterises the adult male sexuality is missing in the female, whose sexuality is bound up in a complex manner with the development of femininity, and particularly with the evolution of a specifically maternal emotion.

Psychoanalysis tends to regard sexuality itself as male, as it does "libido," the concept of motivating energy responsible in humans for both sexual and non-sexual achievements. A basic weakness in the whole of this approach is, as Kate Millet has observed, its male bias. Freud and his followers built up a theory of feminine sexuality to account for the differences they observed between the sexes in their own sexually repressed and male-dominated society. A host of unsupportable assumptions prop up this theory of sexuality in females: the assumption that a female child believes herself to be anatomically inferior to the male (or believes the male to be superior); the assumption that while females envy males their penises, males do not envy females their wombs and their maternity; the assumption that the female child blames her mother (and not her father) for failing to provide her with a penis, and so on. Hence psychoanalytic theory is open to attack on many grounds. Not only was Freudian theory developed within the framework of a patriarchal family system; it fits only a culture in which masculinity and femininity are defined in particular ways. Freud's insistence on the discovery of the missing penis could hardly withstand the realities of preliterate societies where nakedness is the rule; nor is penis envy likely in cultures where little girls are told how lucky they are to have wombs and so to be able to become mothers, and where the male role is consistently devalued. Bruno Bettleheim has described many of the rituals in such societies, which eloquently express the male desire to emulate the achievements of women. The evidence from anthropology shows that the development of sexuality in males and females alike is responsive to a range of social values and rules which govern its legitimate expression, rather than to the biologically constant genital ground-plan of their bodies. Furthermore, penis envy and womb envy may be so named for their symbolic meaning only, and the actual envy men and women have of each other may not be of their genitals and reproductive organs but of their social prestige and economic function. In Freud's time, the feminine role was of low social value, and few women achieved anything of socially recognised value outside the province of home and family.

Differences in the sexuality of male and female have been variously attributed to differences in (a) their anatomies (b) the functioning of their hormones (c) their psychologies (d) their personalities and (e) the cultural learning processes to which they are subjected.

Of these five, only the first two and the last

I submit that love is essentially a much simpler phenomenon—it becomes complicated, corrupted, or obstructed by an unequal balance of power. We have seen that love demands a mutual vulnerability or it turns destructive: the destructive effects of love occur only in a context of inequality. But because sexual inequality has remained a constant—however its degree may have varied—the corruption "romantic" love became characteristic of love between the sexes. . . . Thus "falling in love" is no more than the process of alteration of male vision—through idealization, mystification, glorification— that renders void the woman's class inferiority.

Shulamith Firestone

---

are contrasting explanations, since the psychology and personality of male and female largely depend on culture. In fact the role of anatomy in determining sexuality must remain a purely hypothetical one until some explanation is given on how the two connect. As it stands the statement "anatomy is destiny" offers no real explanation. Freudian theory can be interpreted as a massive attempt to take on the one hand distinctions of anatomy and on the other distinctions of "destiny" (or social role) and propose a series of processes by which one might lead to the other. One example of this is the genesis of penis envy for which the Freudian "explanation" is the little girl's sighting of the male genital and her subsequent envy of men. While these indubitably occur—some little girls do see penises and women do envy men—nothing may follow from the first other than a mere recognition of the anatomical sex difference, while the second may arise not from the first, but instead from an entirely realistic perception of the male's social roles as superior in power, prestige and interest.

In industrial cultures (and in some others too) the sexual relationship between male and female has been subsumed in the general power relationship of the sexes. This—the thesis of Kate Millett's *Sexual Politics*—has far-reaching implications for many areas of sex differentiation, including sexuality itself.

A culture which allots political and economic power to the male and gives him the prestige of playing the public roles, invites a number of responses from the female, to whom these rights and responsibilities are denied. One response is rebellion, epitomised in the emancipation movement of the late nineteenth and early twentieth centuries, and now in the women's liberation movement. But the demand for liberation and the techniques of rebellion are only possible for women who are conscious of rights denied and of the patriarchal bias that history has built into our culture. For the others, one possible response is to compensate for lack of power by obtaining a vicarious emotional satisfaction from exercising control over the powerful (blackmail is one form of this).

Unfortunately, a woman who responds in this way distorts her own personality. She uses her sexuality as a means of attracting males, which is necessary since the "possession" of a male is the only means to power, and since she must have a male to support her if she wishes to bear children (and this wish is the only distinctive part of female sexuality as defined by a patriarchal culture). This use of her sexuality as a means of keeping a male means that she must subordinate her own female desires and needs to those of the male. Inevitably all this distorts the female's own self-image, so that she sees herself as secondary, weak and placatory, and as relying on her sexual charms for a multitude of purposes, including the central one of economic survival.

This distinctively female use of sexuality lies behind the finding that dominant women enjoy sex more than submissive ones. Submissive women are unable to assert themselves sexually and are therefore able to enjoy only one kind of satisfaction, that which is wholly dependent on the technical expertise of the male. They cannot tell their lovers even what they want done to their own bodies, and the awareness of this acts as a barrier to the physical sensation of the experience itself. "Dominant" women on the other hand are not afraid of their sexual aggression, do not interpret it as pseudomasculinity (except in the sense that the norm of sexuality is male, as all norms tend to be male in a male-oriented culture) and are not repulsed by the physical needs and sensations of their own bodies.

Some progressive psychiatric thought is now taking account of the fact that this long conditioning of the female to a particular kind of sexual response (or lack of response) is a facet of the maleness of our culture, and this is leading to the conclusion that some of the so-called sex differences in sexuality are due to conditioning and learning, rather than to innate and pre-cultural factors. The cross-cultural data support this; so does the material quoted earlier in this chapter, showing that the sexual responses of the two sexes are largely determined by their different sexual experiences, which in turn are determined by their cultural roles. So also does the recent biological material, and this is of particular value in helping to finally quash the debate about the vaginal versus the clitoral orgasm. To show that the ultimate sexual response, the orgasm, is physiologically identical in male and female, except for the minor necessary difference of organ and secretion, is a landmark of great importance in the study of human sexuality.

For the study of female sexuality in particular, generalisations from the animal world have been influential and extremely depressing. The infrahuman female primate, says the expert, does not have an orgasm—conclusion, the human female does not have or need an orgasm either? The chimpanzee, on the other hand, does appear to masturbate, which perhaps should cheer feminists up a little. Also, female chimpanzees often take the initiative in sexual liaisons, and so do not confirm the conventional idea of the passivity of the female.

The analogy becomes increasingly ridiculous when we add that the nonhuman female primate has no hymen, menopause, artificial feeding bottle, or voluntary relief from procreation. The males of these species are dominant, aggressive, and sexually assertive, and show no desire or ability to give the female pleasure. This is equally absurd in its application to human culture, enabling the patriarchal world to be supported in its very foundations, justifying the aggressive acts of the male in the bedroom by reference to the jungle, and providing a rationale for aggressive acts in the distinctly human world of social, economic, and political affairs.

To study the evolution of sex differences in sexuality one can, of course, study the chimpanzee, and speculate on the origins of the female orgasm. Is it an evolving trait which is not yet fully established, itself a product of culture? Or is it a "regressive" development, a distinctly human invention which is to be deplored for its tendency to distract females from the central business of maternity? Whatever the answer—and it is doubtful whether we will ever know it—it is surely much more important to study the whole moulding of personality and sexual response by culture, and in different forms of *human* society.

Mary Jane Sherfey, M.D.

A Theory on Female Sexuality

No doubt the most far-reaching hypothesis extrapolated from biological data is the existence of the universal and physically normal condition of women's inability ever to reach complete sexual satiation in the presence of the most intense, repetitive orgasmic experiences, no matter how produced. Theoretically, a woman could go on having orgasms indefinitely if physical exhaustion did not intervene.

It is to be understood that repetitive orgasms leading to the satiation-in-insatiation state will be most apt to occur in parous[1] and experienced women during the luteal phase[2] of the menstrual cycle. It is one of the most important ways in which the sexuality of the primate and human female differs from the primate and human male at the physical level; and this difference exists only because of the female's capacity to produce the fulminating pelvic congestion and edema. This capacity is mediated by specific hormonal combinations with high fluid-imbibing action which are found only in certain primates and, probably, a very few other mammalian species.

I must stress that this condition does not mean a woman is always consciously unsatisfied. There is a great difference between satisfaction and satiation. A woman may be emotionally satisfied to the full in the absence of *any* orgasmic expression (although such a state would rarely persist through years of frequent arousal and coitus without some kind of physical or emotional reaction formation). Satiation-in-insatiation is well illustrated by Masters' statement, "A woman *will usually* be satisfied with three to five orgasms . . ." I believe it would rarely be said, "A man will usually be satisfied with three to five ejaculations." The man *is* satisfied. The woman *usually wills* herself to be satisfied because she is simply unaware of the extent of her orgasmic capacity. However, I predict that this hypothesis will come as no great shock to many women who consciously realize, or intuitively sense, their lack of satiation . . .

It seems that the vast majority of cases of coital frigidity are due simply to the absence of frequent, prolonged coitus. This statement is supported by unpublished data which Masters and Johnson are now accumulating. Following this logical conclusion of their previous research, they began treating a series of couples with severe, chronic frigidity or impotence. All had received prior medical and, often, psychiatric treatment to no avail. For the women, none of whom had ever experienced orgasms after five or more years of marriage, treatment consisted of careful training of the husband to use the proper techniques essential to all women and the specific ones required by his wife. In many cases this in itself was sufficient. In the others, daily sessions were instigated of marital coitus followed by prolonged use of the artificial phallus (three to four hours or more). Thus far, with about fifty women treated, every woman but one responded within three weeks at most and usually within a few days. They began at once to experience intense, multiple

---

[1]"Parous" describes women who have had at least one child.
[2]The luteal phase is the post-ovulatory phase of the menstrual cycle.

orgasms; and once this capacity was achieved after the exposure to daily prolonged coitus, they were able to respond with increasing ease and rapidity so that the protracted stimulation was no longer necessary. It is too early for thorough follow-ups, but initial impressions are most favorable.

Should these preliminary findings hold, an almost total biological etiology of coital frigidity will be proved. The inordinate sexual, orgasmic capacity of the human female will fall in line with that of the other higher primates—and the magnitude of the psychological and social problems facing modern mankind is difficult to contemplate.

Historical Perspective and Cultural Dilemma

The nature of female sexuality as here presented makes it clear that, just as the vagina did not evolve for the delivery of big-headed babies, so women's inordinate orgasmic capacity did not evolve for monogamous, sedentary cultures. It is unreasonable to expect that this inordinate sexual capacity could be, even in part, given expression within the confines of our culture; and it is particularly unreasonable to expect the delayed blooming of the sexuality of many women after the age of thirty or so to find adequate avenues of satisfaction. Less than one hundred years ago, and in many places today, women regularly had their third or fourth child by the time they were eighteen or nineteen, and the life span was no more than thirty-five to forty years. It could well be that the natural synchronization of the peak periods for sexual expression in men and women has been destroyed only in recent years.

These findings give ample proof of the conclusion that neither men nor women, but especially not women, are biologically built for the single-spouse, monogamous marital structure or for the prolonged adolescence which our society can now bestow upon both of them. Generally, men have never accepted strict monogamy except in principle. Women have been forced to accept it; but not, I submit, for the reasons usually given.

The human mating system, with its permanent family and kinship ties, was absolutely essential to man's becoming—and remaining—man. In every culture studied, the crucial transition from the nomadic, hunting, and food-gathering economy to a settled, agricultural existence was the beginning of family life, modern civilization, and civilized man. In the preagricultural societies, life was precarious, population growth slow, and infanticide often essential to group survival. With the domestication of animals and the agriculture revolution, for the first time in all time, the survival of a species lay in the extended family with its private property, kinship lineages, inheritance laws, social ordinances, and, most significantly, many surviving children. Only in that carefully delineated and rigidly maintained large-family complex could the individual find sufficient security to allow his uniquely human potentialities to be developed through the long years of increasingly helpless childhood—and could populations explode into the first little villages and towns.

Many factors have been advanced to explain the rise of the patriarchal, usually polygamous, system and its concomitant ruthless subjugation of female sexuality (which necessarily subjugated her entire emotional and intellectual life). However, if the conclusions reached here are true, it is conceivable that the *forceful* suppression of women's inordinate sexual demands was a prerequisite to the dawn of every modern civilization and almost every living culture. Primitive woman's sexual drive was too strong, too susceptible to the fluctuating extremes of an impelling, aggressive erotism to withstand the disciplined requirements of a settled family life—where many living children were necessary to a family's well-being and where paternity had become as important as maternity in maintaining family and property cohesion. For about half the time, women's erotic needs would be insatiably pursued; paternity could never be certain; and with lactation erotism, constant infant care would be out of the question.

There are many indications from the prehistory studies in the Near East that it took perhaps five thousand years or longer for the subjugation of women to take place. All relevant data from the 12,000 to 8,000 B.C. period indicate that precivilized woman enjoyed full sexual freedom and was often totally incapable of controlling her sexual drive.[3] Therefore, I propose that one of the reasons for the long delay between the earliest development of agriculture (c. 12,000 B.C.) and the rise of urban life and the beginning of recorded knowledge (c. 8,000–5,000 B.C.) was the ungovernable cyclic

sexual drive of women. Not until these drives were gradually brought under control by rigidly enforced social codes could family life become the stabilizing and creative crucible from which modern civilized man could emerge.

Although then (and now) couched in superstitious, religious and rationalized terms, behind the subjugation of women's sexuality lay the inexorable economics of cultural evolution which finally forced men to impose it and women to endure it. If that suppression has been, at times, unduly oppressive or cruel, I suggest the reason has been neither man's sadistic, selfish infliction of servitude upon helpless women nor women's weakness or inborn masochism. The strength of the drive determines the force required to suppress it.

The hypothesis that women possess a *biologically determined*, inordinately high, cyclic sexual drive is too significant to be accepted without confirmation from every field of science touching the subject. Assuming this analysis of the nature of women's sexuality is valid, we must ask ourselves if the basic intensity of women's sexual drive has abated appreciably as the result of the past seven thousand years of suppression (which has been, of course,

[3]"Today it is unfashionable to talk about former more matriarchal orders of society. Nevertheless, there is evidence from many parts of the world that the role of women has weakened since earlier times in several sections of social structure." The evidence given here lends further support to this statement by J. Hawkes and L. Woolley. See *History of Mankind, Vol. I: Prehistory and the Beginnings of Civilization* (New York: Harper & Row, 1963). However, I must make it clear that the biological data presented support only the thesis on the intense, insatiable erotism in women. Such erotism could be contained within one or possibly several types of social structures which would have prevailed through most of the Pleistocene period.

I am indebted to Prof. Joseph Mazzeo of Columbia University for calling my attention to the fact that the first study on the existence of a pre-Neolithic matriarchal society was published in 1861: Bachofen's *Das Mutterrecht*. (Basel: B. Schwabe, 1897). Indeed, Bachofen's work remains an unsurpassed, scholarly analysis of the mythologies of the Near East, hypothesizing both a matriarchal society and the inordinate erotism of women. His entire thesis was summarily rejected by twentieth-century anthropologists for lack of objective evidence (and cultural bias). On several scores, the ancient myths have proved more accurate than the modern scientists' theories. I suspect this will be another instance in which the myths prove faithful reflections of former days.

only partial suppression for most of the time). Just within the very recent past, a decided lifting of the ancient social injunctions against the free expression of female sexuality has occurred. This unprecedented development is born of the scientific revolution, the product of both efficient contraceptives, and the new social equality and emotional honesty sweeping across the world (an equality and honesty which owe more to the genius of Sigmund Freud than to any other single individual). It is hard to predict what will happen should this trend continue—except one thing is certain: if women's sexual drive has not abated, and they prove incapable of controlling it, thereby jeopardizing family life and child care, a return to the rigid, enforced suppression will be inevitable and mandatory. Otherwise the biological family will disappear and what other patterns of infant care and adult relationships could adequately substitute cannot now be imagined.[4]

Should the hypothesis be true that one of the requisite cornerstones upon which all modern civilizations were founded was *coercive* suppression of women's inordinate sexuality, one looks back over the long history of women and their relationships to men, children, and society since the Neolithic revolution with a deeper, almost awesome, sense of the ironic tragedy in the triumph of the human condition.

Summary

Recent embryological research has demonstrated conclusively that the concept of the initial anatomical bisexuality or equipotentiality of the embryo is erroneous. All mammalian embryos, male and female, are anatomically female during the early stages of fetal life. In humans, the differentiation of the male from the female form by the action of fetal androgen begins about the sixth week of embryonic life and is completed by the end of the third month. Female structures develop autonomously without the necessity of hormonal differentiation. If the fetal gonads are removed from a genetic female before the first six weeks, she will develop into a normal female, even undergoing normal pubertal changes if, in the absence of ovaries, exogenous hormones are supplied. If the fetal gonads are similarly removed from a genetic male, he will develop into a female, also undergoing normal female pubertal changes if exogenous hormones are supplied. The probable relationship of the antonomous female anatomy to the evolution of viviparity is described.

From this surprising discovery of modern embryology and other biological data, the hypothesis is suggested that the female's relative lack of differentiating hormones during embryonic life renders her more sensitive to hormonal conditioning in later life, especially to androgens, since some embryonic and strong maternal estrogenic activity is present during embryonic life. This ready androgen responsivity provides the physiological means whereby androgen-sensitive structures could evolve to enhance the female's sexual capacity. In the primates, the marked development of the clitoral system, certain secondary sexual characteristics including skin erotism, and the extreme degree of perineal sexual edema (achieved in part by progesterone with its strong androgenic prop-

----

[4]On the contrary, communal family structures, with men *and* women sharing child care, are not only imaginable, but already in experimental practice.

erties) are combined in various species to produce an intense aggressive sexual drive and an inordinate, insatiable capacity for copulations during estrus.[5] The breeding advantage would thus go to the females with the most insatiable sexual capacity. The infrahuman female's insatiable sexual capacity could evolve only if it did not interfere with maternal care. Maternal care is insured by the existence of the extreme sexual drive only during estrus and its absence during the prolonged postpartum anestrus of these animals.

The validity of these considerations and their relevance to the human female are strongly supported by the demonstration of comparable sexual physiology and behavior in women. This has been accomplished by the research of Masters and Johnson, and a summary of their findings of the actual nature of the sexual response cycle in women is presented. Their most important observations are:

A. There is no such thing as a vaginal orgasm distinct from a clitoral orgasm. The nature of the orgasm is the same regardless of the erotogenic zone stimulated to produce it. The orgasm consists of the rhythmic contractions of the extravaginal musculature against the greatly distended circumvaginal venous plexi and vestibular bulbs surrounding the lower third of the vagina.

B. The nature of the labial-preputial-glandar mechanism which maintains continuous stimulation of the retracted clitoris during intravaginal coition has been described. By this action, clitoris, labia minora, and lower third of the vagina function as a single, smoothly integrated unit when traction is placed on the labia by the male organ during coitus. Stimulation of the clitoris is achieved by the rhythmical pulling on the edematous prepuce. Similar activation of the clitoris is achieved by preputial friction during direct clitoral area stimulation.

C. With full sexual arousal, women are normally capable of many orgasms. As many as six or more can be achieved with intravaginal coition. During clitoral area stimulation, when a woman can control her sexual tension and maintain prolonged stimulation, she may attain up to fifty or more orgasms in an hour's time.

From these observations and other biological data, especially from primatology, I have advanced four hypotheses:

1. The erotogenic potential of the clitoral glans is probably greater than that of the lower third of the vagina . . . The evolution of primate sexuality has occurred primarily through selective adaptations of the perineal edema and the clitoral complex, not the vagina.

2. Under optimal arousal conditions, women's orgasmic potential may be similar to that of the primates described. In both, orgasms are best achieved only with the high degree of pelvic vasocongestion and edema associated with estrus in the primates and the luteal phase of the menstrual cycle in women or with prolonged, effective stimulation. Under these conditions, each orgasm tends to increase pelvic vasocongestion; thus the more orgasms achieved, the more can be achieved. Orgasmic experiences may continue until physical exhaustion intervenes.

3. In these primates and in women, an inordinate cyclic sexual capacity has thus evolved leading to the paradoxical state of sexual insatiation in the presence of the utmost sexual

---

[5]Estrus is that time when a female animal, because of the hormonal milieu, is capable of conception and desirous of copulation. Strictly speaking, true estrus does not occur in the human female.

satiation. The value of this state for evolution is clear: with the breeding premium going to the primate females with the greatest pelvic edema, the most effective clitoral erotism, and the most aggressive sexual behavior, the satiation-in-insatiation state may have been an important factor in the adaptive radiation of the primates leading to man—and a major barrier to the evolution of modern man.

4. The rise of modern civilization, while resulting from many causes, was contingent on the suppression of the inordinate cyclic sexual drive of women because (a) the hyperhormonalization of the early human females associated with the hypersexual drive and the prolonged pregnancies was an important force in the escape from the strict estrus sexuality and the much more important escape from lactation asexuality. Women's uncurtailed continuous hypersexuality would drastically interfere with maternal responsibilities; and (b) with the rise of the settled agriculture economies, man's territorialism became expressed in property rights and kinship laws. Large families of known parentage were mandatory and could not evolve until the inordinate sexual demands of women were curbed.

Finally, the data on the embryonic female primacy and the Masters and Johnson research on the sexual cycle in women will require amendations of psychoanalytic theory. These will be less than one might think at first sight. Other than concepts based on innate bisexuality, the rigid dichotomy between masculine and feminine sexual behavior, and derivative concepts of the clitoral-vaginal transfer theory, psychoanalytic theory will remain. Much of the theory concerning the "masculine" components of female sexuality will also remain but will be based on a different biological conception. Certainly, much of present and past sexual symbolism will take on richer meanings.

It is my strong conviction that these fundamental biological findings will, in fact, strengthen psychoanalytic theory and practice in the area of female sexuality. Without the erroneous biological premises, the basic sexual constitution and its many manifestations will be seen as highly moldable by hormonal influences, which in turn are so very susceptible to all those uniquely human emotional, intellectual, imaginative, and cultural forces upon which psychoanalysis has cast so much light. The power of the psychic processes will stand the stronger. Therefore it may be safely predicted that these new biological findings will not "blow away" Freud's "artificial structure of hypotheses" but will transpose it to a less artificial and more effective level.

In any event, and regardless of the validity of my own conclusions, it is my hope that this presentation of recent major contributions from biology and gynecology bearing on female sexual differentiation and adult functioning will aid in the integration of psychological and biological knowledge and will provide a firm biological foundation upon which all future theories of female psychosexuality must rest.

Anne Koedt

The Myth of the Vaginal Orgasm

Whenever female orgasm and frigidity are discussed, a false distinction is made between vaginal and clitoral orgasm. Frigidity has generally been defined by men as the failure of women to have vaginal orgasms. Actually the vagina is not a highly sensitive area and is not constructed to achieve orgasm. It is the clitoris which is the center of sexual sensitivity and which is the female equivalent of the penis.

I think this explains a great many things: First of all, the fact that the so-called frigidity rate among women is phenomenally high. Rather than tracing female frigidity to the false assumptions about female anatomy, our "experts" have declared frigidity as a psychological problem of women. Those women who complained about it were recommended psychiatrists, so that they might discover their "problem"—diagnosed generally as a failure to adjust to their role as women.

The facts of female anatomy and sexual response tell a different story. Although there are many areas for sexual arousal, there is only one area for sexual climax; that area is the clitoris. All orgasms are extensions of sensation from this area. Since the clitoris is not necessarily stimulated sufficiently in the conventional sexual positions, we are left "frigid."

Aside from physical stimulation, which is the common cause of orgasm for most people, there is also stimulation through primarily mental processes. Some women, for example, may achieve orgasm through sexual fantasies, or through fetishes. However, while the stimulation may be psychological, the orgasm manifests itself physically. Thus, while the cause is psychological, the *effect* is still physical, and the orgasm necessarily takes place in the sexual organ equipped for sexual climax—the clitoris. The orgasm experience may also differ in degree of intensity—some more localized, and some more diffuse and sensitive. But they are all clitoral orgasms.

All this leads to some interesting questions about conventional sex and our role in it. Men have orgasms essentially by friction with the vagina, not the clitoral area, which is external and not able to cause friction the way penetration does. Women have thus been defined sexually in terms of what pleases men; our own biology has not been properly analyzed. Instead, we are fed the myth of the liberated woman and her vaginal orgasm—an orgasm which in fact does not exist.

What we must do is redefine our sexuality. We must discard the "normal" concepts of sex and create new guidelines which take into account mutual sexual enjoyment. While the idea of mutual enjoyment is liberally applauded in marriage manuals, it is not followed to its logical conclusion. We must begin to demand that if certain sexual positions now defined as "standard" are not mutually conducive to orgasm, they no longer be defined as standard. New techniques must be used or devised which transform this particular aspect of our current sexual exploitation.

Freud—A Father of the Vaginal Orgasm

Freud contended that the clitoral orgasm was adolescent, and that upon puberty, when women began having intercourse with men, women should transfer the center of orgasm to the vagina. The vagina, it was assumed, was able to produce a parallel, but more mature, orgasm than the clitoris. Much work was done to elaborate on this theory, but little was done to challenge the basic assumptions.

To fully appreciate this incredible invention, perhaps Freud's general attitude about women should first be recalled. Mary Ellman, in *Thinking About Women,* summed it up this way:

> Everything in Freud's patronizing and fearful attitude toward women follows from their lack of a penis, but it is only in his essay *The Psychology of Women* that Freud makes explicit . . . the deprecations of women which are implicit in his work. He then prescribes for them the abandonment of the life of the mind, which will interfere with their sexual function. When the psychoanalyzed patient is male, the analyst sets himself the task of developing the man's capacities; but with women patients, the job is to resign them to the limits of their sexuality. As Mr. Rieff puts it: For Freud, "Analysis cannot encourage in women new energies for success and achievement, but only teach them the lesson of rational resignation."

It was Freud's feelings about women's secondary and inferior relationship to men that formed the basis for his theories on female sexuality.

Once having laid down the law about the nature of our sexuality, Freud not so strangely discovered a tremendous problem of frigidity in women. His recommended cure for a woman who was frigid was psychiatric care. She was suffering from failure to mentally adjust to her "natural" role as a woman. Frank S. Caprio, a contemporary follower of these ideas, states:

> . . . whenever a woman is incapable of achieving an orgasm via coitus, provided the husband is an adequate partner, and prefers clitoral stimulation to any other form of sexual activity, she can be regarded as suffering from frigidity and requires psychiatric assistance. *(The Sexually Adequate Female,* p. 64.)

The explanation given was that women were envious of men—"renunciation of womanhood." Thus it was diagnosed as an antimale phenomenon.

It is important to emphasize that Freud did not base his theory upon a study of woman's anatomy, but rather upon his assumptions of woman as an inferior appendage to man, and her consequent social and psychological role. In their attempts to deal with the ensuing problem of mass frigidity, Freudians embarked on elaborate mental gymnastics. Marie Bonaparte, in *Female Sexuality,* goes so far as to suggest surgery to help women back on their rightful path. Having discovered a strange connection between the non-frigid woman and the location of the clitoris near the vagina,

> it then occurred to me that where, in certain women, this gap was excessive, and clitoridal fixation obdurate, a clitoridal-vaginal reconciliation might be effected by surgical means, which would then benefit the normal erotic function. Professor Halban, of Vienna, as much a biologist as surgeon, became interested in the problem and worked out a simple operative technique. In this, the suspensory ligament of the clitoris was severed and the clitoris secured to the underlying structures, thus fixing it in a lower position, with the eventual reduction of the labia minora. (p. 148.)

But the severest damage was not in the area of surgery, where Freudians ran around absurdly trying to change female anatomy to fit their basic assumptions. The worst damage was done to the mental health of women, who either suffered silently with self-blame, or flocked to psychiatrists looking desperately for the hidden and terrible repression that had kept from them their vaginal destiny.

Lack of Evidence

One may perhaps at first claim that these are unknown and unexplored areas, but upon closer examination this is certainly not true today, nor was it true even in the past. For example, men have known that women suffered from frigidity often during intercourse. So the problem was there. Also, there is much specific evidence. Men knew that the clitoris was and is the essential organ for masturbation, whether in children or adult women. So obviously women made it clear where *they* thought their sexuality was located. Men also seem suspiciously aware of the clitoral powers during "foreplay," when they want to arouse women and produce the necessary lubrication for penetration. Foreplay is a concept created for male purposes, but works to the disadvantage of many women, since as soon as the woman is aroused, the man changes to vaginal stimulation, leaving her often both aroused and unsatisfied.

It has also been known that women need no anesthesia inside the vagina during surgery, thus pointing to the fact that the vagina is in fact not a highly sensitive area.

Today, with extensive knowledge of anatomy, with Kelly, Kinsey, and Masters and Johnson, to mention just a few sources, there is no ignorance on the subject. There are, however, social reasons why this knowledge has not been popularized. We are living in a male society which has not sought change in women's role.

Anatomical Evidence

Rather than starting with what women *ought* to feel, it would seem logical to start out with the anatomical facts regarding the clitoris and vagina.

The Clitoris is a small equivalent of the penis, except for the fact that the urethra does not go through it as in the man's penis. Its erection is similar to the male erection, and the head of the clitoris has the same type of structure and function as the head of the penis. The anatomist G. Lombard Kelly, in *Sexual Feeling in Married Men and Women,* says:

> The head of the clitoris is also composed of erectile tissue, and it possesses a very sensitive epithelium or surface covering, supplied with special nerve endings called genital corpuscles, which are peculiarly adapted for sensory stimulation that under proper mental conditions terminates in the sexual orgasm. No other part of the female generative tract has such corpuscles. (Pocketbooks; p. 35.)

The clitoris has no other function than that of sexual pleasure.

The Vagina—Its functions are related to the reproductive function. Principally, 1) menstruation, 2) receive penis, 3) hold semen, and 4) birth passage. The interior of the vagina, which according to the defenders of the vaginal caused orgasm is the center and producer of the orgasm, is:

> like nearly all other internal body structures, poorly supplied with end organs of touch. The internal entodermal origin of the lining of the vagina makes it similar in this respect to the rectum and other parts of the digestive tract. (Kinsey, *Sexual Behavior in the Human Female,* p. 580.)

The degree of insensitivity inside the vagina is so high that "Among the women who were tested in our gynecologic sample, less than 14% were at all conscious that they had been touched." (Kinsey, p. 580.)

Even the importance of the vagina as an *erotic* center (as opposed to an orgasmic center) has been found to be minor.

Other Areas—Labia minora and the vestibule of the vagina. These two sensitive areas may trigger off a clitoral orgasm. Because they can be effectively stimulated during "normal" coitus, though infrequently, this kind of stimulation is incorrectly thought to be vaginal orgasm. However, it is important to distinguish between areas which can stimulate the clitoris, though incapable of producing the orgasm themselves, and the clitoris:

> Regardless of what means of excitation is used to bring the individual to the state of sexual climax, the sensation is perceived by the genital corpuscles and is localized where they are situated: in the head of the clitoris or penis. (Kelly, p. 49.)

Psychologically Stimulated Orgasm—Aside from the above mentioned direct and indirect stimulations of the clitoris, there is a third way an orgasm may be triggered. This is through mental (cortical) stimulation, where the imagination stimulates the brain, which in turn stimulates the genital corpuscles of the glans to set off an orgasm.

Women Who Say They Have Vaginal Orgasms

Confusion—Because of the lack of knowledge of their own anatomy, some women accept the idea that an orgasm felt during "normal" intercourse was vaginally caused. This confusion is caused by a combination of two factors. One, failing to locate the center of the orgasm, and two, by a desire to fit her experience to the male-defined idea of sexual normalcy. Considering that women know little about their anatomy, it is easy to be confused.

Deception—The vast majority of women who pretend vaginal orgasm to their men are faking it to "get the job." In a best-selling Danish book, *I Accuse*, Mette Ejlersen specifically deals with this common problem, which she calls the "sex comedy." This comedy has many causes. First of all, the man brings a great deal of pressure to bear on the woman, because he considers his ability as a lover at stake. So as not to offend his ego, the woman will comply with the prescribed role and go through simulated ecstasy. In some of the other Danish women mentioned, women who were left frigid were turned off to sex, and pretended vaginal orgasm to hurry up the sex act. Others admitted that they had faked vaginal orgasm to catch a man. In one case, the woman pretended vaginal orgasm to get him to leave his first wife, who admitted being vaginally frigid. Later she was forced to continue the deception, since obviously she couldn't tell him to stimulate her clitorally.

Many more women were simply afraid to establish their right to equal enjoyment, seeing the sexual act as being primarily for the man's benefit, and any pleasure that the woman got as an added extra.

Other women, with just enough ego to reject the man's idea that they needed psychiatric care, refused to admit their frigidity. They wouldn't accept self-blame, but they didn't know how to solve the problem, not knowing the physiological facts about themselves. So they were left in a peculiar limbo.

Again, perhaps one of the most infuriating and damaging results of this whole charade has been that women who were perfectly healthy sexually were taught that they were not. So in addition to being sexually deprived, these women were told to blame themselves when they deserved no blame. Looking for a cure to a problem that has none can lead a woman on an endless path of self-hatred and insecurity. For she is told by her analyst that not even

We are entitled to keep to our view that in the phallic phase of girls the clitoris is the leading erotogenic zone. But it is not, of course, going to remain so. With the change to femininity the clitoris should wholly or in part hand over its sensitivity, and at the same time its importance, to the vagina.

Sigmund Freud

---

in her one role allowed in a male society—the role of a woman—is she successful. She is put on the defensive, with phony data as evidence, that she'd better try to be even more feminine, think more feminine, and reject her envy of men.

Why Men Maintain the Myth

1. *Sexual Penetration is Preferred*—The best physical stimulant for the penis is the woman's vagina. It supplies the necessary friction and lubrication. From a strictly technical point of view this position offers the best physical conditions, even though the man may try other positions for variation.

2. *The Invisible Woman*—One of the elements of male chauvinism is the refusal or inability to see women as total, separate human beings. Rather, men have chosen to define women only in terms of how they benefited men's lives. Sexually, a woman was not seen as an individual wanting to share equally in the sexual act, any more than she was seen as a person with independent desires when she did anything else in society. Thus, it was easy to make up what was convenient about women; for on top of that, society has been a function of male interests, and women are not organized to form even a vocal opposition to the male experts.

3. *The Penis as Epitome of Masculinity*—Men define their lives primarily in terms of masculinity. It is a universal form of ego-boosting. That is, in every society, however homogeneous

(i.e., with the absence of racial, ethnic, or major economic differences) there is always a group, women, to oppress.

The essence of male chauvinism is in the psychological superiority men exercise over women. This kind of superior-inferior definition of self, rather than positive definition based upon one's own achievements and development, has of course chained victim and oppressor both. But by far the most brutalized of the two is the victim.

An analogy is racism, where the white racist compensates for his feelings of unworthiness by creating an image of the black man (it is primarily a male struggle) as biologically inferior to him. Because of his position in a white-male power structure, the white man can socially enforce this mythical division.

To the extent that men try to rationalize and justify male superiority through physical differentiation, masculinity may be symbolized by being the *most* muscular, the most hairy; having the deepest voice, and the biggest penis. Women, on the other hand, are approved of (i.e., called feminine) if they are weak, petite; shave their legs; have high soft voices.

Since the clitoris is almost identical to the penis, one finds a great deal of evidence of men in various societies trying to either ignore the clitoris and emphasize the vagina (as did Freud), or, as in some places in the Mideast, actually performing clitoridectomy. Freud saw this ancient and still practiced custom as a way of further "feminizing" the female by removing this cardinal vestige of her masculinity. It should be noted also that a big clitoris is considered ugly and masculine. Some cultures engage in the practice of pouring a chemical on the clitoris to make it shrivel up into "proper" size.

It seems clear to me that men in fact fear the clitoris as a threat to "masculinity."

4. *Sexually Expendable Male*—Men fear that they will become sexually expendable if the clitoris is substituted for the vagina as the center of pleasure for women. Actually this has a great deal of validity if one considers *only* the anatomy. The position of the penis inside the vagina, while perfect for reproduction, does not necessarily stimulate an orgasm in women because the clitoris is located externally and higher up. Women must rely upon indirect stimulation in the "normal" position.

Lesbian sexuality could make an excellent case, based only upon anatomical data, for the irrelevancy of the male organ. Albert Ellis says something to the effect that a man without a penis can make a woman an excellent lover.

Considering that the vagina is very desirable from a man's point of view, purely on physical grounds, one begins to see the dilemma for men. And it forces us as well to discard many "physical" arguments explaining why women go to bed with men. What is left, it seems to me, are primarily psychological reasons why women select men, at the exclusion of women, as sexual partners.

5. *Control of Women*—One reason given to explain the Mideastern practice of clitoridectomy is that it will keep the women from straying. By removing the sexual organ capable of orgasm, it must be assumed that her sexual drive will diminish. Considering how men look upon their women as property, particularly in very backward nations, we should begin to consider a great deal more why it is not in men's interest to have women totally free sexually. The double standard, as practiced for example in Latin America, is set up to keep the woman as total property of the husband, while he is free to have affairs as he wishes.

6. *Lesbianism and Bisexuality*—Aside from the strictly anatomical reasons why women might equally seek other women as lovers, there is a fear on men's part that women will seek the company of other women on a full, human basis. The recognition of clitoral orgasm as fact would threaten the heterosexual *institution*. For it would indicate that sexual pleasure was obtainable from either man *or* women, thus making heterosexuality not an absolute, but an option. It would thus open up the whole question of *human* sexual relationships beyond the confines of the present male-female role system.

Susan Griffin

Rape: The All-American Crime

I have never been free of the fear of rape. From a very early age I, like most women, have thought of rape as part of my natural environment—something to be feared and prayed against like fire or lightning. I never asked why men raped; I simply thought it one of the many mysteries of human nature.

I was, however, curious enough about the violent side of humanity to read every crime magazine I was able to ferret away from my grandfather. Each issue featured at least one "sex crime," with pictures of a victim, usually in a pearl necklace, and of the ditch or the orchard where her body was found. I was never certain why the victims were always women, nor what the motives of the murderer were, but I did guess that the world was not a safe place for women. I observed that my grandmother was meticulous about locks and quick to draw the shades before anyone removed so much as a shoe. I sensed that danger lurked outside.

At the age of eight, my suspicions were confirmed. My grandmother took me to the back of the house where the men wouldn't hear, and told me that strange men wanted to do harm to little girls. I learned not to walk on dark streets, not to talk to strangers or get into strange cars, to lock doors, and to be modest. She never explained why a man would want to harm a little girl, and I never asked.

If I thought for a while that my grandmother's fears were imaginary, the illusion was brief. That year, on the way home from school, a schoolmate a few years older than I tried to rape me. Later, in an obscure aisle of the local library (while I was reading *Freddy the Pig*)

I turned to discover a man exposing himself. Then, the friendly man around the corner was arrested for child molesting.

My initiation to sexuality was typical. Every woman has similar stories to tell—the first man who attacked her may have been a neighbor, a family friend, an uncle, her doctor, or perhaps her own father. And women who grow up in New York City always have tales about the subway.

But though rape and the fear of rape are a daily part of every woman's consciousness, the subject is so rarely discussed by that unofficial staff of male intellectuals (who write the books which study seemingly every other form of male activity) that one begins to suspect a conspiracy of silence. And indeed, the obscurity of rape in print exists in marked contrast to the frequency of rape in reality, for *forcible rape is the most frequently committed violent crime in America today.* The Federal Bureau of Investigation classes three crimes as violent: murder, aggravated assault and forcible rape. In 1968, 31,060 rapes were *reported.* According to the FBI and independent criminologists however, to approach accuracy this figure must be multiplied by at least a factor of ten to compensate for the fact that most rapes are not reported; when these compensatory mathematics are used, there are more rapes committed than aggravated assaults and homicides.

When I asked Berkeley, California's Police Inspector in charge of rape investigation if he knew why men rape women, he replied that he had not spoken with "these people and delved into what really makes them tick, because that really isn't my job." However, when

I asked him how a woman might prevent being raped, he was not so reticent. "I wouldn't advise any female to go walking around alone at night . . . and she should lock her car at all times." The Inspector illustrated his warning with a grisly story about a man who lay in wait for women in the back seats of their cars while they were shopping in a local supermarket. This man eventually murdered one of his rape victims. "Always lock your car," the Inspector repeated, and then added, without a hint of irony, "Of course, you don't have to be paranoid about this type of thing."

The Inspector wondered why I wanted to write about rape. Like most men he did not understand the urgency of the topic, for, after all, men are not raped. But like most women I had spent considerable time speculating on the true nature of the rapist. When I was very young, my image of the "sexual offender" was a nightmarish amalgamation of the bogey man and Captain Hook: he wore a black cape, and he cackled. As I matured, so did my image of the rapist. Born into the psychoanalytic age, I tried to "understand" the rapist. Rape, I came to believe, was only one of many unfortunate evils produced by sexual repression. Reasoning by tautology, I concluded that any man who would rape a woman must be out of his mind.

Yet, though the theory that rapists are insane is a popular one, this belief has no basis in fact. According to Professor Menachem Amir's study of 646 rape cases in Philadelphia, *Patterns in Forcible Rape,* men who rape are not abnormal. Amir writes, "Studies indicate that sex offenders do not constitute a unique or psychopathological type; nor are they as a group invariably more disturbed than the control groups to which they are compared." Alan Taylor, a parole officer who has worked with rapists in the prison facilities at San Luis Obispo, Califor-

nia, stated the question in plainer language: "Those men were the most normal men there. They had a lot of hang-ups, but they were the same hang-ups as men walking out on the street."

Another canon in the apologetics of rape is that, if it were not for learned social controls, all men would rape. Rape is held to be natural behavior, and not to rape must be learned. But in truth rape is not universal to the human species. Moreover, studies of rape in our culture reveal that, far from being impulsive behavior, most rape is planned. Professor Amir's study reveals that in cases of group rape (the "gang-bang" of masculine slang) 90 percent . . . were planned; in pair rapes, 83 percent . . . were planned; and in single rapes, 58 percent were planned. These figures should significantly discredit the image of the rapist as a man who is suddenly overcome by sexual needs society does not allow him to fulfill.

Far from the social control of rape being learned, comparisons with other cultures lead one to suspect that, in our society, it is rape itself that is learned. (The fact that rape is against the law should not be considered proof that rape is not in fact encouraged as part of our culture.)

This culture's concept of rape as an illegal, but still understandable, form of behavior is not a universal one. In her study *Sex and Temperament,* Margaret Mead describes a society that does not share our views. The Arapesh do not ". . . have any conception of the male nature that might make rape understandable to them." Indeed our interpretation of rape is a product of our conception of the nature of male sexuality. A common retort to the question, why don't women rape men, is the myth that men have greater sexual needs, that their sexuality is more urgent than women's. And it is the nature of human beings to want to live up to what is expected of them.

And this same culture which expects aggression from the male expects passivity from the female. Conveniently, the companion myth about the nature of female sexuality is that all women secretly want to be raped. Lurking beneath her modest female exterior is a subconscious desire to be ravished. The following description of a stag movie, written by Brenda Starr in Los Angeles' underground paper, *Everywoman,* typifies this male fantasy. The movie "showed a woman in her underclothes reading on her bed. She is interrupted by a rapist with a knife. He immediately wins her over with his charm and they get busy s---ing and f---ing." An advertisement in the *Berkeley Barb* reads, "Now as all women know from their daydreams, rape has a lot of advantages. Best of all it's so simple. No preparation necessary, no planning ahead of time, no wondering if you should or shouldn't; just whang! bang!" Thanks to Masters and Johnson even the scientific canon recognizes that for the female, "whang! bang!" can scarcely be described as pleasurable.

Still the male psyche persists in believing that, protestations and struggles to the contrary, deep inside her mysterious feminine soul, the female victim has wished for her own fate. A young woman who was raped by the husband of a friend said that days after the incident the man returned to her home, pounded on the door and screamed to her, "Jane, Jane. You loved it. You know you loved it."

The theory that women like being raped extends itself by deduction into the proposition that most or much of rape is provoked by the victim. But this too is only myth. Though provocation, considered a mitigating factor in a court of law, may consist of only "a gesture," according to the Federal Commission on Crimes of Violence, only 4 percent of reported rapes involved any precipitative behavior by the woman.

The notion that rape is enjoyed by the victim is also convenient for the man who, though he would not commit forcible rape, enjoys the idea of its existence, as if rape confirms that enormous sexual potency which he secretly knows to be his own. It is for the pleasure of the armchair rapist that detailed accounts of violent rapes exist in the media. Indeed, many men appear to take sexual pleasure from nearly all forms of violence. Whatever the motivation, male sexuality and violence in our culture seem to be inseparable. James Bond alternately whips out his revolver and his cock, and though there is no known connection between the skills of gunfighting and love-making, pacifism seems suspiciously effeminate.

In a recent fictional treatment of the Manson case, Frank Conroy writes of his vicarious titillation when describing the murders to his wife:

> "Every single person there was killed." She didn't move.
> "It sounds like there was torture," I said. As the words left my mouth I knew there was no need to say them to frighten her into believing that she needed me for protection.

The pleasure he feels as his wife's protector is inextricably mixed with pleasure in the violence itself. Conroy writes, "I was excited by the killings, as one is excited by catastrophe on a grand scale, as one is alert to pre-echoes of unknown changes, hints of unrevealed secrets, rumblings of chaos. . . ."

The attraction of the male in our culture to violence and death is a tradition Manson and his admirers are carrying on with tireless avidity (even presuming Manson's innocence, he dreams of the purification of fire and destruction). It was Malraux in his *Anti-Memoirs* who said that, for the male, facing death was *the* illuminating experience analogous to childbirth for the female. Certainly our culture does glorify war and shroud the agonies of the gunfighter in veils of mystery.

And in the spectrum of male behavior, rape, the perfect combination of sex and violence, is the penultimate act. Erotic pleasure cannot be separated from culture, and in our culture male eroticism is wedded to power. Not only should a man be taller and stronger than a female in the perfect love-match, but he must also demonstrate his superior strength in gestures of dominance which are perceived as amorous. Though the law attempts to make a clear division between rape and sexual intercourse, in fact the courts find it difficult to distinguish between a case where the decision to copulate was mutual and one where a man forced himself upon his partner.

The scenario is even further complicated by the expectation that, not only does a woman mean "yes" when she says "no," but that a really decent woman ought to begin by saying "no," and then be led down the primrose path to acquiescence. Ovid, the author of Western Civilization's most celebrated sex manual, makes this expectation perfectly clear: "and when I beg you to say "yes," say "no." Then let me lie outside your bolted door. . . . So Love grows strong."

That the basic elements of rape are involved in all heterosexual relationships may explain why men often identify with the offender in this crime. But to regard the rapist as the victim, a man driven by his inherent sexual needs to take what will not be given him, reveals a basic

> ### Missoula Rape Poem
>
> *There is no difference between being raped*
> *and being pushed down a flight of cement steps*
> *except that the wounds also bleed inside.*
>
> *There is no difference between being raped*
> *and being run over by a truck*
> *except that afterwards men ask you if you*
>   *enjoyed it.*
>
> *There is no difference between being raped*
> *and losing a hand in a mowing machine*
> *except that doctors don't want to get involved,*
> *the police wear a knowing smirk,*
> *and in small towns you become a veteran whore.*
>
> *There is no difference between being raped*
> *and being bitten on the ankle by a rattlesnake*
> *except that people ask if your skirt was short*
> *and why were you out alone anyhow.*
>
> *There is no difference between being raped*
> *and going head first through a windshield*
> *except that afterward you are afraid*
> *not of cars*
> *but of half the human race. . . .*
>
> Marge Piercy

ignorance of sexual politics. For in our culture heterosexual love finds an erotic expression through male dominance and female submission. A man who derives pleasure from raping a woman clearly must enjoy force and dominance as much as or more than the simple pleasures of the flesh. Coitus cannot be experienced in isolation. The weather, the state of the nation, the level of sugar in the blood—all will affect a man's ability to achieve orgasm. If a man can achieve sexual pleasure after terrorizing and humiliating the object of his passion, and in fact while inflicting pain upon

From *I'm Not for Women's Lib . . . But* by Bülbül, Arachne Publishing, Mountain View, Ca.

her, one must assume he derives pleasure directly from terrorizing, humiliating and harming a woman. According to Amir's study of forcible rape, on a statistical average the man who has been convicted of rape was found to have a normal sexual personality, tending to be different from the normal, well-adjusted male only in having a greater tendency to express violence and rage.

And if the professional rapist is to be separated from the average dominant heterosexual, it may be mainly a quantitative difference. For the existence of rape as an index to masculinity is not entirely metaphorical. Though this measure of masculinity seems to be more publicly exhibited among "bad boys" or aging bikers who practice sexual initiation through group rape, in fact "good boys" engage in the same rites to prove their manhood. In Stockton, a small town in California which epitomizes silent-majority America, a bachelor party was given [in the early 1970's] for a young man about to be married. A woman was hired to dance "topless" for the amusement of the guests. At the high point of the evening the bridegroom-to-be dragged the woman into a bedroom. room. No move was made by any of his companions to stop what was clearly going to be an attempted rape. Far from it. As the woman described, "I tried to keep him away—told him of my Herpes Genitalis, et cetera, but he couldn't face the guys if he didn't screw me." After the bridegroom had finished raping the woman and returned with her to the party, far

from chastising him, his friends heckled the woman and covered her with wine.

It was fortunate for the dancer that the bridegroom's friends did not follow him into the bedroom for, though one might suppose that in group rape, since the victim is outnumbered, less force would be inflicted on her, in fact, Amir's studies indicate, "the most excessive degrees of violence occurred in group rape." Far from discouraging violence, the presence of other men may in fact encourage sadism, and even cause the behavior. In an unpublished study of group rape by Gilbert Geis and Duncan Chappell, the authors refer to a study by W.H. Blanchard which relates, "The leader of the male group . . . apparently precipitated and maintained the activity, despite misgivings, because of a need to fulfill the role that the other two men had assigned to him. 'I was scared when it began to happen,' he says. 'I wanted to leave but I didn't want to say it to the other guys—you know—that I was scared.' "

Thus it becomes clear that not only does our culture teach men the rudiments of rape, but society, or more specifically other men, encourage the practice of it.

II

Every man I meet wants to protect me. Can't figure out what from.

—Mae West

If a male society rewards aggressive, domineering sexual behavior, it contains within it-

> *Nowhere is woman treated according to the merit of her work, but rather as a sex. It is therefore almost inevitable that she should pay for her right to exist, to keep a position in whatever line, with sex favors. Thus it is merely a question of degree whether she sells herself to one man, in or out of marriage, or to many men.*
>
> Emma Goldman, *The Traffic in Women* (1917)

---

self a sexual schizophrenia. For the masculine man is also expected to prove his mettle as a protector of women. To the naive eye, this dichotomy implies that men fall into one of two categories: those who rape and those who protect. In fact, life does not prove so simple. In a study euphemistically entitled "Sex Aggression by College Men," it was discovered that men who believe in a double standard of morality for men and women, who in fact believe most fervently in the ultimate value of virginity, are more liable to commit "this aggressive variety of sexual exploitation."

(At this point in our narrative it should come as no surprise that Sir Thomas Malory, creator of that classic tale of chivalry [*Morte d'Arthur*], was himself arrested and found guilty for repeated incidents of rape.)

In the system of chivalry, men protect women against men. This is not unlike the protection relationship which the Mafia established with small businesses in the early part of this century. Indeed, chivalry is an age-old protection racket which depends for its existence on rape.

According to the male mythology which defines and perpetuates rape, [the desire to rape] is an animal instinct inherent in the male. The story goes that sometime in our pre-historical past, the male, more hirsute and burly than today's counterpart, roamed about an uncivilized landscape until he found a desirable female. (Oddly enough, this female is *not* pictured as more muscular than the modern woman.) Her mate does not bother with courtship. He

simply grabs her by the hair and drags her to the closest cave. Presumably, one of the major advantages of modern civilization for the female has been the civilizing of the male. We call it chivalry.

But women do not get chivalry for free. According to the logic of sexual politics, we too have to civilize our behavior. (Enter chastity. Enter virginity. Enter monogamy.) For the female, civilized behavior means chastity before marriage and faithfulness within it. Chivalrous behavior in the male is supposed to protect that chastity from involuntary defilement. The fly in the ointment of this otherwise peaceful system is the fallen woman. She does not behave. And therefore she does not deserve protection. Or, to use another argument, a major tenet of the same value system, what has once been defiled cannot again be violated. One begins to suspect that it is the behavior of the fallen woman and not that of the male, that civilization aims to control.

The assumption that a woman who does not respect this double standard deserves whatever she gets (or at the very least "asks for it") operates in the courts today. While in some states a man's previous rape convictions are not considered admissible evidence, the sexual reputation of the rape victim is considered a crucial element of the facts upon which the court must decide innocence or guilt.

The court's respect for the double standard manifested itself particularly clearly in the case of the People v. Jerry Plotkin. Mr. Plotkin, a

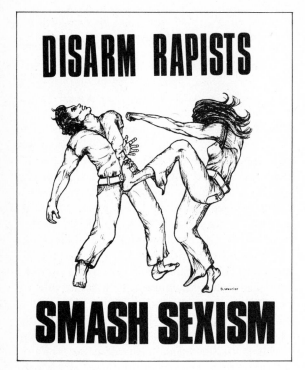

Poster by Betsy Warrior

36-year-old jeweler, was tried for rape [in 1971] in a San Francisco Superior Court. According to the woman who brought the charges, Plotkin, along with three other men, forced her at gunpoint to enter a car one night in October 1970. She was taken to Mr. Plotkin's fashionable apartment where he and the three other men first raped her and then, in the delicate language of the *San Francisco Chronicle,* "subjected her to perverted sex acts." She was, she said, set free in the morning with the warning that she would be killed if she spoke to anyone about the event. She did report the incident to the police, who then searched Plotkin's apartment and discovered a long list of names of women. Her name was on the list and had been crossed out.

In addition to the woman's account of her abduction and rape, the prosecution submitted four of Plotkin's address books containing the names of hundreds of women. Plotkin claimed he did not know all of the women since some of the names had been given to him by friends and he had not yet called on them. Several women, however, did testify in court that Plotkin had, to cite the *Chronicle,* "lured them up to his apartment under one pretext or another, and forced his sexual attentions on them."

Plotkin's defense rested on two premises. First, through his own testimony Plotkin established a reputation for himself as a sexual libertine who frequently picked up girls in bars and took them to his house where sexual relations often took place. He was the Playboy. He claimed that the accusation of rape, therefore, was false—this incident had simply been one of many casual sexual relationships, the victim one of many playmates. The second premise of the defense was that his accuser was also a sexual libertine. However, the picture created of the young woman (fully thirteen years younger than Plotkin) was not akin to the light-hearted, gay-bachelor image projected by the defendant. On the contrary, the day after the defense cross-examined the woman, the *Chronicle* printed a story headlined, "Grueling Day For Rape Case Victim." (A leaflet passed out by women in front of the courtroom was more succinct, "rape was committed by four men in a private apartment in October; on Thursday, it was done by a judge and a lawyer in a public courtroom.")

Through skillful questioning fraught with innuendo, Plotkin's defense attorney James

Martin MacInnis portrayed the young woman as a licentious opportunist and unfit mother. MacInnis began by asking the young woman (then employed as a secretary) whether or not it was true that she was "familiar with liquor" and had worked as a "cocktail waitress." The young woman replied (the *Chronicle* wrote "admitted") that she had worked once or twice as a cocktail waitress. The attorney then asked if she had worked as a secretary in the financial district but had "left that employment after it was discovered that you had sexual intercourse on a couch in the office." The woman replied, "That is a lie. I left because I didn't like working in a one-girl office. It was too lonely." Then the defense asked if, while working as an attendant at a health club, "you were accused of having a sexual affair with a man?" Again the woman denied the story: "I was never accused of that."

Plotkin's attorney then sought to establish that his client's accuser was living with a married man. She responded that the man was separated from his wife. Finally he told the court that she had "spent the night" with another man who lived in the same building.

At this point in the testimony the woman asked Plotkin's defense attorney, "Am I on trial? . . . It is embarrassing and personal to admit these things to all these people . . . I did not commit a crime. I am a human being." The lawyer, true to the chivalry of his class, apologized and immediately resumed questioning her, turning his attention to her children. (She is divorced, and the children at the time of the trial were in a foster home.) "Isn't it true that your two children have a sex game in which one gets on top of another and they—" "That is a lie!" the young woman interrupted him. She ended her testimony by explaining "They

are wonderful children. They are not perverted."

The jury, divided in favor of acquittal ten to two, asked the court stenographer to read the woman's testimony back to them. After this reading, the Superior Court acquitted the defendant of both the charges of rape and kidnapping.

According to the double standard a woman who has had sexual intercourse out of wedlock cannot be raped. Rape is not only a crime of aggression against the body; it is a transgression against chastity as defined by men. When a woman is forced into a sexual relationship, she has, according to the male ethos, been violated. But she is also defiled if she does not behave according to the double standard, by maintaining her chastity, or confining her sexual activities to a monogamous relationship.

One should not assume, however, that a woman can avoid the possibility of rape simply by behaving. Though myth would have it that mainly "bad girls" are raped, this theory has no basis in fact. Available statistics would lead one to believe that a safer course is promiscuity. In a study of rape done in the District of Columbia, it was found that 82 percent of the rape victims had a "good reputation." Even the Police Inspector's advice to stay off the streets is rather useless, for almost half of reported rapes occur in the home of the victim and are committed by a man she has never before seen. Like indiscriminate terrorism, rape can happen to any woman, and few women are ever without this knowledge.

But the courts and the police, both dominated by white males, continue to suspect the rape victim, *sui generis*, of provoking or asking for her own assault. According to Amir's study, the police tend to believe that a woman without a good reputation cannot be raped. The rape victim is usually submitted to countless questions about her own sexual mores and behavior by the police investigator. This preoccupation is partially justified by the legal requirements for prosecution in a rape case. The rape victim must have been penetrated, and she must have made it clear to her assailant that she did not want penetration (unless of course she is unconscious). A [woman's] refusal to accompany a man to some isolated place to allow him to touch her does not in the eyes of the court [make the subsequent act a] rape. She must have said "no" at the crucial genital moment. And the rape victim, to qualify as such, must also have put up a physical struggle—unless she can prove that to do so would have been to endanger her life.

But the zealous interest the police frequently exhibit in the physical details of a rape case is only partially explained by the requirements of the court. A woman who was raped in Berkeley was asked to tell the story of her rape four different times "right out in the street," while her assailant was escaping. She was then required to submit to a pelvic examination to prove that penetration had taken place. Later, she was taken to the police station where she was asked the same questions again: "Were you forced?" "Did he penetrate?" "Are you sure your life was in danger and you had no other choice?" This woman had been pulled off the street by a man who held a 10-inch knife at her throat and forcibly raped her. She was raped at midnight and was not able to return to her home until five in the morning. Police contacted her twice again in the next week, once by telephone at two in the morning and once at four in the morning. In her words, "The rape was probably the least traumatic incident

of the whole evening. If I'm ever raped again . . . I wouldn't report it to the police because of all the degradation. . . ."

If white women are subjected to unnecessary and often hostile questioning after having been raped, third world women are often not believed at all. According to the while male ethos (which is not only sexist but racist), third world women are defined from birth as "impure." Thus the white male is provided with a pool of women who are fair game for sexual imperialism. Third world women frequently do not report rape and for good reason. When blues singer Billie Holliday was ten years old, she was taken off to a local house by a neighbor and raped. Her mother brought the police to rescue her, and she was taken to the local police station crying and bleeding:

> When we got there, instead of treating me and Mom like somebody who called the cops for help, they treated me like I'd killed somebody . . . I guess they had me figured for having enticed this old goat into the whorehouse. . . . All I know for sure is they threw me into a cell . . . a fat white matron . . . saw I was still bleeding, she felt sorry for me and gave me a couple glasses of milk. But nobody else did anything for me except give me filthy looks and snicker to themselves.
>
> After a couple of days in a cell they dragged me into a court. Mr. Dick got sentenced to five years. They sentenced me to a Catholic institution.

Clearly the white man's chivalry is aimed only to protect the chastity of "his" women.

As a final irony, that same system of sexual values from which chivalry is derived has also provided womankind with an unwritten code of behavior, called femininity, which makes a feminine woman the perfect victim of sexual aggression. If being chaste does not ward off the possibility of assault, being feminine certainly increases the chances that it will succeed. To be submissive is to defer to masculine strength; is to lack muscular development or any interest in defending oneself; is to let doors be opened, to have one's arm held when crossing the street. To be feminine is to wear shoes which make it difficult to run; skirts which inhibit one's stride; underclothes which inhibit the circulation. Is it not an intriguing observation that those very clothes which are thought to be flattering to the female and attractive to the male are those which make it impossible for a woman to defend herself against aggression?

Each girl as she grows into womanhood is taught fear. Fear is the form in which the female internalizes both chivalry and the double standard. Since, biologically speaking, women in fact have the same if not greater potential for sexual expression as do men, the woman who is taught that she must behave differently from a man must also learn to distrust her own carnality. She must deny her own feelings and learn not to act from them. She fears herself. This is the essence of passivity, and of course, a woman's passivity is not simply sexual but functions to cripple her from self-expression in every area of her life.

Passivity itself prevents a woman from ever considering her own potential for self-defense and forces her to look to men for protection. The woman is taught fear, but this time fear of the other; and yet her only relief from this fear is to seek out the other. Moreover, the passive woman is taught to regard herself as impotent, unable to act, unable even to perceive, in no way self-sufficient, and, finally, as the object and not the subject of human behavior. It is in this sense that a woman is deprived

---

Fear

When I first heard he was coming after me
I locked my door and hid in the neighbors'
   kitchen.
They were surprised to find me there next
   morning
but they said I could stay, and I did, until
I saw him standing under the window, grinning
one afternoon just as I was pulling the shade.
Next I hung myself on a nail in the back fence
where the snow blew into a pile that covered
   around.
But my head stuck out, he could see my head,
so instead I crawled into the freezer chest,
under the beer, and arranged the ice cubes
so no one could tell. (I spied him beating the snow,
swearing at the fence and the empty nail.)
Now I live in a tent, and I move it every day.

                                   Jody Aliesan

---

of the status of a human being. She is not free to be.

III

Since Ibsen's Nora slammed the door on her patriarchical husband, woman's attempt to be free has been more or less fashionable. In this nineteenth-century portrait of a woman leaving her marriage, Nora tells her husband, "Our home has been nothing but a playroom. I have been your doll-wife just as at home I was papa's doll-child." And, at least on the stage, "The Doll's House" crumbled, leaving audiences with hope for the fate of the modern woman. And today, as in the past, womankind has not lacked examples of liberated women to emulate: Emma Goldman, Greta Garbo and Isadora Duncan all denounced marriage and the double

It is our impression that more constraint has been applied to the libido when it is pressed into the service of the feminine function, and that—to speak teleologically—Nature takes less careful account of its [that function's] demands than in the case of masculinity. And the reason for this may lie—thinking once again teleologically—in the fact that the accomplishment of the aim of biology has been entrusted to the aggressiveness of men and has been made to some extent independent of women's consent.

Sigmund Freud

---

standard, and believed their right to freedom included sexual independence; but still their example has not affected the lives of millions of women who continue to marry, divorce and remarry, living out their lives dependent on the status and economic power of men. Patriarchy still holds the average woman prisoner not because she lacks the courage of an Isadora Duncan, but because the material conditions of her life prevent her from being anything but an object.

In the *Elementary Structures of Kinship*, Claude Levi-Strauss gives to marriage this universal description, "It is always a system of exchange that we find at the origin of the rules of marriage." In this system of exchange, a woman is the "most precious possession." Levi-Strauss continues that the custom of including women as booty in the marketplace is still so general that "a whole volume would not be sufficient to enumerate instances of it." Levi-Strauss makes it clear that he does not exclude Western Civilization from his definition of "universal" and cites examples from modern wedding ceremonies. (The marriage ceremony is still one in which the husband and wife become one, and "that one is the husband.")

The legal proscription against rape reflects this possessory view of women. An article in the 1952-53 *Yale Law Journal* describes the legal rationale behind laws against rape: "In our society sexual taboos, often enacted into law, buttress a system of monogamy based upon the law of 'free bargaining' of the potential spouses. Within this process the woman's power to withhold or grant sexual access is an important bargaining weapon." Presumably then, laws against rape are intended to protect the right of a woman, not for physical self-determination, but for physical "bargaining." The article goes on to explain explicitly why the preservation of the bodies of women is important to men:

The consent standard in our society does more than protect a significant item of social currency for women; it fosters, and is in turn bolstered by, a masculine pride in the exclusive possession of a sexual object. The consent of a woman to sexual intercourse awards the man a privilege of bodily access, a personal "prize" whose value is enhanced by sole ownership. An additional reason for the man's condemnation of rape may be found in the threat to his status from a decrease in the "value" of his sexual possession which would result from forcible violation.

The passage concludes by making clear whose interest the law is designed to protect. "The man responds to this undercutting of his status as *possessor* of the girl with hostility toward the rapist; no other restitution device is available. The law of rape provides an orderly outlet for his vengeance." Presumably the female victim in any case will have been sufficiently socialized so as not to consciously feel any strong need for vengeance. If she does feel this need, society does not speak to it.

Human beings have taken a hostile attitude toward that in themselves which is living, and have alienated themselves from it. This alienation is not of biological, but of social and economic origin. It is not found in human history before the development of the patriarchal social order.

Wilhelm Reich, *The Function of the Orgasm* (1942)

The laws against rape exist to protect rights of the male as possessor of the female body, and not the right of the female over her own body. Even without this enlightening passage from the *Yale Law Review*, the laws themselves are clear: in no state can a man be accused of raping his wife. How can any man steal what already belongs to him? It is in the sense of rape as theft of another man's property that Kate Millett writes, "Traditionally rape has been viewed as an offense one male commits against another—a matter of abusing his woman." In raping another man's woman, a man may aggrandize his own manhood and concurrently reduce that of another man. Thus a man's honor is not subject directly to rape, but only indirectly, through "his" woman.

If the basic social unit is the family, in which the woman is a possession of her husband, the super-structure of society is a male hierarchy, in which men dominate other men (or patriarchal families dominate other patriarchal families). And it is no small irony that, while the very social fabric of our male-dominated culture denies women equal access to political, economic and legal power, the literature, myth and humor of our culture depict women not only as the power behind the throne, but the real source of the oppression of men. The religious version of this fairy tale blames Eve for both carnality and eating of the tree of knowledge, at the same time making her gullible to the obvious devices of a serpent. Adam, of course, is merely the trusting victim of love.

Certainly this is a biased story. But no more biased than the one television audiences receive today from the latest slick comedians. Through a medium which is owned by men, censored by a State dominated by men, all the evils of this social system which make a man's life unpleasant are blamed upon "the wife." The theory is: were it not for the female who waits and plots to "trap" the male into marriage, modern man would be able to achieve Olympian freedom. She is made the scapegoat for a system which is in fact run by men.

Nowhere is this more clear than in the white racist use of the concept of white womanhood. The white male's open rape of black women, coupled with his overweening concern for the chastity and protection of his wife and daughters, represents an extreme of sexist and racist hypocrisy. While on the one hand she was held up as the standard for purity and virtue, on the other the Southern white woman was never asked if she wanted to be on a pedestal, and in fact any deviance from the male-defined standards for white womanhood was treated severely. (It is a powerful commentary on American racism that the historical role of Blacks as slaves, and thus possessions without power, has robbed black women of legal and economic protection through marriage. Thus black women in Southern society and in the ghettoes of the North have long been easy game for white rapists.) The fear that black men would rape white women was, and is, classic paranoia. Quoting from Ann Breen's unpub-

*Today, black women continue to be sexually attacked—and, in some
cases, even murdered—by white men who know that, in all likelihood,
they will never have to face the consequences of their crimes.*

Angela Davis, *Ms.* (June 1975)

---

lished study of racism and sexism in the South,
"The New South: White Man's Country," Frederick Douglass legitimately points out that had
the black man wished to rape white women,
he had ample opportunity to do so during the
Civil War when white women, the wives, sisters, daughters and mothers of the rebels, were
left in the care of Blacks. But yet not a single
act of rape was committed during this time.
The Ku Klux Klan, who tarred and feathered
black men and lynched them in the honor of
the purity of white womanhood, also applied
tar and feathers to a Southern white woman
accused of bigamy, which leads one to suspect
that Southern white men were not so much
outraged at the violation of the woman as a
person, in the few instances where rape was
actually committed by black men, but at the
violation of his property rights. In the situation
where a black man was found to be having
sexual relations with a white woman, the white
woman could exercise skin-privilege, and claim
that she had been raped, in which case the
black man was lynched. But if she did not claim
rape, she herself was subject to lynching.

In constructing the myth of white womanhood so as to justify the lynching and oppression of black men and women, the white male
has created a convenient symbol of his own
power which has resulted in black hostility
toward the white "bitch," accompanied by an
unreasonable fear on the part of many white
women of the black rapist. Moreover, it is not
surprising that after being told for two centuries
that he wants to rape white women, occasionally a black man does actually commit that act.
But it is crucial to note that the frequency of
this practice is outrageously exaggerated in the
white mythos. Ninety percent of reported rape
is intra- not inter-racial.

In *Soul on Ice*, Eldridge Cleaver has described the mixing of a rage against white
power with the internalized sexism of a black
man raping a white woman. "Somehow I arrived at the conclusion that, as a matter of
principle, it was of paramount importance for
me to have an antagonistic, ruthless attitude
toward white women. . . . Rape was an insurrectionary act. It delighted me that I was defying and trampling upon the white man's law,
upon his system of values and that I was defiling his women—and this point, I believe, was
the most satisfying to me because I was very
resentful over the historical fact of how the
white man had used the black woman." Thus
a black man uses white women to take out his
rage against white men. But in fact, whenever
a rape of a white woman by a black man does
take place, it is again the white man who benefits. First, the act itself terrorizes the white
woman and makes her more dependent on the
white male for protection. Then, if the woman
prosecutes her attacker, the white man is afforded legal opportunity to exercise overt racism. Of course, the knowledge of the rape helps
to perpetuate two myths which are beneficial

to white male rule—the bestiality of the black man and the desirability of white women. Finally, the white man surely benefits because he himself is not the object of attack—he has been allowed to stay in power.

Indeed, the existence of rape in any form is beneficial to the ruling class of white males. For rape is a kind of terrorism which severely limits the freedom of women and makes women dependent on men. Moreover, in the act of rape, the rage that one man may harbor toward another higher in the male hierarchy can be deflected toward a female scapegoat. For every man there is always someone lower on the social scale on whom he can take out his aggressions. And that is any woman alive.

This oppressive attitude toward women finds its institutionalization in the traditional family. For it is assumed that a man "wears the pants" in his family—he exercises the option of rule whenever he so chooses. Not that he makes all the decisions—clearly women make most of the important day-to-day decisions in a family. But when a conflict of interest arises, it is the man's interest which will prevail. His word, in itself, is more powerful. He lords it over his wife in the same way his boss lords it over him, so that the very process of exercising his power becomes as important an act as obtaining whatever it is his power can get for him. This notion of power is key to the male ego in this culture, for the two acceptable measures of masculinity are a man's power over women and his power over other men. A man may boast to his friends that "I have 20 men working for me." It is also aggrandizement of his ego if he

has the financial power to clothe his wife in furs and jewels. And, if a man lacks the wherewithal to acquire such power, he can always express his rage through equally masculine activities—rape and theft. Since male society defines the female as a possession, it is not surprising that the felony most often committed together with rape is theft. . . .

Rape is an act of aggression in which the victim is denied her self-determination. It is an act of violence which, if not actually followed by beatings or murder, nevertheless always carries with it the threat of death. And finally, rape is a form of mass terrorism, for the victims of rape are chosen indiscriminately, but the propagandists for male supremacy broadcast that it is women who cause rape by being unchaste or in the wrong place at the wrong time—in essence, by behaving as though they were free. . . .

But rape is not an isolated act that can be rooted out from patriarchy without ending patriarchy itself. The same men and power structure who victimize women are engaged in the act of raping Vietnam, raping Black people and the very earth we live upon. Rape is a classic act of domination where, in the words of Kate Millett, "the emotions of hatred, contempt, and the desire to break or violate personality" takes place. This breaking of the personality characterizes modern life itself. No simple reforms can eliminate rape. As the symbolic expression of the white male hierarchy, rape is the quintessential act of our civilization, one which, Valerie Solanis warns, is in danger of "humping itself to death."

Radicalesbians

The Woman Identified Woman

What is a lesbian? A lesbian is the rage of all women condensed to the point of explosion. She is the woman who, often beginning at an extremely early age, acts in accordance with her inner compulsion to be a more complete and freer human being than her society—perhaps then, but certainly later—cares to allow her. These needs and actions, over a period of years, bring her into painful conflict with people, situations, the accepted ways of thinking, feeling and behaving, until she is in a state of continual war with everything around her, and usually with her self. She may not be fully conscious of the political implications of what for her began as personal necessity, but on some level she has not been able to accept the limitations and oppression laid on her by the most basic role of her society—the female role. The turmoil she experiences tends to induce guilt proportional to the degree to which she feels she is not meeting social expectations, and/or eventually drives her to question and analyze what the rest of her society more or less accepts. She is forced to evolve her own life pattern, often living much of her life alone, learning usually much earlier than her "straight" (heterosexual) sisters about the essential aloneness of life (which the myth of marriage obscures) and about the reality of illusions. To the extent that she cannot expel the heavy socialization that goes with being female, she can never truly find peace with herself. For she is caught somewhere between accepting society's view of her—in which case she cannot accept herself—and coming to understand what this sexist society has done to

her and why it is functional and necessary for it to do so. Those of us who work that through find ourselves on the other side of a tortuous journey through a night that may have been decades long. The perspective gained from that journey, the liberation of self, the inner peace, the real love of self and of all women, is something to be shared with all women—because we are all women.

It should first be understood that lesbianism, like male homosexuality, is a category of behavior possible only in a sexist society characterized by rigid sex roles and dominated by male supremacy. Those sex roles dehumanize women by defining us as a supportive/serving caste *in relation to* the master caste of men, and emotionally cripple men by demanding that they be alienated from their own bodies and emotions in order to perform their economic/political/military functions effectively. Homosexuality is a by-product of a particular way of setting up roles (or approved patterns of behavior) on the basis of sex; as such it is an inauthentic (not consonant with "reality") category. In a society in which men do not oppress women, and sexual expression is allowed to follow feelings, the categories of homosexuality and heterosexuality would disappear.

But lesbianism is also different from male homosexuality, and serves a different function in the society. "Dyke" is a different kind of put-down from "faggot," although both imply you are not playing your socially assigned sex role . . . are not therefore a "real woman" or a "real man." The grudging admiration felt for the tomboy, and the queasiness felt around a sissy boy point to the same thing: the contempt in which women—or those who play a female role—are held. And the investment in keeping women in that contempible role is very great. Lesbian is the word, the label, the condition that holds women in line. When a woman hears this word tossed her way, she knows she is stepping out of line. She knows that she has crossed the terrible boundary of her sex role. She recoils, she protests, she reshapes her actions to gain approval. Lesbian is a label invented by the Man to throw at any woman who dares to be his equal, who dares to challenge his prerogatives (including that of all women as part of the exchange medium among men). who dares to assert the primacy of her own needs. To have the label applied to people active in women's liberation is just the most recent instance of a long history; older women will recall that not so long ago, any woman who was successful, independent, not orienting her whole life about a man, would hear this word. For in this sexist society, for a woman to be independent means she *can't* be a woman—she must be a dyke. That in itself should tell us where women are at. It says as clearly as can be said: women and person are contradictory terms. For a lesbian is not considered a "real woman." And yet, in popular thinking, there is really only one essential difference between a lesbian and other women: that of sexual orientation—which is to say, when you strip off all the packaging, you must finally realize that the essence of being a "woman" is to get f---ed by men.

"Lesbian" is one of the sexual categories by which men have divided up humanity. While all women are dehumanized as sex objects, as the objects of men they are given certain com-

pensations: identification with his power, his ego, his status, his protection (from other males), feeling like a "real woman," finding social acceptance by adhering to her role, etc. Should a woman confront herself by confronting another woman, there are fewer rationalizations, fewer buffers by which to avoid the stark horror of her dehumanized condition. Herein we find the overriding fear of many women toward being used as a sexual object by a woman, which not only will bring her no male-connected compensations, but also will reveal the void which is woman's real situation. This dehumanization is expressed when a straight woman learns that a sister is a lesbian; she begins to relate to her lesbian sister as her potential sex object, laying a surrogate male role on the lesbian. This reveals her heterosexual conditioning to make herself into an object when sex is potentially involved in a relationship, and it denies the lesbian her full humanity. For women, especially those in the movement, to perceive their lesbian sisters through this male grid of role definitions is to accept this male cultural conditioning and to oppress their sisters much as they themselves have been oppressed by men. Are we going to continue the male classification system of defining all females in sexual relation to some other category of people? Affixing the label lesbian not only to a woman who aspires to be a person, but also to any situation of real love, real solidarity, real primacy among women, is a primary form of divisiveness among women: it is the condition which keeps women within the confines of the feminine role, and it is the debunking/ scare term that keeps women from forming any primary attachments, groups, or associations among ourselves.

Women in the movement have in most cases

All women are lesbians except those who don't know it . . . until women see in each the possibility of a primal commitment which includes sexual love they will be denying themselves the love and value they readily accord to men thus affirming their second class status.

Jill Johnston

---

gone to great lengths to avoid discussion and confrontation with the issue of lesbianism. It puts people up-tight. They are hostile, evasive, or try to incorporate it into some "broader issue." They would rather not talk about it. If they have to, they try to dismiss it as a "lavender herring." But it is no side issue. It is absolutely essential to the success and fulfillment of the women's liberation movement that this issue be dealt with. As long as the label "dyke" can be used to frighten a woman into a less militant stand, keep her separate from her sisters, keep her from giving primacy to anything other than men and family—then to that extent she is controlled by the male culture. Until women see in each other the possibility of a primal commitment which includes sexual love, they will be denying themselves the love and value they readily accord to men, thus affirming their second-class status. As long as male acceptability is primary—both to individual women and to the movement as a whole—the term lesbian will be used effectively against women. Insofar as women want only more privileges within the system, they do not want to antagonize male power. They instead seek acceptability for women's liberation, and the most crucial aspect of the acceptability is to deny lesbianism—i.e., to deny any fundamental challenge to the basis of the female. It should also be said that some younger, more radical women have honestly begun to discuss lesbianism, but so far it has been primarily as a sexual "alternative" to men. This, however, is still giving primacy to men, both because the idea of relating more completely to women occurs as a negative reaction to men, and because the lesbian relationship is being characterized simply by sex, which is divisive and sexist. On one level, which is both personal and political, women may withdraw emotional and sexual energies from men, and work out various alternatives for those energies in their own lives. On a different political/psychological level, it must be understood that what is crucial is that women begin disengaging from male-defined response patterns. In the privacy of our own psyches, we must cut those cords to the core. For irrespective of where our love and sexual energies flow, if we are male-identified in our heads, we cannot realize our autonomy as human beings.

But why is it that women have related to and through men? By virtue of having been brought up in a male society, we have internalized the male culture's definition of ourselves. That definition consigns us to sexual and family functions, and excludes us from defining and shaping the terms of our lives. In exchange for our psychic servicing and for performing society's non-profitmaking functions, the man confers on us just one thing: the slave status which makes us legitimate in the eyes of the society in which we live. This is called "femininity" or "being a real woman" in our cultural lingo. We are authentic, legitimate, real to the extent that we are the property of some man whose name we bear. To be a woman who belongs to no man is to be invisible, pathetic, inauthentic, unreal.

The lesbian's yearning for her mother's love is always put in jeopardy through the existence of a male . . . one wonders why [lesbians] are so much resented by men and women. Because of the pride and vanity of the male, only few men would consider lesbians to be serious rivals. Men's dislike of them goes back to a fundamental psychological cause: The need for the mother in a woman. The male wants to be "fed" by the female. He needs ego support throughout his life. A lesbian who "feeds" (loves) another woman puts him and his world into chaos; she is a rival because she takes away maternal support which should be HIS not HERS.

Charlotte Wolff

He confirms his image of us—of what we have to be in order to be acceptable by him—but not our real selves; he confirms our womanhood—as he defines it, in relation to him—but cannot confirm our personhood, our own selves as absolutes. As long as we are dependent on the male culture for this definition, for this approval, we cannot be free.

The consequence of internalizing this role is an enormous reservoir of self-hate. This is not to say the self-hate is recognized or accepted as such; indeed most women would deny it. It may be experienced as discomfort with her role, as feeling empty, as numbness, as restlessness, as a paralyzing anxiety at the center. Alternatively, it may be expressed in shrill defensiveness of the glory and destiny of her role. But it does exist, often beneath the edge of her consciousness, poisoning her existence, keeping her alienated from herself, her own needs, and rendering her a stranger to other women. They try to escape by identifying with the oppressor, living through him, gaining status and identity from his ego, his power, his accomplishments. And by not identifying with other "empty vessels" like themselves. Women resist relating on all levels to other women who will reflect their own oppression, their own secondary status, their own self-hate. For to confront another woman is finally to confront one's self—the self we have gone to such lengths to avoid. And in that mirror we know we cannot really respect and love that which we have been made to be.

As the source of self-hate and the lack of real self are rooted in our male-given identity, we must create a new sense of self. As long as we cling to the idea of "being a woman," we will sense some conflict with that incipient self, that sense of I, that sense of a whole person. It is very difficult to realize and accept that being "feminine" and being a whole person are irreconcilable. Only women can give to each other a new sense of self. That identity we have to develop with reference to ourselves, and not in relation to men. This consciousness is the revolutionary force from which all else will follow, for ours is an organic revolution. For this we must be available and supportive to one another, give our commitment and our love, give the emotional support necessary to sustain this movement. Our energies must flow toward our sisters, not backward toward our oppressors. As long as woman's liberation tries to free women without facing the basic heterosexual structure that binds us in one-to-one relationship with our oppressors, tremendous energies will continue to flow into trying to straighten up each particular relationship with a man, into finding how to get better sex, how to turn his head around—into trying to make the "new man" out of him, in the delusion that this will allow us to be the "new woman." This obviously splits our energies and commitments, leaving us unable to be committed to the construction of the new patterns which will liberate us.

It is the primacy of women relating to

A History of Lesbianism

How they came into the world,
the women-loving-women
came in three by three
and four by four
the women-loving-women
came in ten by ten
and ten by ten again
until there were more
than you could count

>*they took care of each other*
>*the best they knew how*
>*and of each other's children,*
>*if they had any.*

How they lived in the world,
the women-loving-women
learned as much as they were allowed
and walked and wore their clothes
the way they liked
whenever they could. They did whatever
they knew to be happy or free
and worked and worked and worked.
The women-loving-women
In America were called dykes
and some liked it
and some did not.

they made love to each other
the best they knew how
and for the best reasons.

How they went out of the world,
the women-loving-women
went out one by one
having withstood greater and lesser
trials, and much hatred
from other people, they went out
one by one, each having tried
in her own way to overthrow
the rule of men over women,
they tried it one by one
and hundred by hundred,
until each came in her own way
to the end of her life
and died.

>*The subject of lesbianism*
>*is very ordinary; it's the question*
>*of male domination that makes everybody*
>*angry.*

Judy Grahn

---

women, of women creating a new consciousness of and with each other, which is at the heart of women's liberation, and the basis for the cultural revolution. Together we must find, reinforce, and validate our authentic selves. As we do this, we confirm in each other that struggling, incipient sense of pride and strength, the divisive barriers begin to melt, we feel this growing solidarity with our sisters. We see ourselves as prime, find our centers inside of ourselves. We find receding the sense of alienation, of being cut off, of being behind a locked window, of being unable to get out what we know is inside. We feel a real-ness, feel at last we are coinciding with ourselves. With that real self, with that consciousness, we begin a revolution to end the imposition of all coercive identifications, and to achieve maximum autonomy in human expression.

E. K. Childs, E. A. Sachnoff, and E. S. Stocker

Women's Sexuality: A Feminist View

No paper on women's sexuality is complete that does not review our current biological and physiological knowledge about women. The unresolved problems in this area will best be investigated by female researchers. From that research, we understand that most, if not all, women are multiply orgasmic; we believe that women have the right to create their own sexual identities.

We believe that the form the sexual identity takes is completely up to the individual woman, so long as the form she chooses does not oppress any other human being(s) thus, all forms of sexual expression—aside from rape and child molestation—are viable and valid options. We believe that, having settled her own mode of sexual expression, each woman will be able to relate to others—women, children and men—in an unstereotyped and responsible manner.

The Association for Women in Psychology has chosen to make a positive statement. Here, we describe possibilities for every woman to be herself, speaking of individual choice rather than of behavioral categories limiting means of sexual expression. But, we know that choice of sexual expression may change as the woman and her circumstances change. We are also aware that some women label themselves by a sexual category that does not accurately describe their current sexual behavior, what with the complications of life style, sexual identity, and political loyalty. Therefore, our task begins the process of women's defining, knowing and practicing their own sexuality.

Talking about woman's sexuality includes talking about a whole person in interaction with others; e.g., woman with children, with other women and with men as well as with herself. The sexual categories we use refer to descriptions of the possibilities for a woman's sexual behavior, not her identity, which is what a woman calls herself and what she is called publicly. The experiences we cite can involve life styles; and we categorize in terms of the group(s) of people with whom we are to be sexually active. We have a great discomfort with the category labels here; we would prefer another set, articulated around closeness, caring, and pleasure.

However, until we create new ones, let us begin with the old labels: 1. The Celibate; 2. The Lesbian; 3. The Heterosexual; and 4. The Bisexual WOMAN. The model we present here contains many possible ways in which women can relate sexually on the basis of choice rather than on externally defined criteria, and these are expressed in terms of our self-affirmation. Here are contained some examples of maximum control by women over their own lives within a world defined by men.

The self-affirmed woman is a woman who functions as an active member in a partnership of equals—a *total* interaction. That is, an interaction in which the intimacy of the relationship decrees that the woman is free to disagree; that implies that she is free to be active and passive, nurturing and receptive, playful and serious, productive and appreciative. It also implies that the woman is free to be judging and loving. The self-affirmed woman is aggressive and constructive; she has survived her own experience. In a few words, a self-affirmed woman is a woman who:

from **Lesbian Poem**

To learn to love one's woman-self
has been made to seem both
intolerable and difficult.
To learn to love another woman
in one's self is both, and also
worth it.

Robin Morgan

Courtesy of the Trustee of The British Museum

1. can enjoy her own body apart from others—"I have a primary sexual relationship to my-self."
2. can have sexual experiences for her own reasons.
3. can experiment and experience.
4. has her own standards and uses herself as a measure of her own experience.

The self-affirmed woman understands the interpersonal issues found frequently in relationships that are sexual. She knows ways to negotiate, to fight, to settle, and to forgive. She knows when to leave relationships that are too costly. These decisions may have been made after having engaged in alternative modes of sexual expression and discarding those as options, based on an energy conservation priority. Such a woman relates to other women on an affective and appreciative level. She is able to fully experience both women and men on intellectual and emotional levels as peers. She has some social relationships free from sexual distraction. As well, she may be a mother and she can be free to be nurturing and appreciative of children as people. Another positive aspect of this choice is conscious identification with all women, with our mothers and sisters, as well as with our daughters.

I. The Celibate Woman

The Celibate woman is one who consciously decides to refrain from any sexual interaction with others, and perhaps herself. Her decision is in terms of cost; she prefers to use this energy in ways other than sexual; in addition, she may have an idealized love, as for example, nuns.

II. The Lesbian Woman

We prefer to redefine this woman the "Woman Identified Woman." She is a woman who selects another woman, or women—same sex peer(s)—as the person(s) with whom she shares sexual experiences. Being a "Woman Identified

Because the Women's Movement is a plot of women who are lesbians—and a plot of women who are virgins, heterosexuals, celibates, and bisexuals. And we conspirators are all unlearning the absurd prefixes to the word "sexual" and beginning to discover, create, define ourselves as women.

Robin Morgan, Ms. (Sept. 1975)

Woman" permits her to see herself reflected as a mirror in those women she works with and loves. This woman also has the right to become a mother, *and* to retain custody of her children.

III. The Heterosexual Woman

The heterosexual woman is a woman committed to building a structure with a man or men that is based on the assumption of her equality, and that eliminates the possibility of her inferior status in the relationship(s). In many instances she is our mother; and, for example, she selects her own man or men when and if she chooses, and for her own reasons. She may engage in a sexual relationship for the purpose of procreation as well as for pleasure.

IV. The Bisexual Woman

The bisexual woman is a woman who has chosen to relate sexually to both women and men. The Role Model she will present to her children and to others is a new one, not easily classified. Bisexuality has often been considered as only a transitional stage between one mode of sexuality and another. We believe that bisexuality can no longer be trivialized in this manner. Bisexuality is a viable sexual option.

One of several issues which we have failed to confront in this paper is the issue of prostitu-

The Secret Feast by Leonor Fini; reprinted by permission of the artist

tion. Feminists must begin to actively consider the prostitution of women as a social reality.

This Is My Body

Purpose: To experience our bodies in a new way

Directions: Set up a full length mirror in the privacy of your room. Lock you door and undress in front of it. Carefully examine your body. You might talk to yourself while you're looking, telling yourself what you see.

1. Look at your body from all angles, standing, kneeling, sitting with legs apart and together. Look at yourself for a minimum of fifteen minutes.
2. What do you experience while doing this? What feelings about your body do you become aware of? Where do these feelings come from?
3. After you've examined yourself carefully in the mirror for at least fifteen minutes, begin to explore your body with your hands. Run your fingers over your arms, legs, stomach, etc.; feel the muscles, the bones, the fat, and the varied textures of skin. Compare the skin on your inner thigh to that on the soles of your feet, to that on your lips, ears, chest, shins, buttocks. Enjoy the feelings of your hands touching your skin as well as your skin being touched. See if you can't discover something you didn't know before. Do you like any areas better than you thought you would? Can you begin to accept the fact that it's OK to look the way you do?

Again, how do you experience yourself? Record your thoughts and feelings. Then join other class members to form small groups and talk about your experiences.

As a phenomenon, prostitution provides further evidence of the strong positive correlation between women's sexuality and economics. Current legal sanctions against prostitution only serve to force women deeper into criminal environments and to make these women, our sisters, more dependent upon men for protection and less likely to have options for independent action. We believe that decriminalization of prostitution will result in changes which are basic to the quality of life for both women and men. It will result in further freedom to accept ourselves as competent, responsible, reflective and complete persons.

In summary then, self-affirmed women are surviving and exercising control over their own bodies and lives. We, too, need to know about our strengths; we need to start forgiving ourselves and deemphasizing our weaknesses. We must have control of our lives and have both the pleasure and the pain of self-direction. Mythology built around women's sexuality must be disregarded and we must rely upon our own experience and new experiments for direction. Radical Feminism reflects such a choice involving rejection of action based on sex-roles and working together politically for change. In this way we underline our contention that there are no individual solutions: the personal is always the political.

We therefore recommend:

1. that there be an ongoing reexamination and redefinition of women's roles using the best of new biological, physiological and psychological findings.

2. that the expression of sexuality continue to be divorced from reproduction.
3. that we become engaged in the issues around decriminalization of prostitution.
4. that consideration of the expression of sexuality become a function of interpersonal and individual preference. All women must be free to create their own sexual choice based on their own bodies and experiences with no restriction save those expressions which oppress others.

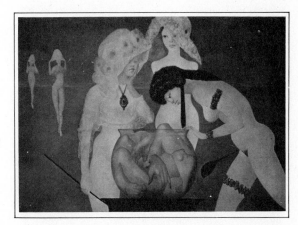

The Strangers by Leonor Fini; reprinted by permission of the artist

For Further Reading

*Boston Women's Health Book Collective.** 1971. *Our Bodies Ourselves.* New York: Simon and Schuster.

*Dodson, B.** 1974. *Liberating Masturbation.* New York: Bodysex Designs.

Garfield-Barbach, L. 1974. *For Yourself.* New York: Stein and Day.

Klaich, D. 1974. *Woman + Woman: Attitudes toward Lesbianism.* New York: William Morrow.

*Millett, K.** 1970. *Sexual Politics.* New York: Doubleday.

Russell, D. 1975. *The Politics of Rape.* New York: Stein and Day.

Wilson, C. and **Connell, N.** 1974. *Rape: The First Sourcebook for Women.* New York: New American Library.

Wolff, C. 1971. *Love Between Women.* New York: Harper Colophon.

Wysor, B. 1974. *The Lesbian Myth, Insights and Conversations.* New York: Random House.

Psychotherapy and Women

Just as women's sexuality has been defined by men, so have mental illness and psychotherapy been considered from a male point of view both in theory and in practice. Phyllis Chesler's "Women as Psychiatric and Psychotherapeutic Patients" presents a feminist interpretation of such topics as why women are labeled "mentally ill" more often and more easily than men, why "mental illness" is self-destructive, and how marriage and psychotherapy can be seen as similar institutions for women.

Of special importance to the psychology of women is self-destructive behavior, which Thomas Szasz (whom Chesler quotes) sees as exemplifying "slave psychology" in which women are "unconsciously 'on strike' against persons (actual or internal) to whom they relate with subservience and against whom they wage an unending and unsuccessful covert rebellion." The symptoms that women display may be seen as indirect indications of social oppression. (In the earlier chapter on "Oppression of the Self," Hacker, Henley and Freeman, and the Bems discuss in greater detail the dynamics involved when members of a minority group internalize their oppression.)

Chesler points out that the definition of the term mental illness differs for men and women, a fact that may account for women being labelled "mentally ill" more often than men. Men who are "mentally ill" go unrecognized as such, since men's style of mental illness is to act out an exaggerated male sex role consisting of aggressive, antisocial, and criminal acts. If these men are Third World or poor, they are imprisoned. White powerful males' "mental illness," however, takes the form of their daily pursuits for worldwide and domestic domination and exploitation. They have the power and the means to arrange the environment to adjust to

their "mental illness" so it appears that they are not "mentally ill" at all. Women's mental illness takes the form of acting out an exaggerated female sex role, which may be characterized as masochistic and hysterical and which exhibits the effects of "slave psychology." Alternatively, women are seen as "mentally ill" if they do not behave according to their role. This has led Chesler to the theoretical proposal (1972) that "what we consider 'madness,' whether it appears in women or men, is the acting out of the devalued female role or the total or partial rejection of one's sex-role stereotype."

In support of Chesler's proposal, clinicians do in fact have different standards of mental health (as is also reported in Betsy Belote's paper). Women are likely to be considered mentally ill if they do not conform to the therapist's standards of mentally healthy females. Likewise, women are mentally ill even if they do conform to the standards of the healthy female because they are no longer healthy according to the norms for a healthy adult person. This is an example of an impossible "no-win" situation in which one loses by choosing either alternative.

Such differential standards of mental health, along with other characteristics of psychotherapists, suggest the patriarchal nature of the psychotherapeutic relationship and how it acts as a means of social control. Women themselves, in therapy as in marriage, seek personal salvation through a male authority figure. Chesler concludes that if psychotherapeutic "treatment does not incorporate a feminist awareness, female patients cannot, by definition, get better."

Masochism and hysteria may also be seen as characterizing women. In Betsy Belote's article, the concept of masochism is reviewed and compared with hysteria and femininity as defined by Broverman's study (1970) with clinicians. Belote concludes that the definition of masochism as presented by social learning theorists seems to be the most accurate description of this phenomenon for women. As with hysteria, the point is that all women display these characteristics to some degree and that it must be so, since femininity so closely corresponds to both masochism and hysteria.

Regarding hysteria, feminists would add that females are seeking emotional responsivity from others because they do not get the emotional response from others (men) that they deserve. Chesler (1972) has indicated that in a patriarchy, women do not receive love and nurturance because men do not nurture women (or anyone else), and other women's attention is directed toward men. Hacker (presented in an earlier chapter) would agree that men are emotionally distant in relationships, as does Firestone, whose analysis of love (1970) indicated that "men are emotional parasites feeding on the strength of women without reciprocation." Furthermore, one way in which men maintain their position of dominance in the interpersonal sphere is through emotional withholding (Henley and Freeman, in the chapter "Oppression of the Self"). From a feminist point of view, taking into account the patriarchal context, women as a class may become "hysterical" because men as a class do not respond.

Emptiness and shallowness are two other common characteristics of the hysterical personality. Women identify with the dominant group (men), exhibiting one of the psychological effects of being a member of a minority group (as described by Hacker). Under such conditions, emptiness and lack of self would be an inevitable psychological consequence. Likewise, women's competition for attention can also be seen as a direct result of being members of an oppressed group, since self-esteem is based on the status and worth conferred by members of the dominant group. This would explain why women prefer the company of men, since men and not women have the ability to bestow worth.

A feminist analysis shows that to be a woman in this society is, in itself, masochistic and is a consequence from which there is no escape. Hysterical, masochistic, and feminine symptoms are methods of coping with an insoluble problem—that of being female in a patriarchy. The least that may be said of this similarity is that all three (femininity, masochism, hysteria) are the result of long-continued, unequal power relationships as described from a superior vantage point, the masculine point of view. They may be more simply seen as signs of distress of a subordinate group resulting from their domination, a condition which before feminism was unlabeled or improperly diagnosed, and therefore made not real. The subordinate group had, therefore, no other alternative but to accept the dominant group's definitions of them—that they were masochistic and hysterical—rather than to realize that their behavior was the result of the effects of patriarchy on women.

Depression, another common symptom of women's distress, occurs as the result of several factors: as an effect of "slave psychology" (see Chesler in this chapter), of anger turned inward because it is culturally unacceptable for women to express anger, of fear of expressing anger for fear of retaliation (see also Gillespie in "Oppression of the Self"), of a sense of loss about the power women never had, of losing

Therapist

*Madness
is an excellent word
for insanity*

*because it also means
anger.*

Jody Aliesan

---

since "women are losers" in a patriarchy (Chesler, 1972). Pauline Bart suggests that an additional cause of depression in women involves the loss of the maternal role. Her article is additionally important because it looks at women of various racial and ethnic backgrounds and is concerned with older women, a group that is often doubly neglected on the basis of age as well as sex.

Middle-aged women may find their depression difficult to understand, since they have tried to gain a sense of worth from a function that, according to society's standards, was supposed to make them feel fulfilled. Not too surprisingly, Bart discovers that the more feminine women are also the more depressed. Masculine women and those who work, although they must cope with the patriarchal world of work, may in the long run be psychologically healthier. Like masochism and hysteria, depression in women has its basis at least to some degree, in social conditions.

This chapter would not be complete without some remarks about anger, since anger can provide an alternative to the traditional modes of expression allowed women—depression, hysteria, masochism, and femininity. Anger may be the result of several factors, many of which are the same as those resulting in depression. One specific source of rage stems from the abundance of "no-win" situations with which women are confronted in their daily lives. Two examples mentioned previously are the Madonna/Whore conflict (see the chapter "Women and Their Sexual Selves") and the impossibility for women to be both mentally healthy *persons* and mentally healthy *women.* In both of these conflicts, women must choose, although they lose either way. The result is both rage and depression. An extension of this concept is that because anger is not part of the female sex role, a woman will not be considered feminine if she expresses anger; but if she does not express anger, she becomes depressed. Her choice is to express anger and receive negative social sanctions for it, or not to express anger and receive positive social sanctions but become depressed. Either alternative seems masochistic, although the style may differ somewhat.

Other sources of rage in women include the fact that women have lived under the domination of men to whom they have related with quiet and controlled subservience. A further source is the accumulation of anger that has been suppressed because it is not included in the female sex role or because of the fear of retaliation. Women feel rage at the recognition that much of their social conditioning cannot be undone and at the injustice to women in a patriarchy with no clear, immediate means to correct the situation. They feel rage at their inability to change the conditions that determine the nature and quality of their lives. Meanwhile, cultural institutions as well as economic, political, and social systems continue their abuse of women.

Phyllis Chesler

Patient and Patriarch: Women in the Psychotherapeutic Relationship

> Like all sciences and valuations, the psychology of women has hitherto been considered only from the point of view of men. It is inevitable that the man's position of advantage should cause objective validity to be attributed to his subjective, affective relations to women . . . the question then is how far analytical psychology also, when its researches have women for their object, is under the spell of this way of thinking.[1]
>
> —Karen Horney

Although Karen Horney wrote this in 1926, very few psychiatrists and psychologists seem to have agreed with and been guided by her words. Female psychology is still being viewed from a masculine point of view. Contemporary psychiatric and psychological theories and practices both reflect and influence our culture's politically naive understanding and emotionally brutal treatment of women. Female unhappiness is viewed and "treated" as a problem of individual pathology, no matter how many other female patients (or nonpatients) are similarly unhappy—and this by men who have studiously bypassed the objective fact of female oppression. Woman's inability to adjust to or to be contented by feminine roles has been considered as a deviation from "natural" female psychology rather than as a criticism of such roles.

I do not wish to imply that female unhappiness is a myth conjured up by men; it is very real. One of the ways white, middle-class women in America attempt to handle this unhappiness is through psychotherapy. They enter private therapy just as they enter marriage—with a sense of urgency and desperation. Also, black and white women of all classes, particularly unmarried women, comprise the largest group of psychiatrically hospitalized and "treated" Americans. This paper will present the following analysis:

1. that for a number of reasons, women "go crazy" more often and more easily than men do; that their "craziness" is mainly self-destructive; and that they are punished for their self-destructive behavior, either by the brutal and impersonal custodial care given them in mental asylums, or by the relationships they have with most (but not all) clinicians, who implicitly encourage them to blame themselves or to take responsibility for their unhappiness in order to be "cured."

2. that both psychotherapy and marriage, the two major socially approved institutions for white, middle-class women, function similarly, i.e., as vehicles for personal "salvation" through the presence of an understanding and benevolent (male) authority. In female culture, not being married, or being unhappily married, is experienced as an "illness" which psychotherapy can, hopefully, cure.

This paper will discuss the following questions: What are some of the facts about women as psychiatric or psychotherapy patients in America? What "symptoms" do they present? Why are more women involved, either voluntarily or involuntarily with mental health professionals than are men? Who are the psychotherapists in America and what are their views about women? What practical implications does this discussion have for women who are in a psychotherapeutic relationship?

General Statistics

A study published in 1970 by the U.S. Department of Health, Education, and Welfare[2] indicated that in both the black and white populations significantly more women than men reported having suffered nervous breakdowns, having felt impending nervous breakdowns,* psychological inertia* and dizziness. Both black and white women also reported higher rates than men for the following symptoms: nervousness,* insomnia, trembling hands,* nightmares,* fainting,*[3] and headaches* (See Table 17-1). White women who were never married reported fewer symptoms than white married or separated women. These findings are essentially in agreement with an earlier study published in 1960, by the Joint Commission on Mental Health and Illness.[4] The Commission reported the following information for nonhospitalized American adults: (1) Greater distress and symptoms are reported by women than by men in all adjustment areas. They report more disturbances in general adjustment, in their self-perception, and in their marital and parental functioning. This sex difference is most marked at the younger age intervals. (2) A feeling of impending breakdown is reported more frequently by divorced and separated females than by any other groups of either sex. (3) The unmarried (whether single, separated, divorced or widowed) have a greater potential for psychological distress than do the married. (4) While the sexes did not differ in the *frequency* with which they reported "unhappi-

ness," the women reported more worry, fear of breakdown, and need for help.

What such studies do not make clear, is how many of these "psychologically distressed" women are involved in any form of psychiatric or psychological treatment. Other studies have attempted to do this. William Schofield[5] found that the average psychiatrist sees significantly more female than male patients. A study published in 1965 reported that women patients outnumbered men patients 3 to 2 in private psychiatric treatment.[6] Statistics for public and private psychiatric hospitalization in America do exist and of course, are controversial. However, statistical studies have indicated certain trends. The National Institute of Mental Health has reported that from 1965–1967 there were 102,241 more women than men involved in the following psychiatric treatment facilities: private psychiatric hospitals, state and county psychiatric hospitals, inpatient psychiatric wards in General and Veterans' Administration hospitals, and General and Veterans' Administration outpatient psychiatric facilities.[7] This figure excludes the number of Americans involved in various forms of private treatment. Earlier studies have reported that admission rates to both public and private psychiatric hospitals are significantly higher for women than for men.[8] Unmarried people (single, divorced or widowed) of both sexes are disproportionately represented among the psychiatrically hospitalized.[9] Thus, while according to the 1970 HEW report, single, white women in the general population report less psychological distress than married or separated white women,[10] women, (as well as men) who are psychiatrically *hospitalized* tend to be unmarried.

Private psychotherapy, like marriage, is an integral part of middle-class female culture.

---

*At all age levels

TABLE 17–1

SYMPTOM RATES BY SEX, SEX AND AGE, AND SEX AND RACE (PER 100)

Symptom and Sex	Total, 18–79 Years	Age							Race	
		18–24 Years	25–34 Years	35–44 Years	45–54 Years	55–64 Years	65–74 Years	75–79 Years	White	Negro
Nervous breakdown										
Male	3.2	1.3	1.8	3.5	3.0	5.4	5.4	1.5	3.2	2.8
Female	6.4	1.0	3.6	5.0	7.3	12.7	10.7	13.1	6.0	10.4
Felt impending Nervous breakdown										
Male	7.7	6.9	7.4	8.6	11.7	6.4	3.1	2.2	7.7	8.2
Female	17.5	14.6	21.6	19.3	18.8	14.5	13.8	10.2	17.8	16.1
Nervousness										
Male	45.1	43.5	47.5	51.9	48.1	37.7	36.6	30.2	47.2	31.3
Female	70.6	61.4	74.4	75.0	72.5	72.6	62.9	65.6	73.2	55.2
Inertia										
Male	16.8	17.2	16.1	17.6	16.3	16.9	18.2	12.1	16.9	17.1
Female	32.5	31.0	34.0	35.2	31.1	29.7	31.9	35.6	33.1	29.5
Insomnia										
Male	23.5	20.4	16.7	20.8	26.8	27.0	35.9	26.5	24.1	20.4
Female	40.4	28.0	33.5	33.7	42.8	53.8	59.0	51.0	40.9	38.9
Trembling hands										
Male	7.0	7.6	6.5	5.4	5.7	8.8	10.0	8.5	6.9	7.1
Female	10.9	10.4	12.2	12.1	10.6	9.3	9.2	13.0	10.6	12.3
Nightmares										
Male	7.6	5.7	9.4	7.7	7.7	8.2	5.8	6.5	6.9	13.0
Female	12.4	12.8	15.8	14.7	9.9	7.5	11.6	11.8	12.3	14.3

Patients entering private therapy betray significantly different attitudes toward men and women therapists. A number of them indicate that they feel sex is important in the therapeutic relationship by voluntarily requesting a therapist of a particular sex.

I have recently completed a study of 1,001 middle-income clinic outpatients (538 women and 463 men) who sought therapeutic treatment in New York City from 1965 to 1969. Patient variables, such as sex, marital status, age, religion, occupation, and so forth, were related to patient requests for a male or a female therapist at the time of the initial interview. These findings are based on a sample of 258 people (159 women and 99 men) who voluntarily requested either a male or a female therapist or who voluntarily stated that they had no sex-of-therapist preference. Twenty-four percent of the 538 women and 14 percent of the 463 men requested a therapist specifically by sex. The findings were as follows:

1. The majority of patients were single (66 percent) and under thirty (72 percent). Whether male or female, they overwhelmingly requested a male rather than a female therapist. This preference was significantly related to marital status in women but not in men (Tables 17–2 and 17–3). This suggests that a woman may be seeking therapy for very different reasons than a man; and that these reasons are generally related to or strictly determined by her rela-

TABLE 17-1 (CONTINUED)

SYMPTOM RATES BY SEX, SEX AND AGE, AND SEX AND RACE (PER 100)

Symptom and Sex	Total, 18–79 Years	Age							Race	
		18–24 Years	25–34 Years	35–44 Years	45–54 Years	55–64 Years	65–74 Years	75–79 Years	White	Negro
Perspiring hands										
Male	17.0	23.2	24.9	17.7	14.7	11.0	7.9	3.0	17.0	16.8
Female	21.4	28.6	27.7	24.2	19.6	15.0	9.2	5.9	22.2	16.0
Fainting										
Male	16.9	17.6	15.7	15.7	18.1	17.3	17.8	17.2	17.5	13.8
Female	29.1	28.5	33.2	29.9	27.0	26.2	29.7	24.8	30.4	20.5
Headaches										
Male	13.7	13.0	12.8	13.8	15.2	15.6	11.3	10.0	13.8	11.9
Female	27.8	24.0	31.6	29.6	29.5	25.9	24.2	19.3	27.5	30.9
Dizziness										
Male	7.1	6.3	3.0	5.0	7.6	10.7	12.8	14.3	6.9	9.2
Female	10.9	8.4	9.5	8.5	10.1	14.3	16.9	16.6	10.3	15.7
Heart palpitations										
Male	3.7	3.3	2.0	2.1	3.9	7.2	6.4	1.5	3.6	4.8
Female	5.8	1.7	3.1	4.7	6.2	9.7	10.4	14.8	5.7	6.4
SCALE MEAN VALUE[1]										
Male										
White	1.70	1.72	1.70	1.72	1.78	1.69	1.66	1.19	1.70	. . .
Negro	1.55	1.25	1.03	1.37	1.79	1.87	2.23	2.99	. . .	1.55
Female										
White	2.88	2.61	3.07	2.93	2.89	2.86	2.82	2.80	2.88	. . .
Negro	2.65	1.91	2.61	2.60	2.52	3.27	3.79	2.62	. . .	2.65

[1]Scale is from 0 to 11.

Source: Study by the U.S. Department of Health, Education, and Welfare, 1970.

tionship (or lack of one) to a man. The number of requests for female therapists was approximately equal to the number of "no preference" requests for both men and women.

2. Single women, under or over thirty, of any religion, requested male therapists more often than married or divorced women did. Married women requested female therapists more often than any of the other sample groups.

3. While all of the male patients regardless of their marital status, requested male therapists rather than female therapists, some differential trends did exist. A higher percentage of divorced men requested male therapists, as compared with either divorced women (53 percent vs. 35 percent), married women (53 percent vs. 41 percent) married men (53 percent vs. 25 percent), or single men (53 percent vs. 44 percent). There was a significant relation between a male patient's request for a male therapist and his age (under thirty) and his religion: specifically, 63 percent of the Jewish male patients (who composed 40 percent of the entire male sample and 73 percent of whom were under thirty) requested male therapists—a higher percentage than in any other group.

4. Some of the most frequent reasons given by male patients for requesting male therapists

By Bülbül, from *I'm Not for Women's Lib . . . But,* Arachne Publishing, Mountain View, Ca.

TABLE 17–2

PERCENTAGE DISTRIBUTION OF PATIENT THERAPIST
PREFERENCE, MARITAL STATUS, AGE, AND RELIGION

	Women (n = 159)	Men (n = 99)	Total
Therapist preference	%	%	%
Male	49 (n = 77)	40 (n = 40)	45 (n = 117)
Female	31 (n = 49)	25 (n = 26)	23 (n = 75)
None	20 (n = 33)	35 (n = 33)	27 (n = 66)
Marital Status			
Single	69 (n = 109)	63 (n = 62)	
Married/living with someone	17 (n = 27)	24 (n = 24)	
Divorced/ separated	14 (n = 23)	13 (n = 13)	
Age			
Under 30	75	69	
Over 30	25	31	
Religion	Jewish Cath.	Jewish Cath.	
	40 19	41 22	
	Prot. None	Prot. None	
	16 25	16 23	

were: greater respect for a man's mind; general discomfort with and mistrust of women; and specific embarrassment about "cursing" or discussing sexual matters, such as impotence, with a woman.[11] Some of the most common reasons given by female patients for requesting male therapists were: greater respect for and confidence in a man's competence and authority; feeling generally more comfortable with and relating better to men than to women; and specific fear and mistrust of women as authorities and as people, a reason sometimes combined with statements about dislike of the patients'

own mothers.[12] In general, both men and women stated that they trusted and respected men—as people and as authorities—more than they did women, whom they generally mistrusted or feared.

Patients who requested a female therapist generally gave fewer reasons for their preference; one over-thirty woman stated that "only a female would understand another female's problems"; another woman stated that she sees "all males as someone to conquer" and is "less open to being honest with them." Almost all of the male patients who *gave reasons* for requesting a female therapist were homosexual.[13] Their main reasons involved expectations of being "sexually attracted" to a male therapist, which they thought would distract or upset them. One nonhomosexual patient felt he would be too "competitive" with a male therapist.

5. Thirty-six percent of the male and 37 percent of the female patients reported generally unclassifiable symptoms during the initial clinic interview. Thirty-one percent of the female and 15 percent of the male patients reported depression as their reason for seeking therapy; 25 percent of the male and 7 percent of the female patients reported active homosexuality; 15 percent of the female and 14 percent of the male patients reported anxiety; 8 percent of the female and 7 percent of the male patients reported sexual impotence; 4 percent of the male and 3 percent of the female patients reported drug or alcoholic addiction. The fact

that twice as many female as male patients report depression, and almost four times as many male as female patients report homosexuality accords with previous findings.

6. Male and female patients remained in therapy for approximately equal lengths of time (an average of thirty-one weeks for males and twenty-eight weeks for females). However, men requesting male therapists remained in therapy longer than other patient groups, an average of forty-two weeks) compared to an average of thirty weeks for females requesting a male therapist; an average of thirty-four weeks for male and thirty-one weeks for female patients requesting a female therapist; an average of twelve weeks for male and seventeen weeks for female patients with a stated "no preference."[14]

In other words, male patients who requested (and who generally received) a male therapist remained in treatment longer than their female counterparts. Perhaps one of the reasons for this is that women often get married and then turn to their husbands (or boy friends) as authorities or protectors, whereas men generally do not turn to their wives or girl friends as authorities, but rather as nurturing mother-surrogates, domestics, sex objects, and perhaps, friends. They usually do not turn to women for expert advice; hence, when they decide they need this kind of help, they tend to remain in therapy with a male therapist. Female patients can transfer their needs for protection or salvation from one man to another. Ultimately, a

TABLE 17–3

THE RELATIONSHIP BETWEEN THERAPIST PREFERENCE AND PATIENT MARITAL STATUS

	Female			Male		
Marital Status	Preference			Preference		
	Male	Female	None	Male	Female	None
Single	54%	30%	16%	44%	28%	29%
Married/living with someone	41%	37%	22%	25%	25%	50%
Divorced	35%	26%	39%	53%	23%	23%

female patient or wife will be disappointed in her husband's or therapist's mothering or saving capacities and will continue the search for salvation *through a man* elsewhere.

Presenting Symptoms

From clinical case histories, psychological studies, novels, mass magazines, and from our own lives, we know that women are often chronically fatigued and/or depressed; they are frigid, hysterical, and paranoid; and they suffer from headaches and feelings of inadequacy.

Studies of childhood behavior problems have indicated that boys are most often referred to child guidance clinics for aggressive, destructive (antisocial), and competitive behavior; girls are referred for personality problems, such as excessive fears and worries, shyness, timidity, lack of self-confidence, and feelings of inferiority.[15] This should be compared with adult male and female psychiatric symptomatology:

The Encounter by Remedios Varo; reprinted by permission of Walter Gruen

"the symptoms of men are also much more likely to reflect a destructive hostility toward others,"[16] as well as a pathological self-indulgence.... Women's symptoms, on the other hand, express a harsh, self-critical, self-depriving and often self-destructive set of attitudes.[17] A study by E. Zigler and L. Phillips, comparing the symptoms of male and female mental hospital patients, found male patients significantly more assaultive than females and more prone to indulge their impulses in socially deviant ways like robbery, rape, drinking, and homosexuality.[18] Female patients were more often found to be self-deprecatory, depressed, perplexed, suffering from suicidal thoughts, or making actual suicidal attempts.[19]

According to T. Szasz, symptoms such as these are "indirect forms of communication" and usually indicate a "slave psychology":

Social oppression in any form, and its manifestations are varied, among them being . . . poverty . . . racial, religious, or sexual discrimination . . . must therefore be regarded as prime determinants of indirect communication of all kinds (e.g. hysteria).[20]

At one point in *The Myth of Mental Illness*, Szasz refers to the "dread of happiness' that seems to afflict all people involved in the "Judaeo-Christian ethic." Although he is not talking about women particularly, his analysis seems especially relevant to our discussion of female psychiatric symptomatology:

In general, the open acknowledgment of satisfaction is feared only in situations of relative oppression (e.g. all-suffering wife vis-à-vis domineering husband). The experiences of satisfaction (joy, contentment) are inhibited lest they lead to an augmentation of one's burden. . . . *the fear of acknowledging satisfaction is a characteristic feature of slave psychology.*

The "properly exploited" slave is forced to labor until he shows signs of fatigue or exhaustion. Completion of his task does not signify that his work is finished and that he may rest. At the same time, even though his task is unfinished, he may be able to influence his master to stop driving him—and to let him rest—if he exhibits signs of imminent collapse. Such signs may be genuine or contrived. Exhibiting signs of fatigue or exhaustion—irrespective of whether they are genuine or contrived (e.g., "being on strike" against one's boss)—is likely to induce a feeling of fatigue or exhaustion in the actor. I believe that this is the mechanism responsible for the great majority of so-called chronic fatigue states. Most of these were formerly called "neurasthenia," a term rarely used nowadays. Chronic fatigue or a feeling of lifelessness and exhaustion are still frequently encountered in clinical practice.

Psychoanalytically, they are considered "charactor symptoms." Many of these patients are unconsciously "on strike" against persons (actual or internal) to whom they relate with subservience and against whom they wage an unending and unsuccessful covert rebellion.[21]*

The analogy between "slave" and "woman" is by no means a perfect one. Women are probably the prototypes for slaves;[22] they were probably the first group of human beings to be enslaved by another group. In a sense, a woman's "work" is in exhibiting the signs and "symptoms" of slavery—as well as, or instead of, doing slave labor in the kitchen, the nursery, and the factory.[23]

Why Are There More Female Patients?

Psychiatrists and psychologists have traditionally described the signs and symptoms of various kinds of real and felt oppression as mental illness. Women often manifest these signs, not only because they are oppressed in an objective sense, but also because the sex role (stereotype) to which they are conditioned is composed of just such signs. For example, Phillips and Segal report that when the number of physical and psychiatric illnesses were held constant for a group of New England women and men, the women were more likely to seek medical and psychiatric care. They suggest that women seek psychiatric help because the social role of women allows them to display emotional and physical distress more easily than

| The Invisible Woman |

*The invisible woman in the asylum corridor
sees others quite clearly,
including the doctor who patiently tells her
she isn't invisible,
and pities the doctor, who must be mad
to stand there in the asylum corridor,
talking and gesturing
to nothing at all.*

*The invisible woman has great compassion.
So, after a while, she pulls on her body
like a rumpled glove, and switches on her
    voice
to comfort the elated doctor with words.
Better to suffer this prominence
than for the poor young doctor to learn
he himself is insane.
Only the strong can know that.*

Robin Morgan

men. "Sensitive or emotional behavior is more tolerated in women, to the point of aberration, while self-assertive, aggressive, vigorous physical demonstrations are more tolerated among men."[24]

It may be that more women than men are involved in psychotherapy[25] because it—along with marriage—is one of the only two socially approved institutions for middle-class women. That these two institutions bear a strong similarity to each other is highly significant. For most women the psychotherapeutic encounter is just one more instance of an unequal relationship, just one more opportunity to be rewarded for expressing distress and to be "helped" by being (expertly) dominated. Both psychotherapy and marriage isolate women from each other; both emphasize individual rather than collective solutions to woman's un-

The Myth of Mental Illness, Thomas S. Szasz, excerpts from pp. 213, 194–195, 263–264. Copyright © 1961 by Hoeber Medical Division of Harper & Row, Publishers, Inc. Reprinted by permission of the publishers.

happiness; both are based on a woman's help-lessness and dependence on a stronger male authority figure; both may, in fact, be viewed as reenactments of a little girl's relation to her father in a patriarchal society;[26] both control and oppress women similarly—yet, at the same time, are the two safest havens for women in a society that offers them no others.

Both psychotherapy and marriage enable women to safely express and defuse their anger by experiencing it as a form of emotional ill-ness, by translating it into hysterical symptoms: frigidity, chronic depression, phobias, and the like. Each woman as patient thinks these symp-toms are unique and are her own fault. She is neurotic, rather than oppressed. She wants from a psychotherapist what she wants—and often cannot get—from a husband: attention, understanding, merciful relief, a *personal solu-tion*— in the arms of the right husband, on the couch of the right therapist.[27] The institutions of therapy and marriage not only mirror each other, they support each other. This is probably not a coincidence, but is rather an expression of the American economic system's need for geographic and psychological mobility, i.e., for young, upwardly mobile "couples" to "survive," to remain more or less intact in a succession of alien and anonymous urban locations, while they carry out the function of socializing chil-dren.

The institution of psychotherapy may be used by many women as a way of keeping a bad marriage together, or as a way of terminating it in order to form a good marriage. Some women, especially young and single women, may use psychotherapy as a way of learning how to catch a husband by practicing with a male therapist. Women probably spend more time during a therapy session talking about their husbands or boy friends—or lack of them—than they do talking about their lack of an independent identity or their relations to other women.

The institutions of psychotherapy and mar-riage both encourage women to talk—often endlessly—rather than to act (except in their socially prearranged roles as passive women or patients). In marriage the talking is usually of an indirect and rather inarticulate nature. Open expressions of rage are too dangerous, and too ineffective for the isolated and eco-nomically dependent women. Most often, such "kitchen" declarations end in tears, self-blame, and in the husband graciously agreeing with his wife that she was "not herself." Even control of a simple—but serious—conversation is usu-ally impossible for most wives when several men, including their husbands, are present. The wife-women talk to each other, or they listen silently while the men talk. Very rarely, if ever, do men listen silently to a group of women talking; even if there are a number of women talking and only one man present, the man will question the women, perhaps patiently, perhaps not, but always in order to ultimately control the conversation from a superior position.

In psychotherapy the patient-woman is en-couraged—in fact directed—to talk, by a thera-pist who is at least expected to be, or is per-ceived as, superior or objective. The traditional therapist may be viewed as ultimately control-ling what the patient says through a subtle system of rewards (attention, interpretations, and so forth) or rewards withheld—but, most ultimately, controlling in the sense that he is attempting to bring his patient to terms with the female role, i.e., to an admission and accep-tance of dependency. Traditionally, the psy-chotherapist, has ignored the objective facts of female oppression. Thus, in every sense, the female patient is still not having a "real" conversation—either with her husband or her therapist. But how is it possible to have a "real" conversation with those who directly profit from her oppression? She would be laughed at, viewed as silly or crazy, and if she persisted, removed from her job—as secretary or wife, perhaps even as patient.

Psychotherapeutic talking is indirect in the sense that it does not immediately or even ultimately involve the woman in any reality-based confrontations with the self. It is also indirect in that words—*any* words—are permitted, so long as certain actions of consequence are totally avoided. (Such is not paying one's bills.)

Who Are the Psychotherapists and What Are Their Views about Women?

Contemporary psychotherapists, like ghetto schoolteachers, do not study themselves or question their own motives or values as easily or as frequently as they do those of their neurotic patients or their culturally deprived pupils. However, in a 1960 study Schofield found that 90 percent of psychiatrists were male; that psychologists were predominantly males, in a ratio of two to one; and that social workers (the least prestigious and least well-paying of the three professional categories) were predominantly females, in a ratio of two to one. The psychologists and psychiatrists were about the same age, an average of forty-four years; the social workers' average age was thirty-eight. Less than 5 percent of the psychiatrists were single; 10 percent of the psychologists, 6 percent of the social workers, and 1 percent of the psychiatrists were divorced. In other words, the majority of psychiatrists and psychologists are middle-aged married men, probably white, whose personal backgrounds were seen by Schofield as containing "pressure

toward upward social mobility."[28] In 1960 the American Psychiatric Association totaled 10,000 male and 983 female members.

What must further be realized is that these predominantly male clinicians are involved in (a) a political institution that (b) has taken a certain traditional view of women. A great deal has been written about the covertly or overtly patriarchal, autocratic, and coercive values and techniques of psychotherapy.[29] Freud believed that the psychoanalyst-patient relationship must be that of "a superior and a subordinate."[30] The psychotherapist has been seen—by his critics as well as by his patients—as a surrogate parent (father or mother), savior, lover, expert, and teacher—all roles that foster "submission, dependency, and infantilism" in the patient: roles that imply the therapist's omniscient and benevolent superiority and the patient's inferiority.[31] (Szasz has remarked on the dubious value of such a role for the patient and the "undeniable" value of such a role for the "helper.") Practicing psychotherapists have been criticized for treating unhappiness as a disease (whenever it is accompanied by an appropriately high verbal and financial output); for behaving as if the psychotherapeutic philosophy or method can cure ethical and political problems; for teaching people that their unhappiness (or neurosis) can be alleviated through individual rather than collective efforts; for encouraging and legitimizing the urban middle-class tendency toward moral irresponsibility and passivity; for discouraging emotionally deprived persons from seeking "acceptance, dependence and security in the more normal and accessible channels of friendship."[32] Finally, the institution of psychotherapy has been viewed as a form of social and political control that offers those who can pay for it temporary relief, the illusion of con-

At the turn of the century, then, in social and political thinking, in literary and artistic culture, there was a tremendous ferment of ideas regarding sexuality, marriage and family, and women's role. Freudianism was only one cultural product of this ferment. Both Freudianism and Feminism came as reactions to one of the smuggest periods in Western civilization, the Victorian Era, characterized by its familycenteredness, and thus its exaggerated sexual oppression and repression. Both movements signified awakening: but Freud was merely a diagnostician for what Feminism purports to cure. . . .

Freudianism was the perfect foil for feminism, because, though it struck the same nerve, it had a safety catch that feminism didn't—it never questioned the given reality.

Shulamith Firestone

trol, and a self-indulgent form of self-knowledge; and that punishes those who cannot pay by labeling their unhappiness as psychotic or dangerous, thereby helping society consign them to asylums where custodial care (rather than therapeutic illusions) is provided.

These criticisms, of course, apply to both male and female therapy patients. However, the institution of psychotherapy differentially and adversely affects women to the extent to which it is similar to marriage, and insofar as it takes its powerfully socialized cues from Freud and his male and female disciples (Helene Deutsch, Marie Bonaparte, Marynia Farnham, Bruno Bettelheim, Erik Erikson, Joseph Rheingold), viewing woman as essentially "breeders and bearers," as potentially warm-hearted creatures, but more often as simply cranky children with uteruses, forever mourning the loss of male organs and male identity. Woman's fulfillment has been couched—inevitably and eternally—in terms of marriage, children, and the vaginal orgasm.[33]

In her 1926 essay entitled "The Flight from Womanhood," Karen Horney says:

> The present analytical picture of feminine development (whether that picture be correct or not) differs in no case by a hair's breadth from the typical ideas that the boy has of the girl.
>
> We are familiar with the ideas that the boy entertains. I will therefore only sketch them in a few succinct phrases, and for the sake of comparison will place in a parallel column our ideas of the development of women.

THE BOYS' IDEAS	OUR PSYCHOANALYTIC IDEAS OF FEMININE DEVELOPMENT
Naive assumption that girls as well as boys possess a penis	For both sexes it is only the male genital which plays any part
Realization of the absence of the penis	Sad discovery of the absence of the penis
Idea that the girl is a castrated, mutilated boy	Belief of the girl that she once possessed a penis and lost it by castration
Belief that the girl has suffered punishment that also threatens him	Castration is conceived of as the infliction of punishment
The girl is regarded as inferior	The girl regards herself as inferior. Penis envy
The boy is unable to imagine how the girl can ever get over this loss or envy	The girl never gets over the sense of deficiency and inferiority and has constantly to master afresh her desire to be a man.
The boy dreads her envy	The girl desires throughout life to avenge herself on the man for possessing something which she lacks[34]

The subject of women seems to elicit the most extraordinary and yet authoritative pronouncements from many "sensitive" psychoanalysts:

SIGMUND FREUD:
(Women) refuse to accept the fact of being castrated and have the hope of someday obtaining a penis in spite of everything. . . . I cannot escape the notion (though hesitate to give it expression) that for woman the level of what is ethically normal is different from what it is in man. We must not allow ourselves to be deflected from such conclusions by the denials of the feminists who

What we call "normal" is a product of repression, denial, splitting, projection, introjection and other forms of destructive action on experience. . . . If our experience is destroyed, our behavior will be destructive. Jack may act upon Jill in many ways. He may make her feel guilty for keeping on "bringing it up." He may invalidate her experience. This can be done more or less radically. He can indicate merely that it is unimportant or trivial, whereas it is important and significant to her. Going further, he can shift the modality of her experience from memory to imagination: "It's all in your imagination." Further still, he can invalidate the content: "It never happened that way." Finally, he can invalidate not only the significance, modality and content, but her very capacity to remember at all, and make her feel guilty for doing so into the bargain.

Ronald D. Laing

---

are anxious to force us to regard the two sexes as completely equal in position and worth.[35]

We say also of women that their social interests are weaker than those of men and that their capacity for the sublimation of their interests is less . . . the difficult development which leads to femininity [seems to] exhaust all the possibilities of the individual.[36]

ERIK ERIKSON:
For the student of development and practitioner of psychoanalysis, the stage of life crucial for the understanding of womanhood is the step from youth to maturity, the state when the young woman relinquishes the care received from the parental family and the extended care of institutions of education, in order to commit herself to the love of a stranger and to the care to be given to his or her offspring. . . . young women often ask, whether they can "have an identity" before they know whom they will marry and for whom they will make a home. Granted that something in the young women's identity must keep itself open for the peculiarities of the man to be joined and of the children to be brought up, I think that much of a young woman's identity is already defined in her kind of attractiveness and in the selectivity of her search for the man (or men) by whom she wishes to be sought.[37]

BRUNO BETTELHEIM:
. . . as much as women want to be good scientists and engineers, they want first and foremost to be womanly companions of men and to be mothers.[38]

JOSEPH RHEINGOLD:
. . . women is nurturance . . . anatomy decrees the life of a woman. . . . When women grow up

without dread of their biological functions and without subversion by feminist doctrines and therefore enter upon motherhood with a sense of fulfillment and altruistic sentiment we shall attain the goal of a good life and a secure world in which to live.[39]

These are all familiar views of women. But their affirmation by experts indirectly strengthened such views among men and *directly* tyrannized women, particularly American middle-class women, through the institution of psychotherapy and the tyranny of published "expert" opinion, stressing the importance of the mother for healthy child development. In their view, lack of—or superabundance of—mother love causes neurotic, criminal, psychiatric, and psychopathic children! The blame is rarely placed on the absence of a father or on the intolerable power struggle at the heart of most nuclear monogamous families—between child and parent, between wife and husband, between the whole economic unit and the struggle to survive in an urban capitalist environment.

Most child development research, like most birth control research, has centered around women, not men: for this is "women's work," for which she is totally responsible, which is "never done," and for which, in a wage-labor economy, she is never directly paid. She does it for love and is amply rewarded—in the writings of Freud et al.

The headaches, fatigue, chronic depression,

frigidity, "paranoia," and overwhelming sense of inferiority that therapists have recorded about their female patients have not been analyzed in any remotely accurate terms. The real oppression (and sexual repression) of women remains unknown to the analysts, for the most part. Such symptoms have not been viewed by most therapists as "indirect communications" that reflect a "slave psychology." Instead, such symptoms have been viewed as hysterical and neurotic productions, as underhanded domestic tyrannies manufactured by spiteful, self-pitying, and generally unpleasant women whose *inability to be happy as women* probably stems from unresolved penis envy, an unresolved Electra (or female Oedipal) complex, or from general, intractable female stubbornness.

In a rereading of some of Freud's early case histories of female "hysterics," particularly his *Case of Dora*, what is remarkable is not his brilliance or his relative sympathy for the female "hysterics";[40] rather, it is his tone: cold, intellectual, detective-like,[41] controlling, sexually Victorian. He really does not like his "intelligent" eighteen-year-old patient. For example, he says: "For several days on end she identified herself with her mother by means of slight symptoms and peculiarities of manner, which gave her an opportunity for some really remarkable achievements in the direction of intolerable behavior." The mother has been diagnosed, unseen, by Freud, as having "housewife's psychosis."[42]

L. Simon reviews the plight of Dora:

> ... she had been brought to Freud by her father for treatment of "... tussis nervosa, aphonia, depression, and taedium vitae." Despite the ominous sound of these Latinisms it should be noted that Dora was not in the midst of a symptom crisis at the time she was brought to Freud, and there

is at least room for argument as to whether these could be legitimately described as symptoms at all. If there was a crisis, it was clearly the father's. Nevertheless, Freud related the development of these "symptoms" to two traumatic sexual experiences Dora had had with Mr. K., a friend of the family. Freud eventually came to explain the symptoms as expressions of her disguised sexual desire for Mr. K., which he saw, in turn, as derived from feelings she held toward her father. Freud attempted, via his interpretations, to put Dora in closer touch with her own unconscious impulses.

... Indeed, the case study could still stand as an exemplary effort were it not for a single, but major, problem having to do with the realities of Dora's life. For throughout his therapeutic examination of Dora's unconscious Freud also knew that she was the bait in a monstrous sexual bargain her father had concocted. This man, who during an earlier period in his life had contracted syphilis and apparently infected his wife ... was now involved in an affair with the wife of Mr. K. There is clear evidence that her father was using Dora to appease Mr. K., and that Freud was fully aware of this. ... At one point Freud states: "Her father was himself partly responsible for her present danger for he had handed her over to this strange man in the interests of his own love-affair." But despite this reality, despite his full knowledge of her father's predilections, Freud insisted on examining Dora's difficulties from a strictly intrapsychic point of view, ignoring the manner in which her father was using her, and denying that her accurate perception of the situation was germane.

... Freud appears to accept fully the willingness of these men to sexually exploit the women around them. One even finds the imagery of capitalism creeping into his metapsychology. Freud's work with Dora may be viewed as an attempt to deal with the exploitation of women that characterized that historical period without even an admission of the fact of its existence. We may conclude that Freud's failure with Dora was a function of his inappropriate level of conceptualization and intervention. He saw that she was suffering, but instead of attempting to deal with the conditions of her life he chose—because he shared in her exploitation—to work within the confines of her ego.[43]

Although Freud eventually conceded (but not to Dora) that her insights into her family situation were correct, he still concluded that these insights would not make her "happy." Freud's own insights—based on self-reproach, rather than on Dora's reproaching of those around her—would hopefully help her discover her own penis envy and Electra complex; somehow this would magically help her to adjust to, or at least to accept, her only alternative in life: housewife's psychosis. If Dora had not left treatment (which Freud views as an act of revenge), her cure presumably would have involved her regaining (through desperation and self-hypnosis) a grateful respect for her patriarch-father; loving and perhaps serving him for years to come; or getting married and performing these functions for a husband or surrogate-patriarch.

Szasz comments on the "hysterical" symptoms of another of Freud's female patients, Anna O., who fell "ill" while nursing her father.

Anna O. thus started to play the hysterical game from a position of distasteful submission: she functioned as an oppressed, unpaid, sick-nurse, who was coerced to be helpful by the very helplessness of a (bodily) sick patient. The women in Anna O.'s position were—as are their counterparts today, who feel similarly entrapped by their small children—insufficiently aware of what they valued in life and of how their own ideas of what they valued affected their conduct. For example, young middle-class women in Freud's day considered it their duty to take care of their sick fathers. They treasured the value that it was their role to take care of father when he was sick. Hiring

---

An Expression

anger
is killing
my face.
it squints all day
despite cool remarks
it thinks the sun
is after it.
it thinks the whole world
is after it!
building armies
above the brow

anger
is killing
my face.
it squints all day
despite cool remarks
it thinks the sun
is after it.
it thinks the whole world
is after it!
building armies
above the brow
just in case.

meanwhile, no one
notices; even suspects
go about private
maneuvers.
one day,
wrinkles will tell
stories like old soldiers
when my lips have nothing
left to say,
pain will lean forward
and speak
for itself.

Susan Efros

a professional servant or nurse for this job would have created a conflict for them, because it would have symbolized to them as well as to others that they did not love ("care for") their fathers. Notice how similar this is to the dilemma in which many contemporary women find themselves, not, however, in relation to their fathers, but rather in relation to their young children. Today, married women are generally expected to take care of their children; they are not supposed to delegate this task to others. The "old folks" can be placed in a home; it is all right to delegate their care to hired help. This is an exact reversal of the social situation which prevailed in upper middle-class European circles until the First World War and even after it. Then, children were often cared for by hired help, while parents were taken care of by their children, now fully grown.[44]*

To Freud, it was to Anna's "great sorrow" that she was no longer "allowed to continue nursing the patient."

We may wonder to what extent contemporary psychotherapists[45] still view women as Freud did, either because they believe his theories, or/and because they are men first and so-called objective professionals second: it may still be in their personal and class interest to (quite unmaliciously) remain "Freudian" in their treatment of women. Two studies relate to this question.

As part of Schofield's 1960 study, each of the psychotherapists were asked to indicate the characteristics of his "ideal" patient, "that is, the kind of patient with whom you feel you are efficient and effective in your therapy." Schofield reports that "for those psychotherapists who did express a sex preference, a preference for females was predominant in all three professional groups." The margin of preference for female patients was largest in the sample of psychiatrists, nearly two-thirds of this group claiming the female patients as "ideal."[46] From 60 to 70 percent of each of the therapist groups place the ideal patient's age in the twenty to forty year range. Very rarely do representatives of any of the three disciplines express a preference for a patient with a graduate degree (M.A., M.D., Ph.D.).

Summarizing his findings, Schofield suggests that the efforts of most clinical practitioners are "restricted" to those clients who present the Yavis syndrome—youthful, attractive, verbal, intelligent, and successful. And, we may add, hopefully female.[47]

A recent study of Broverman et al, supports the hypothesis that most clinicians still view their female patients as Freud viewed his.[48] Seventy-nine clinicians (forty-six male and thirty-three female psychiatrists, psychologists, and social workers) completed a sex-role stereotype questionnaire. The questionnaire consists of 122 bipolar items, each of which describes a particular behavior or trait. For example:

very subjective _____ very objective
not at all aggressive _____ very aggressive

The clinicians were instructed to check off those traits that represent healthy male, healthy female, or healthy adult (sex unspecified) behavior. The results were as follows:

1. There was high agreement among clinicians as to the attributes characterizing healthy adult men, healthy adult women, and healthy adults, sex unspecified.

2. There were no differences among men and women clinicians.

3. Clinicians have different standards of health for men and women. Their concepts of healthy mature men do not differ significantly

---

* The Myth of Mental Illness, excerpts from pp. 213, 194–195, 263–264.

from their concepts of healthy mature adults, but their concepts of healthy mature women do differ significantly from those for men or for adults. Clinicians are likely to suggest that women differ from healthy men by being: more submissive, less independent, less adventurous, more easily influenced, less aggressive, less competitive, more excitable in minor crises, more easily hurt, more emotional, more conceited about their appearance, less objective, and less interested in math and science.

Finally, what is judged healthy for adults, sex unspecified, and for adult males, is in general highly correlated with previous studies of social desirability as perceived by non-professional subjects.

It is clear that for a woman to be healthy she must "adjust" to and accept the behavioral norms for her sex even though these kinds of behavior are generally regarded as less socially desirable. As the authors themselves remark, "This constellation seems a most unusual way of describing any mature, healthy individual."

Obviously, the ethic of mental health is masculine in our culture. Women are perceived as childlike or childish, as *alien* to most male therapists. It is therefore especially interesting that some clinicians, especially psychiatrists prefer female patients. Perhaps their preference makes good sense; a male therapist may receive a real psychological "service" from his female patient: namely, the experience of controlling and feeling superior to a female being upon whom he has projected many of his own forbidden longings for dependency, emotionality, and subjectivity and from whom, as a superior expert, as a doctor, he is protected as he cannot be from his mother, wife, or girl friend. And he earns money to boot!

Private psychoanalysis or psychotherapy is a commodity available to those women who can buy it, that is, to women whose fathers, husbands, or boy friends can help them pay for it.[49] Like the Calvinist elect, those women who can *afford* treatment are already "saved." Even if they are never happy, never free, they will be slow to rebel against their psychological and economic dependence on men. One look at their less-privileged (poor, black, and/or unmarried) sisters' position is enough to keep them silent and more or less gratefully in line. The less-privileged women have no real or psychological silks to smooth down over, to disguise their unhappiness; they have no class to be "better than." As they sit facing the walls, in factories, offices, whorehouses, ghetto apartments, and mental asylums, at least *one* thing they must conclude is that "happiness" is on sale in America—but not at a price they can afford. They are poor. They do not have to be bought off with illusions; they only have to be controlled.

Lower-class and unmarried middle-class women do have access to free or sliding-scale clinics, where, as a rule, they will meet once a week with minimally experienced psychotherapists. I am not suggesting that *maximally* experienced psychotherapists have acquired any expertise in salvation that will benefit the poor and/or unmarried woman. I am merely pointing out that the poor woman receives what is generally considered to be "lesser" treatment.

Given these facts—that psychotherapy is a commodity purchasable by the rich and inflicted on the poor; that as an institution, it socially controls the minds and bodies of middle-class women via the adjustment-to-marriage ideal and the minds and bodies of poor and single women via psychiatric incarceration; and that most clinicians, like most people in a patriarchal society, have deeply antifemale biases—it is difficult for me to make practical suggestions about "improving" therapeutic treatment. If marriage in a patriarchal society is analyzed as the major institution of female oppression, it is logically bizarre[50] to present husbands with helpful hints on how to make their wives "happier." Nevertheless, wives, private patients, and the inmates of mental asylums already exist in large numbers. Therefore, I will make several helpful suggestions regarding women, "mental illness," and psychotherapy.

Male psychologists, psychiatrists, and social workers must realize that as scientists they know nothing about women, their expertise, their diagnoses, even their sympathy is damaging and oppressive to women. Male clinicians should stop treating women altogether, however much this may hurt their wallets and/or sense of benevolent authority. For most women the psychotherapeutic encounter is just one more power relationship in which they submit to a dominant authority figure. I wonder how well such a structure can encourage independence—or healthy dependence—in a woman. I wonder what a woman can learn from a male therapist (however well-intentioned) whose own values are sexist? How free from the dictates of a sexist society can a female as patient be with a male therapist? How much can a male therapist empathize with a female patient? In *Human Sexual Inadequacy* Masters and Johnson state that their research supported unequivocally the "premise that no man will ever fully understand a woman's sexual function or dysfunction . . . (and the same is true for women). . . . it helps immeasurably for a distressed, relatively inarticulate or emotionally

unstable wife to have available a female co-therapist to interpret what she is saying and even what she is attempting unsuccessfully to express to the uncomprehending husband and often to the male co-therapist as well." I would go one step further here and ask: what if the female co-therapist is male-oriented, as much of a sexist as her male counterpart? What if the female therapist has never realized that she is oppressed as a woman? What if the female therapist views marriage and children as sufficient fulfillment for women—except herself?

All women—clinicians as well as their patients—must participate in and/or think seriously and deeply about the woman's liberation movement. Women patients should see female clinicians who are feminists. Female clinicians, together with all women, should create a new or first psychology of women, and as a group, act on it. This might include politically educating and supporting females in mental asylums and in other ghettos of the mind. Perhaps all-female therapeutic communities can be tried as a necessary, interim alternative to female economic and psychological dependence on patriarchal structures such as marriage, psychotherapy, and mental asylums. In such a communal setting, it is not unlikely that friendship, understanding, or objectivity may be desired on a private basis, and that such an interchange might resemble or draw upon psychoanalytic or psychotherapeutic "knowledge" or practice. Who will be—or whether there will be—"experts" of understanding is unknown; who will be—or whether anyone will be—considered "mentally ill" and treated by isolation and ostracism is unknown.

Betsy Belote

Masochistic Syndrome, Hysterical Personality, and the Illusion of a Healthy Woman

Keep me rather in this cage, and feed me sparingly, if you dare. Anything that brings me closer to illness and the edge of death makes me more faithful. It is only when you make me suffer that I feel safe and secure. You should never have agreed to be a god for me if you were afraid to assume the duties of a god, and we all know that they are not as tender as all that.

—*Pauline Reage**

The dynamics of masochism are crucial to an understanding of woman's psychological, social and sexual relationship to man in this culture. From a feminist point of view, it is clear that woman's role is subservient to that of a man's, and it is mainly in relation to a man that she achieves a worthwhile, respected identity, i.e., as wife and mother. Unless she is outstandingly productive or brilliant in a professional field, an unmarried woman is usually considered a failure, or someone to be pitied. Thus, the great majority of women view heterosexual relationships as the most valuable part of life, and throw the greatest part of their mental and emotional selves into developing and maintaining a relationship with a man. Upon entering this relationship, the woman's status and value is increased in the eyes of society, but the price she pays for this kind of acceptance is dear:

It comprises her selfhood, her independence, her autonomy, her freedom to master her life and to find purpose and meaning beyond that of biological reproduction or supporting her husband in his life's work.

*Reage, Pauline. *Story of O.* New York; Grove Press, Inc.

This paper presents a review of the concept of masochism as defined in the psychological literature, and compares its characteristics with those of the hysterical personality and the "healthy" woman. Various approaches to the origin of the phenomenon will be considered: (a) theories which emphasize an instinctual origin of masochism, as first formulated by Freud; (b) theories which stress biological influences; (c) theories which integrate the above-mentioned models with sociocultural concepts and (d) theories which stress an adaptational or socially learned basis of masochism.

The term "masochism" was first conceptualized by Krafft-Ebing in 1882, based on the writings of Sacher-Masoch, the romantic French novelist, on the relationship between sex and cruelty. Krafft-Ebing (1937) described the symptoms, but not the origins of masochism. These include: (1) extreme dependence on the love object; (2) extreme submission to, and lust for the object who is cruel (which over time, changes to lust and desire for the cruelty itself); and (3) an "oversexed" condition in certain individuals who require painful stimulation in order to feel excited. Such individuals were described as being sexually inhibited, and compulsively striving to overcome this inhibition through various adaptive maneuvers.

Instinctual Theory

Krafft-Ebing's (1937) sexual definition of masochism was accepted and elaborated upon by Freud (1953, 1955, 1957, 1961a). He defined it as a primary instinctual drive, and outlined three types: moral, erotogenic and feminine.

Moral masochism is that type which is found in all people as a certain attitude towards life, and is an especially significant factor in the life of social, national and religious bodies. It shares with other types of masochism the unconscious tendency to seek pain and enjoy suffering. Moral masochism is supposedly based on unconscious processes, and guilt related to Oedipal wishes; thus, it is basically sexual in character. Moral masochists receive punishment from their superegos, e.g., by being failures in a career, having unhappy marriages, or misfortunes and disappointments of every kind relating to life and love. Feelings of guilt and corresponding wishes to be punished, which are unconsciously working through the inner authority of the superego, destroy all their plans. A typical example of Freud's moral masochism occurring in everyday life is that of the woman who loses sexual interest in her husband, and due to feeling guilty about her lack of interest, punishes herself by missing a pleasureful opportunity, losing her prized wedding ring, or forcing herself to have sex with him.

Erotegenic masochism was explained by Freud (1961a) in the following way: Physical pain, or emotional fright and horror, produces sexual excitement independent of the attitude towards the inflicting object. Freud did not explain or discuss the relationship between sexual synergism with pain and discomfort and the psychological components of masochism. Neither did his concept of erotogenic masochism explain its psychic genesis, except to say it was instinctual. However, he did indicate that moral and feminine masochism were ultimately grounded in actual erotogenic masochism.

Feminine masochism, according to Freud (1955, 1961a), is an expression of "feminine nature," and therefore not considered aberrant in women. Interestingly, he was concerned with the *men* who suffered this disorder, rather than the women. Freud identified passivity with femininity, and masochism with passivity. Thus, masochism in the male was a primary feminine wish, and therefore a serious violation of sex-role standards. Men who are afflicted with feminine masochism enjoy the fantasy of being sexually abused and impregnated against their wish, which to Freud is a frequent unconscious desire of many women. He stated that men who are masochistic in a feminine style experience feeling loved through punishment. The beating woman represents a composite figure: the loving and loved woman (mother), plus the punishing attitude of the father. The male masochist wants to adopt a passive feminine attitude towards the father, in order to be loved like mother, who was both used and loved by father. Since the male masochist takes the position of a woman with the father, he experiences hostility against the woman (self), who was both preferred by the father and who herself preferred the father to the little boy.

The origin of all three types of masochism in Freud's (1961a) view, is in the instincts of Eros and Thanatos, or, the sexual urge and the death wish (aggression). Eros is seen as a constructive, productive urge; Thanatos as destructive, dissolving and annihilating. The two instincts fight each other throughout life. The sadistic person uses destructive aggression in order to achieve sexual gratification, and thus quell the destructive urge. For example, a man wooing a woman and asserting power over her demonstrates sadism, yet his ultimate goal is Eros, or union with the woman. The origin of masochism is explained by Freud as the death instinct being nurtured by the sadist. According to later psychoanalysts, Freud's hypothesis of the origin of masochism provides a rough framework, but it is grossly reductionistic. The death instinct hypothesis skims over the question of the psychological derivation of masochism and does not acknowledge the existence of social and cultural factors.

Biologically Based Theories

Helen Deutsch (1930), a psychoanalyst, relates masochism in women to sexual anatomy, stating that to be feminine is to be masochistic. To her, masochism in women is characterological, originating in the realization by a little girl that she has no penis. The young girl gives up her active-sadistic orientation attached to the clitoris when she sees that she lacks the anatomical organ that gives meaning to such an orientation. The shock of this realization leaves a lasting influence and her clitoral sadism is turned inwards to become masochism. The supporting evidence Deutsch used in formulating her theory was weak and biased, consisting primarily of other psychoanalysts' observations of sadistic fantasies in neurotic children, and reconstructions out of the analysis of neurotic adults.

Deutsch wanted to understand the significance of femininity, which to her meant "the passive-masochistic disposition of the mental life of women" (1930, p. 48). She states (1944, p. 278) that masochism is an "elemental power in female mental life," and that it is psychobiologically necessary in all women in order to serve towards the preservation of the species. More specifically, it is necessary for all women, according to Deutsch, to enjoy the "pain" of menstruation and childbirth in order to preserve human life. To Deutsch, one of woman's main tasks in life is to govern this masochism, steer it in the right directions, and thereby protect herself and the future of mankind.

Sandor Rado (1933), in his early writings, agreed with Deutsch that the biological and genital endowment of women forces their sexual development into masochistic channels. He explains that little girls become narcissistically shocked following their discovery of the penis; but, he postulated, the effect of the shock varies depending on the little girl's emotional condition. If the shock occurs in the period of early sexual experimentation, it is a particularly painful experience, in addition to a narcissistic blow. It is so because it arouses in the young girl the belief that males can derive more pleasure out of masturbation than females. This awareness of the possibility of a superior pleasure destroys the enjoyment of attainable, but inferior, pleasure. Since, according to Rado, individuals always want what is superior, and lose interest in things that do not match up to their idea of the best, the young girl decathects her own sexuality. However, the extreme mental pain resulting from the discovery of her inferior organ excites her sexually and provides her with a substitute gratification. Thus, the only way she can attain satisfaction is through suffering. She then becomes masochistic in her sexual strivings. The masculinity wish, or a woman's wish to be a man is, to Rado, merely a defense against her basic underlying masochism.

Deutsch's (1930, 1944) and Rado's (1933) views of masochism hold that at root masochism is the result of a woman's genital and reproductive organs in contrast to an instinctual drive (Freud). The problem with the biological view is that it assumes "penis envy" as a phenomenon of *all* women resulting from their awareness of the organ itself, rather than their awareness of the superior position males have in the culture. Young girls likely view the penis as a symbol of power which grants preferential treatment in the society, which may lead them to believe that it gives superior pleasure and consequently to devalue their own genitals. The distinction here, however, is that social and cultural values determine the young girl's attitudes about herself, rather than some arbitrary idea regarding the intrinsic superiority of the penis. The genetic theory also stresses that it is natural and healthy for women to seek pain and to enjoy it (intercourse, menstruation, childbirth) in order to maintain the species, rather than learning to adapt to it because they have no choice. Recent authors (Bardwick, 1971) have pointed out that the great majority of women today choose to avoid the pain of childbirth through use of pain-relieving anesthesias. It therefore seems clear that biological theories of masochism are based on conjectured evidence, and thus are seriously deficient as explanations.

Theories Integrating Biological and Socio-cultural Influences

Theodore Reik (1941) intensively studies Freud's concept of masochism as it applies to both sexes, and followed it with a definition which includes both biological and social-cultural components. He criticized Freud's instinctual formulation of masochism as a primary instinct, on the basis that erotogenic masochism which Freud claimed had a biological, constitutional basis proves to be "nothing but an infantile physiological precondition for the possible development of masochistic sensations later on, if certain psychic elaborations lead up to it" (1941, p. 30). Since no traces of this destructive, self-annihilating instinct have been found in the infant, according to Reik, Freud's explanation is no more than conjecture.

Reik (1941, p. 141) described masochism as a means to an end, rather than an end in itself:

The masochist is a person of strongly sadistic disposition, who has been diverted from his instinctual aim by the vision of punishment. This anxiety prevents his achieving satisfaction, and in his conflict between anxiety and urge for pleasure, he finally decides to get rid of his anxiety by that flight forward. He consequently does not strive for discomfort and punishment as such. He asks for them because they mark the only possible way to untroubled pleasure.

Thus, according to Reik, the masochist does not strive for pain, but for sadistic lust and pleasure, which must be paid for through punishment. He distinguishes the masochism of men from the masochism of women. Biological circumstances such as menstruation, defloration, and childbirth, to Reik, foster an inclination to masochism in women. Cultural factors, such as passive roles women are educated and reinforced to accept, and the suppression of aggressive and violent impulses, favor a vague, mild masochism and a more than mild sadism in women in this culture. He continues by saying that although biological circumstances favor an inclination towards masochism in women, they need not necessarily lead to it. Reik, however, draws a line between the masochism women suffer as a result of cultural roles and their biological state and "masochism as a crude instinctual perversion" in which discomfort, shame, or disgrace are desired. The latter, Reik (1941, p. 212) feels occurs much more often among men:

Masochism as an instinctual aberration and as character seems to disagree with the idea of masculinity and be more in harmony with the idea of the woman. Freud expressed this same opinion by saying masochism sustained an intimate relation to femininity.

The masochistic fantasy in women, to Reik, is supposedly composed of yielding and surrendering themes. In contrast, masochism in men is characterized by ferocity, aggressiveness, vigor, and resoluteness. According to Reik, the difference between male and female experiences of masochism is based on the male's penis, which, he posits, is the carrier of aggression. In another vein, Reik, like Freud, viewed the female superego as weaker and more yielding than the male's. The female conscience therefore experiences guilt less intensely and does not promote self-punishment to the same degree as the male conscience. Female masochism, then, takes the form of enjoyment of passivity, submission and suffering. The woman also enjoys her partner's strength and power, as well as humiliation as a sexual object, and sexual self-humiliation.

Although Reik (1941), as noted above, recognizes the influence of cultural factors and biological circumstances in encouraging the development of "mild masochism" in women, he distinguishes between that and a more perverted masochism which involves suffering pain, being beaten and tied up, and disgraced and humiliated in an extreme way. While he agreed with Freud that to be feminine was to be passive, he did not feel that being passive included being masochistically perverted.

Edmund Bergler (1949) integrated the instinctual and the adaptational views of masochism. He defined two different types: perversion masochism and psychic masochism. Perversion masochism is that type in which the individual experiences bodily pain as pleasurable, while psychic masochism is based on displaced aggression which results in self-punishment and produces unconscious pleasure. The psychic masochist counteracts her own aggression with feelings of guilt and receives libidinal pleasure by being humiliated and defeated. Thus, according to Bergler, the psychic masochist enjoys

pain and seeks it out in order to gratify her libido. Bieber (1966) clarifies that there is a difference between self-injury, which is intrinsic to masochism, and submission to a stronger opponent, as in "normal" male-female relationships, which he does not see as masochistic, in contrast to some feminist positions.

Biological and instinctual theories are not acceptable for reasons stated earlier. However, the socio-cultural aspect which integrationists consider may be useful as explanatory concepts for masochism.

Adaptational Theory

Adaptational theories of masochism present the view that masochism is a socially conditioned defense against deep feelings of fear. This view differs from the instinctual and biological models in that it posits that masochism is *exclusively* learned, socially conditioned behavior.

Karen Horney (1973) was one of the first psychoanalysts to discuss the influence of social and cultural factors in the development of masochism. In her early writings on masochism, she criticized Rado's (1933) biological formulation and provided a major clarification. Horney asserted that Rado's theory implied that the sex life of the majority of women was pathologic, and was in contradiction to Freud's pleasure principle concept (which states that individuals seek satisfaction in every situation). Horney noted that even assuming that little girls do suffer shock from the realization of an unattainable source of pleasure, it does not logically follow that the pain should affect her sexually. She stated that if Rado's formulation was correct it should follow that little boys would perceive their fathers' larger penises as the source of greater pleasure. Horney's final point was that it makes no sense that the little girl's

Woman—Which Includes Man, of Course: An Experience in Awareness

Purpose: To increase awareness of how culture, psychology, and psychotherapy, as well as our thoughts and feelings, come from a Male point of view.

Directions: Close your eyes, find a comfortable position, and relax while someone reads to you the following:

1. Consider reversing the generic term Man. Think of the future of Woman, which, of course, includes both women and men. Feel into that, sense its meaning to you—as a woman—as a man.

2. Think of it always being that way, every day of your life. Feel the everpresence of woman and feel the nonpresence of man. Absorb what it tells you about the importance and value of being woman—of being man.

3. Recall that everything you have ever read all your life uses only female pronouns,—she, her—meaning both girls and boys, both women and men. Recall that most of the voices on radio and most of the faces on TV are women's —when important events are covered—on commercials, and on the late talk shows. Recall that you have no male senator representing you in Washington.

4. Feel into the fact that women are the leaders, the power-centers, the prime-movers. Man, whose natural role is husband and father, fulfills himself through nurturing children and making the home a refuge for woman. This is only natural to balance the biological role of woman who devotes her entire body to the race during pregnancy.

5. Then feel further into the obvious biological explanation for woman as the ideal—her genital construction. By design, female genitals are compact and internal, protected by her body. Male genitals are so exposed that he must be protected from outside attack to assure the perpetuation of the race. His vulnerability clearly requires sheltering.

6. Thus, by nature, males are more passive than females and have a desire in sexual relations to be symbolically engulfed by the protective body of the woman. Males psychologically yearn for this protection, fully realizing their masculinity at this time—feeling exposed and vulnerable at other times. The male is not fully adult until he has overcome his infantile tendency to penis orgasm and has achieved the mature surrender of the testicle orgasm. He then feels himself a "whole man" when engulfed by the woman.

7. If the male denies these feelings, he is unconsciously rejecting his masculinity. Therapy is thus indicated to help him adjust to his own nature. Of course, therapy is administered by a woman, who has the education and wisdom to facilitate openness leading to the male's growth and self-actualization.

8. To help him feel into his defensive emotionality he is invited to get in touch with the "child" in him. He remembers his sister's jeering at his primitive genitals that "flop around foolishly." She can run, climb and ride horseback unencumbered. Obviously, since she is free to move, she is encouraged to develop her body and mind in preparation for her active responsibilities of adult womanhood. The male vulnerability needs female protection, so he is taught the less active, caring virtues of homemaking.

9. Because of his clitoris-envy, he learns to strap up his genitals, and learns to feel ashamed and unclean because of his nocturnal emissions. Instead he is encouraged to dream of getting married, waiting for the time of his fulfillment—when "his woman" gives him a girl-child to care for and carry on the family name. He knows that if it is a boy-child he has failed somehow—but they can try again.

Open your eyes. What did you experience? Record this and share it with the class.

shock reaction to penis awareness should have a lasting, permanent effect driving her to seek suffering throughout her life.

Horney's first hypothesis regarding masochism was that all masochistic strivings are ultimately directed towards getting rid of the self, experienced as conflicted and limited. Furthermore, to her, not all suffering was masochistic, but rather, often merely an accidental by-product of neurotic conflict. Horney (1939) modified this first hypothesis when she attempted to answer the question of whether striving for the relinquishment of self ultimately determines the masochistic process. This modification pointed out two major characteristics of the masochist: first, there is a tendency towards self-minimizing, the result of which is to feel unattractive, insignificant, inefficient, stupid and worthless. The masochist thus tends to be inconspicuous, and to cringe into a corner. Second, the masochist demonstrates a tendency towards personal dependency as a life condition. This type of individual feels as incapable of living without the presence, benevolence, love or friendship of another person as she is of living without oxygen.

> The masochistic [woman] feels [she] cannot do anything on [her] own, and expects to receive everything from the partner: love, success, care, protection. Without ever realizing it, and mostly in contrast to [her] conscious modesty and humility, [her] expectations are parasitic in character. [Her] reasons for clinging to another person are so stringent that [she] may exclude from awareness the fact that the partner is not and never will be the appropriate person to fulfill [her] expectations; . . . (Horney, 1939 p. 251–252).

Masochistic trends, in Horney's view, arise out of the same circumstances which promote perfectionistic and narcissistic trends. All are simply psychological defenses originating from a combination of adverse environmental influences upon the child. These early experiences make her view the world as potentially hostile. The narcissist copes with these negative feelings through self-inflation, the perfectionist by overconformity to standards, while the masochist looks for safety through becoming attached to a person perceived as more powerful and ultimately becoming dependent upon this person.

> By submerging [her] own individuality entirely and by merging with the partner the masochistic [woman] gains a certain reassurance . . . to be compared with that achieved by a small endangered nation which surrenders its rights and its independence to a powerful and aggressive nation and thereby wins protection. One of the differences is that the small nation knows it does not take this step because of its love for the bigger nation, while in the neurotic's mind the process often takes on the appearance of loyalty, devotion or great love. But actually the masochistic [woman] is incapable of love, nor does [she] believe the partner or anyone else can love [her] (Horney, 1939 p. 253).

To Horney, masochistic dependency is replete with hostility (at the inevitable imperfections of the partner). This hostility is expressed in a passive-aggressive manner, i.e., through excessive dependency and moral indignation. She distinguishes between masochistic character structure and masochistic sexual perversions. In short, the masochistic character structure explains the perversion, but the perversion does not explain the character. The perversion is simply the result of the masochistic dependency and unobtrusiveness carried to the extreme.

We should add here that there is a healthy kind of passivity in which the woman responds to frustration and aggression with an elaboration of compromise solutions in thought and fantasy instead of in activity directed outward. This healthy response probably has its origins in the woman's special relationship to her body interior, in her weaker musculature, and in her highly developed verbal skills.

Judith Bardwick

Horney stated that the cultural reality of male supremacy makes it difficult for any woman to escape some degree of masochism. She points out that male doctrines which define the feminine as innately weak, overly emotional, dependent and limited in their ability to work well alone, influence women to act in those ways. Horney also states that the fact that women who display these characteristics are preferred by men as marital partners and lovers is profound reinforcement for women to act in those ways. Since most people want to be approved of and accepted, it follows that most women will adopt the kind of social behavior for which they will be rewarded. As a consequence, great majority of women internalize these feminine characteristics and it is assumed by some theoreticians that this behavior is actually the "nature" of women. Horney (1973, p. 231) explains:

> it therefore seems no exaggeration to say that in such social organizations, masochistic attitudes (or rather milder expressions of masochism) are favored in women while they are discouraged in men. Qualities like emotional dependence on the other sex (clinging vine), absorption in "love," inhibition of the expansive, autonomous development, etc., are regarded as quite desirable in women but are treated with opprobrium and ridicule when found in men.

Wilhelm Reich (1949) also discarded Freud's instinctual concept and replaced it with an adaptive interpretation. He viewed masochism as a defense involving: (1) the choosing of a lesser injury, and (2) a means of punishing significant figures whom the masochist perceived as denying him love in childhood. Reich's argument revolves around the fact that Freud's instinctual hypothesis is in direct contradiction to Freud's pleasure principle theory, a point which had also been made by Horney (1939). Furthermore, Reich proposed that masochism is associated with an excessive need for love based on great fear of being left alone. The masochist also fears success, which symbolizes genital exposure. In regard to the fear of genital exposure, Reich was speaking exclusively of masochism in males.

Clara Thompson (1964) emphasized the manipulative aspects of masochism as it occurs in interpersonal relationships. To her, the masochistic person is attempting to gain the love, security, and dependency which was lacking in childhood. The masochist's behavior demonstrates passive dependency and hostile aggression, suffering, martyrdom. In her view, the masochist provokes guilt in others, who feel compelled to assume burdens of care and responsibility; this mechanism then becomes a transactional device for personal gain. To Thompson, masochism is an adaptive mechanism, or a defense. She described its origins as follows:

> The thumbnail sketch is this—no affection from either parent, parents at war with each other. One of them can be seduced into a show of concern

*Women have the same desires as men, but do not have the same right
to express them.*

Jean Jacques Rousseau

for the child if the child can demonstrate that he
has suffered at the hands of the other, or if he can
create some other situation of suffering. This is
the nearest to love that the child can ever achieve.
Through suffering, he either plays on the sense
of guilt of the parent or parents, and thus gets
some compensatory attention, or he succeeds in
getting them to battle with each other. Again, if
you can't be loved you can at least get attention,
and maybe if you suffer enough you will be forgiven.

This pattern becomes a way of life. There are
two possible lines of development. One is an exaggerated taking of the blame to oneself. There
is usually a quality of insincerity in this attitude.
The patient says 'I deserve to suffer because I am
so bad or so worthless'. . . . The other attitude
is that of the martyr: 'I have given you the best
years of my life, and this is my reward.' Both are
devices to get attention through suffering (1964:
186).

According to Thompson, intimacy is the ultimate goal of the masochistic person. There
is never open hostility, rather anger is expressed by means of making another person
feel guilty, or getting another person to fight
for her own life or actions.

Irving Bieber (1966) sees sadism and masochism as maladaptive, pathological responses
to a threat or a perception of a threat in every
context of experience. He distinguished self-
destructive impulses and acts from those that
are defensive and aiming towards preserving
life, love etc. He considers only the latter to

The Friend

*We sat across the table.
he said, cut off your hands.
they are always poking at things.
they might touch me.
I said yes.*

*Food grew cold on the table.
he said, burn your body.
it is not clean and smells like sex.
it rubs my mind sore.
I said yes.*

*I love you, I said.
that's very nice, he said
I like to be loved,
that makes me happy.
Have you cut off your hands yet?*

Marge Piercy

---

be masochistic and states that while sexual
masochism is relatively uncommon, non-sexual
masochism is demonstrated in most psychiatric
patients (most of whom he fails to mention, are
women).

Masochistic defenses appearing in non-sexual
behaviors are particularly evident in attitudes and
acts felt to be competitive. Fears, whether real or
fancied of antagonizing competitors by successful
performance and fear of evoking competitive or
hostile feelings among rivals tend to induce self
sabotaging tactics (Bieber, 1966, p. 266).

Coming to Save the Blood by Virginia Atkin

Bieber states further that masochism in general is a defensive reaction to a threat, just as submission is a defensive, self-protective posture. He sees passivity, however as pathological, and not a characteristic which is basic to the nature of women:

> Passivity is not a feminine characteristic; it is the manifestation of a chronic inhibition of protective resources and it is pathological for females as for males. Submission is one of the basic social responses of the species to a threat. In Western culture, however, passivity, submissiveness, dependency are more acceptable for females; but such culture themes do not establish these attitudes and behaviors as non-pathological. Rather, they indicate that women are not yet fully emancipated (Bieber, 1966, p. 267).

Rado (1959) revised his earlier (1933) explanation of masochism and began stressing adaptational theory. In his new formulation, both sadist and masochist develop "pain-dependence" early in life in response to disciplinary stress. The individual later pursues punishment as the only means by which he can obtain "license to gratify forbidden desires." The disorder is thus one of the conscience rather than of sexual function.

Simone de Beauvoir (1970) clarifies that masochism exists in a woman only when she chooses to abdicate her will to that of another person, and thus become the possession of that person. She disagrees with Deutsch (1930, 1944) that through being penetrated by a man in the act of intercourse, a woman is masochistic, and states that this act may represent transcendence of self or the unity of self with the lover, rather than abdication. To de Beauvoir, an individual is masochistic when her own ego is viewed as separate from the self and is regarded as being totally dependent upon the will of another.

De Beauvoir holds that masochism is a way of escaping from the conflicts created by woman's "sexual destiny" by wallowing in it, rather than a solution to it. The true solution, to de Beauvoir, is to overcome her passivity and establish an equal relationship with her male partner.

Adaptational theories, unlike instinctual and biological theories of masochism, hold that masochism is socially conditioned, learned behavior. Out of all the theoreticians who hold this view however, only Horney (1939, 1973) actually makes the connection between culturally influenced sex roles and masochism in women. In the view of this researcher, Horney's analysis of masochism is a feminist one, because she has gone to the very root of it by making the connection between the socio-political structure, sex roles and the psychological syndrome itself.

The Hysterical Personality

Almost all of the writers who have discussed the "hysterical personality" agree that it is found almost exclusively in women. In fact it is often described as a caricature of femininity. The *Diagnostic and Statistical Manual of Mental Disorders* (1968) defines it as follows:

> These behavior patterns are characterized by excitability, overreactivity, and self-dramatization. This self-dramatization is always attention seeking and often seductive, whether or not the patient is aware of its purpose. These personalities are also immature, self-centered, often vain, and usually dependent on others.

Freud did not discuss the "hysterical personality," but rather "hysterical conversion." Although the two are different in symptomatolgy, they are similar in dynamics, according to classical psychoanalytic theory, as both disorders entail unresolved Oedipal conflicts, penis envy, and oral fixation which lead to ambivalent, repressed sexuality. In his paper on female sexuality (1961c), Freud discussed the "normal" female. In that paper he asserts that the well-adjusted female is one who accepts the fact that she has no penis, and thus substitutes for this lack by turning her attention to the wish for a baby. In his paper on libidinal types, Freud (1961b) describes the "erotic type" as a person whose main interest in life is focused on love and loving, but above all on being loved. The dread of losing love makes her particularly dependent. Freud's description of the "erotic type" is similar to descriptions of the "hysterical personality," the masochistic woman and the "normal" female in this society.

Wilhelm Reich (1949) pointed out that the "hysterical personality" was very seductive and sexually provocative, yet usually "frigid" in sexual relationships. Reich felt that the "hysterical personality's" actual needs were for affection and nurturance, not sex. Furthermore, to Reich, the hysterical personality is characterized by sharp disappointment reaction, imaginativeness, lack of conviction, compliance, readily giving way to depreciation and disparagement, the compulsive need to be loved, overdependency on others for approval, and powerful capacity for dramatization and somatic compulsion. Reich's major concern however, was with the underlying "oral fixation" of the "hysterical personality," rather than the symptomatology.

Marmor (1953) agreed with Reich that the underlying oral character is the most important variable in determining the "hysterical personality" rather than the symptomatology. The "hysterical personality," to Marmor, is resistant to change, immature, has an unstable, weak ego, is very suggestible and can cease symptomatology quickly, but the underlying character structure does not change: i.e., "If you (therapist) will love and protect me, I will be whatever you want." In this way symptoms may disappear, but the underlying oral dependency remains.

Easer and Leser (1965) noted that the "hysterical personality" is an expression of heightened feminity, and they observed that therapists are often "duped" by it.

Just as a bird that flies about
and beats itself against the cage,
finding at last no passage out
It sits and sings, and so overcomes its rage.

Abraham Cowley (1618–1667)

The rubric [of hysteria] connotes the hysterical woman, hysterical attacks, in short, 'a caricature of femininity.' Hysterics are wont to live up to, in fact, to exaggerate their role. They apply themselves to whatever name one may call them. The psychoanalyst in his countertransference can be aroused by the contagion of the exaggerated effect. He finds himself 'holding the bag' emotionally, provoked into overplaying his role as a therapist, while his patient changes a course and heads down a new emotional alley, perhaps a blind one (p. 391).

Martin (1971) described the extreme dependency needs of the "hysterical personality" and maintained that these needs were illustrative of a symbiotic character structure involving unresolved separation anxiety. In intimate relationships, the love object is depended upon to supplement the "hysterical personality's" deficient ego. The hysterical woman can put up with tremendous hostility emanating from an intimate involvement, but not the loss of the object. It is interesting that this same description is given by Horney (1939, 1973) for the masochistic woman.

Howard Wolowitz (1970) considered the issue of cultural factors contributing to the development of the "hysterical personality." He noted, as did Parsons (1955) that sex-role socialization of men emphasizes mastery-achievement responsibilities. As a consequence, women usually feel strongly inclined to elicit strong positive emotional responses from others, and by so doing, measure their own value and worth. The major contribution of Wolowitz's paper is its development and discussion of the fact that *every* American woman is conditioned to develop an hysterical character in nonpathological, or acceptable form. The cultural factor which creates this "hysterical" response in women is the oppression of being stereotyped as inferior, and the resulting lack of skills, power, and equal opportunity.

Wolowitz also says that the "hysterical personality" has difficulty making friends with same-sexed individuals. These individuals feel more at ease with men if women, as they are less competitive with men. As children, they often have been competitive with their mothers, sisters, female cousins and peers, all for the attention of a male figure. "Hysterical personalities" attempt to find in men the nurturance they missed in their own mothers, and cannot receive from other women due to disappointment in women. However, since most men cannot provide the emotional expressiveness the "hysterical personality" needs, she continues to have an unconscious longing for a maternal figure. "Hysterical personalities" seek responsivity and self-validation from others; therefore, they are high in "other-directedness," and in their frantic effort to gain love and attention, "hysterical personalities," according to Wolowitz, sacrifice feelings of realness and genuineness, losing themselves in the roles that they play. Feelings of falseness, emptiness and loneliness result. Furthermore, they often utilize sex to buy companionship or a sense of immediate

> **Reverse Paranoia** (*as defined by Leonard Roy Frank*): *Affected persons imagine they are safe when, in fact, they are in danger.*
> **Paranoia:** *Affected persons imagine they are in danger when, in fact, they are not.*

worth and power. Traits such as charm, flirtatiousness, provocativeness, exhibitionism and suggestibility, void of genuineness, are the chief instruments utilized in their struggle to get love and attention.

The Female Masochist, the Hysterical Personality, and the Illusion of the "Healthy" Female

While many authors have noted the similarity between the "hysterical personality" and femininity, and masochism and femininity, none have pointed out the relationship among all three of these syndromes.

One of the most striking features of masochism and hysteria as expressed by women is its subtlety and invisibility to the acculturated American. This is so because masochistic and hysterical behavior is so similar to the concept of "femininity" that the three are not clearly distinguishable. That women are accepted and rewarded for exhibiting passivity and dependence in their behavior, affect and cognitive styles has been repeatedly validated (Beller and Neubauer, 1963; Bieri, Bradburn & Galinsky, 1958; Brim Glass, Lavin & Goodman, 1962; Kagan and Moss, 1962· Macoby, 1966; McGuire, 1961; Sears, Whiting, Nolis & Sears 1953; Spangler & Thomas, 1962; Vaught, 1965; Witkin, Dyk, Faterson, Goodenough & Karp, 1962).

While the female sex role is viewed as an inferior one by dominant (male) societal standards, the role is also viewed as "healthy" for

TABLE 1
A Comparison of the Characteristics of Masochism, the "Hysterical Personality," and the "Healthy" Female

Female Masochism*	Hysterical Personality**	Healthy Female***
Absorption in love	Overreactivity	More emotional
Emotional dependence	Excitability	More easily excitable in minor crises
Self-denial	Dependency	Less independent
Fears success		More submissive
Inhibition of expansive, autonomous development		Less competitive / Less aggressive
Low self-esteem	Low self-esteem	
Accepts pain		More easily hurt
Perceives world as hostile	Lack of orgasmic sexual response	Less adventurous
Self-sabotage	Seductiveness	Less objective
Use of weakness and helplessness to woo the other sex		Less interested in math and science

*Horney (1939, p. 229)
**Diagnostic and Statistical Manual of Mental Disorders (1968), Reich (1949).
***Broverman, et al (1970)

women by these same standards. Table 1 demonstrates that the characteristics of a "healthy" female closely parallel the characteristics of the masochistic and hysterical personalities.

The characteristics of the healthy female were derived from a recent study by Broverman, Broverman, Clarkman, Rosencrantz, and Vogel

(1970). Their findings indicated that both male and female psychotherapists adhere to societal stereotypes of women as inferior beings. A questionnaire containing 122 bipolar items describing particular behaviors or traits was sent to a random sample of clinicians of both sexes. They were instructed to check those items which best described a healthy male, healthy female and healthy adult (sex unspecified). The results clearly pointed out the strong sexist bias of both male and female psychotherapists. The typical clinician's concept of the healthy mature man was similar to that of a healthy mature adult in general, while the picture of the healthy mature female differed strongly from both. According to the study, healthy women differ from healthy men in being:

> . . . more submissive, less independent, less adventurous, more easily influenced, less aggressive, less competitive, more easily excitable in minor crises, more easily hurt, more emotional, more conceited about their appearance, less objective, and less interested in math and science (p. 6).

Thus, one can be a healthy male and a healthy adult at the same time but not a healthy woman and a healthy adult. Furthermore, the results indicated that healthy male characteristics are viewed as more socially desirable than healthy female characteristics.

Because the accepted model of the "healthy" female is childlike, inferior, and non-expansive; and the model for the healthy adult is a masculine one, it becomes impossible for any woman to be mature or healthy according to the dominant standards. This puts woman in a most frustrating double-bind: she is damned if she accepts the traditional feminine role, and damned if she does not. The most she can hope for is to find security through adjusting to being inferior, thus becoming masochistic and hysterical as well.

Conclusion

The preceding discussion has attempted to demonstrate the pathology inherent in "normal" femininity through illustrating its similarity to both masochism and the hysterical personality. Moreover, this pathology is invisible, because it is accepted as "normal" by the mainstream of American culture.

The woman who accepts the feminine role is placed in an impossible emotional bind since the role itself is pathological. Furthermore, the woman who rejects the feminine role is considered deviant and therefore unacceptable. This "damned if she does, damned if she does not" proposition ultimately leads many women to their own madness. A feminist analysis is suggested here as one alternative to this bind. Through such analysis women may better prepare themselves to break away from femininity and develop their own personal standards and styles of behavior.

Pauline B. Bart

Depression in Middle-Aged Women

A young man begs his mother for her heart, which a betrothed of his has demanded as a gift; having torn it out of his mother's proferred breast he races away with it; and as he stumbles, the heart falls to the ground, and he hears it question protectively, "Did you hurt yourself, my son?"—*Jewish Folktale.*

I'm glad that God gave me . . . the privilege of being a mother . . . and I loved them. In fact, I wrapped my love so much around them . . . I'm grateful to my husband since if it wasn't for him, there wouldn't be the children. They were my whole life. . . . My whole life was that because I had no life with my husband, the children should make me happy . . . but it never worked out.—*Depressed middle-aged woman*

We have all read numerous case histories in which a child's neurosis or psychosis was attributed to the mother's behavior. Only recently has the schizophrenogenic family replaced the demon double-binding schizophrenogenic mother in theories about the causes of schizophrenia. This inquiry deals with the reverse situation—how given the traditional female role, the children's actions can result in the mother's neurosis or psychosis. This is a study of depressed middle-aged women in mental hospitals. The story of one such woman follows.

The Supermother and Her Plight

Mrs. Gold is a youthful Jewish housewife in her forties. Her daughter is married and lives about twenty miles away; her hyperactive brain-damaged thirteen-year-old son has been placed in a special school even farther away. After his departure she became suicidally de-

pressed and was admitted to a mental hospital.

I asked her how her life was different now and she responded:

It's a very lonely life, and this is when I became ill, and I think I'm facing problems now that I did not face before because I was so involved especially having a sick child at home. I didn't think of myself at all. I was just someone that was there to take care of the needs of my family, my husband and children, especially my sick child. But now I find that I—I want something for myself too. I'm a human being and I'm thinking about myself.

She was dissatisfied with her marriage; their mutual concern for their son held the couple together, but when their son entered an institution, this bond was loosened, although they visited him every Sunday. "My husband is primarily concerned with only one thing, and that is making a living. But there's more to marriage than just that [pause] you don't live by bread alone." Mrs. Gold states that she is not like other women for whom divorce is simple, but she is considering divorcing her husband if their relationship does not improve. Yet, another patient I interviewed later told me Mrs. Gold had cried all the previous night after her husband came to the hospital to tell her he was divorcing her.

Although she believes her life was "fuller, much fuller, yes much fuller" before her children left, she used to have crying spells:

. . . but in the morning I would get up and I knew that there was so much dependent on me, and I didn't want my daughter to become depressed about it or neurotic in any way which could have easily happened because I had been that way. So I'm strong minded and strong willed, so I would pull myself out of it. It's just recently that I couldn't pull myself out of it. I think that if there was—if I was needed maybe I would have, but I feel that there's really no one that needs me now.

She is unable to admit anger toward her children and makes perfectionist demands on herself. "It was extremely hard on me, and I think it has come out now. Very hard. I never knew I had the amount of patience. *That child never heard a raised voice.*"

While she is proud of her daughter and likes her son-in-law, an element of ambivalence is apparent in her remarks. "Naturally as a mother you hate to have your daughter leave home. I mean it was a void there, but, uh, I know she's happy. . . . I'm happy for my daughter because she's happy." Since she had used her daughter as a confidant when the daughter was a teenager, a pattern also present among other women I interviewed, she lost a friend as well as a child with her daughter's departure. Mrs. Gold said she did not want to burden her daughter with her own problems because her daughter was student teaching. The closeness they had now was "different" since her daughter's life "revolved around her husband and her teaching and that's the way it should be." They phone each other every day and see each other about once a week.

Like most depressives she feels inadequate: "I don't feel like I'm very much." Since her son's departure she spent most of her time in bed and neglected her household, in marked contrast to her former behavior. "I was such an energetic woman. I had a big house, and I had my family. My daughter said, 'Mother didn't serve eight courses. She served ten.' My cooking—I took a lot of pride in my cooking and in my home. And very, very clean. I think almost fanatic." She considers herself more serious than other women and could not lead a "worthless existence" playing cards as other women do. She was active in fund-raising for her son's institution, but apparently without the maternal role, the role that gave her her sense of worth, fund-raising was not enough. Formerly, her son "took every minute of our lives" so that she "did none of the things normal women did, nothing." "I can pardon myself for the fact [that he was placed in a school] that I did take care of him for twelve years and he was hyperactive. It was extremely hard on me . . . I never knew I had that amount of patience."

Like most of the women I interviewed, Mrs. Gold is puritanical and embarrassed about sex.

I think anything that gives you pleasure or enjoyment, oh, is good as long as it's, uh, decent, and uh, not with us [slight embarrassment] some women I imagine do things that they shouldn't do, but I'm not referring to anything like that. It's just that I'm not that kind of woman.

Where she is at psychologically and sociologically is dramatically apparent in her response to the question in which she had to rank the seven roles available to middle-aged women in order of importance. She listed *only one role:* "Right now I think *helping my children,* not that they really need my help, but if they did I would really try very hard." Thus, she can no longer enact the role that had given her life meaning, the only role she considered important for her. Her psychiatrist had told her, and she agreed, that a paying job would boost her self-esteem. But what jobs are available for a forty-year-old woman with no special training, who has not worked for over twenty years?

Mrs. Gold combines most of the elements present in the depressed women I interviewed, elements considered by clinicians to make up the personality of involutional depressives: a history of martyrdom with no payoff (and martyrs always expect a payoff at some time) to make up for the years of sacrifice; inability to handle aggressive feelings, rigidity; a need to be useful in order to feel worthwhile; obsessive, compulsive supermother and superhousewife behavior; and generally conventional attitudes.

Why Study Mrs. Portnoy and Her Complaints?

Some of my hip friends ask, "Pauline Bart, what are *you* doing studying depressed middle-aged women?" The question itself, implying that the subject is too uninteresting and unimportant to be worth studying, indicates the unfortunate situation in which these women find themselves. But a nation's humanity may be measured by how it treats its women and its aged as well as by how it treats its racial and religious minorities. This is not a good society in which to grow old or to be a woman, and the combination of the two makes for a poignant situation. In addition, there are practical and theoretical reasons why such a study is important. Women today live longer and end their childbearing sooner than they did in the last century. In other words women are more likely now to reach the "empty-nest" or postparental stage (a term used by those investigators who do not consider this life-cycle stage especially difficult). Depression is the most common psychiatric symptom of adulthood, but, like middle age, it too has been generally ignored by sociologists.[1]

Such a study is theoretically important for several reasons. First, it can illuminate that important sociological concept, role—the concept that links the individual to society— because at this stage a woman loses certain roles and gains others; some roles contract, others expand. Moreover, there is contradictory evidence as to whether middle age *is* a problem for women. Knowing the conditions under which these women become depressed helps us explain these contradictory theories. Why is it that one woman whose son has been "launched" says, "I don't feel as if I've lost a son; I feel as if I've gained a den," while another thinks the worst thing that ever happened to her was

> when I had to break up and be by myself, and be alone, and I'm just—I really feel that I'm not only not loved but not even liked sometimes by my own children . . . they could respect me. If—if they can't say good things why should they, why should they feel better when they hurt my feelings, and make me cry, and then call me a crybaby, or tell me that I—I ought to know better or something like that. My worst thing is that I'm alone, I'm not wanted, nobody interests themselves in me . . . nobody cares.

The *best* times of her life were when she was pregnant and when her children were babies.

One clue to the differing views of middle age is that many of the problem-oriented studies are written by clinicians who are generalizing from their patients, while the studies showing that the postparental stage is no more difficult for most people than any other life-cycle stage, that many people like "disengaging," come from surveys and interviews conducted by behavioral scientists. The patients clinicians see are not a random sample of the population; they are more likely to be middle class and Jewish. This is precisely the group in which I would expect the departure of children to cause stress because the departure of children is more difficult for women whose primary role is maternal—the situation in the traditional Jewish family. If this hypothesis is correct, the difference between the two approaches to middle age may result from clinicians' generalizations about a population that is more susceptible to the stress of middle age—the Jewish mother.

There Is No Bar Mitzvah for Menopause

Émile Durkheim sheds light on the stresses that a mother may feel when her children leave. His concepts of both *egoistic* and *anomic* suicide are relevant to the problems of "the empty nest." According to Durkheim, marriage does not protect women from egoistic suicide, as it does men; rather, the birth of children reduces the suicide rate for women, and immunity to suicide increases with the "density" of the family. "Density" diminishes as the children mature and leave. Few clear norms govern the relationship between a woman and her adult children; consequently, when her children leave the woman's situation is normless or anomic. This normless state is apparent in the responses to my question, "What do people expect a woman to do after her children are grown?" Mrs. West said that while a married woman is supposed to make a home for her husband, she did not know what was expected from a divorced woman like her. "I don't think they expect anything special . . . you just mind your own business. Let them mind theirs. . . ." Another woman said, "My mission in life is completed. I have no place to go." All women ver-

bally denied the obligations of adult children toward their parents. When asked what their children owed them, all the women say "nothing," even though, in fact, they are apparently dissatisfied with their present situation and want more from their children. Much as some of the mothers want to live with their children, they cannot openly state this as a *legitimate* demand.

As financial crises lead to anomic suicides because individuals must change their expectations, women whose children leave must also change their expectations. But not only have these expectations been given legitimacy through years of interaction, there are no guidelines, no *rites de passage* for the mother herself to guide her through this transaction. *There is no bar mitzvah for menopause.*

David Riesman, following the Durkheimian tradition, notes that autonomous persons have no problems when they age, but both the "adjusted," who find meaning in their lives by carrying out culturally defined tasks, and the anomic, whom the culture has been "carrying" but then drops, have difficulties as they grow older and these external "props" are no longer available. Thus, the woman's position dramatically changes; from being overintegrated into society through the props of domestic and maternal roles, she becomes unintegrated or anomic. It is true, as Marvine Sussman claims, that urban kin networks do exist, and that the concept of the isolated nuclear family is false, since kin are turned to in time of trouble.[2] But it is precisely *because* kin, that is, children, can be called upon in time of trouble that secondary gain is possible from depression. When a woman becomes depressed, once again she gets the attention, sympathy, and control over her children she had before they left.

Durkheim constructed a theory of social control and the pathological effects of its break-down. The basis of social control is norms, the factors that control and constrain. However, Durkheim lacked an explicit social psychology, failing to posit any mechanism that could account for the manner in which these constraints are internalized. Role theory furnishes us with such a mechanism.

Role

The most important roles for women in our society are wife and mother. For example, one woman stated that getting married was the only thing she ever did that made her parents think she was worthwhile, compared to her younger brother, a doctor. The wife role may be lost at any time during the adult life cycle through separation, divorce, or widowhood, although the last is most common during old age. However, during the years between forty and fifty-nine, the maternal role is the one most frequently lost.

Two postulates from Ralph Turner's monograph, "Role Theory—A Series of Propositions," are illuminating. "Almost any stabilized role expectation contains some elements of latent feeling that the other ought to continue the same role and role behavior as before. . . . There is a tendency for stabilized roles to be assigned the character of *legitimate expectations*."[3] While ideally a mother should be flexible and change her expectations of her children as they mature, if a woman's personality is rigid, as these women's personalities are, she may expect adult children, even if married, to act largely as they did when they were children and dependent on her. To the extent that they no longer act this way, she is likely to feel resentful; since, as Yehudi Cohen suggests, a woman is not "allowed" to be hostile toward her children, she may turn the resentment inward and become depressed.[4] Turner's second postulate states: "The degree to which ego can legitimately claim the privileges of his role tends to be a function of his degree of role adequacy" since "the actor who performs his role more adequately than could be legitimately expected raises thereby the legitimate expectations of other actors. The mother, for example, by being more patient or working harder than could reasonably be expected, places a moral debt on husband and children which is not satisfied by normal adequacy."[5]

Klayne Kinder, Klayne Tsurus; Grayse Kinder, Grayse Tsurus[6]

Since the women that I predict will be most affected by the departure of their children are the supermothers, the martyrs, the self-sacrificing women who have devoted their lives to their children, they can legitimately expect their children to be more devoted to them, more considerate of them, bring them more satisfaction, than would otherwise be the case. The literature on the Jewish mother quite clearly portrays her as this type of supermother; this supermother is especially likely to be severely affected if her children fail to meet her needs, either by not making what she considers "good" marriages, or by not achieving the career aspirations she has for them, or even by not phoning her every day. The moral debt Turner refers to results in the child's feeling guilty. Therefore, if his mother does become depressed, he is particularly vulnerable, and he may expiate his guilt by becoming the "good" child again. Greenburg's best-selling satire, *How to Be a Jewish Mother*, refers to guilt as the mother's main method of social control;[7] it is no accident that his second book, *How to Make Yourself*

Miserable, begins with the sentence: "You, we can safely assume, are guilty."

Not only is the traditional Jewish mother overinvolved with or overidentified with her children, obtaining narcissistic gratification from them, but the children are viewed as simultaneously *helpless* without the mother's directives and *powerful*—able to kill the mother with "aggravation." As one depressed empty-nest woman says, "My children have taken and drained me." In a sentence completion test, she filled in the blank after the words "I suffer" with "from my children."

Overprotection and overidentification is apparent in the case of another depressed Jewish woman, Mrs. Berg, who moved from Chicago to Los Angeles with her husband four months after her daughter, son-in-law, and granddaughter did "because my daughter and only child moved here, and it was lonesome for her, you know. And I figured we had nobody," except a brother, and "you know how it is. My granddaughter was in Los Angeles. I missed them all." Mrs. Berg and her daughter are "inseparable." "She wouldn't buy a pair of stockings without me." However, the daughter had written to the hospital; in her letter she stated that much as she loved her mother, her need to be kept continually busy was destroying the daughter's own private life, and she had to enter psychotherapy herself.

Mrs. Berg thought that the worst thing that could happen to a woman of her age was for her children to leave home. "Children leaving home to me is a terrible thing, but mine didn't. She waited until she got married." When her daughter did not have a date, this supermother would say to her husband, "Oh, I don't feel so good tonight," so that she and her husband would stay home in case her daughter was lonesome.

I was one of those old-fashioned mothers. I thought that you have to stay home and take care of your child, or when she has a date see what kinda fellow she's going out with . . . today the mothers are a little bit different. We manage a building now and we could write a story—write a book about our life there. The way twenty, twenty-one and twenty-two year olds leave home. Even younger, and share an apartment in Hollywood. I—I oughta write a book on that, when I get the time and the health back.

She thought the best time for a mother was from infancy till the child was eleven or twelve "because after that they become a little self-centered . . . they think about good times and go bowling, go this and that, you know." The best thing for a woman after her children are raised is working. "Keep your hands occupied. Don't think too much. Just be occupied." Her greatest concern is her granddaughter. "It will be the greatest joy of my life when my granddaughter meets somebody and she'll get married."

Role and Self

Role and self-concept are intimately interconnected. When people are given the "Who Are You" test to get at their self-concept, they usually respond in terms of their various roles—wife, doctor, mother, teacher, daughter, and so forth. As a person moves from one life-cycle stage to another, or from one step in a career to another, he or she must change their self-concept because the relevant or significant others, the people with whom they interact, change. A loss of significant others can result in what Arnold Rose called a "mutilated self."[8] Some roles are more central for one's self-image than others; self-esteem comes from role adequacy in these more salient roles. For most people, the social structure determines which roles these are. Because the most important roles for women in our society are the roles of wife and mother, the loss of either of these roles might result in a loss of self-esteem—in the feeling of worthlessness and uselessness that characterizes depressives. For example, one woman said:

> I don't. I don't, I don't feel liked. I don't feel that I'm wanted. I don't feel at all that I'm wanted. I just feel like nothing. I don't feel anybody cares, and nobody's interested, and they don't care whether I do feel good or I don't feel good. I'm pretty useless. . . . I feel like I want somebody to feel for me but nobody does.

Another woman stated: "I don't feel like I'm doing anything. I feel just like I'm standing still, not getting anywhere."

Since mental health or a feeling of well-being is dependent on a positive self-concept, it is therefore dependent on the roles felt to be available to the individual. Women whose identity, whose sense of self, is derived mainly from their role as mothers rather than their role as wives and workers, women whose "significant others" are limited to their children, are in a difficult situation when their children leave. These women's self-conceptions must change; some of these women cannot make this change. They are overcommitted to the maternal role and in middle age suffer the "unintended consequences" of this commitment.

Integration of Psychiatric and Sociological Theory

Psychiatric as well as sociological theory is relevant to a discussion of depression. Depression is usually considered a response to loss, loss of an ambivalently loved person or object

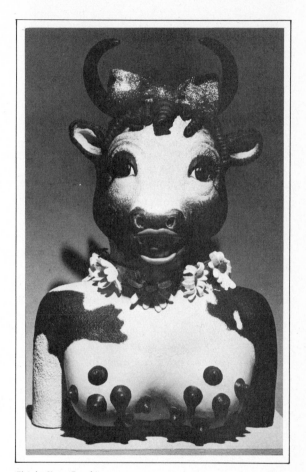

Elsie by Karen Breschi

by the psychoanalytically oriented, loss of a goal or self-esteem by ego psychologists, and loss of meaning by existentialists such as Ernest Becker.[9] Role loss is consistent with all of these approaches.

One possible way of combining the Freudian position which considers depression anger directed inward, the existential position concerning loss of meaning, and the sociological theory I am presenting may be the following.

Le Trajet by Romaine Brooks; courtesy of National Collection of Fine Arts, Smithsonian Institution

Elegy for My Mad Mother

Your pain sleeps like a lioness.
But you prowl my dreams
in your lonely dignity,
your face made terrible by bitterness.

I want to struggle—to run away—
yet my very fear strengthens your grip
*   on me.*
Something in me so passive, paralyzed,
watches, wants you angry, predatory.

Mad Mother, you were brought to the zoo
caged in a screaming ambulance.
They stripped your body & your mind,
then, "tamed," gave you back to us.

I grew old overnight.
I said I could never forgive it.
On my sixteenth birthday Daddy said
*   you were frigid,*
& from the way he said it I knew
*   it was a sin.*

You're trying so hard to be a
*   good girl now—*
you pop your Stellazine every day,
& when you get a crazy thought
you smile, so teasingly naughty.

No time or tears to waste now.
I leave you, loving who you were.
The sleeping lioness is awake now.
It is the witching, the woman's hour.

Rachel Loden

People who are intrapunitive, who turn anger inward against themselves rather than express it, are conforming to the cultural norms, especially if they are women. Since they have been "good" they expect to be rewarded. Therefore, when their husbands or children leave them their lives may seem meaningless; their world may no longer "make sense." Thus introjected anger leads to "proper" behavior which in turn leads to expectations of reward; when this reward does not materialize, but in fact tragedy strikes, they suffer from a loss of meaning and become depressed.

Clinicians use the term "defense mechanism" to describe the way an individual characteristically copes with the problems of living. This construct can be refined by the addition of sociocultural factors. There is a relationship between the utility of a defense and the person's stage in the life cycle. Withdrawal as a defense in a society valuing instrumental activism is likely to cause problems early in life. However, if one *defends by doing*, one can manage very well in our society, barring physical illness, until retirement for men or the departure of children for women. My interview data and certain comments on the hospital charts, for example, "She needed to keep busy all the time," indicated that many of the women had such defense systems. This system had been rewarded by the society at earlier stages in the woman's life cycle; however, later when many women were physically ill, and there was little

Mellaril®
(thioridazine)
for moderate to severe
mixed anxiety-depression*

too anxious to listen...
too depressed to respond

for them to do, this life style was no longer effective.

Methods: Cross Cultural, Epidemiological, and Interview

I used three kinds of data in this study: anthropological, epidemiological, and interviews with projective tests. First, in order to test the hypothesis that depression in middle-aged women was the result of the hormonal changes of menopause, I conducted a cross-cultural study of thirty societies, using the Human Relations Area Files, and intensively studied six cultures, using the original anthropological monographs (becoming the Margaret Mead of menopause).

After I completed this cross-cultural study of the roles available to women after childbearing ceased, I examined the records of 533 women between the ages of forty and fifty-nine who had had no previous hospitalization for mental illness. I used five hospitals, ranging from an upper-class private hospital to the two state hospitals that served people from Los Angeles County. I compared women who had been diagnosed "depressed" (using the following diagnoses: involutional depression, psychotic depression, neurotic depression, manic depressive depressed) with women who had other functional (nonorganic) diagnoses.

Five methods were used to overcome diagnostic biases. First, the sample was drawn from *five* hospitals. Second, "neurotic depressives"

were merged with the "involutional," "psychotic," and "manic depressives" since I suspected that patients who would be called "neurotic depressed" at an upper-class hospital would be called "involutional depressed" at a lower-middle-class hospital, a suspicion that was borne out. Third, a symptom checklist was used in the analysis of data, and I found that depressed patients differed significantly from those given other diagnoses for almost all symptoms. Fourth, a case history of a woman with both depressive and paranoid features was distributed to the psychiatric residents at the teaching hospital for "blind" diagnosis. The woman was called Jewish in half the cases and Presbyterian in the other half. The results showed no differences between the "Jews" and "Presbyterians" in number of stigmatic diagnoses since the most and least stigmatic diagnoses (schizophrenia and neurotic depression) were given to "Presbyterians." Fifth, thirty-nine M.M.P.I. profiles were obtained at one hospital and given to a psychologist to diagnose "blind." He rated them on an impairment continuum. The results supported the decision to combine psychotic, involutional, and neurotic depressives, because the ratio of mild and moderate to serious and very serious was the same for all these groups. But all the schizophrenics were rated serious or very serious.

Next, I conducted twenty intensive interviews at two hospitals to obtain information unavailable from the patients' records, to give

TABLE 6-1

CONDITIONS UNDER WHICH ROLE LOSS IS
INCREASINGLY ASSOCIATED WITH DEPRESSION

Condition	Percent Depressed	Total N (Base)
Role loss	62.0	369
Maternal role loss	63.0	245
Housewives with maternal role loss	69.0	124
Middle-class housewives with maternal role loss	74.0	69
Women with maternal role loss who had overprotective or overinvolved relationships with their children	76.0	72
Housewives with maternal role loss who have overprotective or overinvolved relationships with their children	82.0	44

the women questionnaires used in studies with "normal" middle-aged women, and to administer the projective biography test—a test consisting of sixteen pictures showing women at different stages in their life cycle and in different roles. These interviews provided an especially rich source of information. I did not read their charts until *after* the interviews so as not to have my perception affected by psychiatrists' or social workers' evaluations.

Maternal role loss was recorded when at least one child was not living at home. I considered an overprotective or overinvolved relationship present when a statement such as "my whole life was my husband and my daughter" was written on the woman's record, or if the woman entered the hospital following her child's engagement or marriage. Ratings of role loss and relationship with children and husbands were made from a case history that omitted refer-

ences to symptomatology, ethnicity, or diagnosis; high intercoder reliability was obtained for these variables (an interesting serendipitous finding was that the Jewish coders were more likely to call a parent-child relationship unsatisfactory than non-Jewish coders. The categories were refined so that this difference no longer occurred). A woman was considered Jewish whether or not she was religious if she had a Jewish mother. The attitudes and values I am discussing need not come from religious behavior. For example, Mrs. Gold did not attend religious services and was unsure of her belief in God, but she taught her daughter that "we just don't date Gentile boys," and considered herself very Jewish, "all the way through, to the core."

Results: You Do Not Have to Be Jewish to Be a Jewish Mother, But It Helps

Before embarking on the cross-cultural and epidemiological studies and the interviews and projective tests, I had made a number of hypotheses; some were confirmed and others were refuted.

Depressions in middle-aged women are due to their lack of important roles and subsequent loss of self-esteem, rather than the hormonal changes of the menopause. The cross-cultural studies indicated that women's status frequently rose at this life-cycle stage, that the two societies in which women's status decreased were similar to our own, and that, since middle age was not usually considered an especially stressful period for women, explanations of such stress based on the biological changes of menopause could be rejected.[10]

Role loss *is* associated with depression; middle-aged depressed women are more likely to

TABLE 6–2

EFFECT OF OVERPROTECTIVE OR OVERINVOLVED
RELATIONSHIPS WITH THEIR CHILDREN ON DEPRESSION
FOR WOMEN WITH MATERNAL ROLE LOSS

Relationship	Percent Depressed	Total N (Base)
Overprotective	76.0	72
Not overprotective	58.0	88

Note: No information on 83, of whom 47 were depressed.

TABLE 6–3

RELATIONSHIP BETWEEN ETHNICITY AND DEPRESSION

Ethnicity	Percent Depressed	Total N (Base)
Jews	84.0	122
Non-Jews	47.0	383

have suffered maternal role loss than non-depressed women. Because we are symbolic creatures in which the past and future are ever present, even impending role loss can bring on depression.

I had hypothesized that certain factors—intrinsically satisfying occupations; satisfactory marriages; some children still at home; and children's residence near the mother—would make it easier for the mother when her children left. I had also felt that women who suffered other role loss in addition to maternal role loss and women who had unsatisfactory relationships with the departing children would find role loss much harder to bear. However, neither of these hypotheses was confirmed. Role loss is apparently an all or nothing phenomenon since predictions based on the assumption that such loss is a matter of degree and can be compensated for by the expansion of other roles were not supported.[11]

Certain roles appear to be structurally conducive to increasing the effect of the loss of other roles (see Table 6-1). Women who have overprotective or overinvolved relationships with their children are more likely to suffer depression in their postparental period than women who do not have such relationships (see

Table 6-2). Housewives have a higher rate of depression than working women since being a housewife is really, as Parsons put it, a "pseudo occupation."[12] Not only do housewives have more opportunity than working women to invest themselves completely in their children, but the housewife role is cut down once there are fewer people for whom to shop, cook, and clean. Middle-class housewives have a higher rate of depression than working-class housewives, and those housewives who have overprotective relationships with their children suffer the highest rate of depression of all when the children leave home.

Depression among middle-aged women with maternal loss is related to the family structure and typical interactive patterns of the ethnic groups to which they belong. When ethnic groups are compared, Jews have the highest rate of depression, Anglos an intermediate rate, and blacks the lowest rate. Since in the traditional Jewish family the most important tie is between the mother and the children and the mother identifies very closely with her children, the higher rate of depression among Jewish women in middle age when their children leave is not surprising. Table 6-3 shows that Jewish women are roughly twice as likely to be diagnosed depressed than non-Jewish women; in addition there was a higher ratio of depression to other

Tod und Frau by Kathe Kollwitz; by permission of Prof. Dr. Arne A. Kollwitz, Berlin, and Kornfeld und Klipstein, Bern

mental illness among Jewish women than among non-Jewish women.

However, when family interactive patterns are controlled, the differences between Jews and non-Jews sharply diminish (Table 6-4). Although vertical frequencies show that overprotection or overinvolvement with children is much more common among Jews than among non-Jews, it is clear that *you don't have to be Jewish to be a Jewish mother*. For example, one divorced black woman, who had a hysterectomy, went into a depression when her daughter, her only child, moved to Oregon; the depression lifted when she visited her and recurred when she returned to Los Angeles.

The very small group of Jewish women whose mothers were born in the United States had a depression rate midway between that of Jewish women with mothers born in Europe and Anglo women. One of my hypotheses, that the departure of a son would be more closely associated with depression than the departure of a daughter, could not be tested because in every case when the Jewish women had sons who were only children, the sons still lived with their mothers. As one such woman told me, "My son is my husband, and my husband is my son." Such was not the case for Jewish-only daughters or for sons or daughters in non-Jewish families. (The hypothesis had to be tested with only children because of the way the cards had been punched.)

Black women had a lower rate of depression than white women. The patterns of black female-role behavior rarely result in depression in middle-age. Often, the "granny" or "aunty" lives with the family and cares for the children while the children's mother works; thus, the older woman suffers no maternal role loss. Second, since black women traditionally work, they are less likely to develop the extreme identification, the vicarious living through their children, that is characteristic of Jewish mothers. In addition, there is no puritanical idea in black culture equivalent to that in Anglo and Jewish cultures, that sex is evil and primarily for reproductive purposes or that older women are inappropriate sex objects. The famous black blues singers—women such as Bessie Smith—reached the height of their popularity when they were middle-aged.

Of course, one cannot entirely overlook the possibility that the low black depression rate simply reflects the black community's greater unwillingness to hospitalize depressed black women. Depressives are not likely to come to the attention of the police unless they attempt suicide. Therefore, if the woman or her family do not define her condition as psychiatric, she will remain at home. Only a prevalence study can fully test any hypothesis about the black family.

There were too few Mexican families in the sample to test my hypothesis that Mexican women would have a lower depression rate because Mexican women have larger families and the extended family is very much in operation; in addition, there is a shift in actual, though not in formal, power to the mother from the father as they become middle-aged.

Interviews

The interviews dispelled any of my doubts about the validity of inferences from the hospital charts that these women were overprotective, conventional, martyrs. Even though they were patients and I was an interviewer and a stranger, one Jewish woman forced me to eat candy, saying, "Don't say no to me." Another gave me unsolicited advice on whether I should remarry and to whom, and a third said she would make me a party when she left the hospital. Another example of the extreme nurturant patterns was a fourth patient who insisted on caring for another patient who had just returned from shock while I was interviewing her. She also attempted to find other women for me to interview. The vocabulary of motives invoked by the Jewish women generally attributed their illness to their children. They complained about not seeing their children often enough. The non-Jewish women were more restrained and said they wanted their children to be independent. All the women with children, when asked what they were most proud of, replied "my children"; occasionally, after this, they mentioned their husbands. None mentioned any accomplishment of their own, except being a good mother.

TABLE 6-4

RELATIONSHIP BETWEEN DEPRESSION AND OVERPROTECTION OR OVERINVOLVEMENT WITH CHILDREN FOR JEWISH AND NON-JEWISH HOUSEWIVES WITH MATERNAL ROLE LOSS

Relationship	Jews		Non-Jews	
	Percent Depressed	Total N (Base)	Percent Depressed	Total N (Base)
Overprotective	86.0	21	78.0	23
Not overprotective	75.0	8	60.0	25

Note: No information for 8 Jews, of whom all were depressed and for 38 non-Jews, of whom 21 were depressed.

Two of the Jewish women had lived with their children and wanted to live with them again; their illness was precipitated when their children forced them to live alone. However, living with children was not a satisfactory arrangement for the women in the epidemiological sample, since the few women having this arrangement were all depressed. For example, one woman complained: "Why is my daughter so cold to me? Why does she exclude me? She turns to her husband . . . and leaves me out. I don't tell her what to do, but I like to feel my thoughts are wanted."

Table 6-5 shows the conventionality and rigidity of the women interviewed. In middle age it is necessary to be flexible so that new roles can be assumed. The mother role, "helping my children," is most frequently ranked first or second, although only one of the seven women whose children were all home ranked it first, and one ranked it second. Since it is difficult to help children who are no longer home, women who value this behavior more than any other are in trouble; they are frustrated in behaving in the way that is most important to them. Items that were not chosen are as interesting as those that were; only one woman

By Bülbül, from *I'm Not for Women's Lib . . . But*, Arachne Publishing, Mountain View, Ca.

TABLE 6–5

FREQUENCY OF RANKED CHOICE

Role	1	2	3	4	5	6	7
Being a homemaker	5	—	3	2	2	—	—
Taking part in church, club and community activities	—	1	3	4	1	—	—
Companion to husband[a]	2	2	1	—	1	—	1
Helping parents	1	1	—	1	1	—	—
Sexual partner	—	1	2	—	—	1	—
Paying job	1	3	—	—	—	1	—
Helping children	4	5	2	1	1	—	—

[a]Not including the two unmarried women who ranked this item first.

TABLE 6–6

RESPONSE TO OLD AGE PICTURE

Response	In Story	In Inquiry
Positive	1	1
Negative	6	4
Denial	2	—
Neutral	2	1
Not used	9	—

ranked "helping my parents" first. Her hospitalization followed her mother's move to Chicago after she had remodeled her apartment so that her mother could live with her. No woman listed "being a sexual partner to my husband" first, and only one woman listed it second. Three married women did not include it in their ranking, indicating its lack of importance or their embarrassment or rejection of this role. It is apparent that although eight of the women worked, the occupational role was not important to them; three did not even list it. In short, the women view as important precisely the roles of homemaker and mother that become contracted as the women age. Conversely, they do not consider as important the roles that could be expanded at this time: the sexual partner role, the occupational role, and the organizational role (taking part in church, club, and community activities).

The women interviewed were given the projective biography test—sixteen pictures showing women in different roles and at different stages in their life cycles. The clinical psychologist who devised the test analyzed the protocols "blind" without knowing my hypothesis. He said they were "complete mothers," showing total identification with the maternal role. I content-analyzed the responses to the sexy picture, the pregnancy picture, the old age picture and the angry picture; Table 6-6 shows the responses to the old age picture.

The old age picture shows an old woman sitting in a rocking chair in front of a fireplace. The nine women who did not include this picture in their stories of a woman's life do not want to grow old and inactive. Only one woman used the picture in the story and responded positively to it. Two used it, but denied the aging aspects of it. An example of such denial is the following response: "Here she is over here sitting in front of the fireplace, and she's got

bülbül © 73

her figure back, and I suppose the baby's gone off to sleep and she's relaxing." This woman interpreted every picture with reference to a baby.

Six women did not like the picture (two responses were uncodable). One woman who used the picture in the story said, "And this scene I can't stand. Just sitting alone in old age by just sitting there and by some fireplace all by herself [pause] turning into something like that. And to me this is too lonely. A person has to slow down sometime and just sit, but I would rather be active, and even if I would be elderly, I wouldn't want to live so long that I wouldn't have anything else in life but to just sit alone and you know, just in a rocking chair." Another woman who was divorced and had both her children away from home said, "This could look very much like me. I'm sitting, dreaming, feeling so blue." When she chose that as the picture not liked, she said, "Least of all, I don't like this one at all. That's too much like I was doing. Sitting and worrying and thinking . . ."

In the inquiry period, one more gave a positive response, four gave a negative response, and one response was uncodable. One empty-nest woman who was divorced and living alone did not use the picture in her story. After listing eight other pictures which were like her life, she said, "I don't like to point to that one." One person liked this picture best, but did not perceive the woman as old, while

> **Gesture**
>
> It is a gesture I do
> that grew
> out of my mother
> in me.
>
> I am trying to remember
> what she
> was afraid to say
> all those
>
> years, fingers folded
> against her mouth,
> head turned away.
>
> Beverly Dahlen

six women included this picture among the ones they liked least.

How about Men?

Does this theory explain depression in men? I think it does. Men who have involutional psychosis are usually in their sixties, the retirement age; these are probably men whose occupational roles were "props." Men whose identity comes from their work role will also be depressed on retirement. For example, the director of admissions at the teaching hospital reported that it was not unusual for army of-

The creativity of woman finds its expression in the sphere of living, not only in her biological functions as mother but in the shaping of life generally, be it in her activity as educator, in her role as companion to man, as mother in the home, or in some other form. The development of relationships is of primary importance in the shaping of life, and this is the real field of feminine creative power.

Emma Jung

Wild Women Blues

*I've got a different system
And a way of my own,
When my man starts kicking
I let him find another home.
I get full of good liquor
And walk the street all night,
Go home and put my man out
If he don't treat me right,
Wild women don't worry,
Wild women don't have the blues.*

*You never get nothing
By being an angel child,
You better change your ways
And get real wild.
I want to tell you something
I wouldn't tell you no lie,
Wild women are the only kind
That really get by,
'Cause wild women don't worry,
Wild women don't have the blues.*

Ida Cox

ficers to have involutional depressions on retirement. Rafael Moses and Debora Kleiger's study of involutional depression in Israel found loss of meaning a factor among old pioneers who believed "that the values so dear to them were rapidly disappearing. Current ideals and expectations were now alien to them and the sense of duty and sacrifice as they knew it seemed to exist no longer. They felt different, isolated and superfluous."[13]

What Is to Be Done?

It is very easy to make fun of these women, to ridicule their pride in their children and concern for their well-being. But it is no mark of progress to substitute Mollie Goldberg for Stepin Fetchit as a stock comedy figure. These women are as much casualties of our culture as the children in Harlem whose I.Q.'s decline with each additional year they spend in school. They were doing what they were told to do, what was expected of them by their families, their friends, and the mass media; if they deviated from this role they would have been ridiculed (ask any professional woman). Our task is to make their sacrifices pay off, though in a different way from what they expected. As their stories are told, other women will learn the futility of this life style.

Two psychoanalysts, Therese Benedek and Helene Deutsch, state that menopause is more difficult for "masculine" or "pseudo masculine" women. Benedek describes the "masculine" woman as one whose "psychic economy was dominated—much like that of man's—by strivings of the ego rather than by the primary emotional gratifications of motherliness."[14] Deutsch states that "feminine loving" women have an easier time during climacterium than

*Women are impaled on the cross of self-sacrifice. Unlike men, they are
categorically denied the experience of cultural supremacy, humanity,
and renewal based on their sexual identity—and on the blood sacrifice,
in some way, of a member of the opposite sex. In different ways, some
women are driven mad by this fact. Such madness is essentially an
intense experience of female biological, sexual, and cultural castration,
and a doomed search for potency.*

Phyllis Chesler

Exercises in Assertiveness

Purpose: To enhance our ability to be assertive

Directions: For the following three exercises each person needs a partner.

1. Sit facing one another. One person is designated as the trainee, the other, the trainer. The goal is for the trainer to evoke a response from the trainee. The first phase is accomplished by the trainer simply watching the trainee to make sure that the trainee does not break eye contact or make a facial or bodily movement. When a break occurs, the trainer simply informs the trainee it has occurred and states what she (or he) saw as a break. The second phase is when the trainer tries to provoke the trainee to "break," either by verbal harrassment or body movement (actual physical contact or sudden movement toward the eyes are not allowed). This may be done for as long as 15–30 minutes until the trainee is desensitized. Reverse roles and repeat the exercise.

2. One person is the sender, the other, the receiver. The sender asks a question, and the receiver responds but does not answer the question. The sender must persist until she (or he) gets an answer. If and when the receiver answers, the sender still asks the question to practice asking in the context of emotional discomfort. Continue for 10–15 minutes. Reverse roles and repeat the exercise.

3. Again, one person is the sender, the other, the receiver. The sender says *no* repeatedly, beginning with a fairly low volume and gradually increasing the volume of her voice until she is shouting. The receiver simply listens. Reverse roles and repeat the exercise. (Another variation is to say *yes* instead of *no*.)

What did you experience from these exercises? What feelings emerged? Record your experience and share it with the class.

---

do "masculine-aggressive ones." While she believes in the desirability of "good sublimations" in addition to erotic and maternal qualities, "if their social and professional interests have taken excessive hold of them, these women are threatened in the climacterium by the danger that I call Pseudomasculinity."[15] However, my data show that it is the women who assume the traditional feminine role—who are housewives, who stay married to their husbands, who are not overly aggressive, in short who "buy" the traditional norms—who respond with depression when their children leave. Even the M.M.P.I. masculine-feminine scores for women

---

from **Monster Poem**

Oh mother, I am tired and sick.
One sister, new to this pain called feminist
  consciousness
for want of a scream to name it, asked me last
  week
"But how do you stop from going crazy?" . . .

And I will speak less and less and less to you
and more and more in crazy gibberish you
cannot understand:
witches' incantations, poetry, old women's
  mutterings,
schizophrenic code, accents, keening, firebombs,
poison, knives, bullets, and whatever else
will invent this freedom. . . .

May we go mad together, my sisters.
May our labor agony in bringing forth this
  revolution
be the death of all pain.

May we comprehend that we cannot be stopped.

May I learn how to survive until my part is
  finished.
May I realize that I
        am a
          monster. I am
    a
    monster.
I am a monster.

And I am proud.

                              Robin Morgan

---

at one hospital were one-half a standard deviation *more* feminine than the mean. These findings are consistent with Cohen's theory of depression; he considers depression, in contrast to schizophrenia, an "illness" found among people too closely integrated into the culture.[16]

Ernest Becker's theory of existential depression among middle-aged women is borne out because these martyr mothers thought that by being "good" they would ultimately be rewarded. When there was no pot of gold at the end of the rainbow, their life pattern seemed meaningless. As one woman said:

I felt that I trusted and they—they took advantage of me. I'm very sincere, but I wasn't wise. I loved, and loved strongly and trusted, but I wasn't wise. I—I deserved something, but I thought if I give to others, they'll give to me. How could they be different, but you see, they be different, but you see those things hurted me very deeply and when I had to feel that I don't want to be alone, and I'm going to be alone, and my children will go their way and get married—of which I'm wishing for it and then I'll still be alone, and I got more and more alone, and more and more alone.

The norms of our society are such that a woman is not expected to "fulfill" herself through an occupation, but rather through the traditional feminine roles of wife and mother. More than that, she is not *allowed* to do so. The great discrimination against "uppity women"—women professionals—the cruel humor, not being taken seriously, the lower pay scale, the invisibility (literally and metaphorically), make it suicidal for a woman to attempt to give meaning to her life through her work. (We are told that women are not hired because they put their personal life first, and leave with the first available man. I think the sequence is reversed. It is only after she learns what her situation really is, after she has been treated as a nonperson, that she turns to a more traditional role. If she's lucky she still has that option.)

Until recent years, a common theme of inspirational literature for women, whether on soap operas or in women's magazines, was that they could only find "real happiness" by devoting themselves to their husbands and children, that is, by living vicariously through them. If one's satisfaction, one's sense of worth comes from other people rather than from one's own accomplishments, one is left with an empty shell in place of a self when such people depart. On the other hand, if a woman's sense of worth comes from her own accomplishments, she is not so vulnerable to breakdown when significant others leave. This point is obscured in much of the polemical literature on the allegedly castrating, dominant American female who is considered to have lost her femininity.

It is, after all, *feminine* women, the ones who play the traditional roles, not the career women, who are likely to dominate their husbands and children. This domination, however, may take more traditional female forms of subtle manipulation and invoking of guilt. If, however, a woman does *not* assume the traditional female role and does not expect her needs for achievement or her needs for "narcissistic gratification," as psychiatrists term it, to be met vicariously through the accomplishments of her husband and children, *then* she has no need to dominate them since her well-being does not depend on their accomplishments. In an achievement-oriented society it is unreasonable to expect one sex not to have these needs.

The women's liberation movement, by pointing out alternative life styles, by providing the emotional support necessary for deviating from the ascribed sex roles, and by emphasizing the importance of women actualizing their *own selves*, fulfilling their *own* potentials, can help in the development of personhood for both men and women.

For Further Reading

Agel, J. 1971. *The Radical Therapist.* New York: Ballantine Books.

*****Chesler, P.** 1972. *Women and Madness.* New York: Doubleday.

*****Lederer, W.** 1968. *The Fear of Women.* New York: Harcourt Brace Jovanovich.

Mander, A. V. and **Rush, A. K.** 1974. *Feminism As Therapy.* New York: Random House.

Miller, J. B. 1973. *Psychoanalysis and Women.* New York: Penguin.

Mitchell, J. 1974. *Psychoanalysis and Feminism.* New York: Pantheon.

*****Szasz, T. S.** 1961. *The Myth of Mental Illness.* New York: Harper & Row.

Tennov, D. 1975. *Psychotherapy: The Hazardous Cure.* New York: Abelard-Schuman.

Weissman, M. M. and **Paykel, E. S.** 1974. *The Depressed Woman.* Chicago: Univ. of Chicago Press.

Toward Human Liberation

The liberation of women is all-encompassing. The category of women cuts across racial and class boundaries. Moreover, because sex roles are reciprocally defined, men must change as women do—thus human liberation includes men's as well as women's liberation. In addition, feminists point out that children, another oppressed group, must also be liberated. The liberation of all the members of a society ultimately leads to the liberation of the society itself.

Though many views of the future do not include feminist perspectives, there is some basic agreement among the several feminist views (see Appendix B). The point of view in this chapter, however, is that of the cultural feminist. According to one such feminist (Firestone, 1970), radical change must occur simultaneously on sexual, cultural, and economic levels of society if it is to occur successfully on any one level. In other words, to liberate women and men (and children) from sex roles (sexual revolution), cultural and economic revolutions must also take place. Another way of viewing liberation is that the emergence of Female* psychology involves not only transforming the self and changing interpersonal relationships but requires a drastic change in the social, political, and economic organization of the whole society.

Transformation of the self is difficult because of internalized oppression and the effects of "slave psychology" (see chapters entitled "Oppression of the Self" and "Women and Psychotherapy"). However, internalized oppression and the social conditions that reinforce it daily must be transcended in order to create a new psychology of the self and to establish institutions (or alter existing ones) that support this new self.

Such a radical transformation depends on changing the underlying motivational structure of both society and individuals as described by Slater (quoted in the Introduction). From a cultural feminist viewpoint, it involves creating a new basis for power. Power based on Male principles requires domination and control of another's being and will; power based on the Female principle implies loving and sharing with another being.

The focus of the articles presented in this chapter is change that occurs on personal as well as societal levels. Feminist therapy is included in this chapter rather than in "Women and Psychotherapy" because it is hoped that feminist therapy can assist women (and men) in the human struggle toward both internal and external liberation.

Feminism itself as therapy for much of women's "dis-ease" is discussed by Annette Brodsky and Hannah Lerman in their articles on feminist therapy. Brodsky describes the therapeutic effects of consciousness-raising (CR) groups, and Lerman defines feminist therapy as a combination of the influence of CR groups and humanistic thought. Both agree that the essential elements for positive change are the discovery and expression of anger, the validation of "crazy" feelings, an awareness of the social context (that the personal is the political), and the encouragement of self-nurturance. Two important issues raised regarding feminist therapy are men's role in this process and the goal of creating feminists through feminist therapy.

Since most of what has been written about women and mental health focuses on the dis-

---

*Use of upper case here connotes the psychology defined by women's own experience as distinguished from the lower case term (female) which connotes men's view of women's psychology. See Introduction for detailed explanation.

An-drog-y-ny: *n. from the Greek roots, andro and gynos, meaning "male" and "female"; a condition under which the characteristics of the sexes—and the human impulses expressed by men and women—are not rigidly assigned.*

---

order and lack of health in women, Marcia Perlstein's description of a healthy woman provides a more complete picture. Although it is difficult if not impossible for women to be healthy in this society (since the society itself is not healthy), it still may be helpful for women to have a positive description of a healthy woman, especially since current standards for mental health are different for men and women and have been developed from the male point of view. One of the dangers in presenting such a standard of mental health is that like present standards, it may become oppressive to women. Women have always been compared against external standards rather than being allowed to be their true selves. Another potential danger is that women tend to exhibit a "hysterical" conformity to standards and may imitate this description instead of relying on themselves as the source of their own experience.

A few men are beginning to become aware of the unhealthy aspects of their role as well, realizing that it limits their capacity for humanness. In the context of "men's liberation," both Jack Sawyer and the Berkeley Men's Manifesto describe some of the negative aspects of being men in this society. On a personal level, Sawyer feels that men are limited in their opportunity to play, to show affection, to be weak, or to develop their true selves. He views domination and competition as other negative aspects of the male sex role and sees them as the psychological basis for worldwide exploi-

tation. Although in current sex-role practices, men may lose in competition with other men, at least they can "win" in their relationships with women. The system of sex roles oppresses all. If the women's movement achieves its goals, equality will exist among men as well as between women and men.

Whether men and women are equally oppressed by sex roles is an issue for debate, however. Moderate feminists would probably want to support this position, although it is difficult to determine the extent to which this view may be motivated by identification and sympathy with the oppressor (a common characteristic of minority group consciousness, as discussed in the chapter "Oppression of the Self"). White feminists of more radical leanings may have as much anger at white men labeling themselves "oppressed," as black women feel toward white women for doing the same.

Elaine Walster and Mary Anne Pate's article presents equity theory to explain why women are hard on other women. Walster's theory, which has received much support and validation (Walster, Bercheid, and Walster, 1973), is that people act to preserve equality, though it may be maintained either actually or psychologically. According to her theory, both oppressor and oppressed experience distress, but the oppressed experience much greater distress since they don't have the material benefit that the oppressor does. This theory explains why men belittle women and minimize women's

What is necessary is the ability to call the shots exactly as they are being played; to see our life in all its complexity; to recognize that sometimes we are the victims and sometimes men are the victims, but neither of us is always the victim. . . . What has made men our oppressors is their inability to face the contradictions, but what will allow us to become strong is our increased ability to face the contradictions. That, to me, is feminism carried to its magnificent conclusion.

Vivian Gornick (Ms, July 1972)

---

suffering while refusing to take responsibility for their own actions. It also explains why women justify their own exploitation and inequity especially when they cannot retaliate or demand restitution—it is "less degrading to deny or justify injustice than to face up to one's humiliating position."

Because the psychology of women is based on social, political, cultural, and economic conditions, an analysis of women's current position and how men maintain their position of power is necessary to find ways to change society or create a new and better one. Such an analysis is provided in the article by Barbara Polk. Ac-

cording to her, changes will occur by de- or re-socializing oneself, changing interpersonal interactions, resocializing others, changing male dominance of institutions, and building alternative institutions.

Overall, the articles in this chapter follow from the analysis presented in this book: that the emergence of Female psychology and a balancing of Female and Male principles is necessary to make ourselves happier, healthier human beings (whether male or female) and to redirect the future to make for a more human society.

Annette M. Brodsky

The Consciousness-Raising Group as a Model For Therapy with Women

By now, almost everyone is familiar with a sense of growing unrest among women with many of their traditional sex role stereotypes. There is no evidence that women are more like each other psychologically than men are like each other. In fact, the bulk of evidence on gender role differences points out that the differences between individuals of each sex are greater than differences between men and women (Mischel, 1966). Yet, for a woman in particular, her sex determines to a large degree her future roles in life, dictating limitations on the options for her development, regardless of intellect, activity level, or physical and emotional capacity (Epstein, 1970; Amundsen, 1971). This role confinement has been psychologically frustrating to many women and is a major basis for identification as feminists of many of the therapists on the Feminist Therapist Roster of the Association for Women in Psychology (Brodsky, 1972). Epidemiological studies (Gurin et al., 1960; Chesler, 1971) reveal that women complain more of nervousness, impending breakdown, and attempts at suicide (and they are beginning to achieve this goal more often). They are more frequently seen in therapy, and more likely to be hospitalized for their mental disorders. As Chesler (1971) points out, women are the most "treated" category in our society. The Task Force on Family Law and Policy (1968) concluded that the married woman, in the traditional feminine role of housewife, has the most difficulty psychologically, and the discrepancy between married women and other groups increases with the years of marriage. Bart (1971) noted that depression in middle-

aged women was most likely to occur when there was an overly strong commitment to the mother role so that other forms of individual identity were lacking when the children left home.

Directing women into narrowly confined roles is a long socialization process that starts with the toys and books of young children that encourage specific social models that differentiate instrumental and expressive tools of development (Bardwick, 1971). The realization that women are not to make a significant impact upon the world, that their role in life is not only different from that of their brothers, but qualitatively inferior in terms of the rewards of the society in which they live, occurs in vivid and demonstrable form by high school years. Horner (1970) demonstrates dramatic evidence of the suppression of self-esteem and self-actualization in adolescent girls. The motive to avoid success becomes a powerful inhibition on the academic achievement of girls. The fears of loss of femininity associated with being competitive, the social disapproval of intellectual females, and the actual denial in bright women that a woman is capable of high levels of achievement, were all themes repeatedly related in projective stories of Horner's subjects. Sixty-five per cent of the sample of females, compared to less than ten per cent of the males, showed this phenomenon of avoiding success.

The identity crisis is perhaps most noted in the married, middle-class women who have been over-educated and under utilized. The gulf separating the life style of the upper-middle class housewife and her mate is perhaps wider than any other strata in our society. By definition these women are happy. They have husbands, families, and household help. Why don't they feel fulfilled? Freidan (1963) refers to the uneasiness and disillusionment of the bored middle-class housewives as the "problem that had no name." These women continued to live out their proscribed roles in spite of vague, undefined needs for more variability and needs for more opportunity to reveal individual talents that were often not consonant with the roles of "kinder, kuche, and kirche" (children, kitchen, and church).

With the re-awakening of the feminist movement in the 60's, women began to investigate the problem with no name. Bird (1968) discovered what women in the working world suspected, but dared not voice aloud. That is, when a woman leaves the stereotyped roles, she fights a battle of subtle and often blatant discrimination and resentment. The battle is a lonely one for those who can overcome the initial fears of loss of femininity, social disapproval and disdain of men and women alike for daring to compete in the male domain.

Consciousness-raising (C-R) groups grew out of both the sense of restless constraint noted by Freidan and the awareness of being different and alone noted by Bird. These feelings were finally exposed as a common occurrence and C-R groups developed a very important aspect of the women's movement, the awareness of women that others shared these same self-doubts.

The small group structure of the women's movement was ideally suited to the exploration of personal identity issues. The technique of heightening self-awareness by comparing personal experiences was as basic to the continuance and solidarity of the movement as any other tactic. Women found themselves eliciting and freely giving support to other group members who often were asserting themselves as individuals for the first time in their lives. They gained strength from members who confronted others, and they learned to ask for their own individual rights to adopt new roles and express new behaviors.

The individual changes that occurred in the context of C-R groups were unique from many therapeutic techniques that women had previously experienced. Many C-R group members had previously been in therapy (Newton & Walton, 1971). Many others had considered the entire mental health profession as implying illness and abnormality and had no contact with individual or group experiences until they joined a C-R group.

By education and training, women had been encouraged to be conformists and passive. In their traditional roles, they had been isolated from each other and from events in the larger political and economic world beyond their narrowly confined psychological space. The C-R group offered a sense of closeness or intimacy with other women as opposed to a media-produced sense of competition and alienation from each other. The development of the concept of sisterhood arose as a shared understanding of the unique problems of being a woman in a man's world.

Movement women (Allen, 1971) and professionals (Newton & Walton, 1971) have begun to study consciousness-raising groups for their perspectives on the social movement, and on exploration of new life styles. The present analysis focuses on the psychological impact, with particular reference to the issue of identity crises. In terms of contrast with therapy groups, the C-R group starts with the assumption that the environment, rather than intrapsychic dynamics, plays a major role in the difficulties of the individuals. The medical model of abnormal behavior based on biological, innate causes is not acceptable to these groups. They are struggling to redefine these very concepts that have been seen as assigning women to a helpless patient role, destined as victims of their biological nature to behave in certain ways (Weisstein, 1969; Chesler, 1971).

Women in C-R groups do not react in traditional female interaction patterns that are commonly seen in all-female therapy groups. For example, ask a therapist who has dealt with all-female groups of mothers of patients, institutional groups, etc. The typical response is that women are catty, aggressive, competitive, and much tougher on each other for digressions, than they are toward men.

In C-R groups, women are confronted with acting as individuals. They are encouraged to examine their uniqueness apart from their roles toward others such as wife, mother, or secretary. It appears easier for a woman to reveal taboo subjects and feelings such as not liking the caring of young children, wishing one had never married, feeling more intelligent than one's boss or husband, or being tired of boosting his self-esteem at the expense of her own. Finding that not only are these feelings not abnormal, but common experiences among other women, can have an almost religious conversion reaction in some women (Newton & Walton, 1971).

A sense of trust in other women and a closeness based on common problems that arise from external sources as well as internal deficiencies, serves to bind the groups into continuing, relatively stable units. The attrition rate for the groups I and my colleagues have encountered as well as those studied by Newton & Walton (1971) appear to be lower than those of typical voluntary therapy groups, or sensitivity groups. They appear to move to an intimacy stage rapidly and maintain a strong loyalty. Dropouts occur early, often due to conflict with male relationships that are threatened by changes in dependency behaviors.

The therapeutic processes that occur in these groups are akin to assertive training, personal growth groups, achievement-oriented training or simply self-development groups. In assertive training, the key technique seems to involve the role models provided by other group members. Women as models are more convincing than male authoritarian leaders for whom the assertive role is a cultural expectation. Likewise, achievement needs are raised more readily in an all-woman group. The identification with other women who achieve is more real than transference to a model outside the situation of direct discrimination experiences. In this sense, like Synanon, Recovery, Inc., or Alcoholics Anonymous, in C-R groups some experienced members give strength to the neophyte.

I have seen faculty women return to long forgotten dissertations and take advanced courses, and housewives who have confronted their husbands for more rights or domestic help. Others went through divorces from marriages that had been security traps, and childless women stood up for their right to refuse to have children simply because others thought they should.

One difficulty with the groups comes at a stage when the women try to transfer their new found behaviors outside the group. In a parallel fashion to the sensitivity group member who expects others outside the group to respond as positively as the group, C-R group members often find that the group understands, but the outside world does not change to correspond with the groups' level of awareness. It is at this stage that women tend to become angry with their employers, lovers, and old friends for continuing to act in chauvinistic, stereotyped patterns. A new response from a woman may be either ignored, misunderstood, patronizingly laughed at, or invoke a threatened retaliatory confrontation. Unlike the individual in a more traditional assertive training situation, these women are behaving often in new ways that society usually does not condone. In frustration, women may overreact and as a result, provoke just the response they fear to get. For example, loud demands for better treatment on the job by a previously meek woman may well meet with a backlash response leading to termination of her entire job.

This type of frustration often leads to a period of depression, either of individuals or the group as a whole. They feel that while they can become aware of their situation and make individual changes, they cannot make much of an impact on the outside world. There is little outside reinforcement to carry on their motivation. At this later dropout stage, the faculty woman gets pregnant instead of completing her dissertation, the potential divorcée decides that security is more important after all, the frustrated housewife announces that "Joe thinks this group is making me unhappy and he wants me to quit," or the graduate student cannot find time because she is up nights typing her boyfriend's thesis.

If these regressive tendencies are weathered by the group, the most crucial, and often the most effective, stage of the group experience develops. The women plan to actively alter the environment in a realistic manner to make it more compatible with the developing growth needs of the members. The direction of the group turns from personal, individual solutions

(except for occasional booster-shot sessions as the need arises) to some sort of group action. Actions that groups may take vary according to talents, age and needs. They might consist of organized protests, political lobbying, educational programs, or missionary goals of helping to organize other groups to expand the population of the enlightened. The C-R group works to give a sense of social as well as personal worth to the members, and as a by-product, serves to help modify an environment insensitive to the needs of an increasingly growing population of restless women.

The premise of this paper is that the C-R groups of the women's movement have implications for the treatment of identity problems of women in therapy. The following ways are suggested possibilities for transferring the C-R groups dynamics to use in individual therapy. First, in working with women on identity issues, therapists should be aware of the increasingly wider range of valid goals for healthy functioning of women in terms of roles and personality traits (Maccoby, 1971). For example, exuberance should not be interpreted as aggression because the behavior occurs in a female. Second, a good therapist is aware of the reality of the female patient's situation. Many factors are beyond her control. She cannot realistically expect to attain achievement comparable to a man, unless she has greater intellectual and/or motivational abilities. Discrimination does exist (Amundsen, 1971; Bernard, 1971; Astin, 1969; Epstein, 1970; Bird 1968, etc.). Because of this discrimination, the importance of encouragement through assertive training and independence from others, including the therapist, is paramount to counteract the many years of discouragement through subtle, cultural mores. The therapist can serve as supporter and believer in the patient's competence through the

If we women are ever to pull ourselves out of the morass of self-pity, self-destruction and impotence which has been our heritage for so long as we can remember, then it is perhaps even more important that we be supportive of each other's achievements and successes and strengths, than it is for us to be compassionate and understanding of each other's failures and weaknesses.

Anselma dell'Olio

---

regressive, dropout stages and finally, in the face of individual frustrations he or she can recognize the need for some direct and meaningful activity related to improvment of the societal situations.

Working with women's C-R groups offers a number of insights to a therapist for the particular problems women face in trying to resolve the difficulties of living in a world that revolves around men's work. For example, those women who report patterns of intrusive male behavior often appear to be oversensitive to slights and minor brushoffs. C-R group experiences help women to confirm the reality of such slights, rather than deny their existence or pass them off as projections. For a man, such incidents can be overlooked as exceptional, and not integrated into the broader experience of being taken seriously and accepted as a thinking individual. For a woman, the experience is more a rule, than an exception (unless she is an exceptional woman). Her sensitivity to such slights comes out of an awareness of the situation, and a concomitant frustration in being unable to defend herself in the situation without appearing pompous, uppity, or paranoid.

The accumulation of experiences of being interrupted in conversations, having her opinions ignored or not taken seriously can severely affect a woman's feelings of competence and self-worth. Her desire to be assertive, or to make an impact on the environment is continuously weakened by this lack of affirmation of her self by others.

There are therapists who maintain that women who act insecure or inferior in such situations are doing so in order to get secondary gains from such postures (using feminine wiles) and her verbalizations of a desire for independence or responsibility are not genuine. Such therapists probably do not understand that without role models or encouragement from the environment, these women have no real choice in not accepting the only reality they have been indoctrinated to believe about the capabilities of their sex.

Other major themes that some therapists are apt to misjudge or overlook when dealing with women clients can be briefly mentioned here. Unaware therapists still tend to consider marriage uncritically as a solution for women's problems without realizing that, like with men, divorce or no marriage may often present the best available alternative for the individual. When a woman proposes such a solution, the therapist may become more concerned with her non-traditional life style than with her personal feelings in living out such a style.

Some therapists also automatically assume that a woman's career is secondary to her mate's career. The conflict over "having it both ways," by wanting a career and family is still seen as the wife's burden, not the husband's also. Unusual patterns of division of household tasks, child care, etc. are no longer stigmas that label individuals as deviant. Therapists have been guilty of producing iatrogenic disorders in women who felt comfortable with what they

LOOK CINDERELLA...MAYBE YOU SHOULD SKIP THE BALL,
AND JOIN A CONSCIOUSNESS RAISING GROUP INSTEAD.

By Bülbül, from *I'm Not for Women's Lib...But*, Arachne Publishing, Mountain View, Ca.

were doing until the therapist suggested that they were selfish, unreasonable, or pointed out how no one expected them to accomplish so much and they would be loved and accepted without this unrealistic drive to compete.

Perhaps related to the foregoing is the frustration women have experienced with therapists who can empathize readily with a man who is stifled by a clinging, nagging wife, but who interprets the same complaint from a woman as her being cold and unfeeling for not responding affectionately to an insecure, demanding husband. The crucial issue surrounding such misunderstandings is an unconscious tendency for many therapists to have a double standard for men and women in mental health and adjustment (Broverman, et al., 1970). This attitude restricts their capacity to allow their clients a free expression of the various available roles. Women, after all, have needs for self-esteem, independence, expression of anger and aggression; and men have needs for security, affection and expression of fear and sorrow. While, at present, men may have more diverse models in our society for the development of an adequate masculine role, women's models have been restricted for the most part to housewives or the more narrow traditional feminine occupations.

Perhaps the strongest message to be seen from the success of these C-R groups is that women are capable of using other women as models. Identification of women with role models of their own sex has been largely limited to the traditional homemaker roles or the feminine occupations such as teaching and nursing. The acceptance of more varied roles and personality traits in women will help to integrate a larger portion of women into the "mentally healthy" categories.

Until this happens to a greater extent, perhaps, as Chesler (1971) suggests only women should be therapists for other women. On the other hand, if therapists must have the same experiences as their patients in order to help them, we would be a sorry lot indeed. The important lesson for clinicians, male and female alike, is to make a particular effort to study the facts and reasoning behind the women's movement. We help neurotics, psychotics, children, handicapped, any group of which we are not a member by keeping educated with the current literature written by those in close touch with large numbers of that particular population. In the same vein, any male therapist who has not kept abreast of current theory and issues relating to women, is treating from a position of ignorance. The sample of women in his personal life does not provide sufficient clinical data or theory on which to base therapy. Women have a great need today for allies in their struggles to alter a constricting environment. Legal and political allies are not sufficient. Understanding, enlightened therapists are necessary if we want to avoid psychological casualties of today's transitional cultural changes.

Hannah Lerman, Ph. D.

What Happens in Feminist Therapy

Despite the uniqueness of each and every psychotherapeutic relationship we do find generalizations which can differentiate among schools of psychotherapeutic thought (Fiedler, 1950; Sundland & Barker, 1962). For me, one of the major problems in describing the process of feminist therapy is that it cuts across the usual categories. I know feminist therapists who are Gestalt in terms of the theoretical orientation; I knew behaviorists; I know eclectics, and I even know therapists who are truly feminist therapists who continue to use some psychoanalytic theoretical conceptions in order to explain what they are doing for themselves. Techniques are quite variable and, in my view, relatively unimportant. What most clearly differentiates feminist therapy for me from other types of psychotherapy is a difference in philosophy. My topic is not what feminist therapy *is* but what happens in it. I have to detour briefly into what it is, in my view, before I can intelligently talk about what happens in it.

From the feminist end, feminist therapy is an outgrowth of the theory and philosophy of consciousness-raising, a highly specific technique originally unique to the women's movement which has demonstrated itself to be highly effective in helping women differentiate between that which is purely personal and that which is external and therefore social and political rather than psychological and also in helping women get support from other women in defining themselves for themselves (Kirsh, 1974).

From the therapy or professional end, feminist therapy seems to me to be an outgrowth of eclectic humanistic thought and represents a logical extension of humanistic thinking into the awareness of sex-role issues. I have already indicated that feminist therapists seem to come from all persuasions. I don't think I have met a feminist therapist however, who has not been influenced by humanist principles, regardless of the basis of her theoretical approach to psychotherapy.

Members of Feminist Psychological Associates, the group I am affiliated with in Los Angeles, at first wondered if we indeed were doing anything different than any other humanistically oriented psychotherapist would do. We felt so natural about what we were doing that it was sometimes difficult to imagine that other people weren't doing exactly the same thing. We learned about our difference when we spoke with other humanistically oriented therapists. In extending humanistic principles into the area of sex-role proscriptions, a logical extension really, we found that we were doing something distinctly different from those other humanists who have not explored this area and have left its assumptions unexamined.

On the other hand, within the last year or so, as I have begun to meet and talk to other therapists who label themselves feminist therapists, I have found that we share a common philosophy and even a common language. What is happening is truly exciting in that it seems that therapists throughout the country are independently arriving at the same concepts and changing their modes of interaction with clients. It is truly a grassroots occurrence without a "name" leader. It does feel as though there is a commonality about what feminist therapy is and what happens in it.

I have already said that I view the specific techniques used as much less important than is the philosophy which determines the attitudes with which techniques are used. An example of what I mean that is only tangentially related to feminist therapy but which I think most of you can relate to is the difference between gestalt therapy techniques used in a humanistic and caring way and used in an authoritarian and insensitive way, both of which I have personally experienced.

The first major philosophical position which I see in feminist therapy relates to how the client is viewed vis-à-vis the therapist. The therapist does not take the position of expert about her client. She, on the other hand, views the client as essentially competent and certainly as the person who is most knowledgeable about her own feelings, thoughts and needs. From this perspective, the therapist does not presume to tell the client about herself, diagnose the client or prescribe treatment. Any commitment for psychotherapy arises from an interchange in which the therapist does not assume that her opinions have any greater weight than those of the client. The therapeutic stance, certainly non-authoritarian, could perhaps be related to a true consumerism. The client is seeking certain services which the therapist may be able to offer. A contract is often arrived at, about what the nature of the services (i.e., content, length of the therapy, etc.) will be. Contrary to customary therapeutic practice, the client is encouraged to shop for a therapist, utilizing her impressions and her own judgment to determine if a particular therapist is indeed likely to meet her needs. Frequently, because of the orientation of society and her own socialization, the woman client may at the start feel uncomfortable with the assumption of the competence of her own judgment and attempt to make the therapist contradict this assumption and relate to her instead from a more typical authoritarian expert position. This is an easy pitfall and it bears watching against.

The assumption of competence goes hand in hand with the assumption of personal power. The therapist constantly, at the start of therapy as mentioned above and throughout therapy, attempts to help the woman client validate her own experience rather than to undercut this process through the use of the authority position which the therapist can so easily assume. Women have been trained not to believe that they can have any psychological power, that is, power to determine their own values, needs, actions, thoughts. Instead, they frequently accept that others possess the power to determine this for them, rather than they themselves.

Another important philosophical position which plays a large part in feminist therapy is the tenet of the feminist movement that "the personal is political." We help the woman client to differentiate between what she has been taught and has accepted as socially appropriate and what may actually be appropriate for her. Women have been taught to view difficulties arising out of their socially imposed roles as results of their own personal problems. Helping them differentiate themselves from social proscriptions and roles is likely in itself to go a long way in helping them increase their self-esteem and confidence in themselves. In helping women make these distinctions, feminist therapists are operating very differently from traditional therapists. Where the more usual therapy encourages clients to introspect and thereby learn to know themselves better, feminist therapy helps its clients look outward as well as inward and differentiate clearly what belongs

from **The Common Woman Poems**

VII. Vera, from my childhood

the common woman is as common as the best of bread
and will rise
and will become strong—I swear it to you
I swear it to you on my own head
I swear it to you on my common
woman's
head

Judy Grahn

Positive Strokes

Purpose: To experience receiving acknowledgment and support

Directions:

1. In a group (6–10 people), say good things about yourself for two minutes. The group then gives unqualified feedback by making only positive remarks. Each member of the group takes a turn at this experience. What did you experience? How difficult was it to make positive remarks about yourself and to hear positive remarks from others?
2. Respond to the following questions either by writing your responses or by choosing a partner and taking turns talking to each other.
   (a) What have you done for which you have not yet been acknowledged?
   (b) Is there anyone to whom you want to communicate that?
   (c) Who else do you need to communicate that to?

What did you experience during the exercise? Record your experience and share it with the class.

ful here: I saw a woman who had obtained a Ph.D. in chemistry from a highly renowned program but who had not been able to obtain an academic position despite trying, for three years. She came to me because she was depressed. She learned, after she had been seeing me, about recommendation letters written by her advisor which contained a strangely derogatory statement about her. After we discussed this, it began to become clear to her that while the letters may have had something to do with her job-hunting problems, she was reacting also as if what her advisor said about her was true because he said it. Some of her bad feelings were related to not being able to get the kind of job she wanted. Some, in addition, revolved around her feelings of inadequacy as represented by the fact that she didn't have a job and therefore must be incapable of getting one on her own merits. Distinguishing between the reality of her situation and her feelings about it was highly significant.

Besides enhancing the woman's self confidence and sense of personal power, separating the internal and the external also serves to help a woman learn that she is not crazy. I have learned that most women believe deep down that they are crazy, that is, that their intuitions, their thoughts, their feelings, their needs are crazy. Indeed, in a world in which sensitivity to emotional nuances is discouraged, the expression of feelings downgraded and rationality upheld as the supreme ideal, woman *are* crazy in that sense and directly or indirectly men

to the society and is being imposed and what is internal. This process enhances the individual's sense of her personal power, which I have already mentioned. Perhaps an example is use-

> *The right to vote, or equal civil rights, may be good demands, but true emancipation begins neither at the polls nor in courts. It begins in woman's soul.*
>
> Emma Goldman (1911)

---

especially, but other women as well, are fond of telling them just that in subtle and not so subtle ways. When a therapist helps a woman distinguish more clearly the inside from the outside, there is frequently the equivalent of a sigh of relief. It is extremely important to help a woman validate her feelings, either directly as her therapist, or by serving as a referral service whereby she can get into contact with other women and/or organizations that are dealing with the issues which are most significant for her. Her self-doubt, while internal, is usually a direct result of her training and the circumstances she is in and is likely to lessen as her sense of power and self-definition increases.

The process of assuming one's own power also brings up anger. Anger and dealing with it seems to me to be an essential part of feminist therapy. The experience of it is one of the things that the feminist therapist often has to validate, mostly because few others will. In much of our society, one of the things that others find most difficult to deal with is anger, and there are myriad ways available to discount the feeling and the person feeling it. Owning one's own anger is, I think, for women, an important, perhaps even an essential, step toward personal power. It is especially tricky just because of the effect women's anger has on others, her intimates and her employers. It is, for example, difficult for a truly self-respecting woman to continue to function as a secretary in most places. Difficult and painful choices have to

Dancers by Catherine Bussinger

be made if, and this is usual, her job is economically essential to her. Often, too, similar choices have to be made in the personal realm.

The anger, or often rage, begins at the point where differentiation is being made between the external and the internal. It wells up at the awareness of what the woman has allowed to be done to her without protest. By traditional standards, it is irrational and out of proportion. Its power scares the woman who is beginning to experience it as much as it scares and offends others. The point eventually is to help a woman channel it so it can work for her, rather than repress it or deny it. The interim phase can,

---

Unlearning to Not Speak

Blizzards of paper
in slow motion
sift through her.
In nightmares she suddenly recalls
a class she signed up for
but forgot to attend.
Now it is too late.
Now it is time for finals:
losers will be shot.
Phrases of men who lectured her
drift and rustle in piles:
Why don't you speak up?
Why are you shouting?
You have the wrong answer,
wrong line, wrong face.
They tell her she is womb-man,
babymachine, mirror image, toy,
earth mother and penis-poor,
a dish of synthetic strawberry icecream
rapidly melting.
She grunts to a halt.
She must learn again to speak
starting with I
starting with We
starting as the infant does
with her own true hunger
and pleasure
and rage.

Marge Piercy

model of how women and men develop in our society (Wyckoff, 1973). Using the language of transactional analysis modified somewhat, this model, to explain briefly, suggests that in our society, women are encouraged to overdevelop the nurturing parent function and underdevelop the adult while the reverse is true for men. Both sexes are taught to overdevelop their critical parent. This is comparable to Super Ego or Top Dog. Women highly develop the Intuitive Child, but it is in the service of the Nurturing Parent. Men don't. Both sexes have limited access to their Free Child.

Back to the Nurturing Parent in women. They have been taught, and this training is hooked up with their perceptions of themselves as adequate, that their primary role is nurturing. This means nurturing husband or lover, children, the neighbors and cats and dogs where appropriate. In short, it means nurturing everybody but themselves. In feminist therapy, we encourage them to turn this nurturance around and give some of it to themselves: Be selfish. Be self loving. Choose themselves over others. Allow themselves to do things that make them feel good. The doing of this, i.e., caring enough about themselves to take goodies for themselves, obviously is related to enhancing their sense of self-esteem and worth.

Along with all of these things, modelling also takes place in feminist therapy. The therapist by being who she is can serve as a model for the kind of woman who knows herself and her psychological boundaries, who relates in a human female way and can express her own gentleness along with her own definiteness. Not least, she can share with the client in very important ways about what it means to be a woman in this society. There is a potential bond arising out of a communality of experiences. For this last reason, I think feminist women

however, be hellish—for the woman, for her family, for the therapist. Many women, when they first feel angry, despair about ever relating again with an even emotional tone. It's difficult but it *is* possible.

Another significant aspect of the therapy is encouraging self-nurturance. I am referring to a concept that comes out of the radical therapy

therapists have more to offer other women at this time. I know male feminists and think there is a place for male feminist therapists. I think it is mainly working with men, although perhaps not exclusively.

There are distinct women's issues, which are not usually discussed in individual therapy or groups with men. I first became aware of this for myself when I attended my first all-women's group as a member. Menstruation and childbirth are the first that come to mind. If you made a list, however, it could go all the way from techniques of masturbation to feelings aroused when you change your name when you marry or divorce and include dealing with seduction, rape concerns, physical power issues, being whistled at or otherwise psychologically molested, body image, etc. I'm referring to all the psychological experiences that are unique to women and ignored by men and not mentioned by women around men.

One of the questions Annette Brodsky presented in setting up this symposium was: Is the object of the therapeutic intervention to make clients feminists? Perhaps it may sound to you at this point that my answer would be yes. I would really say yes and no. It would be yes in the sense that what I have said so far is certainly all related to issues of feminist consciousness, by which I mean awareness of the external oppression and the attempt to gain self-definition within it. If that is the sole meaning of feminist, yes indeed I want my clients to become feminists. If you mean that they have to shift their life patterns and goals and espouse the specific tenets of feminism there my answer is no. Women come to therapy with all degrees and types of commitments already established: to specific people, families, ideologies, jobs, life styles and values. The goal is to help them become the best person they

The Lock by Leonor Fini; reprinted by permission of the artist

can be, within the limits of their personal circumstances and the patterns of society in general. If that means they need to become active feminists, fine; if not, fine too.

As a feminist therapist, I have, I think become more acutely aware than ever that therapy has limits and that all human pain is not directly accessible to psychological intervention. We cannot change the world in our offices and

---

For Witches

today
i lost my temper.

temper, when one talks of metal
means strong,
perfect.

temper, for humans,
means angry
irrational
bad.

today i found my temper.
i said,
you step on my head
for 27 years you step on my head
and though I have been trained
to excuse you for your inevitable
clumsiness
today i think
i prefer my head to your clumsiness.

today i began
to find
myself.

tomorrow
perhaps
i will begin
to find
you.

Susan Sutheim

change, you help them become aware of emotional costs and alternatives. Sometimes they make choices you yourself would not make. Sometimes the past influence of society and prior choices already made limit the real possibilities in the present.

Another question that Annette asked was: Can a man be a feminist therapy client? I define feminism as related to a questioning of traditional sex role assumptions with the aim of helping people be people without categorization. From this perspective, of course a man can be a feminist therapy client, and a feminist therapist as I've already mentioned. And since so few male therapists now have the kind of awareness necessary, I feel that women feminist therapists have a great deal to offer men, if they choose to. They may not want to. I have a few male clients now after not having had any for a few years while I was working on my anger toward men. The assumptions of respect, enhancing personal power, etc. hold with men too. The process brings up different issues though, most noticeably the need to help men get in touch with and develop their tender side and feelings in general and let go of all the responsibility involved in being rational and functional and adult at all times.

As I have worked in feminist therapy, it has become more and more real to me and more and more distinct. It differs greatly from traditional therapies and cuts loose from some standard professional assumptions. It is a new field, created as much, I think, by the demand for it as by anything. While some feminists are negative both toward therapists and therapy in general and toward professional women who identify themselves as feminist therapists, feminist therapy belongs to the women's movement and is, I think, a significant outgrowth of our day and time.

many women are already inexorably caught in miserable circumstances when we see them. This awareness has contributed greatly to my feminism. I am referring primarily to economic circumstances and I don't think I have to detail them for you. There are other, sometimes ethical, sometimes familial bonds. If you start with a premise of respect, you don't make people

Marcia Perlstein

What Is a Healthy Woman?

Mental health is a relative notion. For women today it is paradoxically both more elusive and more accessible. The often asked questions—how healthy can women be in a sick society? how healthy can women be given their acculturation? and how healthy can women be given the sexism they will experience?—these are important, but it is possible to put them aside and to ask a different set of questions, queries which encourage us to look inward and to recognize, given a cultural context and a shared history with other women, that each of us has a personal history and our own set of daily and long-term choices. It is in this arena that health is relative—we can feel better about ourselves today than yesterday, better this year than last year.

We can feel as good about ourselves as possible, given the conditions under which we live and try to grow. We are not the externals we must contend with; we are separate individuals. That doesn't mean we don't have responsibility for what's beyond us. We can develop to a point where we are readier to work either independently or collectively to influence our cultural context. But if large-scale political action is to have any meaning at all we must first look inward—toward self-acceptance and a belief in our ability to change and grow.

I would now like to talk about an ideal model toward which one can work. This model assumes neither perfection nor equanimity. It takes into account adversity, regression, negative as well as positive emotions. But of major importance is the notion that making a place

for ourselves and developing process tools for letting go of difficulties as well as learning from them is possible for each of us. And it is within a large personal context of relative health that this is possible. Attempting to hide, minimize, or deny aspects of ourselves is far more destructive than owning and dealing with them. So with that in mind, on to the model.

I see a healthy woman as a complex composite of attitudes, behaviors, and values formerly divided between men and women. An individual healthy woman would be both tough and tender, nurturing and responsive to the nurturance of selected others, alternatingly intellectually rigorous and sensitive. She would have ready access to a wide range of her own feelings including anger, fear, love, joy, pain, etc. She'd be comfortable with herself when that was a choice, but also able to connect with others when that seemed desirable. She would choose the basis on which she connected, the degree of intimacy which she was prepared to involve herself in, and the form of intimacy. She would be clear enough with herself that although she could, at times, identify with others, she would remain separate, would know who she was. A healthy woman would define and facilitate her own productivity; she would work toward maximizing her effectiveness. She would know what supports she needed and reach for the appropriate resources when that seemed desirable. She would by no means be "perfect," whatever that word means. She would accept her total self and work toward changing those aspects which she felt uncom-

Sun Circle by Marie Johnson

fortable with. She would see herself simultaneously as unique yet universal. Let me deal with each of these areas in greater detail.

Access to Herself

A healthy woman would have maximum access to her feelings and needs. In allowing herself to experience a wide range of feelings she would do so without becoming a single emotion, without staying immersed in one aspect of herself to the exclusion of all others.

For example, it is possible to give up a dramatic view of emotion as a style of life (not as an occasional, spontaneous activity, but as an all-encompassing way of experiencing the world). Many women feel that when they are in pain they *are* pain; that that will always be their condition; that they have no choice and are destined by forces outside themselves to continue feeling miserable. It is possible instead to experience painful moments, figure out what is inside oneself and what is outside, see what one has the power to influence and what may be oppressing from outside, and choose to act accordingly. One may choose to continue experiencing the pain for awhile, but recognize that that is a conscious choice. One may choose to band together with others to change our collective condition or may explore other options. In any case, it is possible to think that long-term, deep pain is not very romantic or desirable without, on the other hand, aspiring to totally remove pain from one's life. It is a part of the entire range of emotions which need to be available. Pain is merely one example. I deeply believe that a healthy woman can as easily let go of a feeling as she can experience it in the first place—both are very important.

In having optimum access to herself, a healthy woman is also in touch with her needs; these include sensual, sexual, intellectual, practical and others. She tries to take care of her needs according to her own preferences and knows how to give herself pleasure in a variety of ways. A healthy woman involves herself in specific activities in this regard. Some of these, such as masturbation may involve transcending old superstitions and taboos. She can be with herself in a variety of ways depending upon needs and desires. She is aware that she provides her own sustenance, takes care of herself in basic and major ways and turns to others when she chooses. When a woman truly gets close to herself, she will paradoxically be able to be closer to others when she makes that choice.

Finally, a healthy woman with a good deal of access to herself has a heavy dose of self acceptance, a positive identity (a good sense

Women whose psychological identities are forged out of concern for their own survival and self-definition, and who withdraw from or avoid any interactions which do not support this formidable endeavor, need not "give up" their capacity for warmth, emotionality, and nurturance. They do not have to forsake the "wisdom of the heart" and become "men." They need only transfer the primary force of their "supportiveness" to themselves and to each other—and never to the point of self-sacrifice. Women need not stop being tender, compassionate, or concerned with the feelings of others. They must start being tender and compassionate with themselves and with other women. Women must begin to "save" themselves and their daughters before they "save" their husbands and their sons, . . . [and] the whole world.

Phyllis Chesler

---

of who she is and who she is not). There will be slippage and regression, moments of self doubt, times when one's self gets temporarily confused with another's. However, a healthy woman will recognize these regressions for what they are and take pride in moving them.

The most basic index in this regard may sound like a truism, but for me, intellectually giving lip service to this notion and beginning to experience it on a gut level, have been two different things—a healthy woman deeply, abidingly and overwhelmingly values her own health. She behaves constructively for herself and when she sees her health threatened by either her own self-destructive tendencies or threats from outside herself she moves quickly in favor of her own health. She also looks at signals that all may not be well, tries to understand and deal with them. These may include insomnia, headaches, stomach tension, etc. Thus, the relationship between physical and mental health is clear to a woman actively involved in maintaining access to herself and acting in her own behalf.

Relation to Her Own Work

A healthy woman will see herself as special and important and will therefore regard what she does as important. She will value her own aspirations, try to do something which she finds meaningful and which contributes to her feelings of worth. She will see her own work in the world, her own identity as important as anyone else's. She will pursue ways for getting the emotional and technical support to enable her to carry out the work. Ideally the way in which she earns a living will have some meaning for her, will be part of her work. If this is not possible (considering the economic and cultural realities) she will pursue her work avocationally until the time that her livelihood and interests can be integrated. This may involve exploring and even beginning alternatives to dominant institutions and businesses.

A healthy woman allows herself to dream, reaches towards her dreams in one way or another. She may be comfortable working independently, she may be comfortable working collectively. However, she feels self-confident enough not to have to work competitively. This does not mean that she allows herself to be victimized, merely that she knows her strengths and doesn't have to measure herself next to others. She values first and foremost herself and sees her achievements as part of that self and ideally as part of some broader set of goals outside herself (these will be dealt with in greater depth in the context of global connections).

Connection with Others

A healthy woman sustains herself, gives some meaning to her own existence and looks to others for added meaning and support, but not for basic survival. She is not insatiably needy because she can fulfill her own needs, while

from **From the Prison House**

Underneath my lids another eye has opened
it looks nakedly
at the light

that soaks in from the world of pain
even when I sleep

Steadily it regards
everything I am going through

and more . . .

it sees
the violence
embedded in silence

This eye
is not for weeping
its vision
must be unblurred
though tears are on my face

its intent is clarity
it must forget
nothing

Adrienne Rich

others merely add to her central core. Her connections with others will be direct expressions of her connection to herself. If her access to herself is maximal, her relations with others will probably be deeply mutual and meaningful. She will both be able to give emotionally and to be given to; she will relate sexually according to person and gender preference as another means of experiencing herself and allowing herself to experience another. In her sexual as in emotional experiences she will both know how to ask for pleasure and how to respond to another's needs.

She will be aware of her own needs for both connections and space. No matter how intimately she relates to another she will always serve a sense of where she ends and another person begins. As close as she gets to another, she will not be swept into another's psychological weather.

She will be able to entrust those whom she cares about most with some of her deepest feelings including her anger as well as her love. She will be able to openly express caring, as well as pain in relation to another. In her friendships, she will also be open and responsive to others' emotional places. She will be able to experience in friendships the richness of both similarities and differences among people she chooses to get close to. Similarities will be acknowledged and differences respected. People who really care for each other can agree either to negotiate or can agree to disagree. The old simplistic choice of changing yourself or changing another will only be a small part of a healthy woman's repertoire. She will never change for another; she'll only change when she chooses to; when she experiences some pain or dissatisfaction with an aspect of herself.

Global Connectedness

The three sections preceding this one would all be meaningless without a woman's having some sense of her connections with other women and with all humanity. My definition of a healthy woman includes social responsiveness to the conditions one lives in and to the people around one. It would not be enough to have access to oneself, work which was meaningful and important and relationships which were special and enduring. A part of one's larger self would still be missing. A healthy woman sees herself as part of the whole historical and present flow; as involved with the many social, political, and economic injustices which we are all part of. Knowledge is not enough; this information needs to be acted upon simultaneously to being garnered and understood. As in one's lifework, ideally one's social responsiveness will be integrated with interest and strength, will involve cooperative rather than competitive efforts and will encompass new and viable patterns of behavior. I strongly believe that nobody can define for another what her social responsibilities are. An individual healthy woman must look at her own situation and determine for herself the specific ways in which she chooses to connect to the larger, total picture. The righteousness often associated with women with deep political involvements is often just as narrow as the view held by women who don't see their destiny as being related to that of others.

While it is true that every individual woman must define for herself her own course of action in regard to others, some sort of action is necessary. These notions can't be relegated to a later date, to someone with more time, to a different issue. While it is true that no individual woman can fight every fight, it is also true that ostrich tactics are exceedingly unhealthy. They border on the psychologist's favorite term called "denial." Thus, conditions must be dealt with in one's own way, according to one's own rhythms but they can't be ignored.

Implications

The therapy practiced by and with women who feel some affinity for the model just described is somewhat different from that which we were trained for. However, these implications form

Giving Birth to Myself by Ann Leda Shapiro

another article in itself. The model informs notions of goals and point of view (with emphasis on health rather than pathology); role relationships (lateral, though non-mutual, rather than hierarchical); technique (eg. careful balance between nurturance and challenge, cautious use of identification, etc.); mode (mixture of individual and group contexts); practitioner (trained lay personnel as well as credentialed ones).

Jack Sawyer

On Male Liberation

Male liberation calls for men to free themselves of the sex-role stereotypes that limit their ability to be human. Sex-role stereotypes say that men should be dominant; achieving and enacting a dominant role in relations with others is often taken as an indicator of success. "Success," for a man, often involves influence over the lives of other persons. But success in achieving positions of dominance and influence is necessarily not open to every man, since dominance is relative and hence scarce by definition. Most men in fact fail to achieve the positions of dominance that sex-role stereotypes ideally call for. Stereotypes tend to identify such men as greater or lesser failures, and in extreme cases, men who fail to be dominant are the object of jokes, scorn, and sympathy from wives, peers, and society generally.

One avenue of dominance is potentially open to any man, however—dominance over a woman. As society generally teaches men they should dominate, it teaches women they should be submissive, and so men have the opportunity to dominate women. More and more, however, women are reacting against the ill effects of being dominated. But the battle of women to be free need not be a battle against men as oppressors. The choice about whether men are the enemy is up to men themselves.

Male liberation seeks to aid in destroying the sex-role stereotypes that regard "being a man" and "being a woman" as statuses that must be achieved through proper behavior. People need not take on restrictive roles to establish their sexual identity.

A major male sex-role restriction occurs through the acceptance of a stereotypic view of men's sexual relation to women. Whether or not men consciously admire the Playboy image, they are still influenced by the implicit sex-role demands to be thoroughly competent and self-assured—in short, to be "manly." But since self-assurance is part of the stereotype, men who believe they fall short don't admit it, and each can think he is the only one. Stereotypes limit men's perception of women as well as of themselves. Men learn to be highly aware of a woman's body, face, clothes—and this interferes with their ability to relate to her as a whole person. Advertising and consumer orientations are among the societal forces that both reflect and encourage these sex stereotypes. Women spend to make themselves more "feminine," and men are exhorted to buy cigarettes, clothes, and cars to show their manliness.

The popular image of a successful man combines dominance both over women, in social relations, and over other men, in the occupational world. But being a master has its burdens. It is not really possible for two persons to have a free relationship when one holds the balance of power over the other. The more powerful person can never be sure of full candor from the other, though he may receive the kind of respect that comes from dependence. Moreover, people who have been dependent are coming to recognize more clearly the potentialities of freedom, and it is becoming harder for those who have enjoyed dominance to maintain this position. Persons bent on maintaining dominance are inhibited from developing themselves. Part of the price most men pay for being dominant in one situation is subscribing to a system in which they themselves are subordinated in another situation. The alternative is a system in which men share, among themselves and with women, rather than strive for a dominant role.

In addition to the dehumanization of being (or trying to be) a master, there is another severe, if less noticed, restriction from conventional male sex roles in the area of affect, play, and expressivity. Essentially, men are forbidden to play and show emotion. This restriction is often not even recognized as a limitation, because emotional behavior is so far outside the usual range of male activity.

Men are breadwinners, and are defined first and foremost by their performance in this area. This is a serious business and results in an end product—bringing home the bacon. The process area of life—activities that are enjoyed for the immediate satisfaction they bring—are not part of the central definition of men's role. Yet the failure of men to be aware of this potential part of their lives leads them to be alienated from themselves and from others. Because men are not permitted to play freely, or show affect, they are prevented from really coming in touch with their own emotions.

If men cannot play freely, neither can they freely cry, be gentle, nor show weakness—because these are "feminine," not "masculine." But a fuller concept of humanity recognizes that all men and women are potentially both strong and weak, both active and passive, and that these and other human characteristics are not the province of one sex.

The acceptance of sex-role stereotypes not only limits the individual but also has bad effects on society generally. The apparent attractions of a male sex role are strong, and many males are necessarily caught up with this image. Education from early years calls upon boys to be brave, not to cry, and to fight for

The Phenomenon by Remedios Varo; reprinted by permission of Walter Gruen

what is theirs. The day when these were virtues, if it ever existed, is long past. The main effect now is to help sustain a system in which private "virtues" become public vices. Competitiveness helps promote exploitation of people all over the world, as men strive to achieve "success." If success requires competitive achievement, then an unlimited drive to acquire money, possessions, power, and prestige is only seeking to be successful.

The affairs of the world have always been run nearly exclusively by men, at all levels.

*Where a system of oppression has become institutionalized it is
unnecessary for individuals to be oppressive.*

Florynce Kennedy

The *Generals* by Escobar Marisol; Albright-Knox Art Gallery, Buffalo, N.Y.;
gift of Seymour H. Knox

It is not accidental that the ways that elements
of society have related to each other has been
disastrously competitive, to the point of oppressing large segments of the world's population. Most societies operate on authoritarian
bases—in government, industry, education, religion, the family, and other institutions. It has
been generally assumed that these are the only
bases on which to operate, because those who
have run the world have been reared to know
no other. But women, being deprived of power,
have also been more free of the role of domina-
tor and oppressor; women have been denied
the opportunity to become as competitive and
ruthless as men.

In the increasing recognition of the right of
women to participate equally in the affairs of
the world, then, there is both a danger and a
promise. The danger is that women might end
up simply with an equal share of the action
in the competitive, dehumanizing, exploitative
system that men have created. The promise is
that women and men might work together to
create a system that provides equality to all
and dominates no one. The women's liberation
movement has stressed that women are looking
for a better model for human behavior than
has so far been created. Women are trying to
become human, and men can do the same.
Neither men nor women need be limited by
sex-role stereotypes that define "appropriate"
behavior. The present models for men and
women fail to furnish adequate opportunities
for human development. That one-half of the
human race should be dominant and the other
half submissive is incompatible with a notion
of freedom. Freedom requires that there not be
dominance and submission, but that all individuals be free to determine their own lives
as equals.

Berkeley Men's Center Manifesto

We, as men, want to take back our full humanity. We no longer want to strain and compete to live up to an impossible oppressive masculine image—strong, silent, cool, handsome, unemotional, successful, master of women, leader of men, wealthy, brilliant, athletic, and "heavy." We no longer want to feel the need to perform sexually, socially, or in any way to live up to an imposed male role, from a traditional American society or a "counterculture."

We want to love ourselves. We want to feel good about and experience our sensuality, emotions, intellect, and daily lives in an integrated way. We want to express our feelings completely and not bottle them up or repress them in order to be "controlled" or "respected." We believe it requires strength to let go and be "weak." We want to enjoy masturbating without feeling guilty or that masturbation is a poor substitute for interpersonal sex. We want to make love with those who share our love, male or female, and feel it should not be a revolutionary demand to be either gay, heterosexual, or bisexual. We want to relate to our own personal changes, motivated not by a guilt reaction to women, but by our growth as men.

We want to relate to both women and men in more human ways—with warmth, sensitivity, emotion, and honesty. We want to share our feelings with one another to break down the walls and grow closer. We want to be equal with women and end destructive competitive relationships between men. We don't want to engage in ego battles with anyone.

We are oppressed by conditioning which makes us only half-human. This conditioning serves to create a mutual dependence of male (abstract, aggressive, strong, unemotional) and female (nurturing, passive, weak, emotional) roles. We are oppressed by this dependence on women for support, nurturing, love, and warm feelings. We want to love, nurture, and support ourselves and other men, as well as women. We want to affirm our strengths as men and at the same time encourage the creation of new space for men in areas such as childcare, cooking, sewing, and other "feminine" aspects of life.

We believe that this half-humanization will only change when our competitive, male-dominated, individualistic society becomes cooperative, based on sharing of resources and skills. We are oppressed by working in alienating jobs, as "breadwinners." We want to use our creative energy to serve our common needs and not to make profits for our employers.

We believe that Human Liberation does not stem from individual or social needs alone, but that these needs are part of the same process. We feel that all liberation movements are equally important; there is no hierarchy of oppression. Every group must speak its own language, assume its own form, take its own action; and when each of these groups learns to express itself in harmony with the rest, this will create the basis for an all embracing social change.

As we put our ideas into practice, we will work to form a more concrete analysis of our oppression as men, and clarify what needs to be done in a socially and personally political way to free ourselves. We want men to share their lives and experiences with each other in order to understand who we are, how we got this way, and what we must do to be free.

Elaine Walster and Mary Ann Pate

Why Are Women So Hard on Women?

The coercion of men and women into stereo-typed roles has profound effects on their personalities and attitudes. Once they become aware of the rigid role typing that operates in our society, and conclude that such discrimination is unjust, even more profound and explosive reactions are likely to occur.

Psychological evidence tells us a great deal about how prolonged discrimination affects those involved in inequitable relationships. James Baldwin has argued that the exploiter of other men eventually ends up by suffering more than those he exploits for, in the end, the exploiter loses his humanity. While we cannot say who suffers most in an inequitable relationship, we do know that one crucial outcome of continued inequity is the denigration of the victim both by himself and the exploiter. The reader can best gain an understanding of how this process occurs if we first review the findings which have emerged from equity theory research.

Equity Theory/Theoretical Underpinnings

If it is to survive, a society must develop some system for equitably dividing up community resources. Citizens must agree on rules for deciding who gets what, and these rules must be acceptable to almost everyone.

Although every society eventually reaches a decision about how to apportion resources "equitably," the definition of what is "equitable" varies enormously among groups. Some societies believe that hard work or a distinguished family name entitles one to reward.

Others believe that the ability to sing and tap dance are important assets.

Regardless of the exact system one adopts, it is fairly easy to socialize individuals to behave in an equitable way. In a variety of societies, we find that when an individual inadvertently receives much more reward than he knows he deserves, he will voluntarily share some of his bounty with his deprived friends. His deprived friends, on the other hand, are quick to demand that he give them a fair share of the resources he controls.

Although individuals generally behave equitably they do not inevitably do so. With some regularity, presumably well socialized individuals simply refuse to follow the rules and intentionally exploit others. Or, individuals exploit others unintentionally. Sometimes they are unjust because they are ignorant of equity rules. Sometimes groups within the society disagree about what is fair. Individuals are denounced for being unjust regardless of what they do. Consider the elderly employer who has paid blacks and women less than other workers for the past 35 years. Until now, "No one objected"—at least not to his face. Now he discovers that government agencies insist that such inequities are unfair and illegal. Blacks and women seem to share the government's perception; many old-timers do not. No matter how the employer resolves his dilemma, he will be left with the disturbing feeling that he is behaving and has been behaving inequitably.

Psychologists have discovered that when individuals realize they are in an inequitable relationship—regardless of the reason—both the exploiter and the victim respond in a standard way: First, they *both* experience distress. The more inequitable the relationship, the more acutely distressed they become. The victim usually labels his reaction as anger; the harm-doer labels his feelings as guilt. Regardless of what they call their reaction, the consequences are the same—both the exploiter and the exploited become acutely uncomfortable.

There are only two ways in which they can restore balance to their relationship and eliminate their distress: (1) They can restore actual equity to their relationship, or (2) They can restore psychological equity.

Restoration of Actual Equity

Participants can restore actual equity by acknowledging that an inequity exists and by reallocating resources to eliminate the injustice. For example, the underpaid and overworked secretary (let us label her the "victim"), may be encouraged to "take Monday off" or be given an especially large Christmas bonus by her guilty boss (label him the "exploiter"). Or the secretary may take the initiative. She may demand a raise. (If she has an intractable boss, she may console herself by stealing from the company.)

Sometimes the exploiter is unwilling to give up his undeserved benefits, and the victim is not clever or powerful enough to force him to act fairly. Under such circumstances, the evidence indicates that both participants will distort reality in an effort to convince themselves that their inequitable relationship is, in fact, equitable.

Man's creativity in distorting reality is legendary. Let us consider some of the ways exploiters have found to justify the unjustifiable.

Reactions of the Exploiter

Exploiters have some favorite techniques for justifying their exploitation of others. These include derogation of the victim, minimization of the victim's suffering, and denial of responsibility for the other's deprivation.

Derogation of the victim: If one can convince himself that a victim deserves his lowly state, he can feel a whole lot better about continuing to deprive the other of the things he deserves.

That harm-doers derogate their victims has often been demonstrated. In one experiment, psychologists hired college students to humiliate other students (presumably so the psychologist could discover how people responded after being insulted). This put students in a very uncomfortable position. They were perfectly aware that their fellow students didn't deserve to be humiliated. Yet, they had to insult him or lose the job. Students neatly solved their dilemma by distorting reality. Somehow they managed to convince themselves that the students whom they insulted really were inferior fellows. They convinced themselves that the victim was conceited, stupid, maladjusted, etc., and thus deserved to be hurt. Sykes and Matza (1957) found that juvenile delinquents feel guilty enough about hurting others that they go to the trouble of belittling the victim. They convince themselves (and others) that their victims are really homosexuals, bums, or possess other traits which make them deserving of punishment. In tormenting others, rather than harm-doers. We see this derogation of the victim operating in daily life. The con-man ridicules "suckers" and claims, "You can't cheat an honest man." The owner of a company store insists that the miners he over-charges are "Scum," who would squander their hard-

Credo

If it is not a Manichean universe.
Of course not.
Still it is true that human limited so-far
   consciousness
continues to posit only those two basic choices.
Good.
Evil.
And the third—Indifference.
Which is the Ball in the Tennis Game between the
   Other Two.

the ball isn't bothered, it just sails

Civilizations blaze and one baby
cries, sitting splay-legged in the ruins,

because the Ball is now in one court, now the other.

   the Kafka choice.

On what moral right do I dare attempt
to stop the human species from committing suicide?
None.
Especially since suicide is, we all know, the only
   really
refreshing, new idea with any curiosity about it left
   at all.

Yet if I care to care
force loving into being, then I pry open

all memory's charnel house of sores
that bubble up eternities of searching for metaphors
that could endure what they were being likened to.

What if I were in neither court, and not even the
   ball,
but someone sitting alone in the audience, turning
   my head
first one way and then the other.

So might a schizophrenic sit for forty years,
face poised between shafts of dark and light,
while doctors tried to cure her.

By such will the choice be made.
The mad and the suicidal are the only saints.
The rest of us are merely revolutionaries.

                              Robin Morgan

earned money on liquor if he didn't relieve them of it. The school superintendent, who passes over deserving women in order to promote males to Principal, convinces himself, "Women make lousy administrators; they're emotionally unstable."

Minimization of the victim's suffering: A second way that a person who has injured another can justify his injustice is by denying that the victim was really injured. Researchers have often demonstrated that harm-doers consistently underestimate how much harm they have done to others. Brock and Buss (1962) for example, interviewed college students who had been hired to administer electric shock to other students. It is, of course, very disturbing to have to shock another human being, especially when he does not deserve such punishment. Students rationalized this injustice by distorting how much the victim was suffering. After they had shocked the other student for awhile students began to markedly underestimate the painfulness of the shock they were delivering. Such rationalizations are common. Supervisors of migrant workers were once heard to explain, in all seriousness, that "Mexicans didn't really need much money, since they don't appreciate nice things." The grapeworkers strike soon reduced the plausibility of that rationalization.

When women hear employers explain that "Women really just work for pin money" and thus don't mind making less money than men, they might be forgiven for thinking that that tells one more about the employer's needs than those of women.

Denial of responsibility for the act: If one can convince himself that he is not responsible for existing inequities, he can feel much better about the injustice he observes around him.

In daily life, denial of responsibility seems

to be a favorite strategy of those who are made to feel guilty about exploiting others. War criminals protest vehemently they were "only following orders." Male chauvinists protest that "It's a man's world, and it's not my fault that things are as they are." Such statements often bring considerable satisfaction to those who are enjoying the benefits of the status quo.

Reactions of the Exploited

If an inequitable relationship is distressing to the exploiter it is doubly distressing to his victim. Although an exploiter may have to endure considerable discomfort when he treats others unjustly, he at least has the consolation that he is benefitting materially from his discomfort. The exploited individual has not such comfort—he loses in every way from the inequity.

Like the harm-doer, the victim is naturally eager to restore equity to their one-sided relationship. He can do this in several ways: (1) He can demand restitution. (2) He can retaliate against the harm-doer. (3) He can justify his own exploitation or accept the exploiter's justifications.

Demands for Compensation: Undoubtedly the victim's first response to exploitation is to seek restitution. If he secures compensation, he has restored the relationship to equity and he has benefited materially. It is easy to see why this is a popular response.

Retaliation: A second way victims try to restore equity is by retaliating against the exploiter. Whether or not retaliation is a good strategy is a moot point. Although retaliation does not bring the victim any material benefits, it does at least deprive the exploiter of his illicit benefits. Thus, retaliation may help to dissuade the exploiter from continuing to behave un-

fairly. (In addition, retaliation may bring the victim a certain satisfaction.) Whether or not it is a good strategy, Ross et al. (1971) demonstrate that victims will retaliate against those who have treated them inequitably, when given the opportunity. The more inequitably they believe they were treated, the more they will retaliate. Evidence from Berscheid et al. (1968) suggests that appropriate retaliation will cause the harm-doer (as well, presumably, as the victim) to believe that the previous wrong has been righted, and that the relationship can begin again on a fairer footing. It thus appears that retaliation has as much potential for renewing a relationship as for destroying it.

Justification of the Inequity! Sometimes a victim finds that it is impossible either to elicit restitution or to retaliate against the harm-doer. The important victim is left with only two options: He can acknowledge that he is exploited and that he is too weak to do anything about it, or he can justify his exploitation. Often, victimized individuals find it less upsetting to distort reality and justify their victimization, than to acknowledge that the world is unjust and that they are too impotent to elicit fair treatment (Lerner and Matthews, 1967).

Victimized individuals have been found to restore psychological equity in several ways: Victims sometimes console themselves by imagining that their exploitation has brought them compensating benefits. ("Suffering brings wisdom and purity.") Or, they tell themselves that in the long run the exploiter will be punished as he deserves. ("The mill of the Lord grinds slowly, but it grinds exceedingly fine.") Recent data demonstrate that the victims may also convince themselves that their exploiter actually deserves the excessive benefits he receives. Several experimenters have examined the re-

A woman should not be president; it's not the way God intended it to be. Yes, a woman could become president, but she'd have to become more and more like a man to handle the job. One of our problems today is that women are becoming more like men and men are becoming more like women. That's against God's will.

Anita Bryant

actions of individuals when an unworthy recipient pressures them into performing a difficult favor for him. They found that the abashed favor-doer would try to justify the inequity by convincing himself that the recipient was especially needy or worthy.

In our everyday experience, it is not uncommon to hear women who receive less money than a man for the same work, or who lose a job to a man, to assume that her deprivation is deserved. They say that they realize that the man needs the money more, or needs the job more than they do. Rarely do the women really know about the man's "needs." They do not know whether he has additional income from his wife's salary or whether he does in fact have a family to support. There are thousands of wives around any campus who have given up their own education for the husband who, they will argue, really has a greater need for the degree.

It is distressing to individuals who are desirous of promoting social equality, to see self-denigrating processes in action. As professional women, we frequently see women blaming themselves for problems that are in no way their own. One anecdote should provide insight. A friend of the senior author was interviewed by a department (not her own) at the University of Wisconsin. Her competence was unquestioned. Although she was applying for a job as an Assistant Professor, her work was internationally known and she had published for

more than had the average Full Professors in that department. She also had an excellent reputation as a teacher. Her interviewers perceived her talents. (One of them honestly stated "She wouldn't really fit in here—she's too smart." The comment was uproariously funny because it was true.) In the end, the department decided not to offer her a job. When the decision was criticized, one man countered angrily, "Discrimination is an old Wisconsin tradition." To everyone within the department, the reason for her exclusion was clear. She was talented, but she made the department members uncomfortable.

Within one year, however, the friend had reinterpreted her rejection. She had convinced herself that she had behaved stupidly and thus destroyed her chances for a job. "I had some personal problems at the time," she confided, "and that prevented me from being sensitive to what was going on . . . I came on too strong . . . Probably I was too aggressive . . . I should have been more enthusiastic (about the Chairman's research interest; a project he has since abandoned.) . . . They say they don't hire women, but if I had been convincing enough, I could have changed their minds. At some time everyone reaches a test point. They have to say if I succeed here I'm good. Otherwise I should give up . . . That was my test and I failed; I'm second rate, and I've accepted it." Such self-denigration may have given my friend the illusion that she had some control over her destiny,

from Revolucinations

Men have forgotten how to love,
women have forgotten how not to.
We must risk unlearning
what has kept us alive. . . .

The mask I choose for
my madness and suicide
is revolution.

Robin Morgan

but this illusion of control was purchased at a high cost—self-respect.

Why Women Are So Hard on Women

Reformers who have worked to alleviate social injustice, at great personal sacrifice, are often enraged to discover that the exploited themselves sometimes vehemently defend the status quo. They watch numerous blacks and women offer elaborate rationales for the propriety of their inferior status, and they are incredulous. Those who have suffered the most sometimes are the most reluctant to object to the treatment they have received. Reformers might have more sympathy for and more ability to motivate these Uncle Toms and Aunt Tomasinas if they understood the psychological underpinnings of such reactions. When one is treated inequitably but has no hope of altering the situation, it is often less degrading to deny or "justify" injustice than to face up to one's humiliating position.

Pate has speculated that when one has little hope for change, self-denigration is one's alternative. The more discrimination one has had to accept in a lifetime, the less hope he will have for change; the more entrenched his tendency to denigrate himself will be. This could explain why, in our society, older or already established members of the profession are especially hesitant to accept promised changes. Older, more established women often feel aversion to groups of activist women and tend to be hard on the young women in their field. In every generation there are always those who feel the young should have to struggle as hard for advancement as they did, and begrudge the young benefits they themselves never obtained. The inequity older women have endured, combined with their belief that change is unlikely in their time, leads them to denigrate themselves and to be so hard on younger women. Young women who expect change to occur are more likely to become angry and demand restitution than to denigrate themselves, when faced with inequity. Perhaps failing to understand the damaging self-concepts of their elders who have long suffered discrimination, they may be hostile to the "establishment" women who do not join their cause.

Young and older women should stop being so hard on one another. Both younger and older women must come to understand that they have been treated in discriminatory ways, and to understand the psychological consequences of this treatment. With a greater awareness of their common problems, perhaps they can learn to think constructively about ways of *changing*—rather than *adjusting* to—the discriminatory situations which they meet.

Barbara Polk

Male Power and the Women's Movement

The relationship between females and males in this and virtually every society has been a power relationship—of males over females. The current women's movement, a revitalization of earlier feminist movements, seeks to end or reverse this power relationship. As such, feminists are concerned with analyzing the nature of male power and the condition of women and developing organizations and vehicles for change that are consistent with feminist principles.

In this paper I shall consider four conceptualizations of women's oppression, their assessment of the various modes of male power, and their preferred strategies for changing the status of women in contemporary society. Throughout this paper, it is important to remember that the women's movement is not an organization with officers and a unified theory and set of activities. Instead, it consists of the ideas and activities of women responding to the conditions of their oppression whether as individuals, informal small groups, or large structured organizations. Although I see women who do not consider themselves to be "women's libbers" as part of the movement to the extent that they attempt to restructure their lives in nontraditional ways, here I am concerned with the theory and activities of those women who identify with the movement.

The Contemporary Condition of Women

Many individuals have attempted to account for the historical origins of the near universal oppression of women, grounding their theories in biological differences, evolutionary genetics, economic relationships, and so on. Although these are of interest to most feminists, we are aware that whatever its origins, oppression of women exists in the present and must be combatted now. For that reason most contemporary analyses do not deal in depth, if at all, with why and when questions, but rather attempt to understand the current relationship between the sexes as a basis for action.

Modal Analyses

I see four major approaches to understanding the contemporary condition of women: analyses in terms of sex roles, differences between feminine and masculine culture, male-female power relationships, and economic relationships.* Because the purpose of this paper is not to discuss the conflict and factions within the movement, I present a "modal" analysis of each viewpoint rather than ideal types. Extreme positions within each viewpoint are largely omitted and perspectives overlap to some degree, for in practice, most feminists subscribe to some combination of two or more perspectives. Although I refer to groups or writings which seem to me to fit a particular approach, it should

*A basic tenet of the women's movement is that no one woman can speak for it. This paper expresses my own perspective on the movement, and it is limited by my own experiences, understanding, and biases. It must be read as such. The dozen women who reviewed an earlier draft suggested that I confront that problem directly. Perhaps it is useful to say, then, that by training and because I believe it is most politically effective at this time, I prefer the sex-role approach, heavily modified by acceptance of much of the cultural and power analyses. Although I believe that sexism is deeply embedded in capitalism and that its eradication will require a fundamental change in economic structure, I disagree with the socialist view outlined in this paper.

be kept in mind that in no case is it possible to provide a "pure" example.

Sex-role Socialization. Drawing on social-psychological analysis, this approach views the contemporary oppression of women as the result of the inculcation of socially defined sex roles. This approach is the basic one adopted by most academic social scientists, including Alice Rossi, Cynthia Epstein, and Jessie Bernard, as well as other well-known feminists such as Gloria Steinem, Betty Friedan, Carolyn Bird, and Germaine Greer. It is also the basic orientation of such national groups as the National Organization for Women, Women's Equity Action League, and the Women's Political Caucus. For recent examples of the sex-roles perspective, see Chafetz' excellent book surveying the field (1974) and the articles in Safilios-Rothschild's reader (1972).

The main components of this analysis are:

1. Each society *arbitrarily* views a wide variety of personality characteristics, interests, and behaviors as the virtually exclusive domain of one sex or the other. The fact that societies vary in their definition of feminine and masculine roles is proof that sex roles are based on social rather than on biological factors.

2. The parceling up of human characteristics into "feminine" and "masculine" deprives all of full humanness.

3. Sex roles are systematically inculcated in individuals, beginning at birth, by parents, the educational system, peers, the media, and religious institutions, and are supported by the social sciences and the economic, political, and legal structures of society. Individuals learn appropriate roles through role models and differential reinforcement.

4. Sex roles form the core of an individual's identity. Because self-evaluation is closely linked to sex ("That's a good girl/boy") and to adequacy of sex-role performance, the propriety of the role to which one was socialized becomes difficult to dislodge in adulthood, even when it is seen as dysfunctional. In addition, individuals often link concepts of their adequacy in sex *roles* to their adequacy in *sexual* interactions and vice versa. Thus, a threat to one's role definition is perceived as a threat to one's sexual identity. Such threats are a major mechanism for psychologically locking people into traditional roles.

5. Sex roles are basic roles and thus modify expectations in virtually all other roles. Differential expectations by sex in other roles leads to differential perception of the same behavior in a woman and a man (a businessman is strong-willed; a business woman, rigid). Differential expectations and selective perception limit the extent to which individuals can step outside their sex roles and are major mechanisms for the maintenance of sex roles.

6. Female and male roles form a role system in which the expectations for and behaviors of each sex have implications for the definitions of and behaviors of the other sex. (A man can't be a "gentleman" if a woman will not let him hold the door for her.)

7. The male role has higher status. This status is directly rewarding and provides access to other highly valued statuses and rewards; however, male status also places heavy pressures on men to maintain that status.

8. Males have power over females because of role definitions. "Being powerful" is itself a part of the masculine role definition. In addition, the "rationality" assigned to the male role gives men access to positions of expertise as well as credibility, even when they are not experts.

Conflicting Cultures Approach. This approach focuses on value differences rather than role differences between the sexes. It points out that women who talk only in terms of role differences may seek a solution to their oppression by emulating male roles. The cultural approach is therefore a more overtly feminist analysis, focusing on the positive aspects of feminine culture. Examples of this approach include Firestone (1970), Burris (1971), and Solanas (1968), although the latter is quite different from the view presented here. The main ideas behind this approach follow.

1. Just as roles are dichotomized by sex, so are values. "Masculine" values include competitiveness, aggressiveness, independence, and rationality; "feminine" values include their counterparts: cooperativeness, passivity, dependence, and emotionality. These values are not inherent as male or female (according to most versions of this analysis) but are socially assigned and derived from sex-role definitions. *All* are important qualities of humanness.

2. Masculine values have higher status and constitute the dominant and visible culture of the society. They inform the structure of personal, political, and economic relationships and provide the standard for adulthood and normality (cf. de Beauvoir's [1953] discussion of woman as "the Other").

3. Women are oppressed and devalued because they embody an alternative culture. (In one version of this analysis [Burris, 1971], men are seen as colonizing women's bodies in order to subordinate an alien value system, much as men colonized the land and peoples of other civilizations.)

4. Men are socialized almost exclusively to the masculine value system, but women receive dual socialization because of the dominance of male institutions and because they must comprehend masculine values in order to survive (the slave syndrome). Dual socialization tempts women to try assimilation into the masculine culture, but it also gives women insight into the artificiality of the value dichotomization.

5. Masculine values are largely responsible for the crisis in our society. Competitiveness pits human against human and results in racism, sexism, and colonialism, as well as the rape of the natural environment in the pursuit of economic power: Aggressiveness leads to war. Exaggerated independence inhibits society's ability to solve common problems by failing to recognize the fundamental interdependence among humans and between humans and the physical environment. Excessive rationality is linked to the building of a run-away technological and scientific system incapable of recognizing and granting legitimacy to human needs and feelings.

Power Analysis. This perspective does not deny the importance of sex roles and cultural differences in bringing about and maintaining the oppression of women, but it views them as symptomatic of the primary problem, which is the domination of females by males. Thus, it is more concerned with focusing on the mechanisms of male power than on its origins; e.g., Millett (1970) and Chesler (1972). Its major tenets may be summarized as follows:

1. Men have power and privilege by virtue of their sex. They may and do oppress women in personal relationships, in groups, and on the job.

2. It is in men's interest to maintain that power and privilege. There is status in the ability to oppress someone else, regardless of the oppression one suffers oneself. In addition, power over women in personal relationships gives men what they want, whether that be sex,

smiles, chores, admiration, increased leisure, or control itself.

3. Men occupy and actively exclude women from positions of economic and political power in society. Those positions give men a heavily disproportionate share of the rewards of society, especially economic rewards.

4. Marriage is an institution of personal and sexual slavery for women, who are duped into marrying by the love ethic or economic necessity.

5. Although most males are also oppressed by the system under which we live, they are not oppressed, as females are, *because of* their sex.

6. Feminine roles and cultural values are the product of oppression. Idealization of them is dysfunctional to change.

7. Males have greater behavioral and economic options, including the option of oppressing women. Where individuals have wider options, they are responsible for their choices. In this way, men are responsible, individually and collectively, for their oppression of women.

8. Men oppress women through the use of brute force, by restricting options and selectively reinforcing women within these options, through control of resources and major institutions, and through expertise and access to the media.

Socialist Perspective. This approach holds that the oppression of women is only one aspect of the destructiveness of a generally oppressive economic system and therefore contends that socialism is a prerequisite to feminism. As the basis for outlining this viewpoint, I am using the general orientation of The Socialist Worker's Party and the International Socialists, as discussed with me in conversation, and the writings of Reed (1969). Although I have chosen

Pig Boss by Karen Breschi

to use the viewpoint of socialist organizations heavily dominated by males (thus they are not feminist organizations), women in these groups often form formal or informal caucuses on feminist issues. Closely related are the analyses of the unaffiliated, all-female socialist groups, although these groups generally disagree with the following analysis by affirming the need for an independent women's movement. Their approach is represented by Mitchell (1971). Simone de Beauvoir's work, *The Second Sex,* fits primarily into this category, although the work is so broad that it incorporates the main ideas from all analyses presented here. That de Beauvoir identifies with the socialist perspective on the women's movement as presented here is clear in her autobiography, *Force of Circumstances* (1965).

Big Daddy Draped by May Stevens

1. The oppression of women originated in the concept of private property. Women were defined as property largely because of their ability to reproduce, thereby providing new workers as well as heirs for the elite. Because private property is the institution on which capitalism is founded, the oppression of women is fundamentally linked to capitalist structures and is necessary to their continuation.

2. Sexism is functional to capitalism because it enables capitalists to buy two workers for the price of one. A man is paid a wage; his wife, who is unpaid, provides the necessary services for him to perform his job (even if she, too, has a job).

3. Women provide a cheap reserve labor force for capitalists, thereby holding down wages and increasing profits.

4. Although the rebellion of women against their roles is contrary to the interests of capitalism, an independent women's movement is not, for it separates one oppressed group from others and forestalls a coalition which could overthrow the system.

5. Equality for women is impossible until capitalism is replaced by socialism.

Male Power

These four perspectives on the contemporary condition of women differentially weigh and interpret the current sources of male power but are in general agreement as to what they are. For purposes of this discussion, I shall draw primarily upon the language of the power analysts because they have given the most systematic attention to this issue.

Normative Power. By virtue of their sex and their control of traditional sex-role definitions, men are able to manipulate women's behavior by ignoring, misrepresenting, devaluing, and discrediting women or their accomplishments, especially when women deviate from traditional roles. Some examples are the omission of women's contributions from history texts and the attribution of women's scientific discoveries and artistic achievements to men. In the extreme, the institutionalization of traditional sex-role definitions in the theories of the mental health professions allows males on a day-to-day basis to label female role deviants as "crazy" or to punish their deviations through incarceration (see Chesler, 1972).

Institutional Power. Not only do males have differential amounts of and access to money, education, and positions of influence, they use this control to limit life options for women and extend life options for men. For example, male control of the media, religion, and the educational system is used to influence public opinion and practice. Combined with normative power, males use these public socialization institutions to inculcate traditional role and value systems in both females and males, thereby reducing the probability that females will aspire to or succeed in moving beyond traditional roles.

When women do attempt to change or broaden their roles, they are blocked by male control of the economic institutions. Women lack skills and access to skills through formal education as well as through recognized apprenticeship and trainee programs. Denied access to well-paid jobs, women lack money or access to money through loans which would enable them to change their condition. Thus, dominance of economic institutions by males locks women into traditional roles.

Male dominance of law and politics supports their control through other institutional means. Thus laws are made, interpreted, and enforced with male self-interest in mind. For example, the Supreme Court, with one exception, has refused to apply the Fourteenth and Fifth Amendment guarantees of "equal protection under law" to women, making necessary a *special* constitutional amendment even to establish the legal basis for female equality in society.

The two areas women are said to control, domestic life and education of the young, are delegated to them by men, who retain final authority and monitor the way in which women carry out these roles.

Control of Options Through Reward Power. Men use their institutional and normative power to control women's life choices not only through restricting their options but also through reinforcing choices within them. This is a subtle form of control, as Skinner makes clear; since women do receive some rewards for "appropriate" behavior, those who rebel risk losing real rewards. The recent slight broadening of options is primarily a matter of reinforcing new forms of behavior and does not change the basic control of females by males, i.e., does not change who metes out reinforcement.

The Power of Expertise. In all areas—from international affairs, space technology, and group dynamics to education, child rearing, and female sexuality—the experts are male. This is largely because male dominance of the educational institutions and the media allows males to select which individuals will become experts and which experts shall receive public exposure. For a woman, this means that when she wants information or advice in any field, she must rely for the most part on males whose expertise may serve the interests of male supremacy or male values rather than her own interests.

Psychological Power. Males, having suppressed feminine culture, have access to institutional power partly because they "fit" the value structures of the institutions better than do women (for example, see Epstein's [1971, Chap. 3] discussion of status-set typing, and Chafetz' [1974] illustration of the interaction between sex roles and professional roles, pp. 60–62). The confidence of being "right," of fitting, gives even incompetent men an important source of psychological power over women, who have not been so wholly socialized into the masculine value structure.

World's End by Leonor Fini; reprinted by permission of the artist

Brute Force. Not only are most men stronger than most women but they are trained to have or show confidence in their physical strength. Men physically dominate women by beating wives and girl friends or by rape and threat of rape. Rape is a form of social control (as pointed out by Reynolds, 1971) which serves to restrict women's autonomy and mobility. The threat of rape is reinforced by whistling and other street hassles, which to women, implicitly carry the possibility of physical attack.

Approaches to Change—A New Society

Surrounded by male power, from sources which overlap and reinforce one another,

women find that they must totally transform society to achieve their goal of freedom from oppression. As a result, strategies for change are many and diverse, giving the women's movement the appearance of a lack of direction. However, no one tactic is intended to accomplish the entire task. Groups choose targets and activities partly on the basis of their analyses of women's oppression, partly on the basis of available opportunities for action, and partly according to the personal dispositions of any particular group or collective of women. There is, then, no easy one-to-one match between the perspectives of the participants and the activities of the movement, which I briefly review in the following section.

De- or Resocialization of Oneself

Self-change is important for all perspectives, though in the socialist approach, it is seen as effected through social action. To the extent that sex-role definitions, value systems, and the power which is based on them are socialized characteristics, each of us to some extent participates in those definitions. The most prevalent activity in the women's movement, therefore, has been the small consciousness-raising or rap group in which women piece together an understanding of their oppression and challenge their assumptions about themselves, other women, and men. Within these groups, women find that their experiences, private fears, and self-doubts are not unique but common to many other women and related to their social conditioning. Personal experience thus becomes a basis for political analysis and action.

Most groups focus on building solidarity and support among members, replacing the distrust and dislike of other women with which many enter these groups. In addition, most groups raise questions about appropriate routes to liberation, challenge the notion that liberation means imitating male roles and values, and debate the extent to which individual freedom is possible in the absence of general structural change in the society. In this way, women begin to redefine and change themselves and build a basis for initiating larger changes.

Changing Personal Interactions and Micro-Role Systems

New definitions are useless if not put into action. All perspectives encourage actions to redefine personal relationships and micro-role systems, although they vary to some extent in the kinds of actions they favor. The sex-role analysis focuses heavily on individual change of personal relationships and the broadening of individual life options. The cultural perspective emphasizes decreasing dependence on emotional support from males and substituting strong alliances among women. The power perspective favors direct confrontation with males in all interactions—on the job, in the street, and in personal relationships.

Since, in a sex-role system, definitions are upheld and reinforced by both role actors, when a woman moves outside of traditional definitions, she forces a change in complementary roles. For example, the rap group is often important in providing support for married women seeking more egalitarian sharing of housework and child care, or attempting to return to school, take a job, or resume a career; and for single women attempting to deal with the restrictiveness of a father or boyfriend. Through an analysis of the costs and rewards to both parties in a relationship, the group helps its members find ways of decreasing the rewards (increasing the costs) for male resistance to such changes, while increasing their rewards for more egalitarian behavior.

Toward the Future

Purpose: To become aware of our direction

Directions: Obtain 5 large sheets of paper and colored pens, pencils, or crayons. Sit in a relaxed position. Read the following instructions:

1. Where were you before you were born? Close your eyes for a moment and let an image emerge. Open your eyes and draw it. If an image does not appear, begin to draw and let it come. If there are any thoughts or feelings that emerge, write these down. Repeat this process for the following questions as well.
2. How do you see change happening?
3. What would you like yourself to be? What is your ideal self?
4. What are the barriers to change?
5. What do you need to get through them?

Break into groups of 3 or 4 so that each person can show her (his) drawings, share and discuss what has emerged, and get feedback from others.

The support function of women's groups is a step toward substituting women for men as a basic reference group. This process reduces women's reliance on the kinds of rewards they receive from men. Approval and emotional support is instead sought within the group. In this way, a new set of sisterly relationships are formed, which, for some groups, involves mutual economic support in living communes and sexual gratification in lesbian relationships, making women largely self-sufficient and males almost irrelevant.

Still, almost all women must relate to men in less personal interactions. The power analysts, in particular, help each other develop strategies for confronting rather than ignoring street hassles, for confronting and changing condescending comments and gestures in work and other settings, and for challenging the "servant chores" (making coffee, buying presents, dusting the office, providing a sympathetic ear to the boss) which are a part of many female occupations.

Learning karate and other forms of self-defense as well as engaging in sports activities is one popular feminist strategy for combatting the physical power men have over women. Many women believe that if they develop their strength and learn to understand, use, and have confidence in their bodies, they will be less likely to be attacked physically and more able to defend themselves in the event of an attack. As men are aware that women are able to fight back, the attacker-victim role relationship should become less frequent.

In the attempt to change others through personal interaction and micro-role system change, women undermine several sources of male power. Normative power is further reduced by destroying traditional male roles through withholding cooperation, making them irrelevant, or challenging them directly. To the extent that women provide a support group for one another, they reduce the power of males to define women's options and control their behavior through rewards. Self-defense techniques reduce the threat of brute force. These small-scale attempts at change gradually produce new bases for more egalitarian interaction than traditional practices.

Resocialization of Others

The second most prevalent activity of the women's movement has been use of or attacks on the media in order to extend the resocialization process beyond the boundaries of the movement. These activities have been engaged in primarily by women who use the sex-role perspective, which emphasizes socialization. The cultural approach and the power analysis both caution against dependence on media and media change as main tools of the movement, since the media are dominated by men. As a result, they warn, attempts by women to convey their ideas through the media will tend to distort the message in a way that ridicules or discredits the movement.

Those who use the media view it as a way of reaching and changing women who have not been exposed to rap groups. By publishing books, magazines, and articles, by speaking, producing radio and TV programs, by being interviewed or holding demonstrations covered by the media, women in the movement extend their insights to those outside it. In this way, countless women who do not identify with the movement begin to reevaluate and change their lives.

Women's access to the media also helps reshape men's understanding of the female condition. For those who believe that change can come about through convincing men of the disadvantages of their roles or of masculine values, the media provides a major vehicle for reaching and changing men. Communicating with men in this way provides the beginnings of social legitimation for legal changes and lays the groundwork for a new value system in society.

Much attention is also focused on the socialization of children. A number of groups are publishing feminist books for children and compiling lists of children's literature offering a positive image of women. *Ms.* magazine has even published a children's record, containing liberated songs. In addition, several women's groups throughout the country have formed feminist child care centers or cooperatives.

Some academic women are concerned with building a social science that defines females as full participants in society and creates and supports new definitions of women. This attempt, however, has little support among many active feminists, who point out that the social sciences are male-dominated in membership, substance, and style, thus forcing academic women to work under non- or antifeminist constraints. I myself believe that the most exciting social-psychological analyses in the past five years have taken place in feminist groups. To the extent that this thinking has filtered into academic meetings and writing, it has been a grossly watered down and devitalized version of feminist thought (my own work not excepted). Thus the movement puts little faith in the social sciences' provision of a basis for new images of women and society.

Changing Male Dominance of Institutions

So far, the approaches to change with which I have dealt focus heavily on undermining male normative and cultural power and substituting female group support for male approval. However, these approaches are limited by male control of social institutions, against which women have few resources. The main tactics we employ are legal action, direct action and moral pressure, and skill building.

Growing out of the civil rights movement, several legal changes in the past decade open new options to women. Under law, public accommodations must be available to women, and discrimination in hiring or pay on the basis of sex is illegal in any business or educational institution. These changes formally open the possibilities for women to travel freely, gain skills, and obtain economic and positional resources. However, none of these laws are adequately enforced. It has been incumbent upon

> from **Merced**
>
> *For weeks now a rage*
> *has possessed my body, driving*
> *now out upon men and women*
> *now inward upon myself*
> *Walking Amsterdam Avenue*
> *I find myself in tears*
> *without knowing which thought*
> *forced water to my eyes*
> *To speak to another human*
> *becomes a risk*
> *I think of Norman Morrison*
> *the Buddhists of Saigon*
> *the black teacher last week*
> *who put himself to death*
> *to waken guilt in hearts*
> *too numb to get the message*
> *in a world masculinity made*
> *unfit for women or men*
>
> Adrienne Rich

women to identify discrimination and file suits or complaints with federal, state, or local agencies. This technique is currently in wide use by university women, who are filing complaints against institutions with HEW. In addition, local movement groups give support and advice to individuals seeking redress of employment or pay discrimination cases and rent and loan discrimination.

Another attempt at law enforcement is a current project, coordinated through NOW, to challenge the renewal of TV and radio station FCC licenses on grounds of sexism (discrimination in employment and failure to provide fair and adequate service to a segment of the public).

Women seek to change as well as enforce laws. Campaigns, rallies and marches in support of legalized abortion, welfare rights, and child care attempt to influence public opinion and bring public pressure to bear on legislators.

This tactic is especially favored by socialist groups. In addition, ad hoc groups of women have pressured politicians for new laws—the Equal Rights Amendment, laws on the treatment of female criminals, changes in marriage and divorce laws, laws and procedures governing rape cases, etc.

Direct action includes sit-ins, economic boycotts, moral pressure, and attempts to form women's unions. Sit-ins and boycotts are used to draw attention to illegal and unjust institutional practices as well as to affect the economic position of those against whom they are directed. Groups employing these tactics often negotiate directly over their demands. In addition, these approaches sometimes speed up investigatory or legal action by providing adverse publicity and forcing a business or organization to defend itself publicly.

An example of successful moral pressure is the project of two Wayne State University women who analyzed the Detroit public school system's textbooks, using the latter's own guidelines on treatment of minority groups. As a result of their efforts, Detroit school guidelines now explicitly include females with other groups that must be portrayed fairly in school texts—an incentive for authors and publishers to produce such books.

Attempts to form women's unions in order to collectivize and institutionalize women's power to bargain for better working conditions, equitable pay, and job definitions which allow for promotion are underway in many parts of the country. They are also necessary because unions have been notoriously insensitive to the needs of women. (In Detroit, some UAW leaders crossed picket lines for the first time in their lives when their female staff went on strike.) Some women are organizing unions that cut across occupational types or place of employ-

ment and are attempting to pull employed women and housewives into one union, with demands that include pay for housework. Women's unions are most strongly promoted by groups using a power analysis.

A final, and less direct, way of changing institutions is through skill building. Women's lack of power in institutions stems partly from a lack of knowledge, skills, and confidence. Many feminist projects are devoted to building women's personal and collective resources to enable them to challenge institutional power. Some groups, convinced that all individuals are capable of any activity, given the opportunity to learn and practice, build speaking and writing skills by seeking opportunities for all members to engage in those activities and by assigning members to fill speaking engagements by lot rather than by degree of competence.

Some professional women are actively recruiting women into their ranks. At Wayne State University and elsewhere, women law students accompany recruiters to college campuses, talking to women about careers in law and providing information about the field, entrance requirements, and preparation for Law Board exams. Women from other professions speak at high schools and on college campuses to encourage young women to consider new career opportunities. Within professions, women are beginning to form support groups or caucuses or to change the focus of existing women's professional organizations to consider the roles of women and ways in which they can implement feminine values within their occupations. The entrance of women into prestigious fields such as law, medicine, business, and education not only gives females a basis for power within those institutions but also begins the process of building female expertise as a counter to male expertise, and in some cases begins the systematic introduction of feminine values into institutional structures.

Building Alternative Institutions

Partly as a result of the cultural analysis, which argues that the institutions of society are corrupted by their weddedness to masculine values, and partly for reasons of sheer survival, many women are engaged in building alternative institutions that incorporate feminist values and can thereby serve as models for institutions in a new society. In fact, the women's movement itself may be seen in this light. *The New Woman's Survival Catalogue* (Grimstad & Rennie, 1973) is an excellent resource for locating feminist institutions in the U.S. It also contains information on organizations, publications, and other activities discussed elsewhere in this paper.

The numerous women's self-help medical clinics primarily aim to break down male monopoly of basic medical information. They provide women with information about their bodies that enables them to stay healthy, know when something is wrong, know how to communicate with—and if necessary how to challenge—their doctors or seek alternative care. These clinics operate on the assumption that women lose control of their bodies partly through ignorance. They strive to reduce the distinctions between patients, aides, nurses, technicians, and doctors by teaching each other how to do breast and vaginal self-examinations and basic laboratory tests, and by sharing information on such topics as menopause and nutrition. Self-help groups also collect lists of doctors who are nonchauvinist and those whom women should avoid. Gradually these groups are beginning to negotiate with doctors, hospitals, and clinics for changes in the treatment

Feeling Righteous

The whole thing
came clear to me today
just the way it really is,
man on the top,
woman fighting from the bottom,
and I feel righteous.
I am hearing Nina Simone
sing out her song
you can't keep this woman down
and I feel
righteous.
the sound goes right through
my spine
and down to my toes
and I am
laughing
deep down inside myself because
I feel righteous.
there's nothing
hazy about it now.
the whole thing is
perfectly clear.
there's no way
to keep a righteous woman down.
we will be free; my heart
is free today
and you can hear it sing
the way we're all going to sing
because
we're all going to sing everyday
we're going to sing
every righteous,
goddamn day.

Susan Griffin

of female patients, and more radically, in the structure of the medical professions.

In the field of law, a group of female lawyers in San Francisco is using its expertise to train women in law. If a client wishes, she may work in the office, including the preparation of her

Star Hunter by Remedios Varo; reprinted by permission of Walter Gruen

own legal brief in lieu of some or all of her legal fees. The approach incorporates feminist values into the practice of law by reducing mystification of the law and monopolization of expertise. Status relationships are also equalized as lawyers frequently answer phones and type letters while clients prepare legal briefs.

Another alternative institution is the commune. Although the communal movement is not feminist, many women have seen its potential for providing an alternative to the nuclear family, which power analysts in particular view as a primary oppressive institution. Communes offer women who are already married an opportunity to reduce the sex-role pressures of the nuclear family by sharing work and home roles among several adults; single women find mixed or all-female communes a way of meeting social and economic needs and reducing the pressure on them to marry; single mothers have found that collective living with others in the same position eases child care and economic problems. An important component of all these communal styles is that they increase support among women, who live together rather than in isolated homes, and reduce their dependence on males. Hence they are alternatives especially favored by women using a cultural or power approach.

In the process of working for a feminist revolution, the women's movement has attempted to structure itself around its values for a new society. Since women have been placed in a largely powerless role in society, they are especially sensitive to the degradations associated with powerlessness. Therefore, in seeking change, the movement has sought organizational techniques which do not subject women to oppression within or without the movement. Most groups have been reluctant to recruit actively, depending instead on women coming to the movement when they become aware of their own oppression as women. As mentioned earlier, the media provide indirect recruitment, but most women avoid pressuring or coercing individuals with their views.

Problems with Power and Authority within the Movement Itself

Because feminist values emphasize the right of each women to her own view and choice of activities, a major problem has been the coordination of activities without authoritarian leadership. Granting power to a leader puts other women in a position of subordination similar to the subordination of females to males. Groups have therefore avoided formally or informally institutionalized leadership in a variety of ways. Leadership tasks are often rotated: the person who chairs a meeting, the group that publishes a newsletter, the individuals who speak at a rally or are interviewed by the media are often chosen by lot. Steering committees are selected in representative ways to serve for short time periods. A typical practice is to send two women rather than one to speak before a group or explain a position or action to the press, on the assumption that differences in their perspective, experience, and style will reflect the diversity of the movement.

To avoid domination of group discussion by the articulate, many groups have adopted the disc system, originated by the Feminists of New York: each woman receives the same number of tokens at the beginning of a meeting, yielding one each time she speaks, and remaining quiet when her tokens are gone.

In many cities, feminist groups have organized as coalitions of smaller rap or action groups. Ideally, the coalition form assumes that differences do and will exist and leaves individuals free to support or not support the activities proposed by component groups. It provides a forum for debating ideological differences and coordinating action among those of different persuasions. There are serious criticisms within the movement of each of these organizational forms—but there is also widespread commitment to finding feminist solutions.

In this paper I have attempted to summarize the general perspectives and strategies of the women's movement. In doing so, I have omitted its many controversies—proponents of each approach often differ sharply and sometimes destructively. Each strategy has its detractors, who view it as ineffective, utopian, unnecessarily hostile, retreatist, or trivial. To males—who tend to evaluate a movement by the tightness of its organization, agreement on perspectives, goals, and tactics, and allegiance to a leader or leadership group—the women's movement looks directionless, unorganized, and ineffective. To feminists struggling with new selves and new forms of organization, the means are as important as the goals, and the struggles to coordinate efforts to obtain power for women is itself a small-scale model of a new society, one that accepts and works creatively with and for differences in viewpoint and life experience.

For Further Reading

Fasteau, M. F. 1974. *The Male Machine.* New York: McGraw-Hill.

*Grimstad, K., and **Rennie, S.** 1973. *The New Woman's Survival Catalog.* New York: Coward, McCann and Geoghegan.

Heilbrun, C. 1973. *Toward a Recognition of Androgyny.* New York: Harper and Row.

*Pleck, J. H., and **Sawyer, J.** 1974. *Men and Masculinity.* Englewood Cliffs, N.J.: Prentice-Hall.

*Rush, A. K. 1973. *Getting Clear.* New York: Random House.

*Women Studies Abstracts. Issued Quarterly. Palmyra, N.Y.: Rush Publishing Co.

APPENDIX A: References for Articles

Introductions

Barry, H., Bacon, M. K., and Child, I. L. 1957. A cross-cultural survey of some sex differences in socialization. *Journal of Abnormal and Social Psychology* 55:327–332

Bart, P. 1971. Sexism and social science: from the gilded cage to the iron cage, or, the perils of Pauline. *Journal of Marriage and the Family* 33:734–747

Battle-Sister, A. 1971. Conjectures on the female culture question. *Journal of Marriage and The Family* 33:411–420

Block, J., Von Der Lippe, A., and Block, J. H. 1973. Sex role and socialization patterns: some personality concomitants and environmental antecedents. *Journal of Consulting and Clinical Psychology* 41:321–341

Bowen, D. D. 1971. Reported patterns in TAT measures of needs for achievement, affiliation and power. *Journal of Personality Assessment* 37:424–430

Broverman, I. K., Broverman, D. M., Clarkson, F. E., Rosenkrantz, P. S., and Vogel, S. R. 1970. Sex-role stereotypes and clinical judgements of mental health. *Journal of Consulting and Clinical Psychology* 34:1–7

Broverman, I. K., Vogel, S. R., Broverman, D. M., Clarkson, F. E., Rosenkrantz, P. S. 1972. Sex-role stereotypes: a current appraisal. *Journal of Social Issues* 28:59–78

Burris, B. 1971. Fourth world manifesto. In Koedt, A., Levine, E., and Rapone, A. (Eds.). *Radical Feminism.* New York: Quadrangle/The New York Times Book Co.

Carlson, R. 1971. Where is the person in personality research? *Psychological Bulletin* 75:203–219

Chesler, P. 1972. *Women and Madness.* Garden City, N.Y.: Doubleday

Dan, A. J. and Beekman, S. 1972. Male versus female representation in psychological research. *American Psychologist* 27:1078

Firestone, S. 1970. *The Dialectic of Sex.* New York: Bantam

Galen, D. 1974. Implications for psychiatry of left and right cerebral specialization neurophysiological contact for unconscious processes. Archives, *General Psychiatry* 31:572–583

Hacker, H. M. 1951. Women as a minority group. *Social Forces* 30:60–69

——. 1974. Women as a minority group: twenty years later. *International Journal of Group Tensions* 4:122–141

Johansson, C. B. and Harmon, L. W. 1972. Strong vocational interest blank: one form or two? *Journal of Counseling Psychology* 19:404–410

Koestler, A. 1967. *The Ghost in the Machine.* New York: MacMillan

Lederer, W. 1968. *The Fear of Women.* New York: Harcourt Brace Jovanovich

Maccoby, E. E. and Jacklin, C. N. 1974. *The Psychology of Sex Differences.* Stanford: Stanford University Press

McClintock, M. K. 1971. Menstrual synchrony and suppression. *Nature* 229:244–245

Millett, K. 1970. *Sexual Politics.* New York: Doubleday

Millman, N. 1971. Observations on sex-role research. *Journal of Marriage and the Family* 33:772–776

Milton, G. A. 1959. Sex differences in problem solving as a function of role appropriateness of the problem content. *Psychological Reports* 5:705–708

Montagu, A. 1970. *The Natural Superiority of Women.* New York: Macmillan

Munley, P., Fretz, B. R., and Mills, D. H. 1973. Female college students' scores on the men's and women's Strong vocational interest blanks. *Journal of Counseling Psychology* 20:285–289

Oakley, A. 1972. *Sex, Gender and Society.* New York: Harper & Row

Ornstein, R. E. 1972. *The Psychology of Consciousness.* San Francisco: Freeman.

Paige, Karen E. Women learn to sing the menstrual blues. *Psychology Today* 00:42–46

Patai, R. 1967. *Women in the Modern World.* New York: Free Press

Ramey, E. 1973. Sex hormones and executive ability. *Annals of New York Acad. of Sci.* 208:237–245

Rosenthal, R. 1966. *Experimenter Effects in Behavioral Research.* New York: Appleton-Century-Crofts.

Schultz, D. P. 1969. The human subject in psychological research. *Psychological Bulletin* 72:214–228

Schwabacker, S. 1970. Male vs. female representation in psychological research: an examination of the *Journal of Personality and Social Psychology. Catalogue of Selected Documents in Psychology* 2:20–21

Singer, Judith E., Westphal, M., and Niswander, K. R. 1968. Sex differences in the incidence of neonatal abnormalities and abnormal performance in early childhood. *Child Development* 39:103–122

Slater, Philip. 1970. *The Pursuit of Loneliness.* Boston: Beacon Press

Walster, E., Berscheid, E., and Walster, W. G. 1973. *Journal of Personality and Social Psychology* 25:151–176

Williams, R. J. 1956. *Biochemical Individuality.* New York: John Wiley

Biological Perspectives

Sex Hormones and Executive Ability

Estelle R. Ramey

1. Freud, S. 1933. *New introductory letters on psychoanalysis.* New York: W. W. Norton
2. Freud, S. 1905. *Three Essays on the Theory of Sexuality.* London: Imago Press
3. Ramey, E. R. 1971. What did happen at the Bay of Pigs. *McCall's.* Jan.

4. Salzman, L. 1967. Psychology of the female. *Arch. Gen. Psychiatry* 17:195
5. Public Health Service. 1970. Biological Rhythms in Psychiatry and Medicine. Pub. 2088
6. Beach, F. A. 1958. Neural and chemical regulation of behavior. In *Biological and Biochemical Bases of Behavior.* Madison: Univ. Wisconsin Press
7. Sherfey, M. J. 1966. The evolution and nature of female sexuality in relation to psychoanalytic theory. *J. Am. Psychoanal. Ass.* 14:28
8. Money, J., G. H. Hampson & J. L. Hampson. 1957. Imprinting and the establishment of the gender role. *Arch. Neurol. Psychiat.* 77:333
9. Hampson, J. L. & G. H. Hampson. 1961. The ontogenesis of sexual behavior in man. *In Sex and Internal Secretions.* W. C. Young, Ed. Baltimore: Williams and Wilkins
10. Rado, S. 1940. A critical examination of the concept of bisexuality. *Psychosom. Med.* 2:459
11. Money, J. 1970. Matched pairs of hermaphrodites: Behavioral biology, sexual differences from chromosomes to gender identity. *Engineer. and Science* 33:34
12. Ehrhardt, A. A., N. Greenberg & J. Money. 1970. Female gender identity and absence of fetal gonadal hormones: Turner's Syndrome. *Johns Hop. Med. J.* 126:237
13. Ehrhardt, A. A., R. Epstein & J. Money. 1968. Fetal androgens and female gender identity in the early treated adrenogenital syndrome. *Johns Hop. Med. J.* 122:160
14. Jost, A. 1961. The role of fetal hormones in prenatal development. In *The Harvey Lectures.* Series 55:201. New York: Academic Press
15. Harris, G. W. 1964. Sex hormones, brain development and brain function. *Endocrinology* 75:617
16. Money, J. 1965. Influence of hormones on sexual behavior. *Ann. Rev. Med.* 16:67
17. Conner, R. L., S. Levine, G. A. Wertheim & J. F. Cummer. 1969. Hormonal determinants of aggressive behavior. *Ann. N. Y. Acad. Sci.* 159:760
18. Money, J. & A. A. Ehrhardt. 1968. Prenatal hormonal exposure: Possible effects on behavior in man. In *Endocrinology and Human Behavior.* R. P. Michael, Ed. London: Oxford Univ. Press
19. Money, J. & S. Mittenthal. 1970. Lack of personality pathology in Turner's Syndrome: Relation to cytogenetics, hormones and physique. *Behavior Genetics* 1:43
20. Federman, D. D. 1967. *Abnormal Sexual Development. A Genetic and Endocrine Approach to Differential Diagnosis.* Philadelphia: W. B. Saunders
21. Neumann, F. & W. Elager. 1966. Permanent changes in gonadal function and sexual behavior as a result of early feminization of male rats by treatment with antiandrogenic steroid. *Endokrinologie* 50:209
22. Money, J. 1970. Sexual dimorphism and homosexual gender identity. *Psychol. Bull.* 74:425
23. Lorenz, K. 1935. Der Kumpan in der Umwelt des Vogels. *J. Ornith.* 83:137
24. Schiller, C. H., Ed. 1957. *Instinctive Behavior.* New York: Int. Univ. Press
25. Money, J. W. 1971. Pre-natal hormones and intelligence: a possible relationship. *Impact Sci. on Soc.* 21:285
26. Dalton, K. 1968. Ante-natal progesterone and intelligence. *Brit. J. Psych.* 114:1377
27. Fisher, A. 1966. Chemical and electrical stimulation of the brain in the male rat. In *Brain and Behavior.* R. A. Gorski & R. E. Whalen, Eds. Vol. 3. *The Brain and Gonadal Function.* Berkeley: Univ. Cal. Press

The Premenstrual Syndrome

Mary Brown Parlee

Abramson, M., & Torghele, J. R. 1961. Weight, temperature changes, and psychosomatic symptomatology in relation to the menstrual cycle. *American Journal of Obstetrics and Gynecology* 81:223–232

Altman, M., Knowles, E., & Bull, H. D. 1941. A psychosomatic study of the sex cycle in women. *Psychosomatic Medicine* 3:199–224

Balint, M. 1937. A contribution to the psychology of menstruation. *Psychoanalytic Quarterly* 6:346–352

Bardwick, J. M. 1971. *Psychology of women: A study of biocultural conflicts.* New York: Harper & Row

Benedek, T. 1963. An investigation of the sexual cycle in women's Methodologic considerations. *Archives of General Psychiatry* 8:311–322

Benedek, T., & Rubenstein, B. B. 1939. The correlations between ovarian activity and psychodynamic processes: I. The ovulative phase. *Psychosomatic Medicine* 1:245–270 (a)

Benedek, T., & Rubenstein, B. B. 1939. The correlations between ovarian activity and psychodynamic processes: II. The menstrual phase. *Psychosomatic Medicine* 1:461–485 (b)

Benson, R. C. 1964. *Handbook of obstetrics and gynecology.* Los Angeles: Lange Medical Publications

Borst, C. V. (Ed.) 1970. *The mind/brain identity theory.* New York: Macmillan

Cohen, S. Belensky, I., & Chaym, J. 1965. The study of monoamine oxidase activity by histochemical procedures. *Biochemical Pharmacology* 14:223–228

Cooke, W. R. 1945. The differential psychology of the American woman. *American Journal of Obstetrics and Gynecology* 49:457–472

Coppen, W. R., & Kessel, N. 1963. Menstruation and personality. *British Journal of Psychiatry* 109:711–721

Crane, G. E. 1970. Use of monoamine oxidase inhibiting antidepressants. In W. G. Clark & J. del Giudice (Eds.), *Principles of psychopharmacology: A textbook for physicians, medical students, and behavioral scientists.* New York: Academic Press

Dalton, K. 1954. Discussion on the premenstrual syndrome. *Proceedings of the Royal Society of Medicine* 48:339–346

Dalton, K. 1959. Menstruation and acute psychiatric illness. *British Medical Journal* 1:148–149

Dalton, K. 1960. Effect of menstruation on schoolgirls' weekly work. *British Medical Journal* 1:326–328 (a)

Dalton, K. 1961. Menstruation and crime. *British Medical Journal* 2:1425–1426 (b)

Dalton, K. 1960. Menstruation and accidents. *British Medical Journal* 2:1752–1753

Dalton, K. 1964. *The premenstrual syndrome*. Springfield, Ill.: Charles C Thomas

Dalton, K. 1966. The influence of mother's menstruation on her child. *Proceedings of the Royal Society of Medicine* 59:1014

Eichner, E., & Waltner, C. 1955. Premenstrual tension. *Medical Times* 83:771–779

Ferguson, J. H., & Vermillion, M. B. 1957. Premenstrual tension: Two surveys of its prevalence and a description of the syndrome. *Obstetrics and Gynecology* 9:615–619

Fodor, J. A. 1968. Functional explanation in psychology. In M. Brodbeck (Ed.), *Readings in the philosophy of the social sciences*. New York: Macmillan

Frank, R. T. 1931. The hormonal causes of premenstrual tension. *Archives of Neurology and Psychiatry* 26:1053–1057

Gottschalk, L. A., Kaplan, S. M., Gleser, G. C., & Winget, C. M. 1962. Variations in magnitude of emotions: A method applied to anxiety and hostility during phases of the menstrual cycle. *Psychosomatic Medicine* 24:300–311

Grant, C., & Pryse-Davies, J. 1968. Effects of oral contraceptives on depressive mood changes and on endometrial monoamine oxidase and phosphates. *British Medical Journal* 1:777–780

Greene, R. 1954. Discussion on the premenstrual syndrome. *Proceedings of the Royal Society of Medicine* 48:337–338

Greene, R., & Dalton, K. 1953. The premenstrual syndrome. *British Medical Journal* 1:1007–1013

Hamburg, D. A. 1966. Effects of progesterone on behavior. *Research Publications. Association for Research in Nervous and Mental Diseases* 43:251–265

Hersey, R. B. 1931. Emotional cycles in man. *Journal of Mental Science* 77:151–169

Ivey, M., & Bardwick, J. M. 1968. Patterns of affective fluctuation in the menstrual cycle. *Psychosomatic Medicine* 30:336–345

Janowsky, D. S., Gorney, R., Castelnuovo-Tedesco, P., & Stone, C. B. 1969. Premenstrual-menstrual increase in psychiatric hospital admission rates. *American Journal of Obstetrics and Gynecology* 103:189–191

Janowsky, D., Gorney, R., & Kelley, B. 1966. "The curse"— Vicissitudes and variations of the female fertility cycle: Part I. Psychiatric aspects. *Psychosomatics* 7:242–247

Kane, F. J., Lipton, M. A. & Ewing, J. A. 1969. Hormonal influences in female sexual response. *Archives of General Psychiatry* 20:202–209

Klaiber, E. L., Broverman, D. M., Vogel, W., Kobayashi, Y., & Moriarty, D. 1972. Effects of estrogen therapy on plasma MAO activity and EEG driving responses of depressed women. *American Journal of Psychiatry* 128:1492–1498

Kopell, B. S., Lunde, D. T., Clayton, R. B., & Moos, R. H. 1969. Variations in some measures of arousal during the menstrual cycle. *Journal of Nervous and Mental Diseases* 148:180–187

Lennane, M. B., & Lennane, R. J. 1973. Alleged psychogenic disorders in women—a possible manifestation of sexual prejudice. *New England Journal of Medicine* 288:288–292

Levitt, E. E., & Lubin, B. 1967. Some personality factors associated with menstrual complaints and menstrual attitude. *Journal of Psychosomatic Research* 11:267–270

Lieber, A., & Sherin, C. 1972. The case of the full moon. *Human Behavior* 1:29

Lloyd, C. W. 1970. The ovaries. In R. H. Williams (Ed.), *Textbook of endocrinology*. (3rd ed.) Philadelphia: W. B. Saunders

Luce, G. G. 1970. *Biological rhythms in psychiatry and medicine*. (USPHS Pub. No. 2088) Washington, D.C.: U.S. Department of Health, Education and Welfare

MacKinnon, P. C. B., & MacKinnon, I. L. 1956. Hazards of the menstrual cycle. *British Medical Journal* 1:555

Mandell, A., & Mandell, M. 1967. Suicide and the menstrual cycle. *Journal of the American Medical Association* 200:792–793

McCance, R. A., Luff, M. C., & Widdowson, E. E. 1937. Physical and emotional periodicity in women. *Journal of Hygiene* 37:571–605

McClintock, M. K. 1971. Menstrual synchrony and suppression. *Nature* 229:244–245

Moos, R. H. 1968. The development of a menstrual distress questionnaire. *Psychosomatic Medicine* 30:853–867

Moos, R. H. 1969. Assessment of psychological concomitants of oral contraceptives. In H. A. Salhanick et al (Eds.), *Metabolic effects of gonadal hormones and contraceptive steroids*. New York: Plenum Press (a)

Moos, R. H. 1969. Typology of menstrual cycle symptoms. *American Journal of Obstetrics and Gynecology* 103:390–402 (b)

Moos, R. H., Kopell, B. S., Melges, F. T., Yalom, I. D., Lunde, D. T., Clayton, R. B., & Hamburg, D. A. 1969. Fluctuations in symptoms and moods during the menstrual cycle. *Journal of Psychosomatic Research* 13:37–44

Morton, J. H., Additon, H., Addison, R. G., Hunt, L., & Sullivan, J. J. 1953. A clinical study of premenstrual tension. *American Journal of Obstetrics and Gynecology* 65:1182–1191

Neill, J. D., Johansson, E. D. B., Datts, J. K., & Knobil, E. 1967. Relationship between the plasma levels of leutinizing hormone and progesterone during the normal menstrual cycle. *Journal of Clinical Endocrinology* 27:1167–1173

Nowlis, V. 1965. Research with the Mood Adjective Check List. In S. S. Tomkins & C. E. Izard (Eds.), *Affect. cognition, and personality.* New York: Springer

Paige, K. E. 1971. Effects of oral contraceptives on affective fluctuations associated with the menstrual cycle. *Psychosomatic Medicine* 33:515–537

Pierson, W. R., & Lockhart, A. 1963. Effect of menstruation on simple reaction and movement time. *British Medical Journal* 1:796–797

Rees, L. 1953. The premenstrual tension syndrome and its treatment. *British Medical Journal* 1:1014–1016 (a)

Rees, L. 1953. Psychosomatic aspects of the premenstrual tension syndrome. *Journal of Mental Science* 99:62–73 (b)

Reynolds, L. T. 1966. A note on the perpetuation of a "scientific fiction." *Sociometry* 29:85–88

Ribeiro, A. L. 1962. Menstruation and crime. *British Medical Journal* 1:640

Richter, C. P. 1968. Periodic phenomena in man and animals: Their relation to neuroendocrine mechanisms (a monthly or near monthly cycle). In R. P. Michael (Ed.), *Endocrinology and human behavior.* London: Oxford University Press

Rose, R. M., Gordon, T. P., & Bernstein, P. S. 1972. Plasma testosterone levels in the male rhesus: Influences of sexual and social stimuli. *Science* 178:643–645

Seward, G. H. 1934. The female sex rhythm. *Psychological Bulletin* 31:153–192

Shainess, N. 1961. A re-evaluation of some aspects of femininity through a study of menstruation: A preliminary report. *Comparative Psychiatry* 2:20–26

Sherman, J. A. 1971. *On the psychology of women: A survey of empirical studies.* Springfield, Ill.: Charles C Thomas

Silbergeld, S., Brast, N., & Nobel, E. P. 1971. The menstrual cycle: A double-blind study of symptoms, mood and behavior, and biochemical variables using Enovid and placebo. *Psychosomatic Medicine* 33:411–428

Sommer, B. 1972. Menstrual cycle changes and intellectual performance. *Psychosomatic Medicine* 34:263–269

Southam, A. L., & Gonzaga, F. P. 1965. Systemic changes during the menstrual cycle. *American Journal of Obstetrics and Gynecology* 91:142–165

Southgate, J., Grant, E. C. G., Pollard, W., Pryse-Davies, J., & Sandler, M. 1968. Cyclical variations in endometrial monoamine oxidase: Correlation of histochemical and quantitative biochemical assays. *Biochemical Pharmacology* 17:721–726

Sutherland, H., & Stewart, I. 1965. A critical analysis of the premenstrual syndrome. *Lancet* 1:1180–1193

Thompson, C. 1950. Some effects of the derogatory attitude toward female sexuality. *Psychiatry* 13:349–354

Voitsechovsky, N. V. 1934. [The influence of menstruation upon the nervous and psychic apparatus of women.]

Thesis from the Imperial Military Academy, St. Petersburg, Russia, 1909, No. 6. Cited by G. H. Seward, The female sex rhythm. *Psychological Bulletin* 31:153–192

Whitehead, R. E. 1934. Women pilots. *Journal of Aviation Medicine* 5:47–49

Zimmerman, E., & Parlee, M. B. 1973. Behavioral changes associated with the menstrual cycle: An experimental investigation. *Journal of Applied Social Psychology,* in press

Cultural Variations

A Cross-Culture Analysis of Sex Differences in the Behavior of Children Aged 3 through 11

Beatrice Whiting and Carolyn Pope Edwards

1. Bardwick, J. M. 1971. Psychology of Women: A Study of Biocultural Conflicts. New York: Harper & Row

2. Barry, H., III, Bacon, M. K., & Child, I. L. 1957. A cross-cultural survey of some sex differences in socialization. *J. Abn. & Soc. Psychol.* 55:327–332

3. D'Andrade, R. G. 1966. Sex differences and cultural institutions. In E. E. Maccoby (Ed.), *The Development of Sex Differences.* Stanford, Calif.: Stanford Univ. Press

4. Draper, P. L. November, 1971. Kung bushman childhood: A review of the Barry, Child, and Bacon hypothesis regarding the relation of child training practices to subsistence economy. Paper presented at the annual meetings of the American Anthropological Association, New York

5. Ember, C. R. 1973. The effect of feminine task assignment on the social behavior of boys. *Ethos,* in press

6. Imamura, S. 1965. Mother and Blind Child: The Influence of Child Rearing Practices on the Behavior of Preschool Blind Children. New York: Amer. Found. for Blind

7. Kagan, J., & Moss, H. A. 1962. Birth to Maturity. New York: Wiley

8. Minturn, L., & Lambert, W. W. 1964. Mothers of Six Cultures: Antecedents of Child Rearing. New York: Wiley

9. Munroe, R. L., & Munroe, R. H. 1971. Effect of environmental experience on spacial ability in an East African society. *J. Soc. Psychol.* 83:15–22

10. Nerlove, S. B. 1971. Private communication

11. Nerlove, S. B., Munroe, R. H., & Munroe, R. L. 1971. Effect of environmental experience on spatial ability: A replication. *J. Soc. Psychol.* 84:3–10

12. Whiting, B. B. 1963. Six Cultures: Studies of Child Rearing. New York: Wiley

13. Whiting, B. B., & Whiting, J. W. M. 1971. Task assignment and personality: a consideration of the effect of herding on boys. In W. W. Lambert & R. Weisbrod (Eds.), *Comparative Perspectives on Social Psychology.* Boston: Little, Brown

14. Whiting, J. W. M., Whiting, B. B., & Longabaugh, B. Children of six cultures. In press.

15. Witkin, H. A., Dyk, R. B., Faterson, H. R. Goodenough, D. R., & Karp, S. A. 1962. Psychological Differentiation. New York: Wiley

Matriarchy: As Women See It

Esther Newton and Paula Webster

Leacock, E. 1972. Introduction to Engels. *The origin of the family, private property and the state.* New York: International Publishers.

de Beauvoir, S. 1953. *The second sex.* New York: Knopf.

Borun, M.; McLaughlin, M.; Oboler, G.; Perchonock, N.; Sexton, L. 1971. *Women's liberation: an anthropological view.* Pittsburgh: Know, Inc.

Davis, E. 1970. *The first sex.* New York: Putnam's.

Diner, H. 1965. *Mothers and amazons.* New York: Julian Press.

Firestone, S. 1970. *The dialectic of sex.* New York: Morrow.

Gough, K. 1971. The origin of the family. *Journal of Marriage and the Family.*

Reed, E. 1972. Engels and women's liberation. *International Socialist Review 33:* 4.

Psychological Sex Differences
Psychology Constructs the Female

Naomi Weisstein

Astin, A. W., The functional autonomy of psychotherapy. *American Psychologist,* 1961, *16,* 75–78.

Barron, F. & Leary, T., Changes in psychoneurotic patients with and without psychotherapy. *J. Consulting Psychology,* 1955, *19,* 239–245.

Bregin, A. E., The effects of psychotherapy: negative results revisited. *Journal of Consulting Psychology,* 1963, *10,* 244–250.

Bettelheim, B., The commitment required of a woman entering a scientific profession in present day American society. *Woman and the scientific professions.* The MIT symposium on American Women in Science and Engineering, 1965.

Bleck, J., Some reasons for the apparent inconsistency of personality. *Psychological Bulletin,* 1968, *70,* 210–212.

Cartwright, R. D. & Vogel, J. L., A comparison of changes in psychoneurotic patients during matched periods of therapy and no-therapy. *Journal of Consulting Psychology,* 1960, *24,* 121–127.

Erikson, E., Inner and outer space: reflections on womanhood. *Daedalus,* 1964, *93,* 582–606.

Eysenck, H. J., The effects of psychotherapy: an evaluation. *Journal of Consulting Psychology,* 1952, *16,* 319–324.

Fieldcrest—Advertisement in the *New Yorker,* 1965.

Fried, M. H., Mankind excluding woman, review of Tiger's *Men in groups. Science,* 1969, *165,* 883–884.

Freud, S., *The sexual enlightenment of children.* Collier Books Edition, 1963.

Goldstein, A. P. & Dean, S. J., *The investigation of psychotherapy: commentaries and readings.* John Wiley & Sons, New York: 1966.

Hacker, H. M., Women as a minority group. *Social Forces,* 1951, *30,* 60–69.

Hamburg, D. A. & Lunde, D. T., Sex hormones in the development of sex differences in human behavior. In Maccoby, (ed.), *The development of sex differences,* pp. 1–24, Stanford University Press, 1966.

Hampton, J. L. & Hampton, J. C., The ontogenesis of sexual behavior in man. In Young, W. C., *Sex and internal secretions,* 1966, 1401–1432.

Harlow, H. F., The heterosexual affectional system in monkeys. *The American Psychologist,* 1962, *17,* 1–9.

Hooker, E., Male homosexuality in the Rorschach. *Journal of Projective Techniques,* 1957, *21,* 18–31.

Itani, J., Paternal care in the wild Japanese monkeys, *Macaca fuscata.* In Southwick, C. H. (ed.), *Primate social behavior,* Princeton: Van Nostrand, 1963.

Little, K. B. & Schneidman, E. S., Congruences among interpretations of psychological and anamestic data. *Psychological Monographs,* 1959, *73,* 1–42.

Maccoby, Eleanor E., Sex differences in intellectual functioning. In Maccoby, (ed.), *The development of sex differences,* 25–55. Stanford U. Press: 1966.

Masters, W. H. & Johnson, V. E., *Human sexual response.* Little, Brown: Boston, 1966.

Mead, M., *Male and female: a study of the sexes in a changing world.* William Morrow: New York, 1949.

Milgram, S., Some conditions of obedience and disobedience to authority. *Human Relations,* 1965a, *18,* 57–76.

Milgram, S., Liberating effects of group pressures. *Journal of Personality and Social Psychology,* 1965b, *1,* 127–134.

Mitchell, G. D., Paternalistic behavior in primates. *Psychological Bulletin,* 1969, 71, 399–417.

Money, J. Sexual dimorphism and homosexual gender identity, *Psychological Bulletin,* 1970, *6,* 425–440.

Powers, E. & Witmer, H., *An experiment in the prevention of delinquency.* New York: Columbia University Press, 1951.

Rheingold, J., *The fear of being a woman.* Grune & Stratton: New York, 1964.

Rosenthal, R., On the social psychology of the psychological experiment: the experimenter's hypothesis as unintended determinant of experimental results. *American Scientist,* 1963, *51,* 268–283.

Rosenthal, R., *Experimenter effects in behavioral research.* New York: Appleton-Century Crofts, 1966.

Rosenthal, R. & Jacobson, L., *Pygmalion in the classroom: teacher expectation and pupil's intellectual development.* New York: Holt Rinehart & Winston, 1968.

Rosenthal, R. & Lawson, R., A longitudinal study of the effects of experimenter bias on the operant learning of laboratory rats. Unpublished manuscript, Harvard University, 1961.

Rosenthal, R. & Pode, K. L., The effect of experimenter bias on the performance of the albino rat. Unpublished manuscript, Harvard U., 1960.

Rotter, J. B., Psychotherapy. *Annual Review of Psychology,* 1960, *11,* 381–414.

Schachter, S. & Singer, J. E., Cognitive, social and physiological determinants of emotional state. *Psychological Review,* 1962, *63,* 379–399.

Schwarz-Belkin, M., Les fleurs de mal. In *Festschrift for Gordon Piltdown.* Ponzi Press, New York, 1914.

Storch, M., Reply to Tiger, 1970. Unpublished manuscript.

Tiger, L., Male dominance? Yes. A sexist plot? No. *New York Times Magazine,* October 25, 1970.

Tiger, L., *Men in groups.* New York: Random House, 1969.

Truax, C. B., Effective ingredients in psychotherapy: an approach to unraveling the patient-therapist interaction. *Journal of Counseling Psychology,* 1963, *10,* 256–263.

Psychology of Women

Martha S. Mednick and Hilda J. Weissman

1. Abramowitz, S. I., Abramowitz, C. V., Jackson, C., Gomes, B. 1973. The politics of clinical judgment. *J. Consult. Clin. Psychol.* 41:385–91.

2. Alper, T. G. 1973. The relationship between role orientation and achievement motivation in college women. *J. Pers.* 41:9–31.

3. Astin, H. S., Parelman, A., Fisher, A. 1974. *Annotated bibliography of sex roles.* NIMH–USPHS, ADM 75–166.

4. Astin, H. S., Suniewick, N., Dweck, S. 1971. *Women, a bibliography on their education and careers.* Washington, D.C.: Human Service Press.

5. Babladelis, G. 1973. Sex-stereotyping: students' perceptions of college professors. *Percept. Mot. Skills* 37:47–50.

6. Bardwick, J. M. 1971. *Psychology of Women.* New York: Harper & Row.

7. Bardwick, J. M., ed. 1972. *Readings on the psychology of women.* New York: Harper & Row.

8. Bart, P. 1973. A funny thing happened on the way to the orifice: women in gynecology textbooks. See Ref. 63, 283–88.

9. Beigel, H. 1972. The use of hypnosis in female sexual anaesthesia. *J. Am. Soc. Psychosom. Dent. Med.* 19:4–14.

10. Bem, S. L. 1973. But what can woman become? *Contemp. Psychol.* 18:450.

11. Bem, S. L. 1974. The measurement of psychological androgyny. *J. Consult. Clin. Psychol.* 42:165–72.

12. Bem, S. L. 1975. Sex-role adaptability: one consequence of psychological androgyny. *J. Pers. Soc. Psychol.* In press.

13. Bem, S. L., Bem, D. J. 1971. Training the woman to know her place: the power of a non-conscious ideology. In *Roles women play: readings towards women's liberation,* ed. M. H. Garskoff. Belmont, Calif.: Brooks/Cole.

14. Bernard, J. 1972. *Future of marriage.* New York: World.

15. Bernard, J. 1974. *Future of motherhood.* New York: Dial Press.

16. Block, J. H. 1973. Conceptions of sex roles. *Am. Psychol.* 28:512–26.

17. Block, J., von der Lippe, A., Block, J. H. 1973. Sex role and socialization patterns: some personality concomitants and environmental antecedents. *J. Consult. Clin. Psychol.* 41:321–41.

18. Boserup, E. 1970. *Woman's role in economic development.* New York: St. Martin's.

19. Broverman, I. K., Broverman, D. M., Clarkson, F. E., Rosenkrantz, P. S., Vogel, S. R. 1970. Sex-role stereotypes and clinical judgments of mental health. *J. Consult. Clin. Psychol.* 34:1–7.

20. Broverman, I. K., Vogel, S. R., Broverman, D. M., Clarkson, F. E., Rosenkrantz, P. S. 1972. Sex role stereotypes: a current appraisal. *J. Soc. Issues* 28:59–78.

21. Burghardt, N. R. 1973. *The motive to avoid success in school-aged males and females.* Presented at Am. Psychol. Assoc. Meet. Montreal.

22. Carlson, R. 1972. Understanding women: implications for personality theory and research. *J. Soc. Issues* 28:17–32.

23. Chasseguet-Smirgel, J. 1970. *Female sexuality: new psychoanalytic views.* Ann Arbor: Univ. Michigan Press.

24. Chesler, P. 1972. *Women and madness.* Garden City, N. Y.: Doubleday.

25. Chodoff, P. 1973. Feminine psychology and infantile sexuality. See Ref. 91, 183–200.

26. Constantinople, A. 1973. Masculinity-femininity: an exception to a famous dictum? *Psychol. Bull.* 80:389–407.

27. Crummer, M. L. 1972. *Sex-role identification, "motive to avoid success and competitive performance in college women.* PhD thesis. Univ. Florida, Gainesville. 89 pp.

28. Daly, M. 1973. *Beyond God the father: toward a philosophy of women's liberation.* Boston: Beacon.

29. Deaux, K., Emswiller, T. 1974. Explanations of successful performance on sex-linked tasks: what is skill for the male is luck for the female. *J. Pers. Soc. Psychol.* 29:80–85.

30. de Castillejo, I. C. 1973. *Knowing woman.* New York: Harper & Row.

31. DeMoor, W. 1972. Vaginismus: etiology and treatment. *Am. J. Psychother.* 26:207–15.

32. Dufresne, J. M. M. 1971. *Differential reactions of males to three different female sex roles.* PhD thesis. Univ. Connecticut, Storrs. 199 pp.

33. Ehrlich, C. 1973. The woman book industry. See Ref. 63, 268–82.

34. Eicher, W. 1973. Psychogenesis and treatment of female functional sexual disorders. *Med. Welt* 24:1270–72.

35. Ellis, L. J., Bentler, P. M. 1973. Traditional sex-determined role standards and sex stereotypes. *J. Pers. Soc. Psychol.* 24:28–34.

36. Entwisle, D. R., Greenberger, E. 1972. Adolescents' views of women's work role. *Am. J. Orthopsychiat.* 42:648–56.

37. Feather, N. T., Raphelson, A. C. 1974. Fear of success in Australian and American student groups: motive or sex-role stereotype? *J. Pers.* 42:190–201.

38. Feather, N. T., Simon, J. G. 1971. Attribution of responsibility and valence of outcome in relation to expectations of success based upon selective or manipulative control. *J. Pers. Soc. Psychol.* 18:173–88.

39. Feather, N. T., Simon, J. G. 1973. Fear of success and causal attribution for outcome. *J. Pers.* 41:525–42.

40. Feldman, S. A., Kiesler, S. B. 1975. Those who are number two try harder: the effect of sex on attributions of causality. *J. Pers. Soc. Psychol.* In press.

41. Fisher, S. 1973. *The female orgasm: psychology, physiology, fantasy.* New York: Basic Books.

42. Frieze, I. H. 1975. Women's expectations for and causal attributions of success and failure. See Ref. 90.

43. Furniss, W. T., Graham, P. A. 1974. *Women in higher education.* Washington, D.C.: Am. Counc. Educ.

44. Gadpaille, W. J. 1972. Research into the physiology of maleness and femaleness. *Arch. Gen. Psychiat.* 26:193–206.

45. Gelb, L. 1973. Masculinity-femininity: a study in imposed inequality. See Ref. 91, 363–406.

46. Ginsberg, G. L., Frosch, W. A., Shapiro, T. 1972. The new impotence. *Arch. Gen. Psychiat.* 26:218–20.

47. Gruder, C. L., Cook, T. D. 1971. Sex, dependency and helping. *J. Pers. Soc. Psychol.* 19:290–94.

48. Gump, J. P. 1972. Sex-role attitudes and psychological well-being. *J. Soc. Issues* 28:79–92.

49. Gurin, G., Gurin, P. 1970. Expectancy theory in the study of poverty. *J. Soc. Issues* 26:83–104.

50. Haavio-Mannila, E. 1971. Convergences between East and West: tradition and modernity in sex roles in Sweden, Finland and the Soviet Union. *Acta Sociol.* 14:114–25.

51. Harding, M. E. 1970. *The way of all women.* New York: Putnam.

52. Harris, M. B., Bays, G. 1973. Altruism and sex roles. *Psychol. Rep.* 32:1002.

53. Hawley, P. 1971. What women think men think: does it affect their career choice? *J. Couns. Psychol.* 18:193–99.

54. Helson, R. 1972. The changing image of the career woman. *J. Soc. Issues* 28:33–46.

55. Helson, R. 1973. Heroic and tender modes in women authors of fantasy. *J. Pers.* 41:493–512.

56. Hochschild, A. R. 1973. A review of sex role research. See Ref. 63, 249–67.

57. Hoffman, L. W. 1972. Early childhood experiences and women's achievement motives. *J. Soc. Issues* 28:157–76.

58. Hoffman, L. W. 1974. Fear of success in males and females: 1965 and 1972. *J. Consult. Clin. Psychol.* 42:353–58.

59. Holter, H. 1970. *Sex roles and social structure.* Oslo: Universitetsforlaget.

60. Holter, H. 1971. Sex roles and social change. *Acta Sociol.* 14:2–12.

61. Holmstrom, E. I. 1973. Changing sex roles in a developing country. *J. Marriage Fam.* 35:546–53.

62. Horner, M. S. 1972. Toward an understanding of achievement-related conflicts in women. *J. Soc. Issues* 28:157–75.

63. Huber, J. 1973. *Changing women in a changing society.* Univ. Chicago.

64. Husted, J. R. 1972. The effect of method of systematic desensitization and presence of sexual communication in the treatment of female sexual anxiety by counterconditioning. *Diss. Abstr. Int.* 33:441.

65. Kagan, J. 1964. Acquisition and significance of sex typing and sex role identity. In *Review of Child Development Research,* ed. M. L. Hoffman, L. W. Hoffman. New York: Russell Sage Found.

66. Kando, T. M. 1972. Role strain: comparison of males, females, and transsexuals. *J. Marriage Fam.* 34:459–64.

67. Klein, V. 1946. *The feminine character, history of an ideology,* London: Kegan Paul.

68. Kohlberg, L. 1966. A cognitive-developmental analysis of children's sex-role concepts and attitudes. See Ref. 80, 82–173.

69. Klinger, E. 1969. Fantasy need achievement and performance: a role analysis. *Psychol. Rev.* 76:574–91.

70. Kreps, J. 1971. *Sex in the marketplace: American women at work.* Baltimore: Johns Hopkins.

71. Kresojevich, I. Z. 1972. *Motivation to avoid success in women as related to year in school, academic achievement and success context.* PhD thesis. Michigan State Univ., Lansing. 92 pp.

72. Kriger, S. F. 1972. Nach and perceived parental child-rearing attitudes of career women and homemakers. *J. Vocat. Behav.* 2:419–32.

73. Kronsky, B. J. 1971. Feminism and psychotherapy. *J. Contemp. Psychother.* 2:89–98.

74. Lederer, W. 1968. *The fear of women.* New York: Harcourt Brace Jovanovich.

75. Lipman-Blumen, J. 1972. How ideology shapes women's lives. *Sci. Am.* 226:34–42.

76. Lipman-Blumen, J. 1973. Role de-differentiation as a system response to crisis: occupational and political roles of women. *Sociol. Inq.* 43:105–29.

77. Lirtzman, S. I., Wahba, M. A. 1972. Determinants of coalitional behavior of men and women: sex roles or situational requirements? *J. Appl. Psychol.* 56:406–11.

78. Looft, W. R. 1971. Vocational aspirations of second-grade girls. *Psychol. Rep.* 28:241–42.

79. Looft, W. R. 1971. Sex differences in the expression of vocational aspiration by elementary school children. *Develop. Psychol.* 5:366.

80. Maccoby, E. E., ed. 1966. *The development of sex differences.* Stanford Univ. Press.

81. Maccoby, E. E., Jacklin, C. N. 1973. Sex differences in intellectual functioning. *Proc. 1972 Invitational Conf. Test. Probl.* Princeton: Educ. Test. Serv.

82. Madigan, F. C. 1957. Are sex mortality differentials biologically caused? *Milbank Mem. Fund Quart.* 35:202–23.

83. Maracek, J. 1974. *When stereotypes hurt: responses to dependent and aggressive communications.* Presented at East. Psychol. Assoc. Meet. Philadelphia.

84. Marmor, J. 1968. Changing patterns of femininity. In *The marriage relationship,* ed. S. Rosenbaum, I. Alger. New York: Basic Books.

85. Maxwell, P. G., Gonzalez, A. E. 1972. Traditional and nontraditional role choice and need for failure among college women. *Psychol. Rep.* 31:545–46.

86. McGuinness, E. L. 1974. *Success avoidance and competitive performance.* MS thesis. Rutgers Univ., New Brunswick, N.J. 109 pp.

87. Mednick, M. T. S. 1973. Motivational and personality factors related to career goals of black college women. Report to Manpower Admin., U.S. Dep. Labor, Publ. No. 218969. Springfield, Va.: NTIS.

88. Mednick, M. T. S. 1975. Social change and sex role inertia: the case of the kibbutz. See Ref. 90.

89. Mednick, M. T. S., Tangri, S. S. 1972. New perspectives on women. *J. Soc. Issues* 28(2): 1–250.

90. Mednick, M. T. S., Tangri, S. S., Hoffman, L. W., eds. 1975. *Women: social psychological perspectives on achievement.* New York: Holt, Rinehart & Winston.

91. Miller, J. B. 1973. *Psychoanalysis and women.* Baltimore: Penguin Books.

92. Minturn, L. 1973. *Sex role differentiation in contemporary communes.* Presented at Am. Psychol. Assoc. Meet. Montreal.

93. Mischel, W. 1966. A social-learning view of sex differences in behavior. See Ref. 80, 56–81.

94. Monahan, L., Kuhn, D., Shaver, P. 1974. Intrapsychic versus cultural explanations of the "fear of success" motive. *J. Pers. Soc. Psychol.* 29:60–64.

95. Money, J., Walker, P. A., Higham, E. 1974. My orgasm belongs to daddy. *Contemp. Psychol.* 19:399–400.

96. Morgan, E. 1972. *The descent of woman.* New York: Bantam Books.

97. Moulton, R. 1970. A survey and re-evaluation of the concept of penis envy. *Contemp. Psychoanal.* 7:84–104.

98. Moulton, R. 1973. The myth of femininity: a panel. *Am. J. Psychoanal.* 33:45–49.

99. Nowicki, S. 1973. *Predicting academic achievement of females from a locus of control orientation: some problems and some solutions.* Presented at Am. Psychol. Assoc. Meet. Montreal.

100. Oppenheimer, V. 1975. Woman's occupations. See 90.

101. Orzeck, L. A. 1972. *Stereotypes and expectations: how people react to female and male competitors and cooperators.* PhD thesis. Univ. Colorado, Boulder.

102. Palme, O. 1972. The emancipation of man. *J. Soc. Issues* 28:237–46.

103. Parker, V. J. 1971. *Fear of success, sex-role orientation of the task and competition condition as factors affecting women's performance in achievement-oriented situations.* PhD thesis. Ohio State Univ., Columbus.

104. Peplau, L. A. 1973. *The impact of fear of success, sex-role attitudes and opposite-sex relationships on women's intellectual performance: an experimental study of competition in dating couples.* PhD thesis. Harvard Univ., Cambridge.

105. Putnam, B. A., Hansen, J. C. 1972. Relationship of self-concept and feminine role concept to vocational maturity in young women. *J. Couns. Psychol.* 19:436–40.

106. Puryear, G. R., Mednick, M. S. 1974. Black militancy, affective attachment, and the fear of success in black college women. *J. Consult. Clin. Psychol.* 42:263–66.

107. Ray, L. 1972. The woman's magazine short-story heroine in 1957 and 1967. See Ref. 116, 41–62.

108. Raynor, J. O. 1970. Relationships between achievement-related motives, future orientation, and academic performance. *J. Pers. Soc. Psychol.* 15:28–33.

109. Recely, N. L. C. 1972. *Level of self-esteem and conformity to sex-role stereotypes.* PhD thesis. Univ. Colorado, Boulder. 162 pp.

110. Reik, T. 1960. *The creation of woman.* New York: Braziller.
111. Rice, J. K., Rice, D. G. 1973. Implications of the women's liberation movement for psychotherapy. *Am J. Psychiat.* 130:191–96.
112. Robbins, L., Robbins, E. 1973. Comment on: toward an understanding of achievement related conflicts in women. *J. Soc. Issues* 29:113–37.
113. Rosaldo, M. Z., Lamphere, L. 1974. *Woman, culture and society.* Stanford Univ. Press.
114. Rossi, A. S., Calderwood, A. 1973. *Academic women on the move.* New York: Russell Sage Found.
115. Saario, T., Jacklin, C., Tittle, C. 1973. Sex-role stereotyping in public schools. *Harvard Educ. Rev.* 43:386–416.
116. Safilios-Rothschild, C. 1972. *Toward a sociology of women.* Lexington, Mass.: Xerox Corp.
117. Salzman, L. 1967. Psychology of the female: a new look. *Arch. Gen. Psychiat.* 17:195–203.
118. Sanger, S. P., Alker, H. A. 1972. Dimensions of internal-external locus of control and the women's liberation movement. *J. Soc. Issues* 28:115–29.
118a. Sarason, I. G., Smith, R. E. 1971. Personality. *Ann. Rev. Psychol.* 22:393–446.
119. Schein, V. E. 1973. The relationship between sex-role stereotypes and requisite management characteristics. *J. Appl. Psychol.* 57:95–100.
120. Seward, G. H., Williamson, R. C., eds. 1970. *Sex roles in changing society.* New York: Random House.
121. Seyfried, B. A., Hendrick, C. 1973. When do opposites attract? When they are opposite in sex and sex-role attitudes. *J. Pers. Soc. Psychol.* 25:15–20.
122. Sherfey, M. J. 1972. *The nature and evolution of female sexuality.* New York: Random House.
123. Sherman, J. A. 1971. *On the psychology of women.* Springfield, Ill.: Thomas.
124. Sherman, J. A. 1972. *Social values, femininity and the development of female competence.* Presented at Meet. Am. Assoc. Advan. Sci., Washington, D.C.
125. Sherman, L. J. 1973. A psychological view of women in policing. *J. Police Sci. Admin.* 1:383–93.
126. Simon, J. G., Feather, N. T. 1973. Causal attributions for success and failure at university examinations. *J. Educ. Psychol.* 64:46–56.
127. Sorrentino, R. M., Short, J. A. 1974. Effects of fear of success on women's performance at masculine versus feminine tasks. *J. Res. Pers.* In press.
128. Spence, J. T., Helmreich, R. 1972. Who likes competent women? Competence, sex role congruence of interests, and subjects' attitudes toward women as determinants of interpersonal attraction. *J. Appl. Soc. Psychol.* 2:197–213.
129. Spence, J. T., Helmreich, R., Stapp, J. 1973. A short version of the Attitudes towards Women Scale (AWS). *Bull. Psychon. Soc.* 2:219–20.
130. Spence, J. T., Helmreich, R., Stapp, J. 1975. Ratings of self and peers on sex-role attributes and their relation to self-esteem. *J. Pers. Soc. Psychol.* In press.
131. Stein, A. H., Bailey, M. M. 1973. The socialization of achievement orientation in females. *Psychol. Bull.* 80:345–66.
132. Steinmann, A., Fox, D. J. 1970. Attitudes towards women's family role among black and white undergraduates. *Fam. Coord.* 19:363–68.
133. Stoller, R. J. 1974. Symbiosis anxiety and the development of masculinity. *Arch. Gen. Psychiat.* 30:164.
134. Tangri, S. S. 1972. Determinants of occupational role innovation among college women. *J. Soc. Issues* 28:177–200.
135. Tavris, C. 1973. Who likes women's liberation—and why: the case of the unliberated liberals. *J. Soc. Issues* 29:175–92.
136. Thurber, S. 1972. Defensive externality and academic achievement by women. *Psychol. Rep.* 30:454.
137. Touhey, J. C. 1974. Effects of additional women professionals on ratings of occupational prestige and desirability. *J. Pers. Soc. Psychol.* 29:86–90.
138. Unger, R. K., Denmark, F. L. 1974. *Woman: dependent or independent variable.* New York: Psychol. Dimensions.
139. Unger, R. K., Raymond, B. J., Levine, S. M. 1974. Are women a "minority" group? Sometimes! *Int. J. Group Tensions* 4:71–81.
140. Ward, S. W., Mausner, B. 1973. Behavioral and fantasied indicators of avoidance of success in men and women. *J. Pers.* 41:457–470.
141. Warshay, D. W. 1972. Sex differences in language style. See Ref. 116, 3–9.
142. Weiner, B. 1972. *Theories of motivation.* Chicago: Markham.
143. Weitzmann, L. J., Eifler, D., Hokada, E., Ross, C. 1972. Sex-role socialization in picture books for children. *Am J. Sociol.* 77:1125–49.
144. Wellens, G. J. 1972. *The motive to avoid success in high school seniors: Nach shifts and psychological correlates.* PhD thesis. Illinois Inst. Technol., Chicago. 217 pp.
145. Weston, P., Mednick, M. T. S. 1970. Race, social class and the motive to avoid success in women. *J. Cross-Cult. Psychol.* 1:284–91.
146. White, R. B. 1966. Induced abortions: a survey of their psychiatric implications, complications, and indications. *Texas Rep. Biol. Med.* 24:531–58.
147. Williams, J. H. 1973. Sexual role identification and personality functioning in girls: a theory revisited. *J. Pers.* 41:1–9.

148. Wolf, C., Gunderson, D. 1973. Sex roles in mountain communes: Utopia lost. *Impact* 2:52–60.

Social Construction of the Second Sex

Jo Freeman

1. Rossi, A. "Equality between the sexes: An immodest proposal." In Robert J. Lifton (Ed.), *The woman in America*. Boston: Beacon Press, 1965. pp. 102–103.
2. Bem, S. & Bem, D. "We're all nonconscious sexists." *Psychology Today*, 1970, 4(6), 26.
3. McClelland, D. "Wanted: A new self-image for women." In Robert J. Lifton (Ed.), *The woman in America*. Boston: Beacon Press, 1965, P. 173.
4. Bennett, E. M. & Cohen, L. R. "Men and women: Personality patterns and contrasts." *Genetic Psychology Monographs*, 1959, 59, 101–155.
5. Allport, G. *The nature of prejudice*. Reading, Mass.: Addison-Wesley, 1954. Pp. 142–161.
6. Terman, L. M. & Tyler, L. Psychological sex differences. In Leonard Carmichael (Ed.), *Manual of child psychology*. New York: Wiley & Sons, 1954. Pp. 1080–1100.
7. Smith, S. Age and sex differences in children's opinion concerning sex differences. *Journal of Genetic Psychology*, 1939, 54, 17–25.
8. Goldberg, P. Are women prejudiced against women? *Transaction*, April 1969, 28.
9. Clark, K. & Clark, M. Racial identification and preference in Negro children. In T. M. Newcomb and E. L. Hartley (Eds.), *Readings in social psychology*. New York: Holt, Rinehart & Winston, 1947.
10. Fisher, L. *Gandhi*. New York: Signet Key, 1954.
11. Fanon, F. *The wretched of the earth*. New York: Grove Press, 1963.
12. Myrdal, G. *An American dilemma*. New York: Harper, 1944.
13. De Vos, G. The relation of guilt toward parents to achievement and arranged marriage among the Japanese. *Psychiatry*, 1960, 23, 287–301.
14. Miles, C. C. Gifted children. In Carmichael, *op. cit.*, p. 1045.
15. See: Brown, R. *Social psychology*. New York: The Free Press. P. 162; Reuben Hill and Howard Becker (Eds.), *Family, marriage and parenthood*. Boston: D.C. Heath, 1955. P. 790; Goldberg, *op. cit.*, p. 28; Myrdal, *op. cit.*, Appendix V; and Goode, W. J., *The family*. Englewood Cliffs, New Jersey: Prentice-Hall, 1965. P. 70.
16. Tyler, L. Sex differences. Under "Individual differences" in the *International encyclopedia of the social sciences*, Vol. 7, 1968, New York: The MacMillan Co. Pp. 207–213.

17. Bales, R. F. Task roles and social roles in problem-solving groups. In T. M. Newcomb, E. Maccoby, and E. L. Hartly (Eds.), *Readings in social psychology* (3rd ed.). New York: Holt, Rinehart & Winston, 1958.
18. Maccoby, E. Sex differences in intellectual functioning. In E. Maccoby (Ed.), *The development of sex differences*. Stanford: Stanford University Press, 1966, Pp. 26 ff.
19. Neiman, L. J. The influence of peer groups upon attitudes toward the feminine role. *Social Problems*, 1954, 2, 104–111.
20. Milner, E. Effects of sex-role and social status on the early adolescent personality. *Genetic Psychological Monographs*, 40, 231–325.
21. Lipinski, B. *Sex-role conflict and achievement motivation in college women*. Unpublished doctoral dissertation, University of Cincinnati, 1965.
22. Asch, S. E. Studies of independence and conformity. A minority of one against a unaminous majority. *Psychological Monographs*, 1956, 70, No. 9.
23. Smith, *op. cit.*
24. Goldberg, *op cit.*
25. Bradway, K. P. & Thompson, C. W. Intelligence at adulthood: A twenty-five year followup. *Journal of Educational Psychology*, 1962, 53, 1–14.
26. Stivers, E. N. *Motivation for college of high school boys and girls*. Unpublished doctoral dissertation, University of Chicago, 1959.
27. Pierce, J. V. & Bowman, P. H.: The educational motivation patterns of superior students who do and do not achieve in high school. U.S. Office of Education Project #208, *Co-operative Research Monograph No. 2*, U.S. Printing Office, Washington, 1960, 33–60.
28. Pierce, J. V. Sex differences in achievement motivation of able high school students, *Co-operative Research Project No. 1097*, University of Chicago, December 1961.
29. *Ibid.*, p. 23.
30. *Ibid.*, p. 42.
31. Horner, M. Femininity and successful achievement: A basic inconsistency. In Bardwick, et. al., *Feminine personality and conflict*. Belmont: Brooks/Cole, 1970. See also pp. 97–122 in this text.
32. Terman & Tyler, *op. cit.*, p. 1104.
33. Maccoby, 1966, *op. cit.*, p. 26.
34. *Ibid.*, p. 27.
35. Maccoby, E. Woman's intellect. In Farber & Wilson (Eds.), *The potential of women*. New York: McGraw-Hill, 1963. P. 30.
36. *Ibid.*, p. 31. See also: Sherman, J. A. Problems of sex differences in space perception and aspects of intellectual functioning. *Psychological Review*, July 1967, 74, No. 4, 290–299; and Vernon, P. E. Ability factors and environmental influences. *American Psychologist*, Sept. 1965, 20, No. 9, 723–733.

37. Bronfenbrenner, U. Some familial antecedents of responsibility and leadership in adolescents. In Luigi Petrullo and Bernard M. Bass (Eds.), *Leadership and interpersonal behavior.* New York: Holt, Rinehart, & Winston, 1961. P. 260.

38. Levy, D. M. *Maternal overprotection.* New York: Columbia University Press, 1943.

39. Maccoby, 1963, *op. cit.,* p. 31.

40. Witkin, H. A., Dyk, R. B., Paterson, H. E., Goodenough, D. R., & Karp, S. A. *Psychological differentiation.* New York: Wiley, 1962.

41. Clapp, J. *Sex differences in mathematical reasoning ability.* Unpublished paper, 1968.

42. Sontag, I. W., Baker, C. T., & Nelson, V. A. Mental growth and personality development: A longitudinal study. *Monographs of the Society for Research in Child Development,* 1953, 23, No. 68.

43. Maccoby, 1963, *op. cit.,* p. 33.

44. Kagan, J. & Moss, H. A. *Birth to maturity: A study in psychological development.* New York and London: John Wiley and Sons, 1962. P. 275.

45. *Ibid.,* p. 225.

46. Winterbottom, M. The relation of need for achievement to learning experiences in independence and mastery. In Harold Proshansky and Bernard Seidenberg (Eds.), *Basic studies in social psychology.* New York: Holt, Rinehart & Winston, 1965. Pp. 294–307.

47. Sears, R. R., Maccoby, E., & Levin, H. *Patterns of child rearing.* Evanston, Ill.: Row, Peterson, 1957.

48. Bronfenbrenner, *op. cit.,* p. 260.

49. *Ibid.*

50. Schachter, S. *The psychology of affiliation.* Stanford: Stanford University Press, 1959.

51. Bronfenbrenner, *op. cit.,* p. 267.

52. Douvan, E. Employment and the adolescent. In F. Ivan Nye and Lois W. Hoffman (Eds.), *The employed mother in America.* Chicago: Rand McNally, 1963.

53. Kagan and Moss, *op. cit.,* p. 222.

54. McClelland, D. C. *The achieving society.* Princeton: Van Nostrand, 1961.

55. Kagan and Moss, *op. cit.,* p. 270.

56. Maccoby, 1963, *op. cit.,* p. 37.

57. Sinick, D. Two anxiety scales correlated and examined for sex differences. *Journal of Clinical Psychology,* 1956, 12, 394–395.

58. Maccoby, 1963, *op. cit.,* p. 37.

59. Myrdal, *op. cit.,* p. 1077.

60. Montagu, A. Anti-feminism and race prejudice. *Psychiatry,* 1946, 9, 69–71.

61. Keniston, E. & Keniston, K. An American anachronism: The image of women and work. *American Scholar,* Summer 1964, 33, No. 3, 355–375.

62. Rossi, *op. cit.*

63. Adorno, T. W., et al., *The authoritarian personality.* New York: Harper, 1950.

64. Stephens, W. N. *The family in cross-cultural perspective.* New York: Holt, Rinehart & Winston, 1963.

65. D'Andrade, R. Sex differences and cultural institutions. In Maccoby (Ed.), 1966, *op. cit.,* p. 189.

66. Blood, R. O., & Wolfe, D. M. *Husband and wives.* Glencoe: The Free Press, 1960.

67. Blood, R. O. Long-range causes and consequences of the employment of married women. *Journal of Marriage and the Family,* 1965, 27, No. 1, 46.

68. Goode, *op. cit.,* p. 76.

69. Hill and Becker, *op. cit.,* p. 790.

70. Hallenbeck, P. N. An analysis of power dynamics in marriage. *Journal of Marriage and the Family,* May 1966, 28, No. 2, 203.

71. Blood, *op. cit.,* p. 47.

72. Barry, H., Bacon, M. K., & Child, I. L. A cross-cultural survey of some sex differences in socialization. *Journal of Abnormal and Social Psychology,* 1957, 55, 330.

73. Spiro, M. E. *Kibbutz: Venture in utopia.* Cambridge: Harvard University Press, 1956.

74. D'Andrade, *op. cit.,* p. 191.

75. Goode, *op. cit.,* p. 70.

76. *Ibid.*

77. Barry, Bacon, & Child, *op. cit.,* p. 328.

78. Bronfenbrenner, U. Socialization and social class through time and space. In Maccoby, Newcomb and Hartly, *op. cit.*

79. Bronfenbrenner, U. The effects of social and cultural change on personality. *Journal of Social Issues,* 1969, 17, No. 1, 6–18.

80. Blood, *op. cit.,* p. 47.

Oppression of the Self

Women as a Minority Group

Helen Mayer Hacker

1. Louis Wirth, "The Problem of Minority Groups," *The Science of Man in the World Crisis,* ed. by Ralph Linton (1945), p. 347.

2. Kurt Lewin, "Self-Hatred Among Jews," *Contemporary Jewish Record,* IV (1941), 219–232.

3. *Fortune,* September, 1946, p. 5.

4. P. M. Symonds, "Changes in Sex Differences in Problems and Interests of Adolescents with Increasing Age," *Journal of Genetic Psychology,* 50 (1937), pp. 83–89, as referred to by Georgene H. Seward, *Sex and the Social Order* (1946), pp. 237–238.

5. George A. Lundberg, *Foundations of Sociology* (1939), p. 319.
6. Robert S. and Helen Merrell Lynd, *Middletown* (1929), p. 120, and *Middletown in Transition* (1937), p. 176.
7. Joseph Kirk Folsom, *The Family and Democratic Society* (1943), pp. 623–624.
8. Gunnar Myrdal, *An American Dilemma* (1944), pp. 1073–1078.
9. Helen M. Hacker, Toward a Definition of Role Conflict in Modern Women (unpublished manuscript).
10. As furnished by such books as Helene Deutsch. *The Psychology of Women* (1944–1945) and Ferdinand Lundberg and Marynia F. Farnham, *Modern Woman: The Lost Sex* (1947).
11. David Riesman, "The Saving Remnant: An Examination of Character Structure," *Years of the Modern: An American Appraisal,* ed. by John W. Chase (1949), pp. 139–40.
12. Robert E. Park, "Our Racial Frontier on the Pacific," *The Survey Graphic,* 56 (May 1, 1926), pp. 192–196.
13. William Ogburn and Meyer Nimkoff, *Sociology* (2d ed., 1950), p. 187.
14. Howard Becker, *Systematic Sociology on the Basis of the "Beziehungslehre" and "Gebildelehre" of Leopold von Wiese* (1932), pp. 263–268.
15. Kurt Lewin, *Resolving Social Conflicts* (1948), p. 181.
16. Ruth Benedict, "Continuities and Discontinuities in Cultural Conditioning," *Psychiatry,* 1 (1938), pp. 161–167.
17. Georgene H. Seward, *op. cit.,* pp. 239–240.
18. Mirra Komarovsky, "Cultural Contradictions and Sex Roles," *The American Journal of Sociology,* LII (November 1946), 184–189.
19. Arnold Green, "A Re-Examination of the Marginal Man Concept," *Social Forces,* 26 (December 1947), pp. 167–171.

The Sexual Politics of Interpersonal Behavior

Nancy Henley and Jo Freeman

Argyle, M., Lalljee, M., & Cook, M. The effects of visibility on interaction in a dyad. *Human Relations,* 1968, 21:3–17.
Argyle, M., Salter, V., Nicholson, H., Williams, M., & Burgess, P. The communication of inferior and superior attitudes by verbal and non-verbal signals. *British Journal of Social and Clinical Psychology,* 1970, 9:222–31.
Austin, W. M. Some social aspects of paralanguage. *Canadian Journal of Linguistics,* 1965, 11:31–39.
Brown, R. *Social psychology.* Glencoe, Ill.: Free Press, 1965.
Brown, R., & Ford, M. Address in American English. *Journal of Abnormal and Social Psychology,* 1961, 62:375–85.
Brown, R., & Gilman, A. The pronouns of power and soli-

darity. In T. A. Sebeak, ed., *Style in language.* Cambridge, Mass.: M.I.T. Press, 1960.
Efran, J. S., & Broughton, A. Effect of expectancies for social approval on visual behavior. *Journal of Personality and Social Psychology,* 1966, 4:103–7.
Ellsworth, P. C., Carlsmith, J. M., & Henson, A. The stare as a stimulus to flight in human subjects: A series of field experiments. *Journal of Personality and Social Psychology,* 1972, 21:302–11.
Exline, R. Explorations in the process of person perception: Visual interaction in relation to competition, sex, and need for affiliation. *Journal of Personality,* 1963, 31:1–20.
Exline, R., Gray, D., & Schuette, D. Visual behavior in a dyad as affected by interview content and sex of respondent. *Journal of Personality and Social Psychology,* 1965, 1:201–9.
Goffman, E. The nature of deference and demeanor. *American Anthropologist,* 1956, 58:473–502. Reprinted in E. Goffman, *Interaction ritual.* New York: Anchor, 1967, pp. 47–95.
Goldberg, S., & Lewis, M. Play behavior in the year-old infant: Early sex differences. *Child Development,* 1969, 40:21–31.
Henley, N. The politics of touch. American Psychological Association, 1970. In P. Brown, ed., *Radical psychology.* New York: Harper & Row, 1973.
Hutt, C., & Ounsted, C. The biological significance of gaze aversion with particular reference to the syndrome of infantile autism. *Behavioral Science,* 1966, 11:346–56.
Jourard, S. M. An exploratory study of body accessibility. *British Journal of Social and Clinical Psychology,* 1966, 5:221–31.
Jourard, S. M., & Lasakow, P. Some factors in self-disclosure. *Journal of Abnormal and Social Psychology,* 1958, 56:91–98.
Jourard, S. M., & Rubin, J. E. Self-disclosure and touching: A study of two modes of interpersonal encounter and their interrelation. *Journal of Humanistic Psychology,* 1968, 8:39–48.
Key, M. R. Linguistic behavior of male and female. *Linguistics,* 1972, 88:15–31.
Lakoff, R. Language and woman's place. *Language in Society,* 1973, 2, 1:45–79.
Lewis, M. Parents and children: Sex-Role development. *School Review,* 1972, 80:229–40.
O'Connor, L. Male dominance: The nitty gritty of oppression. *It Ain't Me Babe,* 1970, 1:9.
O'Neill, W. L. *Everyone was brave: The rise and fall of feminism.* Chicago: Quadrangle, 1969.
Ross, E. A. *Principles of sociology.* New York: Century, 1921.
Rubin, Z. Measurement of romantic love. *Journal of Personality and Social Psychology,* 1970, 16:265–73.
Slobin, D. I., Miller, S. H., & Porter, L. W. Forms of address

and social relations in a business organization. *Journal of Personality and Social Psychology,* 1968, 8:289–93.

Sommer, R. *Personal space.* Englewood Cliffs, N.J.: Prentice-Hall, 1969.

Tinbergen, N. Comparative study of the behavior of gulls: A progress report. *Behavior,* 1959, 15:1–70.

Waller, W. W., & Hill, R. *The family: A dynamic interpretation.* New York: Dryden, 1951.

Willis, F. N., Jr. Initial speaking distance as a function of the speakers' relationship. *Psychonomic Science,* 1966, 5:221–22.

Case Study of a Nonconscious Ideology: Training the Woman to Know Her Place

Sandra L. Bem and Daryl J. Bem

Barry, H., III, Bacon, M. K., & Child, I. L. A cross-cultural survey of some sex differences in socialization. *Journal of Abnormal and Social Psychology,* 1957, **55**, 327–332.

Brown, R. *Social psychology.* New York: Free Press, 1965.

Crandall, V. J. & Rabson, A. Children's repetition choices in an intellectual achievement situation following success and failure. *Journal of Genetic Psychology,* 1960, **97**, 161–168.

Dodge, N. D. *Women in the Soviet economy.* Baltimore: The Johns Hopkins Press, 1966.

Flanagan, J. C. Project talent, Unpublished manuscript.

Freidan, B. *The feminine mystique.* New York: Norton, 1963.

Goldberg, P. Are women prejudiced against women? *Transaction,* April 1968, **5,** 28–30.

Goldberg, S. & Lewis, M. Play behavior in the year-old infant: Early sex differences. *Child Development,* 1969, **40,** 21–31.

Gottlesman, I. I. Heritability of personality: A demonstration. *Psychological Monographs,* 1963, **77** (Whole No. 572).

Kagan, J. Acquisition and significance of sex typing and sex role identity. In M. L. Hoffman & L. W. Hoffman (Eds.), *Review of child development research, Vol. 1.* New York: Russell Sage Foundation, 1964, pp. 137–167.

McDavid, J. W. Imitative behavior in preschool children. *Psychological Monographs,* 1959, **73** (Whole No. 486).

Milton, G. A. Five studies of the relation between sex role identification and achievement in problem solving. Technical Report No. 3, Department of Industrial Administration, Department of Psychology, Yale University, December, 1958.

Sears, R. R., Maccoby, E. E., & Levin, H. *Patterns of child rearing.* Evanston, Ill.: Row, Peterson, 1957.

Smith, M. E. The influences of age, sex, and situation on the frequency of form and functions of questions asked by preschool children. *Child Development,* 1933, **3,** 201–213.

Torrance, E. P. *Guiding creative talent.* Englewood Cliffs, N.J.: Prentice-Hall, 1962.

Who Has the Power? The Marital Struggle

Dair L. Gillespie

1. Robert O. Blood, Jr. and Donald M. Wolfe, *Husbands and Wives: The Dynamics of Married Living* (New York: Free Press, 1960), pp. 29–30.
2. *Ibid.,* pp. 19–20.
3. Constantia Safilios-Rothschild, "Family Sociology or Wives' Family Sociology? A Cross-Cultural Examination of Decision Making," *Journal of Marriage and the Family,* 31 (May 1969): 297–98.
4. Blood and Wolfe, p. 22.
5. William Goode, *World Revolution and Family Patterns* (New York: Free Press, 1963), p. 70.
6. *The Family* (Englewood Cliffs, N.J.: Prentice-Hall, 1964), p. 75.
7. *Ibid.,* p. 87.
8. Blood and Wolfe, p. 37.
9. *Ibid.,* p. 29; emphasis mine.
10. *Kinde, Kuche, Kirche As Scientific Law: Psychology Constructs the Female* (pamphlet; New York: New England Free Press, 1969), p. 7.
11. "Marriage," *The Feminist* (New York, 1969), pp. 2–4.
12. Richard T. Gallen, *Wives' Legal Rights* (New York: Dell, 1967), p. 6.
13. Harriet F. Pilpel and Theodora Zavin, *Your Marriage and the Law* (New York: Collier Books, 1964), p. 65.
14. *Know Your Rights: What a Working Wife Should Know About Her Legal Rights* (U.S. Department of Labor, Women's Bureau, 1965), p. 1.
15. Gallen, p. 6.
16. *Women and the Law: The Unfinished Revolution* (Albuquerque: University of New Mexico Press, 1969), p. 41.
17. *Ibid.,* p. 69.
18. Conversation with Ann Leffler, U.C. Berkeley, 1969.
19. *The Second Sex* (New York: Bantam Books, 1968), p. 451.
20. *World Revolution and Family Patterns,* p. 21.
21. Blood and Wolfe, p. 45.
22. *Ibid.,* pp. 40–41.
23. *Ibid.,* p. 39.
24. *Ibid.,* pp. 28, 38.
25. *Blue Collar Marriage* (New York: Vintage Books, 1967), pp. 226–29.
26. *Ibid.,* p. 227.
27. Lynn O'Connor, "Male Dominance, the Nitty-Gritty of Oppression," *It Ain't Me, Babe,* 1 (June 11–July 1, 1970): 9–11.

28. *Women in Divorce* (New York: Free Press, 1956), pp. 120, 123.
29. *Ibid.*, p. 122.
30. Blood and Wolfe, p. 36.
31. Irving Tallman, "Working Class Wives in Suburbia: Fulfillment or Crisis?" *Journal of Marriage and the Family,* 31 (Feb. 1969): 66–69.
32. Blood and Wolfe, p. 34.
33. Andrew Billingsley and Amy Tate Billingsley, *Black Families in White America* (Englewood Cliffs, N.J.: Prentice-Hall, 1968), p. 8.
34. *Negro Women Workers in 1960,* U.S. Department of Labor, Women's Bureau, 1964, pp. 23–25; *Fact Sheet on the Relative Position of Women and Men Workers in the Economy,* U.S. Department of Labor, Women's Bureau, 1965, p. 3: U.S. Department of Labor, Bureau of Labor Statistics, *Employment and Earnings,* vol. 16, no. 7, Jan. 1970, Table A-1 (data under "Negro" heading are for "Negro and Other Races").
35. *Negro Women Workers,* pp. 23–25.
36. *Ibid.*, pp. 13–14.
37. *Marriage and Family Among Negroes* (Englewood Cliffs, N.J.: Prentice-Hall, 1966), p. 69.
38. "The Husband-Wife Power Relationship in Black Families and White Families," Ph.D. Dissertation, Stanford University.
39. Blood and Wolfe, pp. 41–44.
40. David M. Heer, "Dominance and the Working Wife," *Social Forces,* 36 (May 1958): 341–47.
41. Heer, "The Measurement and Bases of Family Power: An Overview," *Marriage and Family Living,* 25 (May 1963): 138.
42. "The Political Economy of Women's Liberation," *Monthly Review,* Sept. 1969, pp. 3–4.
43. *Handbook on Women Workers,* U.S. Department of Labor, Women's Bureau, 1965, pp. 34–35.
44. *Fact Sheet on the Relative Position . . . ,* p. 3.
45. *Handbook on Women Workers,* p. 172.

Ethnic Diversity of Female Experience

Heritage of La Hembra

Anna Nieto-Gomez

1. Adelaida Del Castillo, "Malintzin Tenepal," *Encuentro Femenil,* ed. Anna Nieto-Gomez, (P.O. Box 735, San Fernando, Calif.) Vol. I, No. 2, May, 1974, p. 60.
2. Magnus Morner, "The Conquest of Women," *History of Latin American Civilization,* Lewis Hanke, (Boston: Little, Brown and Co.) 1973, p. 140.
3. Del Castillo, *op. cit.,* p. 74.
4. Morner, *op. cit.,* p. 141.
5. Sylvia Marcos de Robert, "La Mexicana de La Epoca Prehispanica y Colonial," *Boletin Documental Sobre Las Mujeres,* 50 ano, Vol. V, No. 2, Apt. Postal 42, Suc. A., Cuernavaca (MOR) Mexico, May 1975, pp. 23–24.
6. Morner, *op. cit.,* p. 139.
7. Charles C. Cumberland, *Mexico.* (New York: Oxford University Press) 1968, p. 67.
8. Woodrow Borah and Sherburne F. Cook, "Marriage and Legitimacy in Mexican Culture: Mexico and California," *California Law Review,* Vol. 54, Part I, March–May, 1966, p. 962.
9. Cumberland, *op. cit.,* p. 67.
10. *Ibid.*, p. 73.
11. *Ibid.*, p. 70.
12. Morner, *op. cit.,* p. 139.
13. Marcos de Robert, *op. cit.,* p. 26.
14. Anna Nieto-Gomez, "Colonial Women in Mexico," *Regeneracion,* Vol. II, No. 4, ed. Francisca Flores, 1974, pp. 18–19.
15. Cumberland, *op. cit.,* p. 70.
16. Rosemary Radford Ruether, "Misogynism and Virginal Feminism in the Fathers of the Church," *Religion and Sexism,* ed. Rosemary Radford Ruether, (New York: Simon & Schuster) 1974, pp. 164–166.
17. Connie Nieto, "The Chicana and The Women's Rights Movement," *Civil Rights Digest,* Vol. 6, No. 3, Spring, 1974, p. 39.
18. Colin M. Mac Lachlan, "Modernization of Female Status In Mexico: The Image of Woman's Magazines," *Revista Interamericana Review,* Vol. IV, No. 2, p. 248.
19. Maria Del Drago, "The Pride of Inez Garcia," *MS,* Ma May, 1975, p. 54.
20. Shirley Harkness and Cornelia B. Flora, "Women in the News: An Analysis of Media Images in Columbia," *Revista Interamericana Review,* (Universidad Interamericana Puerto Rico), Vol. IV, No. 2, p. 248.
21. Evelyn Stevens, "Machismo and Marianismo"
22. Nieto-Gomez, *op. cit.,* p. 18.
23. Borah and Sherburne, *op. cit.,* 961.
24. *Ibid.*, p. 962.
25. *Ibid.*, p. 960.
26. Morner, *op cit.,* p. 141.
27. Borah and Sherburne, *op. cit.,* p. 961.
28. Morner, *op. cit.,* p. 141.
29. Nieto-Gomez, *op. cit.,* p. 19.
30. Marcos de Robert, *op. cit.,* p. 25.
31. *Ibid.*, p. 25.
32. *Ibid.*, p. 24.
33. Borah and Sherburne, *op. cit.,* p. 962.
34. Marcos de Robert, *op. cit.,* p. 24.
35. Connie Nieto, *op. cit.,* p. 69.

36. Theodora Rodriguez, Interview, May 8, 1975, San Bernardino, California.
37. Nieto-Gomez, Anna, *op. cit.*, p. 18.
38. Ruether, *op. cit.*, pp. 164–166.
39. Bernice Rincon, "La Chicana, Her Role In the Past, and Her Search for a New Role in the Future," Regner Regeneracion, Vol. II, No. 4, ed. Francisca Flores, 1974, p. 39.
40. Harkness & Flora, *op. cit.*, p. 235.
41. Ruether, *op. cit.*, p. 165.
42. Marcos de Robert, *op. cit.*, p. 26.
43. Ruether, *op. cit.*, pp. 164–166.
44. MacLachlan, *op. cit.*,
45. *Ibid.*, p. 244.
46. Ruether, *op. cit.*, p. 164.

The New Asian-American Woman

Irene Fujitomi and Diane Wong

Arkoff, A.; Meredith, G.; and Dong, J. Attitudes of Japanese-American and Caucasian-American students toward marriage roles. *Journal of Social Psychology* 59, 1963, 11–15.

Barnett, L. D. Interracial marriage in Los Angeles, 1948–1959. *Social Forces* 25, 1963, 424–427.

Beal, F. Double jeopardy: to be black and female. In T. Cade (ed.), *The black woman,* New York: Mentor, 1970.

Benedict, R. *The chrysanthemum and the sword.* Boston: Houghton Mifflin, 1946.

Burkhardt, V. R. *Chinese creeds and customs.* Vol. 3. Hong Kong: South China Morning Post, 1960.

Burma, J. H. Current leadership problems among Japanese-Americans. *Sociological and Social Research* 18, 1934, 541–553.

—— Interethnic marriage in Los Angeles, 1948–1959. *Social Forces* 42, 1963, 156–165.

Cade, T. (ed.) *The black woman.* New York: Mentor, 1970.

Dillon, R. *The hatchet men: the study of the Tong wars in San Francisco Chinatown.* New York: Coward McCann, 1962.

Faust, A. K. *New Japanese womanhood.* New York: George H. Doran Co., 1926.

Fei, H. T. *Peasant life in China: a field study of country life in the Yangtze valley.* London: Routledge & Kegan Paul, 1962.

Fried, M. H. *Fabric of Chinese society: A study of the social life of a Chinese country seat.* New York: Praeger, 1953.

Gee, E. Issei: The first women. In *Asian women.* Berkeley: University of California, 1971.

Gidra. Los Angeles ethnic newspaper, Jan. 1971, Apr. 1972, May 1972.

Horner, M. A bright woman is caught in a double bind. *Psychology Today,* Nov. 1969, 36–38.

Jung, B. Chinese immigrant women. In *Asian women.* Berkeley: University of California, 1971.

Kitano, H. L. *Japanese-Americans: the evolution of a subculture.* Englewood Cliffs, N.J.: Prentice-Hall, 1969.

Loomis, A. W. Chinese women in California. *Overland Monthly* II, Apr. 1969, 343–351.

Louie, G. Forgotten women. In *Asian women.* Berkeley: University of California, 1971.

Lowe, P. *Father and glorious descendant.* Boston: Little, Brown, and Co., 1943.

Lundberg, G.; Schrag, D.; Larsen, O.; and Larsen, P. *Sociology.* New York: Harper & Row, 1968.

Lyman, S. M. *The Asian in the West.* Reno: Western Studies Center, University of Nevada, 1971.

Masaoka, J. I forgot my eyes were black. In *Asian women.* Berkeley: University of California, 1971.

Merton, R. K. Intermarriage and social structure: Fact and Theory. *Psychiatry* IV, 1946, 361–374.

Okimoto, D. *American in disguise.* New York: John Weatherhill, 1971.

Skalre, B. L. Intermarriage and the Jewish future. In M. Barron (ed.), *Minorities in a changing world.* New York: Alfred A. Knopf, 1967.

Sung, B. L. *Mountain of gold.* New York: Macmillan, 1967.

Tachiki, A.; Wong, E.; Odo, F.; and Wong, B. (eds.) *Roots: an Asian-American reader.* Los Angeles: Continental Graphics, 1971.

Tinker, J. N. Intermarriage and ethnic boundaries: the Japanese-American case. Paper presented at the meeting of the Pacific Sociological Association, Portland, Ore., Apr. 1972.

Tow, J. S. *The real Chinese in America.* New York: Academy Press, 1923.

Yamamoto, M. Male perspective. In *Gidra.* Los Angeles, Jan. 1971.

Yang, C. K. *A Chinese family in the Communist revolution.* Boston: Massachusetts Institute of Technology Press, 1959.

—— *A Chinese village in early Communist transition.* Boston: Massachusetts Institute of Technology Press, 1959.

Women and Their Sexual Selves

Sexuality

Ann Oakley

Bateson, G. 1947. Sex and culture. *Annals of New York Academy of Science:* XLVII.

Brecher, E. M. 1970. *The sex researchers.* London: Deutsch.

Cohen, A. K. 1956. *Delinquent boys: the culture of the gang.* London: Routledge.

Colby, K. M. 1963. Sex differences in dreams of primitive tribes. *American Anthropologist* **65:**1116–21

Cowie, J.; Cowie, V.; and Slater, E. 1968. *Delinquency in girls.* Heinemann.

Davenport, W. 1965. Sexual patterns and their regulation in a society of the southwest Pacific. In Beach, F. A. (ed.) *Sex and behavior.* New York: Wiley.

Davis, K. 1929. *Factors in the sex life of 2200 women.* New York: Harper.

Devereux, G. 1937. Institutionalized homosexuality of the Mohave Indians. *Human Biology* **9.**

Figes, E. 1970. *Patriarchal attitudes: women in society.* London: Faber.

Ford, C. S. and Beach, F. A. 1952. *Patterns of sexual behavior.* London: Eyre & Spottiswode.

Freud, S. 1950. Female sexuality. *In Collected papers* **V.** London: Hogarth Press.

——. 1962. *Three essays on the theory of sexuality.* London: Hogarth Press.

——. 1964. Femininity. In *New introductory lectures on psychoanalysis.* **XXII.** London: Hogarth Press.

Gagnon, J. H. and Simon, W. (eds.) 1967. *Sexual deviance.* New York: Harper.

Gebhard, P. H.; Raboch, J.; and Geise, H. 1970. *The sexuality of women.* London: Deutsch.

Horney, K. 1967. *Feminine psychology.* London: Routledge.

Jap, P. C. 1963. The female primate. In Farber, J. M. and Wilson, R. H. (eds.). *The potential of woman.* New York: McGraw-Hill.

Kinsey, A. C. et al. 1949. *Sexual behavior in the human female.* Philadelphia: W. B. Saunders.

——. *Sexual behavior in the human male.* Philadelphia: W. B. Saunders.

Malinowski, B. 1932. *The sexual life of savages.* London: Routledge.

Maslow, A. H. 1942. Self-esteem (dominance-feeling) and sexuality in women. *Journal of Social Psychology* **16.**

Masters, W. H. and Johnson, V. E. 1965. The sexual response cycles of the human male and female: comparative anatomy and physiology. In Beach, F. A. (ed.). *Sex and behavior.* New York: Wiley.

——. 1966. Human sexual response. Boston: Little, Brown.

Mead, M. 1935. *Sex and temperament in three primitive societies.* New York: Morrow.

——. 1950. *Sex and female.* London: Penguin.

——. 1961. Cultural determinants of sexual behavior. In Young, W. C. (ed.) *Sex and internal secretions.* London: Bailliere, Tindall and Cox. pp. 1433–79.

Millett, K. 1971. *Sexual politics.* London: Harte-Davis.

Money, J. 1961. Sex hormones and other variables in human eroticism. In Young, W. C. (ed.) *Sex and internal secretions.* London: Bailliere, Tindall and Cox. pp. 1383–1401.

Oliver, B. J. 1967. Sexual deviation in American society. New Haven College and University Press.

Taylor, G. R. 1953. *Sex in history.* London: Thames & Hudson.

Sampson, R. V. 1965. *The psychology of power.* Pantheon.

Schofield, M. 1968. *The sexual behavior of young people.* London: Penguin.

West, D. J. 1968. *Homosexuality.* London: Penguin.

The Myth of the Vaginal Orgasm

Anne Koedt

Bonaparte, M. 1953. *Female sexuality.* New York: Grove Press

Caprio, F. S. 1953, 1966. *The sexually adequate female.* New York: Fawcett Gold Medal Books

Ellis, A. 1958, 1965. *Sex without guilt.* New York: Grove Press

Ejlersen, M. 1968. *I accuse (jeg anklager).* Copenhagen: Chr. Erichsens Forlag

Ellman, M. 1968. *Thinking about women.* New York: Harcourt, Brace & World

Kelly, G. L. 1951, 1965. *Sexual feelings in married men and women.* New York: Pocket Books

Kinsey, A. C. 1953. *Sexual behavior in the human female.* New York: Pocket Books

Masters, W. H. and Johnson, V. E. 1966. *Human sexual response.* Boston: Little, Brown

Psychotherapy and Women

Patient and Patriarch: Women in the Psychotherapeutic Relationship

Phyllis Chesler

1. Karen Horney, "The Flight from Womanhood" (1926), in *Feminine Psychology,* ed. Harold Kelman (New York: W. W. Norton, 1967).
2. "Selected Symptoms of Psychological Distress," U.S. Department of Health, Education and Welfare. Public Health Services, Health Services, and Mental Health Administration. This study is based on data collected in 1960–1962 from a probability sample of 7,710 persons selected to represent the 111 million adults in the U.S. noninstitutional population, aged 18–79.
3. A fascinating and predictable finding in this study was that men with low incomes and females with high incomes reported the highest rate of fainting.
4. G. Gurin, J. Veroff, and S. Feld, *Americans View Their Mental Health* (New York: Basic Books, 1960).
5. William Schofield, *Psychotherapy: The Purchase of Friendship* (Englewood Cliffs, N.J.: Prentice-Hall, 1963).
6. A. K. Bahn, M. Conwell, and P. Hurley, "Survey of

Psychiatric Practice," *Archives of General Psychiatry*, vol. 12 (1965). This data was collected in New York, Washington, D.C., Wisconsin, Kentucky, and California.

7. "Reference Table on Patients in Mental Health Facilities, Age, Sex and Diagnosis," U.S. Department of Health, Education, and Welfare. Health Services and Mental Health Administration, United States, 1965, 1966, 1967. National statistics on "mental illness" are exceedingly troublesome. The data shown for the predominately male, VA psychiatric hospital represent a 100 percent projection based on a 30 percent random sampling of VA hospitals, whereas the data shown for all of the other facilities are raw data, based on the number of hospitals reporting for a given year. From 1965–1967, 1,627 of the *known* psychiatric out-patient facilities, 115 of the known state and county hospitals, 121 of the known private hospitals, and 959 of the known general hospitals did *not* report any patient statistics. Although there are more female than male patients in each of the reporting hospitals, particularly in the private, general and out-patient facilities, there is no way of checking the sex-ratios in the non-reporting hospitals. Further difficulties involved the fact that the criteria for certain of the statistics, such as "first admissions" or "residents at year's end" may (1) count the same patient twice in a given year; (2) may exclude some patients altogether (the "invisible" housewife alcoholic or prostitute-drug addict); (3) may not adequately reflect the phenomena of frequent short- or long-term readmissions and long-term stays that often characterize female patients; (4) are not based on the sex-ratio in the American population at large for the given year; or, more important, (5) are not based on the "real" population the particular patient derived from, e.g., the "population" of white divorced working women with children, or of foreign or native-born migrants, etc. In other words, relevant demographic characteristics such as age, race, marital status, birthplace, social class, education, etc. are not taken into account where they do present a breakdown by "per 100,000" population. (Except in smaller studies which attempt to do just this.) Without such demographic variables we cannot answer such questions as "What is the probability of a black working mother's admission to a psychiatric facility compared with a black working father's, or a white non-working mother's, or with a black non-working father's?"

8. Benjamin Maltzberg, "Important Statistical Data about Mental Illness," *American Handbook of Psychiatry*, Vol. I, ed. Silvano Arieti (New York: Basic Books, 1959).

9. M. A. Dayton, *New Facts on Mental Disorders* (Springfield, Ill.: Charles C. Thomas, 1940); E. Zigler and L. Phillips, "Social Effectiveness and Symptomatic Behaviors," *Journal of Abnormal and Social Psychology* (1960), pp. 231–238; Maltzberg., *op. cit.;* Strole, et al. *Mental Health in the Metropolis: Midtown Manhattan Study* (New York: McGraw-Hill, 1962).

10. A study on the psychiatric "health" of the Manhattan Community conducted by Srole et al., 1962, found higher psychiatric "impairment" among single men when compared with married men, than among single women when compared with married women. Among married people the sexes did not differ in the proportions rated psychiatrically "impaired."

11. One wonders why women are not equally "embarrassed" about discussing their impotence (frigidity) with male therapists.

12. This, as well as the significantly greater female preference for a male therapist, supports Goldberg's 1968 findings of female antifemale prejudice. See P. Goldberg, "Are Women Prejudiced against Women," *Trans-Action,* April 1968, pp. 28–30.

13. There is a definite but not significant tendency toward homosexuality (both active and latent) in the group of men who requested female therapists. This almost suggests that preference for a female—either as an authority figure or as an expert mother figure—requires some break with the dominant sex-role stereotypes of our society.

14. Approximately 80 percent of the male and 76 percent of the female patients who stated a sex preference in requesting a therapist were assigned to therapists of the preferred sex.

15. Jean MacFarlane et al., *A Developmental Study of the Behavior Problems of Normal Children between Twenty-One Months and Thirteen Years* (Berkeley: University of California Press, 1954); L. Phillips, "Cultural versus Intrapsychic Factors in Childhood Behavior Problem Referrals," *Journal of Clinical Psychology* 12 (1956): 400–401; G. M. Gilbert, "A Survey of Referral Problems in Metropolitan Child Guidance Centers," *Journal of Clinical Psychology* 13 (1957): 37–42; D. R. Petersen, "Behavior Problems of Middle Childhood," *Journal of Consulting Psychology* 25 (1961): 205–209; L. M. Terman and Leona E. Tyler, "Psychological Sex Differences," in L. Carmichael, ed., *Manual of Child Psychology* (New York: John Wiley & Sons, 1954).

16. We may note that nearly five million crimes are reported in the United States each year, of which 87 percent are property crimes and the remainder are violent crimes. American adult males have significantly higher rates of arrests for criminal activity; they outnumber women by more than 6:1.

17. Leslie Phillips, "A Social View of Psychopathology," in P. London and D. Rosenhan, eds., *Abnormal Psychology* (New York: Holt, Rinehart & Winston, 1969).

18. Zigler and Phillips, *op. cit.*

19. A government pamphlet entitled *Suicide among Youth* (1970) notes that attempted suicide is far more frequent among girls in the student age bracket than among boys.

The boys attempt fewer suicides but complete more than the girls. Nonwhite males between fifteen and twenty-five have the highest successful suicide rate. Although it is fruitless and irrelevant to attempt to decide whether racism, class conflict, or sexism takes the heaviest toll of physical and psychological life in America, we may, parenthetically (and nevertheless) wonder whether there are more poor and black men in jail and in mental asylums for criminal activity (one measure of racism and class conflict) than there are poor, middle- and upper-class women in mental asylums and in private psychotherapeutic treatment (one measure of sexism). In many ways (physical, economic, and psychological), mental and ex-mental patients suffer more than jailed criminals or ex-convicts. (E. Goffman, *Asylums* [New York: Doubleday-Anchor, 1961.]) For this reason alone—namely, the greater punishment involved in being labeled mentally ill—without looking at any statistics I would personally suspect that more women than men receive the mentally ill rather than the criminal label. And that the kinds of behaviors considered criminal and mentally ill are sex-typed, each sex being conditioned accordingly. Further, that what we consider "madness"—whether it appears in women or men is either (a) the acting out of the female experience or (b) the rejection of one's sex-role stereotype.

20. T. T. Szasz, *The Myth of Mental Illness* (New York: Harper & Row, 1961).

21. *Ibid.* My italics.

22. Frederick Engels, *The Origins of Family, Private Property, and the State* (New York: International Publishers, 1942).

23. Konrad Lorenz, a noted student of animal behavior, has recently been quoted as saying that "there's only one kind of people at a social disadvantage nowadays—a whole class of people who are treated as slaves and who are exploited shamelessly—and that's the young wives. They are educated as well as the men. And the moment they give birth to a baby, they are slaves. They have a 22-hour working day and no holidays and they can't even be ill." *New York Times* interview, July 5, 1970.

24. D. L. Phillips and B. E. Segal, "Sexual Status and Psychiatric Symptoms," *American Sociological Review* (1969): vol. 34.

25. Either actively and voluntarily or when they are involuntarily psychiatrically hospitalized.

26. M. Foucault, in *Madness and Civilization* (New York: Mentor Books, 1967), a brilliant essay on the history of madness in the western world characterizes the organization of mental asylums: "The entire existence of madness, in the world now being prepared for it, was enveloped in what we may call, in anticipation, a 'parental complex.' The prestige of patriarchy is revived around madness. . . . henceforth . . . the discourse of unreason will be linked with . . . the dialectic of the Family. . . . the madman remains a minor and for a long time reason will retain for him the aspect of the Father. . . . He (Tuke, a psychiatrist) isolated the social structure of the bourgeois family, reconstituted it symbolically in the (mental) asylum, and set it adrift in history." Also Freud, in his 1931 essay entitled "Female Sexuality," in *International Journal of Psychoanalysis* 13 (1932), noted how difficult it was for him to "revive the female patient's attachment to the mother . . . but possibly I have received this impression because when I have analyzed women, they have been able to cling to that very father-attachment in which they took refuge from the early phase (of mother-attachment)."

27. Gloria Steinem, "Laboratory for Love Styles," *New York Magazine,* February 1970, quotes one middle-class discussion of psychoanalysts:

> Psychiatrists are the male geishas of our time. I mean, the women who go to analysts usually have empty days on their hands, right? And Freud was too male-chauvinist to figure out we needed professions as well as sex, right? So these analysts get a lot of attractive women in their offices and encourage them to talk about their sex lives and, well, one thing leads to another. Those poor bastards are usually stuck with the wives who put them through medical school anyway, if you see what I mean.
>
> Now, the beautiful part of all this is it's perfect for the woman. She gets sex and someone to listen to her with a little sympathy—the two things she's probably missing in her marriage. Intelligent companionship in the daytime. What husband could object to his wife's appointments with her doctor?

28. Schofield sent basic information questionnaires to randomly selected practitioner members of the American Psychiatric Association, the American Psychological Association, and the National Association of Social Workers. Complete returns were obtained from 140 psychiatrists, 149 psychiatric social workers, and 88 clinical psychologists.

29. Goffman, *op. cit.;* Szasz, *op. cit.;* Schofield, *op. cit.;* Foucault, *op. cit.;* T. J. Scheff, *Being Mentally Ill: A Sociological Theory* (Chicago: Aldine, 1966).

30. Sigmund Freud, "On the History of the Psycho-analytic Movement" (1914), in *Collected Papers of Sigmund Freud,* Vol. I (New York: Basic Books, 1959).

31. Szasz, *op. cit.*

32. Schofield, *op. cit.*

33. The traditional psychoanalytic theories about women, especially Freud's, have been well and fully criticized by Karen Horney, Simone de Beauvoir, Clara Thompson, Natalie Shainess, Betty Friedan, Albert Adler, Thomas Szasz, and Harry Stack Sullivan.

34. Karen Horney, "The Flight from Womanhood," in *Feminine Psychology,* ed. by Harold Kelman (New York: W. W. Norton, 1967). Freud's indirect rejoinder, made in his 1931 essay entitled "Female Sexuality," is as follows:

> It is to be anticipated that male analysts with feminist sympathies, and our women analysts also, will disagree with what I have said here. They will hardly fail to object that such notions have their origin in the man's "masculinity complex," and are meant to justify theoretically his innate propensity to disparage and suppress women. But this sort of psychoanalytic argument reminds us here, as it so often does, of Dostoevsky's famous "knife that cuts both ways." The opponents of those who reason thus will for their part think it quite comprehensible that members of the female sex should refuse to accept a notion that appears to gainsay their eagerly coveted equality with men. The use of analysis as a weapon of controversy obviously leads to no decision.

35. Sigmund Freud, "Some Psychological Consequences of the Anatomical Distinction Between Sexes." *Collected Papers,* Vol. V (London: Hogarth Press, 1956), pp. 196–197.

36. Sigmund Freud, *New Introductory Lectures in Psychoanalysis* (New York: W. W. Norton, 1933).

37. E. H. Erikson, "Inner and Outer Space: Reflections on Womanhood," *Daedalus* 93 (1964):582–606.

38. B. Bettelheim, "The Commitment Required of a Woman Entering a Scientific Profession in Present Day American Society," in *Woman and the Scientific Professions,* an MIT symposium on American Women in Science and Engineering (Cambridge, Mass., 1965).

39. J. Rheingold, *The Fear of Being a Woman* (New York: Grune & Stratton, 1964).

40. S. Freud, *Case of Dora: An Analysis of a Case of Hysteria* (New York: W. W. Norton, 1952). Early in this case history he says: "The demands hysteria make on a physician can be met only by the most sympathetic spirit of inquiry and not by an attitude of superiority and contempt." Unfortunately, Freud does not always maintain this spirit.

41. Like Sherlock Holmes, when Freud has a fact "he doesn't neglect to use it against Dora." He says: "When I set myself the task of bringing to light what human beings keep hidden within them, not by the compelling power of hypnosis, but by observing what they say and what they show . . . no mortal can keep a secret. If his lips are silent, he chatters with his fingertips; betrayal oozes out of him at every pore."

42. Freud was not the only one who disliked Dora. Twenty-four years later, as a forty-two-year-old married woman, Dora was referred to another psychiatrist, Felix Deutsch, for "hysterical" symptoms. Let me quote his description of her:

> The patient then started a tirade about her husband's indifference toward her offerings and how unfortunate her marital life had been. . . . this led her to talk about her own frustrated love life and her frigidity. . . . resentfully she expressed her conviction that her husband had been unfaithful to her . . . tearfully she denounced men in general as selfish, demanding, and ungiving. . . . (she recalled that) her father had been unfaithful even to her mother . . . she talked mainly about her relationship to her mother, of her unhappy childhood because of her mother's exaggerated cleanliness . . . and her lack of affection for her. . . . she finally spoke with pride about her *brother's* career, but she had little hope that her *son* would follow in his footsteps. . . . more than 30 years have elapsed since my visit at Dora's sickbed . . . from (an) informant I learned the additional pertinent facts about the fate of Dora. . . . she clung to (her son) with the same reproachful demands she made on her husband, who had died of a coronary disease—*slighted and tortured by her almost paranoid behavior, strangely enough, he had preferred to die . . . rather than divorce her. Without question, only a man of this type could have been chosen by Dora for a husband.* At the time of her analytic treatment she had stated unequivocally, "men are all so detestable that I would rather not marry. This is my revenge!" Thus, her marriage had served only to cover up her distaste of men. . . . (Dora's) death from a cancer of the colon, which was diagnosed too late for a successful operation, seemed a blessing to those who were close to her. She had been, as my informant phrased it, "one of the most repulsive hysterics" he had ever met. [My italics.] Felix Deutsch, "A Footnote to Freud's 'Fragment of an Analysis of a Case of Hysteria'," *The Psychoanalytic Quarterly* 26 (1957).

43. L. J. Simon, "The Political Unconscious of Psychology: Clinical Psychology and Social Change," unpublished manuscript, 1970.

44. Szasz, *op. cit.*

45. The majority of whom, unlike Erikson or Bettelheim (quoted earlier) are practitioners and not published theorists.

46. Less than one-third of the psychiatrists and one-fourth of the psychologists expressed a preferred sex in their ideal patient.

47. *Ibid.*

48. I. K. Broverman et al., "Sex Role Stereotypes and Clinical Judgment of Mental Health," *Journal of Consulting and Clinical Psychology* 34 (1970): 1–7. This summary

of this study was done by Jo-Ann Gardner, *The Face across the Breakfast Table* (Pittsburgh: Know, Inc., 1970).

49. There are many women who spend most of their salary on their "shrink," and who live with men or with their parents, usually under infantilizing conditions, in order to do so. One wonders who exactly, and how many at that, can pay for private psychoanalytic or psychotherapeutic treatment—treatment that costs anywhere from fifteen to fifty dollars per session, two to five times a week, for anywhere from two to five years. None but a small urban minority can afford such treatment at its supposed "best."

50. But very human—especially when people are clamoring to be helped and "helpers" need to survive economically.

Masochistic Syndrome, Hysterical Personality . . .

Betsy Belote

Bardwick, J. 1971. *Psychology of women.* New York: Harper & Row.

Beller, E. K., & Neubauer, P. B. 1963. Sex differences and symptom patterns in early childhood. *Journal of Child Psychiatry* **2:** 414–33.

Bergler, E. 1949. *The basic neurosis.* New York: Grune & Stratton.

Bieber, I. 1966. Sadism and masochism. In S. Arieti (ed.), *American handbook of psychiatry* **3.** New York: Basic Books.

Bieri, J.; Bradburn, W. M.; & Galinsky, D. M. 1958. Sex differences in perceptual behavior. *Journal of Personality* **26:** (1), 1–12.

Brim, O. G.; Glass, D. C.; Lavin, D. E.; & Goodman, N. 1962. *Personality and decision processes.* Stanford: Stanford University Press.

Broverman, I. K.; Broverman, D. M.; Clarkman, F. E.; Rosencrantz, P. S.; & Vogel, S. R. 1970. Sex-role stereotypes & clinical judgments of mental health. *Journal of Consulting and Clinical Psychology* **34** (1) 1–7.

De Beauvoir, S. 1970. *The second sex.* New York: Bantam.

Deutsch, H. 1930. The significance of masochism in the mental life of women. *International Journal of Psychoanalysis* **11:** 48–60.

Deutsch, H. 1944. *The psychology of women: A psychoanalytic interpretation* Vols. 1 & 2. New York: Grune & Stratton.

Diagnostic and statistical manual of mental disorders. Committee on Nomenclature and Statistics, Washington, D.C.: American Psychiatric Association, 1968.

Easser, B. D., & Lesser, S. R. 1965. Hysterical personality: A reevaluation. *Psychoanalytic Quarterly* **34** (3) 390–405.

Freud, S. 1953. Standard edition of the complete psychological works of . . . Vol. 7. *Three essays on the theory of sexuality.* London: Hogarth Press.

——. 1955. Standard edition of the complete psychological works of . . . Vol. 17. *A child is being beaten.* London: Hogarth Press.

——. 1957. Standard edition of the complete psychological works of . . . Vol. 14. *Instincts and their vicissitudes.* London: Hogarth Press.

——. 1961. Standard edition of the complete psychological works of . . . Vol. 12. *Observations on transference-love (Further recommendations on the technique of psychoanalysis III).* London: Hogarth Press.

——. 1961 (a). Standard edition of the complete psychological works of . . . Vol. 19. *Libidinal types.* London: Hogarth Press.

——. 1961 (b). Standard edition of the complete psychological works of . . . Vol. 21. *Female sexuality.* London, Hogarth.

Horney, K. 1939. *New ways in psychoanalysis.* New York: W. W. Norton.

——. 1973. *Feminine psychology.* New York: W. W. Norton.

Kagan, J. & Moss, H. A. 1962. *Birth to maturity.* New York: John Wiley.

Krafft-Ebing, R. 1937. *Psychopathia sexualis.* New York: Physican and Surgeons Book Co.

Maccoby, E. 1966. *The development of sex differences.* Stanford, Ca.: Stanford University Press.

Marmor, J. 1953. Orality in the hysterical personality. *Journal of the American Psychoanalytic Association,* **1:** 656–71.

Martin, P. A. 1971. Dynamic considerations of hysterical psychosis. *American Journal of Psychiatry* **128:** 6.

McGuire, C. 1961. Sex role and community variability in test performances. *Journal of Educational Psych.* **52.**

Parsons, T. 1955. Family structure and socialization of the child. In T. Parsons & R. F. Bales (eds.), *Family, socialization and interaction process,* Glencoe, Ill.: Free Press.

Rado, S. 1933. Fear of castration in women. *Psychoanalytic Quarterly* **2:** 425–75.

Rado, S. 1956. *Psychoanalysis of behavior.* New York: Grune & Stratton.

Reich, W. 1949. *Character analysis.* New York: Farrar, Straus and Giroux.

Reik, T. 1941. *Masochism in modern man.* New York: Farrar & Rinehart.

Sears, R. R.; Whiting, J.; Nowlis, V.; & Sears, P. 1953. Some child rearing antecedents of aggression and dependency in young children. *Genetic Psychology Monograph* **47:** 135–234.

Spangler, D. P., & Thomas, C. W. 1962. The effect of age, sex, and physical disability upon manifest needs. *Journal of Consulting Psychology* **9:** 313–19.

Thompson, C. 1964. *Interpersonal psychoanalysis.* New York: Basic Books.

Vaught, G. M. 1965. The relationship of role identification and ego strength to sex differences in the rod and frame test. *Journal of Personality* **33:** 271–83.

Witkin, H. A.; Dyk, R. B.; Faterson, H. F.; Goodnough, D.; & Karp, S. A. 1962. *Psychological differentiation.* New York: Wiley.

Wolowitz, H. M. 1972. Hysterical character and feminine identity. In R. Bardwick (ed.), *Readings on the psychology of women.* New York: Harper & Row.

Depression in Middle-aged Women

Pauline B. Bart

1. See my forthcoming chapter on "The Sociology of Depressive Disorders," in *Current Perspectives in Psychiatric Sociology,* eds. Paul Roman and Harrison Trice (Science House, 1971) for a further discussion of this point.
2. Marvine B. Sussman, "Relationships of Adult Children with Their Parents in the United States," in Ethel Shanas and Gordon Streib, eds., *Social Structure and the Family: General Relations* (Englewood Cliffs, N.J.: Prentice-Hall, 1965).
3. Ralph Turner, "Role Theory—A Series of Propositions," *Encyclopedia of the Social Sciences* (New York: Macmillan and the Free Press, 1968). These ideas are incorporated in "Role: Sociological Aspects," *Encyclopedia of the Social Sciences.*
4. Yehudi A. Cohen, "The Sociological Relevance of Schizophrenia and Depression," in Cohen, ed., *Social Structure and Personality* (New York: Holt, Rinehart and Winston, 1961), pp. 477–485.
5. Turner, *op. cit.*
6. Small children, small troubles; big children, big troubles.
7. Dan Greenburg, *How to Be a Jewish Mother* (Los Angeles: Price, Stern, Sloan, 1964).
8. Arnold Rose, "A Social-Psychological Theory of Neurosis," in Rose, ed., *Human Behavior and Social Processes* (Boston: Houghton Mifflin, 1962), pp. 537–549.
9. Ernest Becker, *The Revolution in Psychiatry* (Glencoe: The Free Press, 1964).
10. These results are presented in greater detail in my "Why Women's Status Changes in Middle Age: The Turns of the Social Ferris Role," *Sociological Symposium* 1 (Fall 1969).
11. See *Society, Culture, and Depression* (Cambridge: Schenkman forthcoming) for elaboration of these and subsequent findings.
12. Talcott Parsons, "Age and Sex in the Social Structure of the United States," *American Sociological Review* 7 (1942): 604–606.
13. Rafael Moses and Debora S. Kleiger, "A Comparative Analysis of the Institutionalization of Mental Health

Values: The United States and Israel," unpublished manuscript presented at the American Psychiatric Association meetings, New York, 1965.
14. Therese Benedek and Boris B. Rubenstein, "Psychosexual Functions in Women," in *Psychosomatic Medicine* (New York: Ronald Press, 1952).
15. Helene Deutsch, *The Psychology of Women: A Psychoanalytic Interpretation* (New York: Grune & Stratton, 1945), vol. 2.
16. Cohen, *op. cit.*

Toward Human Liberation

The Consciousness-raising Group as a Model for Therapy with Women

Anne Brodsky

Allen, P. *The small group in women's liberation.* New York: Times Change Press, 1971.

Amundsen, K. *The silenced majority: Women and American democracy.* Englewood Cliffs, N.J.: Prentice-Hall, 1971.

Astin, H. *The woman doctorate in America.* Hartford: Russell Sage Foundation, 1969.

Bardwick, J., & Douvan, E. Ambivalence: The socialization of women. In V. Gornick & B. Moran (Eds.), *Woman in sexist society: Studies in power and powerlessness.* New York: Basic Books, 1971, 147–159.

Bart, P. Depression in middle-aged women. In V. Gornick & B. Moran (Eds.), *Woman in sexist society: Studies in power and powerlessness.* New York: Basic Books, 1971, 99–117.

Bernard, J. *Women and the public interest.* New York: Aldine-Atherton, 1971.

Bird, C. *Born female: The high cost of keeping women down.* New York: McKay, 1968.

Brodsky, A. (Ed.), *Feminist therapist roster of the Association for Women in Psychology.* Pittsburgh: KNOW, Inc., 1972.

Broverman, I. K., Broverman, D. M., Clarkson, F., Rosenkrants, P. & Vogel, S. R. Sex-role stereotypes and clinical judgments of mental health. *Journal of Consulting Psychology,* 1970, 34, 1–7.

Chesler, P. Patient and patriarch: Women in the psychotherapeutic relationship. In V. Gornick & B. Moran (Eds.), *Woman in sexist society: Studies in power and powerlessness.* New York: Basic Books, 1971, 251–275.

Epstein, C. *Woman's place: Options and limits in professional careers.* Berkeley: California Press, 1970.

Friedan, B. *The feminine mystique.* New York: Dell, 1963.

Gurin, G., Veroff, J., & Feld, S. *Americans view their mental health.* New York: Basic Books, 1960.

Horner, M. Femininity and successful achievement: A basic

inconsistency. In J. Bardwick, *Feminine personality and conflict*. Belmont, Calif: Brooks/Cole, 1970, 45–76.

Maccoby, E. Sex differences and their implications for sex roles. Paper presented at American Psychological Association, Sept. 1971, Washington, D.C.

Mischel, W. A social-learning view of sex differences in behavior. In E. Maccoby, *The development of sex differences*. Stanford: Stanford Univ. Press, 1966, 56–81.

Newton, E., & Walton, S. The personal is political: Consciousness-raising and personal change in the women's liberation movement. In B. G. Schoepf (Chw), *Anthropologists look at the study of women*. Symposium presented at the American Anthropological Association, November 19, 1971.

Reeves, N. *Womankind: Beyond the stereotypes*. New York: Aldine-Atherton, 1971.

Report of the Task Force on Family Law and Policy to the Citizen's Advisory Council on the Status of Women, Washington, D. C., 1968.

Weisstein, N. Kinder, kuche, kirche as scientific law: Psychology constructs the female. *Motive*, 1969, 29, 6–7.

What Happens in Feminist Therapy

Hannah Lerman

Fiedler, F. 1950. A comparison of therapeutic relationships in psychoanalytic, nondirective and Adlerian therapy, *J. Consult. Psych.* **14**: 436–45.

Kirsch, B. 1974. Consciousness-raising groups as therapy for women, In Franks, V. and Burtle, V. *Women in therapy: new psychotherapies for a changing society*. New York: Brunner/Mazel Publishers.

Sundland, D. and Barker, E. 1962. The orientations of psychotherapists. *J. Consult. Psych.* **26**: 201–12.

Wyckoff, H. 1973. Between women and men. *Issues in radical therapy*. **1:** 2, 11–15.

Male Power and the Women's Movement

Barbara Polk

De Beauvoir, S. *The second sex*. Trans. by H. M. Parshey. New York: Alfred A. Knopf, 1953; first published in 1949.

De Beauvoir, S. *Force of circumstances*. London: Andre Deutsch, 1965.

Burris, B., in agreement with K. Barry, T. Moon, J. DeLor, J. Parent, and C. Stadelman. *The fourth world manifesto: An angry response to an imperialist venture against the women's liberation movement*. New Haven, Conn.: Advocate Press, 1971.

Chafetz, J. S. *Masculine/feminine or human?* Itasca, Ill.: F. E. Peacock Publishers, 1974.

Chesler, P. *Women and madness*. New York: Doubleday & Company, 1972.

Epstein, C. F. *Woman's place*. Berkeley: University of California Press, 1971.

Firestone, S. *The dialectic of sex*. New York: William Morrow, 1970.

Grimstad, K., & Rennie, S. (Eds.), *The new woman's survival catalogue*. New York: Coward, McCann and Geoghegan/Berkeley Publishing Corporation, 1973.

Millett, K. *Sexual politics*. Garden City, L.I., N.Y.: Doubleday & Co., 1970.

Mitchell, J. *Woman's estate*. New York: Random House, 1971.

Reed, E. *Problems of women's liberation: A Marxist approach*. New York: Merit Publishers, 1969.

Reynolds, J. *Rape as social control*. Unpublished paper presented at the Michigan Sociological Association meetings, Detroit, 1971.

Safilios-Rothschild, C. (Ed.), *Toward a sociology of women*. Lexington, Mass.: Xerox College Publishing, 1972.

Solanas, V. *The scum manifesto*. New York: Olympia, 1968.

WOMEN'S STUDIES PROGRAM
UNIVERSITY OF DAYTON
ST. JOSEPH   414

APPENDIX B: Chart of the Basic Feminist Positions

	Conservative Feminist	**"Politico" Feminist**	**Cultural Feminist**
PROFILE			
Goal	to obtain equal political, economic, and social rights for women within the existing system	to facilitate an economic revolution as a necessary precondition for the establishment of equality between the sexes	to abolish sex distinctions, create new cultural era based on synthesis of Male and Female modes.
Political Position	reformist; seeks changes within the present system	politically radical, seeks to overthrow the present economic system	politically and psychologically radical, concerned with economic and cultural revolution
Methods	organization-minded, emphasis on class-action lawsuits, some consciousness raising, more separation of personal from political	emphasis on organizing women based on consciousness raising, political study groups to analyze women's oppression within (male) left political analyses	emphasis on consciousness raising, political analysis based on personal experiences, re-definition of politics in the Female mode
Constituency	middle class and upper-middle class professionals and career women; some men in organization	working class, middle class, students, political organizers, women from the male left (SDS, civil rights)	middle class, students, women from the (male) left, independents, (women never before involved in politics, lesbians
Activities	seeks to change laws and institutions that condition women to female role. Three major issues are equal pay for equal work, child care, and abortion law reform. Attitude is that women can do anything men can do and that men should be able to stay home and take care of children, too; want greater flexibility and choice of roles desired for both sexes	women's oppression is related to economic class oppression. Women exploited as workers differently on basis of their sex. Women earn less in marketplace and their role in family as unpaid laborer emphasized. Women can be organized around these issues; also health care and child care as these relate especially to women as workers	seeks to create new culture based on Female mode of consciousness or synthesis of Male and Female modes. Consciousness-raising seen as essential. Must be revolution on three levels—sexual, economic, cultural. Women must obtain control of reproduction, economic independence for women and children, integration of them into society, total sexual freedom
ISSUES			
Equal pay, Equal work	legal action required to obtain more jobs for women, equal educational and employment opportunities; equal participation of women at all levels of economic system	analysis of capitalism and an economic revolution is required for women/men to be equal. Not possible for equality between women and men to exist within capitalism.	agrees with the politico feminist position (and in addition there needs to occur simultaneously sexual and cultural revolutions as well). In the future, cybernation of work will allow greater sexual freedom
Child-Care	Child care centers need to be provided so that women can work, or participate in society more easily; women may become more equal to their husbands, if they are also earning money.	women need child-care centers to work to survive economically; availability of child-care centers depends on need for women to be used as labor in the work force. Child-care centers are now provided depending on what capitalism requires, not on what women or children want or need.	oppression of women and children are intertwined. Both need to be economically independent from men and totally integrated into society. Child care centers separate children and segregate them from the rest of society. Child care should not be defined solely as women's responsibility

Chart of the Basic Feminist Positions Cont.

Abortion, Health Care	abortion law repeal is necessary to obtain for women more choice and control over their own bodies. There should be more women physicians.	women can be organized around health-care issues. Delivery of health care is grossly unequal and inadequate for poor women especially; need free clinics, more patient rights, paraprofessionals	agrees with politico feminist; women's health care is in general based on Male principles of efficiency and order, for example. Is essential for women to "seize means of reproduction," and control their own bodies.
Sexuality	maintains heterosexuality as the status quo, and accepts lesbians as special group of women within the group (although this was not always the case)	sexuality greatly repressed to maintain capitalism; heterosexuality regarded as the norm	sexual repression no longer necessary with the elimination of work due to technology. With elimination of sex roles, bisexuality becomes the norm, incest is allowed, and children can be sexual.

CAPITALISM

Analysis	no political or historical analysis of women's oppression. Are more short sighted, aiming toward short-term, immediate, concrete, attainable goals—equal pay, equal work, child-care centers, abortion law reform, etc.	worldwide historical (Marxist) analysis of women's oppression begins with division of labor and subsequent economic organization of the society. Culture based on the economic structure and serves to support and maintain the economic base. Economic structure must be changed, and then culture based on the economic structure will be able to change	worldwide analysis of women as an oppressed group, or class known as the "Fourth World;" biological division of sexes or the inequality between the sexes led to the oppression of one sex by the other; this formed the prototype for subsequent economy class inequalities and oppression. Since patriarchy, the development of culture including capitalism has arisen from the Male mode of consciousness.
Goal	The overthrow of capitalism is not desired. These women tend to benefit more from the current economic system and are therefore more invested in its perpetuation.	the overthrow of capitalism is a necessary and nearly sufficient condition for the goals of feminism to be attained	the overthrow of capitalism is a necessary and far from sufficient condition for the goals to be attained
OTHER VIEWS	men are seen as the source of power; women want to share the power equally with men; and men would also gain from this (they would not have to strive and compete as much, for example)	a few wealthy white men as source of material power—those who own means of production. They buy labor of others, set prices, and wages, etc., control use of what is produced. All of this determines to a large degree the nature and quality of people's lives.	women seen as source of power which they have been feeding to men without acknowledgment or recognition. Women have emotional-psychological power; men have material power; power has thus far been defined in Male mode.

Chart of the Basic Feminist Positions Cont.

Roles	modernization of women's role	redefinition of roles with equal evaluation of men and women	elimination of women's and men's roles altogether
Men	men suffer as much and are trapped as much as women by sex roles and the rigidity with which they are defined	"the system" creates men's sexist attitudes which they can't overcome easily due to their conditioning and the present economic and social structure of society.	men are sometimes seen as "enemy" since they have material economic power over women and won't give it up willingly; few men really trying to overcome sexism since it ultimately benefits them.
Psychological Differences	there may be some "innate" psychological differences between the sexes, but men and women will not be as different from each other psychologically with the increasing flexibility of sex roles.	psychological differences may result from inequalities in the economic system; there may be some innate differences as well. Most important is equal amount of respect and worth for each person regardless of sex.	There are no innate psychological sex differences. Sex roles at present are totally artificial bipolarizations of human psychological traits, and due to inequalities of power.

SOURCES AND FURTHER READINGS

Bird, Caroline, *Born Female,* New York: Pocket Books, 1969.

Friedan, Betty, *The Feminine Mystique,* New York: Dell Publishing Co., Inc., 1964.

Dalla Costa, Mariarosa. *The power of women and the subversion of the community.* Montpelier, England: Falling Wall Press, 1972 (article).

Engels, Frederick, *The origin of the family, private property and the state.* New York International Publishers, 1942.

Gordon, Linda. *Families.* Boston: New England Free Press, 1970 (article).

Mitchell, Juliet. *Woman's Estate.* New York: Vintage, 1973.

From New England Free Press:

Benston, M. 1969. "The Political Economy of Women's Liberation"

Gordon, L. 1970. "Families"

Tax, M. 1970. "Woman and Her Mind: The Story of Everyday Life"

Firestone, Shulamith. *The Dialectic of Sex.* New York: William Morrow and Co., Inc., 1970.

Koedt, Anne, Levine, Ellen, and Rapone, Anita. *Radical Feminism.* New York: Quadrangle, 1973.

Project Editor: Barbara L. Carpenter
Sponsoring Editor: Michael Zamczyk
Designer: Judith Olson
Artist: Marta Thoman

67890/54321